The Challenges of Educating People to Lead in a Challenging World

Educational Innovation in Economics and Business

Volume 10

The titles published in this series are listed at the end of this volume.

The Challenges of Educating People to Lead in a Challenging World

Edited by

Michael K. McCuddy

Valparaiso University,
Valparaiso, IN, U.S.A.

Herman van den Bosch

Open Universiteit Nederland,
The Netherlands

Wm. Benjamin Martz (Jr.)

Northern Kentucky University,
Highlands Heights, KY, U.S.A.

Alexei V. Matveev

City University of New York,
Staten Island, N.Y., U.S.A.

and

Kenneth O. Morse

Waikato University,
Hamilton, New Zealand

Springer

A C.I.P. Catalogue record for this book is available from the Library of Congress.

ISBN-10 1-4020-5611-7 (HB)
ISBN-13 978-1-4020-5611-6 (HB)
ISBN-10 1-4020-5612-5 (e-book)
ISBN-13 978-1-4020-5612-3 (e-book)

Published by Springer,
P.O. Box 17, 3300 AA Dordrecht, The Netherlands.

www.springer.com

Printed on acid-free paper

Contents

Contributing Authors

Andrew Ashwin, *Biz/ed, Institute for Learning and Research Technology, University of Bristol, Bristol, UK.* a.ashwin@bristol.ac.uk

Graham Benmore, *Southampton Business School, Southampton Solent University, Southhampton, UK.* graham.benmore@solent.ac.uk

Alessandro Biscaccianti, *Baobab Architecture, Dijon, France.* baobab.architecture@wanadoo.fr

Herman van den Bosch, *School of Management of the Open University of the Netherlands, Heerlen, the Netherlands.* herman.vandenbosch@ou.nl

Marjolein C. J. Caniëls, *School of Management of the Open University of the Netherlands, Heerlen, the Netherlands.* marjolein.caniels@ou.nl

Tim Cappelli, *Manchester Institute of Telematics and Employment Research, Manchester Metropolitan University, Manchester, UK.* t.cappelli@mmu.ac.uk

Nicole van Emmerik, *International Business School, Hogeschool Brabant, Breda, the Netherlands.* nw.vanemmerik@avans.nl

Anne-Marie De Jonghe, *University of Southampton, CHEMPAS School of Management, Highfield Southampton, UK.* anne-marie.dejonghe@skynet.be

Deborah Dewolfe Waddill, *Restek Consulting, Vienna, Virginia, USA.* deb.waddill@cox.net

Stewart Falconer, *Napier University, Edinburgh, Scotland.* s.falconer@napier.ac.uk

Greet Fastré, *University of Maastricht, Faculty of Economics and Business Administration, Maastricht, the Netherlands.* g.fastré@educ.unimaas.nl

Blanca J. Garza Flores, *Monterrey Institute of Technology, Campus Estado de México, México*

Anita Van Gils, *University of Maastricht, Faculty of Economics and Business Administration, Maastricht, the Netherlands.* a.vangils@os.unimaas.nl

Aurora González Turnbull, *Monterrey Institute of Technology, Campus Estado de México, México.* aturnbul@itesm.mx

Meredith Godat, *Faculty of Business, Queensland University of Technology, Brisbane, Queensland, Australia,* m.godat@qut.edu.au

Jan Hellberg, *Lund University, Lund, Sweden.* jan.hellberg@med.lu.se

Ard Huizing, *Universiteit van Amsterdam Business School, Department of Business Studies, Information Management Section, Amsterdam, the Netherlands.* a.huizing@uva.nl

Marc Humbert, *Grenoble Ecole de Managemement, Grenoble, France.* marc.humbert@esc-grenoble.fr

Rik Maes, *Universiteit van Amsterdam Business School, Department of Business Studies, Information Management Section, Amsterdam, the Netherlands.* r.e.maes@uva.nl

Wm. Benjamin Martz, Jr., *University of Colorado at Colorado Springs Colorado Springs, USA.* wmartz@mail.uccs.edu

Michael K. Mc.Cuddy, *College of Business Administration, Valparaiso University, Valparaiso, Indiana, USA.* mike.mccuddy@valpo.edu

Kenneth O. Morse, *Waikato Management School, University of Waikato, Hamilton, New Zealand.* kndjmorse@aol.com

Thomas C. Neil, *Allen University, Columbia, South Carolina, USA.* penguin@sc.rr.com

Jan Nijhuis, *University of Maastricht, Faculty of Economics & Business Administration, the Netherlands.* J.nijhuis@os.unimaas.nl

Hans Otting, *Christelijke Hogeschool Nederland, Leeuwarden, the Netherlands.* hotting@chn.nl

Wendy L. Pirie, *College of Business Administration, Valparaiso University, Valparaiso, Indiana, USA.* wendy.pirie@valpo.edu

Kieren Pitts, *Biz/ed, Institute for Learning and Research Technology, University of Bristol, Bristol, UK.* kieren.pitts@bristol.ac.uk

Jennifer Radbourne, *Faculty of Business, Queensland University of Technology, Brisbane, Australia.* jradbour@usc.edu.au

Rysia Reynolds, *Southampton Business School, Southampton Solent University, UK.* . rysia.reynolds@solent.ac.uk

Raymond Ruijten, *Research & Evaluation Office, Breda Business School, Hogeschool Brabant, Breda, the Netherlands.* ruyten.msm@avans.nl

David Russell, *Manchester Institute of Telematics and Employment Research, Manchester Metropolitan University, Manchester, UK.* d.russell@mmu.ac.uk

Rubén D. Santiago Acosta, *Monterrey Institute of Technology, Campus Estado de México, México*

Johann Seiwald, *Wirtschaftsuniversität Wien, Wien, Austria.* johann.seiwald@bmi.gv.at

Morgan M. Shepard, *University of Colorado at Colorado Springs, USA.* mshepher@uccs.edu

Aileen M. Sibbald, *Napier University Business School, Napier University, Scotland, UK.* am.sibbald@napier.ac.uk

Anke H. J. Smeets-Verstraeten, *School of Management of the Open University of the Netherlands, Heerlen, the Netherlands.*

Jackie Stephens, Nottingham Trent University, Nottingham, UK. jackie.stephens@ntu.ac.uk

Dirk Tempelaar, *University of Maastricht, Faculty of Economics & Business Administration, the Netherlands*, d.tempelaar@ke.unimaas.nl

Thomas H. P. Thijssen, *Via Nova Academy and PrimaVera Research Group, Universiteit van Amsterdam, the Netherlands*. hamint@wxs.nl

John Troy, *Napier University Business School, Napier University, Scotland, UK*. j.troy@napier.ac.uk

Sergio Vasquez Bronfman, *ESCP-EAP (European School of Management), Paris, France*. vasquez@escp-eap.net

Fons T. J. Vernooij, *Vrije Universiteit, Amsterdam, the Netherlands*. mail@fons-vernooij.nl

Kate Whiteley-De Graaf. *School of Advertising, Marketing and Public Relations, Faculty of Business, Queensland University of Technology, Brisbane, Queensland, Australia*. k.degraaf@qut.edu.au

Robert Williams, *University of Plymouth, Devon, Newton Abbot, UK*. rjwilliams@plymouth.ac.uk

Wichard Zwaal, *Christelijke Hogeschool Nederland, Leeuwarden, the Netherlands*. wzwaal@chn.nl

Acknowledgments

The editorial team for this book wishes to thank the contributing authors for working with us to produce a product of the highest intellectual quality possible. We also wish to thank Richard G. Milter, Editor-in-Chief of the EDiNEB/Springer Verlag Book Series; Wim Gijselaers, President of the EDiNEB Foundation; and Ellen Nelissen, EDiNEB Network Coordinator for their support. A very deeply-felt expression of gratitude goes to Henny Dankers at Maastricht University for the assistance and support she provided in preparing this volume for publication.

Editorial Team

The editorial team for Volume 10 of the hard copy text series, *Educational Innovation in Economics and Business*, consisted of five EDiNEB members who gave very generously of their time and talent to bring this book to fruition. This volume reflects the best papers presented at the EDiNEB X Conference in Salzburg, Austria and the EDiNEB XI Conference in Maastricht, The Netherlands. Michael McCuddy served as editor for the volume. Herman van den Bosch served as an associate editor for both sets of submitted papers and helped the editor in several other ways. Ben Martz served as an associate editor for both sets of submitted papers, while Alexei Matveev served as an associate editor for the Salzburg papers and Ken Morse served as an associate editor for the Maastricht papers. The expertise and commitment that these people brought to the editorial process is evident in their brief biographical descriptions, which follow.

Michael K. McCuddy

Michael McCuddy holds The Louis S. and Mary L. Morgal Chair of Christian Business Ethics and is a Professor of Management at Valparaiso University in the USA. He serves on EDiNEB's Editorial Board and has been a frequent contributor of chapters to the EDiNEB book series. After earning a Ph.D. (1977) from Purdue University he embarked on his teaching and research career. He is interested in issues associated with innovative education as well as various aspects of personal and business ethics. His current research focuses on the teaching of ethics, the issues and implications associated with teaching-centered versus learning-centered models of education, managerial and leadership skill development, linkages between freedom and ethics in a global context, and the role of stewardship in personal and professional ethics. He has written numerous instructional supplements and cases for management, organizational behavior, and ethics textbooks. He has authored or co-authored a wide range of conference papers, journal articles, and book chapters that address a variety of educational issues and ethical topics. He also served as project director for a four-year curriculum development project at Valparaiso University that was funded by the Lilly Endowment.

Herman van den Bosch

Herman van den Bosch, Dean of the School of Management at the Open University of the Netherlands and Professor in Learning in Business Administration, specializes in distance learning. He has a long history of involvement in innovative education at the university and pre-university levels. He earned an MA in Geography from the University of Nijmegen, The Netherlands, in 1972. He also has taught at the University of Nijmegen, specializing in educational aspects of geography with respect to learning at school as well as in museums and documentary films. His Ph.D. thesis in 1980 explored the role of geography in the development of a global attitude among schoolchildren. Beginning in 1982, he specialized in the efficacy of educational methods. Between 1988 and 2001, he served as director of the School of Policy Sciences, which in 2001 was renamed the Nijmegen School of Management. In this position he was responsible for overseeing the problem-based curriculum. In 2001, he assumed his present position as Dean and Professor in Learning in Business Administration at the Open University of the Netherlands. His publications focus on the development of academic competencies, problem-based learning, management of educational institutions, and information and communications technology (ICT) in education.

Wm. Benjamin Martz, Jr.

In 2006, Ben was appointed Chair of the Information Systems Department at Northern Kentucky University's College of Informatics. Prior to this appointment, he was on the faculty at Chico State and the University of Colorado at Colorado Springs. His teaching interests include e-business, software development, groupware and team-based problem solving. He received his B.B.A in Marketing from the College of William & Mary; his

M.S. in Management Information Systems (MIS) and his Ph.D. in Business, with an emphasis in MIS, from the University of Arizona. Ben was one of the founding members, as well as President and COO, of Ventana Corporation – a technology, spin-off firm from the University of Arizona - incorporated to commercialize the groupware software product GroupSystems. In 1994, GroupSystems won PC Magazine's Editor's Choice award for best Electronic Meeting System software. Ben has published his groupware research in *MIS Quarterly*, *Decision Support Systems*, and the *Journal of Management Information Systems* and his student learning environment research in the *Decision Sciences Journal of Innovative Education, Journal of Cooperative Education* and *Journal of Computer Information Systems*.

Alexei V. Matveev

Alexei V. Matveev (Ph.D., Ohio University) is an Assistant Professor of Management with the Department of Business, The City University of New York, College of Staten Island (USA). His research focuses on innovation in management education and practice, including problem-based learning, effective cross-cultural management, and high-performance multicultural teams. He has worked as a management consultant with Deloitte Touché and The World Bank on international development and corporate restructuring projects in Eastern Europe. He has conducted consulting projects and addressed professional audiences in Austria, Canada, Croatia, Germany, Mexico, Portugal, Russia, Scotland, Sweden, the United Kingdom, and the United States. His research and consulting activity has materialized in a number of journal articles, professional papers, and grants on interactive learning, multicultural team performance, international research methodology, and management education in Russia.

Kenneth O. Morse

Dr. Kenneth O. Morse has been a member of the EDINEB editorial board for the several years. Prior to his recent retirement from academe, he was a Senior Lecturer in International Management at the Wailkato Management School, Hamilton, New Zealand. As a learning facilitator, he mentored in the areas of international business operations, international marketing, and cross-cultural communication. His research field focuses on learning techniques and practices, especially related to electronic learning across national borders. He recently received a New Zealand national information technology award for his contributions to New Zealand's transnational e-learning practices. Upon his retirement from active teaching, he returned to the USA to pursue a different helping career. Drawing on years of experience with Asian students, Ken and his spouse are involved in developing a contingent of missionaries for Asia who themselves are Asians presently residing in America.

Preface

This book represents the final publication, Volume 10, of the hard copy text series *Educational Innovation in Economics and Business*. The series, originally published under Kluwer Academic Press, began as a collection of the best papers provided at the inaugural EDiNEB Conference held in Maastricht in December of 1993. That conference, and subsequent book, provided the impetus for the development of both a conference series and a book series nurtured by Wim Gijselaers and his foundation team at Maastricht University (then the University of Limburg).

Both the conference series and the book series continue to thrive. In addition to Maastricht (the Netherlands), annual conference meetings of the EDiNEB Network have been complemented by such venues as Uppsala (Sweden), Orlando, Cleveland, and Newport Beach (USA), Edinburgh (Scotland), Bergen (Norway), Nice (France), Guadalajara (Mexico), Salzburg (Austria), Antwerp (Belgium), and, by the time of this printing, Lisbon (Portugal). These locations have added their share of culture and spirit to the innovative drive and collaborative efforts of the authors across the ten volumes of this book series.

Although the hard copy version of this book series will conclude with this volume, the publication will continue in the form of an online e-book series, and as hard copy version (although in a different set-up). One of the limitations of the current hard copy editions was an inability to quickly move the research findings and best practice illustrations to the public forum. It is our intent that our new approach will provide much quicker access to quality articles after they have been processed through peer review. Articles, or chapters, published in our new series will continue to be measured for quality using the peer review process. The new series will also accept submissions for review that have not been linked to specific conference presentations. That is, the new series will draw from both conference papers and an open call for articles.

The quality review process that has been used by the current book series actually begins as each conference abstract is initially screened by a selection committee before acceptance into the program for that annual meeting. Following the conference a double-blind peer review process is used to evaluate the best papers submitted for review by the presenting authors. The list of reviewers and editors is listed on the EDiNEB website. The selection decisions are made by the book editors in consideration of their own reviews and the feedback from the reviewers. Once the best papers are selected, a thorough and systematic review and enhancement process is undertaken with those authors willing to subject their papers to that process. It is only after this comprehensive approach that we are able to provide the chapters in this book for your enlightenment.

Like previous volumes in the *Educational Innovation in Economics and Business* series, this volume is genuinely international in terms of its coverage. The contributions for this volume have been selected from two separate conferences of the EDiNEB Network. This volume's editor, Michael K. McCuddy, and his associate editors have done a superb job working with the authors to produce a compilation of chapters that meets the high quality standards of the EDiNEB Network and Springer Verlag. They have also demonstrated excellence in integrating the chapters around five key themes which illustrate innovation in business education with a view toward enhancing the learning experience. It should provide value to anyone engaged directly in business education, defined broadly to embrace management, finance, marketing, economics, informational studies, and ethics, or who has responsibility for fostering the professional development of business educators. The editors have fully aligned this book to the EDiNEB objective of encouraging and inspiring others as well as illustrating innovative practices in business education.

I wish you well as you open your mind to the encouragement and inspiration offered in abundance on the pages to follow.

Richard G. Milter, Editor-in-Chief
EDiNEB/Springer Verlag Book Series
Educational Innovation in Economics and Business

PART I

INTRODUCTION

Chapter 1

THE CHALLENGES OF EDUCATING PEOPLE TO LEAD IN A CHALLENGING WORLD

Michael K. McCuddy
Valparaiso University, College of Business Administration, Valparaiso, Indiana, USA

1. THE CHALLENGES OF CONTEMPORARY EDUCATION

The early 21st century is an exciting time, a challenging time for the individuals and institutions engaged in educating people to be responsible and productive participants in all kinds of social institutions, and especially in business organizations. Why are the challenges so great for the education of business professionals and business leaders? There are many answers to this question.

Business is perhaps the most pervasive social institution that people encounter during the course of their lives. For the typical person, work consumes more time than any other single activity, except perhaps sleep. Businesses have the potential for being major players, even dominant forces, in producing sweeping economic, social, and even political change (*HBR on Corporate Responsibility*, 2003; Paine, 2003). Such a pervasive and powerful human enterprise requires talented, competent, and dedicated people — leaders and followers alike — to effectively address the increasingly complex and profound challenges that face the global economy.

We live and work in an increasingly complex, globalized economy. Business organizations must now deal with diverse cultural, legal, economic, and political considerations in their international operations. Similarly complex decision environments often accompany the domestic operations of business organizations. Globalization has brought about more intense competition while simultaneously creating opportunities for substantive collaboration. Global sourcing, foreign investment, and other competitive

M.K. McCuddy et al. (eds.),
The Challenges of Educating People to Lead in a Challenging World, 3–30.

factors can affect even small business organizations. All of these elements — and more — create challenges for businesses and their leaders, and for those who educate people to assume responsible roles in business.

Life in business organizations is fast-paced — even frenetic in some cases — and change can occur with near-blinding rapidity. All members of business organizations must understand the need for change and have the competencies to either initiate change or effectively respond to it. Leaders in particular must hone their competencies for initiating and guiding change efforts.

An increasingly demanding challenge for people at all levels of business organizations — indeed, in walks of life — is the impact of technology. Technology continues to be developed in wide-ranging arenas and at an increasingly rapid pace. Technological developments create opportunities and threats for both business enterprises and educational enterprises. Both business and education must properly and effectively embrace the technology revolution or risk becoming anachronistic dinosaurs. Yet, businesses and education must not forget the human beings that the technology is designed to serve. Remaining profoundly committed to humanity in business and education while eagerly embracing the potential of technology is an enormous challenge for people, and especially leaders, in our modern world.

A crisis of ethics and values has permeated many sectors of the global economy in the past few years, bringing to the forefront the unsavory side of life in our economic, social, and political institutions. Perhaps never before in the history of humankind has the awareness of moral crisis been greater. In large part, this is due to the rapidity with which information now traverses the globe. In part, this also is due to more and more people worldwide having the growing opportunity — perhaps luxury — of questioning the operations of various organizations and institutions. Whatever the explanatory reasons, more and more of the world's population demand ethical decisions and actions from organizations and their leaders. In turn, educators and educational institutions are challenged to help these leaders — and their followers — to develop the necessary perspectives and competencies for pursuing ethical courses of action.

All of these factors create profound challenges and raise important questions for educators and the educational establishment. What competencies, capacities, attitudes, and perspectives do learners need to develop so they can be contributing, productive members of organizations and society? How do we deal with the resource challenges that increasingly constrain the educational enterprise? How do we make the learning process more effective? How do we best use technology to effectively deliver content and meaningfully engage learners in the educational process? How do we develop people to become effective leaders of businesses and other organizations in an increasingly complex and values-driven world that is changing rapidly and often contentiously? How do we accommodate the needs of learners throughout their lives? How do we accomplish all of this in a multicultural and global environment?

This volume tackles these questions and more, providing perspectives and insights from educators around the globe. Representing a combination of the best papers from the EDiNEB X and EDiNEB XI Conferences, this volume focuses on two sets of challenges: (a) the challenges being encountered by the teaching and learning enterprise itself as it seeks to educate future business leaders and other business professionals; and (b) preparing leaders and other professionals to effectively address their own future challenges in the modern workplace.

EDiNEB X, which focused on *The Impact of Culture and Education on Learning Practices*, is more closely aligned to the first set of challenges. It focuses on what people learn and how they learn, both of which are crucial elements in personal and professional success and satisfaction. It also focuses on the nature of the learning enterprise and the factors that influence it. As stated in the EDiNEB X call for papers, "Our cultural and educational environments also impact our lives and our learning. ... Professional educators and leaders of educational programs need to appreciate and understand the impact of culture and education on teaching practices and on learning platforms."

EDiNEB XI focused on *The Changing Face of Globalization: Its Impact on Educating Future Leaders*. As indicated in the call for papers, the conference focus was intended to encourage "a discussion of broad and innovative perspectives on cultural, economic, social, ethical, and technological forces that affect corporate leaders and educators in their efforts to prepare competent future leaders of the 21st century." Although the EDiNEB XI focus is clearly on educating future leaders to meet their own set of challenges, globalization and all its implications create a bridge back to the first set of challenges.

The title of this introductory chapter, *The Challenges of Educating People to Lead in a Challenging World*, clearly identifies the two sets of challenges that bind the two conference themes together. The Editor and Associate Editors of this volume encourage, you, the reader, to keep these two sets of challenges foremost in your mind as you peruse and reflect upon the ensuing chapters.

The remainder of the book is organized into five parts, with each part containing from five to seven chapters. Each set of chapters is organized around a particular theme that provides insight into the global teaching/learning enterprise as it is evolving early in the 21st century. Part II of the book examines *The Teaching/Learning Conundrum: Issues, Challenges, and Prospects*. Part III focuses on *Assessing the Dimensions and Characteristics of Learning and Learners*. Part IV discusses *Developing Competencies for Career Success: Issues and Practices*. Part V explores *Using Technology to Facilitate Teaching and Learning*. Part VI describes *Teaching and Learning Insights from Unique Applications*.

2. PART II: THE TEACHING/LEARNING CONUNDRUM: ISSUES, CHALLENGES, AND PROSPECTS

As we reflect on the past and present and look forward to the future, the roles of teaching and learning in academe continue to dominate educators' thinking and concerns. Part II of the book explores the perpetual enigma of what teachers can and should do as opposed to what learners can and should do. Part II focuses on various aspects of change in the teaching/learning enterprise. It begins with three chapters (Chapters 2 to 4) that provide broad conceptual and philosophical perspectives regarding teacher-centered learning versus student-centered learning, and the challenges associated with changing from the former paradigm to the latter paradigm. The next two chapters (Chapters 5 and 6) focus on more targeted concerns in shifting from an emphasis on teaching to an emphasis on learning. The final two chapters (Chapters 7 and 8) bring Part II full circle by exploring the issues, implications, and impediments associated with sustaining change in the teaching/learning enterprise.

2.1 Chapter 2, "Learning on Demand" — The Education Objective for the Knowledge Economy

Ken Morse argues that globalization has changed the world in many ways, which in turn has changed and continues to change the face of education. Morse asserts that never before in the history of education has there been such an emphasis on learning and the ability to learn. This emphasis on learning and learning to learn results from the need for rapid adaptation to constantly changing work environments, social conditions, and information availability.

The changes bought about by globalization have created and continue to create numerous and varied problems for society, institutions, businesses, and their members. In turn, these changes have generated a profound need for people to develop and refine their problem-solving skills. The increased need for problem-solving skills places a premium on both knowing and knowing how to learn, with the latter being an ascendant skill for success in both work and social environments. In short, the need for problem-solving skills creates a profound need for *learning on demand.*

Morse points out that learning on demand dramatically contrasts with the assembly line approach that dominated much of 20th century education and which is still all too prevalent in the early 21st century. He maintains that academic institutions and academic personnel need to shift their focus from teaching to learning — a paradigmatic shift that is already in progress — and to refocus from learning "what to learn" to learning "how to learn." According to Morse, developing the skill of learning on demand offers future university graduates the best opportunity to succeed in learning organizations and in the changing global environment. The implications for the delivery of education are that learning must trump teaching; the process must shift from being teacher-centric to being student- or learner-centric; and professors must change their philosophies and methods, moving from being a "sage-on-the-stage" to being a "guide-on-the-side."

2.2 Chapter 3, The Model of Cooperative Contextual Change: A Process for Implementing Problem-based Learning

Alessandro Biscaccianti and Thomas C. Neil introduce a model that provides both a foundation and a structure for transforming a curriculum via problem-based learning. They argue that PBL is a radical departure from the traditional "teaching approach" because the teacher does not dominate the relationship based on his/her expertise and position. Instead, the teacher becomes a facilitator of the learner's inquiry and resolution of issues raised within a specific context. In short, the introduction of PBL into a curriculum represents a significant organizational change process — and, like any change initiative, that process is constrained by a variety of factors, including resistance to change, lack of commitment, misunderstandings, and opting out.

Biscaccianti and Neil propose the Model of Cooperative Contextual Change (M3C) as a method for effectively implementing PBL into a curriculum while simultaneously overcoming barriers to organizational change. The model focuses on dynamic stability to foster personal and group change and to create the conditions for sustaining a learning community. The premise of dynamic stability specifies that each individual, as well as the group, must be presented with anchors that provide a sense of security as the tide of change rises. These anchors help people to embrace and accept change. Acceptance of change requires people to make an explicit commitment to become involved in the process of emotional and intellectual learning and to assume responsibility for personal and team actions. Biscaccianti and Neil conclude this chapter with a case illustration of the M3C being used to transform the curriculum at the academic institution where Neil teaches.

2.3 Chapter 4, Dealing with Dilemmas in Contemporary Higher Education: Universitat Oberta de Catalunya

Anne-Marie De Jonghe explores two important dilemmas encountered in contemporary higher education institutions. One dilemma — the preservation of cultural heritage versus constructivist learning — reflects the tension between professor-centered and student-centered views of academe. The preservation of cultural heritage, or the professor-centered view, emphasizes research and the "sage on the stage" mode of instruction where students play a passive role in the educational process. In sharp contrast is the constructivist learning, or student-centered view, that reflects four important trends — the concept of student as customers, the increasing focus on learning, the changing role of professors, and the changing concept of the student — that are redefining educational processes. The second dilemma — academic community versus flexible, lifelong learning — reflects the tension between campus teaching, which enables the creation of academic communities, and distance teaching and learning, which offers the opportunity to reach a more diverse student population but where creating a community becomes more difficult. Physical campuses enable and encourage the advantages of being an interacting academic community. Distance teaching and learning, enabled and supported by information and communication technologies, permits the provision of education services to a more diverse and dispersed student population.

De Jonghe discusses issues related to these two dilemmas, and then describes how one university addressed them. She presents the case of Universitat Oberta de Catalunya (UOC), a distance e-based university, located in Barcelona, Spain. UOC uses a virtual and asynchronous teaching model that allows students to learn in an effective way without being impeded by barriers of space or time. Among other features, the UOC educational approach unbundled the tasks of professors and built a user-friendly communication area and a cultural learning environment on the Web. Details are provided regarding the design and operation of UOC, and how the decisions and actions in these arenas actually resolved the dilemmas. De Jonghe argues that the UOC experience provides valuable lessons for other educators, asserting that the relevance of UOC's learning and organizational model goes far beyond the world of e-learning and the geographical area of Catalunya or Spain.

2.4 Chapter 5, From Teaching to Learning: A Tempus Tacis Project as a Catalyst for Change in Post-Soviet Georgia

Jackie Stephens and Jan Hellberg describe a change effort instituted at two universities in post-Soviet Georgia. Under the central governance of the former Soviet Union, universities were required to deliver courses that would maintain and enhance the practical workings of a centrally planned economy. The content and approach of education was dictated; teachers did not have any control over course content or instructional methods, and students were passive recipients of information. However, with the break-up of the Soviet Union, two Georgian universities — Grigol Robakhidze University and Batumi State University — began exploring the viability of student-centered education. Under the tutelage of educators at Nottingham Trent University, UK and Lund University, Sweden, Academic Quality Assurance Centers were established at the Georgian universities and training was provided to teachers involved in the student-centered educational experiment.

Stephens and Hellberg, representing Nottingham Trent University and Lund University, respectively, discuss how the experiment was carried out at Grigol Robakhidze University and Batumi State University. In an attempt to provide some assessment of the experiment's impact, Stephens and Hellberg also report extensively on interview and questionnaire data collected from the participating teachers. The data reveal that the participating teachers expressed frustration and dissatisfaction with the teacher-centered approach of the Soviet system and positive attitudes toward the student-centered approach used in the experiment. Interestingly, more change occurred in attitudes toward student-centered education than in actual professorial and student behaviors aimed at implementing it. This, of course, represents an effort at changing a strongly embedded cultural phenomenon — and changes in cultural attitudes are arguably easier to effect than changes in cultural behaviors. The authors also discuss some of the implications of this change differential.

2.5 Chapter 6, Lifelong Learning in Higher Education: Is There a Gap Between the Idea and its Application in Higher Education?

Aileen M. Sibbald and John Troy discuss the vision of the Scottish Parliament for lifelong learning among the Scottish populace, examine the literature regarding major issues associated with the development of a lifelong learning strategy, and report on survey results regarding beliefs about and practices of lifelong learning in the Business School at Scotland's Napier University. Sibbald and Troy point out that lifelong learning is an educational concept being touted as a panacea for future economic development in modern industrial societies. They then explore five major issues — the individual as a learner, participation and equity, learning and working, funding learning, and delivering learning — that must be addressed in universities' development of lifelong learning strategies.

Using Scottish and other United Kingdom universities as a context, and emphasizing that almost all these universities have lifelong learning as part of their "vision" statements, Sibbald and Troy pose the question: "Is lifelong learning an area where cooperation rather than competition is more appropriate?" In attempting to answer this question, Sibbald and Troy report the results of a survey conducted among the academic staff at the Business School of Napier University in Scotland. The survey results focus on the major issues and perceived problems associated with lifelong learning, and indicate that, among the respondents, there is an apparent gap between the vision for lifelong learning and its actual application. Recommendations are made concerning reduction of this gap between vision and application, as well as for addressing the lifelong learning agenda at a macro-economic level in Scotland.

2.6 Chapter 7, Implementing and Sustaining Educational Innovations

Michael K. McCuddy and Wendy L. Pirie explore educational innovation from the perspective of organizational change and development, and propose a model that explains both the adoption of educational innovations and the failure to sustain educational innovations. Adapting and extending the well-known Lewinian model of change, they examine the implementation and sustainability of educational innovations in institutions of higher learning. Their model explores *openness to educational innovation*, *innovation activities*, and *consequences of innovation* — both personal and organizational.

McCuddy and Pirie report survey results that both test the proposed model and provide some insight into EDiNEB members' attitudes and beliefs regarding educational innovation. Although the results reflect a relatively small sample, considerable support for the model is presented. The results also indicate that the motivating factors for initiating and continuing educational innovations are intrinsic and student oriented, and that the primary impediments to innovation are institutional and collegial. With regard to these primary impediments, over 90 percent of the respondents reported they had discontinued or curtailed their efforts at educational innovation. Given the disconcerting nature of these latter findings, and given the fact that they reflect a sample of people who are committed to educational innovation, a rosy future for educational innovation can be justifiably questioned.

2.7 Chapter 8, Willingness to Innovate: Use, Misuse, and Abuse of Student Evaluations of Instruction

Michael K. McCuddy and Wendy L. Pirie explore why educational innovation is valued by some but not all academics, and why even some of those academics who have a strong interest in innovative education appear to be reluctant to actually innovate. So what inhibits innovative education? The authors assert that one major culprit is the student ratings system being widely used throughout the world.

McCuddy and Pirie contend that student ratings are inherently flawed as performance appraisal instruments, and consequently such ratings systems are potentially detrimental to innovative education. In exploring this fundamental contention, the evaluative and developmental lenses of performance appraisal are used to examine the challenges associated with student ratings and their impact on innovation. In an effort to transform the typical student evaluation system into a more useful evaluative and developmental tool, the authors propose an alternative approach — one based on behaviorally anchored rating scales — for utilizing student ratings.

Another important feature of this chapter is the discussion of the dangers that are inherent in the *student-as-customer* model of education and assessment of teachers' instructional performance. McCuddy and Pirie argue that society, not the students, are the real customers for the output of educational institutions and that instructional evaluation systems should be geared more to serving society's interests than students' interests.

3. PART III: ASSESSING THE DIMENSIONS AND CHARACTERISTICS OF LEARNING AND LEARNERS

With the increasing emphasis being placed on learning and learners in contemporary education circles, educators are in need of information and insights regarding: (a) the dynamics of the learning process; (b) the attitudes, beliefs, needs, and behaviors of learners; and (c) how the learning process can be designed to accommodate lifelong learners' attitudes, beliefs, needs, and behaviors. Chapters 9 and 10 explore some of the important aspects of the dynamics of the learning process. Chapter 9 reports on a study designed to empirically ascertain the impact of constructivist educational principles on different learner-centered approaches for effectively engaging learners. Chapter 10 proposes a theoretical framework for analyzing and understanding learning processes that occur in creating new business ventures. Chapters 11 and 12 explore students' attitudes and beliefs toward particular academic disciplines and particular careers. Chapter 11 examines student attitudes and beliefs about quantitative, analytical courses as well as more qualitative, management-oriented courses. Chapter 12 explores cross-cultural differences in students' attitudes and beliefs regarding the entrepreneurial lifestyle. Chapters 13 and 14 deal with two different challenges that accompany the world's growing emphasis on lifelong learning. Chapter 13 tackles the challenge of developing online learning materials that are useful for a variety of users, when the actual users and their specific learning needs are unknown to the developer. Chapter 14 discusses an approach for evaluating the prior experiential learning of people who are seeking to enhance their career potential through academic credentialing.

3.1 Chapter 9, The Identification of Constructivist Pedagogy in Different Learning Environments

Hans Otting and Wichard Zwaal explore the nature of the constructivist framework and how that framework could be manifested in four different educational settings: problem-based learning, action learning, project work, and workplace learning. Noting that relatively few attempts have been made to research constructivism in educational practice, Otting and Zwaal designed a study to ascertain whether the principles of constructivist pedagogy actually exist in problem-based learning, action learning, project work, and workplace learning.

They examined three different BA programs — International Hospitality Management, Leisure Management, and Retail Management — at one university. Each BA program used one or more of the four educational approaches. Students and instructional designers from each of the three programs participated in the study, responding to a 30-item questionnaire that measured the presence of constructivist pedagogy. The study's findings revealed that problem-based learning could be considered to be the almost ideal application of constructivist principles, because it supports active and cooperative knowledge construction and focuses on problem solving and in-depth understanding. Consequently, they advise educational designers to continue capitalizing on the constructivist principles of PBL.

3.2 Chapter 10, Learning in Venture Creation: Development of Competence in Translating Business Ideas into Practice

Johann Seiwald, draws on the fields of organizational learning and entrepreneurship to develop a theoretical framework for analyzing the learning processes of new venture creators. Taking a practice-based perspective on these learning processes, Seiwald argues that their complex, dynamic, and interrelated nature must be analyzed in the context in which they occur. To integrate learning processes and learning contexts, the author proposes a theoretical framework with four major conceptual elements: venture creating as translation, activities and activity systems, institutional rules, and learning process and knowing.

Seiwald also presents a case study of an Austrian start-up organization that illustrates how new venture creators translate their business ideas into a concrete business. This case study shows that the venture creation process is a practical learning process which involves a wide variety of different activity systems, and which is influenced and mediated by institutional knowledge and the social stock of knowledge about organizations. Important implications for entrepreneurial education through direct experience are explored in six separate but not unrelated areas: learning of interconnected practices of the organization and the communities and activity systems in which the organization operates; learning and positioning within the organizational environment; learning and organizing the internal structure; learning in exercising the managerial role; balancing contradictions in different communities and different activity systems; and self-reflective and implicit assumptions about the nature of knowledge and learning.

3.3 Chapter 11, Commonalities in Attitudes and Beliefs Toward Different Academic Subjects

Dirk Tempelaar and Jan Nijhuis explore students' attitudes and beliefs toward two analytical courses — Quantitative Methods and Finance and Accounting — and three management-oriented courses — Business Strategy, Marketing Management, and Organization and Human Resource Management. The courses are part of the program of study pursued by students in International Business at the University of Maastricht.

Tempelaar and Nijhuis use the Survey of Attitudes Toward Statistics (SATS) developed by Schau, Stevens, Dauphinee and DelVecchio (1995) to assess student attitudes and beliefs regarding the Quantitative Methods Course. The SATS assesses four major factors: *Affect* (positive and negative feelings concerning the subject matter); *Cognitive Competence* (attitudes about intellectual knowledge and skills concerning the subject matter); *Value* (measuring attitudes about the usefulness, relevance, and worth of the subject matter in personal and professional life); and *Difficulty* (attitudes about the difficulty of the subject). Tempelaar and Nijhuis also adapted the SATS for application in the other four courses.

Using structural equation modeling to analyze the data they collected, Tempelaar and Nijhuis confirmed earlier empirical results that students' attitudes and beliefs vary across academic subjects. They also discovered a common underlying factor across the courses. Drawing on these results the authors discuss possible implications for course interventions as well as evaluations.

3.4 Chapter 12, Multicultural Perceptions of the Entrepreneurial Lifestyle

Ben Martz, Tom Neil, Alessandro Biscaccianti, and Robert Williams, report on a research project that was undertaken to explore possible cultural differences in student perceptions of entrepreneurship. Based on the argument that the perceptions of entrepreneurs will be influenced by the way a culture rewards or encourages entrepreneurship, the authors hypothesize that the more positively a culture supports entrepreneurship, the more likely that students will have positive perceptions of the entrepreneurial lifestyle and will gravitate toward it as a career choice.

Exploratory in nature, the study examined questionnaire responses of over 900 students in American, French, and United Kingdom universities. The survey, which was developed based upon several of the characteristics identified in previous entrepreneurship studies, contains 29 statements related to the entrepreneur's lifestyle, education and ability, acceptance of risk, reputation, and aspirations. In general, the American students perceived the entrepreneurial lifestyle to be more favorable than did either the French or UK students. Among the educational implications of the findings are the identification of some of the cultural characteristics: (a) that educators should pay attention to when designing a curriculum or program; (b) that serve as "signal towers" into possible changes in perceptions of the entrepreneurial lifestyle; (c) that promote discussions in multicultural programs and classes; and (d) that provide "touch points" for a class in entrepreneurship.

3.5 Chapter 13, Developing Learning Materials for the Unknown Online Learner

Andrew Ashwin and Kieren Pitts draw on knowledge about learning and learning styles in developing an approach to improve the effectiveness and efficiency of e-learning in economics and business when the user of those materials cannot be easily identified. Known as Biz/ed, the approach seeks to meet the needs of a variety of learning styles for a wide-ranging, indeterminate e-learning clientele. In this context, Biz/ed is also designed to meet the needs of students at schools, colleges, and universities; the needs of educators; and the needs of people studying independently or within corporate training programs.

The Biz/ed model is founded on the belief that that students and trainees want to learn and that they will use on-line resources to help them in that learning. Ashwin and Pitts discuss the rationale and pedagogy behind the development of the learning materials used in Biz/ed, explaining how it pinpoints different learning styles and provides resources to help address those learning styles. They also describe what students and trainees will learn through the resources provided by Biz/ed and the relevance of such learning with respect to individual and organizational needs. Finally, Ashwin and Pitts provide practical illustrations of these resources and describe the benefits and limitations of technology in supporting the learning process.

3.6 Chapter 14, 'Credit Where Credit's Due': Piloting the Accreditation of Experiential Learning — A Case Study

Stewart Falconer and John Troy argue that lifelong learning enables individuals to continue developing personal and technical skills, knowledge, and understanding to ensure their employability and personal fulfillment while meeting the needs of a changing economic environment. Employers also benefit from lifelong learning by having people at their disposal in the numbers and of the quality they require to meet their objectives. Obviously, lifelong learning demands that higher education institutions develop innovative approaches for providing relevant knowledge. Perhaps less obvious is that lifelong learning also challenges higher education institutions to develop appropriate methods for evaluating people's prior experiential learning and awarding academic credit for it.

Falconer and Troy report on how the School of Accounting and Economics at Napier University in Edinburgh, Scotland has successfully addressed the challenge of accrediting prior learning for lifelong learners wishing to pursue the four-year Scottish BA Honors Financial Services degree. Based on a review of the learning outcomes for the first two years of this degree program, the authors developed a questionnaire to guide prospective students in providing a reflective account of the experiential learning they had accumulated during their careers. Included in the chapter is a detailed description of this process for accrediting experiential learning. Falconer and Troy indicate their early experience in using this process has been very positive.

4. PART IV: DEVELOPING COMPETENCIES FOR CAREER SUCCESS: ISSUES AND PRACTICES

Contemporary businesses expect new entrants to the workforce to arrive with a variety of developed competencies that will allow them to become productive contributors to the organization in a fairly rapid fashion. Businesses also demand the ongoing refinement of existing competencies and the development of new ones among the members of their current workforces. The education world has responded to these expectations and demands by developing curricula that stresses competency development in a variety of skill domains. Chapter 15 addresses the need for developing generic competencies within the educational environment, and reports on efforts to develop five broad categories of generic competencies. Although competency development often occurs in a face-to-face, classroom or behavioral laboratory context, Chapter 16 persuasively demonstrates that competency development need not be restricted to the these educational venues. Rather, competency development can be effectively facilitated in a distance learning environment. The remaining chapters in Part IV address specific areas of competency development. Chapter 17 focuses on the critical need for learners to develop an appreciation for and competency in ethical leadership. Chapter 18 focuses on developing critical thinking skills among both those who speak English as a first language and those who speak English as a second language. Chapter 19, the final chapter in Part IV, explores competencies that are critical for entrepreneurial success as well as how those competencies can be developed.

4.1 Chapter 15, Teaching for Life — Generic Capabilities that Link University Learning with Workplace Learning

Jennifer Radbourne asserts that business schools are under increasing pressure to enhance the learning capability and employability of graduates. Her discussion focuses on the importance of helping students develop the competencies needed to embark on successful careers in Australian organizations. Drawing on relevant literature, Radbourne identifies five categories of generic skills that appear to be essential for career success. These categories are: leadership and management skills; interpersonal and communication skills; social justice skills; adventurous decision making skills; and technical, professional, and cognitive skills.

Radbourne reports on four linked projects that took place over six years (1998-2003) at the Queensland University of Technology (QUT) in Australia. The linked projects are based on the hypothesis that *by teaching business students generic skills and capabilities for effective performance in the workplace, they are being taught learning that lasts.* To test this hypothesis, the projects focused on analyzing the effectiveness with which generic skills and capabilities were imparted through QUT's business curriculum. The first project involved a survey of business graduates and employers to ascertain the importance of selected skills and abilities. The second project changed the curriculum by embedding activities that would help develop the important skills and abilities identified in the survey. The third project was a second survey to determine how well the curricular changes were working. The fourth project used focus groups of graduates five years after their degree completion to explore the effectiveness of the university and the workplace in terms of learning these selected skills and abilities. The results of the four projects lend support to Radbourne's hypothesis.

4.2 Chapter 16, How Distance Education Can Sustain the Development of Competencies

Herman van den Bosch provides a powerful illustration of how distance learning can go beyond traditional learning objectives, such as the transmission of information, to embrace innovative learning objectives, such as the emphasis on competency development that is embedded in problem-based and project learning. This emphasis on competency development reflects educators' efforts to respond to employers' demands for "graduates who are able to operate in complex environments, *i.e.*, environments characterized by ill-defined problems, contradictory information, informal collaboration and abstract, dynamic and highly integrated processes" (Westera, 2001). In this chapter, Van den Bosch explores the challenges of adapting the competency development emphasis from the campus-based, face-to-face learning environment to the distance learning environment.

In analyzing the campus-based learning environment, Van den Bosch identifies six curricular design features that are essential for the development of competencies. These essential curricular design features include the following: (a) learning is based on tasks, representing the pursued competencies; (b) learning becomes more realistic by applying cases; (c) giving feedback is a major role of the teacher; (d) learning is a collaborative act; (e) students have to search actively for information; and (e) education should afford different learning paths. The author then extends these curricular design elements to the distance learning environment. He shows how each element can be adapted to the distance learning environment and identifies important issues that need to be addressed when operationalizing each element. Professor Van den Bosch goes on to illustrate the application of these curricular elements to distance learning by describing the design and implementation of a 'Basics of Marketing' course at the Open University of the Netherlands. He demonstrates that distance education — where learning occurs at the student's own pace and speed and anywhere there is Internet access — need not be restricted to information transmission. Rather, distance education can be applied effectively to the competency development of distance learners.

4.3 Chapter 17, The Ethical Education of Future Leaders: An Approach for Helping Students Become Authentic Ethical Role Models

Michael K. McCuddy, addresses the need for the ethical education of everyone who intends, at some point in time, to assume a leadership role in modern organizations. He argues that all people, who would become effective and respected leaders at any level in our global society's economic and social institutions, must learn to be an *authentic ethical role model* for their followers.

McCuddy maintains that for anyone to become an authentic ethical role model, four key requirements must be fulfilled. First, becoming an authentic ethical role model requires people to become acutely aware of their own moral orientation and how they are developing as moral individuals. Second, it requires people to be aware of how their personal moral orientation fits in with broader community expectations, values, and norms. Third, it requires people to examine how their personal moral orientation affects their decisions and actions on various organizational issues. Finally, it requires people to explore how their decisions and actions will affect relationships with and the interests of the organization's various stakeholders.

The chapter describes how these four key requirements are addressed in a course typically taken by two groups of students: fourth year students in an undergraduate business program and masters students in several different programs in the arts and sciences. The chapter also provides details regarding how the topical coverage, course assignments, and daily class activities foster the students' exploration of their ongoing development as moral beings.

4.4 Chapter 18, Developing Critical Thinking Skills Online to Facilitate a Discursive Multicultural Classroom

Meredith Godat and Kate Whiteley-De Graaf discuss how to foster critical thinking competencies among students for whom English is their native tongue as well as for those who speak English as a second language. The development of critical thinking skills requires students to be actively engaged in the learning process rather than being passive recipients of information. Moving from passive to active learning is an ongoing, and sometimes difficult, challenge in educating students throughout the globe. This challenge seems to be compounded when dealing with students who are accustomed to rote learning — for instance, Middle-Eastern and Asian students — as well as for those who are pursuing educational programs taught in a language other than their native tongues. These are the types of educational challenges with which Godat and Whiteley-De Graaf are grappling.

The authors respond to their particular mix of local challenges by focusing on the development of critical thinking competencies through the use of a scaffolding (or layering) process that enables students to preview and review learning materials prior to engaging in guided discussion activities, both online and face-to-face in the classroom. They describe the procedures for and the challenges of translating critical thinking processes from the online discussion environment to the face-to-face discussion environment.

Based on the results of quantitative and qualitative assessments of their experiment, Godat and Whiteley-De Graaf provide several important insights about developing critical thinking skills in a multicultural environment. Of particular note is the finding that appropriately designed and facilitated online discussion forums can facilitate the development of critical thinking skills for both students whose first language is English and those whose first language is not English. Another important insight is that well-executed online discussion forums can facilitate the effectiveness and richness of subsequent face-to-face discussions. The authors point out that presenting students with questions that are designed to elicit deep cognitive learning processes is a key factor in ensuring that critical thinking takes place in either online or face-to-face discussions.

4.5 Chapter 19, Competence Development in Entrepreneurship: The Role of University Education

Greet Fastré and Anita Van Gils discuss the importance of entrepreneurial behavior in the contemporary global business environment. Based on their review of entrepreneurship research, the authors identify six categories of competencies — opportunity, relationship, conceptual, organizing, strategic, and commitment — that are related to improved entrepreneurial performance. Although several of these and other competencies can be taught, most universities have not yet adopted the competency approach in their curricula. According to the authors, two notable exceptions are education sciences and human resource management, where the added value of this approach has been demonstrated in different learning contexts.

Using the six categories of entrepreneurial competencies as a point of departure, Fastré and Van Gils analyze the curricula of two universities (one in Belgium and one in the Netherlands), each of which have a different approach to entrepreneurial education. Their findings reveal differing perceptions between the respondents of the two universities regarding the importance of entrepreneurial competencies. In the Belgian university, strategic and conceptual competencies are perceived as more important; in the Dutch university, relationship and commitment competencies are perceived as more important. Fastré and Van Gils suggest these results imply that a competency-based approach to curriculum development should consider specific job, national, or cultural contexts. They further assert that copying entrepreneurial programs offered at international universities, instead of building curricula based on the competencies required for a specific job, national, or cultural context, could result in a wrong program focus.

5. PART V: USING TECHNOLOGY TO FACILITATE TEACHING AND LEARNING

Technology presents both opportunities and threats for educators and educational enterprises. Technology provides opportunities to develop new and innovative ways of addressing the learning needs of the world's population. At the same time, technology threatens the operations and/or existence of tradition-bound educational institutions and educators. Part V of the book provides some insightful commentary regarding the bridging of traditional classroom education and contemporary online education. Chapter 20 addresses the teaching/learning challenges of competency development via distance education; it describes a highly integrated approach for combining (a) software systems that support various aspects of distance education into (b) a single Web-based distance teaching/learning system that emphasizes competency development. Drawing on the concept of diffusion of innovation and other variables that influence teaching and learning in classroom and online environments, Chapter 21 explores faculty responses to adopting an instructional format that blends the classroom and online approaches. Chapter 22 describes the development of a project that combines different instructional technologies within a virtual learning environment to provide professional development opportunities to a specific sector of the United Kingdom economy. Chapter 23 focuses on the challenges of using a technology-based platform to facilitate redesigning a curriculum to shift from a teacher-centered approach to a learning-centered (or student-centered) approach to education. Chapter 24 examines the transferability of proven classroom methods for action-learning-oriented management education and development activities to an online action learning environment. The concluding chapter of Part V, Chapter 25, focuses on socialization cues as a possible explanatory factor in student test-taking performance in a classroom environment as compared to an online environment.

5.1 Chapter 20, LMS, LCMS, and E-Learning Environments: Where Did the Didactics Go?

Marjolein Caniëls, Anke Smeets-Verstraeten, and Herman van den Bosch initially identify three groups of software systems — Learning Management Systems (LMS), Learning Content Management Systems (LCMS) or authoring tools, and e-learning environments — that provide a specific kind of electronic support to educational institutions. Each of these systems has shortcomings that need to be overcome. The authors report on the design and implementation of a fourth generation Web-based distance teaching/learning system that overcomes the shortcomings of existing software tools and enables the application of competency-based learning within distance education. The system, currently named Sophia, provides an all-in-one solution in that LMS, LCMS, and e-learning environments are integrated into one software system. In other words, authoring tools and administrative tools are integrated within an e-learning environment where students and teachers interact.

Caniëls, Smeets-Verstraeten, and Van den Bosch observe that the adoption of modern technologies, such as the Internet, is often used to revitalize out-dated learning principles rather than to implement contemporary principles of competency-oriented learning. They have identified six characteristics, which together create conditions that enable students to develop competencies. These characteristics are incorporated into the design and implementation of Sophia. The authors also show how Sophia helps faculty members to develop instructional strategies that enable the translation of classroom education into Web-based education while creating opportunities for students to develop their competencies.

5.2 Chapter 21, Adoption of Blended Learning by Faculty: An Exploratory Analysis

Marc Humbert reports on the experiences of faculty members at the Grenoble Ecole de Management (GEM) in developing and teaching courses that flexibly combine face-to-face education with various forms of Information and Communication Technology (ICT). Drawing on its considerable experience in using ICT to support traditional courses, GEM made the decision to generalize and structure this experience and develop blended learning for all courses. Humbert presents the first results of the adoption of blended learning by a sample group of 37 faculty members at GEM.

Humbert's analysis draws on a conceptual framework that includes the diffusion of innovation model proposed by Rogers (1995), the Myers-Briggs Type Indicator (MBTI), and Grasha's (1994) cluster typology of teaching styles. Rogers' model identifies five distinct groups of innovation adoption — Innovators, Early Adopters, Early Majority, Late Majority, and Laggards — based on when they embrace innovation. Humbert analyzes the blended learning adoption process at GEM in light of these five categories. The MBTI provides information regarding the personality orientations of introversion and extraversion, which have demonstrated relevance to teaching effectiveness in online and classroom environments. Grasha's cluster typology reflects the typical educational orientations and strategies implemented by college instructors. The four clusters are: (1) the expert/formal authority cluster; (2) the personal model/expert/formal authority; (3) the facilitator/personal model/expert cluster; and (4) the delegator/facilitator/expert cluster. Due to small sample size, Humbert stresses the tentative nature of any conclusions regarding the explanatory power of the MBTI or teaching styles dimensions for the adoption of blended learning at GEM. Humbert also discusses barriers to technology adoption, as GEM's faculty perceives them.

5.3 Chapter 22, Digital Media U, the Sectoral University: Applying the Concept of a Corporate University to a Business Sector

Tim Cappelli and David Russell discuss an innovative application of the corporate university concept to providing continuing professional development education to professionals working within the digital media sector of the British economy. Research has identified diverse training and development needs in the digital media sector; these needs range from short just-in-time learning to longer-term professional development.

Dubbed Digital Media U (DM-U), the program, run by the Manchester Institute of Telematics and Employment Research at Manchester Metropolitan University, functions in collaboration with a group of major business partners and educational institutions. DM-U emphasizes work-based learning along with a range of on-line, instructor-led, and blended courses that are accessed and managed through a virtual learning environment. The innovative architecture of DM-U also provides various entry levels and pathways through the learning materials and resources; it also includes the learning and knowledge management systems that were developed by the program's project partners.

Cappelli and Russell discuss the research upon which the DM-U project is based and describe the progress made with the completed stages of the program. As a work-in-progress, DM-U still has much to accomplish. It is intended to become a self-sustaining venture that provides a model for continuing professional education that could be used in any business sector or subsector.

5.4 Chapter 23, Design and Implementation of Various Web-Based Courses Which Involve a Didactic Technique: The ITESM Model

Aurora González Turnbull, Rubén D. Santiago Acosta, and Blanca J. Garza Flores discuss the transformation of ITESM's educational approach from one that was teacher-oriented to one that is student-oriented. This transformation, which was conceived and executed as a means of helping to fulfill ITESM's mission, sought to assist students in acquiring and/or developing certain attitudes, abilities, and values deemed necessary for making sucessful contributions to the Mexican economy and society.

The redesigned educational model used at the Instituto Tecnologico y de Estudios Superiores de Monterrey (ITESM) required significant changes in courses, professors' roles, and students' roles. The redesigned courses drew on the educational resources and materials used previously but emphasized implementation on a technology-based platform that supported much different student and professorial roles. Professors moved from being the "sage on the stage" to being a consultant. This change was facilitated by a multi-phased training program for the development of teaching abilities that helped professors become proficient in using the student-centered learning approach. Students moved from being passive recipients of information to being active participants in the redesigned educational model. Teamwork and participative problem solving, along with other important student-centered learning activities, helped students to develop the desired attitudes, abilities, and values. The entire transformation process was facilitated and supported by an Education Committee; this committee also provides ongoing support for ITESM's redesigned educational model.

5.5 Chapter 24, Action E-learning: An Exploratory Case Study Examining the Impact of Action Learning on the Design of Management-level Web-based Instruction

Deborah DeWolfe Waddill describes her experiences with an experimental online course offered to a volunteer group of twelve United States government senior level managers. The experimental course modified an action learning course that had been conducted face-to-face in a classroom, transforming it into an action e-learning course. Action learning enjoys substantial support as an effective method for management education and development in face-to-face learning approaches. Waddill sought to ascertain the transferability of this proven educational approach to the online environment.

She uses an assessment method that is based upon Kirkpatrick's (1994) Four Levels of Evaluation, which seeks to determine the answers to four questions: What were the students' perceptions of the learning approach to the course? What was learned? Was the learning being used and if so, how? Did the learning have a positive effect on the host organization? Drawing on several sources of qualitative data, Waddill addresses these questions and concludes that action learning is an effective delivery method in a Web-based environment that incorporates asynchronous communication.

5.6 Chapter 25, Online Internet Testing: Lower Perceived Performance by Students

Wm. Benjamin Martz and Morgan M. Shepherd review literature comparing distance education with traditional, on-campus education and conclude that the research is inconclusive. Some studies show significant differences between the two environments and other studies reveal no significant differences between the two environments. One important category of factors in this debate seems to be socialization cues. Consequently, Martz and Shepherd explore the role that socialization cues might play in differences between students' performance in courses taught in an online environment versus an on-campus environment.

Rather than focusing on the course level, the authors focus on a micro aspect of the course — test taking. Specifically, Martz and Shepherd hypothesize that *due to the lack of socialization cues in the distance education environment, distance education students would be less satisfied with their performance on a quiz than would traditional classroom students.* Their paper reports the results of research comparing two sections of a graduate programming class, where one was an on-campus class and the other an online class. After controlling for a number of factors, very few differences between the two environments were uncovered with respect to students' perceptions and satisfaction.

6. PART VI: TEACHING AND LEARNING INSIGHTS FROM UNIQUE APPLICATIONS

Part of the excitement of innovative education derives from the variety of interesting — indeed, intriguing — applications that occur. Part VI presents five different unique applications of teaching and learning innovation. Three of these applications invoke the consideration of profound issues such as: knowing versus doing versus being; the educational impacts of globalization; and the application of business wisdom to society's social services challenges. Chapter 26 provides an intriguing analysis of corporate education, focusing on the needs to learn how to do something or to be something as opposed to the need to learn about something (which all too often is the presumed need in corporate education). The chapter also provides an example of corporate education that is designed to directly address the 'need to do.' Chapter 27 discusses five major globalization implications that are affecting how universities compete and cooperate in the worldwide educational marketplace, and describes how three educational experiments have incorporated insights that were derived from these globalization implications. Chapter 28 takes a model of organizational culture and cultural change that was developed in the private sector context, then adapts it to the public sector context of social services in The Netherlands. The chapter also describes a social services experiment based on this adaptation, and reports on the educational insights provided by this adaptation.

The last two chapters of Part VI take a bit narrower educational focus than the preceding three chapters — narrower in terms of addressing the course level as opposed to the program, organizational, or societal level; and narrower in terms of embracing less sweeping principles regarding human beings and their collective interactions. Chapter 29 explores the various educational challenges associated with integrating learning of a foreign language with learning the content of business courses that utilize problem-based learning. Chapter 30 develops the approach of enquiry-based learning, which builds on problem-based learning, and applies it to one instructional module in human resource management. The chapter also discusses how students may misperceive the true purpose of enquiry-based learning and problem-based learning with respect to competency development for career success in the contemporary business world.

6.1 Chapter 26, Bridging the Knowing-Doing Gap: Powerful Ideas for Innovative Learning Design and the Use of IT in Corporate Education

Sergio Vasquez Bronfman, addresses a vexing challenge in professional, continuous, and corporate education (PCCE) — namely, helping people to learn to how to perform their tasks and jobs well while working in their companies. The author presents convincing arguments that PCCE often focuses on knowing (*i.e.*, learning about something) rather than doing (*i.e.*, learning how to do something) or being (*i.e.*, learning to be something, such as a negotiator, a communicator, a researcher in the field of history, a doctor, a software designer, etc.). Vasquez Bronfman attributes the gap between knowing and doing to *infocentrism* and *technocentrism,* both of which misinterpret how people learn and, especially, how they learn to become and develop themselves as professionals.

Emphasizing that learning must link to daily activities, the author describes a corporate educational framework that emphasizes innovative learning design and the use of information technology. This educational framework is based on the work of well-known educational thinkers, and it helps to bridge the gap between what is taught in courses and the reality people face daily at their workplaces. Vasquez Bronfman also describes how this framework has been implemented in some online courses that were designed and implemented for la Caixa, a Spanish savings bank. Vasquez Bronfman concludes this chapter with a discussion of *practicentrism* — a pedagogical perspective for educational design that emphasizes what is necessary when one needs to learn "to do" something and/or learn "to be" somebody.

6.2 Chapter 27, Educating Professionals: Leveraging Diversity in Globalizing Education

Ard Huizing, Rik Maes, and Thomas Thijssen base their analysis on the premise that globalization will lead to increased cultural diversity in educational settings, and that this diversity can be leveraged into enhanced learning capabilities for all those involved. The chapter also theorizes that leveraging diversity can and will be used by universities while competing and cooperating globally. Huizing, Maes, and Thijssen further argue that globalization is a very broad issue that leaves ample room for individual universities, faculties, business schools, and sections to construct their own responses to globalization and, in that way, to help shape their futures.

In developing support for their arguments, Huizing, Maes, and Thijssen describe five categories of globalization implications for higher education and illustrate how each of these five categories have been operationally manifested in three educational experiments in the Section of Information Management of the University of Amsterdam. The five categories of implications, through which higher education institutions can potentially enhance their efforts to create a sustainable future, are: (1) a need to harmonize education structures, programs, procedures, and agreements across countries; (2) a need to meet more varied and changing learning requirements; (3) a need for generative learning; (4) a need for grounding education upon a social learning theory; and (5) a need for personal and social identification. The authors then describe three experiments — one from the Section of Information Management's regular programs, one from its continuing education offerings, and one from its derived programs — that have applied ideas and concepts from the five categories of globalization implications. Finally, Huizing, Maes, and Thijssen discuss the lessons to be gained from these experiments, emphasizing insights gained in each category of globalization implications.

6.3 Chapter 28, Social Entrepreneurship and Cultural Change: The Relevance of a Public Sector Experiment for Innovative Education

Thomas J. P. Thijssen and Fons T. J. Vernooij use Robert Quinn's (1995) 'Competing Values Model' to examine private sector experiences with innovation and to ascertain how they can be adapted to innovations in the area of social services for the poor in the Netherlands. The 'Competing Values Model' emphasizes the notion that successful organizations achieve balance among four types of culture: purpose, people, process, and performance. Using this perspective, Thijssen and Vernooij review evidence showing progression towards a better balance among the four types of cultures in Netherlands' social services sector. Unfortunately, these social sector experiments lacked an overall vision and strategy.

Using the insights provided by Quinn's model and the review of the aforementioned experiments, Thijssen and Vernooij then report on the first phase of the Zeeland experiment. This phase was designed around an overall vision and strategy of social entrepreneurship and the use of participatory research and collaborative learning in helping individuals who existed in a state of poverty and social exclusion. The first-phase results revealed the development of an organizational culture with balance among purpose (vision), people (role of all participants geared toward benefiting the client), processes (clear steps towards social integration), and performance (the improvement of the perspective of individual clients). Drawing on these results, Thijssen and Vernooij discuss educational implications in terms of the competencies needed for collaborative learning and the similarities between bureaucratic social service agencies and educational institutions.

6.4 Chapter 29, Integrating Language Learning within PBL: Principles and Practices

Raymond Ruijten and Nicole van Emmerik discuss the teaching and learning challenges associated with foreign language courses that supplement programs largely consisting of PBL-based content courses. The authors argue that Content-Based foreign language Instruction (CBI) is a viable approach for addressing these challenges. After reviewing the nature and models of CBI, Ruijten and Van Emmerik describe how the Breda Business School attempted to optimize integration of its language learning goals with the content learning objectives of its PBL-based core programs. The authors then describe the results of a study that was undertaken to ascertain the efficiency and effectiveness of innovative CBI courses in English, French, and German that are offered in the first year of International Business School Breda, which is one of the departments of Breda Business School.

The research study addressed three main questions: (1) How well did the innovative language courses link up with the PBL courses? (2) How well did the courses fit the functional needs of students of various linguistic backgrounds? (3) How well did the courses stimulate a self-directed learning approach from the students? The research results demonstrate that the implementation of Content-Based foreign language Instruction was a quite difficult process, with the desired effect not being achieved in at least two ways: (1) problems in striking the right balance between language and content learning objectives; and (2) problems in making the program suitable to the needs of all the students. Based on an assessment of their experience, Ruijten and Van Emmerik offer some key recommendations to other educators who may be contemplating the implementation of Content-Based foreign language Instruction.

6.5 Chapter 30, Any Problems? PBL Experience with First Year Business Undergraduates

Rysia Reynolds and Graham Benmore use problem-based learning (PBL) as the foundational context for introducing the concept of enquiry-based learning (EBL). They assert that PBL focuses on getting students used to finding solutions to problems, whereas EBL focuses on investigating phenomena, topics, or issues rather than problems. Based on this conceptual framework, Reynolds and Benmore developed and implemented an active learning approach for one instructional unit within the BA (Hons) in Human Resource Management at the Southampton Business School. This instructional unit was organized around six HRM issues: the historical development of HRM, the employment relationship, individual differences, organizational cultures, employee well-being, and managing people effectively.

The authors describe how their PBL/EBL approach was implemented; discuss, in the light of literature, the experiences of students and staff with the experimental approach; and explore the possibilities and implications of future development of this approach. The authors point out an important perceptual risk with PBL/EBL: even though students seem to be aware of some of the educational purposes of PBL/EBL, they may misperceive the central purpose as being the promotion of teamwork. Reynolds and Benmore emphasize the importance of getting students to realize that PBL/EBL is a method for enriching learning and fostering the development of numerous skills — including but not limited to problem solving, communication, decision making, and, yes, teamwork — that the students will need for success in the modern business world.

7. A FINAL HOPE OF THE EDITORIAL TEAM

The Editor and Associate Editors hope that the preceding overview of the book provides the necessary guidance for readers to place all the chapters into proper perspective regarding the challenges facing the modern teaching/learning enterprise as it prepares future leaders and other business professionals to face their own career challenges.

REFERENCES

Grasha, A. F. (1994). A matter of style: The teacher as expert, formal authority, personal model, facilitator, and delegator. *College Teaching, 42,* 142-149.

_____. (2003). *Harvard Business Review on Corporate Responsibility.* Boston, MA: Harvard Business Review Publishing Corporation.

Kirkpatrick, D. (1994). *Evaluating Training Programs: The Four Levels.* San Francisco: Berrett-Koehler.

Paine, L. S. (2003). *Value Shift: Why Companies Must Merge Social and Financial Imperatives to Achieve Superior Performance.* New York, NY: McGraw-Hill.

Quinn, R. E. (1995). *Becoming a Master Manager: A Competency Framework.* New York: John Wiley & Sons.

Rogers, E. M. (1995). *Diffusion of Innovations.* New York, NY: Free Press.

Schau, C., Stevens, J., Dauphinee, T. L., & Vecchio, A. D. (1995). The development and validation of the survey of attitudes toward statistics. *Educational and Psychological Measurement, 55* (5), 868-875.

Westera, W. (2001). Competences in education: A confusion of tongues. *Journal of Curriculum Studies, 33* (1), 75-88.

PART II

THE TEACHING/LEARNING CONUNDRUM: ISSUES, CHALLENGES, AND PROSPECTS

Chapter 2

"LEARNING ON DEMAND"

The Education Objective for the Knowledge Economy

Ken Morse
Waikato Management School, University of Waikato, Hamilton, New Zealand

1. INTRODUCTION

Improvements in information and communication technology (ICT) have allowed greater access to inexpensive information than at any time in the history of mankind. Development of the printing press in 1456 meant that, from about the year 1500 onwards, material contained in documents laboriously created by scribes could be typeset into books made readily available to all who could afford them. Thus, the information doubling period decreased from 1,000 years, prior to this development, to a mere 250 years. The increasing availability of written materials also provided the impetus to improve human literacy, leading to the commensurate development of widespread education systems. Later, development of the telegraph, the wireless radio, and the telephone provided a further increase in information distribution and thus availability, such that by the early 20th century the information doubling period had decreased from 250 years to less than 100 years. The post-WWII developments of television, Xerox photocopying, and paperback book publication further reduced the postwar information doubling period to a mere 25 years. The advent of computers and the Internet have seen that information doubling period fall to an estimated 10 years in the mid-1990s, with speculation that the next doubling could take as little as 5 years (Gupta, 2000; Editors, 1999).

The increased availability of information and increasingly reduced cost led to demands for greater literacy — the ability to read and enumerate — as both a social goal and an economic response. By the latter half of the 19th century, governments increasingly adopted a goal of universal literacy — a

M.K. McCuddy et al. (eds.),
The Challenges of Educating People to Lead in a Challenging World, 33–49.

goal that drove an increasing demand for education services. This social response had direct effects on labor markets, as literate workers became more productive employees, raising the economic benefits to societies of having literate citizens (Todaro, 1994). Commensurate with this social development has been the increasing number of university graduates — supposedly creating more learned societies (Jones, 2004). The social response by governments to the ready availability of information has put pressure on firms to improve the efficiency of not only the use of more literate and more learned workers, but also to more efficiently collect, analyze and use the ever more rapidly growing body of readily available information (Jimenez, 2000; Bloch, 1998).

Adding to the external pressure on firms have been the phenomenal developments in a wide range of technologies in the last four decades of the 20th century. Improved transportation systems (jet aircraft, containerization, interstate highways), which embody not only greater speed but also much improved carrying capacity, have been complemented by a quantum leap in information handling and complementary marketing data mining technologies that make a previously unknown quantity of customer-based market information available in vastly reduced time increments. One result of this technology diffusion has seen markets become increasingly globalized, such that firms must compete not only with domestic counterparts, but also with competitors from the far-flung corners of the world (Kotabe & Helsen, 2001; Hill, 2000).

Stemming from changes in information availability, transportation capability and marketing data, globalization has changed the face of the world. Globalization — the process of the world becoming a single place — has shifted the economic emphasis from comparative advantages based on resources to competitive advantages based on knowledge and innovation (Porter, 1990; Porter, 2001). Economic advantages based on low cost labor have given way to the necessity for nations, and firms, to more rapidly innovate to create new products, a continuous shortening of the product life cycle, and the increasing need for progressively more rapid innovation (Hill, 2000; Vernon, 1997; De Meyer, 1997). These changes have had a major impact not only on firms, but on managers and employees as well.

Beginning in the 1970s and gaining momentum in the 1980s and 1990s, the typical structure of management has undergone a complete change. "Downsizing" and "rightsizing" have resulted in flatter organizations with fewer levels of information flow and decision-making (Gupta, 2000). Increasingly, flatter organizations resulted in fewer managers, but more interaction between managers across structural lines. One of the most dominant resultant intra-organizational initiatives of the past decade has been the development of team-based work systems, quite simply because teams in general have provided firms with significant gains in productivity (Townsend, DeMarie, & Hendrickson, 1998). As a result of these structural developments, more interpersonal skills and an increasing emphasis on teamwork and co-operative problem solving in organizations has been required (Donnellon, 1996). With increasing importance, intra-organizational communication, teamwork, and interaction have become necessary to insure increased speed of response to ever more rapid environmental changes, decreasing product life cycles, and cost and communication efficiencies.

Improvements in transportation capability and faster communications capability, coupled with improved information handling capability leading to increased globalization of markets, have exacerbated the pressure on firms to maximize benefits from knowledge development and management responsiveness while minimizing costs associated with the administration of business activity. Moreover, gobalization is pressuring societies to adjust to the changed reward structure resultant from both ICT and economic changes.

Much has been written relative to the development of a "knowledge economy" (Norris, 2001; Drucker, 1998) — more than can be addressed in this discussion. However, the essential societal responses have been to increase the availability of technology in the classroom, and to expose learners to the technology of information search at an early age. Unfortunately, the responses have been slow, and such measures are unlikely to have a major impact until current learners become future managers — a long-term response (Butterfield, 2002). Recognizing this delay, many in the education industry have looked to use innovative techniques to prepare current learners — from the 18-year-old secondary school graduate to the adult re-entry learner — with the requisite skills to adapt to this rapidly changing competitive environment (Taylor, 2000; Weil & McGill, 1989; Brookfield, 1986). Our effectiveness has had mixed results so far (Vasquez Bronfman, 2004; Russell, Calvey & Banks, 2004).

Ready availability of information of myriad sorts, universal literacy, and technology improvements to rapidly access such information — a veritable information explosion — has resulted in the condition known as "information overload" (Gupta, 2000). Sadly, however, ready availability of information does not necessarily translate into more or better knowledge — but by its sheer quantity in fact renders development of knowledge, and its complementary distribution, both more difficult and more expensive (Porter, 2001; Drucker, 1998). Furthermore, the growing need for cooperation, information sharing, and collective problem solving and decision making has thus given greater impetus to the need for teamwork and the commensurate development of teamwork skills in the face of an expanding lack of complete knowledge relative to the issues at hand. Such development emphasizes interpersonal skills, communication skills and negotiation skills while highlighting the need for broad knowledge of firm capabilities and limitations, as well as customer expectations and requirements. This range of required skills continues to expand rapidly as knowledge/technology/ response all accelerate in today's globalized markets (Kidger, 2002; Nixon, 2001a; Nixon, 2001b; Wright & Burns, 1998).

Thus, for both individuals and firms to reap the benefits of participation in this vastly changed competitive environment, they must assimilate techniques which allow them the greatest flexibility in finding and then using relevant information/knowledge in the shortest possible time at the lowest possible cost. How to do this becomes the key issue for remaining competitive in today's environment — both for the firm and for the individual.

2. EDUCATION CHANGES

As intimated above, environmental changes are changing the face of education as well as that of the workplace and general society. Never before in the history of education has there been such an emphasis on learning and the ability to learn. Rapid adaptation to constantly changing work environments, changing social conditions, and information availability put a premium on knowing, but also on "knowing how to find out." Thus, knowing how to learn is an ascendant skill for success in both work and social environments.

The role of the faculty is to teach. This single fundamental statement has set the foundation for the academic delivery model that was the hallmark of the 19th and 20th centuries. From this foundation flows the lecture-based model, providing a platform for the sage-on-the-stage which was the standard delivery mode of "*teaching in the post World War II era*" (Latchman & Latchman, 2001). In this model, the faculty by virtue of their academic qualifications as faculty, are presumed to be expert and are thus given the responsibility to transmit this expertise to the learner. This model tends toward unidirectional communication from the teacher to the learner, with little required of the learner except to passively absorb the "golden words" of the sage-on-the-stage (McCuddy, Pirie, Schroeder, & Strasser, 2002).

But over the past three decades, this model has fallen into some disrepute, especially in light of the changes taking place in the environment external to academia. A large body of research beginning in the late 1970s, calls into question the efficacy of lectures and the resultant sage-on-the-stage performance. Beginning with Bell Laboratories in 1975, studies have identified through quantitative measurement that less than 11% of lecture material is retained by recipients. Citing this and other studies, Dryden and Vos (1993, p. 37) report "*We learn ten percent of what we hear, fifteen percent of what we read, but eighty percent of what we experience.*" A number of successive studies have repeatedly validated these results (Latchman & Latchman, 2001). Yet the sage-on-the-stage remains the predominant academic delivery mode.

Likewise, another literature stream is increasingly calling into question the learning value of that mainstay of student assessment — the individual essay/term project (Winter, 2003; Lea, 1999; Brockbank & McGill, 1998; Messer-Davidow, & Shumway, 1993; Barnett, 1992). As with the lecture mode of delivery, the unidirectional nature of the exercise tends to preclude interactive learning — the learner is engaged with the content of the essay, the reiteration of other's research, and the mechanics of one-way communication. That feedback is provided, regardless of the depth or quality of that feedback, appears to be of little value as it is not reinforced by further iterations of the research/writing exercise. Thus, this assessment is increasingly seen as a one-of-a-kind, all-or-nothing performance rather than a learning experience.

Further, yet another mainstay of assessment — the examination — is likewise drawing increasing questioning as a learning device (Dixon, 2000; Wiggins, 1992). There is increasing recognition that typical examinations, even difficult examinations, over-assess content at the expense of knowledge and understanding. These critical flaws explicit in this delivery model point directly to the implicit center of learning — the faculty. The presumption is that if faculty teach, students will learn.

The demonstrated positive result of this model is the "efficient" delivery of content with a finite resource base. This might be termed the "Fordist" model of education (Reich, 1993), in that the assembly line technique is adopted to improve economic efficiency. This has become increasingly viable as a small number of teaching resources can be spread over a larger and larger number of buyers (students), increasing total revenues and leading to an affordable education for all (Jones, 2004). However, included among the major drawbacks is the lack of dialog between faculty and students, especially interactive dialog. Thus, little in the way of reflective learning is produced; rather a reliance on repetition of practice leads to storage of information which, given the earlier discussion of information growth, rapidly renders that information storage obsolete.

Education literature over the past two decades increasingly shows that learning is achieved on a number of levels, and is dependent on the level of involvement of the learner in the process. Surface learning occurs when the learner is provided a rudimentary familiarity with the subject matter, similar perhaps to Bloom's taxonomic identification (knowledge) of "being familiar with" material (Bloom, Krathwohl, & Masia, 1964). The knowledge level of learning includes those behaviors that emphasize remembering — either by recognition or recall — ideas, material, or phenomena (Bloom *et al.*, 1964, p. 62). Deeper levels of learner involvement — more engagement with both subject matter and knowledgeable experts — result from discourse, the interaction of the three different learning components — the material, the expert, and the learner – similar perhaps to Bloom's taxonomic identification of "synthesis," defined as "a recombination of parts with new material reconstructed into a new, well integrated whole" (Bloom *et al.*, 1964, p. 162). Familiarity with content, coupled with discourse between actors leads to critique — the critical thinking expected of global leaders and practitioners in a rapidly changing world. Critical thinking relies on a combination of learner self-confidence and the ability to rearrange the three learning components into a body of knowledge compatible with the learner's world and world view – in taxonomic terms similar to Bloom's "evaluation," defined as "making judgments about the value, for some specific purpose, of ideas, works, solutions, methods and materials, involving the use of criteria as well as standards for appraising the extent to which particulars are accurate, effective, economical or satisfying" (Bloom *et al.*, 1964, p. 185).

Key factors in this analysis are the environment, the role and the engagement of the learner. That is, to move from surface learning to critical thinking requires the greater involvement of the learner in the process — at the expense of both the teacher, and the content or material. Deep learning represents a search for understanding of the underlying algorithms of knowledge in its general sense, rather than the accumulation of information for the sake of information (Biggs, 1987; Pask, 1986; Entwistle & Ramsden, 1983). Drawing on a wide range of educational resources to indicate a relationship between levels of learning and the cognitive framework for teaching and learning, Miller and McDaniel (2003) have highlighted the relationships as indicated in Figure 1.

The upper branch illustrates the actions associated with content interaction — materials such as lectures, readings, audio and video presentations, cases, simulations, and images — that engage the absorptive abilities of the learner. Content interaction is associated with materials and cognitive tools that tax the least level of effort on the part of the learner — reading, watching, and listening — all by their very nature passive activities. The focus of content interaction is building a repertoire of information that can be recalled for use at some obscure point in the future (Kolb, 1984; Bloom *et al.*, 1964). Content interaction is supplemented by lectures and tutorials that expand the relationship between discreet content and, while discussion may take place, that discussion is limited to the nature of the content and associative examples under tutorship of the sage-on-the-stage. Assessment mechanisms such as examinations and written essays — based on content retention and comprehension — provide the only active involvement of the learner, in a recall and restatement of the content role.

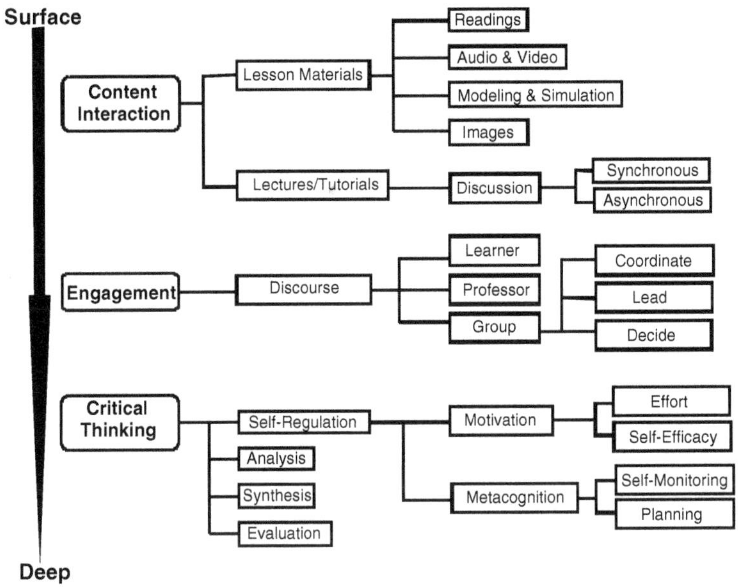

Figure 1. Cognitive Framework for Teaching and Learning

Turning to the center branch of Figure 1, more engagement is associated with discourse, which by definition includes interaction and expression on the part of all participants. In this engagement type of learning, the learner becomes an active participant in the learning activity rather than a passive recipient (Dixon, 2000). Engagement involves the learner in dialog, interaction, questioning, and hypothesizing in not only a participant role, but also in a leadership and/or a decision-making role in conjunction not only with faculty but also all other members of the referent group (Entwistle & Ramsden, 1983). Unlike content interaction, much of this engagement activity takes place at spurious and random times and in locations that defy the standardized scheduling of discrete educational activities (Mellander, 2001). Learning at this level is a spontaneous activity that does not fit well into discrete scheduling segments — either temporal or spatial. Thus, group dynamics and group interaction is a key component of the increasing depth of learning, requiring extensive participative effort on the part of the learner, whose assessment is based on both discourse and critical analysis rather than content interaction (Dixon, 2000). It is at this level that the faculty role shifts from that of sage-on-the- stage to that of becoming the guide-on-the-side (McCuddy *et al.*, 2002).

Finally, critical thinking emulates the deepest form of learning, as the learner is engaged with self in an activity of determination of right/wrong and acceptable/unacceptable to develop a synthesis of their understanding of the issue/subject. Much of the learning at this level is centered on the reflective practices of the learner, guided by an innate curiosity and/or an external environmental motivator to solve a problem which had not, in the past, been a part of the learner's experience (Gibbs, 1988; Kolb, 1984). Requiring the greatest level of self-discipline and self-motivation as noted by the repeated references to "self" along this branch of Figure 1, critical thinking results in lessons learned "for life" — the deepest of all learning. Assessment is through success provided by the solutions generated, and the experiences that result from this learning are cumulative, and are mutually reinforcing. (Tickle, 2001; Kay, 2001; Panitz, 1998).

In light of this continuum, the critique of the historical learning model stands in good stead. Much of the sage-on-the-stage performance is targeted at content interaction or the surface level of learning, supported by a range of content interaction tools and techniques. But little of the deeper levels of learning are breached by this delivery method. In an attempt to revitalize the content interaction learning model, technology has more recently been adapted as an additional tool. One of the newest changes to delivery is the robust and rapid expansion of "e-delivered" materials. At this content interaction level reside the majority of applications associated with e-delivery. The key advantages are the spatial and temporal freedom allowed the learner to interact *with the content* of the various materials, while the major disadvantages are less face-to-face content/interaction with the sage-on-the-stage and thus less discourse (Morse, 2003). While enhancing the breadth of delivery, and catering to an anytime/anyplace delivery scheme, this technology adaptation is little more than the next step in the efficient delivery of content. The conclusion that such adaptations are simply more efficient means to deliver content is justified if the content of many of the e-delivered materials are examined. The mode appears to be "electronic" revision of the lecture content, delivered in the lecture style (Kozma, 2003; Barnett, Harwood, Keating, & Saam, 2002; Bork & Britton, 2002; Bastiaens, Nijhof, Streumer, & Abma, 1997). The learner (seeker of knowledge) is little better off than with the sage-on-the-stage model, else the convenience of the delivery. Institutions, on the other hand, benefit from the breadth of delivery with similar, or perhaps fewer, human resources, as the marginal costs for such delivery is minimal, if not non-existent (Kozma, 2003; Barnett *et al.*, 2002).

On the other hand, discourse, by its very nature, involves interaction (potentially possible in the e-environment generally) and engagement (possible in the synchronous e-environment — not the asynchronous one!) (Morse, 2003). Moreover, it is appropriate to ask — how does this contribute to "critical thinking" — the practice of reflective contemplation — which is not a content dependant activity.

Not only does developing research in a wide range of disciplines increasingly substantiate not only the failure of the historical unidirectional teaching model, but it simultaneously points to the alternative center of learning — learners — which lies on the diametric opposite horizon, and has caused an increasing level of confusion, confrontation and even conflict as we attempt to reconcile education theory with practice (Barnett *et al.*, 2002; Panitz, 1998). As we move through the 21st century, it is clear that there is a growing tension between education, personal development, and training (Malik & Morse, 2001). The outcome of this increased tension is the emergence of a transition from teacher-centric to learner-centric education, an approach that has been referred to as the guide-on-the-side (McCuddy *et al.*, 2002). In this approach, learning is seen as a joint activity, rather than a production process as has been the case of the predominant 20th century Fordist model of education.

The educational literature indicates that learners learn in various ways — and there has been much research into learning styles. Some learners are passive, others are active, but as indicated by Dryden and Vos (1993), most effective learning is based on the various forms of experiential learning — action learning, problem-based learning, simulation and gaming, etc. (Morse & Malik, 1999). Early work in learning styles was published by David Kolb (1984) when he developed the learning style inventory (LSI) system. Successive works have further refined this concept to confirm and at the same time extend the conceptual understanding of alternate learning styles (Gibbs, 1988, Pask, 1986). More recently, extensive investigation of learning styles has been related to depth of learning and learning effectiveness relative to personality type (Tickle, 2001). This conclusion is based on the work of a number of researchers, including Marton (1975), Biggs (1978), Entwistle and Ramsden (1983), Biggs (1987), Pask (1986), and Schmeck, (1988), who collectively related the level of academic learning to the learner's motivation to learn, which is a direct input into learning style. They conclude that deeper learning is the result of the motivation and the engagement of the learner in discourse and evaluation of information and processes (Tickle, 2001). This corroborates Miller and McDaniel's contention (Figure 1) that deeper learning occurs in direct interaction with discourse and critical thinking — essential inputs to the process of problem solving. Thus it is essential to define, and then describe the concept of "Learning on Demand." The discussion now turns to that purpose.

3. THE CONCEPT: LEARNING ON DEMAND

As with any concept, a fundamental definition provides the foundation for the discussion. The earliest identifiable notation of this concept in the literature occurs in Panitz (1998) who suggests:

> "Learning on demand is the process in which technology is used to enable and encourage workers, managers, and executives to learn and acquire new skills while resolving the organization's problems, the learning process takes place in context and on demand" (Panitz, 1998, p. 19).

The key is the last phrase — in context and on demand. Another, broader definition is worth noting here:

> "Learning on demand is not just learning from pre-packaged courses but also of combinations of skills specified by the individual learners themselves, and at the times and places convenient to them" (Student post, MINT501B, October 2003).

Consistent with the conception of deeper learning identified earlier, these definitions highlight both the learner-centeredness and the contextual combinations of skills required by the learner. The keys here are convenience, need, and learner definition — polar opposite motivation forces of the driving factors behind the efficient delivery of teaching in the Fordist model of education.

The changes in our global environment, the explosion of information availability, and the pace of technological change have rendered obsolete the content-based delivery model of teaching. For the learner, the only future certainty is change: change that occurs faster and faster; change that is continual; change that is broader — encompassing an increasingly wider range of interests across a spectrum of differing activities.

As the foregoing has illustrated, the shift from unidirectional teaching to multi-directional learning has grown in both relevance and importance over the past few decades. But that shift is only a step in the right direction. If, as anticipated, the information doubling time can be as little as five years, and presumably even shorter as technology continues apace, a second step must be taken — a step which puts the learner in the driver's seat, so-to-speak. The upper branch of Figure 2 illustrates the problem by describing the process by which the learner identifies a learning need.

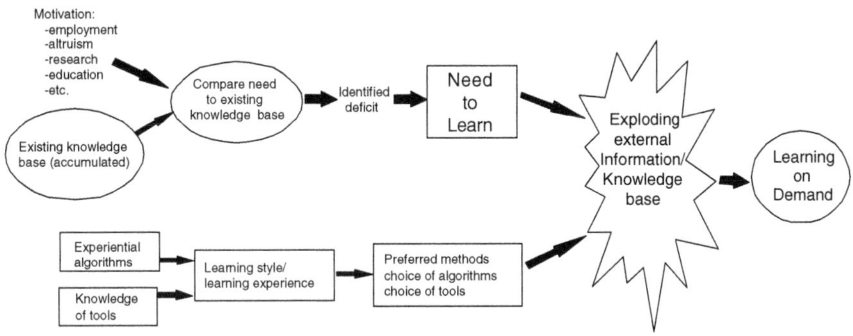

Figure 2. The Learning on Demand Framework

Beginning from a base of existing knowledge, the learner's motivation causes them to compare their existing knowledge base (what they currently know, including archival content) to determine if they have the appropriate information and/or knowledge. When this is not extant in the existing knowledge base, the learner identifies a need to learn from their external environment. For the learner, the problem to be solved becomes "what next?" — how do I gain the information/knowledge that I need — NOW!

Problem solving requires adherence to a series of well-ordered steps. Beginning with the sense that a problem exists (*i.e.*, lack of information or knowledge), the problem is identified and a framework (set of boundaries) is established to identify initial search parameters. Because of the immediate nature of the information/knowledge need, the learner then applies previously learned algorithms to the framework to seek the information and/or knowledge they need, after which analytical techniques (analysis) is applied to identify potential solutions to the problem, from which a choice of applied solution is made. This discovery must be made in the face of an unknown future — unknown in terms of both complexity and uncertainty (Barnett *et al.*, 2002). The lower branch of Figure 2 indicates the learners' accumulated store of past learning techniques, the algorithms used in the past, the heuristics which allowed those algorithms to function, and the methods which have been successful in the past in accumulating new information/knowledge. Those algorithms/heuristics are modulated by the learners' learning style and past learning experience to yield a preferred set of learning methods, algorithms, and tools. These are then applied to the need-to-learn as identified in the upper branch. These preferred tools are then applied to the exploding body of knowledge in the external environment — and are applied to attempt to assuage the learning need.

Because at the time the "need-to-learn" is identified, the learner must select algorithms, heuristics, and tools immediately, there is generally insufficient time to, at that point, assimilate new learning methods. Thus, the determination of "the learning method" has already been done when it is time to learn — prior to the "learning on demand" requirement. Therefore, the learner must develop self-confidence, resilience, openness, courage, engagement (and a willingness to let go), stillness, and reflection in order to become competent, capable contributors to their environment and the society — including employment — around them. Self-confidence is a self-reinforcing activity, an outgrowth of success, an outcome of positive reinforcement from both employment and the society around them. "A good learning program will give everyone an opportunity to make decisions, test their skills, take risks and fail — in a protected environment" (Mellander, 2001, p. 170). For faculty, the requirement is to challenge, reinforce, mentor, coach, and even cheerlead in the learner development process, building and reinforcing self-confidence in the process.

4. THE IMPLICATIONS

There are a number of key implications that devolve from the above observations. The first has been recognized by the teaching profession for the last few years, and continues to drive the development of teaching practices. That observation is that learning is less dependant on content than it is on the interaction of the learner with the learning process. We have already seen a number of colleagues argue that teaching should not be content-based, but should be an attempt to change the algorithms/heuristics of the learner (seeker of knowledge). This entails a shift from identifying and delivering "what to learn" to identifying and informing "how to learn" as a first priority.

From this conclusion comes the contention that it is not teaching, but learning that should be the focus of the activity of the teacher — that is, teachers must shift their focus from teaching to learning. Thus, it becomes increasingly important for the teacher to shift from the role of the sage-on-the-stage to the guide-on-the-side, as suggested in earlier research (McCuddy *et al.*, 2002). But such a shift has major implications for learners, for faculty, and for institutions regarding the development of learning.

Learning is a spontaneous activity — not easily amenable to scheduling either temporally or spatially, as it may not be limited to finite "blocks of time" such as class periods, semester hours, or terms, or even, perhaps, discrete disciplines or identifiable physical locations, all of which seem to be arbitrary divisions for the sake of efficiency rather than learning. Given the key learners' need as specified by the Learning on Demand framework — any time any place learning — educational programs should deliver not content, but should coach creative active learning and problem solving through collegial guidance; through coaxing learning within a friendly, learning supportive environment, both physical and personal. Further, given the dynamics of change facing learners in the future, increasing multidisciplinary and cross-disciplinary coaching/collegial guidance would seem more appropriate. The discipline is simply a framework; the subject is simply a touchstone — a stable point of contact. The choice of pedagogy should be driven by these characteristics: challenge, interaction, mentoring, and positive reinforcement, all of which lead to growing self-confidence. To accomplish this requires a shift in teaching attitudes, which would place much less emphasis on "covering material" but more emphasis on demonstrating and practicing the associated problem-solving algorithms/heuristics.

"When the right conditions are in place, ... learning takes place continuously and people respond successfully and effectively to new challenges and opportunities over and over again" (Mellander, 2001, pp. 165-166). As learning takes place continuously, it is important to develop the skills of learning, not simply the learner's retention ability. However, to facilitate learning, it is essential to match the skills of how to learn with the critical time component, such that those skills are already available to the learner when those learning skills are required. Thus learning skills must be available *when required,* not developed *when convenient* — a repertoire of learning skills that can be applied to accomplish results through Learning on Demand.

"Recognizing that students construct knowledge from existing knowledge, teachers need to find out what existing knowledge their students possess. Failure to do so may result in students developing concepts very different from the ones the teacher intends" (Eisenkraft, 2003, p. 57). It is thus the responsibility of faculty to not simply posit content *en masse*, but to develop learning skills individually. Of course, to engage in dialog, discourse, coaching, and mentoring takes more time on the part of faculty, a requirement in direct conflict with the efficiency requirements of the 20th century Fordist model of university education.

5. CONCLUSIONS

Learning on Demand is as much a result of the changes in the current information environment (speed, quantity, etc.) and the resultant information overload as it is the thirst for knowledge and understanding. Both give rise to the need for individuals and organizations to solve problems. Thus, consistent with the earlier definition, problem solving is the key driver of learning on demand. Therefore, programs of instruction based on problem solving (Problem-Based Learning, Action Learning, Experiential Learning) are driven by the need for learners to understand the problem setting and the problem-solving process (Morse & Malik, 1999).

It is the skill of "learning on demand" which offers future university graduates the best opportunity to succeed in learning organizations, to support innovation, and to develop competitive advantages, and thus successfully respond to the changing global environment. But for learners to accumulate this vitally important skill — to be able to make the model work for them, there must first be some changes. Building on the learning to learn patterns with which they enter the university, they must learn ***how*** to learn, how to build their inventory of algorithms, heuristics, and problem solving tools before they are needed, not after the fact. Thus, developing students' ability to "learn on demand" is the only acceptable teaching objective for the 21st century.

REFERENCES

Barnett, M., Harwood, W., Keating, T., & Saam, J. (2002). Using emerging technologies to bridge the gap between university theory and classroom practice: Challenges and successes. *School Science and Mathematics*, *102* (6), 299-313.

Barnett, R. (1992). *Improving Higher Education.* Buckingham, UK: Open University Press.

Bastiaens, T. J., Nijhof, W. J., Streumer, J. N., & Abma, H. J. (1997). Working and learning with electronic support systems: An effectiveness study. *Training for Quality*, *5* (1), 10-14.

Biggs, J. B. (1987). *Student Approaches to Learning and Studying.* Australian Council for Educational Research, Hawthorne, NSW, Australia.

Biggs, J. B. (1978). Individual and group differences in study processes. *British Journal of Psychology*, *48*, 266-279.

Bloom, B. S., Krathwohl, D. R., & Masia, B. B. (1964). *Taxonomy of Educational Objectives: The Classification of Educational Goals by a Committee of College and University Examiners.* London: Longman.

Bloch, B. (1998). Globalization's assault on the labor market: A German perspective. *European Business Review*, *98* (1), 13-24.

Bork, A., & Britton, D. R., Jr. (2002). The Web is not yet suitable for learning. *IEEE Computer*, *31* (6), 115-116.

Brockbank, A., & McGill, I., 1998. *Facilitating Reflective Learning in Higher Education.* Buckingham, UK: Open University Press.

Brookfield, S. D. (1986). *Understanding and Facilitating Adult Learning.* Buckingham, UK: Open University Press.

Butterfield, S. (2002). (March). *Highways and Pathways: Exploring New Zealand's E-Learning Opportunities.* Minister of Education — E-Learning Advisory Group, Wellington, New Zealand.

Class Forum. (2003). Student post MINT 501B, University of Waikato, Hamilton, New Zealand.

De Meyer, A. (1997). Management of international R&D operations. In H. Vernon-Wortzel & L. Wortzel (Eds.), *Strategic Management in a Global Economy*, 3rd ed. (pp. 419-429). New York, NY: John Wiley & Sons, Inc.

Dixon, F. (2000). The discussion examination: Making assessment match institutional strategy. *Roeper Review, 23* (2), 104-108.

Donnellon, A. (1996). *Team Talk: The Power of Language in Team Dynamics*. Boston, MA: Harvard Business School Press.

Drucker, P. (1998). From capitalism to knowledge society. In D. Neff (Ed.), *The Knowledge Economy* (pp. 15-34). Boston, MA: Butterworth-Heinemann Publishers.

Dryden, G., & Vos, J. (1993). *The Learning Revolution*. Wellington, NZ: Profile Publishers.

Editors. (1999, June 26-July 2). The net imperative: Business and the Internet. *The Economist, 351* (8125), 6-44.

Eisenkraft, A. (2003). Expanding the 5E model. *The Science Teacher, 70* (6), 56-59.

Entwistle, N. J., & Ramsden, P. (1983). *Understanding Student Learning*. London, UK: Croom Helm.

Gibbs, G. (1988). *Learning by Doing: A Guide to Teaching and Learning Methods*. London, UK: Kogan Page.

Gupta, I. (2000). *Information Systems: Success in the 21st Century*. Upper Saddle River, NJ: Prentice Hall International, Inc.

Hill, C. W. (2000). *International Business*. Boston, MA: Irwin/McGraw Hill.

Jimenez, M. (2000). Global Change, economic restructuring and labor market issues in Mexico City. *International Journal of Manpower, 21* (6), 464-480.

Jones, B. (2004). *Degrees For Everyone*. Christchurch, New Zealand: Hazard Press Publishers.

Kay, J. (2001). Learner control. *User Modeling and User-Adapted Interaction, 11*, 111-127.

Kidger, P. (2002). Management structure in multinational enterprises. *Employee Relations, 24* (1), 69-85.

Kolb, D. A. (1984). *Experiential Learning: Experience and the Source of Learning and Development*. Boston, MA: McBer and Company.

Kotabe, M., & Helsen, K. (2001). *Global Marketing Management* (2nd ed.). New York, NY: John Wiley & Sons, Inc.

Kozma, R. (2003). Technology and classroom practices: An international study. *Journal of Research on Technology in Education, 36* (1), 1-14.

Latchman, H., & Latchman, S. (2001). Lectures on demand in ALN: Enhancing the online learning experience. *Journal of Asynchronous Learning Networks, 5* (1), 85-98.

Lea, M. (1999). Academic literacies and learning in higher education. In C. Jones, J. Turner, & B. Street (Eds.), *Student Writing in the University: Cultural and Epistemological Issues* (pp. 103-124). Amsterdam, The Netherlands: John Benjamin Publishers.

Malik, S. D., & Morse, K. (2001). Trainer, mentor, educator: What role for the business faculty in the 21st century. In T. A. Johannessen, A. Pedersen & K. Petersen (Eds.), *Educational Innovations in Economics and Business VI* (pp. 273-282). Dordrecht, The Netherlands: Kluwer Academic Publishers.

Marton, F. (1975). On Non-verbatim Learning: I. Level of processing and level of outcome. *Scandinavian Journal of Psychology, 16*, 273-279.

McCuddy, M., Pirie, W., Schroeder, D., & Strasser, S. (2002). Issues in team teaching: Point and counterpoint. In T. A. Johannessen, A. Pedersen & K. Petersen (Eds.), *Educational Innovations in Economics and Business VI* (pp. 63-74). Dordrecht, The Netherlands: Kluwer Academic Publishers.

Mellander, K. (2001). Engaging the human spirit: A knowledge evolution demands the right conditions for learning. *Journal of Intellectual Capital*, *2* (2), 165-171.

Messer-Davidow, E., & Shumway, D. (Eds.). (1993). *Knowledges: Historical and Critical Studies in Disciplinarity*. Charlottesville, VA: University of Virginia Press.

Miller, M., & McDaniel, E. (2003, November 15). *Discovering a cognitive framework for teaching and learning that resonates with faculty*. Presented at the 9th Annual Sloan-C Asynchronous Learning Networks Conference, Orlando, Florida.

Morse, K. (2003). Does one size fit all? Exploring asynchronous learning in a multicultural environment. *Journal of Asynchronous Learning Networks*, *7* (1), 37-55.

Morse, K., & Malik, S. D. (1999). "Who's on first?" Exploring the concepts of problem-based learning, experiential learning and lifelong learning. *Developments in Business Simulation and Experiential Learining*, *26*, 303-309. Reprinted in Hugh M. Cannon (Ed.), *The Bernie Keys Library* (2nd ed.). Available from http://www.ABSEL.org.

Nixon, B. (2001a). The big issues — part 1, *Industrial and Commercial Training*, *33* (3), 89-93.

Nixon, B. (2001b). The big issues — part 2, *Industrial and Commercial Training*, *33* (4), 126-130.

Norris, R. (2001). *The Knowledge Economy*. Minister for Information Technology — IT Advisory Group, Wellington, New Zealand. Available from http://www.lnowledge.gen.nz or http://www.moc.govt.nz/itag/publish.htm.

Panitz, B. (1998). Learning on demand. *ASEE Prism*. April, 18-24.

Pask, G. (1986). Learning strategies, teaching strategies, and conceptual or learning style. In R. R. Schmeck (Ed.), *Learning Strategies and Learning Styles* (pp. 167-192). New York, NY: Plenum Publishers.

Porter, M. E. (1990). *The Competitive Advantage of Nations*. New York, NY: The Free Press.

Porter, M. E. (2001). Strategy and the Internet. *Harvard Business Review*, *79*, 62-78.

Reich, R. B. (1993). *The Next American Frontier*. New York, NY: The New York Times Book Company.

Russell, D. M., Calvey, D., & Banks, M. (2004). Business process, experience and memory: Educational approaches and technology tools for the global workforce. In R. Ottewill, L. Borredon, L. Falque, B. MacFarlane, & A. Wall (Eds.), *Educational Innovations In Economics and Business: Pedagogy, Technology and Innovation* (pp. 19-40). Dordrecht, The Netherlands: Kluwer Academic Publishers.

Schmeck, R. R. (Ed.). (1988). *Learning Strategies and Learning Styles*. New York, NY: Plenum Publishers.

Tickle, S. (2001). What have we learnt about student learning? *Kybernetes*, *30* (7/8), 955-969.

Taylor, K. (2000). *Developing Adult Learners: Strategies for Teachers and Trainers*. San Francisco, CA: Jossey-Bass Publishers.

Todaro, M. P. (1994). *Economic Development*. White Plains, NY: Longman Group, Inc.

Townsend, A., DeMarie, S., & Hendrickson, A. (1998). Virtual teams: Technology and the workplace of the future. *Academy of Management Executive*, *12* (3), 17-29.

Vasquez Bronfman, S. (2004). Linking pedagogical innovation and information technology to enhance business education. In R. Ottewill, L. Borredon, L. Falque, B. MacFarlane, & A. Wall (Eds.), *Educational Innovations In Economics and Business: Pedagogy, Technology and Innovation* (pp. 77-92). Dordrecht, The Netherlands: Kluwer Academic Publishers.

Vernon, R. (1997). Where are the Multinationals Headed? In H. Vernon-Wortzel & L. Wortzel (Eds.), *Strategic Management in a Global Economy*, 3rd ed. (pp. 3-18). New York, NY: John Wiley & Sons, Inc.

Weil, S. W., & McGill, I. (Eds.). (1989). *Making Sense of Experiential Learning: Diversity in Theory and Practice*. London, UK: Open University Press.

Wiggins, G. (1992). Creating tests worth taking. In K. Canley, F. Linder, & J. McMillan, (Eds.), *Educational Psychology Annual Editions*. Guilford, CT: Dushkin/McGraw Hill.

Winter, R. (2003). Contextualizing the patchwork text: Addressing the problems of coursework assessment in higher education. *Innovations in Education and Teaching International*, *40* (2), 112-122.

Wright, D., & Burns, N. (1998). New organization structures for global business: An empirical study. *International Journal of Operations & Production Management*, *18* (9/10), 896-923.

Chapter 3

THE MODEL OF COOPERATIVE CONTEXTUAL CHANGE

A Process for Implementing Problem-based Learning

Alessandro Biscaccianti[1] and Thomas C. Neil[2]
[1]*Baobab Architecture, Dijon, France;* [2]*Allen University, Columbia, South Carolina, USA*

1. INTRODUCTION

The contemporary and forecasted economic context is seen as experiencing dynamic change, which requires learning as a continuous endeavor. When confronted with a new context, which requires changing one's perceptions and behaviors and engaging in 'new' learning, people may believe they don't 'control' the change (Watzlawick, Weakland, & Fisch, 1974). Widespread and/or intense contextual change can destroy cultural, social, and/or psychological anchors. Under these conditions, individuals are more likely to continue habituated behaviors and retain biased perceptions because of the need to maintain intellectual and emotional stability. Maintaining a sense of stability is understandable. Stabilizing anchors are necessary if individuals, groups, and communities are to focus their energy on discovering and implementing positive responses to dynamic change (Watzlawick, Weakland, & Fisch, 1974). For the change initiator/ facilitator/teacher the issue is how to present and maintain 'anchors' that facilitate rather than hinder 'new' approaches to, processes of, and objectives for learning. In this chapter, Change Initiator, Facilitator, and Teacher as well as Learner and Student are used interchangeably.

The simultaneous experiencing of change and stability appears to be in contradiction, yet isn't. Dynamic stability exists in the physical realm as exhibited by a spinning top. Teachers and Learners must recognize that the paradox of dynamic stability does exist in the human condition. Individuals experience passive as well as dynamic change in some aspect of their life

M.K. McCuddy et al. (eds.),
The Challenges of Educating People to Lead in a Challenging World, 51–71.

even while retaining the majority of their behaviors. Weight gain is often a passive change, but once recognized the individual may institute a dynamic change to experience weight reduction. In regard to 'new' learning, dynamic stability is an essential condition for the individual and the system, because 'new' perceptions and behaviors must be substituted for 'old' ones.

Dynamic stability requires the existence of four intellectual and emotional anchors:

- The explicit identification of what is at stake in the learning process for everyone and the providing of persistent direction in achieving it (Fisher, Ury, & Patton, 1981).
- The co-construction and the co-optation of the ground rules, which are necessary for handling the interfaces between the elements of the system and enforcing the rules consistently (Axelrod, 1984; Grant, 2001).
- Systemic relationships, which are necessary for initiating and regulating actions and ensuring their use at all hierarchical levels throughout the organization (Hersey & Blanchard, 1972a, 1972b, 1972c; Hersey, 1984);
- The implementation of a solution-oriented mindset (De Bono, 1985).

This chapter will first discuss learning from a systemic approach and the establishment of dynamic stability to facilitate 'new' learning. Next, the establishment of a community of learners built upon the principles of the Model of Cooperative Contextual Change (M3C) is presented. Third, determining the learner's status in regard to autonomy and the accepting of responsibility is discussed. Finally, application of the M3C is presented through a 'living example.'

2. A SYSTEMIC APPROACH TO LEARNING

Learning initiatives often use instability, the dynamic of change, to induce people to modify their habituated perceptions and responses to specific contexts. However, as mentioned above, misinterpreted change, absent intellectual and/or emotional understanding, can generate fear, doubt or anxiety. When people are in a 'constricted thinking' state, they become intellectually and emotionally preoccupied with their instability. As a result, their energies are spent fighting against the forces of change and maintaining anchors that provide "safe harbor" against the vagaries of uncertainty.

If an individual feels confident, calm, and centered, she/he is more likely to support and engage in externally induced change initiatives (Anderson & Ackerman Anderson, 2001). Therefore, even as the individual is made aware of the need for learning (Anderson & Ackerman Anderson, 2001), conditions of stability and emotional safety are required. Theories of change usually present stability as the antithesis of change rather than as a complementary condition (Watzlawick, Weakland & Fisch, 1974; Haley, 1973, 1976). Table 1 shows the interdependence between the event of change and the type of condition (stability or instability) of the system during the change process:

Table 1. Impact of Stability and Instability During the Change Process

Condition	No Change	Change
Stability	Gradual Decline	Evolution
Instability	Disruption	Chaos

The systemic approach to change was developed, in part, by the therapists at the School of Palo Alto (Watzlawick, Helmick Beavin, & Jackson, 1967; Watzlawick, Weakland, & Fisch, 1974; Watzlawick, 1983; Haley, 1973, 1976). Two levels of change, *first-order* and *second-order*, were identified as individuals experienced the processes of changing their behaviors as well as perceptions of the context. A parallel can be established with the process of learning, because learning involves not only acquiring 'new' but also altering 'old' knowledge.

First-order learning occurs when a system experiences internal changes, regardless of number or magnitude, which alter existing outcomes. The supposition, underlying first-order learning, is that if a 'new' behavior is exchanged for an 'old' behavior, traditional values, norms, beliefs, and protocols can be retained.

Second-order learning requires a paradigm shift in the enactment of contexts (an alteration of the 'why' something happens), which is then reflected in the transformation of behavioral patterns, generating new outcomes. Second-order learning may be experienced as a discontinuity or a logical progression. As a discontinuity, its manifestation may seem uncontrollable, even incomprehensible, especially when responding to an external force. As a logical progression, the individual may experience a sudden illumination that to others appears as illogical and paradoxical.

Second-order learning concerns itself with the consequences of new behaviors in reference to the altered or emerging context. It does not focus on the presumed causes of existing behaviors, which are based on the historical context. Certainly, *why* has always played a central role in the history of science. However, from the transformational perspective the crucial questions are '*What happens now?*' '*How do we make it happen in the future?*' and not '*Why did it happen?*' (Watzlawick, Weakland, & Fisch, 1974).

Resolution of an issue may be attempted at the substance level of the problem, even though the issue is on the relational-emotional level (Watzlawick, Helmick Beavin, & Jackson, 1967). At the substance level, priority is given to the technical side of the learning, focusing on quantifiable issues such as the subject taught, the number of hours taught, the assessment's features, and the qualification of the teacher and of the learners. There is a tendency to ignore the relational dimensions that incorporate the emotional interfaces of the learner and facilitator as well as learner and learning materials (Arendt, Landis, & Meister 1995; New & Singer, 1983; Huston, 1992; Tissier, & Verne, 1989; Levine, 1997). Relational-emotional interfaces require investing in the communication, training and follow-up necessary to create the conditions for learning to become successful. Learners' inputs, initially required for establishing the conditions for transferring knowledge and skills, are neglected, which creates disillusion, skepticism and irritation (Weinbach, 1984). A technical learning approach tends to minimize the emotional resistance to new learning. As a result, the individual's initial behaviors and ways of relating are approximations of the desired ways of acting associated with the 'new' solution. However, because the 'player' is only 'acting out roles,' a gradual regress to the 'old' ways of behaving and relating is more likely to occur in the absence of understanding and reinforcement (Schein, 1985).

Second-order learning requires behaving differently in relationship to an issue, consistently and over-time. Therefore, the individual and the system must re-frame the elements of the evolving or anticipated context. However, context re-framing is difficult because the perceiver must step out of her/his 'point-of-view' and adopt an alternative perspective at both the intellectual and emotional levels. In essence, the individual must modify the mental model and the emotions associated with the context (perceived reality). Mental models are sets of implicit and tacit assumptions and beliefs that drive behaviors (Senge, Kleiner, Roberts, Ross, & Smith, 1994). Transformational learning begins with making explicit the mental model(s) used to frame the existing issue and its context as well as the supportive emotions. Articulation requires the identification of the information selected from the context, explaining how the information is put together to interpret the perceived issue, and the anticipated consequences from the selected action. A facilitator, using adroit reflective as well as initiating statements, helps the individual understand the enacted context, reframe it to match the desired stake and, as a consequence, modify the associated behaviors and emotions (Schein, 1985).

Re-framing changes the meaning attributed to the situation, and therefore, the anticipated consequences. However, the facts associated with the situation are not altered. Re-framing requires changing the conceptual and/or emotional setting or viewpoint in relation to which a situation is experienced. When a conceptualization is placed into another frame of reference, which fits the facts of the situation equally well, its entire meaning is changed (Watzlawick, Weakland, & Fisch, 1974).

The art of re-framing requires that teachers understand the role interpersonal communications plays in the transmission and sustaining of mental models and associated behaviors and emotions. The teacher elicits from the individual 'the way things are' to initiate transformational learning. 'The way things are' reveals the individual's underlying resistance to a new context and is used to reference the re-framing and introduce second-order learning. In a learning context, the teacher focuses on both the individual and the group. The teacher facilitates the individual's analysis of her/his role in the group. For the group, the analysis incorporates the interfaces with each other. The issues created by the mutual relationships and the interdependencies it generates are identified. The group focuses on the global functioning of the system and how it can evolve, not on each individual's behavior. Each individual is expected to reframe her/his specific role and interfaces in light of the new context. In this manner, the entire system is re-framed and each individual is provided with the support of the group as 'new' ways of behaving are adopted (Schein, 1985).

3. ESTABLISHING DYNAMIC STABILITY

As mentioned above, dynamic stability must exist to create the conditions favorable for successful learning (Desikachar, 1999). Dynamic stability is both a process and a state of being, which allows the learner and the learning group to modify their functioning while retaining and enlarging their identity. As a process, dynamic stability encourages alterations in behavior and relationships, which facilitate achieving the common, explicit stake (learning). As a state of being, dynamic stability provides the security of identity, even as the group and the individual evolve.

The Model of Cooperative Contextual Change, M3C, recognizes that when confronted with change, individuals, who are experiencing a sense of community, are more likely to commit to learning new ways of perceiving and behaving. The construct "community of practice" supports the "legitimatization of participation." Legitimizing participation allows the individual to engage in new behaviors under the support of others with similar needs, values, and goals. The M3C focuses on legitimizing participation through four sequential, developmental conditions, which are necessary for developing dynamic stability: *the Explicit Stake, Co-built and Co-opted Ground-rules, Systemic Relationships, and the Solution-oriented Mindset.*

3.1 The Explicit Stake

The Stake is the most valuable tangible or intangible asset that an organization, unit, group, and individual want to protect with their change/learning initiative. Understanding the criticality of this asset — the Stake — is essential in any change/learning initiative. The *explicitness of the Stake* sensitizes learners to their context and the potential consequences of the change/learning initiative with the goal of ensuring that the process of constant regeneration occurs. The process of constant regeneration is essential for any community confronted with complex uncertainty. Aware of the positive consequences of a successful 'change', individuals are more likely to accept 'suggestions' and actively seek 'understandings' that can be integrated into the learning initiative (Watzlawick, Weakland, & Fisch, 1974).

3.2 Co-Built and Co-opted Ground-Rules

Ground-rules clarify the interfaces between and among the elements of the organization, the philosophy underlying relationships, and the different roles and associated responsibilities that are required during the change process. *Ground-rules* are used to identify and manage the drifting of function, the rationale for trade-offs that are made to satisfy divergent interests, the decision-making process, and the way actions will be taken to protect the cohesiveness of the group (Grant, 2001). The process of constructing procedural agreement through a collaborative effort not only generates 'new' meaning (Wenger, 1998; Van de Bossche, Gijselaers, & Segers, 2004) but also a commitment to becoming a team.

Ground-rules define the way the actions are carried out within the context of the learners' group as well as the rules of engagement between the group and the external environment. To ensure the progress of learning, sustainable cooperation must exist within the group. Therefore, an essential *ground-rule* is that, in interacting, learners will treat each other with respect as persons while acknowledging that disagreement may exist in the activities linked to their roles in the learners' group (Rosenberg, 1999; Grant, 2001; Choo & Bontis, 2002).

3.3 Systemic Relationships

As the organization takes on 'new' perspectives, it must remain aligned as to its *Explicit Stake*. Alignment requires the existence of systemic relationships among the learners, which incorporates the regulating and initiating responsibilities assigned to the individual.

Regulating responsibility requires each learner to ensure that the activities, necessary to protect the *Explicit Stake*, are performed consistent with the Ground- rules. Regulating responsibility speaks to the contribution of each learner to the viability of the system (Anderson & Ackerman Anderson, 2001). Initiating responsibility grants to each individual the responsibility for initiating actions, which protect the *Explicit Stake*, as well as those actions, which improve it. If the learner recognizes a deviation from or a potential improvement to the *Explicit Stake*, she/he must present the findings and/or recommendations to the learners' group (Senge *et. al.*, 1994). The construct Drive-ship was developed to integrate, regulate and initiate responsibilities for individuals acting to sustain dynamic stability within the re-conceptualized organization. The Driver role adds meaning and long-term value to each individual's actions, because of the emphasis on improving the efficiency and effectiveness of the whole system (Anderson & Ackerman Anderson, 2001). A more complete explanation of Drive-ship and the Driver role is provided in Section 4.

3.4 The Solution-Oriented Mindset

As learners acquire new knowledge and skills, errors and mistakes in omission and commission will occur, resulting in an initial degradation of efficiency and effectiveness. Accepting this reality requires institutionalizing the right and the responsibility of error-based learning. However, if the individual commits repetitive errors, causality must be determined. If the necessary competence or relevant information is lacking, re-training or changes in information processing must be made. If the individual has failed to accept regulating and initiating responsibilities, ground-rule sanctions must be invoked.

The *solution-oriented mindset* is the required decision-making approach for resolving any issues and/or initiating improvements generated through regulating and initiating responsibility.

Adopting a *solution-oriented mindset* generates one benefit and three conditions:

- Individuals capable of distinguishing between presenting a solution rather than offering an explanation as to why the issue exists (Watzlawick, Weakland, & Fisch, 1974; Watzlawick, 1983);
- The offered solution must go through the process of co-building and co-opting (Schutz, 1958, 1982, 1984);
- The offered solution must meet the requirement of protecting the *Explicit Stake* (Fisher, Ury, & Patton, 1981, 1991);
- The offered solution must be ecologically optimal. An ecological solution promotes the well being of the community without reducing

the well being of any of the parts (De Saint Paul & Tenebaum, 2002; Fisher, Ury, & Patton, 1981, 1991).

Introducing the condition of dynamic stability and the four modules provides organizational members with answers to two critical questions. First, *"What activities will I, individually and as a member of a team, be responsible for within our 'new' organization?"* The assigning of regulating and initiating responsibilities provides the individual with the intellectual anchor that encourages discussing contributing to the Explicit Stake. Van de Bossche *et al.* (2004) suggest that negotiating the resolving of conflicted meaning through discussion brings about mutually shared understandings. Second, *"How will we get along?"* Each individual needs to experience acceptance and the psychological safety net provided by the community of learners during the process of change (Van de Bossche *et al.*, 2004). As the individual understands her/his value in contributing to achieving the stake within the new organizational context, the emotional anchor emerges.

Sustaining dynamic stability requires that individuals be responsive to the existing context and proactive to the anticipated/forecasted context. Therefore, the emergence of intellectual and emotional anchors increases the probability of accepting responsibility for personal and team actions (Anderson & Ackerman Anderson, 2001). A *responsive orientation* effectively and efficiently integrates the incremental change(s) required to resolve existing issues as well as issues emerging in the moment. The responsive orientation is a maintenance function essential for learning in the moment. A *proactive orientation* prepares for future changes that have an increased probability of occurrence. Proactivation institutes planning (forward thinking) and actions (anticipatory learning) regarding future contexts to decrease the probability of unexpected instability (Denison & Mishra, 1995; Collins, 2001). The proactive orientation is an adaptive function that reduces intellectual uncertainty and emotional anxiety, thereby facilitating continuous learning.

4. THE DRIVE-SHIP PARADIGM — ESTABLISHING AUTONOMY STATUS

The four conditions previously discussed generate the need for organizational members, who willingly strive to achieve autonomy. A person reaches a state of autonomy — when control of self is achieved and reliability is demonstrated across diverse contexts. The autonomous individual enters into agreements with others to achieve goals that are beneficial to the community, to the others and to self. The autonomous individual accepts the Drive-ship role, which requires leading as necessary and following when appropriate. In this sense, the autonomous individual is self-regulating but is responsive to the social relationships within the diverse communities she/he has membership.

In traditional change/teaching models, the *change initiator/teacher* assumes the role of authority, leader/manager, dispensing knowledge, directing activities, and establishing goals to direct reports and docile students. In this context, direct reports' and students' perception of their role is as passive followers or recipients. As a consequence, they may be reluctant to accept responsible for determining or having influence over what knowledge they require, how they are supposed to learn, or behave in a proposed 'learning community' context, *i.e.*, become autonomous learners. The M3C uses the construct, *Drive-Ship* to represent the mutual responsibility of all members, regardless of assigned role, in sustaining and improving the community. In regard to the Drive-Ship paradigm, each community member accepts responsibility, in regard to regulating and initiating activities, which ensure the viability of the Explicit Stake. As a consequence, any member may assume the Driver role based on the presenting context requirements, *i.e.*, a domain expert can override a non-expert superior. A Driver and Colleagues establish relationships based on 'judged reliability' and 'negotiated autonomy'. The Driver provides guidance to Colleagues in reference to the activities necessary for protecting the Driver's stake. The Drive-ship paradigm provides organizations with a coherent governance process, which offers a sense of stability during the experiencing of change. Drive-ship provides each member with an emotional anchor grounded in community responsibility and individual autonomy. Drive-ship answers the question of "What am I responsible for in regard to my own stake and the Explicit Stake as the organization evolves?"

Senge *et al.* (1994) suggest that 'learning' cannot endure unless sparked by the individual's own ardent interest and curiosity. This supposition contains two essential learning outcomes. First, the individual must experience a positive, emotional involvement during the learning process, which increases the probability of follow-through. Second, the individual, upon completion of the 'learning,' will exhibit a degree of competence, appropriate for the designated goal(s). If this supposition is valid, then judging an individual's commitment and competence during and after any change/learning initiative is essential. Within the M3C, commitment refers to a Learner's explicit and voluntary willingness to engage in the 'new' learning process and in acquiring the competencies that will sustain the 'new' community. The 'new' competencies are intellectual — discerning variations, patterns, redundancies, and relationships — and extrapolation and emotional intelligence — self-awareness, understanding of system dynamics, and reflective thinking. (Becker, 1960; Herzberg, 1959, 1968;

Kanter, 1968; Porter, Steers, Mowday, & Boulian, 1974; Salancik, 1977; Wiener, 1982). The Drive-ship paradigm requires the determination of two behavioral constructs, 'Judged Reliability' and 'Negotiated Autonomy.'

4.1 'Judged Reliability'

Judged Reliability is a qualitative process based on a Driver's ability, through appropriate interpersonal communication, to discern a colleague's commitment and competencies, which influence performance and outcome (achieving the stake).

*Judged Reliability = f (Performance * Outcome*
Where
Performance = f (Competence Commitment)*
and
Outcome = f (Commitment Performance)*

The Judged Reliability Matrix was constructed based on Barjou (1999), Hersey and Blanchard (1969), and Hersey (1984), referencing the influence that commitment and competence have on the stability of outcomes and performance. This matrix is presented in Table 2.

Table 2. The Judged Reliability Matrix

		Level of Competence	
Level of Commitment		**Low**	**High**
	High	**Cell 1** Performance = Unpredictable Outcome = Uncertain Reliability = Unstable	**Cell 2** Performance = Predictable Outcome = Positive Reliability = Stable
	Low	**Cell 3** Performance = Predictable Outcome = Negative Reliability = Stable	**Cell 4** Performance = Unpredictable Outcome = Uncertain Reliability = Unstable

Cell 1 — The individual's high level of commitment but low level of competencies generates unpredictable performance and uncertain outcomes resulting in unstable reliability. In this context, demonstrable behaviors are as follows: shows interest; seeks instructions on how to perform activities; and asks for help to improve performance. The highly committed individual will require reassurance regarding her/his contribution.

Cell 2 — The individual is interested in the activity's outcome and seeks to leverage her/his competencies to ensure an acceptable outcome. In this context, observable behaviors include the following: is enthusiastic about the activity and is loyal in relationships with others; is self-confident in accepting responsibility for goal achievement; leverages all needed competencies to perform the activity; and willingly engages others in achieving the stake.

Cell 3 — The individual is not interested in the activities, which may reflect the lack of competency and/or valuing of the stake. The individual demonstrates behaviors that reflect no interest in the activity, avoidance of responsibilities, and is focused more on difficulties than on opportunities and solutions.

Cell 4 — The individual is fully capable of successfully carrying out the activity but the low level of commitment becomes an obstacle to other's actions and performance. The individual's observable behaviors include: expressed self-confidence; seeking of freedom in decision-making and execution of activities; argumentative in presenting own ideas; disdains others' contributions; and work relationships are highly dependent on emotional state at any given moment.

4.2 'Negotiated Autonomy'

Although Judged Reliability is sufficient for engaging team/group members, the need to consider the importance of the Driver's stake is essential in an interdependent relationship. Task and outcome interdependence have been shown to significantly influence collaborative behavior in association with achieving superior task performance (Wageman, 1995). Group potency — the collective belief that the group can be effective — is dependent upon each group member's commitment to task and degree of self-efficacy (Van den Bossche *et al.*, 2004) in-conjunction with functional autonomy. The construct 'Negotiated Autonomy' was developed to clarify the conditions under which a Driver assigns and a Colleague accepts responsibility for completing stake-related activities.

Negotiated Autonomy = f (Judged Reliability Driver's Stake)*

Combining the four-cell Judged Reliability with the importance (Low-High) of the Driver's stake produces the eight-cell Negotiated Autonomy matrix shown in Table 3.

Table 3. Degree of Autonomy

		Judged Reliability			
Importance of Stake		Unstable	Stable	Stable	Unstable
	High	Low Autonomy	Limited Sufficient Autonomy	Limited Autonomy	Limited Sufficient Autonomy
	Low	Limited Autonomy	Sufficient Autonomy	Sufficient Autonomy	High Autonomy

The matrix indicates the Degree of Autonomy resulting from the negotiation between the Driver and Colleague. Within each cell, the Colleague and Driver agree on the behaviors and responsibilities, which will comprise their relationship.

Low Degree of Autonomy. Because accomplishing the Driver's stake is high, time with the learner is primarily spent organizing and structuring the learner's activities. The Driver's communication 'quantifies' and 'specifies' through a factual explanation of the duties, activities, and outcomes the learner must produce (Blake & Mouton, 1985). This structured approach is designed to shape the individual's commitment and competence. The learner's perceptions regarding commitment may be influenced through incremental success. Competence acquisition is supported through developmental sequencing of behaviors and near-time feedback (Watzlawick, Helmick Beavin, & Jackson, 1967).

Limited Degree of Autonomy. The learner performs the activity in a basic but more secure way, starts asking questions and seeks a better understanding of the context of the activity. The teacher decreases the time allocated to activity organization and monitoring. The communication of the teacher starts focusing on deep understanding.

Sufficient Degree of Autonomy. The learner is able to organize most of the activity and is ready to propose possible solutions. The learner needs more time to exchange ideas with the teacher and less help in the execution of the activity. The teacher focuses more on 'Socratic' exchanges and is available on an 'as needed' basis.

High Degree of Autonomy. The learner no longer needs help in the developmental sequencing of activities nor in the execution of marginal activities. In regard to essential activities, timely feedback and progress review protocols are established. Communication focuses on providing guidance to optimize the Learner's performance.

Limited/Sufficient Autonomy. In cell 2a and 4a, because of the unpredictability of performance and a high stake, the Driver negotiates initial limited autonomy with frequent feedback on progress from the Learner. If acceptable progress is sustained, sufficient autonomy is instituted.

Van de Bossche *et al.* (2004) show that constructive conflict negotiating can influence positively the effectiveness and the success of a learning process. In essence, Negotiated Autonomy provides for the Driver and Learner the opportunity to establish a mutually beneficial relationship that protects each individual's stake as well as the organization's stake.

Regardless of the Learner's Negotiated Autonomy, the Driver focuses on: (a) creating a context that facilitates performing the activity correctly; (b) reducing anxiety regarding performance failure through structuring of the activity; and (c) fostering learning by incremental success (Kotter, 1995).

4.3 The Autonomy Curve Protocol

The Autonomy Curve protocol was developed to illustrate how the Driver and the Learner might interact with each other. Table 4 details the features of the Autonomy Curve Protocol and suggests the types of possible interactions.

In any interdependent relationship, each individual plays a role and expects the counterpart to play a complementary role, consistent with the context (Watzlawick, Helmick Beavin, and Jackson, 1967). In the Drive-Ship paradigm, the Driver must be aware that playing the appropriate role has a high symbolic value for the stability and the soundness of the relationship with the Learner. The Driver must also provide the appropriate type of guidance required by the Negotiated Autonomy of the relationship.

Table 4. Driver-Learner Relationships

Features	**Relationship Low**	**Relationship Limited**	**Relationship Sufficient**	**Relationship High**
Drive-Ship Style	Teaching	Training	Delegating	Empowering
Role Learner Expects Teacher to Play	Instructor	Tutor	Coach	Mentor
Guidance Learner Needs	Direction	Support	Participation	Orientation
Type of Goals to be Set	Instructions	Sequential Steps	Tasks	Missions
Type of Control to be Used	Complete	Systematic	Focused	Random

5. APPLICATION OF M3C: THE LIVING EXAMPLE

One might think, that the decision to implement an 'innovation' such as PBL, which has generated documented, positive results and been introduced in a variety of educational venues, would be well accepted by professional educators. However, an 'innovation,' such as PBL, requires an alteration to the 'status quo,' which may generate conditions so 'disruptive' that the 'innovation' has minimal, positive outcomes at best or at worst is abandoned. Although the inevitability of the 'innovation' might be granted, individuals and groups may become embroiled in debating both the merits of this 'new' learning and the 'best' process for implementation (Weinbach, 1984). The M3C was used to improve performance through the introduction of new methodologies, in several business settings, two of them documented by case studies (Biscaccianti, 2004; Biscaccianti, Neil, & Renard, 2004).

Because the M3C has its theoretical roots in organizational change and was structured to incorporate constructs, such as communities of practice, the learning organization, and knowledge acquisition and transfer, it seems eminently applicable to institutions of higher learning. What follows is the description of an initiative to re-structure an undergraduate business program through the implementation of the M3C. The initiative is projected for five years with the first year devoted in large part to context assessment. Documentation occurs throughout the initiative for use in assessing progress and achievement of goals and to provide researchable case material.

In September 2004, one of the authors introduced *5 Years to Excellence*, a plan to achieve a "Sovereignty-Based Learning System" within a Division of Business and Economics. *5 Years to Excellence* incorporates a cascading change initiative from the institutional strategic level, to the operational division level, and then to the pedagogical student level. At the institutional strategic level, the concern is ensuring support of the institutional vision and mission. At the operational division level, the focus is on introducing the four modules of the M3C implementation process — Context Assessment, Community Norming, Contextual Drive-Ship Initiation, and Cooperative Innovation. Beyond the division level, the focus is on developing relationships that support the Division's stake within the university's mission.

5.1 Institutional Strategic Level

In October 2003, Thomas C. Neil, Ph.D. (co-author), met with the president of Allen University to discuss an entrepreneurial consortium that could involve Allen University and five other small higher education institutions within South Carolina. At that time, the president was not interested in becoming a member of such a consortium. However, he did express interest in the concepts and purposes underlying the consortium. In April 2004, the president asked the co-author if he would be interested in a position at Allen. After meeting with the president and explaining how the existing Division of Business and Economics could be improved, Dr. Neil accepted the chair position.

5.1.1 Context Assessment

The decision to accept the chair position was based on two significant factors. First, Allen University's president was seen as highly committed to implementing excellence into the university pedagogy. He had assumed the presidency three years earlier and initially focused on establishing a sound financial foundation. The president was now ready to focus on academics, in part for re-affirming accreditation, and was seeking professionals, who shared in and were committed to a vision of excellence. (In addition to the co-author, a new chair for the Division of Math and Natural Science was hired.) Second, the co-author was seeking the opportunity to demonstrate the validity of specific 'innovative' learning constructs and concepts related to a 'Learning System' rather than a traditional 'Teacher-Oriented' system.

Preliminary analysis revealed a small institution, less than 1,000 undergraduates, with five majors and a liberal arts foundation. Students entering the university vary significantly in quality of academic preparation and attitude toward learning. The existing business administration major had the typical course requirements, *e.g.*, Accounting, Finance, Management, Marketing, and Policy. The learning process was sequential only to the extent some courses had prerequisites, a historical precedent existed, and the sequence seemed to be 'this is what everyone else is doing.' Assessments of learning outcomes followed traditional models of objective quantification — true/false, multiple choices, and verifiable problems with simple solutions. Faculty within the Division of Business did not coordinate learning materials nor seek synergy by working with other faculty to integrate known knowledge and skills generated in previous courses. Business faculty relations with other departments, whose faculty were responsible for general core courses, were limited. For this reason, other departments' objectives and syllabi for the core courses were obtained for review. Because new chairs were appointed to other divisions, significant alterations in terms of goals, procedures, processes, and relationships are expected. Relationships will be established with directors of support services to determine service levels and requirements.

5.1.2 Establishing the Stake

The *5 Years to Excellence* plan, in draft form was presented to the president for review. The draft was then presented for review and discussion to the academic dean, the other departmental chairs and departmental faculty. Resources within Allen University were to be identified, *i.e.*, information technology as well as potential external resources. For example, Centers of Excellence in Teaching and Instruction, a national organization, has two centers within South Carolina.

5.1.3 Community Norming

Community Norming at the strategic level involves the other departmental chairs and their respective faculty. Initially, the goal is to establish a community of practice to facilitate an open discussion of pedagogical approaches. A goal of the community of practice process is establishing ground-rules regarding improving the entire learning system, both pedagogical and support.

5.1.4 Drive-Ship

The president had already begun the process of initiating and regulating actions that support his vision and mission. In addition, the vice-president of academic affairs (dean) and the chairs of other divisions began to initiate actions in response to the president's initiative. The co-author, through the Community Norming process, began identifying individuals interested in working directly or tangentially with the Business Division.

5.1.5 Cooperative Innovation

The existence of institutional as well as individual efforts in learning innovation were documented. New organizational practices regarding integrating student services into the academic process has begun.

5.2 Division of Business — Operational Level

5.2.1 Context Assessment

Business faculty identified concerns with as well as strengths of the division, *i.e.*, personal maturation and academic foundation preparation. Wide variation existed in the academic preparation of incoming students. At the institutional level, student attitudes toward learning and the responsibility it entails are a developmental area. The majority of students come from families lacking a history of participation in higher education. The size of classes, the culture being developed by the president, and the faculty's desire for a quality program are potential positive factors. Information on each business course is collected: existing syllabi, examples of assessment instruments, required textbooks, required reading materials, core concepts-constructs-theories, and student outcome results.

5.2.2 Establishing the Stake

Introducing the *5 Years to Excellence* plan at the strategic level began the process of stake identification. The Stake for the Division of Business consists of providing a learning system that enables students to achieve *Personal and Professional Sovereignty*, the acceptance of responsibility for self-learning.

5.2.3 Community Norming

The faculty is being asked to develop ground rules, which support the 'new' learning system and its Stake. The 'new' system is based in part on the principles of PBL and other interactive learning models. Additional components include but are not limited to student portfolio assessment, peer review of teaching, developmental sequencing of courses, integration of learning materials, and cross-functional referencing. A goal for the Division's faculty is to become a Learning Community and serve as a model for the other divisions.

5.2.4 Drive-Ship

Initially, the chair will direct the implementation process as the identification of reliability among the faculty continues. The chair expects that the relationship with the faculty will result in their accepting the role of Driver and will engage the students in the same process of Drive-ship. Since the chair will be teaching courses, observations of student attitudes and behaviors in regard to accepting personal and professional responsibility for learning can be made.

5.2.5 Cooperative Innovation

Division faculty will be encouraged and supported in collaborative efforts to achieve the Stake through novel ideas. External learning innovators will be invited on campus to engage faculty.

5.2.6 Pedagogical Student Level

Faculty will be asked to assume the role of Driver with the students. The principles of M3C and Drive-Ship will be used to shape the process of integration and follow students through their academic career. The students are expected to apply the 'new' knowledge and skills in their interactions with their peers, the faculty, and the administration.

6. CONCLUSION

Is the M3C and the Drive-Ship paradigm a viable model for initiating and sustaining learning innovation into a formal learning system? Based on the first year results as described above, the initiating stage was successful. The Living Example documents (a) the implementation of *5 Years to Excellence* within the Division of Business and Economics and (b) consequences resulting from conditions and changes in other parts of the university. For example, in teaching 1st year and 4th year students during the Fall 2004 semester, the co-author discovered a lack of foundation skills in reading comprehension, quantitative analysis, and systems thinking. These findings must be considered in regard to implementing all elements of the 5-year plan. A team consisting of the dean and the chairs of Math and Natural Science, Humanities and Social Science, and Business and Economics began meeting on a regular basis to discuss a program to improve the General Education core courses, beginning in the fall 2005.

In regard to sustaining the M3C change initiative, a decision made in April 2005 is enlightening. The existing dean asked to return to the position of chair, Division of Education, because it required guidance during re-affirmation of accreditation. The president selected a new vice president of academic affairs (dean) from outside the University. The new dean stated his emphasis was on preparation for re-affirming accreditation and stopped all initiatives. This Living Example demonstrates the influence "new," key decision-makers can have on existing organizational change initiatives. In this regard, the Division of Business and Economics' 5-year plan is on hold until the new dean presents his own strategic plan.

The M3C has demonstrated the capacity to establish a condition of dynamic stability, which encourages the individual to accept responsibility for protecting both the organization's as well as her/his stake. The M3C requires the Driver of the change initiative to be explicit in describing the nature of the change process and the benefits and costs that will accrue to the individual, the team, group, and the organization. In addition, the Driver must accept the necessity of establishing the individual's emotional security.

Emotional security evolves through the co-building and co-opting of ground-rules, systemic relationships, and collaborative efforts to protect the stake, which delineate the individual's future role in the changing organization. By satisfying the intellectual and emotional needs of the individual, the success of the change initiative is enhanced.

REFERENCES

Anderson, D., & Ackerman Anderson, L. (2001). *Beyond Change Management.* San Francisco, CA: Jossey-Bass, Pfeiffer.

Arendt, C. H., Landis, R. M., & Meister, T. B. (1995). The human side of change — part 4, *IEE Solutions*, May, 22-26.

Axelrod, R. (1984). *The Evolution of Cooperation.* New York, NY: Basic Books.

Barjou, B. (1999). *Manager par Projet: Methodes et Comportements pour Animer Hors Statut Hierarchique* (2nd ed.). Paris: ESF Editeur.

Becker, H. S. (1960). Notes on the concept of commitment. *American Journal of Sociology, 66* (1), 32-40.

Biscaccianti, A. (2004). Foundations and Implementation of the Model of Cooperative Contextual Change and its Impact on Executives and Team's Performance. DBA Dissertation, International School of Management, Paris.

Biscaccianti, A., Neil, T. C., & Renard, P. (2004). The model of cooperative contextual change: Establishing the conditions for continuum improvement. Presented at Educational Innovation in Economics and Business XI, Maastricht, The Netherlands.

Blake, R. R., & Mouton, J. S. (1985). *The Managerial Grid III: The Key to Leadership Excellence.* Houston, TX: Gulf Publishing Company.

Collins, J. (2001). Good to great. *Fast Company*, October (51), 90-100.

Choo, C. W., & Bontis, N. (2002). Knowledge, intellectual capital, and strategy: Themes and tensions. In C. W. Choo & N. Bontis (Ed.), *The Strategic Management of Intellectual Capital and Organizational Knowledge* (pp. 3-22). New York, NY: Oxford University Press.

De Bono, E. (1985). *Six Thinking Hats.* Toronto, Ontario: Key Porter Books Ltd.

De Saint Paul, J., & Tenenbaum, S. (2002). *L'Esprit de la Magie. La Programmation Neuro-Linguistique. Relation à soi, relation à l'autre, relation au monde.* Paris: InterEditions-Dunod.

Denison, D. R., & Mishra, A. K. (1995). Toward a theory of organizational culture and effectiveness. *Organization Science: A Journal of the Institute of Management Sciences, 6* (2), 204-224.

Desikachar, K. (1999). *Stability in Change: Notes of the seminar.* Reims, France: Association Viniyoga.

Fisher, R., Ury, W., & Patton, B. (1981). *Getting to Yes.* Boston, MA: Houghton Mifflin Company.

Fisher, R., Ury, W., & Patton, B. (1991). *Getting to Yes.* Boston, MA: Houghton Mifflin Company.

Grant, R. M. (2001). Knowledge and organization. In I. Nonaka & D. J. Teece (Eds.), *Managing Industrial Knowledge* (pp. 145-169). London: Sage Publications.

Haley, J. (1973). *Uncommon Therapy.* New York, NY: Norton.

Haley, J. (1976). *Problem-Solving Therapy, New Strategies for Effective Family Therapy*. San Francisco, CA: Jossey-Bass.

Hersey, P. (1984). *The Situational Leader*. Escondido, CA: Center for Leadership Studies.

Hersey, P., & Blanchard, K. H. (1969). Life cycle theory of leadership. *Training and Development Journal*, May, 26-34.

Hersey, P., & Blanchard, K. H. (1972a). The Management of Change, Part1. *Training and Development Journal*, January, 6-10.

Hersey, P., & Blanchard, K. H. (1972b). The Management of Change, Part2. *Training and Development Journal*, February, 20-24.

Hersey, P., Blanchard, K. H. (1972c). The Management of Change, Part3. *Training and Development Journal*, March, 28-33.

Herzberg, F. (1968). *Work and the Nature of Man*. London: Staples Press (reprinting of World Publishing Co., New York, NY, 1966).

Herzberg, F. (1959). *Motivation to Work*. New York, NY: John Wiley & Sons.

Huston, L. A. (1992). Using total quality to put strategic intent to motion. *Planning Review, 20* (5), 21-23.

Kanter, R. M. (1968). Commitment and social organization: A study of commitment mechanisms in utopian communities. *American Sociological Review, 33* **(4)**, 499-517.

Kotter, J. P. (1995). Leading change: Why transformation efforts fail. *Harvard Business Review, 73* (2), 59-67.

Levine, G. (1997). Forging successful resistance. *Bobbin, 39* (1), 164-166.

New, J. R., & Singer, D. D. (1983). Understanding why people reject new ideas helps to convert resistance into acceptance. *Industrial Engineering, 15* (5), 50-57.

Porter, L. W., Steers, R. M., Mowday, R. T., & Boulian, P. V. (1974). Organizational commitment, job satisfaction and turnover among psychiatric technicians. *Journal of Applied Psychology, 59* **(5),** 603-609.

Rosenberg, M. (1999). *Nonviolent Communication: A Language of Compassion*. Del Mar, CA: PuddlerDancer Press.

Salancik, G. R. (1977). *Commitment is too easy*. Organizational Dynamics, Summer, 62-80.

Schein, E. (1985). *Organizational Culture and Leadership*. San Francisco, CA: Jossey-Bass.

Schutz, W. C. (1958). *FIRO: A Three Dimensional Theory of Interpersonal Behavior*. New York, NY: Holt Rinehart & Winston.

Schutz, W. C. (1982). *Profound Simplicity*. San Diego, CA: Learning Concepts.

Schutz, W. C. (1984). *The Truth Option: A Practical Technology for Human Affairs*. Berkeley, CA: Ten Speed Press.

Senge, P. M., Kleiner, A., Roberts, C., Ross, R. R., & Smith, B. J. (1994). *The Fifth Discipline Fieldbook: Strategies and Tools for Building a Learning Organization*. New York, NY: Doubleday.

Tissier, D. & Verne, E. (1989). *Management Situationnel 1. Les Voies de l'Autonomie et de la Délégation*. Paris: INSEP.

Van den Bossche, P., Gijselaers, W. H., & Segers, M. S. R. (2004). Effects of social factors on shared cognition and teamwork in collaborative learning environments, presented at the Annual Meeting of the American Educational Research Association, San Diego, CA, April: 12-26.

Wageman, R. (1995). Interdependence and group effectiveness *Administrative Science Quarterly, 40* (1), 145-180.

Weinbach, R. W. (1984). Implementing change: Insights and strategies of the supervisor. *Social Work, 29* (3), 282-286.

Wenger, E. C. (1998). *Communities of Practice: Learning, Meaning, and Identity*. Cambridge, UK: Cambridge University Press.

Wiener, Y. (1982). Commitment in organizations: A normative view. *Academy of Management Review*, *7* (3), 418-428.

Watzlawick, P. (1983). *The Situation is Hopeless but not Serious (The Pursuit of Unhappiness)*. New York, NY: Norton.

Watzlawick, P., Helmick Beavin, J., & Jackson, D. D. (1967). *Pragmatics of Human Communication. A Study on Interactional Patterns, Pathologies, and Paradoxes*. New York, NY: W.W. Norton and Company.

Watzlawick, P., Weakland, J., & Fisch, R. (1974). *Change: Principles of Problem Formation and Problem Resolution*. New York, NY: W.W. Norton and Company.

Chapter 4

DEALING WITH DILEMMAS IN CONTEMPORARY HIGHER EDUCATION

Universitat Oberta de Catalunya

Anne-Marie De Jonghe
University of Southampton, CHEMPAS School of Management, Highfield Southampton, UK

1. DILEMMAS IN CONTEMPORARY HIGHER EDUCATION

Contemporary Higher Education Institutions (HEI) are confronted with several dilemmas. In this chapter we will discuss two of these dilemmas.

1.1 First Dilemma: Preservation of Cultural Heritage versus Constructivist Learning

One of these dilemmas is the tension between being a professional organization, which protects academic values according to disciplinary rules, and being a modern, constructivist organization with a focus on learning in which the relationship with the student is central.

One side of the dilemma implies a professor-centered view and a focus on research. Teaching often comes in second place. In traditional education, the teacher is the central agent or even the "authority." He controls both the content of the subject and the way it is taught. Teaching often means "lecturing." The student plays a passive role and is expected to absorb and reproduce what has been taught.

The other side of the dilemma refers to the growing importance of the student and becomes evident when looking at four important trends affecting the academic world: the concept of the student as a customer, the increasing

M.K. McCuddy et al. (eds.),
The Challenges of Educating People to Lead in a Challenging World, 73–93.

focus on learning, the changing role of the professor, and the changing concept of the student.

Traditional universities are struggling with the "customer" concept. Is the student a customer or a client for learning services? Jarvis, Holford, and Griffin (2003) observe that education is no longer a welfare provision, or a meeting of social needs. Education has to be seen as a road to wealth production. This can be interpreted in two ways. Education can be seen as a commodity to be sold by the provider (courses for sale). Education can also lead to economic wealth for the consumer (a way to the job market). It has become a matter of market provision.

According to Naudé (2004) the student is often a "consumer" and companies and larger networks are the real "customer." Armstrong (2003) suggests a student-as-client model where the university is like a professional firm and the student as a client paying a fee to receive the service. Following Webster's *Third New International Dictionary* (1986), he distinguishes between a customer "purchasing a commodity or a service" and a client "engaging the professional advice or services of another."

While this discussion is still going on and partly as a result of it, many HEI are changing their approach from being faculty centered to being learning centered. This focus on the learning process of the student is not only a consequence of a more market-oriented approach, but also based on new insights about learning processes. It challenges the traditional professor-student relationships. The classic paradigm of teaching as lecturing is being questioned. Traditional professors are not trained in the modern visions on student learning processes. De Wolf (2001) points out that respected experts in a particular field are not always good teachers. Those involved in teaching will have to learn new techniques and tools.

One of these techniques is the use of learning contracts. Jarvis, Holford, and Griffin (2003, p. 105) point out that contracts could be seen as a mechanism "for introducing a measure of order and predictability" in a fast changing world, which is unpredictable and risky because it is organized on a market basis. They are the basis of the relationship between two parties.

The use of "contracts" in learning processes originated in self-directed learning. Knowles (1986), an influential North-American writer on adult education, introduced the concept of a learning plan as a basis for self-directed learning. It has become common practice in many types of education (adult education, higher education, professional education, training, etc.).

What will be the role of the expert if the learner will play a more active role? The new focus requires familiarity with the goals of the students and assessment of their needs (or "wants" if one only sees the pressures from the market). Processes for student coaching become necessary, curricula and course content have to be adapted, and evaluation processes have to be reviewed. Faculty members will become coaches, advisors, and designers of the learning experience, the processes, and the environments. Students will become active learners, responsible for their own learning and outcomes (Kallenberg, Van der Grijspaarde, Ter Braak, & Van Horzen, 2000). In his book *The Rise of the Network Society*, Castells (1996) emphasizes the continuing importance for the development of learners of the close personal contact with experienced experts, even in a network society.

Traditionally, universities have been focusing on the professor as a researcher (research universities) and/or as a teacher (teaching universities) and not so much on the student and his needs. Several authors (Griffin, 1987, Jarvis, Holford, and Griffin, 2003) state that the meaning of "needs" has changed. It indicates no longer "a generalized need of potential students" but it refers to "special needs" of different groups in society. The European Community's policy on life-long learning emphasizes social inclusion and hopes that special needs will be fulfilled through good governance.

Increasingly universities will have to take into account that student populations are changing and becoming older (Bourgeois, Duke, Guyot, & Merrill, 1999). Trends in student population show that more and more students are not coming straight from high school any more. A major redefinition of the concept of "college student" is taking place. In the USA, only 17 % of the traditional college students are between 18 and 22 years old (Duderstadt, 2000). Many students are working adults responsible for earning their own money and for whom relocating to a campus is difficult and expensive.

Methods for adult learning will have to be applied not only for the traditional occasional adult learner but also for the changing (older, with special needs) student population and the life-long learners. Adult learning is typically by trial and error, in dialogue. Web-based learning makes it possible to structure one's own learning process. It allows non-traditional instruction via a new medium.

1.2 Second Dilemma: Academic Community versus Flexible, Life-long Learning

Another dilemma is the tension between campus teaching, which enables the creation of academic communities and distance teaching which offers the opportunity to reach a more diverse student population (*e.g.*, working students, students with a dysfunction) but where it seems more difficult to create a community.

One of the classic boundaries of the traditional university is the campus. A conventional university campus has classrooms, libraries, laboratories and lecture rooms. The campus model arose out of the need to regroup the intellectual sources. Throughout the history of the universities the campus has been important, although there are different types of campuses (*i.e.*, city campuses, multi-campuses, secluded campuses).

Some argue that a real campus has some advantages like social control since it permits checking if students are doing their work personally. A campus has also a symbolic role. A campus allows for face-to-face interaction and group socialization; it is a community of practice with informal, implicit knowledge going around; it is a "rite of passage" before work and family responsibilities (based on Cornford & Pollock, 2003, pp. 38-51).

Taking a cultural approach to learning, the psychologist Crook (2002) states that the temporal organization of study, the place of study, the student's participation in a community, and his learning materials are four aspects of the traditional culture of HEI. Accordingly, he believes that the virtualization of universities leads to a disturbance of these four aspects.

Crook (2002) suggests that the functional geography of a campus may help students to focus on studying. It makes it easier to differentiate from recreational interests while a computer offers the possibility for recreation and study. However, students studying at universities located in cities have always dealt with the tension between recreation and study. The coming generations of students, familiar with computers from their childhood on, are also used to multi-tasking.

In order to have the advantages of a real campus, lateral interaction between the learners ("the actors") is necessary. Cornford and Pollock (2003) apply concepts from actors' network theory in order to reflect on online education in a new way. In their view, online education can be seen as the construction of an actor network: the binding of people (lecturers, authors, technicians, librarians, graphic artists, publishers, assessment experts, administrators, students), text (textbooks, course lists, examination papers), and machines and other physical objects (computers, offices, telecommunication network).

Castells (1996, 2000, p. 403) refers to a culture of real virtuality to indicate the new communications systems. According to him, the experience of reality has always been virtual because it is perceived through symbols, referring to some meaning beyond the semantic definition of the symbol. The new environment created by electronic media is also a reality communicated through symbols but with totally different concepts of space and time.

Liberati (2004) points out that Internet users have "created their own rules of interaction as a basis for their own virtual culture" in order to build successful online relationships. In face-to-face relationships, messages (what is said) also consist of nonverbal cues (how it is said). Communication rules are dependent on the context: who are we communicating with, in what role, in which position, what is the perceived power relationship? In a cross-cultural context these rules may vary. Virtual teamwork will be based on the normal rules of teamwork but needs also to take into account "Internet etiquette."

The planning function for campuses becomes more and more complex. The campus forms a drain on resources and a constraint on the reach of the university (time and space). Do students need a campus? While Crook (2002) agrees that groups of students, such as life-long learners, may be motivated to deal with disturbances of traditional culture of HEI and even prefer the flexibility of virtualization, he also believes that traditional (school-leaving) undergraduates may have a different appreciation of the features of virtualization. Crook (2002) rightly points out that although now traditional students are regarded as customers, their opinion is rarely considered. The poor attention to student feedback could explain why many traditional universities experience difficulties when implementing e-learning.

Traditional universities are struggling with the concept of Information and Communication Technology ICT. Several studies describe negative experiences with ICT use (in education and administration) in traditional universities as it often results in more work for the professors, inflexible technology barriers, and an inappropriate organization model, all in the face of significant investment costs. Access and equity are not ensured, quality assurance is a problem, and the focus is on teaching and not on research and service to society.

Although these obstacles are known and ICT use is considered overrated, many traditional universities still consider ICT as the way of the future, pressured by cost, efficiency, and effectiveness. More effective systems for financing and delivering learning services have to be found (Duderstadt, 2000). Some universities see ICT as an opportunity for the university to overcome the boundaries of the campus and enter into the global higher education market. Nevertheless, investments in traditional campuses and infrastructure are continued.

Nowadays the coordinating and communicating power of digital network technologies allows people to communicate and to share information without barriers of space and time. But is education the creation, the assembling, the storing, the transmitting, and the processing of information for which a campus is no longer necessary? Or does a campus provide for a wide range of educational resources, which are not constrained as much by space and time limits?

Many traditional universities seem to be struggling with the link between Information Technology (IT) and their missions. IT is seen as a technical tool, not embedded in the mission. As pointed out by Graves, Henshaw, Oberlin, and Parker (1997, p. 432), "linking IT strategically to the mission is a largely unmet mission." In business, those problems have been experienced since the introduction of ICT. Cleary, a fit between technological infrastructure and strategic intent is necessary. The ICT system needs to have the organizational architecture capability to manage the problems or the situations that organizations experience (Sauer & Willcocks, 2003).

1.3 How to Cope with Dilemmas?

In next section of the chapter we will describe the case of the Universitat Oberta de Catalunya (UOC), located in Barcelona (Spain), as an interesting illustration of the two dilemmas identified above. In earlier research (De Jonghe, Dutta, Van Poeck, & Verdin, 2003a; and De Jonghe, 2003b) we compared strategies in traditional higher education with those implemented in new Higher Education Institutions (HEI) such as UOC.

UOC is a "green-field university" (a new start-up from scratch), a distance e-based university, which is going beyond the futuristic concept of a virtual university. It is really building a new university concept based on a rather unique strategy. It has a student-centered vision and teaches through ICT with a lot of attention to the creation of an academic community on the Web but it also wants to do research. It is not only based on (sometimes theoretical or futuristic) possibilities offered by the new technologies (as pointed out by Robin and Webster (2002)) but on a quite different approach. UOC takes into account the broader economic (cost of higher education, complexity of tasks), social (influence of IT, inclusion of special groups), political (role of nations in the global world), and managerial (adapted organizational structure and management style) issues related to higher education.

In so doing, UOC's relevance reaches far beyond the world of distance education or e-learning and beyond the geographical area of Catalunya or Spain. As a sign of success, UOC already has won several national and international awards.

This chapter uses information gathered from on-site visits, extensive semi-structured as well as unstructured interviews with the main actors in the period 2002-2003, internal and published documents, and the UOC Website. Further literature review has been undertaken with respect to strategic and organizational issues related to traditional and virtual higher education and with respect to learning issues in both environments.

We explored why UOC is so different from other traditional distance education. The purpose was not to generalize from the case but to get some understanding of the rather new research area of learning by using technology. We wanted to identify some important features, understand them, and conceptualize them for further study.

Since the end of the 20th century changes in the economy and people's non-working lives increased the demand for life-long learning. In many respects, UOC addresses the challenges of adult education and life-long learning as identified in recent reports and conferences (*e.g.*, the Conference on the European Research Area organized by the European Commission, Liège (B), May 25-28, 2004).

In what follows we describe the UOC case in more detail.

2. THE UOC CASE

2.1 A Public-Private Construction

In this section, we describe how a demand by the Catalan government resulted in negotiations, allowing UOC to obtain some real autonomy while setting up an appropriate governance structure.

In the early 1990s, the Catalan government had been eager to address the detected need in the region for distance education, while overcoming problems related to distance and physical handicaps. At first, the Catalan government negotiated with the Spanish authorities for control of UNED (the national distance university of Spain, based in Madrid) in Catalonia. However, as UNED's faculty members were not too keen on devolving to Catalonia, the Catalan government decided to start its own distance education. As a result, UOC became one of the eleven public universities of Catalonia.

In 1993, Gabriel Ferraté, a man with a clear vision and considerable experience, was asked to set up this Catalan distance university. He had been an engineer and entrepreneur early in his career, and later became a rector of traditional universities as well as a business and political leader.

Ferraté accepted the Catalan government's offer to start a distance university from scratch, provided that he could do it "his way." His more than 20 years of experience in traditional universities had given him a clear vision on which course he wanted this new institution to follow. He wanted to set up a university for the people, unhampered by the legacies of traditional universities. A contract with the government was agreed upon and performance indicators established.

He had discovered that public organizations were often in a disadvantaged position to make timely decisions because of many obstacles like government rules and lengthy debates at all levels and in different committees. Therefore, if he wanted to combine effective decision making with governmental support, he had to push the legal forces to the limits by inventing a completely new and complex legal public/private framework, allowing easy adaptation and reaction to the demanding needs of an evolving society.

In 1994, the Foundation for the Universitat Oberta de Catalunya (FUOC) was established, consisting of only four private partners. This private founding would allow for a more efficient company-like structure and organization. The Catalan Autonomous Government was added immediately afterwards (becoming a majority member) to enable public financing (of the Catalan degrees). This governance structure was key to setting up a new organizational model and strategy. The organizational and legal framework was consolidated in the academic year 2002-2003.

In short, UOC could build a specific relationship with the government through an inventive legal framework, allowing a company-like managerial model and effective decision making.

The next section discusses UOC's focus on the customer relationship with the student and the organization of learning services.

2.2 The Innovative Approach to Student Learning at UOC

2.2.1 At UOC the Student is a Client

UOC students are part of a changing student population and life-long learners for whom Web-based learning has become a solution. Their age ranges between 18 and 70, with one-third between 25 and 29 years old, 95% employed, 60% single, 55% male, and 83% without children.

UOC built a client-focused university, where the students are at the center, receiving an excellent service. It uses a unique pedagogical model, focusing on the client relationship with students.

One clear choice that has been made from the beginning is the use of a virtual and asynchronous teaching model, allowing students to learn in an effective way without being impeded by barriers of space or time and offering flexible learning, which suits their lifestyle.

"Our first aim is to make sure that each person can satisfy his or her learning needs. Therefore, we use information technologies, allowing us to overcome barriers of space and time. Furthermore, we offer full support to each student by using an educational design, based on personalization of the student" (Mission statement UOC, October 2002).

In Figure 1, four models of education are presented with relation to coincidence in space and time. UOC uses a model in which barriers of space or time are overcome: the Asynchronous Teaching Model through the virtual campus.

Coincidence in Space	No	Tele-Education	Virtual Campus
	Yes	Traditional Campus	Support Center
		Yes	No
		Coincidence in Time	

Figure 1. Asynchronous Teaching Model

Besides the virtual campus there are regional support centers without lecture rooms but with a UOC representative. They play an important role in this service-oriented model. They often collaborate to promote a dynamic variety of extra-academic activities. At the same time, they have to investigate the needs of the students and the public, in order to facilitate further improvements of the UOC institution. They attract new candidates. They provide physical space if necessary. They are used for organizing exams — increasingly replaced, however, by continuous assessment.

Face-to-face meetings bring students and teaching staff together at the beginning (presentation meeting) and at the end of each semester (synthesis meeting). Those meetings consist of academic activities (such as counseling and tutoring sessions; lectures) and complementary activities (such as workshops and cultural activities). The academic activities are attended by 35% of enrolled students.

Hereafter, we will describe other aspects of the UOC model enabling it to offer excellent service to its students. Students are in close contact with tutors and counselors. Some professors have a management role. The advantages of the campus are integrated in the virtual campus (section 2.2.4).

2.2.2 The Central Position of the Student and Their Relationships with Tutors and Counselors

UOC makes sure to approach its students in a very different way. It treats them as if they were clients, deserving an education of the highest quality. So a student-centered learning process has been adopted and replaces the dominant and even exclusive focus of traditional universities on a professor-centered teaching process. In order to do this, UOC brings other roles into the learning model shown in Figure 2: "tutors" who are subject-based and "counselors" who are student-based.

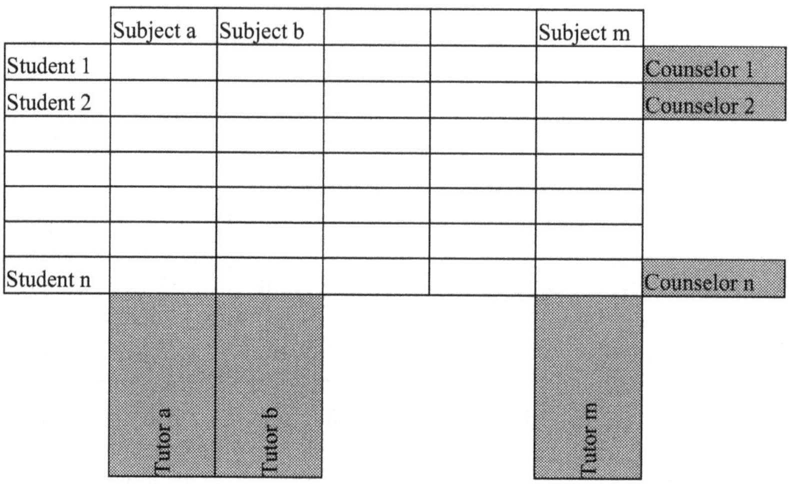

Figure 2. The Role of Tutors and Counselors at UOC

2.2.2.1 Tutors

"Tutors" are (external) specialists in a specific study subject. They are usually faculty members at other universities or professionals (*e.g.*, lawyers or business executives) working for UOC on a freelance basis. They guide, stimulate, and assess the student's learning process with respect to a certain subject. In general, a tutor would be responsible for a group of up to 70 students, which is the maximum for one tutor (see Figure 2). Although "tutors" are not required to be constantly online, or do not follow a specific time schedule, all students' messages or enquiries are to be answered within 48 hours.

The relationship student-tutor is based on a well-structured working plan, offering the student a clear vision on how the semester (typically 13 class weeks) would look in terms of course content, workload, study material, and assessments. The working plan could be considered as a "learning contract."

The assessment is part of a continuous learning philosophy, as it is made up of series of programmed activities that take place throughout the entire semester, reducing the weight of the final exam.

Given the crucial role of the "tutor" within the student's learning process, special attention is given to their selection. The UOC professors (as will be explained below) are then responsible for selecting those external candidates who possess a unique combination of experience and open-mindedness.

Tutors (either academics or professionals) are always 'recruited' on the basis of a six-months contract, which would be either indirect, which is means through the institution where the tutor is employed full-time, or direct in the case of a high-level professional. In general, as UOC has been founded with help of the Catalan Government, agreements with regard to the use of professors from other universities as counselors/tutors for UOC were relatively easy to establish. Such contracts are needed, given the tremendous interest shown by traditional university professors to collaborate.

Tutors, once recruited, originally receive one year of training on the pedagogical principles, the tasks, and the working climate at UOC. Recently, the decision was made to shorten the time span of this training to six months, in order to give the tutors all of the required information "right from the start." In general, tutors belong to a particular team, thereby stimulating group learning and easing the training process (learning by doing).

2.2.2.2 Counselors

"Counselors" are also mostly external collaborators. They are selected on the basis of demonstrated academic or professional experience in the field of the studies being counseled. They are fully informed about the working plan and ultimately become the personal counselor and primary spokesperson for the student throughout his entire educational process at the UOC.

Counselors will help the student through the first contacts with the virtual campus and monitor the students' progress through the rest of the program. Counselors, which could be compared with personal coaches, are an important factor in the UOC approach to student care and services. The counseling classroom is the space in the virtual campus where the student can stay in permanent contact with his or her counselor.

Although the compensation of the external staff is shared between the individual and the institution (payment of overhead) where he or she is affiliated, it is nonetheless clear that special attention has been given towards motivation of the personnel by the use of variable payments. Tutors and counselors, for instance, are rewarded with a fixed salary on the one hand, and a variable part, in function of the number of credits and students, on the other hand.

2.2.3 The Role of the Professor: A Management Role?

"We wanted to create a university for the students to learn, NOT for the professors to teach — therefore we need very good professors!" (Gabriel Ferraté, November 2002).

Not only does UOC need outstanding "professors," but also professors capable of fulfilling a different role, while paradoxically enough not performing any of the "traditional teaching" tasks.

Faculties at UOC are different from traditional faculties. With regard to the official degrees, UOC consists of six different study fields: economics and business studies; psychology and educational sciences; law and political science; humanities, language and literature; computer science; and multimedia, information; and communication sciences. Each study field is headed by a "Director of Studies."

In addition, each study field has two or more "Program Directors," in charge of a particular program and of a number of "professors." Originally, a professor is a specialist in a certain academic field, but at UOC (s)he is in charge of coordinating the work of the various tutors, and taking part in the design of the syllabus.

The directors, the program directors and the professors are internal members of UOC's academic staff, while the authors who provide course material (as described in the next paragraph), the tutors, and the counselors are always outside-members (*i.e.*, are not employees of UOC).

In the case of authors, a direct contract is drawn, in which it is stipulated that the delivered course material would become property of the UOC. At times, the delivered material is sold afterwards to the university in which the author is employed on a full-time basis. Existing material of course remains the property or right of the original author.

In the first place, the professor-manager has to design the course concept and negotiate with different authors that could provide interesting course material. Course materials can consist of books or manuals, CD-ROMs, videos, or Web pages. The design of the course concept and providing students with the best materials is very important and to be considered as crucial in the service relationship with the student-client. Secondly, the professors are responsible for finding tutors (mostly professors at other universities) and for coordinating and directing the overall progress.

As a result, at UOC a student receives an excellent service as he or she is being supported by a team of three sets of specialists ("tutors," "counselors," and "professors"), each of them performing specialized tasks. The student then in some ways can be seen at the center of what we could call a 'learning matrix organization'!

Given the fact that only professors with the "right" attitude would feel at ease in this revolutionary teaching environment, once again, special care has been taken with regard to the selection process. The HR staff of UOC first sets up a ranking of applicants, purely on the basis of their educational qualification, as mentioned in the CVs. The top three (four) are then invited to have an interview with a selection panel, consisting of one internal HR person, one external psychologist, and one internal person specialized in the field. However, as very bright people often do not have complete CVs, reducing their chances of selection, it is the task of the manager-professor to detect those flaws in the selection system. In the case of the non-degree programs, the professor is an external professional (not an academic). In this selection process, more weight is attached to previous experience.

2.2.4 The Virtual Campus: As Close to a Real Campus as You Can Get

In this section we give a brief overview of some of the main features of the UOC campus concept on the Web.

The design of the campus is at the core of the pedagogical model of UOC. "Our campus is a real campus, a special place where we try to stimulate all the useful functions of a face-to-face campus"(Gabriel Ferraté, April 2003).

This unique campus could be seen as the principal communication area for teaching, communication, tutorial, and student support, as well as for cultural, social, and personal communication. It therefore provides most academic and non-academic services found on a traditional university campus. Several characteristics mainly define its success.

Firstly and as already mentioned above, it allows an asynchronous approach towards education, which is one of UOC greatest advantages as most UOC students need great flexibility towards the organization of their study time.

Secondly, all students are trained in and accustomed to the use of PCs, Internet, and multi media material. Before enrolling, they get access to a special place, the introduction classroom to the virtual campus, where they are familiarized with the main spaces and functionalities of the campus and the virtual learning environment. Student acceptance is indeed an important factor for successful implementation of instructional technologies (Martins, 2004).

Thirdly, psychological aspects of learning (Crook, 2002) are integrated in the virtual communication system. The model clearly avoids student isolation, traditionally associated with distance education, by providing a 'virtual space,' uniting all members of the UOC community. Interaction and communication between UOC members takes place in this space.

The virtual communication system permits access to many services such as mentioned hereafter: the "class room" space (consisting of four blocks: planning, communication, documentation, and evaluation); formal and informal communication; administrative services; the library (with use of internal and external databases); to student co-operatives; and the club UOC, a community of people (30,000 people after 6 years) with a common interest in learning and knowledge. Access is also possible to the "campus for peace," which is a development co-operation program through which UOC provides technology transfer, virtual training, and consultancy in order to fulfill its ethical commitment to society (*e.g.*, Camps, Isabel Sales, & Uribe-Echevarria, 2004). "Art nodes" is another interesting space, which focuses on the study of the intersection between art, science, and technology.

Fourthly, the concept of the "meta-campus" is being promoted as a space where relationships with universities worldwide can be developed.

2.3 Technology to the Service of the Student

UOC launched its teaching activities in 1995 by means of a pilot course with 200 students, which was very positively evaluated and which motivated the staff to continue and expand their activities. As the Internet was only at its infancy at that time, the access to virtual education was made possible through "FirstClass" software (developed and sold by Open Text) and e-mail based solutions. During the pilot year, specialists would be sent to students' homes to fix technical problems, giving them a very special service. This service, of course, was not only meant to pamper the first students, it also provided a good learning opportunity for their own technical staff. The following year (1996-1997), the number of students grew to 1,500. At this point, UOC developed its own wholly Web-based application known as Virtual Campus 2.0. UOC made it a top priority not to install software on their students' home PCs. Since the new Virtual Campus was accessed through a Web browser, the students did not need any application software on their PCs. Home visits were abolished; instead students could contact an independent call center or browse a CD-Rom with technical explanations. Students benefited from a special deal from Telefónica, the telecom company, offering attractive conditions to UOC. Thus, when in 1997, the Internet was being adopted in large numbers in Catalonia, UOC was well prepared to take fully advantage of its potential. As a result, the student numbers exploded to almost 10,000 in 1998.

In the following years new services were added, and those already existing were extended. The 'Supracampus' (regrouping virtual campus environments of different teaching communities) was developed. New links to the Internet were provided (UUNET, IBERNET) and the UOC turned into an Internet Autonomous System (September 2000).

With more than 250,000 different users each month and an hourly average of 2,800 visits, www.uoc.edu has already become the most visited specialized Web site of Spain and one of the five most important educational Web sites of the world. The registered users (staff, students, collaborators) are about 35,000.

After two years of preparation, a new virtual campus was realized in 2002-2003 with more added values, in terms of simplicity, clarity, user-friendliness, and the number of interactive courses. Input was received from a focus "client" group (students). Satisfaction further improved and incidents were reduced. The main focus of UOC is concentrated on its pedagogical model; the technology mainly serves then to make it all operational.

2.4 The Organizational Model

The UOC model (see Figure 3) shows a balance between the academic dimension, the resource dimension, and the programs and projects dimension.

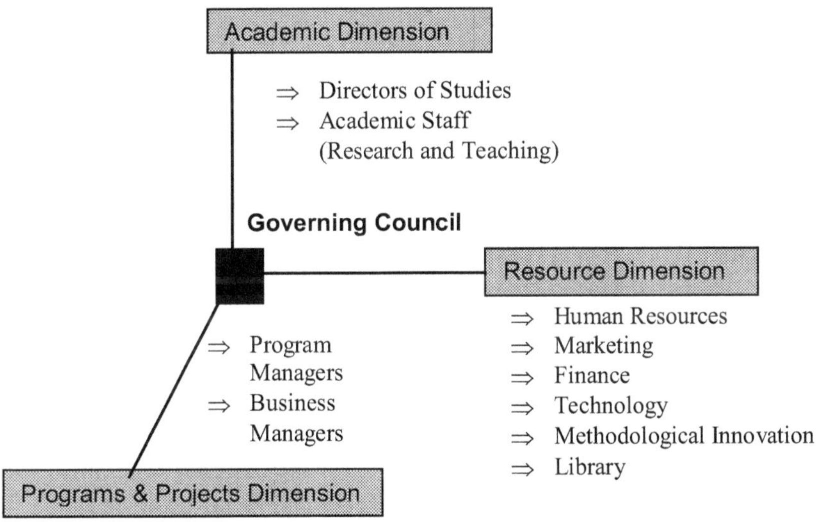

Figure 3. Organizational Model

The academic staff constitutes a first axis in this unique organizational framework. In general, they are responsible for the delivery of both the official and the non-official degrees (the latter being the Post-Degree Programs, the Extension Courses, and the Business Training Programs).

The second axis of the organizational framework refers to the resource dimension, reflecting UOC's own internal resources (e.g. human resources, marketing, finance, technology, methodological innovation, and the library services). Consisting of over 400 persons, it has the goal of offering the highest level of services, both to the students and the teaching staff, to the general public and the governmental institutions.

The third axis of the organizational framework includes the managers of the university, representing the business units with a bottom line responsibility. They act as facilitators, constantly trying to translate UOC's strategy and the visionary ideas of the rector into realistic targets.

Overlooking these three dimensions is the Governing Council, comprising the rector, the general manager, and the five vice rectors. The council has the objective of continuously balancing the university towards a stable equilibrium between the three different dimensions.

A network of different private companies is available to help UOC to achieve its unique mission. The complex nature of UOC's daily reality has made collaboration with other institutions indispensable in achieving the best results. Gradually, over time, this need resulted in different strategic alliances and equity stakes in other organizations, leading to the development of the UOC Group. This network, in which UOC plays a very active role, offers mixed or shared activities to assist the university in achieving its objectives of service, quality, and universality.

3. HOW DOES UOC DEAL WITH THE DILEMMAS AND TENSIONS CONFRONTING CONTEMPORARY EDUCATION?

UOC was able to deal with the dilemmas mentioned in the first section of the chapter in a constructive way. Hereafter, we discuss the performance of UOC and the way it handled the dilemmas.

UOC has been able to perform well in a very short period of time. It succeeded in improving its financial situation rapidly over time. The quality of the education received at UOC, definitely contributed to its superior performance. Yearly assessment of the quality of teaching and of the services offered at UOC is very positive.

We disagree with observers such as Aslaksen (2002, p. 91), who merely mention UOC as "a type of institution which resembles in many ways traditional distance education or correspondence institutions in the sense that it practices guided independent learning, through electronic course delivery and the use of electronic communication tools."

Such observations in our view are focusing too much on the technical aspects and do not reflect the clear strategic concept and dramatically different way of operating behind the entire set-up of the UOC, both in terms of its learning model and its organizational model.

3.1 How did UOC deal with the first dilemma mentioned in section 1.1?

One side of the first dilemma implies a professor-centered view and a focus on research. The other side of this dilemma refers to the central relationship with the student.

At UOC, a clear choice has been made in putting the students first. The tasks of the professors have been deconstructed and organized in a different way. The unbundling of the complex and multiple tasks of professors has been put into practice. Unbundling can take place at different levels: individual (separation of research and teaching in one person), organizational (research and teaching are not in the same place), or inter-organizational network growth (outsourcing) (Duderstadt, 2000; De Boer, Huisman, Klemperer, Van der Meulen, Neave, Theiens, & Van der Wende, 2002). At UOC teaching and research is separated. The teaching services are also delivered by several persons and no one professor is responsible for all the aspects of it.

After some experiments with different systems, a teaching staff charter has been drafted recently in order to regulate the professional and academic development of professors at UOC. Besides research professors, professors involved in teaching activities are given the possibility of doing research. UOC's research program is multi-disciplinary.

The Internet Interdisciplinary Institute (IN3) focuses on the impact of ICT and its implication for knowledge and society. It has worked together with more than 100 European institutions (universities, research institutions, and technology companies) in joint research projects, many of them sponsored by the European Commission. The project "Internet Catalonia" (seven sector studies on the information society in Catalonia), is supported by the regional government.

3.2 How did UOC deal with the second dilemma mentioned in section 1.2? OK

The second dilemma is the tension between campus teaching and distance teaching. Is it possible to create the advantages of a real (geographical) campus on the Web?

We evaluate the UOC approach, which exists in linking IT strategically to the mission and we elaborate on the importance of the campus concept on the Web. Clearly, UOC is trying to preserve a liberal — in the sense of education as a (world) citizen based on higher values — university by trying to integrate all the aspects of a "university of culture" (Readings, 1996) into its online campus concept. It is not an elitist form of liberal education but a new type of liberal education trying to create a community, which transcends the boundaries of time, space, class, gender, and nation.

The UOC approach acknowledges the importance of a campus setting in the education process. It uses an innovative campus concept in an online education context. More specifically, UOC integrated the four important psychological elements (Crook, 2002) important for learning in its strategy:

- Time: Asynchronous learning suited the customers well given their preoccupation with other aspects of their life such as work.
- Space: The design of the campus on the Web features all the important functions of a real campus. UOC was able to create a new learning space, the campus on the Web, without neglecting other learning spaces such as instruction, documents, information, communication, collaboration, exploration, and multimedia (based on Peters, 2002).
- Community: Learning communities arise through academic programs but also through social, extracurricular, and cultural activities. The learning community leads to a community of practice, which shares ideas and values. The campus on the Web and the classroom on the Web make it possible to create communities on the Web for learning and for other activities (Garrido, 2003).
- Materials: The design of the syllabus and the provision of other learning materials is an important task for UOC.

UOC acknowledged the importance of the community feeling. It tried to create a cultural environment on the Web, offering an attractive alternative to the traditional bricks-and-mortar learning environments.

Nunez Masteo's (2004) research about sociability at UOC's virtual forum confirms that metaphors in the electronic communication arena served the students. They were able to understand one thing in terms of another. Different metaphors responded to various interests in the social space generated by the forum.

A Web-based satisfaction survey by a market research firm yielded the following results. Overall satisfaction of the students with the various aspects of UOC's pedagogical model is around a value of 4 — on a 1 (low satisfaction) to 5 (high satisfaction) scale — as was the satisfaction with specific study and learning support. Grau Valldosera and Fornieles Deu (2004) show that UOC students are highly committed to online satisfaction surveys. The participation rate and the quality of their response are high.

UOC's approach also shows that distributed education can be more than an informational process as seen in a technical process-oriented view of the business process re-engineering model where core value-adding processes are made as lean and efficient as possible. The virtual campus implies the use of adapted technology.

4. CONCLUSION

Throughout this chapter we have tried to show the process that UOC went through in creating an online university. We also tried to emphasize the fact that they see themselves as a real university, which we can explain by seeing the virtual university as an actors' network and a learning and social community on the Web. This social transformation could take place by combining a vision of service to the student with the technological means of the moment. This is clearly a case in which technology has been strategically linked to the mission. A strategy, which consists of a unique value proposition to the market, requires the adaptation of the organizational model.

UOC proposes a true paradigm shift: the modern university should be a virtual university where the changing needs and expectations of students are at the center of attention. Paradoxically, this is quite different from the usual concept of a 'distance university,' which emphasizes the "distance" as being far from a building and from the traditional professor giving a lecture, referring to an institution- or professors-centered vision (of the past?) (Heydinger, 1997).

UOC tried to create an attractive cultural environment for flexible learning through the Web by taking into account the psychological elements, which are important while learning. As a newcomer it could implement this learning strategy combining such key success factors as: clear vision and strategy, a reinvented relationship with the government, an adapted organizational model, an effective network organization, and a strong leader with a highly motivated team.

UOC shows how the relationship with the national (regional) government can be reinvented without losing the ties with national culture and while becoming part of a global network. This contradicts findings such as those by Robins and Webster (2002) who state that the university as a "national institution" is "in crisis." Readings (1996) also argues that the national model of the university is "in ruins" given the developments due to globalization. He indicates that the relation between nation-state, national culture, and higher education is breaking down. UOC tries to build a global university by its global campus on the Web.

UOC plays an innovative role in the field of e-learning. It was able to create a new type of university. There may be no political will yet to question the continuity between traditional secondary and tertiary education, but a virtual university such as UOC shows the way to an attractive alternative.

REFERENCES

Armstrong, M. J. (2003). Students as clients: A professional services model for business education. *Academy of Management Learning and Education, 2* (4), 371-377.

Aslaksen, K. O. (2002). Imagine Global U — European Union and international initiatives as an incentive for international virtual cooperation. In B. Wächter (Ed.), *The Virtual Challenge to International Cooperation in Higher Education: A Project of the Academic Cooperation Association* (pp. 89-97). Bonn: Lemmens.

Bourgeois, E., Duke, C., Guyot, J. L., & Merrill, B. (1999). *The Adult University*. Society for Research into Higher Education (SRHE) and Open University Press, Buckingham, UK and Philadelphia, PA.

Camps, R., Isabel Sales, F., & Uribe-Echevarria, A. (2004). Absoo: Sharing for education. An e-learning experiment in education for development, http://www.uoc.edu/dt/eng/20402.html, accessed June 7, 2004.

Castells, M. (1996). *The Rise of the Network Society*. Malden: Blackwell.

Castells, M. (2000). *The Rise of the Network Society*, Malden: Blackwell.

Cornford, J., & Pollock, N. (2003). *Putting the University Online: Information, Technology and Organizational Change*. Society for Research into Higher Education (SRHE) and Open University Press, Buckingham, UK and Philadelphia, PA.

Crook, C. (2002). The virtual university: The learner's perspective. In K. Robins & F. Webster (Eds.), *The Virtual University? Knowledge, Markets and Management* (pp. 105-125). Oxford, UK: Oxford University Press.

De Boer, H., Huisman, J., Klemperer, A., Van der Meulen, B., Neave, G., Theiens, T., & Van der Wende, M. (2002). Academia in the 21st century. An analysis of trends and perspectives in higher education and research. A technical report written for the Dutch Council on Science and Technology Policy (also available on the Web) Adviesraad voor het Wetenschaps-en Technologiebeleid (AWT), Den Haag, http://www.utwente.nl/cheps/publications/, accessed August 19, 2003, pp. 62-72.

De Jonghe, A. M., Dutta, S., Van Poeck, E., & Verdin, P. (2003a). Universitat Oberta de Catalunya, A University without Distance: INSEAD Case Study, INSEAD, Fontainebleau, France.

De Jonghe, A. M. (2003b). UOC (Universitat Oberta de Catalunya). A case of dramatic change: Leapfrogging traditional universities. Working paper University of Bath, School of Management.

De Wolf, H. (2001). Universities in the network society. In H. J. Van der Molen (Ed.), *Virtual University? Educational Environments of the Future*. London: Portland Press. http://www.portlandpress.com/pp/books/online/vu/contents.htm, accessed September 2, 2003.

Duderstadt, J. J. (2000). *A University for the 21st Century*. Ann Arbor, MI: The University of Michigan Press.

European Commission. (2004). Conference: The Europe of Knowledge 2020. A Vision for University Based Research and Innovation. Liège, Belgium, April 25-28.

Garrido, A. (2003). Learning as an identity of participation in the processes of online communities, http://www.uoc.edu/in3/dt/20110/index.html, accessed October 3, 2003.

Graves, W. H., Henshaw, R. G., Oberlin, J. L., & Parker, A. S. (1997). Infusing information technology into the academic process. In M. W. Peterson, D. D. Dill, L. A. Mets, & Associates (Eds.), *Planning and Management for a Changing Environment* (pp. 432-452). San Francisco, CA: Jossey-Bass.

Grau Valldosera, J., & Fornieles Deu, A. (2004). Online satisfaction surveys: A practical experience, http://www.edu/dt/20400/index.html, accessed June 8, 2004.

Heydinger, R. B. (1997). Principles for redesigning institutions. In M. W. Peterson, D. D. Dill, L. A. Mets, & Associates (Eds.), *Planning and Management for a Changing Environment* (pp. 106-123). San Francisco, CA: Jossey-Bass.

Griffin, C. (1987). *Adult Education as a Social Policy*. London: Croom Helm.

Jarvis, P., Holford, J., & Griffin, C. (2003). *The Theory and Practice of Learning* (2nd ed.). Kogan Page, London and Sterling, VA.

Kallenberg, A. J., Van der Grijspaarde, L., Ter Braak, A., & Van Horzen, C. J. (2000). Leren en Doceren in het Hoger Onderwijs (Learning and Teaching in Higher Education). Utrecht: Lemma BV.

Knowles, M. (1986). *Using Learning Contracts*. San Francisco, CA: Jossey-Bass.

Liberati, D. (2004). Building successful online relationships. In G. M. Piskurich (Ed.), *Getting the Most from Online Learning* (pp. 131-144). San Francisco, CA: John Wiley & Sons.

Martins, L. L. (2004). A model of business school students' acceptance of a web-based course management system. *Academy of Management Learning and Education, 3* (1), 7-26.

Naudé, P. (2004). Some ideas on marketing, presentation to DBA Program. University of Bath Management School, May 27.

Nunez Masteo, F. (2004). Internet metaphors: Revista digital d'humanitats, nr 6, http://www.uoc.edu, accessed June 7, 2004.

Peters, O. (2002). *Distance Education in Transition*. Biblioteks und informationssystems de Universitat Oldenburg, Oldenburg.

Readings, B. (1996). *The University in Ruins*. Cambridge, MA: Harvard University Press.

Robins, K., & Webster, F. (2002). The virtual university? In K. Robins & F. Webster (Eds.), *The Virtual University?* (pp. 1-19). Oxford, UK: Oxford University Press.

Sauer, C., & Willcocks, L. (2003). Establishing the business of the future: The role of organizational architecture and information technologies. *European Management Journal, 21* (4), 497-508.

Webster's *Third New International Dictionary*. (1986).

Chapter 5

FROM TEACHING TO LEARNING

A Tempus Tacis Project as a Catalyst for Change in Post-Soviet Georgia

Jackie Stephens[1] and Jan Hellberg[2]
[1]*Nottingham Trent University, Nottingham, United Kingdom;* [2]*Lund University, Lund, Sweden*

1. INTRODUCTION

Quality assurance is, among other things, concerned with initiating, maintaining and managing change, but not in a random way. Change that leads to improved quality is directed towards defined goals and undertaken in a systematic way. For this to take place in an organization within higher education there is a need for continuity and expertise. In many universities and other institutions within the higher education sector, Academic Quality Assurance Centers (AQACs) are established with the aim of supporting the academic staff in their pursuit of excellence. AQACs typically track development and research on teaching and learning in higher education and are active in such research and development.

Georgia is an example of a post-Soviet country that has been working hard at developing higher education since gaining independence in 1991. For example, private universities have emerged alongside the State provided ones. However there has been no strong tradition of establishing AQACs as described above. The need for systematic change aimed at improving higher education has been recognized within both the public and the private institutions, and the European Union has given its support to their work through the TEMPUS program. This study was undertaken within one such TEMPUS project entitled *The Establishment of Academic Quality Assurance Centers at Grigol Robakhidze University, Tbilisi, and Batumi State University, Batumi, Georgia.* In addition to these two Georgian universities, there were two partners from Western Europe: Nottingham Trent University,

M.K. McCuddy et al. (eds.),
The Challenges of Educating People to Lead in a Challenging World, 95–113.

UK and Lund University, Sweden. As the project title implies, the main goal was to establish AQACs with the support from the two western universities.

The project was started in early spring 2001 and was concluded with a Symposium in Tbilisi, Georgia in July 2003. All objectives and activities that were planned to support the establishment of the AQACs were accomplished. This study reports on an investigation to discover whether academic staff, with the support of program activities, have changed their views and their teaching and learning practices. Specifically, has any eventual change resulted in movement in the intended direction from a teacher-centered to a more student-centered approach?

2. A PARADIGM SHIFT

Several signs point to the fact that a paradigm shift has been taking place within higher education for some years; this is a shift that can be described as changing from teaching to learning (Barr & Tagg, 1995). Essentially, it reflects a move from providing instruction to producing learning, or expressed another way, a change from a teacher-centered to a student-centered approach to teaching. Interestingly, Barr and Tagg found that when teachers discuss what they want to offer their students, two things are obvious: firstly, there is a clear, general agreement that the students should be allowed to develop their critical thinking and have freedom to construct their knowledge according to their personal learning styles, and, secondly, practice bears evidence to the contrary.

One explanation of this discrepancy is that institutions of higher education are very rigid in their structure and organization, making it very difficult to change practice. When Barr and Tagg wrote their article they were optimistic about the rate of change. This optimism was based, amongst other things, on the fact that the majority of teachers within higher education agree on what constitutes the best learning situation for the students.

Three years after the first article, Barr published another article (Barr, 1998). It was initiated by the fact that he could see very little change from 1995 to 1998. What were the obstacles? The teachers seemed to agree, but still very little happened in practice. What caused the process of changing from one paradigm to another to take so long? Barr identified difficulties both on an individual level and on an organizational level. On an individual level, describing an optimal situation for student learning and agreeing with colleagues about what constitutes an optimal situation is insufficient; rather, the individual teacher is required to think *within* it rather than about it. When that happens the paradigm becomes the context rather than the content. This is a major change for a teacher who has spent his/her academic life in a paradigm where the main task is to provide instruction (*i.e.*, to lecture), rather than thinking about the broader developments within the context of higher education. Trowler (1998) also adds that the way in which an academic specializes in his/her discipline strongly affects his/her professional culture and consequent responses to innovations such that, having spent all his/her academic life adapting to this culture, events that require adjustments may be met with resistance.

On an organizational level, Barr (1998, p. 19) observed that a shift requires changing from closed, self-sealing static institutions to open, continuously learning and changing organizations — organizations with their fundamental structures and processes significantly altered. In other words, this is no ordinary change but a transformation. All change has to be accomplished against a (natural) resistance to change, and when the change required is better described as a transformation, it is to be expected that the resistance may be significant.

The main argument for a shift from teaching to learning is the increase in the quality of learning that the students achieve within the learning paradigm. There is an abundance of evidence that the quality of learning within the learning paradigm is superior to what is achieved within the old paradigm. This is often generalized as a dichotomy between "deep" and "surface" learning and what constitutes contexts that favor one or the other (see, for example, Marton & Säljö, 1976; Marton, 1988; Biggs, 1989; Trigwell & Prosser, 1991; Kember & Gow, 1994).

Findings of significance for the study reported here are those stating a strong correlation between how the teachers look upon learning and how the students approach their studies. Essentially, if the quality of learning that the students achieve is to be improved, then the way that teachers look upon learning needs to be changed. These ideas are summarized in the model suggested by Trigwell, Prosser, and Taylor (1994) based upon their phenomenographic research, whereby they distinguished five qualitatively different approaches to teaching that teachers follow:

A. A teacher-focused strategy with intentions of transmitting information to students.
B. A teacher-focused strategy with the intention that students acquire the concepts of the discipline.
C. A teacher/student interaction strategy with the intention that students acquire the concepts of the discipline.
D. A student-focused strategy aimed at students developing their conceptions.
E. A student-focused strategy aimed at students changing their conceptions.

Approaches D and E result in deep learning among the students while approaches A and B favor surface learning. Approach C represents an intermediate approach. In other words, for the students to achieve high quality (deep) learning it is necessary for the teachers to take the latter approaches, a view also supported by more recent studies (see for example, Trigwell, Prosser, & Waterhouse, 1999; Kember & Kwan, 2000).

In Trigwell, Prosser, and Taylor's (1994) model there are several factors that influence what approach a teacher takes; one very strong factor is the teacher's prior experience. Prior experience determines to a great extent both how the situation is perceived and what approach to teaching and learning the teacher takes. In line with Dall´Alba (1991), Trigwell *et al.* could see that the teacher's more complete, extended conception of teaching holds more complete understandings of learning. Another factor they highlight (Prosser & Trigwell, 1997) is that both the factual situation and the teacher's perceptions of his/her teaching situation can influence the approach taken. Prosser and Trigwell (1997) also identified other characteristics that are associated with the adoption of student-focused strategies, including teachers perceiving their workload as not being too high and class sizes not too large, teachers having some control over what they teach and how they teach it, and the variation in student characteristics not being too large. These characteristics formed the basis for the 'Perception of Teaching Environment Inventory' (Prosser & Trigwell, 1997) (see Appendix B).

The teacher's perception of his/her teaching situation is of great significance in this project. Georgian higher education was part of the Soviet system and the majority of the teachers active today were both educated and, to a great extent, active as teachers within that system. It was centrally governed with universities required to deliver courses that would serve to maintain and enhance the practical workings of a centrally planned economy. Teaching was extensively didactic, and teachers were allowed very little freedom to deviate from what was centrally decided and declared as correct with regard to both teaching style and content (Machabeli, 2002). In the post-Soviet year of 1991, the reforms within Georgian higher education started but, being a slow process, it was not until 2001 that several Georgian universities showed a heightened interest in improving the quality of higher education. This project is a result of this heightened interest.

3. THE PROJECT

The awareness of the need to change to a more student-centered approach was high, as reflected in the fact that both Grigol Robakhidze University (GRU), a private institution, and Batumi State University (BSU) decided to establish AQACs to support the teachers. The design of the project aimed not only at supporting the organization, the structure of the centers, and the training of those staff members who were given the task to establish and develop the centers, but also at engaging as many teachers as possible in activities meant to illustrate what kind of support a center can provide, both to an individual teacher and groups/teams of teachers. Study visits to both Nottingham Trent University and to Lund University were also arranged for those staff chosen to be part of the centers.

The rationale behind this design was that it was not only important to establish AQACs, but also to ensure that, ideally, all faculty members would approve of the design and recognize how they could benefit from it. As has been discussed above, the key to increased quality in students' learning is the approach to teaching and learning taken by the teachers. Consequently, the project was built ensuring that the teachers, together with students, participated in activities designed to expose them to a broad variety of learning situations aimed at demonstrating student-focused strategies. Also, time to reflect and discuss these experiences in peer groups was an essential part of the program. This approach is supported by the work of Sorcinelli (2002) in that one of her ten principles of good practice for establishing centers for support includes 'building stakeholders by listening to all perspectives.' In other words, it is of critical importance to create a situation where all concerned can see the benefits of such an establishment from both an individual and an organizational perspective.

Another complementary activity was to work on course design, engaging in such tasks as building a modular structure based upon the United Kingdom credit point system, writing module specifications, and defining student workload. The rationale behind this approach was to provide concrete experiences of practical consequences of the new way of thinking. That is, the rationale was to create opportunities for the teachers to experience what it takes to change the teaching and learning situation for their students in order to facilitate high quality learning.

Theoretical aspects were also introduced in connection with the different activities as well as examples of concrete implementations based on the student-centered thinking. The necessity of clarifying the different ways of thinking about teaching and learning was highlighted by presenting and discussing the "personal theories of teaching" advocated by Fox (1983). The argument made was not for uniformity between teachers, but for constructive discussion among colleagues about teaching and learning — an approach that requires trust and openness among members of the group. Problem- based learning was presented as an example of a working concept true to the student focus idea (*e.g.*, Schmidt, 1993). The SOLO taxonomy (Biggs & Collis, 1982) was also presented and applied in practical situations in order to illustrate means of assessing whether students' learning outcomes reached desired levels of quality.

The duration of the project was two years and in this period each of the Georgian universities worked actively together with representatives from Nottingham and Lund for a total of eight weeks at the respective locations in Georgia. Added to this were study visits for a total of seven teachers from each of the two Georgian universities, covering three weeks in Sweden and six weeks in England. These teachers were to have a special responsibility for the establishment of the respective AQACs as well as being teachers at their respective institutions.

4. OUR APPROACH

This study was undertaken to investigate whether the support provided within the project and its specific design had resulted in a change among the participating teachers towards a more student-centered approach to teaching and learning. An interpretative approach was adopted, with the main research method being semi-structured interviews with a group of lecturers teaching English in the universities. The subjects were eight teachers, four from GRU and four from BSU, who represented the total population of the English language area within the Departments of Philology: four from each of the universities. Restricting the sample to this subject area was purposive in two ways: subjects who could speak English were chosen, so avoiding the methodological and practical complexities of using an interpreter; and both subject groups had developed and tested modules within the time period covered by the project.

The subjects were interviewed both individually and as two focus groups, one at each university. The group from each location included the head of the subject area and teachers of varying age and length of teaching experience. The combination of individual interviews and focus groups was chosen as the former allowed the subjects confidentiality and time when talking about, for example, their own previous experience, while the latter allowed them not only to feed off each others' comments but also to express a wider range of thoughts through those colleagues with more advanced English language skills. All interviews were semi-structured with questions aimed at investigating the teachers' prior experience, their conceptions of their teaching and their students' learning, and their teaching environment. In order to gain insight to their prior experience, the teachers were asked to reflect on both the Soviet and post-Soviet systems within universities. Questions regarding their conceptions of teaching were based upon the Prosser *et al.* (1994) and Dall'Alba (1991) categorizations of teaching concepts (referred to above in section 2 of this chapter) and summarized in Appendix A), and questions regarding their teaching environment were based upon the subscales of Prosser and Trigwell's (1997) 'Perception of Teaching Environment Inventory' (see Appendix B). For confidentiality, the teachers were identified as T1 to T8.

In order to measure the ways teachers approach their teaching in a particular situation, Trigwell and Prosser (1996) developed an 'Approaches to Teaching Inventory' (see Appendix C), using the characteristics of the two 'extreme' approaches described above in section to create the sixteen items on the inventory. This Inventory is composed of two scales with four subscales. One scale is the conceptual change/student-focused (CCSF) approach scale and the other is the information transmission/teacher-focused (ITTF) approach scale. The approach to teaching in a particular context is shown by comparing the scores obtained on the two scales. Trigwell and Prosser take pains to point out that responses to the Inventory are relational and are specific to the context in which they are collected; teachers who adopt one approach in one context may not adopt the same one in a different context. So in addition to undertaking interviews, the subjects were also asked to complete the 'Approaches to Teaching Inventory'[1] in relation to the specific context of teaching English to first year students.

During our sessions with the teachers, debate was actively encouraged and so we were also able to reflect on their contributions as participant observers and utilize our observations in our findings.

5. THEIR STORIES

5.1 Teaching in the Soviet System

Six of the eight teachers interviewed had been students in the Soviet system, the remaining two entering the profession more recently. Of the six, two had also taught in that period. Their reported experience supports the picture painted by Machabeli (2002) of a centrally imposed and controlled system. For example, they describe standardized curricula, a "*national framework*" within each subject area: "*They got a program from Russia and had to do a very detailed teaching plan. They were then inspected to make sure the plan was followed*" (T1 and T5).

Control through unannounced 'inspections' seemed to be a strong feature of the system. "*The purpose was checking and the disposition was not*

[1] Used with permission from the authors.

friendly. They were critical. Not peer observation" (T1). Even capable and experienced teachers "*lived in fear*" (T5) of these inspections as discussions would follow within the university "*and the teacher could be sacked*" (T5).

The centralized system served to not only control *what* the teachers taught, but also *how* they taught it. "*Guidelines on how to do it*" (T5) were provided and there were "*no modern techniques — any creative thinking was done at home. The teacher only checked and did not generate what was going on*" (T1). The consequence for how English was taught was that it was "*traditional translation with emphasis on accuracy rather than getting into the spirit of it. From the learner's perspective it was directive*" (T1). Teacher T1 referred to an occasion when she was inspected: "*Students were taking an active part in the discussion. It was taken as a lack of discipline … it was considered very bad because the students were very, very, very active and noisy. I was criticized and advised to go on a methodological course. Frustrating!*"

So the experience of our subjects in this period suggests that even if the teachers had prior conceptions of what constituted the kind of teaching that encourages deep learning in the students, their perceived, and actual, lack of control in their teaching environment did not encourage them to actually adopt such approaches. The consequence was a tendency towards teacher-centered teaching.

5.2 Teaching in Post-Soviet Georgia

Following independence from the USSR, centralized control was relaxed and training for teachers became available, with much of it being supplied and funded by British and American organizations. Our subjects described the effect as liberating: "*It was like having a weight lifted*" *(T1)* and the different perspectives on teaching showed that "*We can do miracles*" *(T5).*

So the change in the political context and the ensuing training seem to have provided impetus for the teachers to change their perceptions of their teaching situation. In particular, they had more control over their teaching both in terms of *what* and *how* they taught. Apart from all students having to study Georgian history and culture, the requirement for standardized curricula was removed. Teacher T5 concluded that: "*Teachers and students are more open, there is more creativity. Teaching and learning styles have changed to match that*" (T5).

Centralized, external inspections were replaced by each university's own internal system, *e.g.*, senior staff would check or, in the larger State universities, a committee would have responsibility: "*We are free to choose style [referring to teaching] but we have a Method Commission, [which is] a council who estimates how we do things*" (T7).

The emphasis of these internal systems also changed from policing to one of support: "*They don't **tell** us — it is more support. We discuss how it could be better*" (T6) (Subject's own emphasis). This more supportive environment and the training to increase awareness of what teaching is about seems to have either changed teachers' conceptions of teaching or encouraged the teachers to allow their prior conceptions of teaching to show through. In both cases the effect was a shift towards what Dall'Alba (1991) described as more complete conceptions.

Teachers indicated that their conceptions of teaching were now more focused on the students and their understanding. For example, when asked the purpose of the degree, replies included: "*To give them problem-solving skills…as in a real situation, in everyday life they do have to use knowledge gained here at university to solve practical problems that arise with working English*" (T1). The more complete conceptions were also demonstrated through their views of their role. For example: "*I don't think that my role is just to control how they pronounce and so on. It is helping them develop their listening skills and help* (sic) *them in understanding different forms of English*" (T2).

So change had begun. What further change, if any, did the project instigate?

6. DID THE PROJECT INFLUENCE CHANGE?

As discussed earlier, the deregulation of Post-Soviet higher education brought a need to ensure that quality can be both assured and demonstrated. Prompted by the UK approach, the English courses have been redesigned into a modular structure based on a system of credit points. Module specifications have been written and include, amongst other things, student workload and learning outcomes. While it was expected that such changes would require different administrative processes and procedures (*e.g.*, new committee structures), the resultant, the positive effect on conceptions of teaching and perceptions of the teaching situation was quite far reaching and not anticipated by us.

Firstly, there was a further shift towards more complete conceptions of teaching. A more student-centered focus and willingness to develop or even change students' conceptions became apparent. But why did changing to a modular structure give added impetus for change? Teacher T1 gave the following explanation: "*We needed formal recognition. The project gave management a kick. We were ready with methodology, but…we needed a new mindset, a framework*" (T1). She went on to explain that the authoring of learning outcomes for the module specifications was a difficult task, but was key to changes in teachers' and students' conceptions. "*I needed to restructure in my mind... The most important thing for me — now I know the outcomes for* **students.** *Students, not only teachers have changed.*"

The change in teachers' conceptions showed through in their new approach to teaching — encouraging more independent and experiential learning in the students. For example, teacher T6 introduced buzz groups: "*The students translate in groups then discuss with other students who give feedback. I explained the process first. They didn't understand and were nervous.*" Teacher T7 involved students in the assessment process: "*Students marked their own presentations.*"

Secondly, there were further changes in their perceptions of the teaching situation. In particular, there was strengthened teamwork that, in turn, fostered individual and team control over the teaching situation. Teachers T8 and T6 commented as follows: "*Module teams help organize the work. We get together and discuss*" (T8). "*For example, we discussed the choice of text book and it was positive, more positive than before. We felt we were sharing more. We felt more involved*" (T6). One of the subject heads also observed how her role had changed for the better: "*There are small teams and team leaders so they can help me oversee it all*" (T5). This shift from a 'top-down' to a more transparent, 'bottom-up' form of control, along with increased openness and readiness on the part of the teachers to actively seek out areas for improvement, also seems to have lead them to suggest and welcome peer support and the sharing of good practice. These activities can be viewed as forms of voluntary self-regulation and control. Teacher T6 describes her experience of sharing good practice: "*We share experience. Go to each others' lectures. Do the best one...* [Referring to her buzz groups] *I would tell colleagues and someone else has watched and copied.*"

They also claimed that the new framework encouraged self-reflection. Teacher T1 suggested that learning outcomes gave the following advantage: "*At the end of the module we will be able to look and say 'I did this OK. I did that quite OK. That was not so good.'* "

Furthermore, these new forms of control, combined with the conception of the student as being central, also placed *students* within the new framework for control. As Teacher T7 reports, student evaluation was actively sought and reacted to as appropriate: "*The new thing is getting the view of the student. Students felt that they should not approach and tell changes to the teacher. Now they are encouraged.*" Prior to the project some evaluation was sought, but it was limited in both style and content: "[Student] *evaluation is now at module level. Previous evaluation was oral, just about the teacher's personality and not so frank*" (T5).

In addition to the teachers now having some control over what they do and how they do it, they also viewed their class sizes as "*comfortable*" (All teachers). Teacher T6 described the situation when she felt that her class was too large and "*they split it into two*," again indicating this teacher's increased influence and control. However, the issue of academic workload and associated payment is an area that has not changed. Teachers have to prepare for classes, workshops, etc., but are "*only paid for contact time*" (T7). When asked if this was fair, T7 responded, "*I don't know. It is not my business. Administration gives us some hours — no more, no less.*"

So for all our subjects the project has encouraged more complete conceptions of teaching as well as improved perceptions of the teaching situation. These are aspects that Trigwell *et al.* (1994) and Prosser *et al.* (1997) identify as being necessary for approaches to teaching to be student-centered. So have approaches to teaching changed?

7. FROM TEACHING TO LEARNING?

Six of the eight teachers completed the Trigwell *et al.* (1996) Approaches to Teaching Inventory (see Appendix C). The scores for each inventory scale are summarized in Table 1.

Table 1. Scores from the Approaches to Teaching Inventory (Trigwell *et al.*, 1996)

	Conceptual Change/Student Focused Approach*	Information Transmission/Teacher Focused Approach*
T1	30	21
T2	30	32
T4	25	31
T5	30	32
T6	26	28
T7	25	27

*Maximum score per scale is 40

The approach to teaching taken by each person is indicated by comparing the scores obtained on the two inventory scales; the higher score indicates the teacher's preferred approach. From Table 1 it can be seen that the teachers interviewed were, on the whole, more teacher-centered than student-centered in approach. The exception to this was teacher T1 who had a higher score for the student-centered approach.

At first glance these results may seem disappointing in that most of the teachers do not seem to have changed to the kind of approach that encourages deep learning in the students — despite having more complete conceptions of teaching and an increased awareness of a range of teaching techniques. However, it must be remembered that a particular context — *i.e.*, teaching English to first year students — is being investigated and each teacher's perceptions of this particular situation will have influence. Their perceptions may be that these new students are not yet sufficiently mature to engage in such independent activities and have to be introduced gradually to this approach. This view is supported by the earlier quotation: "*Students were reticent at first, but are now starting to be more independent*" (T8).

Similarly, they may feel that the students have little useful prior knowledge as they are new, inexperienced, and from a range of different backgrounds. Consequently, they may decide that the students will not be able to undertake activities that question and challenge ideas, and so they adopt the more information transmission, teacher-centered strategies. Teacher T1, on the other hand, may have more confidence in the abilities of her students.

During our participation in the project, we observed on many occasions that the teacher was viewed as being the key source of knowledge for the student. In Dall'Alba's (1991) terms, this conception of teaching would be in either the 'limited' or the 'intermediate' category of conceptions. While this view can be argued to be a direct consequence of the deeply ingrained Soviet approach, the teaching situation is also a limiting factor. Alternative learning resources (*e.g.*, books and electronic sources) are not readily available — something over which the teachers would not have control. Also, contact hours are high. Teachers are paid for contact hours only, so this feature of the teaching situation does not encourage more independent learning and, consequently, the more complete conception of teaching.

It was argued earlier that having less 'top-down' control has been a factor of the teaching situation that has encouraged more complete conceptions. However, a key control from the top that has remained very significant is that whereby a teacher's performance is judged on students' results, "*If assessment is bad, the Administration asks why*" (T7, tone reflected seriousness). Again, this may not encourage the more complete conceptions.

Over the duration of this study, the facts of the teaching situation seemed very much the same in each university. However, discussion did suggest that certain factors in the teaching situation, such as the expansion of the modular structure to other subjects and the development and usage of the AQAC, are more advanced in the private university and could act as catalysts for change in the medium rather than the longer term. For example, both culture and practice could be influenced in a way that facilitates increased use of independent learning. It is, perhaps, no surprise that the private university seems a little closer to embracing further changes as smaller, newer, less traditional institutions are typically able to adapt to change more quickly, bringing about the fundamental organizational changes that Barr (1998) suggested are necessary.

So despite significant positive movement towards more complete conceptions of teaching, the approaches adopted by most of this group of teachers, in the specific context of teaching English to first year undergraduates, remain teacher-centered. Our findings suggest that this is a consequence of actual and perceived limitations in the teaching context, echoing Prosser and Trigwell's (1999, p. 177) emphasis of the centrality of context: "Teachers who adopt one approach in one context may not adopt that same one in a different context."

8. CONCLUSIONS

The main idea behind this project, besides actually supporting the universities in the establishment of AQACs, was to make it possible for all faculty members to see how they could benefit from having access to this kind of center. The individual teachers were also supported in getting to know more about modern theories of learning and associated implementation in the learning situation. In particular, they were encouraged to take the next step of embracing the ideas and trying them in their own teaching.

However, two aspects are noteworthy. One is the very strict, strong and uniform prior experiences shared by the faculty from the Soviet period. It is bound to have a very strong influence on how the individual teacher perceives the new ideas and situations — even more so when finding himself or herself in a group situation among peers with similar experiences. This may work against being open to new ideas, resulting in some resistance to change.

The other aspect is a more positive one. The fact that both universities have sought and actively worked for this project shows that the thinking is changing and is grounded in an awareness of the need to change and develop aspects of the learning situation. One example of this openness was the fact that students were invited to work together with the teachers during all training sessions, both in Batumi and Tbilisi. So there is evidence of some movement away from being closed, self-sealing static institutions toward being the more open, continuously learning organizations that Barr (1998) suggests more readily embrace change.

We are convinced that the project has assisted in changing conceptions of teaching, with the concrete experience of creating module specifications and other quality assurance documentation seeming to act as a catalyst for this change. However, it was also evident that change is a gradual process, and each individual had progressed differently on the journey from the less complete conceptions, where the teacher's awareness is only of him/herself, towards more complete conceptions where his/her awareness has been expanded to include him/herself, the content, and students' understanding of the content (Martin & Ramsden, 1993). Even with complete conceptions, the most advanced teacher may choose to use a very teacher-centered approach if it is judged to be the most effective in the circumstances. Indeed, we felt it important that the teachers appreciated the fact that what they had been doing up until the time of the project was absolutely legitimate and that the new ideas were only complements and extensions to what they had already used and mastered. Without these complements and extensions the paradigm shift from teaching to learning would not be possible.

APPENDIX A: SUMMARY OF RESEARCH ON CONCEPTIONS OF TEACHING FROM A RELATIONAL PERSPECTIVE

	Dall'Alba (1991)	**Prosser et al (1994)**
	Bringing about conceptual change	Helping students change conceptions
	Exploring ways of understanding from particular perspectives	Helping students develop conceptions
Complete Conceptions	Developing the capacity to be expert	
	Developing concepts and their interrelations	Helping students acquire: D: teacher's knowledge C: Concepts of the syllabus
Intermediate Conceptions	Illustrating the application of theory to practice	
	Transmitting information	
Limited Conceptions	Imparting information	Transmitting: B: Teacher's Knowledge A: Concepts of the syllabus

Source: McKenzie (1995).

APPENDIX B: PERCEPTIONS OF TEACHING ENVIRONMENT INVENTORY SUB-SCALES, DEFINING ITEMS, AND SCORING

Sub-scale	Comment	Defining Item
Control of Teaching	Focus on the amount of material included in the first year curriculum and the very little room for variation and diversity in what is taught and how it is taught.	The department allows me considerable flexibility in the way I teach in this topic. (scored positively)
Appropriate class size	Focus on the extent to which appropriate class size influences the nature and amount of interaction between student and lecturer.	I stick closely to my notes when teaching large classes. (scored negatively)
Enabling student characteristics	Focus on the increasing variation in the ability of the students, the language background and gender.	Students have such variable skills that I find it hard to know what they know and what they don't know. (scored negatively)
Departmental support for teaching	Focus on the lack of balance between the valuing of teaching and research at the departmental level.	This department's view of teaching makes it less rewarding to focus much attention on teaching. (scored negatively)
Appropriate academic workload	On the amount of time spent on teaching and/or assessment and its interference with time for research.	Increasing workload makes it difficult for me to maintain my enthusiasm for teaching this topic. (scored negatively)

Source: Prosser & Trigwell (1997).

APPENDIX C: APPROACHES TO TEACHING INVENTORY

This inventory is designed to explore the way that academics go about teaching in a specific context or subject. This may mean that your responses to these items may be different to the responses you might make on your teaching in the other contexts or subjects.

Please describe the context here:...

For each item please circle one of the numbers (1-5). The numbers stand for the following responses:

1. This item was **only rarely** true for me in this subject.
2. This item was **sometimes** true for me in this subject.
3. This item was true for me **about half the time** in this subject.
4. This item was **frequently** true for me in this subject.
5. This item was almost **always** true for me in this subject.

Please answer each item. Do not spend a long time on each; your first reaction is probably the best one.

		Only Rarely				Almost Always
1	I design my teaching in this subject with the assumption that most of the students have very little useful knowledge of the topics to be covered.	1	2	3	4	5
2	I feel it is important that this subject should be completely described in terms of specific objectives relating to what students have to know for formal assessment items.	1	2	3	4	5
3	In my class/tutorial for this subject I try to develop a conversation with students about the topics we are studying.	1	2	3	4	5
4	I feel it is important to present a lot of facts in classes so that students know what they have to learn for this subject.	1	2	3	4	5

5	I feel that the assessment in this subject should be an opportunity for students to reveal their changed conceptual understanding of the subject.	1	2	3	4	5
6	We take time out in classes so that the students can discuss, among themselves, the difficulties that they encounter studying this subject.	1	2	3	4	5
7	In this subject I concentrate in covering the information that might be available from a good textbook.	1	2	3	4	5
8	I encourage students to restructure their existing knowledge in terms of the new way of thinking about the subject that they will develop.	1	2	3	4	5
9	In lectures for this subject, I use difficult or undefined examples to provoke debate.	1	2	3	4	5
10	I structure this subject to help students to pass the formal assessment items.	1	2	3	4	5
11	I think an important reason for giving lectures in this subject is to give students a good set of notes.	1	2	3	4	5
12	When I give this subject, I only provide the students with the information they will need to pass the formal assessments.	1	2	3	4	5
13	I feel that I should know the answers to any questions that students may put to me during this subject.	1	2	3	4	5
14	Formal teaching time is made available in this subject for students to discuss their changing understanding of the subject.	1	2	3	4	5

15	I feel that it is better for students in this subject to generate their own notes rather than always copy mine.	1	2	3	4	5
16	I feel a lot of teaching time in this subject should be used to question students' ideas.	1	2	3	4	5

Thank You

Source: Prosser & Trigwell, 1999, pp. 176-179.

REFERENCES

Barr, R. B., & Tagg, J. (1995). From teaching to learning — A new paradigm for undergraduate education. *Change, 27* (6), 12-25.

Barr, R. B. (1998). Obstacles to implementing the learning paradigm — What it takes to overcome them. *About Campus*, *3* (4), 18-25.

Biggs, J. B., & Collis, K. F. (1982). *Evaluating the Quality of Learning: The SOLO Taxonomy (Structure of the Observed Learning Outcome)*. New York: Academic Press.

Biggs, J. B. (1989). Approaches to the enhancement of tertiary teaching, *Higher Education Research and Development, 8* (1), 7-25.

Dall´Alba, G., 1991, Foreshadowing conceptions of teaching. *Research and Development in Higher Education, 13*, 293-297.

Fox, D. (1983). Personal theories of teaching. *Studies in Higher Education, 8* (2), 151-64.

Kember, D., & Gow, L. (1994). Orientations to teaching and their effect on the quality of student learning. *Journal of Higher Education*, *65* (1), 58-74.

Kember, D., & Kwan, K. (2000). Lecturers´ Approaches to Teaching and Their Relationship to Conceptions of Good Teaching. *Instructional Science, 28*, 469-490.

McKenzie, J. (1995). Changing Conceptions of University Teaching, unpublished Doctoral Assessment paper. University of Technology, Sydney, cited in M. Prosser & K. Trigwell (1999), *Understanding Learning and Teaching: The Experience in Higher Education.* Buckingham: SRHE and Open University Press.

Machabeli, I. (2002). *Country Report: Georgia.* Report presented at the 3rd Regional Conference "Legal Framework for Quality Assurance in Education," November 21-22, 2002, Department of Science, Academic Recognition and Mobility, Ministry of Education, Tbilisi, Georgia.

Martin, E., & Ramsden, P. (1993). An expanding awareness: How lecturers change their understanding of teaching. *Research and Development in Higher Education, 15,* 148-155.

Marton, F. (1988). Describing and improving learning. In R. R. Schmeck (Ed.), *Learning Strategies and Learning Styles* (pp. 54-82). New York: Plenum Press.

Marton, F., & Säljö, R. (1976). On qualitative differences in learning: 1. Outcome and process. *British Journal of Educational Psychology, 46,* 4-11.

Prosser, M., Trigwell, K., & Taylor, P. (1994). A phenomenographic study of academics' conceptions of science learning and teaching. *Learning and Instruction, 4*, 217-231.

Prosser, M., & Trigwell, K. (1997). Relations between perceptions of the teaching environment and approaches to teaching. *British Journal of Educational Psychology*, *67*, 25-35.

Prosser, M., & Trigwell, K. (1999). *Understanding Learning and Teaching. The Experience in Higher Education.* Buckingham: SRHE and Open University Press.

Schmidt, H. G. (1993). Foundations of problem-based learning: Some explanatory notes. *Medical Education*, *27,* 422-432.

Sorcinelli, M. D. (2002). Ten principles of good practice in creating and sustaining teaching and learning centers. In K. H. Gillespie (Ed.), *A Guide to Faculty Development: Practical Advice, Examples and Resources* (pp. 9-23). Bolton: Anker Publishing Company, Inc.

Trigwell, K., & Prosser, M. (1991). Improving the quality of student learning: The influence of learning context and student approaches to learning on learning outcomes. *Higher Education, 22*, 251-266.

Trigwell, K., & Prosser, M. (1996). Congruence between intention and strategy in science teachers' approach to teaching. *Higher Education, 32*, 77-87.

Trigwell, K., Prosser, M., & Taylor, P. (1994). Qualitative differences in approaches to teaching first year university science. *Higher Education, 27*, 75-84.

Trigwell, K., Prosser, M., & Waterhouse, F. (1999). Relations between teachers' approaches to Teaching and Students' Approaches to Learning. *Higher Education, 37*, 57-70.

Trowler, P. R. (1998). *Academics Responding to Change: New Higher Education Frameworks and Academic Cultures*. Buckingham: SRHE and Open University Press.

Chapter 6

LIFELONG LEARNING IN HIGHER EDUCATION

Is There a Gap Between the Idea and its Application in Higher Education?

Aileen M. Sibbald and John Troy
Napier University Business School, Napier University, Scotland, UK

1. INTRODUCTION

The concept of lifelong learning first came to prominence in the 1970s when the United Nations Educational, Scientific and Cultural Organization (UNESCO) adopted it. It was argued that lifelong education should be part of the fundamental policy and underlying concept to be used for the educational policies of both developed and developing countries since it contributed to economic development and equality of opportunity in society.

Its emphasis was that "education should last the whole life for all individuals and not just be tacked on to School or University for a privileged or specialized few" (Field, 2000). This view sets out the parameters under which lifelong learning — the creation of opportunities for all, at all levels of education — should be a right of all citizens in all societies at all times.

The origins of lifelong learning can be traced back to the writings of Dewey, Lindeman and Yeaxlee in the early part of the twentieth century (Tight, 1998). Emphasis was on adult education provided by the Church, Trade Unions and Co-operative Guilds, where opportunity had not existed before this time. As we examine the concept in the early part of the 21st century we find that not only has the definition of lifelong learning become wider, the complexity of the language leads to a lack of a shared view of what constitutes lifelong learning. Edwards, Raggat, Harrison, McCollum, and Calder (1998) point out that "there is a lack of a shared language and

M.K. McCuddy et al. (eds.),
The Challenges of Educating People to Lead in a Challenging World, 115–129.

understanding which is central to the difficulty of deciding what constitutes the literature on lifelong learning," and Gustavsson (2002) suggests that "the problem with lifelong learning is that it is used as a vision but is rather empty of content ... with no steer on how it may be transformed into practice" (our emphasis). Despite the lack of a shared view of lifelong learning, its importance for economic development, social justice, and citizenship has been highlighted in numerous policy papers across the globe.

While lifelong learning policies target fairness, opportunity and inclusion amongst their objectives, the importance of the economic dimension cannot be underestimated. The link between investment in education and longer-term economic growth targets has long been established, even if difficult to quantify. The ability to achieve targets for capacity planning through educational investment represents a major opportunity for governments that have a longer-term vision of the importance of this objective.

This can also be evidenced at the micro-economic level. A recent study that we carried out in relation to a departmental project in Mauritius (Napier University, 2000) highlighted the short-term impact of improving the teaching qualifications of secondary teachers in terms of the impact on student performance. While this research only covered a short time span (three years), it did emphasize the importance of lifelong learning policies as a strategic economic weapon in dealing with capacity building objectives.

This chapter emphasizes the ways in which Institutions of Higher Education can play an important role in supporting Government Policy. This chapter seeks to explore how successful one Institution has been in supporting lifelong learning policies. In particular, it explores the question: *"How can a lifelong learning vision be put into workable practice, which will enable policy makers (at the aggregate level) and implementers (at the operational level) to evaluate whether or not a lifelong learning strategy is working?"*

The chapter is presented in two distinct parts:

- A brief review and evaluation of the macro-economic and political vision of lifelong learning (as applied to the University sector) in Scotland; and
- An analysis and evaluation of the gap between theory and practice within the Business School at one Institution (Napier University in Scotland).

2. THE VISION

The vision of the Scottish Parliament is for a "Smart, Successful Scotland, where creating, learning and connecting faster is the basis for sustained productivity, growth, competitiveness and prosperity" (The Scottish Executive, 2001). This is a laudable aim especially as the key element in the approach is "entitlement" (The Scottish Parliament, 2002a) to widen access to all at all different levels of the educational spectrum.

This vision attempts to take account of research expressed by, amongst others, Hughes and Tight (1998, p. 185) who noted that "while some of the richer nations are naturally much closer than others to creating something like a lifelong learning society, in all cases substantial proportions of the population remain excluded or under-involved." Where, therefore, is the chain in linking the principle of lifelong learning to "entitlement" and more importantly action and application in terms of the University sector in Scotland?

Presently, there are fourteen Universities in Scotland and four in the Southeast of Scotland where Napier University is based. Napier's mission statement indicates that the intention is for the University to be "the lifelong learning University in the Southeast of Scotland" (Napier University, 2001).

How does this fit the vision of the Scottish Parliament for the Scottish economy as a whole? The answer is, of course, that it does not and cannot without a coordinated policy that looks at the relative strengths, weaknesses, and opportunities available to the sector on both a regional and, more importantly, national basis.

A national policy requires coordination to achieve global targets for lifelong learning but the "market" for program provision/training is a competitive one where individual universities compete for (largely) the same students while offering (in most cases) similar programs of study. In other words we have a product (lifelong learning) where the over-riding strategy is one of widening access and opportunity in the pursuit of providing a public good. However, in the application of providing this public good we are faced with a competitive market environment.

In other words, the strategy on lifelong learning is in danger of repeating the mistakes of the traditional approaches to the education sector in Scotland and the rest of the UK from the 1980s — competition in the provision of what should be a public good or social service.

In order to achieve meaningful targets for national success in the provision of lifelong learning, what is required is a change in culture which will lead to different universities specializing in different types of lifelong learning provision and, more importantly, abandoning others. This can avoid the problem of over-provision in lifelong learning and it is a policy that may well be directed to full-time provision as well.

While these 'aggregate' barriers to lifelong learning policies exist, the question still remains as to how it may be applied at the level of the individual unit of provision — an individual university.

3. LIFELONG LEARNING AND HIGHER EDUCATION

The concept of lifelong learning dominates much of the educational debate and policy discussion in Scotland. However, while its importance for economic development, social justice, citizenship, and quality is recognized, a lack of a shared vision is considered to inhibit the delivery of such policies (Aspin & Chapman, 2000; Slowey, 2000). Given the lack of a shared vision, a key element of the research reported in this chapter was to identify those issues that needed to be addressed in the development of a lifelong learning strategy. Edwards *et al.* (1998) identified five 'big issues,' as follows:

- The individual as a learner.
- Participation and equity.
- Learning and working.
- Funding learning.
- Delivering learning.

The literature review focused on these 'big issues' and an overview of what this means for the development of a Higher Education strategy is given below.

3.1 The Individual as a Learner

As the volume of knowledge and information available to learners increases within the *knowledge-based economy*, the focus within education is shifting from the content of learning to the learning process. Greater emphasis is being placed on developing skills in students that will enable them to assimilate and apply new knowledge and information as it appears.

The notion of a job for life is disappearing. As technology changes rapidly, so does the skills-base required of the workers. More and more employees are required to develop new skills or skills which are transferable. In this environment therefore, individuals must take responsibility for being able to adapt as needs require. As highlighted by the UK Department for Education & Employment, "individuals are urged to invest in lifelong learning to develop their personal competitiveness" (DfEE, 1995). Therefore the focus in education should be on responding to the needs of individual learners. However is this a realistic goal? A declining resource base in education restricts the opportunity to develop programs of study that meet the needs of **each** individual.

As noted by Edwards *et al.* (1998), there is a "fundamental tension between responding to individual needs and the agendas of other stakeholders such as Government, Employers, Funding Bodies, Institutions, and Professional Bodies." Therefore, there are other factors which influence what Higher Education (HE) Institutions are able to deliver and who has access to them.

Various initiatives have been developed within HE that can support the needs of learners to some extent — for example, the Credit Accumulation & Transfer Scheme (CATS) and the process of Accreditation of Prior Learning. As more flexible approaches to learning are developed, this will make it easier for students to move in and out of learning to suit their individual needs and, in turn, go some way to meeting the needs of learners.

3.2 Participation and Equity

Studies in participation, such as McGivney (1990) and Sargant (1996), found that those with "minimal initial education, manual workers, adults from lower socio-economic groups and old people" were consistently under-represented in learning (Edwards *et al.*, 1998). Historically the pattern of enrollment in HE is different between the social classes (*e.g.*, pupils whose parents are from second/third generation unemployed are less likely to go onto HE than those whose parents are themselves graduates). Despite this, Napier University has in fact participated in a number of initiatives that have been successful in promoting social inclusion. Examples include delivery of bridging modules to support student articulating from Further Education into Higher Education, the Lothian and Edinburgh Equal Access Program for Schools (LEAPS) [a body which aims to ensure that all students with an ability to succeed on degree courses get the opportunity to go on to university in spite of economic or social barriers that might disadvantage them], an Employers Forum for widening access, and a student retention project which aims to identify where students are having difficulties.

A key government policy priority within both the UK and Scotland has been to widen access to Higher and Further Education. While this has been successful, particularly for mature learners, there is evidence that there is still under-representation from different social groups (Watt & Paterson, 2000). Hughes & Tight (1998, p. 185) note, "while some of the richer nations are naturally much closer than others to creating something like a lifelong learning society, in all cases substantial proportions of the population remain excluded or under-involved."

Widening access is a priority that will not disappear. It has been argued that investing in Adult learners is beneficial from a number of perspectives including active citizenship, social exclusion, living standards and employability. Further, Higher Education has a duty to help meet this challenge and to do so effectively major reorganization of the traditional university learning context is needed. As a result, academic staff should be more adaptable and flexible when it comes to program provision. To support this there needs to be institutional change, curriculum change, a shift from teaching to learning and enhanced staff development within HE (Edwards *et al.*, 1998).

3.3 Learning and Working

The majority of Napier students are drawn from a fairly local population, namely the Lothian regions of Scotland. This is an area in which the labor market is currently strong with a fast growing number of vacancies. Skills shortages are emerging, particularly in the area of financial services and call centers. Despite this there are pockets of high unemployment in certain areas within Edinburgh, and a challenge to Napier University, amongst others, is to help to spread prosperity within the city. Through the Scottish Executive's *Future Skills Unit*, action is being taken to address some of these discrepancies. However, an important factor to take into consideration is that there could be there a potential mismatch between the needs of employers and the desire of the unemployed to be trained/re-trained into those areas where there are specific skills shortages (Edwards *et al.*, 1998).

Joint working between Scottish Further Education (FE) Institutions, *learndirect™ scotland*, training providers and regular liaison with the Enterprise Networks, and the Scottish Further & Higher Education Funding Councils (SFEFC/SHEFC), is one way to ensure that Higher Education can help to meet the needs of industry. However, further action will need to be taken to attract learners in those areas where there are skills shortages. Perhaps this could be achieved by targeting financial support in particular areas, either by the government or other stakeholders.

3.4 Funding Learning

The Independent Committee of Inquiry into Student Finance in 1999 (ICISF, 1999) confirms that financial consideration is a strong deterrent to participation in HE. In response to this, the SHEFC has developed a series of linked initiatives that aim to stimulate Scottish Universities to promote part-time study opportunities and to widen access to HE in Scotland by removing some of the financial barriers experienced by those adults with low incomes who wish to study on a part-time basis. More recently, the Enterprise and Lifelong Learning Committee of the Scottish Parliament has recommended that "part-time learners should have the same access to fee support as full-time learners with pilot projects to target groups such as low wage earners and single parents" (Scottish Parliament, 2002b).

3.5 Delivering Learning

The environment within which HE Institutions are operating is one in which HE is no longer the sole provider of knowledge. Universities are no longer exclusive bodies of knowledge or providers of skills training. Information Communications and Technology (ICT) developments enable new kinds of distance learning as well as new modes of study and dissemination of knowledge. These are all potential threats to HE and as a result, all HE Institutions are repositioning themselves (Williamson, 1998). As Slowey (2000) writes, "new forms of knowledge creation and dissemination, greater access to information sources, use of new media and new channels of communication, development of complex partnerships with both external providers and user groups, and the growing role of education markets are all factors that have a major impact on where how and when students learn."

In the new knowledge-based learning age, universities need to grasp opportunities as they present themselves and respond quickly if they are to remain competitive. Operating within a climate of declining resources means that alternative and innovative ways of providing education need to be found. Forming partnerships with other providers is one way of providing high quality education at a lesser cost than if the whole product was to be delivered by one Institution.

Gallagher and Thomson (1999) highlight the many benefits being accrued by the Further and Higher Education sectors through the agreements that have been established between many of the Institutions. Increasingly, the focus is on the creation of links between HE Institutions, particularly Scottish Institutions where the local market is small. In a climate of diminishing resources, greater sharing of expertise and innovation is beneficial to institutions and their students.

To accommodate the needs of lifelong learners, HE Institutions have to become much more open, flexible and responsive to the different circumstances and motivations of the much more heterogeneous student body. The number of non-traditional students is rapidly increasing (as compared to traditional 17-22 year-olds in full-time education). Slowey (2000) suggests that perhaps this differentiation between traditional and non-traditional student is no longer appropriate. However, in many HE Institutions the "non-traditional" students are not seen as core educational business and are considered to require a substantial amount of student support. Despite this, in session 2001/02 41% of the student population at Napier University was non-traditional (*i.e.*, aged 25 and over).

Another reason to move away from concentrating efforts on the "traditional student" is the aging population in the UK. The Office of

Science & Technology (Scase, 1999) predicts that in the first decade of the 21st century population will increase little. Like many other European countries, the UK population will be static or fall. An aging population will arise from a fall in the birth rates combined with increased life expectancy, with the result that by 2010 there will be a fall in the population of people under 25 and an increase in the middle-aged and people over 65. Institutions need to bear this in mind in their long-term planning of educational provision; they will need to consider the appropriateness of the modes of delivery and programs of study to meet the needs of an aging population.

However, being more open, flexible and responsive to the needs of all learners requires the support of senior management. Staff members need to be given adequate training and support to develop the flexible delivery of their materials, and also on how to support the "non-traditional" learner.

An important question in terms of the academic provision within HE is: "Does it match the needs and expectations of lifelong learners?" Another important question is: "Are institutions fully aware of the needs of their market and what is being sought or required?" Many learners may wish shorter programs or non-credit bearing programs. In many HE Institutions there is a separate Continuing Professional Development Unit with the responsibility to help develop such provision. Slowey (2000) considers that availability of such units in HE is an indicator of their commitment to playing a part in the broad system of lifelong learning. However, since the establishment of these units, has such provision moved from the peripheries of the institution towards core units? As early as 1982, Hoggart, Stephens, Taylor, and Smethurst suggested that such units suffered as a result of their status as separate units outside regular academic programs and called for the integration of continuing education within the routine work of the departments.

Williamson (1998) has suggested that to survive universities need to meet a wider variety of education and training needs than they currently do. In order to reduce their vulnerability they must be seen as having a unique place in the cultural life of society as a whole. He further states that "The university of the future must embrace the agenda for lifelong learning and to do so requires a new kind of academic leadership, one that is more clued up about the changes taking place in society and determined to shape the direction of such change in democratic ways" (Williamson, 1998, p. 130). If universities are to be able to meet the changing needs for knowledge, research, and lifelong learning and continue to rely primarily on government funding, then they themselves need to be responsive to new circumstances, new kinds of students, and new forms of study and research. Universities must therefore be more critical of themselves and of their old ways of doing things and as a result be more responsive to any need to change. The Council of Europe (2000) also noted that having moved into the *Knowledge Age*, not only must individuals adapt to change with different patterns of learning, living and working but also equally established ways of doing things must change. Is the Napier Business School repositioning itself effectively, or is it continuing to do “more of the same”?

3.6 Key Indicators of Lifelong Learning

From the review of the literature on lifelong learning it is clear that the term encompasses many forms of learning and has wide reaching implications for HE. To facilitate the research, fifteen key indicators of lifelong learning were identified from the literature review as important to the Higher Education sector in Scotland, as set out in Table 1.

Table 1. Key Indicators of Lifelong Learning

	Indicators
1	Involving industry in program content and design.
2	Accreditation of work-based learning.
3	Developing top-up programs which award substantial credit for prior learning.
4	Widening access through non-traditional routes.
5	Providing programs of study with academic content that is sought by the learner.
6	Providing programs of study other than traditional undergraduate/postgraduate degrees.
7	Providing learning opportunities for learners in Southeast Scotland.
8	Collaboration with other providers of education/training in the provision of programs.
9	Linking with Secondary Schools to promote progression of learners to HE.
10	Linking with FE Colleges to promote progression of learners to HE.
11	Delivering programs at times that suit mature learners/people in employment.
12	Providing programs of study that do not require physical attendance at the University.
13	Providing support for learners from non-traditional backgrounds.
14	Staff development (to keep apace with the changing learning environment).
15	Keeping a database of graduates, for future promotion of programs.

4. THE ‘APPLICATION’ OF LIFELONG LEARNING

The second part of this paper provides some results from a survey carried out amongst staff in the Business School of Napier University during 2002. The objective of the research was to determine whether or not there was a gap between the University’s vision for lifelong learning and the actual practice within the Business School of Napier University.

4.1 Research Methodology

A qualitative method (rather than a quantitative one) was considered to be the most suitable, as qualitative methods of research are capable of providing a rich source of data that might not be discovered from purely quantitative methods (Hammersley, 1993), although the limitations in its scope must be recognized. The specific information required to address the Research Question that *there is no gap between the University's vision for lifelong learning and actual practice within the Napier University Business School* was as follows:

1. What does staff understand by the term 'Lifelong Learning'?
   - How does staff define lifelong learning?
   - What does staff think is the role of HE in lifelong learning?

2. What does staff perceive as the importance of lifelong learning: underpinning economic prosperity, or social (developing a democratic, informed participative society), or both?
   - What does lifelong learning mean for Napier University?
   - Does staff consider the lifelong learning vision to be achievable?
   - What does staff think is meant by the vision statement?
   - Does staff think that there is adequate central support to deliver this vision?

3. What does lifelong learning mean for the Business School?
   - Does staff feel that the programs that are being delivered in their School meet the needs of today's student (in terms of academic content, skills training, flexibility in place, and pace)?
   - Is the Business School delivering lifelong learning opportunities? (For example, programs developed/delivered with Industry, Accreditation of Learning in the Workplace and development of joint programs, links with Schools to develop desire to learn throughout life and to highlight opportunities available to students from all backgrounds, links with FE Colleges, and opportunities for mature learners or links with the local community.)
   - What does staff feel inhibits such developments; is it financial, no desire to do so, no reward to Schools to develop these, the view that it is not the responsibility of HE?
   - Does staff feel they receive adequate staff development to keep apace of the challenging learning environment? (For example, support for and delivery to flexible learners/distance learners; to

prepare for the diverse range of academic ability to students as access is widened.)

- Does Napier do enough to entice graduates back to Napier for further learning?
- Does Napier provide opportunities for learning that are being sought by learners or is it dictating what is offered?
- Does staff feel that the Vision for lifelong learning is being met in their school, if not what needs to be done to achieve this?

Using this information, a questionnaire was designed and distributed to all of the academic staff in the Business School. The response rates were poor — only 42% of members of academic staff from the School of Accounting & Economics (*i.e.*, 19 respondents from a possible 45), 17% from the School of Marketing & Tourism (*i.e.*, 5 from 29), and 16% from the School of Management (*i.e.*, 6 from 38). While these figures were disappointing there are two observations that can be made:

- The School of Accounting and Economics is the one in the Business School that has the highest level of involvement in flexible learning programs designed for non-standard entrants.
- The staff of this School is more actively involved in the promotion of new approaches to learning (including membership in ED*i*NEB!).

The questionnaire was also used to develop an understanding of what staff considered to be the key indicators in the pursuit of a lifelong learning policy (as identified in section 3.6 of this chapter). In addition, the research sought to measure the extent to which staff felt that their School was effective in carrying this out.

4.2 Research Findings

The findings from the research indicated that the top six key indicators of lifelong learning for Higher Education were as follows:

- Involving industry in program content and design.
- Linking with FE Colleges to promote progression of learners to HE.
- Providing programs of study other than traditional undergraduate/postgraduate degrees; widening access through non-traditional routes.
- Delivering programs at times that suit mature learners and/or people in employment.
- Providing support for learners from non-traditional backgrounds.
- Staff development.

The research findings further indicated that there was a high level of agreement that certain issues were important for the delivery of lifelong learning opportunities within Higher Education, and indeed all of the indicators identified were considered important. However, when we looked at the effectiveness of Schools in the delivery of these, a large proportion of respondents felt their School was ineffective in a lot of these.

Looking at the effectiveness of delivery across the Business School, the results indicated very low effectiveness. Only in one area, 'providing learning opportunities for South-East Scotland,' did over 70% of respondents consider delivery to be effective. For the majority of the indicators, only 40-48% of respondents considered delivery to be effective. These findings suggest that the Business School should review its activities in relation to delivery of the lifelong learning vision to ensure that the rhetoric is translated into organizational action.

Williamson (1998, p. 130) states that "The university of the future must embrace the agenda for lifelong learning and to do so requires a new kind of academic leadership, one that is more clued up about the changes taking place in society and determined to shape the direction of such change in democratic ways." If universities are to be able to meet the changing needs for knowledge, research, and lifelong learning, and continue to rely primarily on government funding, then they need to be responsive to new circumstances, new kinds of students, and new forms of study and research. Universities must therefore be more critical of themselves and of their old way of doing things and as a result be more responsive to any need to change. The Council of Europe (2000) noted that having moved into the *Knowledge Age,* not only must individuals adapt to change with different patterns of learning, living and working, but also equally established ways of doing things must change.

While it is clear from the responses to the questionnaire that academic staff members have an awareness of the importance of lifelong learning and the role of Higher Education in its delivery, the findings on effectiveness demonstrate that Napier University has failed to translate its lifelong learning vision into action. Hoyle (1988) suggests that there are three possible reasons why missions in educational strategy fail; namely through failure to convert the mission statement into practice, failure to involve/convert staff, and failure to interpret the environment correctly. Therefore, Napier should undertake further research to determine and rectify the failure to deliver the Vision outlined in section 2 of this chapter.

5. THE FUTURE

The framework for this research centered on a micro-level analysis of lifelong learning (specifically one Faculty within one Scottish University) and the conclusions and recommendations that could be drawn from the data collected. The emphasis of this research was on the examination of the gap between theory and practice at a micro-level. The research has highlighted the role of a university in supporting lifelong learning, particularly as it relates to the development of the Scottish economy and increasing participation in learning, two of the main pillars of the lifelong learning.

However, while working on the research it became clear that there were wider and deeper issues which could be addressed in the future both at a localized level (*i.e.*, lifelong learning in Napier University) and also for the broader context of HE within the Scottish economy. Accordingly, it would be valuable to conclude the research with a short examination of possible future trends at the macro-environment level.

For Napier University, the framework developed for this research could be applied to the other Faculties to determine whether common issues arise across the University or not. Although the scope of such a study was beyond the reference point for this research, it could serve as a starting point for similar work to be carried out in the other Faculties.

While this type of analysis might give the senior management of Napier University an insight into a 'gap analysis' on a University-wide scale, one must consider the implications of <u>all</u> HE Institutions having a lifelong learning policy for <u>all</u> areas of their activity. Therefore, the future scope should examine whether or not Napier University is **"the"** lifelong learning University in Southeast Scotland, or indeed should wish to be.

A recent article in the *Scotsman* applauds the achievements of graduates and highlights the fact that the government target of 50% for the population's participation in mass higher education has been achieved in Scotland. However, it suggests that "increased participation by itself is too crude a measure of development of personal and professional skills at one level and potential contribution to the economy and society at another" (Scotsman, 13 July, 2002). This would suggest that there needs to be a planned approach to the provision of lifelong learning with all interested parties contributing to any strategy and implementation policies.

This is to sound a note of caution. If all HE Institutions embark on a policy of lifelong learning with all their programs, there will soon be a provision over-supply that would be wasteful in terms of resource allocation at a micro-economic level. What is needed is an 'educational audit' of lifelong learning and future activities to permit planning rather than competition. The recent inquiry into lifelong learning undertaken by the Scottish Parliament has highlighted the fact that there is no coordinated strategy for lifelong learning and it is seeking to redress this through the outcomes of the inquiry. It is therefore important that all interested parties participate in this inquiry to ensure that their concerns and ideas for the future can be taken into account in future government strategy and policy in Scotland.

6. CONCLUSIONS

The research findings highlighted a number of positive and encouraging factors for the future. In particular:

- There is a wide range of lifelong learning activity across the Business School Faculty.
- There is a good awareness of the opportunities and threats to the development of lifelong learning activity, which when addressed will enable the gap to be reduced.
- There is a willingness amongst a number of key members of the academic staff to keep lifelong learning as a major part of the Faculty strategy.

On a negative note, however, a number of staff are not as supportive of the lifelong learning vision, primarily because they believe that inadequate human and financial resources are being made available to support this.

In terms of the research question posed that *there is no gap between the University's vision for lifelong learning and actual practice within the Napier University Business School*, the simple conclusion is that there is a gap between the vision of the University and the actual level of current and planned activity in the field of lifelong learning. The main features of this are centered on issues such as resources and support from central support and administrative units. There are major, not minor, costs involved in setting up flexible learning programs, and the real opportunity costs of these are only now being taken into account. This is an encouraging development as it will give a more realistic view as to how University targets are set in the future.

REFERENCES

Aspin, D. N., & Chapman, J. D. (2000). Lifelong Learning: concepts and conceptions. *International Journal of Lifelong Education* (Jan-Feb 2000). *19* (1), 2-19.

Council of Europe. (2000). *Lifelong Learning for Equity and Social Cohesion: a New Challenge to Higher Education, Progress Report*. Strasbourg: Council of Europe.

DfEE. (1995). *Lifetime Learning: A Consultation Document*. Sheffield: Department for Education & Employment (DfEE).

Edwards, R., Raggat, P., Harrison, R., McCollum, A., & Calder, J. (1998). *Recent Thinking in Lifelong Learning: A Review of the Literature*. Research Report No. 80. Norwich: Her Majesty's Stationery Office (HMSO).

Field, J. (2000). Governing the ungovernable: Why lifelong learning policies promise so much yet deliver so little. *Educational Management & Administration*, *28* (3), 249-261.

Gallagher, J., & Thomson, C. (1999). Further education: Overlapping or overstepping, *Scottish Journal of Adult and Continuing Education*, *5* (1), 9-24.

Gustavsson, B. (2002). What do we mean by lifelong learning and knowledge? *International Journal of Lifelong Education*, *21* (1), 13-23.

Hammersley, M. (Ed.). (1993). *Educational Research: Current Issues*. London: Paul Chapman Publishing Ltd, in association with The Open University.

Hoggart, R., Stephens, M., Taylor, J., & Smethurst, R. (1982). Continuing education within universities and polytechnics. In D. D. A. Bligh (Ed.), *Professionalism and Flexibility in Learning*. Guilford, Surrey: Society for Research into Higher Education.

Hoyle, E. (1988). Micropolitics of educational institutions. In A. Westoby (Ed.), *Culture and Power in Educational Organizations* (pp.255-69). Oxford: Open University Press.

Hughes, C., & Tight, M. (1998). The myth of the learning society. In S. Ranson (Ed.), *Inside the Learning Society* (Chapter 15). London: Cassell.

ICISF, (1999). The Independent Committee of Inquiry into Student Finance: final report (commonly known as The Cubie Report). Edinburgh: Independent Committee of Inquiry into Student Finance.

McGivney, V. (1990). *Education's for Other People: Access to Education for Non-participative Adults*. Leicester: National Institute of Adult Continuing Education (NIACE).

Napier University. (2000). Report to the Tertiary Education Commission/Ministry of Education (TEC/MoE) — Mauritius. Edinburgh: Napier University.

Napier University (2001). Strategic Plan 2001-2005.

Sargant, N. (1996). Learning and leisure. In R. Edwards, A. Hanson, & P. Raggat (Eds.), *Boundaries of Adult Learning*. London: Routledge.

Scase, R. (1999). *Britain Towards 2010: The Changing Business Environment*. London: Department of Trade & Industry.

Scottish Executive. (2001). A Smart Successful Scotland: Ambitions for the Enterprise Networks, http://www.scotland.gov.uk/library3/enterprise, accessed November 28, 2002.

Scottish Parliament. (2002a) *Interim Report on Lifelong Learning*, http://www.scottish.parliament.uk, accessed November 12, 2002.

Scottish Parliament. (2002b). Final Report on Lifelong Learning, http://www.scottish.parliament.uk/officialreport, accessed November 12, 2002.

Slowey, M. (2000). The United Kingdom. In H. G. Schuetz, & M. Slowey, (Eds.), *Higher Education & Lifelong Learners: International Perspectives on Change* (Chapter 6). London: RoutledgeFalmer.

The Scotsman. (2002, July 13). Universities must be freed to pursue excellence, p. 13.

Tight, M. (1998). Lifelong learning: Opportunity or compulsion? *British Journal of Educational Studies*, *46* (3), 251-263.

Watt, S., & Paterson, L. (2000). Pathways and partnerships: Widening access to higher education. *Journal of Further and Higher Education*, *24* (1), 107-116.

Williamson, B. (1998). *Lifeworlds and Learning*. Leicester: National Institute of Adult Continuing Education (NIACE).

Chapter 7

IMPLEMENTING AND SUSTAINING EDUCATIONAL INNOVATIONS[2]

Michael K. McCuddy and Wendy L. Pirie
College of Business Administration, Valparaiso University, Valparaiso, Indiana, USA

1. INTRODUCTION

Concerns about the lack of institutional and collegial support for implementing and sustaining educational innovations have frequently been mentioned in various forums at the annual EDiNEB Conferences. This raises two questions: (1) Is there, in fact, a lack of support for educational innovation? and (2) If so, why is there a lack of support? One possible answer is that these concerns reflect an organizational change process gone awry. However, little seems to have been done to systematically and formally document the educational innovation process from the perspective of managing organizational change, let alone systematically exploring how the change process has gone awry.

This chapter seeks to examine the implementation and sustainability of educational innovations by adapting Kurt Lewin's (1951) three-phase model of change (*i.e.*, unfreezing, change, and refreezing). The Lewinian model is widely accepted in the organizational change and development (OCD) discipline, with applications existing in many different business and institutional settings (see for example: Argyris, 1970; Beer & Walton, 1990; Bertsch & Williams, 1994; Cummings & Worley, 1997; McWhinney, 1989;

[2] We wish to acknowledge and thank Barbara Aarestad and David Moews for their suggestions, contributions, and involvement in the early stages of this paper. We also wish to thank the EDiNEB Network, and especially Richard G. Milter and Ellen Nelissen, for supporting the survey by providing access to the EDiNEB membership mailing list.

M.K. McCuddy et al. (eds.),
The Challenges of Educating People to Lead in a Challenging World, 131–148.

and Smither, Houston, & McIntire, 1996). We believe this model can be adapted to help explain and understand the phenomenon of implementing and sustaining educational innovation in institutions of higher learning. We propose a model of educational innovation (see Figure 1) that both parallels and adapts the unfreezing, change, and refreezing phases of Lewin's model. We use different labels for the three phases, however. *Openness to educational innovation* corresponds to unfreezing, *innovation activities* correspond to change, and *consequences of innovation* relate to refreezing. In addition, we expand the consequences of change beyond the usual focus of the Lewinian model. We also add a feedback loop; this reflects the fact that the resulting consequences of change may impact the future openness to innovation.

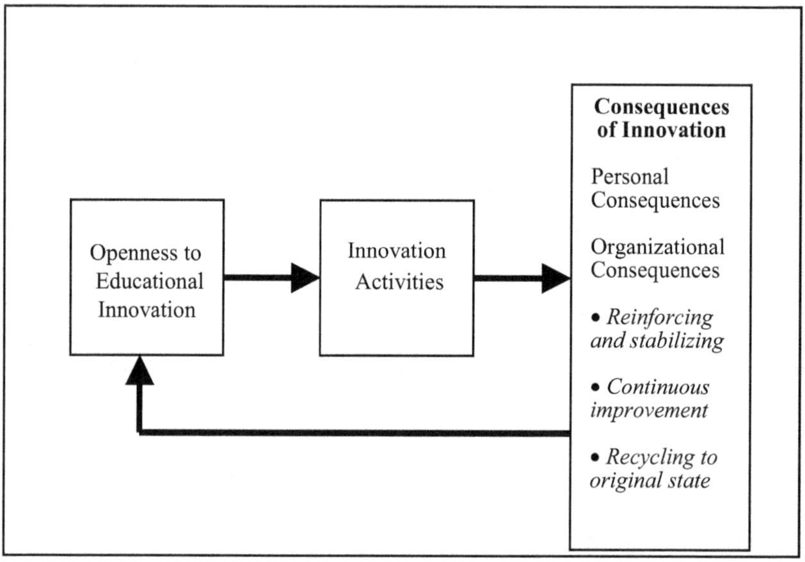

Figure 1. A Proposed Model of Educational Innovation

Like unfreezing, *openness to educational innovation* reflects the conditions and forces that create and motivate the need for change, or restrain them. Similar to change, *innovation activities* refer to the actions that are undertaken to address the need for change. New systems, processes, procedures, and behaviors are developed and implemented in order to produce the desired change. *Consequences of innovation* adapt and extend the refreezing phase. We identify both personal and organizational consequences of innovation. *Personal consequences*, which reflect benefits or detriments to the individual innovator, may have an enduring impact on the sustainability of change at the organizational level. *Organizational consequences*, however, appear to be more likely to foster sustainable change for the institution, or to repress it.

We propose three different paths by which organizational consequences can evolve. Like Lewin's refreezing, *organizational consequences of innovation* involve reinforcing and stabilizing the new behaviors within the organization. Unlike refreezing, however, *organizational consequences* go beyond reinforcing and stabilizing by specifying two other possible institutional outcomes of the educational innovation process. One of these outcomes is a process of continuous improvement wherein the educational institution encourages and supports ongoing educational innovation that builds on, extends, and adapts prior innovations. Another possible consequence of educational innovation is a recycling of the institution to the conditions that were in place when the educational innovation was originally initiated. Educational innovations, while initially being supported and endorsed by some segments of the institution, end up being jettisoned over the long term as institutional forces and collegial sentiments undermine innovation. In short, this category of innovation consequences reflects a return to the "same old, same old" way of doing things. In our view, it is this latter path that underlies concerns about the lack of support for educational innovations. Ultimately, we contend that the consequences result in feedback to the participants that impacts their willingness to continue to experiment with educational innovation.

Because of the unique nature of educational institutions in comparison to other types of organizations, a feedback loop is an essential component of the education innovation model. The feedback loop is critical in the educational change process due to faculty governance and academic freedom. If administrators cannot impose changes, it is imperative that they provide appropriate feedback and reinforcement in order for meaningful changes to be sustained and to help create motivation and supporting conditions for future changes.

Using the results of an e-mail survey of the EDiNEB Network membership, we assess the utility and viability of our adaptation of Lewin's model. The survey results provide insights regarding how change has been implemented and sustained in the educational context. The proposed model and the survey results will hopefully provide EDiNEB Network members with useful information, insights, and ideas for their efforts in implementing, improving, and sustaining educational innovations at their respective institutions.

2. SURVEY METHODOLOGY

2.1 Questionnaire

A questionnaire was designed to collect data on EDiNEB members' experiences with educational innovation. The questionnaire, which is displayed in Appendix A, contains 19 questions, 12 of which have some form of structured response and seven of which are open-ended. Seven of the structured response questions (1 through 7) describe the characteristics of the respondents. Two questions — number 8, which is structured, and number 12, which is open-ended — address the *openness to educational innovation* component of our proposed model. Three questions (9, 10, and 11) pertain to the *innovation activities* component of the model. Questions 9 and 10 have structured responses whereas question 11 is open-ended. Questions 13 through 19 are relevant to the *consequences of innovation* component. Question 14, which is open-ended, and Question 15, which has structured responses, provide a general characterization of innovation outcomes. Question 13, a structured response item, addresses *personal consequences of innovation*. Questions 16 through 19, all of which are open-ended, concern *organizational consequences of innovation*.

2.2 Survey Sample

The survey was sent via e-mail to the entire membership roster of the EDiNEB Network. A total of 198 individuals were e-mailed the questionnaire in early December 2002. Of these 198 e-mails, 31 were returned as undeliverable due to full e-mail boxes, incorrect e-mail addresses, or the person no longer being affiliated with the institution for which the e-mail address existed. Consequently, the effective size of our potential respondent pool was reduced to 167 EDiNEB Network members. A follow-up e-mail was sent to EDiNEB Network members in mid-January 2003.

2.3 Analysis Protocol

The data for all questions with structured responses were summarized with frequency distributions. In addition, means and ranges were computed, where appropriate. The responses to the open-ended questions were content analyzed to identify key themes and categories.

3. SURVEY RESULTS

3.1 Respondent Characteristics

Twenty-eight responses were received from the potential respondent pool of 167, a response rate of 16.8 percent, which is not vastly different from the typical response pattern of a conventional "snail mail" survey where non-respondents can reach as high as 90 percent (Clover & Balsley 1979, p. 96). The respondents can be characterized in a variety of ways, based on answers to questions 1 to 7. Eighteen of the respondents represented public college or universities, and another eight respondents came from private colleges and universities. The other two respondents were from the non-academic world. Of those in the academic realm, two respondents described their institutions as having a liberal arts focus, ten respondents were from comprehensive institutions, five represented masters granting institutions, and nine were from doctoral institutions. The vast majority of the respondents were from either The Netherlands (n = 9) or the United States of America (n =11). Responses were also received from the United Kingdom (n = 3), Mexico (n = 2), Australia (n = 1), New Zealand (n = 1), and South Africa (n = 1).

The size of the respondents' academic institutions can be described via several measures. Table 1 provides information on the size of the undergraduate student population at the respondents' institutions. The overall average size of the undergraduate population for the 26 academic institutions is 10,335 students, and the range is from 575 students to 45,000 students. Table 2 presents data on the size of the graduate student body at the respondents' institutions. The overall average size of graduate student body for the 23 academic institutions with graduate programs is 2,658, with a range of 50 to 7,000 students.

Table 1. Size of Undergraduate Student Body at Respondents' Institutions

Number of Undergraduate Students	Number of Institutions	Average Size Per Category
1 to 4,999	11	2,082
5,000 to 9,999	5	7,263
10,000 to 14,999	4	12,375
15,000 to 19,999	1	15,000
20,000 to 24,999	1	20,000
25,000 to 29,999	2	25,000
30,000 to 34,999	1	30,000
35,000 and greater	1	45,000

Table 2. Size of Graduate Student Body at Respondents' Institutions

Number of Graduate Students	Number of Institutions	Average Size Per Category
1 to 999	5	215
1,000 to 1,999	8	1,500
2,000 to 2,999	2	2,500
3,000 to 3,999	0	0
4,000 to 4,999	1	4,000
5,000 to 5,999	4	5,000
6,000 to 6,999	2	6,025
7,000 to 7,999	1	7,000

The sample can also be characterized in terms of the number of undergraduate and graduate students majoring in business and in economics. Table 3 presents data regarding the undergraduate majors while Table 4 provides information on the graduate majors. For the relevant respondent institutions, the average number of undergraduates majoring in business is 1,451 and the average number of undergraduates majoring in economics is 202. The respective ranges for the undergraduates are 400 to 6,000 and 20 to 800. For the reported graduate programs, the average number of business majors is 616 and the average number of economics majors is 236. The respective ranges for the graduate students are 15 to 3,000 and 5 to 800.

Table 3. Number of Undergraduate Students in Business and Economics at Respondents' Institutions

	Undergraduate Business Students		Undergraduate Economics Students	
Number of Majors	Number of Institutions	Average Size Per Category	Number of Institutions	Average Size Per Category
1 to 999	11	639	14	202
1,000 to 1,999	7	1,457	0	0
2,000 to 2,999	4	2,148	0	0
3,000 to 3,999	1	3,000	0	0
4,000 and greater	1	6,000	0	0

Table 4. Number of Graduate Students in Business and Economics at Respondents' Institutions

	Graduate Business Students		Graduate Economics Students	
Number of Majors	Number of Institutions	Average Size Per Category	Number of Institutions	Average Size Per Category
1 to 999	16	282	7	236
1,000 to 1,999	2	1,250	0	0
2,000 to 2,999	1	2,300	0	0
3,000 to 3,999	1	3,000	0	0

3.2 Openness to Educational Innovation

Openness to educational innovation is captured in questions 8 and 12. This openness to change corresponds, albeit not identically, to the unfreezing stage in the Lewinian model. The questions reflect why a need for change was felt (question 12) and how strongly the respondent answers that need (question 8) as opposed to the change leader's task of creating a felt need for change, and the process by which the change is made.

The motivation to experiment with innovative educational approaches, as reflected in the open-ended responses to Question 12, can be categorized as resulting from four sources. The innovation is driven by: (1) personal characteristics of the respondent, which is an intrinsic motivation; (2) a concern for the student; (3) a change in the environment; or (4) institutional imperatives.

A sampling of responses for each category is as follows:

Intrinsically (self) motivated:

- "How else do you stay intellectually alive?"
- "Naturally creative."
- "I like variety."

Student motivated:

- "Looking for better learning solutions. More effective learning (anytime, anywhere)."
- "Concern regarding the development of student skills."
- "Improve the students' learning process."

Environmentally motivated:

- "Change in technology."
- "Serendipitous environmental influences: growing interest/technical ability in eEducation."
- "The availability of computing resources has made me interested in developing computer-based projects."

Institutionally motivated:

- "We want to be a dynamic school working in the frontline of educational quality."
- "It's what the alumni survey said should be done."
- "Reduction of costs."

Although a single respondent may indicate more than one motivating factor, a concern for the student is expressed in 19 of the 28 responses, thereby demonstrating a strong student orientation across respondents. The other sources of motivation are approximately equally prevalent. Eight responses indicated an intrinsic motivation. Eight responses indicated an institutional imperative. Seven responses reflected a change in environment as motivating the innovation.

Two dominant descriptions of the respondents' attitudes toward educational innovation emerged from Question 8. A few respondents chose more than one alternative on this question. The overwhelming majority (n = 23) of our sample describes themselves as enthusiastic initiators of major educational innovations. Five of the respondents report being receptive to major changes that are initiated by others. Only one respondent indicated some degree of resistance to change. Clearly, most of the people sampled are active participants in change, which is not surprising given the source of our sample.

3.3 Innovation Activities

Innovation activities are captured in questions 9, 10, and 11. The activities correspond to the change leader's task of implementing change. Further, the activities very closely approximate identifying new and more effective behaviors, choosing appropriate changes, and taking action.

Consistent with the finding that there was a strong concern for the student as the primary motivating factor for educational innovation, the focus of the educational innovation efforts, as indicated in responses to Question 9, was directed more toward the student and methods of learning than toward the teacher/instructor/professor. Twenty responses indicated that the focus was the student and method of learning; two responses indicated the focus was the teacher and the material presentation, and six responses indicated a joint focus.

Of the actual innovation activities pursued by the respondents (see Question 10), instructional methods seem to dominate. The distribution was approximately equal among the mode of learning for a specific topic (n = 23), method of delivery (n = 25), and alteration of student and professor roles (n = 26). Assessment of the individual student's competencies and/or performance characterized 18 of the innovations. Assessment of the curriculum and changes to it were reflected in 11 and 17 of the responses, respectively. Once again, the individual student orientation asserts a powerful influence on the types of innovations that occur. The innovations tend to be more micro in nature. There seems to be little innovation with a global or macro orientation. This is consistent with a perceived lack of institutional support.

Responses to Question 11 can be categorized in two ways: (a) micro versus macro innovations, and (b) type of innovation. Given a student orientation toward educational innovation and a relatively low indication of institutional imperatives, it is not surprising that micro innovations dominated with 21 responses, compared to seven responses that were macro in nature. Four types of innovations were indicated with a high degree of frequency: experiential learning (n = 14), e-learning and technology-driven learning (n = 12), problem-based learning (n = 11), and team learning (n = 12). Both integration and student assessment were indicated in six responses, and the use of cases was indicated in two responses. The low number associated with the use of cases is probably reflective of the fact that, given the long history of case usage in business schools, such activity is at best on the fringe of innovation. In turn, this might be suggestive of an institutional environment that is not particularly supportive of true innovation.

3.4 Consequences of Innovation

The consequences of innovation correspond to the refreezing stage, and extend it. Responses to questions 14, 15, 16, and to an extent 19 reflect the acceptance of the change and continuity of the new behaviors. Questions 13, 17, 18, and to an extent 19 reflect the existence of positive reinforcements and performance-contingent rewards, as well as the extent to which necessary support is provided.

In describing how they assessed the success or failure of their educational innovations (see Question 14), an overwhelming majority of the respondents indicated they relied on student oriented assessment measures. Sixteen respondents used student feedback — formal and informal — and 12 respondents rely on student outcomes, such as skills assessments, course grades, and feedback from employers, among others. Seven respondents mentioned the term "evaluation" without elaborating on the source or the focus of the evaluation. While the focus of these evaluations was not delineated, it is reasonable to surmise that they likely included one or more of the following: student evaluations, institutional/accrediting evaluations, or professorial appraisals. Other methods of assessing success or failure were publications (n = 1), personal observations/reactions (n = 2), and anecdotes (n = 1). Some respondents indicated the use of multiple assessment measures, so the total number of responses exceeds 28.

The respondents were also asked to characterize their educational innovations as being a complete success, partial success, or complete failure (see Question 15). Nine respondents described their innovations as a complete success, 17 indicated a partial success, and two respondents indicated both a partial and complete success reflecting different innovation targets. For example, one respondent indicated innovation was a complete success in the MBA program but only a partial success in the undergraduate program. Interestingly, not a single respondent admitted to a complete failure of an educational innovation. One respondent who characterized the innovation as a complete success observed, "However, success doesn't mean it has spread." Two of the respondents who characterized their innovation as partially successful provided illuminating elaborative comments. One respondent said, "We know we have been successful, and are recognized by the external community and our profession (organization development). But we have severe problems in our own school because of an unsupportive, unleaderly like dean." The second respondent indicated the innovation was "too expensive in the long run' and that "people have to stress their own research more and more." Taken together, these comments reveal the existence of a potential deterrence to innovation even when there is some degree of success.

For educational innovators, the consequences of these activities may be personal or institutional/organizational. One of the survey questions (Question 13) provides information regarding the personal consequences of innovation. Four survey questions (16, 17, 18, and 19) yield data relevant to the organizational consequences of innovation.

3.4.1 Personal Consequences of Innovation

Numerous different personal consequences of educational innovation exist. These personal consequences most likely occur in some form of encouragement or recognition. Table 5 identifies the frequency with which the respondents have received various forms of encouragement or recognition. As is obvious from the data, many respondents mentioned multiple personal consequences. Interestingly, the most frequently cited personal consequences have either a professional focus (*i.e.*, recognition/encouragement within the professional academic disciplines or by one's colleagues) or a student focus (*i.e.*, recognition by one's students). Of the 152 separate citations of personal consequence factors by the 28 respondents, 94 of them (or 61.8 percent) reflected the professional focus and student focus. In contrast, 32 separate citations (or 21.1 percent) had an administrative or institutional focus (*i.e.*, being recognized or encouraged by administration through publicity or favorable salary, promotion, or tenure decisions). Another 26 citations (or 17.1 percent) reflected recognition or encouragement from external sources such as the business community, accrediting agencies, or funding agencies.

Clearly, an approximate 3 to 1 ratio of encouragement/recognition from the teaching profession and from students relative to either the employing institution or external constituents sends a powerful signal to professional academics regarding the perceived value of their educational innovations. Those involved in doing it — other professionals — and those who are the recipients of it — students — are the ones who predominantly provide the encouragement and recognition for educational innovation. Of course, not everyone's colleagues are supportive of educational innovation. One respondent, who interestingly described the educational innovation as being a complete success, observed that the "Benefits of my innovations have been denied by colleagues. Extension of my innovations has been blocked by colleagues." This respondent went on to indicate that the faculty voted against institutionalizing this innovation even after its demonstrated success. This observation is a precursor to a pattern that we will see emerging in the discussion of the organizational consequences of innovation in the next section.

Table 5. Frequency of Occurrence of Different Forms of Encouragement or Recognition

Forms of Encouragement or Recognition	N
Professional Focus:	
My innovations have resulted in conference presentations.	24
My innovations have resulted in journal articles.	20
My innovations have been praised by colleagues.	15
My innovations have been adopted by colleagues.	17
Student Focus:	
My innovations have been recognized by students on evaluations or in other forms.	18
Administrative/Institutional Focus:	
My innovations have been publicized by administration.	7
My innovations have been recognized in salary decisions.	8
My innovations have been recognized in promotion decisions.	9
My innovations have been recognized in tenure decisions.	8
External Constituent Focus:	
My innovations have been recognized by members of the business community.	10
My innovations have resulted in recognition by professional accrediting agencies.	7
My innovations were supported by grants.	9

A potentially informative comparison occurs with a breakdown of personal consequences by reported level of success with educational innovations (see Question 15). In comparing the personal consequences for the 17 respondents who described their innovations as a partial success to those for the nine respondents who described their innovations as a complete success, a larger percentage of the latter group reported experiencing positive consequences on every dimension in Table 5. The most dramatic difference was that 55.6 percent of those reporting complete success had some concrete reward from administration in the form of salary, promotion, and/or tenure versus 41.2 percent of those reporting partial success. Further analysis of this breakdown is not warranted since the small sample size precludes any meaningful statistical comparisons.

Unfortunately, we must note that our survey data also reveal a disconcerting phenomenon with respect to feedback from administrators and external constituents. These findings suggest that the institutions and external constituents fail to adequately support educational innovations through favorable personal consequences to the initiators of such innovations. This is disconcerting in that these are some of the very same organizations that the media portrays as seeking, perhaps even demanding, educational innovation.

3.4.2 Organizational Consequences of Innovation

The institutional/organizational consequences of innovation were explored by asking the respondents to indicate the extent to which they have continued with their innovation(s) (Question 16), the key factors that motivate them to continue (Question 17) or that deter them from continuing (Question 18), and the perceived likelihood of the innovation continuing if they would leave their employing institutions (Question 19).

In content analyzing the responses to Question 16, six distinct categories regarding the continuation of innovations became apparent. A few respondents had two responses to this question, each reflecting different innovations or categories of innovations. Consequently, more than 28 responses are reported. Two respondents reported the complete continuation of their innovation; another 10 respondents described their innovation efforts as ongoing but not at 100 percent. Eight respondents have continued with their innovations, but in a limited way — limited in scope, time, or faculty commitment. Seven indicated they have only continued with innovations over which they have specific control. Four people indicated that innovations did not become a regular part of the educational program due to the lack of administrative/institutional support. One person admitted to stopping the innovation. All but two of the 32 separate responses reflect less than full commitment to continued innovation. Clearly, continuing to vigorously pursue educational innovations is a debatable proposition when 93.8 percent of those who have chosen to innovate apparently have experienced sufficient roadblocks that they have contracted their innovation efforts.

Some of the comments made in response to Question 16 are particularly enlightening regarding restricted or limited continuation of educational innovations or discontinuation of them. One respondent indicated, "Only those that I can control have continued, those that require support of administration have failed." Another respondent, with a corroborating observation, said, "I have continued my innovation efforts within specific courses. I have discontinued innovation efforts on a program basis." Still another respondent observed, "We are moving forward but are hampered in our progress by an administration which doesn't support us." An additional respondent bemoaned the diversion of resources to other institutional areas with the consequent under-resourcing of a proven team-teaching approach.

These observations are consistent with the lack of recognition and encouragement provided by administration, as noted in the discussion of personal consequences.

The same types of factors that influence openness to educational innovation also affect the motivation to continue with innovations (Question 17). However, the relative weightings on the factors change as the innovation process unfolds. Initially, a student orientation dominated (*i.e.*, 19 of 42 separate citations) and the other three factors had approximately equal influence; together they had approximately the same level of influence as the student orientation. When the decision to continue with innovation is made, personal or intrinsic motivation is slightly higher (*i.e.*, 14 of 37 separate citations) than the student-oriented motivation (*i.e.*, 13 of 37 separate citations). Personal satisfaction appears to be a much stronger driver of continuing innovation whereas student orientation initiated the process. Institutional support also increases in importance with regard to continuing innovation (*i.e.*, 8 of 37 separate citations), and environmental conditions decreased in relative importance (*i.e.*, 2 of 37 separate citations). The critical role of institutional support for sustaining educational innovations is powerfully demonstrated by one respondent's observation about the motivation for continuing. According to this respondent, "Leadership support [is needed] to do something right for the students. Without leadership support and resources, it's not worth my time and effort!" Another respondent indicated that "Enthusiastic support has come from [the] Dean and other administrators."

The responses received to open-ended Question 18 can be organized into six broad categories. Three of these categories relate to institutional support. These are a failure to provide resources (n = 9); a failure to recognize innovation in promotion, tenure, and compensation decisions (n = 10); and a failure to exhibit leadership (n = 6). Another key factor indicated as a deterrent to continuing innovation was lack of support from fellow faculty members (n = 11). The other two deterrence factors relate to individual concerns with the time (n = 7) and effort (n = 4) involved in innovation.

On Question 19, those who indicated that the innovation would continue without them identified two primary reasons for the continuation: (1) the innovation had been formally adopted by the institution (n = 11), and (2) the innovation had been adopted by other faculty members (n = 8). For those who indicated that the innovation would not likely continue in their absence, the primary reasons were lack of collegial support (n = 8), the change was very specific to the skills and interests of the innovator (n = 6), and lack of institutional support (n = 3). Once again, it is very apparent that for innovation to be sustained, institutional and faculty support are required.

3.5 Feedback Loop

The consequences of the innovation observed by the respondent feeds back to and impacts on their future openness to innovation. The phrase ‘once burnt, twice shy’ seems apropos. Some respondents perceived little positive reinforcement or even encountered negative responses to their innovations, and as a result are reluctant to forge ahead.

Responses to questions 16, 17, and 18 reflect the willingness and extent to which the respondents continue with innovation and the factors that motivate and deter them from continuation. As mentioned in the previous section, almost three-fifths of those who have chosen to innovate in the past have either reduced or discontinued their efforts. This does not bode well for the future of educational innovation.

4. CONCLUDING OBSERVATIONS

We recognize that the small sample size upon which our analysis and conclusions are based potentially limits the degree to which these results can be extrapolated beyond the sample. However, the EDiNEB Network exists to disseminate the results of innovative educational efforts in economics and business, so the reservations being expressed by participating individuals are extremely powerful. The information provided by respondents is remarkable in its content and consistency. Twenty-three of the 28 people who were motivated to respond to our survey, described themselves as enthusiastically initiating major changes. If over 90 percent of such individuals report that their innovative efforts have either been curtailed or discontinued, what might we expect to be reported by those individuals who were not motivated to respond or who are not members of the EDiNEB Network? The respondents’ disconcerting and alarming experiences with educational innovation may reflect the tip of an iceberg, rather than being representative experiences of a few heretical outliers. If this is how people at the forefront of educational innovation are reacting, what might we expect from others who are not at the forefront?

Our survey results provide considerable support for the proposed model of educational innovation. Openness to educational innovation derives primarily from an intrinsically motivated faculty with a strong student orientation. These faculty members create and undertake various innovative student-oriented activities to enhance learning experiences. While the students’ learning experiences are often successful and beneficial to their development, the innovations are not necessarily adopted by the educational institution. A variety of institutional factors serve as forces for maintaining the status quo rather than for fostering meaningful change. Consequently, faculty members' innovation efforts are discouraged — accompanied by a recycling to some approximation of the state that existed prior to attempting the innovation. When innovation becomes institutionalized, it is through adequate resourcing, effective administrative leadership, and acceptance and adoption by colleagues. This institutionalization reinforces and stabilizes the educational innovation and even creates the motivation for continuous improvement. Unfortunately, these favorable outcomes characterize the minority of educational innovation efforts, whereas the deterrence of innovative efforts — through both institutional resistance and negative personal consequences to the innovators — typify the outcomes of the majority of efforts at educational innovations.

Perhaps a major reason for the lack of institutional support for educational innovation is that the majority of faculty members' efforts and interests are focused on areas other than educational innovation. Our data suggest that even faculty members with an innovation inclination soon learn that their academic success — indeed survival — more often than not may be tied to factors that are unrelated to innovative education. With such a disincentive, what might the future hold for innovative education?

We suggest that educational innovation is a pipe dream unless there is massive transformation of existing institutional and collegial structures. Institutions must cease giving lip service to educational innovation and replace it with authentic support for educational innovation. In conjunction with authentic institutional support, a critical mass — perhaps even a majority — of faculty members who actively initiate and warmly embrace educational innovation is necessary for true change to be implemented and sustained. Innovation might be tried but it will not be sustained with only a small cadre of willing and supportive faculty.

It appears that while the business community complains of academe's failure to provide students with knowledge of real-world issues and to help them develop real-world skills, the administrations of academic institutions face different pressures. For instance, one respondent noted an increasing concern with providing cheaper education — a not surprising phenomenon in these days of cutbacks in funding to higher education. Cheaper education is not necessarily relevant and useful education, nor is it necessarily innovative education. All of this has repercussions for initiating and sustaining educational innovations.

APPENDIX A: QUESTIONNAIRE USED IN E-MAIL SURVEY

Concerns about the lack of a supportive infrastructure for implementing and sustaining educational innovations have frequently been mentioned in various forums at the annual EDiNEB Conferences. However, little seems to have been done to systematically and formally document the educational innovation process from the perspective of managing change. It is critical to share information regarding how change has been implemented and sustained in an educational context. Therefore, we ask you to take a few minutes of your time to thoughtfully respond to this questionnaire. We will summarize the results for a presentation at the 2003 EDiNEB Conference.

1. Which of the following best describes your institution?
   ____ Public college or university.
   ____ Private college or university.
   ____ Corporate training.
   ____ Other (please specify) ____

2. Would you classify your institution as __________?
   ____ Liberal Arts
   ____ Comprehensive
   ____ Master's
   ____ Doctoral

3. In which country is your institution located? ____________________________

4. Approximate number of undergraduate students at your institution: _____
   Approximate number of graduate students at your institution: _____

5. Approximate number of undergraduate students majoring in business: _____
   Approximate number of undergraduate students majoring in economics: _____

6. Approximate number of graduate students majoring in business: _____
   Approximate number of graduate students majoring in economics: _____

7. Are the business and economics units separate at your institution?
   _____ Yes _____ No

8. Which of the following best describes your attitude toward educational innovation?
   ____ I resist educational innovation; the traditional ways work just fine. (If you chose this alternative, submit your questionnaire now and do not answer the remaining questions.)

____ I change if I have to, but I do not initiate change.
____ I experiment with minor changes.
____ I am receptive to major changes initiated by others.
____ I bore easily and make changes just to do something different.
____ I enthusiastically initiate major changes.

9. Which of the following more accurately describes the focus of your educational innovation effort(s)?
____ Directed more toward the teacher and what/how material is taught and presented.
____ Directed more toward the student and methods of learning.
____ Other (please specify) ________________________________

10. How would you characterize the innovations with which you have experimented? (check all that apply)
_____ Instructional methods that alter the mode of learning for a specific topic.
_____ Instructional methods that change how the professor delivers material.
_____ Instructional methods that substantially change the roles of students and the professor.
_____ Assessment of the individual student's competencies and/or performance.
_____ Assessment of the curriculum.
_____ Curricular changes.
_____ Other (please describe) ________________________________

11. Briefly describe the innovations you have been involved with (*e.g.*, problem-based learning, experiential learning, team learning, assessment center, etc.).

12. What motivated you to experiment with innovative educational approaches?

13. Have you experienced any of the following forms of encouragement or recognition for your innovation? (check all that apply)
_____ My innovations have been recognized in salary decisions.
_____ My innovations have been recognized in promotion decisions.
_____ My innovations have been recognized in tenure decisions.
_____ My innovations have been recognized by students on evaluations or in other forms.
_____ My innovations have been praised by colleagues.
_____ My innovations have been adopted by colleagues.
_____ My innovations have been publicized by administration.
_____ My innovations have resulted in conference presentations.
_____ My innovations have resulted in journal articles.
_____ My innovations have resulted in recognition by professional accrediting agencies.
_____ My innovations have been recognized by members of the business community.
_____ My innovations were supported by grants.

_____ Other (please specify) ______________________________________

14. How did you assess the success or failure of your innovations?

15. How successful was your innovation?
    _____ It was a complete success.
    _____ It was a partial success.
    _____ It was a complete failure.

16. To what extent have you continued with your innovation(s)?

17. What are the key factors that motivate you to continue with innovation?

18. What are the key factors that deter you from continuing with innovation?

19. Do you think any of the changes that you have been instrumental in effecting would continue if you were no longer with your institution? Why or why not?

REFERENCES

Argyris, C. (1970). *Intervention Theory and Method: A Behavioral Science View*. Reading, MA: Addison-Wesley.

Beer, M., & Walton, E. (1990). Developing the competitive organization: Intervention and strategies. *American Psychologist, 45* (2), 154-161.

Bertsch, B., & Williams, R. (1994). How multinational CEOs make change programs stick. *Long Range Planning, 27* (5), 12-24.

Clover, V. T., & Balsley, H. L. (1979). *Business Research Methods*, 2nd ed. Columbus, OH: Grid Publishing, Inc.

Cummings, T. G., & Worley, C. G. (1997). *Organization Development and Change*, 6th ed. Cincinnati, OH: South-Western College Publishing.

Lewin, K. (1951). *Field Theory in Social Science*. New York: Harper and Row.

McWhinney, W. (1989). Meta-praxis: A framework for making complex changes. In A. M. Mohrman Jr., S. A. Mohrman, G. E. Ledford Jr., T. G. Cummings, & E. E. Lawler III (Eds.). *Large-Scale Organizational Change* (pp. 154-199). San Francisco, CA: Jossey-Bass.

Smither, R. D., Houston, J. M., & McIntire, S. D. (1996). *Organization Development: Strategies for Changing Environments*. New York: HarperCollins College Publishers.

Chapter 8

WILLINGNESS TO INNOVATE

Use, Misuse, and Abuse of Student Evaluations of Instruction

Michael K. McCuddy and Wendy L. Pirie
College of Business Administration, Valparaiso University, Valparaiso, Indiana, USA

1. INTRODUCTION

In this paper we discuss the potential implications of commonly used student ratings of teacher performance on faculty members' willingness to pursue innovative educational practices. Our fundamental contention is that student ratings of teaching are potentially detrimental to innovative education. In exploring this fundamental contention, we first examine the inherent evaluation and developmental challenges associated with student ratings. Next, we discuss the common uses, misuses, and abuses of student ratings from both an evaluative perspective and a developmental perspective. We then propose an alternative approach — one based on behaviorally anchored rating scales — for utilizing student ratings. This proposed approach can potentially limit the misuses and abuses of student ratings, and can promote their viability as useful and accepted tools for both evaluative and developmental purposes, especially for the latter. Finally, we conclude the paper with a statement of our beliefs regarding the dangers associated with adhering to a *student-as-customer* mode of teacher ratings — dangers which can discourage innovative educational efforts and pervert the educational process as well as undermine students' acquisition of the competencies they will need to function effectively in modern society.

M.K. McCuddy et al. (eds.),
The Challenges of Educating People to Lead in a Challenging World, 149–168.

2. THE CHALLENGES OF STUDENT EVALUATION OF INSTUCTION

Student evaluation of instruction seems to have spread like the plague throughout academe — a devastating plague that destroys the motivation of professional academics to pursue innovative education. Our basic thesis is that student ratings of teaching, as commonly used in most academic institutions, are subject to misuse and abuse and are detrimental to innovative education. Both misuse and abuse involve improper use of student ratings, but abuse is much more deliberate in nature in that it reflects a knowing subversion and malicious intent. Further, student rating forms, as currently structured in many, if not most, academic institutions are likely to fail in providing effective evaluation and promoting faculty development — which are the common justifications for their use. Instead of student evaluation of instruction being an effective instrument to promote development and innovation, it is potentially "an instrument of doom."

An evaluation instrument, be it a performance appraisal used, say in business, or a student evaluation used in academe, theoretically has evaluative and developmental purposes, sometimes called summative and formative uses, respectively. To be meaningful for evaluative purposes, the instrument must be developed within the context of the essential skills that are required for success in a given set of activities. For the instrument to be effective, these essential skills must be clearly identified and described. Further, the usefulness of the evaluation instrument and process is limited by the capabilities of an evaluator to assess these skills accurately and meaningfully.

To be meaningful for developmental purposes, constructive feedback should be provided to help foster a person's growth and development. This feedback can be supportive or corrective in nature, but always must be provided out of concern for the individual being assessed. The usefulness of the feedback provided is limited both by the competency and commitment of the evaluator and by the structure of the evaluation instrument.

Student evaluation of instruction, as it is commonly used in many institutions, does not meet the above-specified criteria for being a useful evaluative or developmental instrument. Further, by its very nature, student evaluations have the unintended consequence of discouraging innovative education. Continued use of student evaluations, without drastic alterations, is destined to fail in meeting the intended purposes and will continue to be detrimental to innovation. We therefore argue that either student ratings should not be used, or if they must be used, they need to be significantly revamped. This revamping should consider the definition of effective teaching, the essential skills of the teachers' job, the appropriate training of the evaluators, and the need to encourage, or at least not discourage, innovative educational methods.

3. COMMON USES, MISUSES, AND ABUSES OF STUDENT EVALUATIONS

The three groups of stakeholders in the student evaluation of instruction process at most institutions are faculty, students, and administrators. The original purpose of student evaluations was purportedly to provide developmental feedback from students to faculty. This feedback was intended to assist faculty in creating a positive learning environment and in modifying and enhancing course content and delivery. Subsequently, administrators saw an opportunity to utilize student feedback for evaluation of faculty for promotion, tenure, and salary adjustment decisions — a purpose for which student feedback was not originally intended. This has resulted in the modification of student rating forms to generate simplistic quantitative measures of uncertain reliability and validity.

- Interestingly, Chen and Hoshower (2003) report that students place greater importance on teacher and course improvement than on providing information to be used in administrative decisions regarding promotion, tenure, and salary, or in student decisions about instructor and course selection. Students are more willing and effective participants in the process if they perceive the outcome to be better teaching and courses. As Chen and Hoshower note, however, "The usefulness of student evaluation data is severely undermined unless students willingly provide quality input" (2003, p. 72). The inference is that if students do not see the rating system as primarily developmental in nature, they will not take the process seriously nor respond in a conscientious manner.

Faculty members have likewise been impacted by the transition of the student evaluation of instruction from emphasizing constructive feedback and development to a rating measure impacting the determination of faculty rewards. The result is an emphasis on placating and pleasing the students rather than on nurturing their desire and capacity to learn. As noted by Kolstoe (1975), faculty may mistakenly allow students a voice in the content to be covered. "This is nonsense for the reason that, particularly at the lower division levels, the students do not know enough about either the subject or related areas to judge the importance of information impinging on other information. This requires the mature judgment of a scholar" (Kolstoe, 1975, p. 69). As a result of some faculty leading students to believe that their input as to content is relevant, other faculty, who determine content based on knowledge of the discipline, may be criticized inappropriately by students. The following actual comments from student evaluations of instruction at our institution illustrate this phenomenon: "I would rather learn about 5 chapters than cram in 25 chapters." "Speed is not essential. I would have rather finished 8 chapters thoroughly rather than go through 24." Student preferences for an easier workload or less intellectual rigor should not be a determining factor in the content of any course — at any institution.

The transformation of the student evaluation system from a developmental to an evaluative emphasis has even resulted in attempts by faculty to manipulate student ratings. Recent research and personal anecdotes support this contention. Simpson and Siguaw (2000) find that teachers engage in activities — such as hosting student parties, having a fun class immediately preceding evaluations, and making the exam process much easier — to influence student ratings. We are personally aware of a situation in which a faculty member held an ice cream social for the students at the time student evaluations were administered. In another situation, home-baked cookies were brought into class on the day that evaluations were administered. Certainly, the resulting environment in both situations was less than conducive for generating genuinely useful developmental feedback based on thoughtful and reflective consideration of the course and instruction. These are examples of what has become known as gaming for the purpose of improving student ratings (Martin, 1998; Newton, 1988; Wright, Whittenton, & Whittenberg, 1984).

University administrators typically use student-rating forms as input into promotion, tenure, and salary decisions but there is no reason that administrators cannot be active participants in the continuous quality improvement process for which the forms were initially intended. Teaching colloquia, seminars, etc. could be supported by administration in efforts to facilitate teaching improvement. Also, the rating results, in aggregate for the academic unit rather than for individual faculty, should be considered to see if any systemic changes are required to facilitate the learning process. The focus should be on the learning process and environment, not on simply teaching via the lecture mode.

Student rating systems are often geared toward the "talking head" conception of education, not toward innovative education. Centra observes that "the typical student rating form is devised to reflect effectiveness in lecture, lecture discussion and other teacher-centered methods" (1993, p. 47). This is not surprising given that teaching is commonly connoted to equate with lecturing. Kolitch and Dean (1999) found that evaluation instruments typically emphasize a model of teaching than revolves around knowledge transmission rather than one that is based upon student involvement and critical problem solving.

Even when there appears to be an understanding that teaching goes beyond lecturing, one often returns to the idea of teacher as "talking head." In the chapter 'On Being a Teacher' Kolstoe notes, "A teacher can do little other than set conditions for allowing others to learn. ... The consequence of this observation attests to the functioning of the teacher as a manipulator of the learning environment" (1975, p. 61). Seemingly, this enlightened perspective would encourage innovation in manipulating the learning environment. However, it is weakened when Kolstoe continues by discussing the use of cassette tapes and video recorders in monitoring teacher performance in terms of "voice, mannerisms, and appearance" — an apparent reversion to the "sage on the stage" perspective. The idea that lecturing is teaching and vice versa is all too pervasive in academe. This perspective is illustrated and reinforced by the following two statements from actual student evaluations at one institution: "She needs to lecture the material." "Teaching equals lecturing."

The use of student rating forms that are geared toward lecturing furthers the belief that teaching is lecturing. The use of such forms exacerbates the problem created when only the teacher is considered without taking into account either student responsibility or the learning process as a whole. Kolstoe (1975) identifies two key elements of teacher effectiveness: preparation and communication skills. He also identifies two key elements of student effectiveness: well-identified goals and self-discipline. This recognition that there are two responsible parties is critical. Learning is a function of both the student and teacher. The responsibility for the learning process is often misperceived to be exclusively within the purview of the teacher. Yet in our experience, many if not most truly innovative teaching approaches recognize that genuine learning will result only when both students and faculty fulfill their responsibilities.[3] To be useful, student evaluation of instruction should also indicate how the student perceived him/herself fulfilling his/her responsibilities. This should not simply be limited to soliciting their grade but should require reflection on preparation and commitment as well. A student's attitude can greatly impact his/her perception of an instructor's performance and thus should be factored into any evaluation.

3 By genuine learning we are referring to learning that results in retention, assimilation, critical thinking, and application of knowledge in the context of life-long learning. Genuine learning is not simply learning material on a short-term basis for regurgitation in an exam setting.

3.1 The impact of Student Ratings from an Evaluative Perspective

If no responsibility for learning is assigned to the student, the implications of using student-rating forms for promotion, tenure, and salary decisions are clear. Faculty members are more likely to be motivated to engage in activities that ensure high ratings rather than concerning themselves with the learning outcomes. As a result, educational quality as a whole may suffer. Wilson (1998) pointed out that in 1973 only 30% of colleges and universities had students evaluate faculty. Now the use of student-rating forms is ubiquitous. Further, research drawn upon by Wilson (1998) shows that in order to get higher ratings, faculty may lower their standards for student performance, offer a less rigorous course, and try to entertain rather than educate. Perhaps it is no coincidence that grade inflation became a significant issue simultaneously with the prevalent use of student-rating forms to evaluate teaching effectiveness. Nonetheless, the most striking aspect of Wilson's article is the clear delineation of the *student-as-customer phenomena*, particularly given the way student ratings are currently and commonly used by administrators.

Another question raised by the Wilson article is: "Do student ratings actually reflect teaching quality?" A situation was described wherein a professor changed his teaching style to court students. While ratings did improve, the students did no better on exams, so the professor concluded that in spite of higher ratings his teaching was no more effective. In a reverse situation, the authors of this paper have experimented with team learning and found that student performance improved but teaching ratings deteriorated (Christ, Christ, Graham, McCuddy, & Pirie, 2004). As one of the authors commented in a different forum, "All I know is that I am glad that I didn't try to actually teach until I had tenure."

Perhaps the problem is that student rating forms are designed for simplicity of calibration — "designed to be analyzed by a computer, which responds with a numerical rating for each professor" (Wilson, 1998, p. A12) — and do not focus on appropriate measures of teaching effectiveness. "Student ratings can make or break the careers of instructors on grounds unrelated to objective measures of student learning, and for factors correctable with minor coaching" (Wilson, 1998, p. A12). Clearly, student-rating forms should be redesigned to better reflect appropriate measures of teaching rather than being designed for simplicity of calibration. In critiquing student-rating forms, Saroyan and Amundsen (2001) argue that an inherent limitation of these forms is their reliance on the students' judgment of overt teaching actions. Teaching, however, is a much more complicated process and should not be evaluated on the basis of delivery of instruction alone. Although students are often asked to evaluate preparation and learning, their competence and capability in this area is questionable.

In general, the literature indicates that students do not have sufficient knowledge or expertise to assess an instructor's level of knowledge, the currency and relevance of course material, or whether a course is adequately comprehensive (Cashin, 1983; Centra, 1993; Lowman, 1984; Seldin, 1993). In reviewing studies that address the issues of reliability and validity of student evaluations of teaching effectiveness, Hobson and Talbot (2001) conclude that there is strong support for their reliability but mixed and questionable evidence for their validity. Using student evaluations as the sole measure of teaching effectiveness is potentially very damaging to the motivation and morale of professors. This is of particular concern since the vast majority of professors believe that students are not qualified to evaluate many of the features and aspects of high-quality teaching (Bures, De Ridder, & Tong, 1990; Reckers, 1996). Thus, while students may consistently evaluate a phenomenon that they think is teaching effectiveness, they do not truly know what teaching effectiveness is.

The perception of teaching effectiveness is premised on a belief as to what teaching is. According to Saroyan and Amundsen (2001) the conceptions of teaching can be ordered along a continuum into five broad categories: "imparting information, transmitting structured knowledge, teacher student interaction, facilitating understanding, and conceptual change" (p. 345). When a professor defines teaching as transformative learning, students must accept this meaning of teaching if they are to be competent evaluators and if they are to have any validity as judges in the view of the professor. This is particularly critical if any developmental use is intended.

3.2 The Impact of Student Ratings from a Developmental Perspective

Students seem to recognize and value the developmental perspective of performance appraisal and feedback. Chen and Hoshower (2003), for instance, observe that students place greater importance on teacher and course improvement than on evaluation. Wilson (1998, p. A12), quoting a student, reports: "I always try to be thoughtful about what I write. If I'm able to tell my professors what I like and dislike, I'm ultimately going to get a better education." The inference is that if students do not see the rating system as primarily developmental in nature, they will not take the process seriously nor respond in a conscientiousness manner. If the focus of ratings becomes evaluative rather than developmental, the feedback from students is less likely to be useful and teachers will be less concerned about the learning process and more concerned about managing their ratings.

However, a difficulty with using student input for developmental purposes is that even with the best of intentions students lack the expertise and training to offer constructive feedback. If one thinks of student rating forms as analogous to appraisals in industry with both developmental and evaluative purposes, there are some key differences. Well-constructed appraisal forms are linked to specific skill sets and meet the criteria of reliability and validity. Further, those who are doing the appraisal are appropriately trained in assessing those skills. McKeachie (1997) comments on the fact that students are not trained in rating teaching — and even questions their ability to assess their own learning experiences.

If student-rating forms are to be useful, they should focus on specific skill sets. Tamblyn (2000) identifies and elaborates on seven qualities that he considers to be keys for success in teaching: knowledge of the material, respect for the student, concern for the learner, flexibility, passion for teaching, motivational skills, and a willingness to take risks and make mistakes. Palmer (1998) and Zarra (2003) identify excellent teachers as those that have a vocation to teach and a passion for teaching. Through this passion the teacher brings the subject to life and engages the student in the learning process. An implicit requirement is knowledge of the subject matter.

Sometimes students and faculty agree regarding the skill sets that are perceived to be important for effective teaching; sometimes these two groups do not agree. Hoppes and Chesbro (2003) identified four qualities that both students and faculty agreed were essential to teaching effectiveness in a professional school: ability to relate theory and practice, communication skills, preparation and organization, and subject knowledge. They also found that students and faculty differed regarding the importance of five qualities of teacher effectiveness. For some of the qualities the difference was due to the subjective interpretation of the quality's meaning. For instance, friendliness and respect for students was rated as very important by students because they emphasized the word respect whereas faculty focused on the word friendliness and rated it less important. Other qualities, where a difference of opinion existed, highlight the diametrically opposed expectations that faculty and students have in the learning process. Faculty rated the *ability to challenge intellectually and encourage independent thought* very highly whereas students placed very little importance on this.

Collectively, the works of Hoppes and Chesbro (2003), Palmer (1998), Tamblyn (2000), and Zarra (2003) have two very important implications for the teaching/learning enterprise. First, these works indicate that a passion for active learning and all that it implies are essential elements of effective teaching. Second, these works reveal some degree of discrepancy between students and faculty regarding preferences for qualities that reflect active learning as opposed to those that reflect passive learning — with faculty opting for the former and students the latter. Clearly, if the purpose of a university is to serve the *student-as-customer*, then the set of skills necessary to be a satisfactory professor is very different than those necessary to assist a student in becoming a valuable member of society.

It is essential that the expectations and even the definition of teaching are clearly articulated and agreed upon for the student-rating form to be a useful instrument. The expectation of teaching can range from transmitting knowledge with the student as a passive learner to facilitating learning with the student as an active learner. The teaching styles used in meeting each set of expectations will vary. The teaching styles will range from straight lecture to various discussion formats to active student involvement in problem-solving activities to largely self-directed learning under the general guidance of a mentor.

We must make a distinction between teaching and facilitating learning. Facilitating learning will challenge professors and students to devise the best methods for the transfer of knowledge and development of skills. What might be called the *cliché of teaching* focuses on the passive transfer of knowledge from professor to student — whether or not it is the best method. McKeachie (1997) suggests that the majority of students prefer a passive learning style. Consequently, any movement to student-centered learning — an arguably superior approach to learning that facilitates retention, understanding, and the student's ability to engage in lifelong learning — is likely to meet with hostility. This is true even if student performance on exams is superior to that experienced when passive learning is accommodated (Christ *et al.*, 2004).

3.3 The Impact of Student Ratings from an Innovative Education Perspective

Schneider, Hanges, Goldstein, and Braverman (1994) endorse a consumer model of education. They argue that teaching is a service and that students are consumers of this service. Further, Wiesenfeld (1996) observes that many students use a "disgruntled consumer approach" in evaluating teachers. We think the consumer model of education puts student ratings of teaching on an inappropriate pedestal, which in turn does a majestic disservice to efforts to pursue innovative education. To easily gain a fundamental grasp of the inappropriateness of the student-as-customer model for educational innovation, all one needs to do is thoughtfully answer the following question: "Why do people seek to have a college education?"

Ask any group of undergraduates why they are going to college and most of them will state that they are seeking to acquire the skills necessary to get a good job upon graduation and to have a reasonable start on a fulfilling career. Very few of them will say they are attending college primarily, let alone solely, out of the love for learning. For these few, the Schneider *et al.* (1994) consumer model of education is appropriate — they indeed are the consumers; they seek knowledge and learning for its own sake, not for its instrumental value with respect to jobs and careers. The vast majority of college students are not the real consumers; rather they are products being processed — or from a more humanistic viewpoint, they are people for whom value is hopefully being added through the educational process. (Perhaps colleges and universities should cease charging tuition and start charging a value added tax!) The ***real customers*** for the output of educational institutions are prospective employers: businesses, not-for-profit organizations, and government agencies — indeed, society itself. These are the entities that expect, cajole, demand, and require innovative educational practices. Why? Because these true consumers of educational outputs know all too well that the lecture method of teaching does incredibly little in guiding the development of the skills and competencies that are so essential in contemporary workplaces.

A commonly perceived — and indeed misperceived — conception of teaching is that it occurs primarily, if not solely, when the professor operates in the mode of "sage on the stage." According to this perspective, teaching does not occur unless an experienced knowledgeable person is spewing forth his/her accumulated wisdom to enlighten and enrich a grateful audience. Unfortunately, all too often the evaluation form that is used further reinforces this belief. The only innovation that is valued in the "sage on the stage" mode is devising methods of delivering better and/or more efficient and/or more entertaining lectures. This, in turn, may have little, if any, substantive impact on students' acquisition of knowledge and /or skills. In discussing the deficiencies and limitations of student ratings of teaching effectiveness, Martin (1998, p. 1079) makes the case that student evaluations "... tend to distract all participants and observers from the learning mission of the university, and insure the sub-optimization and further decline of the higher education system."

"Given the present transition from teacher-centered to student-centered learning there is the likelihood of a mismatch between teachers' styles and students' preferences. So, when teachers choose to adopt strategies and activities that could enhance students' learning experiences, in response to the mandate given to higher education, some students might not value this. Teachers might be unfairly judged and could receive low ratings for choosing to adopt innovative strategies" (Penny, 2003, p. 407). Moreover, based on 90 different curriculum and teaching innovation projects at universities in Hong Kong, Kember (2000) concludes that the commonly-used student ratings of teaching that emphasize the teacher-centered lecture and entertainment mode of instruction are inappropriate for fostering innovative teaching.

Facilitating learning is being the "guide on the side" rather than the "sage on the stage." By it very nature, facilitating learning leads to innovation because faculty assume a much different role in the educational process — and this different role requires the development and execution of new ways of engaging students in the acquisition of the competencies they need for successful functioning within contemporary workplaces. As Martin observed, "This new student-centered active learning model changes the orientation of a high quality teacher from the relatively narrow master of content and dynamic oration to an infinitely more complex master of content, organization, facilitation and guidance in the process of building students' capacity for self-discovery. Moving from the old teacher-centered lecture mode to the student-centered active learning mode requires experimentation which is extremely risky in an environment where faculty are evaluated, compared and ranked on the basis of student opinions" (1998, pp. 1081-1082).

Saroyan and Amundsen (2001) indicate that due to the limitations of current student rating forms, teachers may choose teaching styles and activities that are not intended to foster learning but rather because of student preferences, and for the facility and ease of the professor. They contend that as a teacher becomes more competent pedagogically, the student will have a much more prominent role in the teaching and learning process. Interestingly, these teachers will then be evaluated poorly by students if the students in fact prefer a more passive role. In such an environment, there is in fact a disincentive to innovate or move along the pedagogical continuum. When advances are made towards transformational learning, these are often quickly reversed in the face of poor student evaluations. This might be in spite of actual improved performance on the part of students. In one instance, the authors of this paper are aware of an entire department discontinuing a teaching innovation because the students did not like it; this was done in spite of superior grades and understanding of the material on the part of the students.

4. A PROPOSED SOLUTION TO THE STUDENT RATINGS CONUNDRUM — AN ALTERNATIVE THAT PROMOTES AND REINFORCES INNOVATIVE EDUCATION

In the modern world, the true purpose of education in general and higher education in particular is to prepare students to be effective, responsible, contributing members of society. This cannot be accomplished effectively through the mere transfer of knowledge from the "sage on the stage" to passive student recipients. Rather, active involvement of students in the learning process, with faculty appropriately fulfilling the role of "guide on the side" offers much potential for fulfilling education's true purpose. Everything possible must be done to facilitate the attainment of this true purpose — indeed, the future of humanity depends on it.

One important aspect of "doing everything possible" is to either jettison student rating systems or to revamp them so that innovative education is fostered and reinforced rather than being discouraged and marginalized, if not outright eliminated. Saroyan and Amundsen conclude that despite the popularity of student course ratings, "it is time to examine the usefulness of these instruments and to carefully consider the extent to which they actually contribute to the improvement of teaching" (2001, p. 349). We suspect that outright elimination of student ratings of teaching is unlikely to be warmly embraced by either academic administrators or professors who subscribe to the *student-as-customer* model of education. Pressure for educational accountability also makes the viability of eliminating student ratings quite unlikely. Given these "educational facts of life," the best approach is to transform the student-ratings process into an exercise that is consistent with and promotes innovative education, and is within the realm of students' evaluative capabilities.

One suggestion is to use the Teacher Behavior Inventory that evaluates teachers on the basis of 60 low-inference teaching behaviors using a Likert-type scale (Saroyan & Amundsen, 2001). Another alternative that has some merit is to use the Instructional Development and Effectiveness Assessment (IDEA) developed at Kansas State University. The IDEA system is touted to be "the only widely used student evaluation that uses student learning as the major criterion for teaching effectiveness" (Hobson & Talbot, 2001, p. 29). An additional alternative is to design and use a rating form reflecting teacher and student behaviors along Saroyan and Amundsen's (2001) aforementioned instructional continuum of "imparting information, transmitting structured knowledge, teacher student interaction, facilitating understanding, and conceptual change" (p. 345). Such a rating form should be devised as a series of Behaviorally Anchored Rating Scales (BARS) to appropriately capture behavioral differences among the five steps on the continuum. We assert that movement from the teacher-oriented instructional option of *imparting information* toward the opposing student-oriented instructional option of *conceptual change* is a movement toward innovative education.

While we embrace the labels and sequential ordering of Saroyan and Amundsen's (2001) instructional continuum, we believe it necessary to define those labels to adequately illustrate the conception of the different teaching behaviors that we allude to in this paper. In this spirit, we have developed the following operational definitions — ones that facilitate the proposed development of a BARS approach to student ratings.

- **Imparting information:** The professor takes information and conveys it to students with minimal thought to reorganizing and/or applying material from the text. This approach is a basic, no-frills "show and tell" approach, and requires minimal effort on the part of the professor. An excellent example of this is the use of PowerPoint slides provided by a textbook publisher. The professor appears prepared while putting forth little real effort.
- **Transmitting structured knowledge:** The professor, based on his/her underlying knowledge, recasts the material into a different framework or order in the hope of clarifying the material for the students. This approach often expands upon the textual material and requires some thought and effort on the part of the professor.
- **Teacher-student interaction:** The professor expects students to be involved through discussion, questions and answers, and in-class work during or after the professor's primary presentation. This approach is still teacher oriented but the students are required to assume some responsibility for class activities — or at least to be awake! The professor must be well-prepared in order to respond to students' inquiries and comments.
- **Facilitating understanding:** The students assume responsibility for being prepared for class, and the professor is more actively involved in helping students to understand and/or apply material than in transmitting it. This approach requires considerable preparation and effort on the part of the professor to get students involved, and requires advance preparation on the part of the students to take full advantage of the available learning opportunities.
- **Conceptual change:** The students are responsible for their initial exposure to the material and thus have greater responsibility in the learning process, while the professor serves as a facilitator to help them

grasp the material and gain confidence in their own abilities to acquire new knowledge. This approach fosters independent, life-long learning. It is the most demanding approach for both the students and the professor.

It is important to note that as one moves along this continuum, the work efforts of both students and faculty increase. Students often perceive that, as their work effort and responsibility for learning increase, the professor's effort and responsibility declines. As a result, when a professor operates toward the student-oriented instruction end of the continuum but is evaluated using a traditional student rating system, the professor is unjustly chastised for lack of preparation and effort.

The proposed BARS approach to student ratings can be particularly informative if there are differences regarding where the students place themselves versus where the professors strive to be on the continuum. For this reason, we believe that the initial questions should focus on assessing conceptions of teaching. The most fundamental flaw in existing student ratings is a failure to recognize that the students' responses are premised on a concept of teaching that may in fact be diametrically opposed to the professor's concept, or even to what the institution might desire. A further useful variant of this approach is to alter the questions slightly to elicit responses from the professor. This approach addresses the criticism that student rating forms do not take into account the different objectives and expectations of faculty and students. Comparing students' responses with the professor's response could provide very useful diagnostic information regarding the planning and execution of innovative educational approaches.

Listed below is a reasonable sampling of the types of questions that can be used in our proposed BARS approach. The questions that appear in regular print represent the student form of the proposed questionnaire. The italicized questions represent the professor form of the questionnaire. One of the strengths of this approach is that both forms have the same behavioral anchors. The relevant anchors are listed below each set of questions, with the exception of the first two sets of questions where the same anchors are used for both sets.

- Which of the following statements best describes your understanding of teaching? *Which of the following statements best describes your understanding of teaching?*

- Which of the following statements best describes your perception of your teacher's concept of teaching? *Which of the following statements best describes your perception of your students' concept of teaching?*

1. The teacher discusses material virtually verbatim from the text, with little adaptation and/or application.
2. The teacher expands on material in the text drawing on his/her own insights, and if relevant shows how to apply the material.
3. The teacher presents the fundamental concepts and then engages students in a general discussion of the material or in answering focused questions about the material.
4. The students read the material in preparation for class and the teacher helps the students to understand and/or apply knowledge they have acquired.
5. The students study the material to acquire basic knowledge prior to class and the teacher guides the students' development of competence and confidence in using the material to solve problems.

- Which of the following statements best describes your teacher's articulation of objectives for the course? *Which of the following statements best describes your articulation of objectives for the course?*

1. The course objectives specify the content to be covered.
2. The course objectives specify the content to be covered and how it may be applied.
3. The course objectives specify the content to be covered and expectations for student participation in class activities.
4. The course objectives focus on developing student understanding of and/or ability to apply the course material.
5. The course objectives focus on the intellectual and behavioral changes that the students may expect.

- Which of the following statements best describes your goals for this course? *Which of the following statements best describes your perceptions of the students' goals for this course?*

1. Students should listen to the teacher's lecture and take exams that focus on factual recall of what the teacher said.
2. Students should listen to the teacher's lecture and take exams that test for understanding and application of the material.
3. Students should listen to the teacher's lecture, engage in some discussion based on their understanding of the material, and complete appropriate tests and assignments to demonstrate their understanding of the material.
4. Students should read the material and be ready to participate in teacher-guided class activities and assignments that enhance

understanding and application of the material. Students should then complete appropriate tests and assignments to demonstrate their understanding of the material.

5. Students should take substantial initiative for learning the material and applying it to a variety of problem situations through appropriate analyses and projects. Students will complete appropriate tests and assignments to demonstrate their understanding of and ability to apply the material.

- Which of the following statements describes your typical level of preparation for class? *Which of the following statements describes the students' typical level of preparation for class?*

1. Attends class.
2. Attends class regularly, ready to listen and take notes.
3. Attends class regularly, ready to listen, take notes, and participate.
4. Attends class regularly, ready to participate after reading any assigned material.
5. Attends class regularly, ready to participate after reading and making an effort to understand any assigned material.

- Which of the following statements describes your perception of your teacher's typical level of preparation for class? *Which of the following statements describes your typical level of preparation for class?*

1. The teacher puts forth little effort to prepare — *e.g.*, reads from the text or reiterates material from the text.
2. The teacher puts forth some effort to prepare — *e.g.*, expands on and explains material in the text.
3. The teacher puts forth reasonable effort to prepare — *e.g.*, explains and expands on material in the text; and requires students to participate,
4. The teacher puts forth substantial effort to prepare and enhance students' understanding of material — *e.g.*, expects students to come to class prepared and helps them gain an understanding of the material.
5. The teacher puts forth considerable effort to prepare and create learning opportunities — *e.g.*, gives assignments to help students prepare for class, expects students to come class prepared, and uses class time to help students gain an understanding of the material and/or to apply it.

- Which of the following statements best describes your perception of your teacher's expectations regarding your typical level of preparation for class? *Which of the following statements best describes your expectations regarding the students' level of preparation for class?*

    1. The student should attend class and not be disruptive.
    2. The student should attend class regularly, and be ready to listen and take notes.
    3. The student should attend class regularly, and be ready to listen, take notes, and participate.
    4. The student should attend class regularly, and be ready to participate after reading any assigned material.
    5. The student should attend class regularly, and be ready to participate after reading and making an effort to understand any assigned material.

- Which of the following statements describes your typical level of activity during class? *Which of the following statements describes the typical student's level of activity during class?*

    1. The student sits quietly.
    2. The student takes notes.
    3. The student listens, asks questions, and responds to questions.
    4. The student is involved in a guided application of the material.
    5. The student initiates discussion in order to understand and/or apply the material.

- Which of the following statements best describes your perception of your teacher's expectations regarding your typical level of activity during class? *Which of the following statements best describes your expectations regarding the typical student's level of activity during class?*

    1. The student should sit quietly.
    2. The student should take notes.
    3. The student should listen, ask questions, and respond to questions.
    4. The student should be involved in a guided application of the material.
    5. The student should initiate discussion in order to understand and/or apply the material.

These suggested questions and behavioral anchors provide reasonable examples of what might be used in a BARS approach to student ratings that would be compatible with and facilitative of innovative educational activities. These examples are sufficiently general to be applied in a wide range of educational institutions and learning situations. Of course, other questions can be developed for use in this BARS framework. These additional questions could address issues such as: the use of technology and library resources, relationships with students, the number of hours students commit to the course, and fairness and rigor of grading mechanisms. Regardless of the questions used in a BARS system, they can — and indeed probably should — be adapted to fit the needs of the specific institutions and learning situations.

5. CONCLUDING OBSERVATIONS

As we stated earlier, the true purpose of education — liberal and professional — is to prepare students to be effective, responsible, contributing members of society. We believe the most effective way to achieve this purpose is through the use of various learning-focused and student-centered methods that are within the purview of innovative education. Unfortunately, the *student-as-customer* mode of teacher evaluation undermines innovative educational efforts. Innovative education must be encouraged, supported and reinforced through an evaluation mode that provides a viable alternative to the standard Likert-type rating scales that are used at many, if not most, academic institutions.

The continued use of these types of rating scales promulgates and supports the myth of the *student-as-customer* mode of teacher evaluation. Consequently, academic administrators with a solitary focus on the bottom line continue to embrace these methods even though they profess the value of innovative educational practices. Indeed, drawing on the faculty handbook at our own institution, administration encourages the development of new technologies to enhance the learning environment. However, at our institution — as elsewhere — the current Likert-type rating scale system that values teacher-centered education continues to be used in spite of the professed primary concern with improving teaching effectiveness. The real impetus seems to be the provision of easily determined metrics for inputs into promotion, tenure, and salary decisions, even though this is considered to be a secondary purpose of evaluating teaching.

Perhaps academic administrators truly expect and desire innovative education, but their reliance on the *student-as-customer* teacher rating system rewards something quite different. The omnipresence of this approach promulgates many misuses and abuses. As Steven Kerr wrote in his classic article entitled "On the Folly of Rewarding A, While Hoping for B," managers and administrators must structure reward systems to actually reward desired behaviors rather than just hoping that they will occur. For those who are interested in the future of education, two overarching questions must be asked: "Do we desire learning, or do we desire appeasing students?" "Do we wish to produce contributing members of society in the long term, or happy students in the short term?"

REFERENCES

Bures, A. L., De Ridder, J. J., & Tong, H. M. (1990). An empirical study of accounting faculty evaluation systems. *The Accounting Educators' Journal*, 68-76.

Cashin, W. E. (1983). Concerns about using student ratings in community colleges. *New Directions for Community Colleges*, *11*, 1, 57-65.

Centra, J. A. (1993). *Reflective Faculty Evaluation*. San Francisco: Jossey-Bass.

Chen, Y., & Hoshower, L. B. (2003). Student evaluation of teaching effectiveness: An assessment of student perception and motivation. *Assessment & Evaluation in Higher Education, 28*, 1, 71-88.

Christ, L. F., Christ, M. Y., Graham, A. S., McCuddy, M. K., & Pirie, W. L. (2004). Using team learning in the classroom: Experiences and lessons. In R. Ottewill, L. Borredon, L. Falque, B. Macfarlane, & A. Wall (Eds.), *Educational Innovation in Economics and Business VIII: Pedagogy, Technology and Innovation* (pp. 129-146). Dordrecht: Kluwer Academic Publishers.

Hobson, S. M., & Talbot, D. M. (2001). Understanding student evaluations. *College Teaching*, *49*, 1, 26-31.

Hoppes, S., & Chesbro, S. (2003). Elements of instruction in allied health: Do Faculty and students value the same things? *Journal of Allied Health, 32*, 3, 167-172.

Kember, D. (2000). *Action Learning and Action Research: Improving the Quality of Teaching and Learning*. London: Kogan Page.

Kerr, S. (1975). On the folly of rewarding A, while hoping for B. *Academy of Management Journal*, *18*, 769-783.

Kolitch, E., & Dean, A. V. (1999). Student ratings of instruction in the USA: Hidden assumptions and missing conceptions about 'good' teaching. *Studies in Higher Education*, *24*, 1, 27-42.

Kolstoe, O. P. (1975). *College Professoring: Or Through Academia with Gun and Camera.* Carbondale: Southern Illinois University Press.

Lowman, J. (1984). *Mastering the Techniques of Teaching*. San Francisco: Jossey-Bass.

Martin, J. R. (1998). Evaluating faculty based on student opinions: Problems, implications and recommendations from Deming's theory of management perspective. *Issues in Accounting Education*, *13*, 4, 1079-1094.

McKeachie, W. J. (1997). Student ratings: The validity of use. *American Psychologist*, *52*, 1218-1225.

Newton, J. D. (1988). Using student evaluation of teaching in administrative control: The validity problem. *Journal of Accounting Education*, *6*, 1-14.

Palmer, P. J. (1998). *The Courage to Teach*. San Francisco: Jossey-Bass.

Penny, A. R. (2003). Changing the agenda for research into students' views about university teaching: Four shortcomings of SRT research, *Teaching in Higher Education*, *8*, 3, 399-411.

Reckers, M. P. (1996). Know thy customer. *Journal of Accounting Education*, 179-185.

Saroyan, A., & Amundsen, C. (2001). Evaluating university teaching: Time to take stock. *Assessment & Evaluation in Higher Education*, *26,* 4, 341-353.

Schneider, B., Hanges, P. J., Goldstein, H. W., & Braverman, E. P. (1994). Do customer service perceptions generalize? The case of student and chair ratings of faculty effectiveness. *Journal of Applied Psychology*, *79*, 685-690.

Seldin, P. (1993). The use and abuse of student evaluation of professors. *The Chronicle of Higher Education*, *40,* 1, A40.

Simpson, P. M., & Siguaw, J. A. (2000). Student evaluations of teaching: An exploratory study of the faculty response. *Journal of Marketing Education*, *22*, 3, 199-213.

Tamblyn, P. (2000). Qualities of success: Lessons from a teaching career. *Education Canada*, *40*, 1, 16-19.

Wiesenfeld, K. (1996). Making the grade. *Newsweek*, 16.

Wilson, R. (1998). New research casts doubt on value of student evaluations. *Chronicle of Higher Education*, *44,* 19, A12+.

Wright, P., Whittenton, R., & Whittenberg, G. E. (1984). Student ratings of teaching effectiveness: What the research reveals. *Journal of Accounting Education*, *2*, 5-30.

Zarra III, E. J. (2003). Taking it to the next level: Components of excellent secondary educators. Paper presented at the Annual Meeting of the American Association of Colleges for Teacher Education, New Orleans.

PART III

ASSESSING THE DIMENSIONS AND CHARACTERISTICS OF LEARNING AND LEARNERS

Chapter 9

THE IDENTIFICATION OF CONSTRUCTIVIST PEDAGOGY IN DIFFERENT LEARNING ENVIRONMENTS

Hans Otting and Wichard Zwaal
Christelijke Hogeschool Nederland, Leeuwarden, the Netherlands

1. INTRODUCTION

The present society is often considered as a knowledge or learning society in which the continuous advancement of the level of knowledge has become an important political and economic issue (Dijstelbloem & Schuijt, 2002; WRR, 2002). Increasing global competition and technological advancement have a decisive impact on the rate of product innovation in organizations and, by consequence, influence the work environment, the task complexity, and the expected performance of every individual employee. Knowledge and learning, rather than capital, are becoming the main resources of the new global economy in which the use and creation of knowledge are considered as the most important factors for sustained economic growth. Therefore, companies in the global knowledge economy focus on the improvement of their knowledge base and highly value lifelong learning activities. Successful companies are the ones that learn effectively, because they understand that knowledge is becoming their most valuable asset and therefore focus on knowledge creation and knowledge sharing for sustainable economic success (Nonaka, 1991; Davis & Botkin, 1994a, 1994b; Nonaka & Takeuchi, 1995; De Geus, 1997; Choo, 1998; Drucker, 1999). The business sector has discovered the value of knowledge and their interest in knowledge and learning is growing. In a knowledge society, learning is the key factor for the production and diffusion of knowledge. A knowledge economy requires continuous learning, because the shelf life of

M.K. McCuddy et al. (eds.),
The Challenges of Educating People to Lead in a Challenging World, 171–196.

knowledge is getting shorter and knowledge rapidly becomes obsolete. Therefore, the new workplace competencies companies require focus on learning to learn, communication and collaboration, creative thinking and problem solving, technological literacy, global business literacy, leadership development, and career self-management (Meister, 1998). These requirements form a tremendous challenge to higher education for developing the competencies that students really need.

The contours for new ideas about knowledge and learning in higher education as a consequence of the aforementioned shift to a knowledge society are beginning to take shape. Graduates should not only possess a wide range of competencies, but must also be able to apply their knowledge and skills to a wide range of problem situations. The new workplace competencies, which are required by the growing knowledge intensity in today's society, demand a review of the perspective from which education, knowledge and learning should be approached. The teaching environment, with its emphasis on giving information, is gradually developing into a powerful learning environment that supports constructive knowledge acquisition processes (De Corte, 1995; 2000; Dochy, Segers, Van den Bossche, & Gijbels, 2003). The focus of education should shift from transmission of information and knowledge to a conception of learning as a self-organized and continuous process of constructing and reconstructing new knowledge on the basis of prior knowledge.

A constructivist conception of education not only emphasizes the cognitive aspects of learning, but also takes the development of the whole person of the learner in his social and cultural environment into consideration (Bereiter, 1994; Billett, 1996, Anderson, Greeno, Reder, & Simon, 2000; Von Glasersfeld, 1999). In constructivism, learning can be seen as an active search for meaning that takes place in interaction with the environment. Thus, constructivism is a viewpoint of knowledge and learning, which is founded on the premise that individuals construct their own understanding of the world. Constructivism is first and foremost a way of thinking about the formation of knowledge. Knowledge is a human creation that is dependent on the learner as the source of all explanations of reality. Constructivist views of learning emphasize learning processes in which students actively construct knowledge for themselves in interaction with rich and authentic learning environments. Therefore, pedagogical practices like project work, workplace learning, and action learning, which stress active and collaborative learning activities, might also fit in a constructivist framework. However, little research has focused on the characteristics of constructivist pedagogy in connection with different learning environments.

Research on innovations in economics and business education and the effects of problem-based learning on student performance is well-documented (Milter, Stinson, & Gijselaers, 1998; Borghans, Gijselaers, Milter, & Stinson, 2000; Bentzen-Bilkvist, Gijselaers, & Milter, 2002; Dolmans, Gijselaers, Moust, De Grave, Wolfhagen, & Van der Vleuten, 2002). However, empirical research that places problem-based learning and related educational innovations in a constructivist framework is considerably less available (Hay & Barab, 2001). Therefore, this study intends to contribute to the empirical research on problem-based learning in a constructivist framework and tries to identify the major elements of constructivist pedagogy in different educational settings.

2. CONCEPTUAL FRAMEWORK

2.1 The Constructivist Perspective

Constructivism is a perspective on knowledge that is based on the assumption that knowledge is not a representation of the world outside the human mind. "It holds that knowledge is under all circumstances constructed by individual thinkers as an adaptation to their subjective experience" (Von Glasersfeld, 2000, p. 4). Knowledge does not simply transfer from a knowledgeable person to someone who lacks knowledge. Knowledge cannot be simply given to another individual. Constructivism challenges the view that education is a process that can be characterized as 'filling the empty heads of students.' Learning is an active knowledge construction process. The principle of active knowledge construction has fundamental consequences for pedagogical practice and the role of the lecturer. The lecturer is not the person who possesses true knowledge, who has all the right answers, and persuades the students to see things his way. On the contrary, the lecturer must be considered as a person who is genuinely concerned with the student's beliefs and thinking processes, functions as a facilitator of the student's learning process, and encourages students to take responsibility for their own learning. Students are invited to contribute to dialogues, are given opportunities to express their specific interests, and to specify their own learning goals.

A constructivist view of learning emphasizes a learning process in which students actively construct knowledge for themselves. Learning can be seen as an active search for meaning that takes place in interaction with the environment. "Learning in constructivist terms is:

- both the process and the result of questioning, interpreting, and analyzing information;

- using this information and thinking process to develop, build, and alter our meaning and understanding of concepts and ideas; and
- integrating current experiences with our past experiences and what we already know about a given subject" (Marlowe & Page, 1998, p. 10).

Constructivism is not a unified concept and different interpretations of constructivism can be found (Phillips, 1995; Steffe & Gale, 1995; Ernest, 1995; Prawat, 1996; Geelan, 1997; Phillips, 2000; Otting, 2000). Although the interpretations of constructivism differ from one another, common beliefs like the focus on authentic tasks, the embeddedness of tasks in a challenging and complex task environment, are shared (Savery & Duffy, 1996).

2.2 Different Educational Settings

In this section of the chapter, we describe and discuss four different educational settings that fit in a constructivist framework: problem-based learning, action learning, project work, and workplace learning.

2.2.1 Problem-Based Learning

Problem-based learning (PBL) was first introduced in medical education at McMaster University (Canada) in the late 1960s (Barrows & Tamblyn, 1980). Soon after, other medical schools (University of Newcastle, University of New Mexico, Maastricht University) adopted problem-based learning. In the Netherlands, Maastricht University was the first to integrate problem-based learning in the medical curriculum. Since then, several higher education institutions introduced problem-based learning as an alternative to the more traditional forms of teaching.

Dochy, Heylen, & Van de Mosselaer, (2000) describe learning in a problem-based learning environment as an active, cumulative, constructive, context-bound, self-regulated, purposeful, and meaningful process. Moreover, they consider a cognitive conflict as the stimulus for learning, emphasize knowledge development in a social context, and stress the need for rehearsal and training for the development of expertise.

Problem-based learning is an educational philosophy for designing curricula and an instructional method that uses problems as a context for students to acquire and apply knowledge (Gijselaers, 1995). Problem-based learning is characterized by a modular, thematic, interdisciplinary approach (Bouhuijs, 1993). It is an integrated system for student learning in which students are confronted with real-life problems that need to be discussed and solved. Acquisition of an integrated body of knowledge related to the problem and the development and application of problem solving skills are the main educational objectives of problem-based learning (Barrows & Tamblyn, 1980). The problems that form the basis of the study activities are usually descriptions of real-life situations or events, which have to be analyzed by a small group of students under supervision of a tutor. The learning process starts with the activation of the students' prior knowledge. Students use a systematic procedure to analyze the problem, to formulate learning objectives, to collect additional information, and to acquire new and relevant knowledge.

The role of the tutor is essential for the progress of learning in the PBL tutorials. Tutors stimulate the learning processes and allow discussions to proceed. They promote a relaxed atmosphere and encourage the cooperation among students. They observe the group activities, ask stimulating questions, and intervene if the group functioning is impeded. The interventions of the tutor can make the difference in the success or failure of the PBL tutorial (Moust, Bouhuijs, & Schmidt, 1997; Hendry, Frommer, & Walker, 1999).

In PBL, the quality of student learning is largely dependent on the quality of the problems. If a problem is too simple, it will not stimulate the learning process. If the problem is too complex and unstructured, students will have difficulties to solve the problem on their own and will need help from an expert tutor. PBL-tasks should match the student's level of prior knowledge (Schmidt & Gijselaers, 1990; Dochy, 1992; Jacobs, Dolmans, Wolfhagen, & Scherpbier, 2003). PBL tasks have to lead to problem-solving activities and should stimulate a positive learning climate. Otting and Peeters (1986) distinguish between the objective and subjective characteristics of problems. The objective characteristics of a problem relate to the educational aims and contents of the problem. It should not pass unnoted that there might be a discrepancy between the responsibility of the instructional designers who have to take responsibility for the quality of the curriculum and the basic aim of problem-based learning: students take responsibility for their own learning. The design of a problem-based curriculum should neither fully prescribe what all the students should know nor give the student complete freedom. The development of self-directed learning skills and subject matter coverage are not necessarily incompatible goals in a problem-based curriculum (Dolmans, 1994). However, one should not overestimate the degrees of freedom for students in a problem-based curriculum. The subjective characteristics of a problem concern the motivational, attitudinal, and personal aspects. A problem should be attractive to students; it should stimulate a variety of learning activities, not only cognitive learning, but also social learning. It is essential that instructional designers take both the subjective and objective characteristics of the problem into account.

Problem-based learning requires a lot of knowledge, experience, creativity, and insight in the student's learning process. It is not enough for the student to master theory; it is of eminent importance to apply the knowledge in practice. Knowledge in problem-based learning is of both theoretical and practical relevance. Problem-based learning tries to bridge the gap between theory and practice. Schmidt (2001) considers problem-based learning as emblematic of a constructivist approach to education.

From two often-cited reviews of problem-based learning (Albanese & Mitchell, 1993; Vernon & Blake, 1993), it can be concluded that the effects of problem-based learning are difficult to measure because of the lack of methodologically reliable research. The reviews suggest that problem-based learning in medical education has a positive effect on clinical performance and skills. Recently, Dochy *et al.* (2003, p. 533) performed a meta-analysis on the effects of problem-based learning and came to the same conclusion: "the review reveals that there is a robust positive effect from PBL on the skills of students." Moreover, they report a remarkable finding. "Students in PBL gained slightly less knowledge, but remember more of the acquired knowledge" (Dochy *et al.*, 2003, p. 533). This finding is in line with Capon and Kuhn's study (2004, p. 74), which concluded that the benefit of problem-based learning does not lie in superior acquisition of new concepts, but that "the answer to what's good about problem-based learning is that it promotes sense making."

2.2.2 Action Learning

Action learning was developed in the 1970s by Reg Revans (1971, 1991, and 1998) as a different approach to management education and as an alternative for the more traditional approaches to education in British business schools. Action learning recognizes the learning potential of the learner and uses prior experience as an important source for learning. Pedler (1991, p. XXII) defines action learning as "an approach to the development of people in organizations which takes the task as the vehicle for learning. It is based on the premise that there is no learning without action and no sober and deliberate action without learning." The emphasis in the learning process in not on the acquisition of facts, not on book learning and intellectualizing, but rather on a process of restructuring existing knowledge and past experience. Action learning is widely used and acknowledged as a practical and effective approach to leadership and organizational development (Revans, 1971; 1991; Gasparski & Botham, 1998; Dotlich & Noel, 1998; Marquandt, 1999; Weinstein, 1999; McGill & Beaty, 1995; Donnenberg, 1999).

The recognition of ignorance is the key to action learning. In a condition of ignorance, risk, and confusion, the main task of the learner is to pose questions. Learning (L) is the sum of programmed knowledge (P) and questioning insight (Q): the learning equation is L = P + Q (Revans, 1997). Programmed knowledge, the already existing knowledge and the knowledge of solutions to problems in the past, can be found in great quantities. In a static environment, this programmed knowledge provides solutions for well-known problems. However, in a society that is characterized by rapid and constant change, yesterday's solutions do not work and can even create an entirely wrong mental set. To solve new problems, to become aware of ignorance, and the ability to ask penetrating questions are essential (Reid, 1997). Action learning is a cooperative and social process in which people learn with and from one another. In the regular meetings of the group (the action learning set), the students discuss their individual projects. Students learn more effectively by working together on similar problems as 'comrades in adversity' (Mumford, 1997). Learning is a process in which learners acquire the ability to behave and to function as community members. They are becoming practitioners that learn about the significance of knowledge in the context of the community. The attention is drawn away from abstract knowledge and cranial learning about practice to learning in a communal context. Working, learning and innovating are closely related (Brown & Duguid, 1991).

Three main components of action learning can be distinguished:

1. **Learning and action.** Students or participants accept responsibility for acting on a particular issue or problem and work together on a specific company project. The emphasis in action learning is on learning, not just on the taking of action. This emphasis on learning distinguishes the action-learning project from other projects. By giving the participant in the action learning program the opportunity to manage a project in an organization, two aims are targeted: the enhancement of the development of the company and the improvement of the learning capacity of the individual person, the team, and the organization.
2. **Action in the real world.** The specific nature of the problem or task requires that action must be undertaken in the real world. Students are given authority to take action on the problem. In the process of finding, selecting, describing, and defining the action learning project the relevance of the project for educational and business goals must be discussed. The optimization of action learning goals and processes is demonstrated by the mutual relation of educational and business goals, and the interrelationship of learning and action. In the project, a balance must be maintained between the practical use of the project for the company and the learning opportunities for the individual student. In the

action learning process, learning and action are closely interrelated. There is no learning without action and no action without learning. The opportunities to learn and the concern for practical benefits must be in balance. The integration of work with learning in the project minimizes the problem of transfer of learning.

3. **The action learning set.** An action learning set is a learning situation in which a group of people work together and support each other. The set is the home base of its members. The action learning set consists of six to eight people who meet on a regular basis. The set members have the task to help one another in an unthreatening and supportive way. They learn from one another's experiences. "Action learning is a continuous essay in understanding and explaining one's actions, in a community of fellow learners" (Morris, 1994, p. 536). The group members are concerned with learning and with work. They are involved in a constant effort to balance the commitment to action (the focus on the progress of the project and the orientation on results) and to learning (the acquisition and evaluation of new information).

Action learning emphasizes that the main objective of working together as a team is to learn and work as a team. The success of the team's learning activities depends on the individual learning of all team members. Every group member learns individually and socially. Sharing the right answers is not enough; essential concepts and ideas must be explained to the other team members. According to Slavin (1991) three concepts are central to team learning: team rewards, individual accountability, and equal opportunities for success.

In order to bridge the gap between theory and practice and to improve on the practical management competencies of students, action learning is widely used. In a university context, most of the educational programs can be characterized as work-based and therefore, specific attention has to be given to the interrelationships between work and learning. Boud, Solomon, & Symes (2001) distinguish six ideal characteristics of work-based programs that, in our opinion, perfectly fit in an action learning framework:

1. A partnership between an external organization and an educational institution is established to foster learning.
2. Learners are in some contractual relationship (employee, trainee) with an external organization.
3. The program is based on the needs of the workplace and of the learner and not on the disciplines. In the professional curriculum, work is the curriculum.
4. Recognition and accreditation of prior knowledge and experience, and the identification of the learning the students wish to engage in, represent the starting point for the program.

5. The most significant element of a learning program is the action learning project. Action learning projects are oriented to the challenges of the actual work and the future needs of the learner and the organization.
6. The learning outcomes of the programs have to be assessed within a standardized framework.

Implementing action learning not only entails the design of the curriculum from a student perspective, but also recognizes the opportunities and constraints for learning in the workplace. The action learning projects, which address crucial work-related issues, are important means for realizing realistic educational outcomes.

Does action learning work? Research on the educational outcomes of action learning is limited. For instance, De Winter Hebron and De Winter Hebron (1998) researched the potential learning effects of the action learning program in the Warsaw School of Agriculture. Their research showed a remarkable improvement on the pretest-posttest results in knowledge of different aspects of management. Cunningham (1991) interviewed 32 out of the 41 participants of the program 'Action Learning for Chief Executives' and found in his research that most participants benefited greatly from the program. Research generally reflects the two main fields for the application of action learning: the training of managers in a wide range of industries and management education programs in universities. The action learning literature mainly focuses on the introduction of action learning in management education and training and do not go into detail about the learning results. The introduction and application of action learning in different academic and industrial settings shows a persistent and on-going discussion about the opportunities and limitations of action learning and confronts educational experts with the resistance to change of those involved in conventional learning situations (McLaughlin & Thorpe, 1993; O'Hara, Webber, & Reeve, 1996; Peattie, 1996; Gasparski & Botham, 1998; Bourner, Cooper, & France, 2000).

2.2.3 Project Work

Project work finds its origin in the pragmatic educational philosophy of Dewey. Dewey (1907) wants to shift the center of gravity in education from the teacher and the textbook to the student. Education focuses on learning activities and prepares students for active participation in the life of a democratic society. Free inquiry in projects emphasizing process over product characterizes a Deweyan approach to education. Students are confronted with real world problems, which offer opportunities for exploration, discovery, and problem solving. Education is not a passive process but a process of active participation in social activities.

Project work is a form of cooperative education, in which students work in small groups on the solution to problems that originate from organizations outside the school context and by consequence have a high reality value. Smith and Dodds (1997) describe a number of conditions for projects:

1. A good project creates change, is bounded in scope, has a limited time scale and offers distinctive payoffs.
2. Projects can be centered on one department level or focus on a combination of departments. A project in one department must involve opportunities for gaining broader understandings than the confines of the department.
3. The project must provide a means for exploring a significant problem area relevant for the company and leading to involvement and responsibility for action.
4. The project should include all aspects of project management and project planning. It is an opportunity to demonstrate a broad range of competencies and skills.

A project is more than a process of data collection and interpretation in a specific domain. Taking action, communicating, managing, and implementing are integrating parts of the process. Handling relationships with stakeholders, developing and maintaining internal and external networks, and working with others in a team context are important features of project management. Writing a project report and stating some general recommendations without taking action is not enough. "So long as there is no serious intention to act upon a report, it will be received with the greatest enthusiasm and unanimity; only when the path to practical action is opened is any danger seen to arise. This is because praising reports demands only eloquence, whereas taking action upon them calls for commitment" (Revans, 1971, p. 27). Therefore, coherent assessments of the learning process, the cooperation among students, the actions of the students, and the project results are necessary.

2.2.4 Workplace Learning

The interest in workplace learning has increased due to the heightened awareness that workplace competencies may contribute to business competitiveness. In the contemporary workplace, knowledge and learning are of crucial importance because knowledge and learning become connected with productivity and employee performance. Recently, learning in the workplace has become integrated in schools and workplace learning has become a formal component of education for developing work-related competencies (Boud & Solomon, 2001).

Two ways to approach the workplace inside school can be distinguished (Barab & Duffy, 2000). The first approach is the educational approach that focuses on the creation of a practice field in which the student engages in the kinds of problems, practices, or tasks that he might encounter in industry. In a practice field, students are engaged in the kind of activities that might take place in the real world. They work on problems and tasks as if they were derived from the real world. One of the best examples of this kind of practice is problem-based learning in which authentic and constructed problems are used as a driver for student learning. In professional education, the professional practice often works with a laboratory-like professional situation. In hospitality education, for instance, practice is being taught in a food lab or instruction kitchen and students demonstrate their skills on separate units. These kinds of practices generally focus on individualized ways of learning.

The second approach originates from anthropology and considers learning as a function of taking part in a specific community. In a community of practice, students learn on the job and from working together. On the job learning is implicit, informal, tacit, and social, and so natural that one has to realize that any learning takes place at all. Students as beginning practitioners acquire the relevant skills by participating in practice. Teachers and students work closely together and are dependent on each other. "This interdependence promotes an atmosphere of joint responsibility, mutual respect, and a sense of personal and group identity" (Brown, 1994, p. 10). Learning is largely a process of becoming a member of the community of practice. "Learning viewed as situated activity has as its central defining characteristic a process that we call *legitimate peripheral participation"* (Lave & Wenger, 1991, p. 29, italics in original). This is a process of increasing participation in the socio-cultural practice of a community by which students become members of that community.

"Viewing learning as legitimate peripheral participation means that learning is not merely a condition for membership, but is itself an evolving form of membership" (Lave & Wenger, 1991, p. 53). Learning is an integral aspect of practice and concerns the whole person. "The central issue in learning is *becoming* a practitioner not learning *about* practice" (Brown & Duguid, 1991, p. 48). The specific characteristics of the workplace cannot be simply replicated in a school. "It is a fundamental challenge for design — for both the school and the workplace — to redesign the learning environment so that newcomers can legitimately and peripherally participate in authentic social practice in rich and productive ways — to, in short, make it possible for learners to 'steal' the knowledge they need" (Brown & Duguid, 1993, p. 11).

In learning theory, emphasis is placed on authentic human performance in differing social and educational contexts. Social and cooperative learning in real-world contexts and the attention to authentic tasks and work environments emphasizing meaningful learning are the issues that are brought to the center of educational reform (Glaser, Ferguson, & Vosniadou, 1996; Cognition and Technology Group at Vanderbilt, 1996). The value of learning in the workplace is based on the premise that the exposure of students to structured work experiences might enhance the acquisition and application of an integrated body of knowledge and skills. In the workplace, work experiences and learning experiences are closely connected. Characteristic for learning in the workplace is the balance that must be maintained between the demand-driven nature of the workplace and the learning opportunities for students. Although, it is easily asserted that work and learning go hand-in-hand in the workplace, the dynamics of the workplace often cause dysfunctional work or learning outcomes. Therefore, careful attention has to be given to the dynamic balance between work and learning, between the demand-driven business environment and the focus on student-centered learning. The workplace as a constructivist learning environment demands a dynamic balance between flexibility and desired outcomes, between student learning and labor productivity.

Outside school, the quality of the workplace is rather vulnerable to changes in the organizational environment and the emphasis on productivity. During work placements, students often experience that work comes first and learning comes in second place. As a result of the varying work circumstances, continuous tensions between the learning that actually takes place and the learning that should take place can be noticed. The workplace and real-life tasks are considered as authentic examples of constructivist learning environments which provide students with opportunities for learning that are not fully specified by the curriculum. In a professional work practice, students learn by actively participating in practice.

The value of the integration of learning and work in the workplace is based on the premise that structured work experiences can be used to enhance the acquisition of knowledge and skills. Research shows that the quality of learning, to a large extent, is dependent on the quality of the workplace (Onstenk, 1997; 2003; Van de Klink, 1999).

3. PROBLEM STATEMENT AND RESEARCH QUESTIONS

Over the last decade, constructivism as a theory of knowledge has been discussed as a new approach to education. Constructivism is one of the main themes in the educational discourse (Steffe & Gale, 1995; Matthews, 1998; Phillips, 2000). However, there is little evidence that constructivist theory has been of significant relevance to pedagogical practice. The growing interest in constructivism has concentrated on theory and has neglected to consider educational practice. Despite the fact that "constructivists believe that theory and practice are fundamentally interlinked" (Mir & Watson, 2000), relatively few attempts have been made to research constructivism in educational practice. That is why this study aims to investigate the principles of constructivist pedagogy in different educational practices: *Can we find evidence for constructivist pedagogy in four different educational settings?*

The question is approached from two different angles: the student perspective and the point of view of instructional designers. With reference to the students perspective we formulated the following research question: *Is there a difference in the degree of constructivism as perceived by students between the four educational settings studied?* From the point of view of the instructional designers, the following research question was formulated: *Is there a difference in the degree of perceived implementation of constructivist principles between instructional designers involved in each of the four educational settings studied?* Finally, a comparison is made between the perception of students and the opinion of the instructional designers. This leads to the research question: *Is there a difference in the perceived degree of constructivism between students and instructional designers?*

4. METHOD

4.1 Programs

In the present study, students from three different BA programs participated: International Hospitality Management, Leisure Management, and Retail Management. Within these programs, four different learning conditions were distinguished: problem-based learning (PBL), problem-based learning combined with workplace learning (PBL & WPL), action learning (AL), and project work (PW).

Problem-based learning was first introduced in the programs of the institution in 1987. Since then PBL has been applied to curricula varying from hospitality and tourism management to teacher education and creative therapy.

In several modules of the hospitality management program, students are involved in two activities: PBL (3 weeks) and workplace learning (3 weeks). The workplace is a commercially operated hotel with 28 bedrooms, a conference center, three restaurants, and kitchens. Students learn from experience by participating in all hospitality operations and services. In this learning environment, hospitality management students take responsibility for all operations.

Action learning is used as the main educational method in the second year of a retail management program. The retail industry provides jobs, assignments, and projects for the students; and the teachers of the retail program facilitate the action learning program.

In the third year of their study, leisure management students are assigned to a specific project. The commercial research and consultancy department of the institution is responsible for the acquisition of the projects, the facilitation of the projects, and the quality control. The projects are on a profit or non-profit basis and can be described as authentic and challenging. The projects have to achieve results and the findings of the research are really important for the customers. The students are assigned as project members of the research community and perform their day-to-day work in a research setting outside school.

4.2 Subjects

A total of 237 students and 14 instructional designers from three different programs in economics and business of a university of professional education participated in the study. Table 1 provides information on the students who participated in the study.

Table 1. Division of Students over Learning Conditions (N=237)

	PBL	PBL & WPL	Action Learning	Project Work	
1st year	42	27			69
2nd year	41	34	24		75
3rd year	35	19		15	93
	118	80	24	15	

4.3 Instrumentation

A questionnaire, which was developed by Tenenbaum, Naidu, Jegede, and Austin (2001), was used as an instrument to identify constructivist pedagogy in four different learning environments. Tenenbaum *et al.* (2001) conducted their study in two separate stages. In the first stage, they used qualitative methods to identify the essential features and instructional principles of constructivist pedagogy. They used the characteristics of constructivism for the second stage of their research, which was largely quantitative and aimed at the elaboration of the key features of constructivism. A questionnaire with a preliminary set of 150 items was developed to measure constructivist pedagogy. The 150-item questionnaire was subjected to a principal component analysis followed by Oblimin rotation with eigenvalue > 1.00, to determine the number of factors. This process resulted in seven factors, which together accounted for 69.5% of the variance (Tenenbaum *et al.*, 2001). After three additional reduction procedures 30 items remained in the short version of the constructivism questionnaire. In an additional procedure the short version of the questionnaire was administered to 271 students and a confirmatory factor analyses was used for validation of the factor structure. Confirmatory factor analysis showed that six of the seven factors are highly correlated and seem to share one underlying dimension. Tenenbaum *et al.* (2001) believe that the factor 'conceptual conflicts and dilemmas' is a unique factor, which probably represents constructivist pedagogy more than the other factors. In the final questionnaire, which was used in this research, the word 'unit' was replaced by 'module' because a module is used as the basic unit in our educational system. Factors and items are shown in Table 2. All items were scored using a 5-point Likert-scale with the following scale-anchors: 1 = not at all; 2 = a little; 3 = somewhat; 4 = much; 5 = very much.

4.4 Design and Data Collection

The present study can be classified as a descriptive, cross-sectional field-study with an ex post facto design. Data were collected during a six-week period in May/June 2003, among a sample of students from four different educational settings (see Table 1). In the PBL condition, seven modules were included. Five modules met the criteria of the PBL/WPL condition. One module is entirely built on project work and one module was in an action learning format. For each of the 14 modules of this study, the module coordinator, who was responsible for the design of the module, was approached to fill out the questionnaire from the instructional designer's perspective. The participation of the students and instructional designers was voluntary. Subjects were asked to spend a maximum of 15 minutes to fill out the 30-item questionnaire on constructivist education adapted from Tenenbaum *et al.* (2001).

4.5 Statistical Analysis

The data were transmitted to the statistical software program SPSS and analyzed using descriptive statistics, t-tests and analysis of variance.

Table 2. Factors and Items in the Tenenbaum Constructivism Survey (Tenenbaum et al., 2001)

Factor 1: Arguments, discussions, debates
The module encouraged originality of ideas.
The module allowed for constant exchange of ideas between student and teacher.
Multiple perspectives of situations were often presented in the module.
I learned to develop mind tools in this module (*e.g.*, critical thinking).
The module allowed for arguments, discussions and debates.
Factor 2: Conceptual conflicts and dilemmas
The module posed some dilemmas for me.
The module caused confusion among conceptual ideas for me.
The module caused conflicts for me among various concepts.
Factor 3: Sharing ideas with others
The module allowed for social interaction.
The module comprised a variety of learning activities.
I was given sufficient opportunities to express myself.
I was given sufficient opportunities to share my own experiences with others.
Factor 4: Materials and resources targeted toward solutions
The module taught me how to arrive at appropriate answers.
The module resources effectively conveyed information to be learned.
The module included relevant examples.
Factor 5: Motivation toward reflections and concept investigation
The module enabled me to use knowledge acquired for abstract thinking.
The module taught me to investigate concepts.
The module motivated me to think reflectively.
The module encouraged me to examine several perspectives of an issue.
The module motivated me for further learning of related subjects.
The ideas in the module motivated me to learn.
Factor 6: Meeting students' needs
I felt pleased with what I learned in the module.
The module took into consideration my needs and concerns.
The module helped me to pursue personal goals.
The module helped me to benefit from my learning difficulties.
The module allowed for the negotiation of the instructional goals and objectives.
Factor 7: Making meaning, real-life examples
The module addressed real-life events.
The module was rich in examples.
The module focused more on making meaning of the learned concepts rather than just answering questions.
The learning environment encouraged me to think.

5. RESULTS

5.1 Constructivism in Four Educational Settings

Research question 1: Is there a difference in the degree of constructivism as perceived by students between the four educational settings studied?

Table 3 summarizes the mean scores, standard deviation, and sample sizes for the students' constructivism responses in each of the four educational settings.

Table 3. Mean Constructivism Scores by Students in Four Educational Settings (N=237)

	PBL	PBL & WPL	Action Learning	Project Work
Mean	3.07	2.91	2.92	2.97
Std. Dev.	.31	.22	.44	.54
N	118	80	24	15

The overall mean score on the 30-item constructivism questionnaire for students is 2.99 with a standard deviation of .32. The reliability of the 30-item scale, indicated by Cronbach's alpha, is .67. ANOVA indicates that a significant difference exists between the mean scores assigned by students in each of the four learning conditions ($F(3,233) = 4.83$; $p = .003$). This result is caused by the significant contrast between the PBL and the PBL/WPL conditions. None of the other conditions showed significant differences.

The results of our study show that the overall mean score assigned by students (2.99 on the five-point constructivism scale) cannot be considered as strong evidence for the existence of constructivist pedagogy in the modules in this study. Although we lack comparative results from other universities, at least we can assume that a mean score of almost 3 on a five-point scale leaves ample room for improvement. However, the results of our study clearly show that the PBL condition has a significantly higher mean score on the constructivism scale than the other three settings.

The profiles of the four educational settings in Table 4 show that the dominant factors in PBL are factors 3 (sharing ideas with others) and 5 (motivation toward reflections and concept investigation). Most dominant in PBL&WPL, project work, and action learning are factors 3 (sharing ideas with others) and 7 (making meaning, real-life examples). These results suggest an overlap between these three educational settings.

ANOVA on the results of Table 4 indicate significant differences between educational conditions on all factors, except for factor 4 (materials and resources targeted toward solutions) and 6 (meeting students' needs). A significant difference can be observed between PBL and PBL&WPL on factor 1 (arguments, discussions and debates). Factor 2 (conceptual conflicts and dilemmas) reveals significant differences between PBL and project work and between PBL&WPL and project work. Factor 7 (making meaning, real-life examples) shows a significant contrast between project work and PBL&WPL.

Table 4. Mean Factor Scores by Students in Four Educational Settings

	PBL (n=118)	PBL & WPL (n=80)	Action Learning (n=24)	Project Work (n=15)	F (3,233)	Sign.
Factor 1	3.05	2.78	2.95	3.05	3.55	.015
Factor 2	2.95	2.91	2.56	2.31	5.82	.001
Factor 3	3.17	2.98	3.26	3.35	2.83	.039
Factor 4	3.02	2.88	2.74	2.76	2.24	.085 ns
Factor 5	3.12	2.93	2.83	3.00	3.47	.017
Factor 6	3.02	2.94	2.85	2.71	2.28	.080 ns
Factor 7	3.11	2.95	3.16	3.42	4.34	.005

5.2 Implementation of Constructivist Principles by Instructional Designers

Research question 2: Is there a difference in the degree of implementation of constructivist principles between instructional designers involved in each of the four educational settings studied?

Table 5 summarizes the mean scores, standard deviation, and sample sizes for the instructional designers' constructivism responses in each of the four educational settings.

Table 5. Mean Constructivism Scores by Instructional Designers (N=14)

	PBL	PBL & WPL	Action Learning	Project Work
Mean	3.39	3.39	2.93	2.87
Std. Dev.	.37	.78	-	-
N	7	5	1	1

ANOVA on the results in Table 5 indicates that no significant difference exists between the mean scores assigned by instructional designers in each of the four learning conditions ($F(3, 10) = .417$; $p = .745$).

ANOVA on the results of Table 6 indicates that instructional designers significantly differ in their opinion on factor 1 (arguments, discussions, and debates) ($F = 3.74$; $p = .04$).

Table 6. Mean Factor Scores by Instructional Designers (N=14)

	PBL (n=7)	PBL & WPL (n=5)	Action Learning (n=1)	Project Work (n=1)	F (3, 10)	Sign.
Factor 1	3.40	3.64	1.60	2.40	3.74	.049
Factor 2	3.33	2.53	3.67	3.67	1.05	.413 ns
Factor 3	3.46	4.05	3.75	1.50	2.85	.091 ns
Factor 4	3.14	3.00	3.00	4.67	.69	.582 ns
Factor 5	3.40	3.20	3.17	2.67	.25	.861 ns
Factor 6	3.29	3.08	2.80	3.00	.14	.935 ns
Factor 7	3.61	4.00	3.00	3.00	3.61	.053 ns

5.3 Comparison Between Students and Instructional Designers

Research question 3: Is there a difference in the perceived degree of constructivism between students and instructional designers?

The overall mean on the 30-item constructivism scale is 2.99 for students (N = 237) and 3.32 for instructional designers (N = 14). This difference is significant (t = -2.25; p = .04), which implies that instructional designers differ from students regarding the degree to which they perceive their module to comply with constructivist principles.

As shown in Table 7 instructional designers generally perceive their modules to be more complying to constructivist principles than students do. Only project work shows a reversed outcome: students rate this condition as more constructivist than instructional designers. Although the mean constructivist score assigned by students and instructional designers differs in each of the four educational settings, only one of scores is statistically significant: compared with students, instructional designers rate the PBL modules as significantly more conforming to constructivism.

Table 7. Mean Constructivism Scores by Students and Instructional Designers in Four Educational Settings

	Students (n=237)	**Instructional Designers (n=14)**	
PBL	3.07	3.39	t (123) = -2.61; p = .01
PBL & WPL	2.91	3.39	ns
Action Learning	2.92	2.93	ns
Project Work	2.97	2.87	ns

Although the difference between students and instructional designers in the PBL&WPL condition is even larger than in the PBL condition, this difference is not significant, because the number of subjects involved in the PBL&WPL condition is small, and the difference in variance is much larger, than in the PBL condition.

Table 8 reports results comparing students and instructional designers on the seven factors. The perception of students and instructional designers differs significantly with respect to factor 1 (arguments, discussions, debates) ($F = 4.11$; $p = .04$), factor 3 (sharing ideas with others) ($F = 5.69$; $p = .018$) and factor 7 (making meaning, real-life examples) ($F = 16.64$; $p = .000$).

Table 8. Comparison Between Students and Instructional Designers on the Seven Components

	Overall Mean (n=251)	Students (n=237)	Instructional designers (n=14)	F (1, 249)	Sign.
Factor 1	2.97	2.95	3.29	4.11	.044
Factor 2	2.87	2.86	3.10	1.51	.221 ns
Factor 3	3.15	3.13	3.55	5.69	.018
Factor 4	2.94	2.93	3.19	2.13	.146 ns
Factor 5	3.04	3.02	3.26	2.64	.105 ns
Factor 6	2.97	2.96	3.16	2.02	.157 ns
Factor 7	3.11	3.08	3.66	16.64	.000

6. CONCLUSION AND DISCUSSION

The main research question for the present study was: *Can we find evidence for constructivist pedagogy in four different educational settings?* This question was approached both from the perspective of the students and the instructional designers. Students, on average, perceive the presence of the main aspects of constructivist pedagogy in the different educational settings. Although the instructional designers positively assess the application of constructivist principles in the modules, even their mean score leaves ample room for improvement. The theoretical framework of constructivism has not yet filtered through to the practice of educational designers. It is not surprising that educationalists that adhere to constructivist views of education still have a lot of work to do in convincing teachers and students of the benefits of constructivist pedagogy.

Especially two conditions, PBL and PBL&WPL, show significant differences in the degree of perceived constructivism. These differences could be the result of two elements. First, the specific way in which workplace learning in a hospitality environment is designed (the structures in the workplace) and, second, the formalized and standardized work procedures and instructions for the students (the procedures in the workplace). These structures and procedures focus on conformance of behavior and limit the degrees of freedom for students toward self-management in the workplace and thereby limit the opportunities for self-directed learning. Considered on its own, the workplace as an authentic learning environment is obviously an insufficient guarantee for constructivist learning to take place.

Contrary to the students, instructional designers perceive no significant differences between the four educational settings. For an explanation, we can either look at characteristics of the perceiver or at the object of perception. Instructional designers might be biased and primarily observe or stress the similarities between the four educational settings. Alternatively, we could hypothesize that instructional designers always apply the same set of principles, which would lead to similar educational formats, under different names. Particularly when the PBL paradigm constitutes the overarching educational philosophy, like in the university in this study, this will create some shared characteristics between educational settings. Another explanation for the different perceptions of students and instructional designers could be attributed to diverse interpretations of the concepts used in the questionnaire. Finally, a statistical explanation could be that because of the small number of instructional designers, the power of the testing procedure is rather low.

Instructional designers generally perceive their PBL modules to be more constructivist than students. Only project work shows a reversed outcome: students rate this condition as more constructivist than instructional designers. A possible explanation is that students and instructional designers assign different weights to different aspects of constructivism. This raises important and interesting questions about the nature and dimensions of the epistemological beliefs that students and instructional designers hold.

The present study was limited to four educational settings within one single university. A second limitation was that only students from the programs in the sector 'economics and management' were included in the study and that the sample was not equally composed of first, second, and third year students. A third limitation is related to the instrumentation applied. We used the questionnaire developed by Tenenbaum *et al.* (2001) since it was specifically developed for measuring constructivist pedagogy and therefore the construction of a new instrument seemed unnecessary.

The generalization of the results of this study is limited. We suggest that the study should be extended to different programs and be repeated in other universities, particularly universities that apply constructivist pedagogy in their curriculum. Replication of the study would serve several purposes. First, it would contribute to the determination of benchmarks for constructivism in higher education. Second, it would offer opportunities to cross-validate and test the construct validity of the constructivism questionnaire of Tenenbaum *et al.* (2001). Another line of research in extension of the present study might concern the investigation of the effectiveness and efficiency of constructivist pedagogy compared to traditional educational approaches. The assumption, implicit in the present study, that application of constructivist principles will lead to a more desirable educational payoff, will also need explicit testing in additional studies.

Problem-based learning is consistent with constructivist views of learning. PBL can be considered as the almost ideal application of constructivist principles, because PBL supports active and cooperative knowledge construction, and focuses on problem solving and in-depth understanding (Savery & Duffy, 1996; Camp, 1996; Dolmans, Wolfhagen, Van der Vleuten, & Wijnen, 2000). For the moment, considering the result of this study that PBL proved to be perceived as most complying to constructivist pedagogy, we would advise educational designers to continue capitalizing on the constructivist principles of PBL.

REFERENCES

Albanese, M. A., & Mitchell, S. (1993). Problem-based learning: A review of literature on its outcomes and implementation issues. *Academic Medicine, 68* (1), 52-81.

Anderson, J. R., Greeno, J. G., Reder, L. M., & Simon, H. A. (2000). Perspectives on learning, thinking, and activity. *Educational Researcher, 29* (4), 11-13.

Barab, S. A., & Duffy, T. M. (2000). From practice fields to communities of practice. In D. H. Jonassen, & S. M Land (Eds.), *Theoretical Foundations of Learning Environments* (pp. 25-55). Mahwah, NJ: Lawrence Erlbaum Associates.

Barrows, H. S., & Tamblyn, R. M. (1980). *Problem-Based Learning.* New York: Springer.

Bentzen-Bilkvist, A., Gijselaers, W. H., & Milter, R. G. (Eds.). (2002). *Educational Innovation in Economics and Business VII. Educating Knowledge Workers for Corporate Leadership: Learning into the Future.* Dordrecht: Kluwer Academic Publishers.

Bereiter, C. (1994). Constructivism, socioculturalism, and Popper's world 3. *Educational Researcher, 23* (7), 21-23.

Billett, S. (1996). Situated learning: Bridging sociocultural and cognitive theorizing. *Learning and Instruction, 6* (3), 263-280.

Borghans, L. Gijselaers, W. H., Milter, R. G. & Stinson, J. E. (Eds.). (2000). *Educational Innovation in Economics and Business V. Business Education for the Changing Workplace.* Dordrecht: Kluwer Academic Publishers.

Boud, D., & Solomon, N. (2001). Repositioning universities and work. In D. Boud & N. Solomon (Eds.), *Work-based Learning: A New Higher Education?* (pp. 18-33). The Society for Research into Higher Education & Open University Press, Buckingham.

Boud, D., Solomon, N., & Symes, C. (2001). New practices for new times. In D. Boud & N. Solomon (Eds.), *Work-based Learning: A New Higher Education?* (pp. 3-17). The Society for Research into Higher Education & Open University Press, Buckingham.

Bouhuijs, P. (1993). *Problem-Based Learning as an Educational Strategy*. Maastricht: Network Publications.

Bourner, T., Cooper, A., & France, L. (2000). Action learning across a university community. *Innovations in Education and Training International*, *37* (1), 2-9.

Brown, A. L. (1994). The advancement of learning. *Educational Researcher*, *23* (8), 4-12.

Brown, J. S., & Duguid, P. (1991). Organizational learning and communities-of-practice: Toward a unified view of working, learning, and innovation. *Organization Science*, *2* (1), 40-57.

Brown, J. S., & Duguid, P. (1993). Stolen knowledge. *Educational Technology*, March:10-15, available at http://www2.parc.com/ops/members/brown/papers/stolenknow.html.

Camp, G. (1996). Problem-based learning: A Paradigm shift or a passing fad. *Medical Education Online*, *1* (2), available at http://www.med-ed-online.org/volume1.htm.

Capon, N., & Kuhn, D. (2004). What's so good about problem-based learning? *Cognition and Instruction*, *22* (1), 61-79.

Choo, C. W. (1998). *The Knowing Organization. How Organizations Use Information to Construct Meaning, Create Knowledge, and Make Decisions*. New York: Oxford University Press.

Cognition and Technology Group at Vanderbilt. (1996). Multimedia environments for enhancing learning in mathematics. In S. Vosniadou, E. De Corte, R. Glaser, & H. Mandl (Eds.), *International Perspectives on the Design of Technology-Supported Learning Environments* (pp. 285-305). Mahwah, NJ: Lawrence Erlbaum Associates.

Cunningham, I. (1991). Action learning for chief executives. In M. Pedler (Ed.), *Action learning in Practice* (pp. 319-340). Aldershot: Gower.

Davis, S. M., & Botkin, J. W. (1994a). *The Monster under the Bed. How Business is Mastering the Opportunity of Knowledge for Profit*. London: Simon & Schuster.

Davis, S. M., & Botkin, J. W. (1994b). The coming of knowledge-based business. *Harvard Business Review*, *72* (5), 165-170.

De Corte, E. (1995). Fostering cognitive growth: A perspective from research on mathematics learning and instruction. *Educational Psychologist*, *30* (1), 37-46.

De Corte, E. (2000). Marrying theory building and the improvement of school practice: a permanent challenge for instructional psychology. *Learning and Instruction*, *10* (3), 249-266.

De Geus, A. (1997). *The Living Company: Growth, Learning and Longevity in Business*. London: Nicholas Brealey Publishing.

Dewey, J. (1907). *The School and Society*. Chicago: University of Chicago Press.

De Winter Hebron, C., & De Winter Hebron, D. J. (1998). Applying action learning principles to academic seminars: A study in praxiological action. In W. W. Gasparski & D. Botham (Eds.), *Action Learning. Praxiology: The International Annual of Practical Philosophy and Methodology, Volume 6* (pp. 105-127). New Brunswick: Transaction Publishers.

Dochy, F. J. R. C. (1992). *Assessment of Prior Knowledge as a Determinant for Future Learning: The Use of Prior Knowledge State Tests and Knowledge Profiles*. Utrecht: Uitgeverij Lemma.

Dochy, F., Heylen, L., & Van de Mosselaer, H. (2000). *Coöperatief Leren in een Krachtige Leeromgeving: Handboek Probleemgestuurd Leren in de Praktijk*. Leuven: Acco.

Dochy, F., Segers, M., Van den Bossche, P., & Gijbels, D. (2003). Effects of problem-based learning: A meta-analysis. *Learning and Instruction, 13* (5), 533-568.

Dolmans, D. H. J. M. (1994). *How Students Learn in a Problem-Based Curriculum*. Maastricht: Universitaire Pers.

Dolmans, D. H. J. M., Wolfhagen, I. H. A. P., Van der Vleuten, C. P. M., & Wijnen, W. H. F. W. (2000). Probleemgestuurd Onderwijs in het Hoger Onderwijs: Een Hype of een Paradigmaverandering? In J. Van der Linden & E. Roelofs (Eds.), *Leren in dialog. Een discussie over samenwerkend leren in onderwijs en opleiding*. Groningen: Wolters-Noordhoff.

Dolmans, D. H. J. M., Gijselaers, W. H., Moust, J. C., De Grave, W. S., Wolfhagen, I. H. A. P., & Van der Vleuten, C. P. M. (2002). Trends in research on the tutor in problem-based learning: Conclusions and implications for educational practice and research, *Medical Teacher, 24* (2), 173-180.

Donnenberg, O. (Ed.). (1999). *Action Learning: Ein Handbuch*. Stuttgart: Klett-Cotta.

Dotlich. D. L. & Noel, J. L. (1998). *Action Learning. How the World's Top Companies are Re-creating their Leaders and Themselves*. San Francisco: Jossey-Bass Publishers.

Drucker, P. F. (1999). *Management Challenges for the 21st Century*. Oxford: Butterworth Heinemann.

Dijstelbloem, H., & Schuijt, C. J. M. (Eds.). (2002). *De Publieke Dimensie van Kennis. WRR Voorstudies en Achtergronden V110*. Den Haag: Sdu uitgevers.

Ernest, P. (1995). The one and the many. In L. P. Steffe & J. Gale (Eds.), *Constructivism in Education*. Hillsdale: Lawrence Erlbaum Associates.

Gasparski, W. W., & Botham, D. (Eds.). (1998). *Action Learning. Praxiology: The International Annual of Practical Philosophy and Methodology, Volume 6*. New Brunswick: Transaction Publishers.

Geelan, D. R. (1997). Epistemological anarchy and the many forms of constructivism. *Science & Education, 6* (1-2), 15-28.

Gijselaers, W. H. (1995). Perspectives on problem-based learning In W. H. Gijselaers, D. T. Tempelaar, P. K. Keizer, J. M. Blommaert, E. M. Bernard, & H. Kasper (Eds.), *Educational Innovation in Economics and Business Administration: The Case of Problem-Based Learning* (pp. 39-52). Dordrecht: Kluwer Academic Publishers.

Glaser, R., Ferguson, E. L., & Vosniadou, S. (1996). Introduction: Cognition and the design of environments for learning. In S. Vosniadou, E. De Corte, R. Glaser, & H. Mandl, H. (Eds.), *International Perspectives on the Design of Technology-Supported Learning Environments*. Mahwah: Lawrence Erlbaum Associates.

Hay, K. E., & Barab, S. A. (2001). Constructivism in practice: A comparison and contrast of apprenticeship and constructionist learning environments. *The Journal of the Learning Sciences, 10* (3), 281-322.

Hendry, G. D., Frommer, M., & Walker, R. A. (1999). Constructivism and problem-based learning. *Journal of Further and Higher Education, 23* (3), 359-371.

Jacobs, A., Dolmans, D., Wolfhagen, I., & Scherpbier, A. (2003). Validation of a short questionnaire to assess the degree of complexity and structuredness of PBL problems. *Medical Education, 37* (11), 1001-1007.

Lave, J., & Wenger, E. (1991). *Situated Learning: Legitimate Peripheral Practice*. Cambridge, UK: Cambridge University Press.

Marlowe, B. A., & Page, M. L. (1998). *Creating and Sustaining the Constructivist Classroom*. Thousand Oaks, CA: Corwin Press.

Marquandt, M. J. (1999). *Action Learning in Action: Transforming Problems and People for World-Class Organizational Learning*. Palo Alto, CA: Davies-Black Publishing.

Matthews, M. R. (Ed.). (1998). *Constructivism in Science Education: A Philosophical Examination*. Dordrecht: Kluwer Academic Publishers.

McGill, I., & Beaty, L. (1995). *Action Learning: A Guide for Professional, Management and Educational Development*. London: Kogan Page.

McLaughlin, H., & Thorpe, R. (1993). Action learning — a paradigm in emergence: The problems facing a challenge to traditional management education and development. *British Journal of Management*, *4* (1), 19-27.

Meister, J. C. (1998). *Corporate Universities: Lessons in Building a World-Class Work Force*. New York: McGraw-Hill.

Milter, R. G., Stinson, J. E., & Gijselaers, W. H. (1998). *Educational Innovation in Economics and Business III: Innovative Practices in Business Education*. Dordrecht: Kluwer Academic Publishers.

Mir, R., & Watson, A. (2000). Strategic management and the philosophy of science: The case for a constructivist methodology. *Strategic Management Journal, 21* (9), 941-953.

Morris, J., (1994). Action learning: The long haul. In J. Prior (Ed.), *Gower Handbook of Training and Development* (pp. 524-537). Aldershot: Gower.

Moust, J. H. C., Bouhuijs, P. A. J., & Schmidt, H. G. (1997). *Probleemgestuurd Leren*. Groningen: Wolters-Noordhoff.

Mumford, A. (1997). Putting learning styles to work. In A. Mumford (Ed.), *Action Learning at Work*. Aldershot: Gower.

Nonaka, I. (1991). The knowledge-creating company. *Harvard Business Review, 69* (6), 96-104.

Nonaka, I., & Takeuchi, H. (1995). *The Knowledge-Creating Company: How Japanese Companies Create the Dynamics of Innovation*. New York: Oxford University Press.

O'Hara, S., Webber, T., & Reeve, S. (1996). Action learning in management education. *Education and Learning*, *35* (8), 16-21.

Onstenk, J. (1997). *Lerend Leren Werken: Brede Vakbekwaamheid en de Integratie van Leren, Werken en Innoveren*. Proefschrift. Delft: Eburon.

Onstenk, J. (2003). *Werkplekleren in de Beroepskolom: Naar een Integratie van Binnen- en buitenschools Leren*. Onderwijsraad, Den Haag.

Otting, H.. (2000). Constructivisme als uitgangspunt voor een onderwijsconcept. *Tijdschrift voor Hoger Onderwijs, 18* (3), 146-161.

Otting, H., & Peeters, J. M. (1986). *Probleemgestuurd Onderwijs: Eindverslag*. Deventer: AMA.

Peattie, K. (1996). Action learning in action. The teaching company scheme. *Management Learning*, *27* (1), 87-112.

Pedler, M. (Ed.). (1991). *Action Learning in Practice*. Aldershot: Gower.

Phillips, D. C. (1995). The good, the bad, and the ugly, The many faces of constructivism. *Educational Researcher*, *24* (7), 5-12.

Phillips, D. C. (2000). An opinionated account of the constructivist landscape. In D. C. Phillips (Ed.), *Constructivism in Education: Opinions and Second Opinions on Controversial Issues. Ninety-ninth Yearbook of the National Society for the Study of Education, Part 1* (pp. 1-16). Chicago: The University of Chicago Press.

Prawat, R. S. (1996). Constructivisms, modern and postmodern. *Educational Psychologist, 31* (3/4), 215-225.

Reid, M. (1997). The IMC experience. In A. Mumford (Ed.), *Action Learning at Work* (pp. 42-54). Aldershot: Gower.

Revans, R. W. (1971). *Developing Effective Managers: A New Approach to Business Education*. London: Praeger.

Revans, R. W. (1991). Action learning: Its origins and nature. In M. Pedler (Ed.), *Action Learning in Practice* (pp. 3-15). Gower, Aldershot.

Revans, R. W. (1997). The learning equation. In A. Mumford (Ed.), *Action Learning at Work* (pp. XXI-XXII). Aldershot: Gower.

Revans, R. W. (1998). *ABC of Action Learning: Empowering Managers to Act and to Learn from Action*. London: Lemos & Crane.

Savery, J. R., & Duffy, T. M. (1996). Problem based learning: An instructional model and its constructivist framework. In B. G. Wilson (Ed.), *Constructivist Learning Environments: Case Studies in Instructional Design* (pp. 135-148). Englewood Cliffs, NJ: Educational Technology Publications.

Schmidt, H. G. (2001). Probleemgestuurd onderwijs: Historie van een constructivistische aanpak van hoger onderwijs. *Onderzoek van Onderwijs, 30* (4), 47-49.

Schmidt, H. G., & Gijselaers, W. H. (1990). Causal modeling of problem-based learning. Paper presented at the Annual Meeting of the American Educational Research Association, Boston, MA.

Slavin, R. E. (1991). Synthesis of research on cooperative learning. *Educational Leadership, 49* (5), 71-82.

Smith, B., & Dodds, B. (1997). *Developing Managers through Project-Based Learning*. Aldershot, Gower.

Steffe, L. P., & Gale, J. (Eds.). (1995). *Constructivism in Education*. Hillsdale: Lawrence Erlbaum Associates.

Tenenbaum, G., Naidu, S., Jegede, O., & Austin, J. (2001). Constructivist pedagogy in conventional on-campus and distance learning practice: An exploratory investigation. *Learning and Instruction, 11* (2), 87-111.

Van de Klink, M. R. (1999). *De Effectiviteit van Werkplekopleidingen*. Proefschrift. Universiteit Twente, Enschede.

Vernon, D. T. A., & Blake, R. L. (1993). Does problem-based learning work? A meta-analysis of evaluative research. *Academic Medicine, 68* (7), 550-563.

Von Glasersfeld, E. (1999). Piaget's legacy: Cognition as adaptive activity. In A. Riegler, M. Peschl, & A. Von Stein (Eds.), *Understanding Representation in the Cognitive Sciences: Does Representation Need Reality?* (pp. 283-287). Kluwer Academic/Plenum Publishers, New York.

Von Glasersfeld, E. (2000). Problems of constructivism. In L. P. Steffe & P. W. Thompson (Eds.), *Radical Constructivism in Action: Building on the Pioneering Work of Ernst von Glasersfeld* (pp. 3-9). London: RoutledgeFalmer.

Weinstein, K. (1999). *Action Learning: A Practical Guide*. Aldershot: Gower.

WRR (Wetenschappelijke Raad voor het Regeringsbeleid). (2002). *Van Oude en Nieuwe Kennis: De Gevolgen van ICT voor het Kennisbeleid. Rapporten aan de Regering*. Den Haag: Sdu uitgevers.

Chapter 10

LEARNING IN VENTURE CREATION

Development of Competence in Translating Business Ideas into Practice

Johann Seiwald
Wirtschaftsuniversität Wien, Wien, Austria

1. INTRODUCTION: LEARNING AND VENTURE CREATION — A NEGLECTED RESEARCH AREA

"Life-long learning" (OECD, 1996; Van Leeuwen & Van Praag, 2002), the learning organization (Senge, 1991), the organizational knowledge-base (Blackler, 1995; Gherardi, 1996; Von Krogh, Roos, & Kleine, 1998; Pawlowsky, 2001) or effective management of organizational competences and knowledge (Blackler, 1995) are considered as central resources and competitive advantages for all types of organizations as well as for successful individuals. Learning and knowledge management became buzzwords that resulted in a rise, within several disciplines, of publications exploring these activities; this increased level of publication arose within the 1990s and continued in the beginning of the third century (Easterby-Smith, 1997; Easterby-Smith & Araujo, 1999).

There is rising interest in research on newcomers in organizations, specific contexts, or social roles (*e.g.* Hill, 1992; Orr, 1996; Gherardi, Nicolini, & Odella, 1998; Richter, 1998). The above cited studies concentrate on the learning processes of new members of communities of practice (Lave & Wenger, 1991; Brown & Duguid, 1996) or of social actors in new positions (*e.g.*, management positions: Hill, 1992). Learning processes in the field of new venture creators, however, are highly underrepresented, not only in the research fields of organizational learning

M.K. McCuddy et al. (eds.),
The Challenges of Educating People to Lead in a Challenging World, 197–224.

but also in the literature of entrepreneurship. Despite studies on the influence of outside-assistance on new venture creation (Chrisman, 1999; Chrisman & McMullan, 2000), the learning processes have not been studied in depth. An exception in this respect is Starr and Fondas' (1992) model of entrepreneurial socialization.

New venture creators face the problem of "liability of newness" (Singh, Tucker, & House, 1986) and the challenge to secure the survival of the newly established organization. Nevertheless, the importance of learning and experience of new venture creators is often emphasized in the literature (*e.g.*, Miles & Randolph, 1980; Crossan, Lane, & White, 1999; Reuber & Fischer, 1999). Miles and Randolph (1980, p. 44f.) argued that the processes of learning in new settings are especially important, "if not [the] most important link, between organizational creation and maturity or failure."

This paper aims at the development of a conceptual framework for the analysis of learning processes of new venture creators, considering the specific social relationships and the type and social nature of the activity in which new venture creators are involved. The theoretical framework has to consider the fact that the learning processes take place in an emergent context with underdeveloped social structures in wide areas of social relationships. Furthermore, the learning process is embedded into an institutional context that guides and constrains the learning processes and simultaneously provides opportunities for the new venture creators.

The focus of the paper is how new venture creators, as social actors, learn to do their jobs that are embedded in a network of various actors and institutional rules. In a case study of an Austrian innovative firm, the concepts will be applied and the theoretical framework will serve as the means to simultaneously analyze context and processes.

Using the argumentation of Frank and Lueger (1997), the empirical research design follows an interpretative approach that has potential to provide insight into situational interpretations because the background against which certain developments occur can establish which factors become significant and explain why decisions were made. For this purpose, stories of new venture creators, employees as well as other key actors in the venture process are reconstructed and analyzed. Stories refer to institutional and cultural rules, and express what is seen as legitimate, appropriate or moral at different places in different spaces. "Stories achieve their meanings by explicating deviations from the ordinary in a comprehensible form — by providing the 'impossible logic'" (Bruner, 1990, p. 47). Therefore, stories contrast normality with deviation so that an insight into the learning process of 'normality' can be developed.

The main data are narrative interviews (Lueger, 2000; Froschauer & Lueger, 2003) of the above-mentioned actors; these are enriched by documentary material (such as business reports, internal organizational communications, charts) and observations. The case study was selected by the principle of theoretical sampling. The main motive for the case selection was the fact that the new venture creators had not acquired practical experience in venture creation and management, thereby isolating this development process from the transfer of experiences between practical contexts.

2. AN ACTIVITY SYSTEM BASED MODEL OF PRACTICE-BASED THEORIZING

Practice-based theorizing focuses upon how people engage in doing "real work" (Cook & Brown, 1999, p. 387). Consequently, the research focus lies on the interaction of actors with the social and physical features of context in the everyday activities (Jarzabkowski, 2003. p. 23). The learning processes are embedded in the social contexts, social processes, and practices. The duality and separation of thinking, learning, acting, working, or innovation are criticized as those processes are seen as taking place simultaneously (Brown & Duguid, 1996; Cook & Yanow, 1996; Czarniawska, 1997; Gherardi, 1999). People "perfink" — they perceive, feel, and think at once (Bruner, 1986, p. 69). Following a practice-based perspective, learning is a social rather than an individual psychological process. For our better understanding, the learning processes in organizations and organizational networks and not the individual and cognitive processes are of interest; of special interest are the social structures, contexts, and practices that constitute the learning processes.

An emerging central issue in learning in organizations is how to be a practitioner, not merely learning about a practice. This approach draws attention away from abstract knowledge and canonical processes and situates it in the practices and communities in which knowledge takes on significance (Brown & Duguid, 1996, p. 48). Learning is regarded as an interactive process of networking that takes a range of factors outside the control of any organization into consideration and which "are associated with the network of relationships conducted both through, canonical, institutionalized links between organizations and non-canonical, informal links established between individuals in organizational fields" (Araujo, 1998, p. 330).

In practice-based theorizing, the organization itself is not seen as the actor of organizational learning; "people and 'communities of practice' are those that learn; organizations change and their change is sometimes brought about by the incorporation of learning, but it may also occur in other forms, for example through contagion, through variation and selection, through conflict, through problem solving, or through turnover in their members" (Gherardi, 2000a, p. 3938). Learning is an inseparable and integral part of all organizational practices. Learning of and within organizations does not halt at the organizational boundaries of formal organizations (Gherardi, 1999, p. 113).

A main part of the studies concentrates on already established practices as well as the development and the diffusion of such practices. The development of emergent practices and emergent communities is a rather neglected research topic. Whereas the theory of communities of practices mainly focuses on already established communities and practices, activity theory also draws the attention to emergent practices and communities (Blackler & Mc Donald, 2000).

The main concepts of activity theory (Engeström, Miettinen, & Punamäki, 1999; Blackler, 1993, 1995; Engeström, 2000) are the "activity system" (depicted in Figure 1) defined as the context of actions (Blackler, 1993, p. 867) and the concept of mediation. Within an activity system, subjects operate in relationship to their communities as being engaged in their activities. Actions are discrete, have clear endings and beginnings, and exist over short time-scales. Activities, however, are the more general concepts and describe collective phenomena that are complex patterns of practice that endure over long time periods (Blackler, Crump, & McDonald, 2000, p. 280). Activities give hints for targets and motives that are socially and historically embedded. The relationship between subject, object and community are mediated by rules, division of labor, and instruments. These factors are interwoven in a complex web of mutual interactions (Blackler, 1993, p. 875). Mediational tools are "devices through which a person experiences, senses and feels the world and also shapes action in the world" (Holman *et al.*, 1997, p. 140).

Practice-based theorizing regards the new venture creators as social actors in their concrete social positions, in combination with the specific contexts and the corresponding social practices. The level of analysis is not restricted to the single new venture creator. Learning is no longer regarded as an isolated phenomenon restricted to certain areas of life (Gherardi, 2001, p. 133) and is analyzed as inherent in social practices so that the practical learning process can be explained.

Taking the collective activity system as the unit of analysis makes the social and the individual dimension of learning manageable. Individual biographies are considered, but regarded as socially constructed and are analyzed in connection to the communities. That is necessary, as competence in specific communities is socially constructed and historically embedded

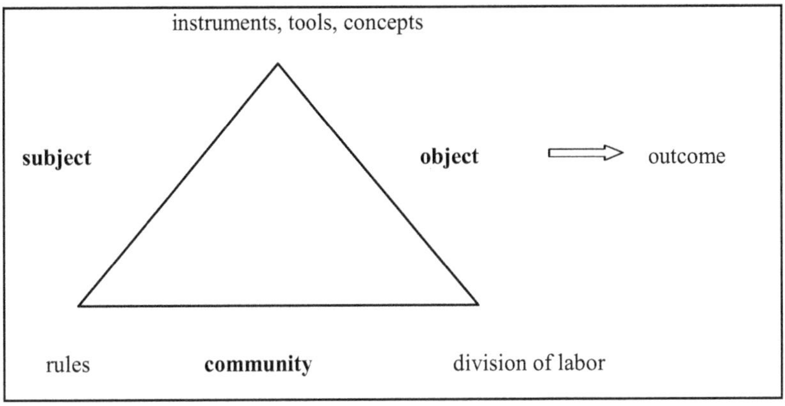

Figure 1. Basic Model of an Activity System (Blackler, 1993)

(Wenger, 2000, p. 226). Competence, therefore, is not the individual knowledge or know-how developed by the venture creators but the interplay of individual knowledge and the specific assumptions concerning competence of the community in the specific activities that venture creators enact in performing their actions.

3. LEARNING IN VENTURE CREATING—A PRACTICE-BASED THEORIZING APPROACH TO NEW VENTURE CREATION

Starting with a definition of new venture creation that emphasizes the social embeddedness of venture creation and considering both the innovative and the realization aspect, a model for analyzing new venture creation as activity systems is presented. The conceptual elements of this model are summarized in Table 1 and then discussed in detail in the following sections of the chapter. The influence of institutional aspects on learning processes is described as well.

3.1 Venture Creating as Translation

In the entrepreneurship literature, a wide range of definitions for venture creations is given. It is primarily seen as an innovative and creative activity (*e.g.*, Stevenson & Jarillo, 1990). Venture creating, however, is a process that can not be reduced to the formal act, due to its wide consequences for the development of organizations, but also because the pre-organizational stage is an implicit part of the creation process (Learned, 1992). In contrast to life-cycle models, a definition of venture creating is chosen that does not

Table 1. Conceptual Elements

Venture creating as translation	Venture creating is regarded as a translation process of business ideas into actions and "commercially viable business forms."
Activities and activity systems	Venture creating is a heterogeneous activity and highly context specific due to the variety of ideas and business areas of the single venture. The different practices constitute different activity systems that are overlapping in the sense that they are related to each other in a complex web. The outcomes of one system provide inputs to another.
Institutional rules	Institutionalized knowledge is widely "taken for granted" knowledge about social practices, which is regarded as embedded in the environmental context, history-dependent, stable, but provisional. It serves as lenses, through which actors view the world, and as classification systems and "meaning systems" that provide a collective sense for actions.
Learning process and knowing	Learning involves the active participation of the venture creators in different activities with concrete individuals, the development of knowing competence, belonging and positioning in the discourse, and practical activities.

regard the phenomenon from a temporal perspective and considers the context-bound nature of new venture creation.

Generally, the creation of new ventures starts with an idea for this new venture whereby these ideas need not result from rational decision-making processes. They can arise spontaneously or through various types of creative acts, can be developed during work processes or be planned systematically. There is a wide range of possibilities for the emergence of ideas. These ideas have a more or less complex and long story, are influenced by diverse factors. They are developed and further developed by several actors who contribute in different ways. Nevertheless, the ideas themselves and the idea development processes are diverse; in order for a venture to be successful, the ideas have to be translated into actions. Venture creating is the transformation of business ideas into "a commercially viable business form" (Anderson, 2000, p. 92). The business ideas are not static and are modified within the venture creation process.

This translation process is crucial as new ventures are embedded into a network of diverse actors (Larson & Starr, 1993) that influence the development. The concept of translation emphasizes that in different contexts, different logics of action (concepts of activity) prevail so that ideas have to be translated into that logic for ideas to be viable in that context (Anderson, 2000, p. 92). This process is complex and again embedded into a complex network of practices, communities, and environments. "Many ingredients are necessary in the translating of an idea into a viable business and it is the 'baking' — the packages of resources and the strategy adopted — that determines future viability" (Birley, 1996, p. 33).

3.2 Learning in a Web of Activities and Activity Systems of New Venture Creators

New venture creators act in a context of an emergent organization that is regarded as a set of activity systems. The model shown in Figure 2 is based on an activity theory approach and is used as an analytical framework for the development of insights about the learning processes and contexts. Venture creating is not a homogenous and unified activity and practice, but is highly context specific as new ventures, their ideas and business areas of the single ventures vary greatly.

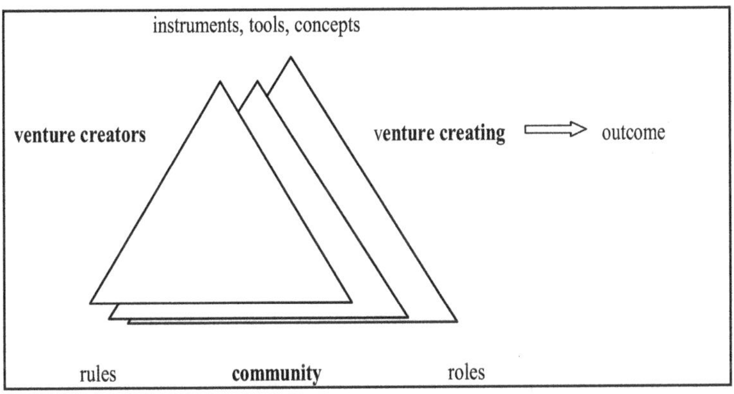

Figure 2. Model of an Activity System for Venture Creating

Consequently, an exhaustive list of new venture activities is not given, but the activities "venture creating," "organizing," and "managing" are used to describe the phenomenon. The activities are not distinct categories due to their overlapping and interrelated nature, but each activity mentioned highlights distinct aspects of the overall activity.

The activity of new venture creating comprises actions to establish a new venture that are located in the activity system. Thereby, a considerable variety of tasks and functions have to be fulfilled. Venture creating is the translation of a business idea into business and includes both the creative and entrepreneurial act as well as the successful realization of the venture. Therefore, venture creating is the translation of ideas developed in an activity system into other activity systems in order to ensure the viability of the business idea. New venture creators have to manage the boundaries between the single activity systems. Venture creating is a muddling-through process that is accompanied, should problems arise, by permanent reframing activities to see the world from a different point of view in order to enable successful actions (Czarniawska, 1997, p. 477) rather than a simplistic rationalistic linear planning process.

Managing emphasizes the being-in-relation-to-others (Cunliffe, 2001, p. 361) aspects of new venture creation. This activity refers to relational acts and the establishment of relationships with internal actors (co-workers, partners) as well as environmental actors and reference groups (Larson & Starr, 1993). Managing is a "creative intellectual activity" comprising decision-making (logical component) as well as creative thinking (Spender, 1989), and involves the coping and developing of strategies with insecurity involved in venture creating processes (Sjoestrand, 1997).

Organizing is "an ordering activity, consisting in assuring that appropriate people and objects arrive at an appropriate place at an appropriate time" (Czarniawska, 1997, p. 476). The management of formal organizational activities is a central aspect of venture creating, but organizing is a more complex activity shaping social relationships to human and non-human actors (Gherardi, 1999, p. 114; Watson, 2001, p. 223).

New venture creators, therefore, act in a network of "interconnected practices" (Gherardi & Nicolini, 2002) and act in "communities of knowing with overlapping and differentiated membership" (Araujo, 1998, p. 326). The practices constitute activity systems that form the specific context for the actions of translating the business ideas into practice. In order to take into consideration that the learning processes, areas, and contexts differ between the organizations and that new venture creators learn a variety of practices, different venture creators are regarded as actors in a network of interdependent, loosely coupled (Spender & Grinyer, 1996), and overlapping activity systems (Blackler *et al.*, 2000). The outcomes of one system provide inputs to another (Blackler, 1993. p. 871). Different activity systems follow different logics of action and therefore create a source of potential conflicts that might arise in the relationship between the different activity systems (Blackler, 1993, p. 871).

3.3 Institutional Rules and Knowledge

While socialization processes of new organizational members are organized according to the organization's principles in the form of a "situated learning curriculum" (Gherardi *et al.*, 1998) and, as a consequence, are more formalized in an existing organizational context, the socialization of venture creators in their contexts of activity depends on local as well as societal influences. "Others on stage already have a sense of what the play is about, enough of a sense to make negotiations with newcomers possible" (Bruner, 1990, p. 34).

In order to take the institutional and environmental embeddedness into consideration, the conceptual elements drawn from the practice-based theorizing framework will be enriched by new institutional ideas in order to capture the specific nature and context of new venture creation (suggested by Blackler, 1993; Spender & Grinyer, 1996).

Originally, new venture creators have abstract, general knowledge about the activities and practices of management and new venture creation. The knowledge base between different new venture creators may vary heavily as they have quite diverse work backgrounds and experiences. The new venture creators, however, enter a context that they partly know and they partly do not know. In order to make it possible for newcomers to engage in the activities, institutionalized knowledge provides "lenses through which actors view the world and the very categories of structures, action, and thought" (DiMaggio & Powell, 1991, p. 13), act as classification systems (Douglas, 1986) and "meaning systems" that provide a collective sense for actions (Scott, 1994. p. 57). Institutions prescribe legitimate social practices and by the same time define proscribed practices (Hinings & Greenwood, 1988, p. 53ff.). The institutional order, therefore, is a "set of social practices legitimate in a given time and place" (Czarniawska, 1997, p. 481). Institutions provide actors with pre-produced "pretested" (Tolbert & Zucker, 1996) and widely "taken for granted" knowledge about social practices, which is regarded as embedded in the environmental context, history-dependent, stable, but provisional.

In this context, two types of institutionalized knowledge can be distinguished: knowledge that is rather specific for distinct organizational fields (such as industry recipes (Spender, 1989)) and the "social stock of knowledge" (Forssell & Jansson, 1996). This social stock of knowledge is institutionalized in the sense that "'everyone' has some abstract knowledge about how the activity is organized" (Forssell & Jansson, 1996, p. 99) and that they are "widely known and enduring" (Forssell & Jansson, 1996, p. 95). Therefore, new venture creators acquire a general, abstracted knowledge about organizations, how organizations work, and which business practices have to be done (*e.g.*, business organizations are profit-oriented, are controlled by return on investment, and managed by the principle of efficiency) (Forssell & Jansson, 1996). For our purposes, this social stock of knowledge is already acquired during other socialization stages and therefore seen as given.

Acquisition of more specific institutionalized knowledge is not a pure adoption and adaptation process. Institutions do not fully determine organizational activities. Rather, "they represent a 'tool kit' or repertoire from which actors select different pieces for constructing lines of action" (Swidler, 1986, p. 277). Within the restrictions set by the (also ambiguous and ambivalent) environmental requirements, new venture creators choose among those types of institutionalized knowledge the ones that fit with the organizational core identity. Institutionalized knowledge acts as "templates for organizing" (DiMaggio & Powell, 1991). Institutions serve as means and tools for transferring and translating venture ideas from one activity system into other relevant activity systems. "Institutions are exchange networks through which properly packaged and blackboxed representations of ideas onto/into action are passed on constantly" (Czarniawska & Joerges, 1998, p. 228).

Knowledge can be global, but knowing is situated and local. Therefore the translation of general models and abstract, codified types of knowledge is the crucial process in the construction of new knowledge (Brown & Duguid, 2001a). This knowledge has to be put into the logic of the specific activity system. The transfer of knowledge and practices within a specific interaction context, therefore, is not a mechanistic, simplified transfer of knowledge in the form of organizational structures, procedures or products, but is rather a "translation of the general idea adapted to local circumstances" (Brunsson, 1998, p. 263) or a "local edition of the general idea" (Brunsson, 1998, p. 263). Standardized models or presentations of practices, and not the experiences and practices themselves, are the basis for imitation (Sevon, 1998). Rationalizations of experiences are imitated (Sahlin-Andersson, 1996, p. 78). The experiences are disembedded from the temporal and local context and form a "context free prototype" (Sahlin-Andersson, 1996, p. 80).

The embedding conditions of activity systems are quite different because "distinct practices create distinct embedding conditions" (Brown & Duguid, 2001a, p. 204) so that processes of disembedding and reembedding knowledge in local practices is a critical factor in knowledge transfer (Brown & Duguid, 2001a, p. 205). Therefore, it is important to consider practices as well as communities to analyze why and how knowledge, practices, or business models are translated into the logic of the specific activity systems.

3.4 Learning Process and Knowing

Starr and Fondas (1992, p. 72) emphasize the importance of active involvement of the entrepreneur in entrepreneurial activities and that "most entrepreneurial experience can only be learned on-the-job in practical start-up operations." New venture creators learn through active "engagement"

(Wenger, 1998, p. 95) in ongoing practices. Learning a practice thus involves the active participation of the venture creator in different activities with concrete individuals who recognize this participation as competence. Acquiring the competence to act within the activity system is a creative process with the result that venture creators "do more than they yet know how to do" (Blackler, 1993, p. 879).

Learning is not restricted to the acquisition of the different types of knowledge that new venture creators need to do their job. The main part is to acquire the ability of competent knowing, "the epistemic work done as part of action or practice" (Cook & Brown, 1999, p. 387). They develop the ability to use and recombine acquired knowledge in the different contexts into a coherent pattern of action and so to take a "context-dependent synthesis of different types of knowledge" (Spender, 1994, p. 395). A considerable part of social collective knowledge is not transferred via language, but is communicated in an indirect manner through shared practices and the participation in these practices (Spender, 1995, p. 170). In this indirect process they learn to act competently (Gherardi & Nicolini, 2002) and to consider the "unarticulated background" (Tsoukas, 1996, p. 17) that is inherent in specific practices.

During their learning path of becoming experts in doing their job in the activity systems, the primary "focal awareness" to some problems is gradually displaced by "subsidiary awareness" (Gherardi, 2000b, p. 214). "What once required conscious, deliberate, and explicit thought no longer does. What once would have taken much deliberation and planning becomes the obvious thing to do" (Crossan *et al.*, 1999, p. 525). Learning in practice involves the ability of behaving as a competent member in a discursive community (Gherardi & Nicolini, 2002, p. 421). As new venture creators engage in a variety of "interconnected practices" which constitute different activity systems, they have to shape the boundaries between the different practices and different activity systems. The practices and outcomes of practices in the single activity systems have to be translated into the logic of other activity systems. Translation is a process that supports transfers of organizing and learning experiences from one context to another (Czarniawska, 1997, p. 480). Thereby, they have to consider "aesthetic rationality" (Sjoestrand, 1997) and the different modes of representing ideas in different activity systems.

The "process of becoming a practitioner" (Richter, 1998; Brown & Duguid, 2001b; Watson, 2001) is a social process not restricted to new venture creators as individuals but rather related to the communities. "People become managers or engineers not only by modeling themselves on managers or engineers (Ibarra, 1999), but also by gaining the acceptance and recognition of managers or engineers. Learning, in all, involves acquiring identities that reflect both how a learner sees the world and how the world sees the learner" (Brown & Duguid, 2001a, p. 200). Learning, therefore, is both belonging and positioning oneself in a discourse (Gherardi & Nicolini, 2002, p. 421).

Sense-making of experiences is a central process for learning, whereby especially the "frames applied to history" (Levitt & March, 1996, p. 522) influence what is being learned. Sense-making is a social process (Lueger, 2000) wherein process venture creators refer to the classification and categorization systems of institutions (Douglas, 1986) and therefore the individual experience can be connected with the activities. The main competence, however, is to translate the conclusions drawn from their experience into competent actions within the activity systems.

4. LEARNING AND TRANSLATING FOR ECONOMIC SUCCESS

The following case study will illustrate a successful new venture that demonstrates the learning process of new venture creators as "learning the ropes" (Louis, 1980).

4.1 Context — The Story of an Idea that Became a Business

The "Fotoinitiative LOMOgraphische Gesellschaft" was established as an association in 1991 and subsequently became a successful Austrian company. The phases of the company's development are listed in Table 2 and will be further explained below.

4.1.1 The First Steps

The life story of the company is centered around a small little camera called LOMO. The LOMO is a technically astonishing, gorgeous little Russian compact camera. It comes from St. Petersburg and is the only one able to use *Professor Radionov's extra-special and totally sexy lens.*

The fascination with the LOMO is best described by the company on its official homepage: "It is the close-up/long range/night vision and ever-watchful glass eye from Russia with THE RELENTLESS WINK. It is your constant friend and helper, a trusty companion in all situations and for all walks of life, with precisely those qualities required to make every day more exciting and varied and, in doing this, the mundane more bearable, simpler."

Two Austrians who were fond of that LOMO camera decided to promote the dissemination of LOMO photography and founded the non-profit organization "Fotoinitiative LOMOgraphische Gesellschaft" in 1991. For them, LOMOgraphy was a new photography culture, more than taking photos, a modern form of art expression. It was fun, a life-style; photos as a social event.

Table 2. Development Steps of LOMO

Development Steps	Characteristics
The first steps (phase 1)	• Foundation of a non-profit-organization in 1991 • Promotion of a new form of photography art • Project of self-realization for the new venture creators
Business transformation (phase 2)	• Transformation into a private limited company in 1995 due to rising sales • Business adventures • Lack of conventional business organization • Emerging problems
Expansion (phase 3)	• Continuing Success • Increase in number of employees • LOMO is still trendsetter
Development of a professional organization (phase 4)	• Business orientation • Support by organization specialist • Focused business activities • Economic evaluation of ideas

They developed the idea during their studies. One venture creator studied business administration and worked as a research assistant at the Institute for Empirical Sociology; this individual also worked for a parliament member responsible for public relations and as a free-lance photographer. The other founder, a law studies graduate who completed a postgraduate course in European law, had acquired practical experience while working for lawyers and occasionally worked as a journalist for "Der Falter," the Viennese magazine for young urban people.

When asked about the primary target of the project, one of the founders answered: *"We just began a project without intending to make a business. For us it was a project of self-realization, a fun, creative organization of our leisure time. Each of us wanted to enjoy the feeling of being an artist, so we began to organize exhibitions and parties. And then the project became more and more successful. Originally, we pursued absolutely different career targets. Due to the project's success, though, we had to decide at a certain point, 'Do we want to work full-time for the project or should we give it up?'"*

The idea of LOMO was strongly promoted by mass media and the concept spread. The product as well as the company became famous. This led to the beginning of the LOMO movement and many orders for the cameras were placed with the company. As a consequence, the considerable number of orders could no longer be handled by the small group of association members who donated their leisure time.

4.1.2 Business Transformation

The ongoing success of LOMO, increasing popularity, and rising sales prompted the founders to go professional. The strong response to the idea induced the founders to create a business-oriented organization as opposed to an association. In 1995, the former club was officially changed into a private limited company. *"Fun became true reality."* While the founders continued to develop, promote, and elaborate on the LOMO-idea, the change into a profit-oriented organization led to numerous changes in organizational practices. From the company's inception onwards, the founders worked in a highly intuitive and spontaneous manner. Realizing interesting ideas and promoting the LOMO-idea for the "LOMO-society" were the key concepts. The realization of interesting projects and having fun were the central motives for their engagement in the business.

One of the founders confessed that, *"we did not know anything. We just knew that both of us had a certain thirst for independence and that it is more fun to realize our own ideas than working for other employers and realizing their ideas. That was our main objective."*

This period was characterized by many "business adventures." They had many ideas and their thirst for action was unquenchable. Although they focused on business-related ideas connected with profit targets, they aimed to promote the idea of LOMO. Their way of action remained more or less the same but circumstances changed with the organizational transformation. With the establishment of a business organization, they faced additional stakeholders and their relationship to environmental actors changed, in particular the capital market. While an association, the company did not require capital, as sales were not the main target. In the transforming phase, however, they needed financial resources in order to finance the establishment of an appropriate organization and to pre-finance the expenses for their stock of LOMO products.

Although the founders had not yet built up a conventional business organization (an accounting system, a logistics system, a division of labor within the company, etc.), the organizational stakeholders, who provided financial resources, demanded certain conditions for granting a loan. The founders, however, underestimated the importance of controlling their financial situation. The young company's unbalanced financial situation and the resulting increasing debts caused major financial problems, which resulted in the need for additional financial resources. Banks, however, rejected the venture creator's demands, as their financial standing and financial organization did not conform to the bank's requirements for granting a loan. These difficulties caused a psychologically difficult situation for the founders and led them to rethink their current position and organization.

In their over-eagerness to realize new, interesting and innovative ideas, the venture creators engaged in many additional "business adventures" that were more or less coupled with photography: LOMO Slideshows, LOMOTV, LOMOMusic, LOMOParties, and LOMOTravelling. Although many projects were integrated into the original concept of LOMO and had a high market response, some ideas, such as LOMOTravelling, proved highly inefficient for the company.

The founders utilized their contacts for the diffusion of their concept and tried to extend the level of awareness. The numerous travels abroad were so successful that LOMOgraphie became an international movement. By 1995, the first "LOMO Botschaften" (the international branches of LOMOgraphie, literally translated as: LOMO Embassies) were established in various European and American cities.

4.1.3 Expansion

Despite some difficulties and inappropriate decisions and investments, the company remained very successful and grew. A growing team of employees, secretaries, IT-specialists, and graphic artists now supported the former "two-man show." With an increasing number of employees, the work practices changed as work had to be coordinated in a different manner.

The development of principles of how to structure day-to-day work was one of the main challenges in this phase. The highly intuitive and informal working patterns prevailed even into this phase, although business coordination rules, albeit highly informal and implicit, were developed. The two founders also acquired knowledge about appropriate business practices and introduced a planning and accounting system; a logistics system to carry out their orders; and the development of an explicit, written, and coherent strategic profile. Furthermore, the founders also started to change their decision-making routines. Decisions, still driven by intuition, were beginning to be based on data. Objectified information was generated for legitimizing their decisions and the founders emphasized a more systematic approach to decision making.

Due to the owners' and employees' numerous contacts, they got early exposure to new innovations, trends, and developments, and had the opportunities to take advantage of their knowledge. They described themselves as "trendscouts." LOMO was one of the first Austrian companies to have a homepage and was already conducting e-business by 1994. As the Internet's popularity and usage soared, the project was developed further with considerable competitive advantage for LOMO.

4.1.4 Development of a Professional Organization

With the rising number of international branches and Internet activities, the complexity of the business increased. The company developed a profile and a strategy for its business and defines itself as a trading, public relations, event marketing, and publishing company. Its main field remains the worldwide trading of the Russian LOMO camera, whereby the company has exclusive worldwide rights for sales. The founders tried to develop a coherent strategy and stick to it by concentrating on its core competence, namely, LOMOs and related marketing activities. The strategy encompasses not only strategic management, but also the optimization of the general processes of the organization. As evidenced by the company's move to a bigger office, the whole organization of the company is being differentiated and shaped more professionally.

In order to develop organizational structures that enable more strict, controllable, and coordinated processes, an organization specialist was recruited. The expert had been responsible for organizing activities and developing organizational structures for larger companies. Recommended by a member of the Chamber of Commerce, she regarded working at LOMO as a challenge: developing professional organizational structures for a growing, creative organization. The tension between creativity and a transparent, formal organizational structure had to be solved. The task was to organize activities in such a way that they are appropriate for a professional business (logistics, departmentalization, job descriptions, etc.) without destroying the creative power and spirit of the organization.

Targets and values of the organization and the founders changed as a result of the intensive integration into the business context. The spirit of adventure, of promoting the LOMO idea is still part of the organizational vision, but more business-related targets, such as the e-commerce shop or the establishment of a public limited company offering shares, became more important. With the change in targets, business practices and strategy, the organizational concept of the customer has undergone a radical change. While in the beginning, the idea of promoting LOMO was the center of the company's concept, the members of the LOMO society and their needs and wishes were the center of the company's attention. With the continuous adoption of profit targets and practices, however, different segments of customers were attracted, and the concept of the LOMO society was no longer appropriate for all. Originally, customers were more or less integrated into the activity system of "developing the idea of LOMOgraphie." Now, however, customers are seen as external actors with demands that have an impact on the company.

Despite all the organizational (procedural and structural) and economic changes, the venture creators have not lost their spirit of finding creative solutions. Unconventional ideas are also evaluated from an economic point of view in order to elaborate the concept of LOMO while solving business problems. A financial analysis proves that the organization boasts a healthy business base. Sales were increased steadily during the last five years, and in 1999, the turnover nearly doubled. Despite the expansion and internationalization and the resulting high cost of investments, the organization recorded profits since 1997.

4.2 Research Results

The venture creators faced many changes during the development of the company. The transformation process of a non-profit company into a profit organization, of a creative adventure into a successful venture, of an intuitively muddling-through strategy into the enactment of a professional-intentional strategy, has led to a variety of changes in internal organizational interaction and interaction with external actors. Learning processes are particularly interconnected, interwoven and critical for a successful transformation process, especially when venture creators have a lack of knowledge and competence at acting professionally in some activity systems.

4.2.1 Learning of Interconnected Practices

In the first phase, the materialization of the idea "Promoting LOMOgraphy" was central. Institutional context mainly influenced the learning need of the new venture creators; especially it defined the activity systems in which they had to act in order to realize their business targets, and the challenge was the enactment of appropriate practices during their "generative dance" between the different activity contexts. The main activity system and therefore the constitutive actors for the organization in the beginning of the company were the "LOMO community" and interaction with people interested in LOMO. With the foundation of a private limited company, the relevant communities and reference groups for the venture creators changed. Operating in a profit area means learning to be a manager in activity systems such as "financing business," "professional organization of business activities," or "strategy formulation."

Acting, thinking, working, and behaving like a manager was an absolutely new experience for the founders despite their management education. During their work for different companies and projects they had acquired practical experience in many fields, but they did not have first-hand knowledge for solving business problems. The process was characterized by a trial-and-error pattern, but the two founders eventually learned how to be managers. In addition, the constituents and relevant activity systems changed — not just the members of the association and the consumers. Learning was further complicated by the non-integration into a specific industry. As a consequence, the founders oriented themselves towards existing reference companies and tried to translate distinct practices into their local logic.

The highly intuitive, creative, and spontaneous behavior of the founders in the early years of the profit organization led to the negative feedback of environmental agents, which was a result of the contradiction of local and internal organizational activities and environmental requirements within external activity systems. The fact that the founders did not have an appropriate practical management background led to a dramatic change in organizational routines. The implementation of an accounting system can be seen as a materialized result of a learning process, but the learning process itself is broader and not so specific. The founders learned to act in accordance to the requirements of the activity systems; they learned to be venture creators and managers of a new venture. They also learned that they had to manage financial resources and that the instrument of accounting is a necessary element of a company.

As the institutional context represents a reference system, learning about institutional requirements and standards has to be brought to the founders' attention. Focal awareness (Gherardi, 2000a) enables an active reflective process about environmental information and experience. Awareness on managerial issues became focused as subsidiary awareness on the habitual practice of organizational activities was questioned, as demanded by environmental feedback and rejection of the further supply of resources. The interruption of habitual activities hindered unreflected reproduction of organizational activities and structures, and, as a consequence, enabled learning and change.

Learning is not restricted to the instrumental dimension and to business practices. It also encompasses a general understanding of an organization as a profit-oriented enterprise, including targets, managerial tasks, and other role-constituting characteristics. This means that knowledge of the communities of the activity systems, which served as a reference system, was acquired in a process of active involvement in the activity context. This knowledge provides venture creators with a basis according to which organizational activities and outcomes are being evaluated.

4.2.2 Learning and Positioning

One decisive question is: In which activity systems can the organization succeed in the long-term? It refers to the question in which contexts the situated LOMO concept of the founders is appropriate so that the scope of action is broad enough in order for a creative concept to be competitive. In the case of the travel agency sector, in which highly standardized products are sold, the fun and action aspects of the product cannot substitute for price competition. In the core business, LOMO has discretionary definition power over the products and, as a result, customers are integrated constituents of the product. In highly institutionalized fields with restricted possibility for differentiation and clear expectations of processes and products, however, LOMO solutions are inadequate, as price differences between LOMO and its competitors cannot be compensated for by LOMO's creativity and reputation. The founders learned to find a context that enabled a successful translation of the idea so the primary competence of LOMO could be unfolded.

The translation activities of the LOMO idea of the founders takes place in the contradiction between local, organizational internal activity systems (*e.g.*, decision making within the organization) and activity systems that coordinate actions with environmental actions (*e.g.*, selling products, financing business activities). In order to resolve the conflict between creativity and intuition on the one hand, and rationality and environmental expectations on the other hand, the ideas were transformed into an environmentally acceptable form. Decisions about business ideas, therefore, were translated into the logic of other activity systems. Appropriate "labeling" (Sjoestrand, 1997) such as "strategy or "business plan" is essential in this process.

4.2.3 Learning and Organizing

Although the venture creators had to develop formal organizational structures to meet the requirements of environmental actors (such as banks, customers, or investors) and describe their organizational structure according to the principles of professional organizations, ideas often arose spontaneously, were highly unconventional and intuitive, and were not always based on rational reasoning. Generally accepted instruments that were seen as elements of professional, modern profit organizations (such as business plans, accounting, and strategy planning), therefore, served as ex-post-decision legitimation in order to act appropriately in the relevant activity systems and so as to secure access to environmental resources.

As a result, formalized organizational structure based on the concept of departmentalization and division of labor were implemented. As the primary internal activity system was based on an informal, flexible and intuitive structure of daily activities, the historically grown structure had to be translated into a viable form of formal organization in the internal activity system. Learning processes not only refer to the acquisition of institutionalized knowledge but also to the translation into an appropriate organizational model that is functional for organizational coordination. New solutions also had to be culturally viable so that historically developed structures were not destroyed. The new venture creators had to learn to balance the contradictions that arise within and between the activity systems.

Learning to be a venture creator means coping with difficult and dissatisfying situations. For the founders, solving emerging problems was primarily a psychological difficulty. The technical dimension could be resolved with adequate knowledge, but emotional learning was mainly necessary in order to regain the self-assurance for action. Through reflection on and sense-making of certain situations, problems were identified and clarified ex-post so that the situations could be de-emotionalized. For future action, self-consciousness could be regained. The acquired knowledge stock, as well as the security that difficult situations in the past were solved successfully, provided a basis for preventing these problems in future.

4.2.4 Learning in Managing

Gradually, the founders entered into their new manager's role away from the role of a new venture creator. It has to be emphasized that there is no clear cut between the two stages. The need for institutionalized knowledge (such as instrumental knowledge in personnel management and organizing, as well as professional management in general) was recognized. In phase 4, institutionalized knowledge is no longer anymore directly acquired by the founders but rather by integrating experts responsible for the professionalizing of the whole organization. The hired organization specialist in phase 4 claims: "For the Lomographs, in my opinion, the biggest learning process is the huge step into internationalization and professionalism." The arrangement of necessary jobs, not active working, is regarded as the management's main task. Learning to manage, in this sense, means identifying and defining appropriate knowledge fields that have to be integrated into the organization and finding experts who are able to integrate this type of knowledge into the existing framework.

With increased involvement in business and institutional contexts, the loosely-joined relationship between organizational action (highly informal and intuitive) and formal organizational structure develops into a tighter relationship, although many formal instruments and structural elements are translated in a way that have a symbolic character rather than pure functional reasons for the implementation.

4.2.5 Balancing Contradictions

The above description of the learning processes and learning patterns of the new venture creators demonstrates the complexity of learning processes that encompass a variety of activity systems. Different learning processes take place at different times, partly simultaneously and partly serial, with different communities in different activity systems. The common feature is the actor of learning: the new venture creators as social actors and the community of the venture creators.

In general, three main factors have influenced the content of the founder's learning: the emergent path of development; the distinct features of the activity and institutional context; as well as the experience, competence, and knowledge base of the founders. Learning content and modes vary according to institutional, historical, and activity contexts.

In the entire learning process, the tension between routinized and "traditional" patterns of interaction of the new venture creators and new ideas and activities resulting from the interaction in new activity systems had to be balanced (*e.g.*, contradiction between the fun logic within the "LOMO community" and the business focus the activity system "financing business" or the internal activity system "LOMO organization" in phase 2 and 3 with the activity system "professional organization of business activities"). The transformation of the business idea of an earlier phase had to be transferred into the logic of new activity contexts; combining the old with the new was the central task. Translation of ideas into the new logic was central for sustaining their identity as innovative venture creators. Nevertheless, the identity of the venture creators shifted to innovative managers. The process demanded a simultaneous demarcation of the past and identification with the history that made possible the translation of the past into the changed present and future.

In the course of the new venture's history, the founders translated their ideas into new contexts several times wherein the idea was changed, re-formulated, and further developed (especially when the business idea developed in the activity system constituting the two founders was transformed into the activity systems of "financing business," "professional organization of business activities," and "strategy formulation").

Chronologically, the first, and most dramatic, translation was that of the original LOMO idea of the activity system of the two founders into a business-oriented activity system. The second translation was the change from a founder-oriented organization to a small company with employees who were not directly involved in the founding process, from the activity system of the founders in phase 1 to the activity system of the founders and core employees in phase 2. The establishment of a founder-independent, standardized organization was the third important translation process — from established activity systems within the organization to emerging activity systems in a complex organization.

4.2.6 Self-reflective and Implicit Assumptions about Knowledge and Learning

Implicitly and explicitly the new venture creators conceive learning as a social process of interaction with environmental actors. Learning and acquiring knowledge were not regarded as technical processes of gaining access to theoretical, abstract and universal knowledge. To the contrary, learning is situated within the social networks. Knowledge, therefore, can only be acquired in social interactions that involve feedback and experiential learning. The main resource for learning is direct experience which is expressed in the following quote of one of the founders: *"Meanwhile, I realized that learning primarily has to do with experience. The best and quickest way to learn might be negative experience and this fact can be shown in our whole history [...]."*

The focus on situational knowledge was central in the constitution of the organization phase 2, as knowledge acquired in past actions is the basis for future interpretation of actions. It provides the venture creators with the "knowledge at hand" that allows for risk-bearing action, as this knowledge base reduces uncertainty.

One of the founders explained the importance of experience: *"[...] you gain a lot of experience in everything that you are doing, such as how, as a manager, to deal with risks. That is a central question."* The focus on direct experience enables active experimenting, such as innovating products or marketing activities, normally limited by restrictions of the activity and institutional contexts. The situational logic of the knowledge concept enables the integration of creativity and commerce. Creativity, the "old" logic of the activity systems of the organization, was based on a muddling-through strategy with highly unconventional and intuitive patterns of action, and on the motives of fun and self-actualization. The enacted and emerging logic of the commercialization and professionalism within internal organizational activity systems demanded an absolutely new way of organizing. When abiding by environmental requirements and rules, the organization's profit-orientation and coordinated actions involve a formalized structure that stands in contrast to the logic of the internal activity system in phases 1 through 3.

As institutionalized knowledge is being translated into the local logic of internal activity systems and transformed into situational knowledge, the two contrasting logics can be integrated. For institutionalized knowledge to be viable in the organization, a social process of interaction between the founders and the experts, who bring in "new knowledge," has to take place. The solution is often framed as a "compromise." In this learning process, the mutual understanding of the contrasting logics is necessary in order to find a compromise. Suggestions, therefore, have to be framed according to the situated logic in order not to be rejected. Ideas and suggestions that do not fit the situational logic are often not articulated, as rejection is anticipated. Knowledge simultaneously constrains and constitutes novel action in organizations (Hargadon & Fanelli, 2002, p. 294). So the situational understanding of knowledge within the internal activity systems implicitly defines the reproduction mode for innovative knowledge.

5. CONCLUSION

"I don't know how much you really can teach a person [about management]. It's like teaching someone how to ride a bike. You can go through the motions. You can understand perfectly well what it is you need to do — that you get on the bike, hold on to the handlebars, move your feet so that you turn the pedals just so, and go down the road to that tree over there. But that still doesn't teach you how to balance [...]" (Hill, 1992, p. 209).

The described case emphasizes the context-bound nature of learning processes as well as the practical character of knowledge. Besides the individual experiences and therefore the basic competence that the venture creators have acquired through anticipatory socialization (Starr & Fondas, 1992), the activity systems in which the venture creators engage, vary as far as the object of venture creation as well as the historical stages of the organizations are concerned. For making clear recommendations, more detailed qualitative, and in further consequence quantitative research, is needed in order to develop a more precise and detailed understanding of the phenomenon.

In general, learning can occur in different places and times as well as in many manifestations. Learning, however, is always influenced by the respective practices and activity contexts. Two phenomena stand out in their influence on what is being learned and how it can be learned:

- The historical path of the development of an organization.
- The institutional context in which the organization is embedded.

As shown above, different phases can be distinguished in the development of the company. Starting with an idea and its materialization (Czarniawska & Joerges, 1996), the idea was translated into different activity systems and in the historical development of the organization. Working practices, structures, problems, and experience all influenced what has already been learned and what has not been learned. The case shows that the relevant fields of activity and the focus of learning changed during the creation process. The founders were confronted with some problems, came into contact with distinct practices and communities, and learned to act within the activity systems so that the activity in question was enacted. Thereby, in general the founders had a rudimentary understanding of the activities in question, they disposed of the "social stock of knowledge" (Forssell & Jansen, 1996) and had an abstracted, generalized idea about the practice and the activity systems. They lacked, however, the competence of knowing.

The institutional context also comes into play. New venture creators are conceived of as being embedded into a variety of activity systems. Institutional circumstances define what an organization is and ought to be, and, therefore, unfold its consequences for the practices and learning processes of new venture creators. With a change in the reference systems, the competence to act in new activity systems and to enact useful practices becomes critical.

As mentioned above, there is a research interest in the influence of outside assistance of venture creation and their success. The explication of any recommendation demands a solid understanding of the learning process and the practices. This paper tries to provide a conceptual possibility for regarding the process and understanding a complex phenomenon.

REFERENCES

Anderson, A. R. (2000). Paradox in the periphery: an entrepreneurial reconstruction? *Entrepreneurship & Regional Development, 12* (2), 91-109.

Araujo, L. (1998). Knowing and learning as networking. *Management Learning, 29* (3), 317-336.

Birley, S. (1996). Start-up. In P. Burns & J. Dewhurst (Eds.), *Small Business and Entrepreneurship*, 2nd ed. (pp. 20-39). London: Macmillan Business.

Blackler, F. (1993). Knowledge and the theory of organizations: Organizations as activity systems and the reframing of management. *Journal of Management Studies, 30* (6), 863-884.

Blackler, F. (1995). Knowledge, knowledge work and organizations: An overview and interpretation. *Organization Studies, 16* (6), 1021-1046.

Blackler, F., & McDonald, S. (2000). Power, mastery and organizational learning. *Journal of Management Studies, 37* (6), 833-851.

Blackler, F., Crump N., & McDonald, S. (2000). Organizing processes in complex activity networks. *Organization, 7* (2), 277-300.

Brown, J. S., & Duguid P. (1996). Organizational learning and communities of practice: Toward a unified view of working, learning and innovation. In M. D. Cohen & L. S. Sproull (Eds.), *Organizational Learning* (pp. 40-57). Thousand Oaks, CA.: Sage.

Brown, J. S., & Duguid P. (2001a). Knowledge and organization: A social-practice perspective. *Organization Science, 12* (2), 198-213.

Brown, J. S., & Duguid, P. (2001b). Structure and spontaneity: Knowledge and organization. In I. Nonaka & D. J. Teece (Eds.), *Managing Industrial Knowledge: Creation, Transfer and Utilization* (pp. 44-67). London: Sage.

Bruner, J. (1986). *Actual Minds, Possible Worlds*. Cambridge, MA: Harvard University Press.

Bruner, J. (1990). *Acts of Meaning*. Cambridge, MA: Harvard University Press.

Brunsson, N. (1998). Homogeneity and heterogeneity in organizational forms as the result of cropping-up processes. In N. Brunsson & J. P. Olsen (Eds.), *Organizing Organizations* (pp. 259-278). Bergen-Sandviken: Fagbokvorlag.

Chrisman, J. J. (1999). The influence of outsider-generated knowledge resources on venture creation. *Journal of Small Business Management, 37* (4), 42-58.

Chrisman, J. J., & McMullan, W. (2000). A preliminary assessment of outsider assistance as a knowledge resource: The longer-term impact of new venture counseling. *Entrepreneurship Theory and Practice, 24* (1), 37-53.

Cook, S.D., & Brown, J. S. (1999). Bridging epistemologies: the generative dance between organizational knowledge and organizational knowing. *Organization Science, 10* (4), 381-400.

Cook, S. D., & Yanow, D. (1996). Culture and organizational learning. In M. D. Cohen & L. S. Sproull (Eds.), *Organizational Learning* (pp. 430 – 459). Thousand Oaks, CA: Sage.

Crossan, M. M., Lane, H. W., & White, R. E. (1999). An organizational learning framework: From intuition to institution. *Academy of Management Review, 24* (3), 522-537.

Cunliffe, A. L. (2001). Managers as practical authors: Reconstructing our understanding of management practice. *Journal of Management Studies, 38* (3), 350-371.

Czarniawska, B. (1997). Learning organizing in a changing institutional order. *Management Learning, 28,* (4), 475-495.

Czarniawska, B., & Joerges, B. (1998). Winds of organizational change: How ideas translate into objects and actions. In N. Brunsson & J. P. Olsen (Eds.), *Organizing Organizations* (pp. 197-236). Bergen-Sandviken: Fagbokvorlag.

Czarniawska, B., & Sevón, G. (1996). *Translating Organizational Change*. Berlin: Walter de Gruyter.

Dierkes, M., Antal, A. B., Child, J., & Nonaka, I. (2001). *Handbook of Organizational Learning and Knowledge*. Oxford: Oxford University Press.

DiMaggio, P. J., & Powell, W. W. (1991). Introduction. In W. W. Powell & P. J. DiMaggio (Eds.) (pp. 1-38). *The New Institutionalism in Organizational Analysis*. London: The University of Chicago Press.

Douglas, M. (1986). *How Institutions Think*. New York: Syracuse University Press.

Easterby-Smith, M. (1997). Disciplines of organizational learning: Contributions and critiques. *Human Relations, 50* (9), 1085-1113.

Easterby-Smith, M., & Araujo, L. (1999). Organizational learning: Current debates and opportunities In M. Easterby-Smith, J. Burgoyne, & L. Aurajo (Eds.), *Organizational Learning and the Learning Organization: Developments in Theory and Practice* (pp. 1-21). Thousand Oaks, CA: Sage.

Engeström, Y. (2000). Comment on Blackler *et al.* Activity theory and the social construction of knowledge: A story of four umpires. *Organization, 7* (2), 301-310.

Engeström, Y., Miettinen, R., & Punamäki, R. (1999). *Perspectives on Activity Theory*. Cambridge: Cambridge University Press.

Forssell, A., & Jansson, D. (1996). The logic of organizational transformation: On the conversion of non-business organizations. In B. Czarniawska & G. Sevón (Eds.), *Translating Organizational Change* (pp. 93 – 116). Berlin: Walter de Gruyter.

Frank, H., & Lueger, M. (1997). Reconstructing development processes. *International Studies of Management and Organization, 27*, (3), 34-63.

Froschauer, U., & Lueger, M. (2003). *Das qualitative Interview. Zur Praxis interpretativer Analyse sozialer Systeme*. Wien: Wiener Universitätsverlag.

Gherardi, S. (1996). Organizational learning. In M. Warner (Ed.), *International Encyclopedia of Business and Management* (pp. 3934-3942). London: Routledge.

Gherardi, S. (1999). Learning as problem-driven or learning in the face of mystery? *Organization Studies, 20* (1), 101-124.

Gherardi, S. (2000a). Organizational learning. In M. Warner (Ed.), *International Encyclopedia of Business and Management,* 2nd ed. (pp. 3934-3942). London: Routledge.

Gherardi, S. (2000b). Practice-based theorizing on learning and knowing in organizations. *Organization, 7* (2), 211-223.

Gherardi, S. (2001). From organizational learning to practice-based knowing. *Human Relations*, *54* (1), 131-139.

Gherardi, S., & Nicolini, D. (2002). Learning in a constellation of interconnected practices: canon and dissonance? *Journal of Management Studies*, *39* (4), 419-436.

Gherardi, S., Nicolini, D., & Odella, F. (1998). Toward a social understanding of how people learn in organizations. *Management Learning*, *29* (3), 273-297.

Hargadon, A., & Fanelli, A. (2002). Action and possibility: Reconciling dual perspectives of knowledge in organizations. *Organization Science*, *13* (3), 290-302.

Hill, L. (1992). *Becoming a Manager: How New Managers Master the Challenges of Leadership*. Cambridge, MA: Harvard Business School Press.

Hinings, B., & Greenwood, R. (1988). The normative prescription of organizations. In L. G. Zucker, *Institutional Patterns and Organizations: Culture and Environment* (pp. 53-70), Cambridge, Ballinger.

Holman, D., Pavlica, K., & Thorpe, R. (1997). Rethinking Kolb's theory of experiential learning in management education: The contribution of social constructionism and activity theory. *Management Learning*, *28* (2), 135-148.

Jarzabkowski, P. (2003). Strategic practices: An activity theory perspective on continuity and change. *Journal of Management Studies*, *40* (1), 23-55.

Larson, A., & Starr, J. A. (1993). A network model of organization formation. *Entrepreneurship Theory and Practice*, *4* (17), 5-15.

Lave, J., & Wenger, E. (1991). *Situated Learning: Legitimate Peripheral Participation.* Cambridge: Cambridge University Press.

Learned, K. E. (1992). What happened before the organization? A model of organization formation. *Entrepreneurship Theory and Practice*, *3* (16), 39-47.

Levitt, B., & March, J. G. (1996). Organizational learning. In M. D. Cohen & L. S. Sproull (Eds.), *Organizational Learning* (pp. 516-540). Thousand Oaks, CA: Sage.

Louis, M. R. (1980). Surprise and sense making: What newcomers experience in entering unfamiliar organizational settings. *Administrative Science Quarterly*, *2* (25), 226-251.

Lueger, M. (2000) *Zur Praxis Interpretativer Feldforschung. Forschungsorganisierung - Beobachtung – Materialanalyse*. Wien: Wiener Universitätsverlag.

Miles, R. H., & Randolph, W. A. (1980). Influence of organizational learning styles on early development. In J. R. Kimberly & R. H. Miles (Eds.), *The Organizational Life Cycle: Issues in the Creation, Transformation, and Decline of Organizations* (pp. 44-82). San Francisco, CA: Jossey-Bass Publishers.

OECD. (1996). *Lifelong Learning for All*. Paris, Organization for Economic Cooperation and Development.

Orr, J. (1996). *Talking About Machines: An Ethnography of a Modern Job*. Ithaca, NY: Cornell University Press.

Pawlowsky, P. (2001). The treatment of organizational learning in management science. In M. Dierkes, A .B. Antal, J. Child, & I. Nonaka (Eds.), *Handbook of Organizational Learning and Knowledge* (pp. 61 – 88). Oxford: Oxford University Press.

Powell, W. W., & DiMaggio, P. J. (1991). *The New Institutionalism in Organizational Analysis*. London: The University of Chicago Press.

Reuber, R. A., & Fischer, E. (1999). Understanding the consequences of founders' experience. *Journal of Small Business Management*, *37* (2), 30-45.

Richter, I. (1998). Individual and organizational learning at the executive level. *Management Learning*, *29* (3), 299-316.

Sahlin-Andersson, K. (1996). Imitating by editing success: The construction of organizational fields. In B. Czarniawska & G. Sevón (Eds.), *Translating Organizational Change* (pp. 69-92). Berlin: Walter de Gruyter.

Scott, W. R. (1994). Institutions and organizations: Toward a theoretical synthesis. In W. R. Scott & J. W. Meyer (Eds.), *Institutional Environments and Organizations: Structural Complexity and Individualism* (pp. 55-80). Thousand Oaks, CA.: Sage.

Scott, W. R., & Meyer, J. W. (1994). *Institutional Environments and Organizations: Structural Complexity and Individualism*. Thousand Oaks, CA: Sage.

Senge, P. M. (1990). *The Fifth Discipline*. New York: Currency Doubleday.

Sevón, G. (1998). Organizational imitation in identity transformation. In N. Brunsson & J. P. Olsen (Eds.), *Organizing Organizations* (pp. 237-258). Bergen-Sandviken: Fagbokvorlag.

Singh, J. V., Tucker, D. J., & House, R. J. (1986). Organizational legitimacy and the liability of newness. *Administrative Science Quarterly*, *31* (2), 171-193.

Sjoestrand, S.-E. (1997). *The Two Faces of Management: The Janus Factor*. London: International Thomson Business Press.

Spender, J.-C. (1989). *Industry Recipes: An Enquiry into the Nature and Sources of Managerial Judgment*. Cambridge: Blackwell.

Spender, J.-C. (1994). Knowing, managing and learning. A dynamic managerial epistemology. *Management Learning*, 25 (3), 387-412.

Spender, J.-C. (1995). Organizations are activity systems, not merely systems of thought. In P. Shrivastava & C. Stubbart (Eds.), *Advances in Strategic Management: Challenges from within the Mainstream* (pp. 153-174). London: JAI Press.

Spender, J.-C., & Grinyer, P. H. (1996). Organizational renewal: Deinstitutionalization and loosely coupled systems. *International Studies of Management and Organization*, *26* (1), 17-40.

Starr, J. A., & Fondas, N. (1992). A model of entrepreneurial socialization and organization formation. *Entrepreneurship Theory and Practice*, *16* (1), 67-76.

Stevenson, H. H., & Jarillo, J. C. (1990). A paradigm of entrepreneurship: Entrepreneurial management. *Strategic Management Journal, 11* (5), 17-27.

Stewart, R. C., Hardy, C. & Nord, W .R. (1996). *Handbook of Organization Studies.* London: Sage.

Swidler, A. (1986). Culture in action: Symbols and strategies. *American Sociological Review, 51* (2), 273-286.

Tolbert, P. S., & Zucker, L. G. (1996). The institutionalization of institutional theory. In S. R. Clegg, C. Hardy, & W. R. Nord (Eds.), *Handbook of Organization Studies* (pp. 175-190). London: Sage.

Tsoukas, H. (1996). The firm as a distributed knowledge system: a constructionist approach. *Strategic Management Journal, 17* (Winter special issues), 11-25.

Van Leeuwen, M. J., & Van Praag, B. (2002). The costs and benefits of lifelong learning: The case of the Netherlands. *Human Resource Development Quarterly, 13* (2), 151-168.

Von Krogh, G., Roos, J., & Kleine, D. (1998). *Knowing in Firms: Understanding, Managing and Measuring Knowledge.* London: Sage.

Warner, M. (1996). *International Encyclopedia of Business and Management.* London: Routledge.

Warner, M. (2000). *International Encyclopedia of Business and Management*, 2nd edition. London: Routledge.

Watson, T. J. (2001). The emergent manager and processes of management pre-learning, *Management Learning, 32* (2), 221-235.

Wenger, E. (1998). *Communities of practice: learning, meaning, and identity.* Cambridge: Cambridge University Press.

Wenger, E. (2000). Communities of practice and social learning systems. *Organization, 7* (2), 225-246.

Zucker, L. G. (1988). *Institutional Patterns and Organizations: Culture and Environment.* Cambridge: Ballinger.

Chapter 11

COMMONALITIES IN ATTITUDES AND BELIEFS TOWARD DIFFERENT ACADEMIC SUBJECTS

Dirk Tempelaar and Jan Nijhuis
University of Maastricht, Faculty of Economics & Business Administration, the Netherlands

1. INTRODUCTION

The growth of student-centered learning as a paradigm in education at the expense of teacher-centered learning, has caused an important shift in research in learning processes: from the investigation of the impact of different instructional regimes, to the research of the influence of student characteristics and learning context on the learning process. An important element in this type of research refers to the interaction of student characteristics and context: different students perceive one and the same learning context in different ways, and develop, on the basis of these perceptions, different approaches to learning. This interaction is the focus of the so-called process stage in Presage-Process-Product or 3P models of learning.

An intriguing issue in developing 3P models of learning is the demarcation of Presage versus Process: what students' characteristics are so stable that they are dominantly outside the control of teachers, curriculum developers, student advisors or other staff (and thus belong to the Presage), and what students' characteristics are, to an important extent, influenced by contextual factors (thus belonging to the Process). In this contribution, we focus on a specific but important aspect of student characteristics: attitudes and beliefs of students toward different subjects. Most research studies investigating the role of academic affective factors on learning have concluded that students' affect toward different subjects demonstrates strong

M.K. McCuddy et al. (eds.),
The Challenges of Educating People to Lead in a Challenging World, 225–249.

variability, indicating that these affects should be regarded as Process variables (see *e.g.*, Marsh & Yeung, 1996). However, in most of these studies self-concept is an important ingredient of the affective variables that have been investigated. Since self-concept is known to be dependent upon students' success in earlier learning experiences, the variability of affect scores is more or less implied by variation in earlier learning experiences. Focusing on a more restricted set of affective factors, attitudes and beliefs toward different subjects may increase the perspective of finding commonalities between subjects.

The study reported in this chapter reflects students who attend the problem-based program of International Business Study at the University of Maastricht. Over a period of two years, several questionnaires were administered, each measuring attitudes and beliefs to different academic subjects: statistics, business strategy, finance and accounting, marketing management, and organization. These parallel questionnaires were all based on the SATS instrument, the 'Survey of Attitudes Toward Statistics,' that was adapted to the several subjects. From a methodological point of view, data from these questionnaires were used to create a latent variables attitudes model that not only allows investigation of the existence of commonalities between subject affects, but also determination of the size of these common elements relative to the size of subject-specific affects.

2. METHODOLOGICAL BACKGROUND OF THIS STUDY

2.1 Modeling Student Learning

The 'Presage-Process-Product modeling approach of classroom learning' was developed by Biggs (1993, 1999) and elaborated by Prosser & Trigwell (1999). According to this 3P modeling approach, learning is seen as a progression from Presage (teaching context) through Process (teaching acts) to Products (class achievement). The approach distinguishes several building blocks in explaining learning outcomes (see Figure 1, adapted from Prosser & Trigwell, 1999).

The Presage building block containing student-based factors develops from an individual differences perspective in psychology on student learning. Relevant factors include abilities, prior knowledge, motivation, personality facts, learning styles, stabilized learning approaches, and so on. The second building block builds on traditional staff-developmental models, and focuses on teacher behavior. The third building block, strategies for handling the task, derives from information processing psychology, focuses on the process, the efficiency with which basic cognitive strategies are developed. The complete model integrates teaching-based, student-based, and process-based approaches to learning, and in addition to that, allows for feedback from Process to Presage, and from Product to Process and Presage. Since feedback and feedforward processes are rather different in nature, an important issue, both from a research and an applied educational point of view, is the demarcation of the several building blocks: "What, for example, belongs to students' characteristics, and is to be regarded as rather stable and independent of the context, and what belongs to students' perceptions of this context?"

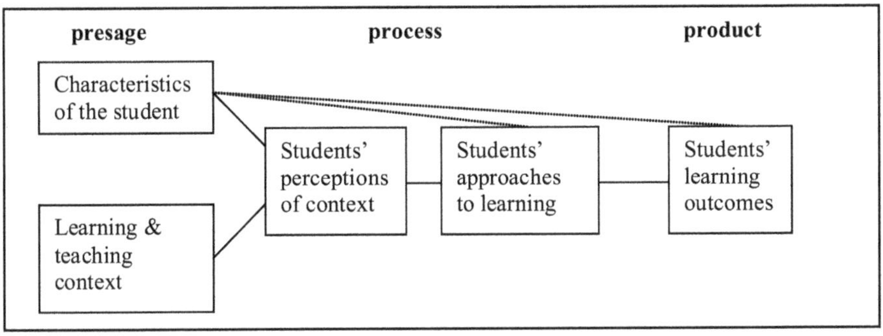

Figure 1. 3P or Presage-Process-Product Model of Classroom Learning

A related perspective on this demarcation issue can be cast into the 'aptitudes for learning' approach developed by Snow (Snow, Corno, & Jackson, 1996; Snow, & Jackson, 1993). According to this approach, human learning is determined by a wide range of psychological constructs. A common classification of these constructs is the dichotomy of personality versus intelligence; however, Snow advises avoiding these 'cloudy concepts as too complex and vague'. Instead, he proposes distinguishing among the three modes of mental functioning: cognition, conation or volition, and affection. Each of these modes is primarily defined by an enumeration of the several processes it includes; see Figure 2, adapted from Snow, Corno, and Jackson (1996). As a first step of this enumeration, the three modes can be subdivided into two underlying sub-domains for each mode: temperament and emotion for affection; motivation and volition for conation; and procedural and declarative knowledge for cognition. As a second step, Figure 2 lists the constructs that constitute the sub-domains.

According to this taxonomy, attitudes can be of different kinds: some are (more) affective in nature, others (more) conative. Similar remarks refer to beliefs and values. This leaves us with the empirical question: "Is it possible to unravel constructs like attitudes into these different constituent parts?"

'Personality'			'Intelligence'		
Affection		Conation		Cognition	
Temperament	Emotion	Motivation	Volition	Procedural knowledge	Declarative knowledge
General and special personality factors		Achievement orientations	Action Controls	Skills	Domain knowledge
Values		Self-directed orientations	Other-directed orientations	Strategies Tactics	
	Attitudes	Values, Attitudes, Interest, Beliefs	Personal Styles		Beliefs

Figure 2. Taxonomy of Individual Difference Constructs in Aptitudes for Learning Approach, Adapted from Snow, Corno, and Jackson (1996)

2.2 Subjects of the Study

Active learning, or the related concept of student-centered learning, can be implemented through different educational methods. Problem-based learning is one manifestation of student-centered learning and the one adopted at the University of Maastricht (UM) with its several faculties and schools since the school's founding in the late 1970s. In 1984 the Faculty of Economics was established as part of the University of Maastricht. The faculty offers English-language International Business and Economics programs, as well as a Dutch one. All programs are characterized by a student-centered educational approach known as problem-based learning. Students develop their knowledge and skills while working on problems in small groups. This is the dominant instructional mode, and only in a limited number of service courses are these tutorial sessions supplemented with more traditional lectures. The first-year service courses in Quantitative Methods (QM) are an example of such a hybrid educational approach. The three QM courses cover subjects from mathematics, statistics, and computer skills. The material is often regarded as being difficult and unattractive by most of our students.

QM is a series of required service courses for our students; its' nature of being obligatory is certainly responsible for most of the audience. The 'more attractive' courses from the perspective of our students are without doubt the business and economics courses; they really deal with the topics students expect in a business school. Table 1 contains the undergraduate program of the study of International Business. As is apparent from the structure, the program is organized according to a semester system with four 8-week courses per semester, always two in parallel. Courses printed in bold are the courses for which students' attitudes toward the subject were investigated.

Table 1. Undergraduate Program of International Business Study

	Courses in Undergraduate Study of International Business	
Semester 1, Block 1	Organization & Marketing	**Quantitative Methods 1**
Semester 1, Block 2	International Business	Quantitative Methods 2
Semester 2, Block 3	Economic & Social Sciences	Quantitative Methods 3
Semester 2, Block 4	Finance & Accounting I	Financial Inf. Systems
Semester 3, Block 1	**Business Strategy**	International Economics
Semester 3, Block 2	**Finance & Accounting II**	Quantitative Methods 4
Semester 4, Block 3	**Marketing Management**	Business Informatics
Semester 4, Block 4	International Business Law	**Organization & HRM**

Of the approximately 1,000 students participating in first-year courses, a great majority are first-year students (900). The remaining students are 'repeat' students who did not manage to pass that specific course the year before. The 900-student inflow can be decomposed according to nationality: about 600 Dutch students, 240 German students, and 60 students of other nationalities. That decomposition is important since huge differences exist between secondary school systems in Europe. All Dutch first-year students entering our school having participated in a final, national exam in at least seven subjects, including either basic mathematics (calculus oriented), or advanced mathematics (algebra and geometry oriented), or both. In contrast, German pupils have four subjects in their final exam: two at an advanced level, two at a basic level. Having chosen mathematics in their final exam ('Abitur'), either at advanced level ('Leistungskurs') or at basic level ('Grundkurs'), their mathematical schooling is somewhat comparable to that of Dutch students in the two different groups. However, a sizeable proportion of German freshmen did not select mathematics at any level for their final exam, and their level of mathematical schooling is of a really different order compared to that of Dutch students. Besides that, the share of statistics and probability theory in mathematical courses will differ from state to state in Germany, while in the Netherlands those two topics are incorporated in basic mathematics (preparing for social sciences), but not in advanced mathematics (preparing for sciences).

With regard to prior knowledge in economics and business, similar differences exist. Students with a Dutch educational background have mostly taken introductory courses in business, or economics, or both. Inflow with a foreign diploma, in general, does not have the opportunity to achieve any prior education in these two subjects.

2.3 Students' Attitudes and Beliefs Toward Academic Subjects

In the context of mathematics education, the study of affective factors in learning processes has a long tradition and has given rise to terms like 'mathematics anxiety' that seem to be reserved for the mathematics domain only. In conceptualizing the affective domain of mathematics education, McLeod (1992) distinguishes between emotions, attitudes, and beliefs. Emotions are fleeting positive and negative responses triggered by one's immediate experiences while studying mathematics. Attitudes are relatively stable, intense feelings that develop as repeated positive or negative emotional responses are automated over time. Beliefs are individually held ideas about mathematics, about oneself as a learner of mathematics, and about the social context of learning mathematics that together provide a context for mathematical experiences. In many studies of learning processes, the focus is on beliefs and attitudes, rather than emotions, which are transient and hard to measure directly, but serve as a source for the development of attitudes and are thus measured indirectly (see, for example, Gal & Garfield, 1997). A large body of literature on the role of attitudes and beliefs toward statistics has developed, borrowing ideas from the research in mathematics education, in which one question keeps reappearing: "Are attitudes and beliefs toward learning statistics distinct from the more general ones, such as toward learning mathematics, or toward exams in general?" Gal and Ginsburg (1994) and Gal and Garfield (1997) are examples of this line of research. The issues investigated in this research are a natural continuation of this question: "Are attitudes and beliefs toward statistics distinct from other attitudes and beliefs, such as those toward business subjects for students studying business?"

The area of research on developing instruments to assess attitudes and beliefs toward statistics is well developed. In the 1980s, several instruments were developed, all using statements for which respondents mark their agreement or disagreement on 5-point or 7-point, Likert-type scale. These include the Statistics Attitude Survey (see Roberts & Bilderback, 1980; Roberts & Saxe, 1982), the Statistical Anxiety Rating Scale (see Cruise, Cash, & Bolton, 1985), the Statistical Anxiety Inventory (see Zeidner, 1991), and the Attitudes Toward Statistics (see Wise, 1985). As each of these instruments had some drawbacks, Schau, Stevens, Dauphinee, and DelVecchio (1995) developed the Survey of Attitudes Toward Statistics (SATS) in the 1990s. In our research, we opted for the SATS instrument on the grounds of the theoretical reasons that led to its development and the fact its statistical properties are well documented.

In their review article, Gal and Garfield (1997) distinguish several reasons to take affective factors into account. Attitudes and beliefs about statistics influence the learning and teaching of statistics, and the willingness of students to enroll in elective statistics courses. There is, however, more than this process consideration. Amongst the goals of education, the development of problem-solving capabilities, literacy and related communication skills, and data-analyzing skills becomes increasingly important. To reach those goals, it is important to remove negative attitudes and beliefs — and in doing that, we should assess and monitor students' attitudes.

Gal and Garfield (1997) distinguish among three different sources for attitudes and beliefs toward statistics: previous experience with statistics in school-related contexts, 'notions' on what statistics means based on out-of-school-lives, and attitudes toward mathematics that are merely transferred to statistics. A proper definition of the several aspects of students' ideas, feelings and reactions about academic subjects, and the learning of them, is, however, still a challenging issue. As Gal and Garfield (1997, p. 40) remark, researchers in statistical education have used the terms 'attitudes' and 'beliefs,' and also the linkage of the two, without paying much attention to an explicit definition of the terms and the distinction between them. In applying McLeod's terminology to education in statistics and several business subjects, we will follow Gal and Garfield (1997) in focusing on beliefs and attitudes, rather than emotions, which are transient and hard to measure directly, but serve as a source for the development of attitudes and are thus measured indirectly. Beliefs are relatively stable and resistant to change; it takes time to develop them, and cultural factors play an important role in their development. They possess a larger cognitive component and less emotional intensity than attitudes. Attitudes toward an academic subject represent an accumulation of emotions and feelings experienced over time in the context of learning that and related subjects. They are rather stable with moderate intensity, having a smaller cognitive component than beliefs. Attributes are expressed along a positive-negative continuum, and may represent feelings, for example, toward a topic or activity.

An examination of research on learning business subjects suggests that, although the role of student attitudes in learning has been investigated, these attitudes do not refer to specific business subjects, but instead to more general aspects. Examples are research of students' attitudes toward academic group work, toward different instructional formats, toward school or university in general, or to instructional tools as computers (see for example, Gardner & Korth, 1998; Ruggiero, 1998).

2.4 SATS: Survey of Attitudes Toward Statistics

To assess student attitudes and beliefs regarding statistics, Schau *et al.* (1995) developed the Survey of Attitudes Toward Statistics (SATS). The SATS contains 28 items to identify attitudes about statistics. The SATS scales, each accompanied by two examples of items, one positively and one negatively worded, are (see Gal & Garfield, 1997, p. 44):

- Affect: measuring positive and negative feeling concerning statistics: *I like statistics; I am scared by statistics.*
- Cognitive Competence: measuring attitudes about intellectual knowledge and skills when applied to statistics: *I can learn statistics; I have no idea of what's going on in statistics.*
- Value: measuring attitudes about the usefulness, relevance, and worth of statistics in personal and professional life: *I use statistics in my everyday life; I will have no application for statistics in my profession.*
- Difficulty: measuring attitudes about the difficulty of statistics as a subject: *Statistics formulas are easy to understand; Statistics is highly technical.*

The SATS has two forms, with minor differences in wording: a 'pre' form for students who have not yet taken a statistics course, and a 'post' form for administration during or after a course. Since most students were already familiar with the subject statistics, it was decided to administer the post version.

In total, attitudes and beliefs inventories based on the SATS instrument were administered for five different subjects (see also Table 1): Statistics, International Business Strategy, International Finance and Accounting II, International Marketing Management, and International Organization and Human Resource Management (HRM) (since all courses in the International Business studies have 'International' as first part of the their name, it will be skipped in all further references). The Statistics questionnaire was administered in the very first week of the first semester; the questionnaires for the several business subjects were administered in the third and fourth semester (see once again Table 1 for the exact timing). The Statistics SATS, being part of a larger collection of inventories, was administered using a 5-point, Likert- type scale, contrary to the original SATS. The practical reason to do so was based on the wish to have one item format for all entry questionnaires. Anchors were, however, the same: 'strongly disagree' (left-hand anchor), 'neither disagree nor agree' (center anchor), and 'strongly agree' (right-hand anchor).

All 984 students in the first-year programs of the Economics studies and International Business studies participated in the administration of the SATS

Statistics in the first semester. Since the investigation of the robustness of SATS outcomes over several subgroups (see next section) was one of the aims of the analysis, it was decided to keep all students in the sample. Based on the notion of robustness over subgroups, we can anticipate the empirical results of the next section: outcomes for both studies will be similar (for all variables, the hypothesis of invariance over studies will not be statistically rejected), justifying the assumption that characteristics of students from both studies can be regarded as equal.

3. ATTITUDES AND BELIEFS TOWARD STATISTICS

As a prelude to our empirical results, we will summarize findings in other reported applications. Schau *et al.* (1995) and Gal and Garfield (1997) report that scores on the four scales vary in their interrelationship. Scores on Affect and Cognitive Competence are strongly related; scores on Value and Difficulty are moderately related to Affect and Cognitive Competence but unrelated to each other. Internal consistencies of all scales where found to be adequate, ranging from .6 to above .8 (see for example, Hair, Anderson, Tatham, & Black, 1998, for a discussion of cut-off points). In a confirmatory analysis comparing factor models of dimensions 1 to 4, Dauphinee, Schau, and Stevens (1997) concluded that the four-factor model had the best statistical properties, both in an absolute and relative (that is, corrected for degrees of freedom) sense; however, improvement over a three-factor model was limited (we will return to this issue in the next section). In the four-factor structural equation model developed in Dauphinee, Schau, and Stevens (1997), the factors are not based upon separate items but on two to three item parcels or testlets. 'Item parcelling' is the technique, applied in many large scale SEM studies, to replace dozens of items all loading on one factor, by a restricted number (two to four) parcels or mini-scales loading on that factor. Each parcel is found by aggregating related items. Item parcelling has several advantages, such as reducing the dimension of the factor model, and improving the reliability of the measured variables. We will refer to Dauphinee, Schau, and Stevens (1997) once again, this time not for its discussion of SATS, but as one of the prime references of item parcelling in applied educational psychology. We apply item parcelling in *our* study, and base the choice of parcels on the ones developed in Dauphinee, Schau, and Stevens (1997).

Descriptive statistics for several subgroups of students in the studies Economics and International Business are contained in Table 2.

Table 2. Average Scores for Scales of Affect, Cognitive Competence, Value, and Difficulty in Several Categories of Students

	Dutch UM students			German UM students			All	All
	Female (n=204)	Male (n=353)	Total (n=557)	Female Total (n=92)	Male (n=125)	(n=217)	Female (n=386)	Male (n=560)
AFFECT	3.26	3.49	3.40	3.14	3.24	3.19	3.19	3.39
COGNC	3.36	3.65	3.54	3.47	3.61	3.55	3.38	3.62
VALUE	3.66	3.70	3.68	3.81	3.78	3.79	3.69	3.71
DIFFIC	2.68	2.80	2.76	2.56	2.62	2.59	2.62	2.74

All mean scores for Affect (AFFECT), Cognitive Concept (COGNC), and Value (VALUE) are far above (and statistically significantly different from) the neutral level of three: students of different background have positive attitudes and beliefs in these aspects (of 32 hypothesis tests, 30 result in p-values smaller than .0005, the other two in .006 and .039). In contrast, all mean scores for Difficulty (DIFFIC) are below the neutral level, expressing that students perceive the subject as difficult (the naming of the Difficulty-scale is somewhat counter intuitive: all scales are defined such that higher values correspond to more positive attitudes and feelings; a name like 'lack of perceived difficulty' would better catch this meaning). The table demonstrates that students can evaluate themselves as rather cognitively competent in learning statistics (mean score of 3.52 on the 5-point scale), and at the same time regard statistics as a somewhat difficult topic.

Table 2 suggests that both gender and nationality effects may be present. Performing independent samples t-tests confirms this impression: male students have significantly higher scores on Affect, Cognitive Competence, and Difficulty (all p-values less than .001, given the very small values of all standard errors: in the range of 0.01 to 0.05); for Value, no difference exists. In comparing Dutch and German students, once again three scales demonstrate significant differences. German students score significantly higher in Value, but significantly lower in Affect and Difficulty than Dutch students, while the score on Cognitive Concept is invariant across nationalities. Figure 3 illustrates these patterns of gender and nationality effects in a graphical way, demonstrating several 95% confidence intervals for scale means. In this graph, all students with a non-Dutch secondary diploma (most of them of German nationality) are integrated in one category.

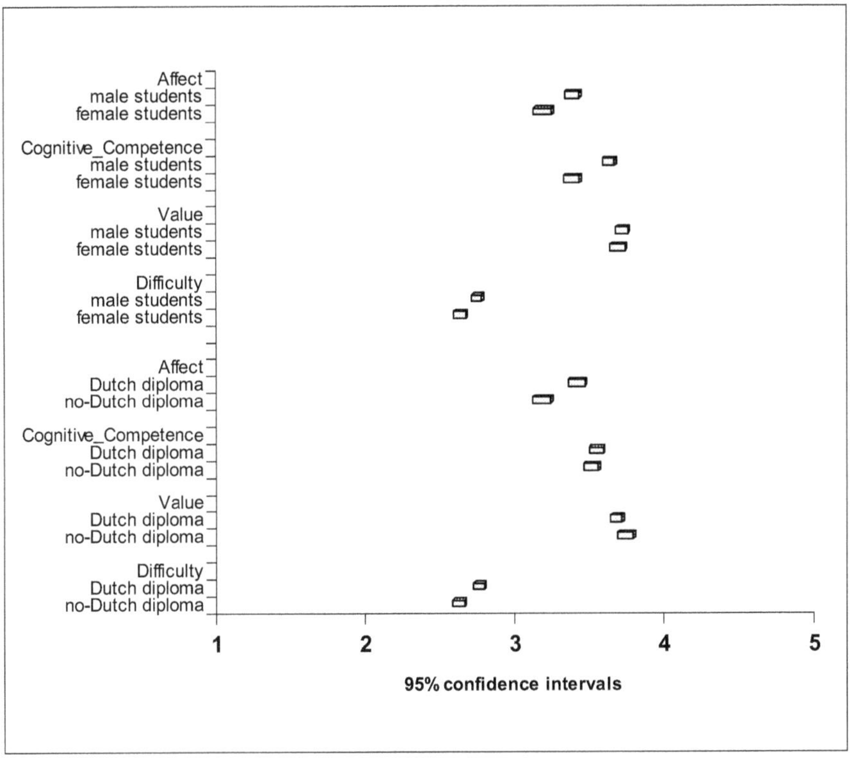

Figure 3. 95% Confidence Intervals of Mean Attitude Scores for Male Versus Female Students and Students with a Dutch Diploma Versus Students with a Non-Dutch Diploma

With regard to the correlation structure of the four attitudes scales, our findings support the results reported in Gal and Garfield (1997): Affect and Cognitive Competence are strongly related; Value and Difficulty are moderately related to Affect and Cognitive Competence but are not interrelated. See Table 3 for the correlations between the several scales for all students.

The internal consistency is evaluated by calculating the Cronbach alpha coefficients for internal consistency; their values are also given in Table 3. In the last column, reference values are given based upon Schau *et al.* (1995) and Dauphinee, Schau, and Stevens (1997). The values given in that column specify a range derived from several studies and samples. The alpha coefficients of all scales are, although somewhat lower than the reference values, satisfactory. Not removing extreme cases from the data set, as in some other studies, may be a possible explanation for the differences compared to the reference values.

Table 3. Correlations Between the Four Attitude Scales, and Cronbach Alpha Coefficients for Internal Consistency with Reference Values from Schau *et al.* (1995).

	Correlations				Cronbach Alpha Reliabilities	
	AFFECT	COGNC	VALUE	DIFFIC	This Study	Schau *et al.*
AFFECT	1.00				.80	.81 - .85
COGNC	.70	1.00			.72	.77 - .83
VALUE	.35	.38	1.00		.76	.80 - .85
DIFFIC	.50	.49	.10	1.00	.62	.64 - .75

Several studies of gender differences in attitudes toward statistics are reviewed in Dauphinee, Schau, and Stevens (1997). Although the general conclusion of all these studies tends to be the same, there are some restrictions in comparing their outcomes since different researchers used different instruments, each having different scales. Roberts and Saxe (1982), using the one-dimensional Statistics Attitude Survey developed by Roberts and Bilderback (1980), concluded that male students exhibit, on average, more positive attitudes than female students, both at the beginning and at the end of an introductory statistics course. This is, in short, also the general conclusion of other research, but then with much more nuance brought forward by the use of multi-dimensional attitude scales. In an application of Wise's (1985) Attitudes Toward Statistics, Waters, Martelli, Zakrajsek, and Popovich (1988) found that male students have more positive course attitudes than female students, whereas no gender differences exist with respect to the other attitude scales. These outcomes resemble our conclusions as reported in Table 3. Dauphinee, Schau, and Stevens (1997) study a different aspect of gender effects: not the invariance of means, but the invariance of factorial structures. We will extend our study in that direction in the next paragraph, in which a measurement model of attitudes is discussed.

As a preliminary step to confirmatory factor analysis on the SATS-data, we proceed with the analysis by 'item parcelling': forming parcels or mini-scales by aggregating item scores. Nine item-parcels are formed in exactly the same way as described in Dauphinee, Schau, and Stevens (1997): two parcels for Affect (AFFPARC1 and AFFPARC2), two parcels for Cognitive Concept (COCPARC1 and COCPARC2), three parcels for Value (VALPARC1, VALPARC2, and VALPARC3), and two parcels for Difficulty (DIFPARC1 and DIFPARC2). Based on these parcels, a measurement model for four latent variables AFFECT, COGNC, VALUE and DIFFIC was estimated in different subsamples: females and males, and Dutch and German students.

The structure of these models appeared to be extremely stable: no cross-loading emerged (in more than one subsample), and all latent factors, except for VALUE and DIFFIC, have significant positive correlations. The correlation between VALUE and DIFFIC is also positive, but not significantly in all samples, and thus was restricted to be zero. The final model, estimated on the total sample, is depicted in Figure 4 and Table 4.

The structure of this final model is identical to that of the final model described in Dauphinee *et al.* (1997), confirming the robust character of the SATS inventory. To allow an impression of the similarities of both models, the correlation structure of latent errors is reproduced from Dauphinee *et al.* (1997) in Table 4.

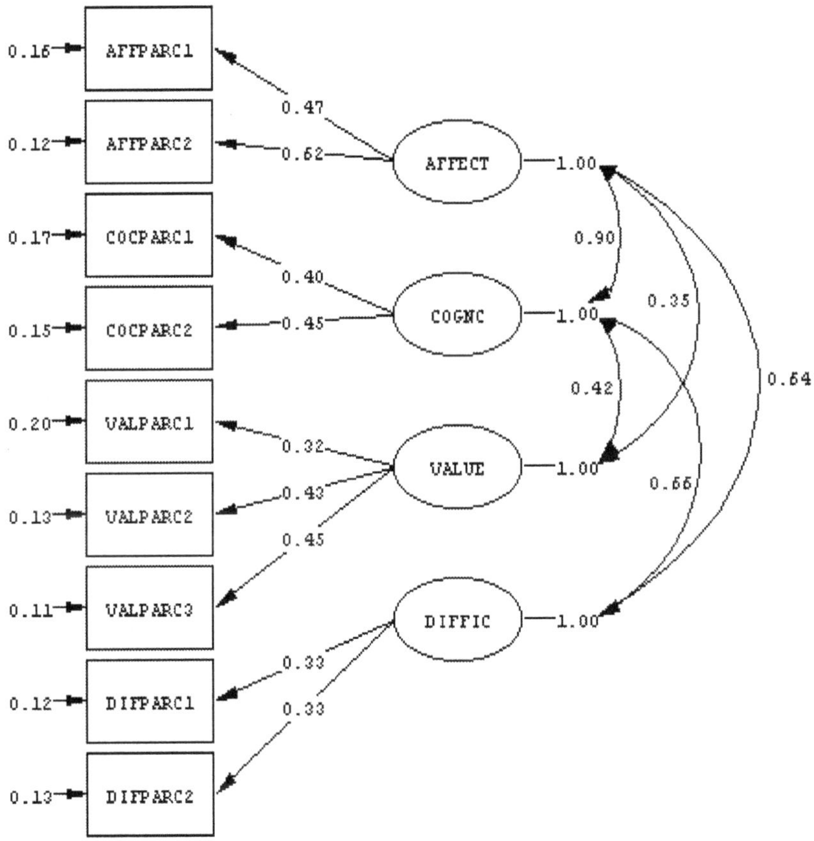

Figure 4. Factor Model with Unstandardized Factor Loadings

Table 4. Final Measurement Model of Attitudes and Beliefs: Completely Standardized Factor Loadings and Correlation of Latent Errors (Including Reference Values)

Completely standardized factor loadings				
	AFFECT	COGNC	VALUE	DIFFIC
AFFPARC1	0.76			
AFFPARC2	0.87			
COCPARC1		0.70		
COCPARC2		0.77		
VALPARC1			0.58	
VALPARC2			0.76	
VALPARC3			0.80	
DIFPARC1				0.69

Correlation matrix of latent errors (reference values, in brackets, from Dauphinee *et al.* 1997)				
	AFFECT	COGNC	VALUE	DIFFIC
COGNC	0.90 (0.94)			
VALUE	0.35 (0.32)	0.42 (0.39)		
DIFFIC	0.64 (0.73)	0.66 (0.64)	- (-)	

We continue the analysis by investigating gender and nationality effects. We perform sequentially more restrictive tests of model invariance as in Dauphinee *et al.* (1997). In that article a factor structure and factor loadings were found that were invariant across gender, but the hypothesis of invariance with regard to factor variances and covariances had to be rejected. The latter was caused by females having a much higher variance in Value scores, and a much smaller correlation between Value and Affect scores, than males. In our sample, we were not able to reproduce these empirical findings. In testing for a nationality effect, the last and most restrictive test was significant, indicating that the hypothesis of invariant factor structure and error correlations cannot be rejected, but that the variability in scores on the several parcels is different for Dutch and German students. Differences appeared to be in the Value and Difficulty parcels, the variability being much larger in German students than in Dutch students.

A very last step in testing for gender and nationality effects is to perform a test on latent means. Dauphinee *et al.* (1997) do not report on this type of test, so no reference values are available. In testing for gender effect, we find large differences for three of the four latent variables: for the latent variables AFFECT, COGNC, and DIFFIC, the means of male students are significantly higher than that of female students (p-values all smaller than .001), while for the remaining latent variable, VALUE, no significant difference in means exist. For the nationality case, the following pattern arises: in comparison to German students, Dutch students score significantly higher in AFFECT and DIFFIC, significantly lower in VALUE, and similarly in COGNC. These outcomes are similar to the ones achieved in performing independent samples *t*-test on scale means.

These conclusions seem to add to the validation of the SATS-instrument and the factor model based on that instrument. In contrast to findings in Dauphinee *et al.* (1997), the model created on the whole sample appears to be valid for all relevant subsamples, even though these subsamples show large differences in characteristics, and even though our sample is extremely large (in comparison to other studies). However, these differences are best interpreted as differences in latent means, while the factorial structure is invariant. This leaves the question of: "Why are there large differences in the means?" The difference in means across nationalities can easily be explained by the better match between secondary and higher education. The introduction to statistics in Dutch secondary schools could explain the higher scores in Affect and Difficulty of Dutch students, while the strong study orientation of German students explains their high Value score. However, we are at a loss to provide a good explanation behind the large gender effect.

4. ATTITUDES AND BELIEFS TOWARD BUSINESS SUBJECTS AND STATISTICS

One year after the administration of the SATS Statistics, attitudes and beliefs toward four different international business subjects were assessed for a subset of the students. This subset consists of students in the study of International Business (so excluding Economics students) who passed their propedeutic exam (in the Dutch tertiary education system, the first year program is finished with an exam, called the propedeutic exam, that serves as an entry exam for the second year program; students failing this propedeutic exam redo the first year program as 'repeat students'). To assess students' attitudes and beliefs toward Business Strategy, Finance and Accounting, Marketing Management, and Organization and Human Resource Management (HRM), the SATS inventory was adapted by replacing the subject name Statistics by each of the four subject names mentioned. In addition to that, two items were slightly reformulated, to accommodate the different nature of business subjects. The statement 'Statistics formulas are easy to understand' was rephrased as 'Techniques of Business Strategy are easy to understand,' and the statement 'Statistics involves massive computations' as 'Business Strategy involves a lot of technical aspects' (similar for the other subjects). The inventories were administered using the original 7-point Likert scale; to make the outcomes comparable to the Statistics outcomes, all scores were re-expressed in terms of a 1-5 scale. This re-expression using a linear transformation was performed so as to pertain to the three anchors (so 1=>1, 4=>3, and 7=>5, preserving left-hand, centre, and right-hand anchors). To eliminate any confounding factors in the comparison between subjects, the data on which the Statistics attitudes and beliefs are based are restricted to those students for which data is available for the other courses. Table 5 contains descriptive statistics for all four attitudes and beliefs scales in all five subjects, including the relevant sample size.

Table 5. Means, and Standard Errors Per Attitude Scale Per Subject, and Sample Size n, for Subjects: Statistics (1.1QM), Business Strategy (2.1BS), Finance and Accounting (2.2FA), Marketing Management (2.3MM), and Organization and Human Resource Management (2.4OHRM)

Attitude Scales	Affect		Cognitive Competence		Value		Difficulty		Size
Subjects	Mean	St.err.	Mean	St.err.	Mean	St.err.	Mean	St.err.	N
1.1QM	3.23	0.03	3.47	0.03	3.70	0.03	2.62	0.02	346
2.1BS	4.02	0.04	4.09	0.04	4.04	0.04	3.24	0.04	349
2.2F&A	3.00	0.06	3.29	0.05	3.54	0.04	2.23	0.04	320
2.3MM	3.95	0.05	3.96	0.04	3.97	0.05	3.17	0.04	267
2.4OHRM	3.91	0.04	3.87	0.04	3.81	0.04	3.35	0.04	281

The descriptive statistics displayed in Table 5 show a clear pattern. For the subjects Business Strategy, Marketing Management, and Organization and HRM, students express positive attitudes and beliefs: all scale means are far (and statistically significant given the small values of the standard errors; all t-values of testing against the neutral level are larger than 4.3, all p-values smaller than .0005) above the neutral level of 3. On top of that, differences in scale means between the three subjects are very small. In contrast, the descriptives for both Statistics and Finance and Accounting are much less positive, and even negative for the scale Difficulty. Although these two subjects, perceived as the most analytical subjects of the program, both have less positive attitudes, scores are not identical: Finance and Accounting tends to have an even tougher reputation than Statistics.

Since LISREL estimates are based upon the correlation structure of the several items, a further impression can be achieved by studying the correlation structure of the several attitude scales per subject. These are expressed in Table 6.

Table 6. Correlations Between Attitude Scales Per Subject, for Subjects: Statistics (1.1QM), Business Strategy (2.1BS), Finance and Accounting (2.2F&A), Marketing Management (2.3MM), and Organization and Human Resource Management (2.4OHRM)

1.1QM	AFFECT	COGNC	VALUE	DIFFIC
AFFECT	1.00			
COGNC	0.71	1.00		
VALUE	0.35	0.40	1.00	
DIFFIC	0.53	0.54	0.13	1.00

2.2F&A	AFFECT	COGNC	VALUE	DIFFIC
AFFECT	1.00			
COGNC	0.78	1.00		
VALUE	0.47	0.49	1.00	
DIFFIC	0.50	0.52	0.10	1.00

2.1BS	AFFECT	COGNC	VALUE	DIFFIC
AFFECT	1.00			
COGNC	0.62	1.00		
VALUE	0.54	0.50	1.00	
DIFFIC	0.30	0.44	0.05	1.00

2.3MM	AFFECT	COGNC	VALUE	DIFFIC
AFFECT	1.00			
COGNC	0.63	1.00		
VALUE	0.50	0.49	1.00	
DIFFIC	0.27	0.43	0.01	1.00

2.4OHRM	AFFECT	COGNC	VALUE	DIFFIC
AFFECT	1.00			
COGNC	0.60	1.00		
VALUE	0.61	0.36	1.00	
DIFFIC	0.26	0.55	-0.03	1.00

Table 6 confirms the similarity of the three management-oriented subjects, in contrast to the two analytical subjects. Two striking differences are: the correlation between Value and Difficulty, the smallest correlation of the four attitudes scales for Statistics, completely disappears in the right-hand side of Table 6: for the management-oriented subjects, Value and Difficulty are unrelated concepts. And the very high correlation between Affect and Cognitive Competence for both analytical subjects gets much smaller for the management-oriented subjects, whereas the correlation of Affect and Value rises for the later subjects.

Table 7. Factor Loadings of Parcels for 1st Order Latent Factor Models Per Subject, for Subjects: Statistics (1.1QM), Business Strategy (2.1BS), Finance and Accounting (2.2F&A), Marketing Management (2.3MM), and Organization and Human Resource Management 2.4OHRM)

1.1QM	Parcel1	Parcel2	Parcel3
AFFECT	0.81	0.87	
COGNC	0.70	0.76	
VALUE	0.56	0.80	0.86
DIFFIC	0.63	0.73	

2.2F&A	Parcel1	Parcel2	Parcel3
AFFECT	0.84	0.91	
COGNC	0.85	0.81	
VALUE	0.64	0.84	0.88
DIFFIC	0.77	0.84	

2.1BS	Parcel1	Parcel2	Parcel3
AFFECT	0.72	0.85	
COGNC	0.76	0.83	
VALUE	0.65	0.79	0.82
DIFFIC	0.76	0.79	

2.3MM	Parcel1	Parcel2	Parcel3
AFFECT	0.82	0.80	
COGNC	0.84	0.76	
VALUE	0.75	0.84	0.86
DIFFIC	0.80	0.80	

2.4OHRM	Parcel1	Parcel2	Parcel3
AFFECT	0.76	0.84	
COGNC	0.78	0.80	
VALUE	0.79	0.81	0.90
DIFFIC	0.87	0.74	

The next step in the statistical analysis of the subject attitudes is the estimation of a four-factor, first-order confirmatory factor model for each of the subjects separately. For all subjects, the same model structure was imposed: factors were allowed to covary, except for attitudes Affect and Value, for which the covariation was set to zero. Outcomes of the estimation of these first-order models are summarized in Tables 7 and 8, containing factor loadings and the correlation structure of the latent factors.

Table 8. Correlations Between Latent Factors Per Subject, for Subjects: Statistics (1.1QM), Business Strategy (2.1BS), Finance and Accounting (2.2F&A), Marketing Management (2.3MM), and Organization and Human Resource Management (2.4OHRM)

1.1QM	AFFECT	COGNC	VALUE	DIFFIC
AFFECT	1.00			
COGNC	0.91	1.00		
VALUE	0.36	0.45	1.00	
DIFFIC	0.65	0.67	-	1.00

2.2F&A	AFFECT	COGNC	VALUE	DIFFIC
AFFECT	1.00			
COGNC	0.91	1.00		
VALUE	0.48	0.53	1.00	
DIFFIC	0.59	0.62	-	1.00

2.1BS	AFFECT	COGNC	VALUE	DIFFIC
AFFECT	1.00			
COGNC	0.80	1.00		
VALUE	0.67	0.63	1.00	
DIFFIC	0.37	0.56	-	1.00

2.3MM	AFFECT	COGNC	VALUE	DIFFIC
AFFECT	1.00			
COGNC	0.81	1.00		
VALUE	0.59	0.56	1.00	
DIFFIC	0.34	0.52	-	1.00

2.4OHRM	AFFECT	COGNC	VALUE	DIFFIC
AFFECT	1.00			
COGNC	0.83	1.00		
VALUE	0.73	0.47	1.00	
DIFFIC	0.38	0.72	-	1.00

This structural equation modeling step confirms the conclusions of the descriptive analysis: judged on the basis of students' attitudes and beliefs, the program contains two kinds of subjects — analytical subjects and management-oriented subjects. Analytical subjects, such as Quantitative Methods and Finance and Accounting, give rise to attitudes where:

- The covariation between the latent factors Affect and Cognitive Competence is so strong that these attitudes nearly collapse (correlations above 0.90). This is in agreement with the finding of

Dauphinee, Schau, C., and Stevens (1997), where the four-factor models induced minor improvements over the three-factor model.

- The correlation between Affect and Value is relatively low: students can dislike the subject, but still regard it as highly important.

The management oriented subjects give rise to attitudes where:

- The latent factors Affect and Cognitive Competence demonstrate less covariation; the correlation is in the order of 0.8, a figure low enough to make the two factors really different.
- The correlation between Affect and Value is relatively high: the liking of the subject is a strong predictor of the attached importance of the subject, and vice versa.

5. A SECOND-ORDER FACTOR MODEL

As a last step in this modeling tour, a second-order factor model was estimated with a common 2nd order factor for each of the attitudes, explaining the corresponding subject-specific 1st order attitude factors. The correlation structure of the 2nd order factor was chosen to be identical to the correlation structures of the 1st order models: all attitudes were allowed to covary, except for Value and Difficulty. No cross-loadings were allowed. Figure 5 depicts the estimated model graphically, with the four 2nd order latent factors on the left-hand side, explaining the 20 subject-specific 1st order factors in the middle of the graph, and with the 45 subject-specific item-parcels used as indicator variables on the right-hand side.

Tables 9-11 contain numerical output on the estimated 2nd order factor model. In Table 9, the completely standardized factor loadings or regression coefficients that explain 1st order factors by the corresponding 2nd order factors are indicated. The table demonstrates an already rather familiar pattern: factor loadings of the management-oriented subjects are different, and in this case much higher, than those of the analytical subjects.

Table 10 depicts the correlation structure of the 2nd order factors. The values are very similar to those in the right-hand side of Table 8: the 1st order correlation structure of the factors of the management-oriented subjects.

The last table, Table 11, provides the explained variation in the 1st order factors by the 2nd order factors, expressed as the percentage value of R^2.

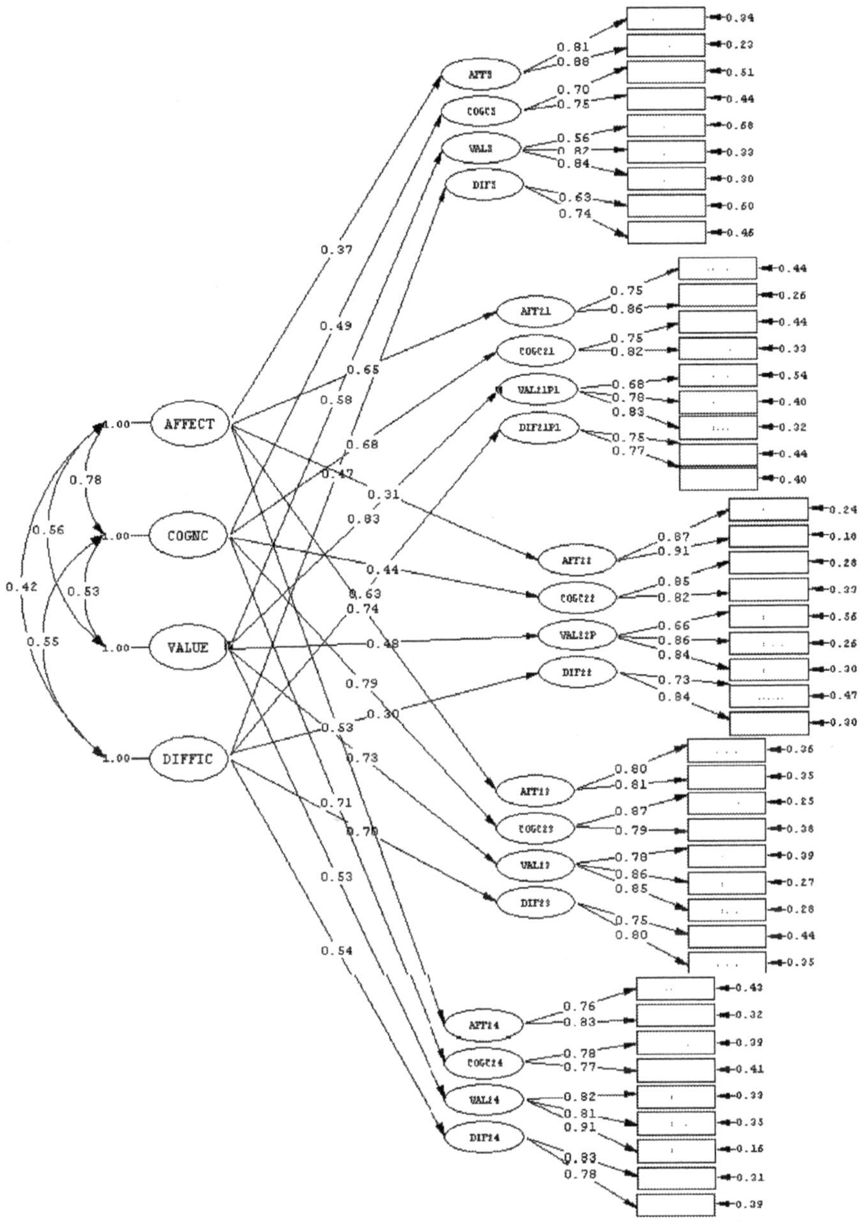

Figure 4. Final Measurement Model of Attitudes and Beliefs: Factor Model with Unstandardized Factor Loadings

Table 9. Completely Standardized Factor Loadings of 1st Order Factors on 2nd Order Factors, for Subjects: Statistics (1.1QM), Business Strategy (2.1BS), Finance and Accounting (2.2FA), Marketing Management (2.3MM), and Organization and Human Resource Management (2.4OHRM)

Subjects	AFFECT	COGNC	VALUE	DIFFIC
1.1QM	0.35	0.47	0.54	0.48
2.1BS	0.61	0.65	0.82	0.61
2.2F&A	0.31	0.45	0.45	0.37
2.3MM	0.76	0.80	0.73	0.67
2.4OHRM	0.56	0.71	0.56	0.53

Table 10. Correlations Between 2nd Order Latent Factors

	AFFECT	COGNC	VALUE	DIFFIC
AFFECT	1.00			
COGNC	0.78	1.00		
VALUE	0.56	0.53	1.00	
DIFFIC	0.42	0.55	-	1.00

Table 11. Explained Variation of 1st Order Factors by 2nd Order Factors, for Subjects: Statistics (1.1QM), Business Strategy (2.1BS), Finance and Accounting (2.2FA), Marketing Management (2.3MM), and Organization and Human Resource Management (2.4OHRM)

Subjects	AFFECT	COGNC	VALUE	DIFFIC	Average
1.1QM	14	24	34	22	24
2.1BS	41	46	67	39	48
2.2F&A	9	19	23	9	15
2.3MM	56	64	53	49	56
2.4OHRM	28	50	31	30	35
Average	30	41	42	30	35

Once again, the different kinds of subjects quite clearly manifest themselves: the figures for the management-oriented subjects are quite different from those of the analytical subjects. Another pattern appears: the explained variation in the factors Cognitive Competence and Value is much higher than that in the other two factors, Affect and Difficulty.

Summarizing all outcomes, the following picture emerges:

- There exist strong commonalities in students' attitudes and beliefs toward different subjects. Averaged over all attitudes and all subjects, somewhat more than one-third of the variation of subject-specific attitudes can be explained by deeper, subject-independent attitudes of students.

- The degree of commonality is different for diverse attitudes. The attitudes Cognitive Competence and Value have the strongest common components, irrespective of the subject. And for all subjects, the attitudes Affect and Difficulty have the strongest subject-specific components.
- Strong differences exist in the importance of the common attitudes vis-à-vis the subject-specific attitudes, between the two kinds of subjects. In the management-oriented subjects, roughly half of all variation is explained by the common component. In contrast, only about 20% of the variation in attitudes is explained by a shared attitude component, while the major part is subject-specific in the case of the analytical subjects.

6. CONCLUSIONS

From a substantive point of view, the Marsh and Yeung (1996) study aims to test two different "straw person hypotheses": that different academic affects associated with the same subject can be incorporated into a single subject-specific factor, implying that distinctions among different academic affects are not very important; and that affect in different academic subjects is quite distinct from affect in other subjects, implying that one cannot hope to describe affect with general affect factors only. Marsh and Yeung (1996) succeed in testing and rejecting both hypotheses, as we do in this study. However, Marsh and Yeung (1996, p. 684) were somewhat limited in their analysis by the restricted richness of their data set: "*Unfortunately, however, data available in the NELS88 are not very strong for testing this hypothesis. Stronger tests of this hypothesis would require well-validated multi-item scales instead of single-item scales and the inclusion of a more diverse set of academic affects.*" All these requirements — multi-item scales, well validated, for a range of affects — are provided by the SATS and the application of it to a diversity of subjects (be it of tertiary level, instead of secondary).

The outcomes of our study confirm those of the Marsh and Yeung (1996) study:

- Affect has two important components: one general, context independent, and one subject-specific, both of them of significant size; and
- Affect is multidimensional, that is, it is constituted of a range of different constructs.

This study, through the richness of its data, provides relevant details within this broad outline (*e.g.*, in management-oriented subjects, four different attitudes are clearly apparent; in the analytical subjects, the attitudes Affect and Cognitive competence tend to get indistinguishable).

What is the educational implication of these findings? Contrary to the general perception of lecturers, who expect their students to have similar attitudes toward and to get similar ratings in different subjects, Marsh and Yeung (1996) find that students demonstrate different affects to different subjects. Recognition of this variation should lead to more effective teaching is the rather positive conclusion of the Marsh and Yeung (1996) study. The outcomes of our study confirm their findings: the hypothesis of invariant affects toward different subjects is to be rejected. Our study, however, also reveals a common underlying factor in these subject-specific affective factors. This conclusion that affects are a mixture of a trait-like stable component and a state-like subject-specific component has promising potential educational implications for interventions directed at adjusting negative affects. Such interventions should typically consist of a combination of interventions within courses, with the lecturer stimulating and enthusing students for specific academic disciplines, and interventions over several courses, *e.g.*, empowering students with low self-concepts (the cognitive competence component of affects). Extreme interventions — that is only within a course or solely outside specific courses — are expected to be less efficient as interventions operating at both levels.

Much further research is needed into affective factors in education. An intriguing question is the relationship between personality styles and (the common component of) attitudes toward subjects. Although intriguing, outcomes of this type of research might not offer that much to the perspectives of intervention. It is difficult to imagine (negative) attitudes being more stable than those explained by personality, and for that reason it is difficult to imagine what interventions could be successful in adjusting those negative affects. A research question that combines both relevancy and perspectives for educational interventions refers to the relation between attitudes and student learning approaches; it is this research area on which both authors are presently working.

REFERENCES

Biggs, J. B. (1993). From theory to practice: A cognitive systems approach, *Higher Education Research and Development*, *12*, 73-86.

Biggs, J. (1999). *Teaching for Quality Learning at University*, The Society for Research into Higher Education & Open University Press, Buckingham.

Cruise, R. J., Cash, R. W., & Bolton, D. L. (1985). Development and validation of an instrument to measure statistical anxiety, *American Statistical Association Proceedings of the Section on Statistics Education*, 92-97.

Dauphinee, T. L., Schau, C., & Stevens, J. J. (1997). Survey of attitudes toward statistics: Factor structure and factorial invariance for women and men, *Structural Equation Modeling: A Multidisciplinary Journal*, *4* (2), 129-141.

Gal, I., & Garfield, J. B. (1997). *Curricular Goals and Assessment Challenges in Statistics Education*. In I. Gal, & J. B. Garfield, *The Assessment Challenge in Statistical Education* (pp. 1-13). Voorburg: IOS Press.

Gal, I, & Ginsburg L. (1994). The Role of Beliefs and Attitudes in Learning Statistics: Towards an Assessment Framework. *Journal of Statistics Education,* 2 (2).

Gardner, B. S., & Korth, S. J. (1998). A framework for learning to work in teams. *Journal of Education for Business*, *74* (1), 28-33.

Hair, J. F., Anderson, R. E., Tatham, R. L., & Black, W. C. (1998). *Multivariate Data Analysis* (5th ed.). Upper Saddle River, NJ.: Prentice-Hall.

Marsh, H. W., & Yeung, A. S. (1996). The distinctiveness of affects in specific school subjects: An Application of confirmatory factor analysis with the national educational longitudinal study of 1988. *American Educational Research Journal*, *33* (3), 665-689.

McLeod, D. B. (1992). Research on affect in mathematics education: A reconceptualization. In D. A. Grouws, (Ed.), *Handbook of Research on Mathematics Teaching and Learning*, a project of the National Council of Teachers of Mathematics (pp. 575-596). New York: Macmillan.

Prosser, M., & Trigwell, K. (1999). *Understanding Learning and Teaching: The Experience in Higher Education*. The Society for Research into Higher Education & Open University Press, Buckingham.

Roberts, D. M., & Bilderback, E. W. (1980). Reliability and validity of a statistics attitude survey. *Educational and Psychological Measurement*, *40*, 235-238.

Roberts, D. M., & Saxe, J. E. (1982). Validity of a statistics attitude survey: A follow-up study. *Educational and Psychological Measurement*, *47*, 907-912.

Ruggiero, V. R. (1998). *Changing Attitudes, a Strategy for Motivating Students to Learn*. Boston: Allyn & Bacon.

Schau, C., Stevens, J., Dauphinee, T. L., & DelVecchio, A. D. (1995). The development and validation of the survey of attitudes toward statistics. *Educational and Psychological Measurement*, *55* (5), 868-875.

Snow, R. E., Corno, L., & Jackson, D. (1996). Individual differences in affective and conative functions. In D. C. Berliner & R. C. Calfee (Eds.), *Handbook of Educational Psychology* (pp. 243-310). New York, Simon & Schuster Macmillan.

Snow, R. E., & Jackson, D. N. (1993). Assessment of Conative Constructs for Educational Research and Evaluation: a Catalogue. CSE Technical Report 354, CRESST, Los Angeles.

Wise, S. L. (1985). The development and validation of a scale measuring attitudes towards statistics. *Educational and Psychological Measurement*, *45*, 401-405.

Zeidner, M. (1991). Statistics and mathematics anxiety in social science students: Some interesting parallels. *British Journal of Educational Psychology*, *61*, 319-328.

Chapter 12

MULTICULTURAL PERCEPTIONS OF THE ENTREPRENEURIAL LIFESTYLE

Ben Martz[1], Tom Neil[2], Alessandro Biscaccianti[3], and Robert Williams[4]
[1]University of Colorado at Colorado Springs, USA [2]Allen University, Columbia, South Carolina, USA [3]Burgundy School of Business, France [4] University of Plymouth, Devon, Newton Abbot, UK

1. INTRODUCTION

The area of entrepreneurship has been suggested as a key factor for business over the years. Business schools around the world offer courses and even complete degrees emphasizing entrepreneurship. However, the perception of an entrepreneur differs across cultures. The entrepreneurial lifestyle is perceived, rewarded, acknowledged, etc. differently across cultures based upon cultural norms. This paper presents results from a set of data collected over two years in three countries: United States, United Kingdom, and France. The analysis of over 900 questionnaires found support for the basic conjecture that the perception of entrepreneurship differs between countries and in the direction predicted by the Total Entrepreneurship Activity (TEA) report; the US students perceived the entrepreneurship lifestyle better than did students from France or the UK. The final section of the paper highlights the cross-cultural differences that were found and offers some ideas on why they occur.

2. BACKGROUND

One driver for this study is to compare the interest in entrepreneurship across cultures. This idea can be traced back to several researchers who saw

M.K. McCuddy et al. (eds.),
The Challenges of Educating People to Lead in a Challenging World, 251–271.

culture as a key factor in business and economic growth. McClelland (1961, p.11) pointed to the need to study sociological explanations for economic forces such as "technology advances, population growth, and energetic entrepreneurship." In the first chapter of his book, *The Achieving Society*, entrepreneurship is identified as one of four key forces and further traces several well-known economic theorists and their premises on the subject. Ultimately, the key point made is that the forces underlying economic development might well reside outside the economic sphere.

Drucker goes further in his vision when he states that: "Innovation and entrepreneurship are thus needed in society as much as in the economy" (1985, p. 254). His contention is that the search for innovation will keep the society and the economy self-renewing. One of the key challenges Drucker points to in his vision for individuals is the need, the requirement, for continuous learning and relearning.

This is a follow up study to the original research study that compared the perception of entrepreneurs held by students across three cultures: America, France and United Kingdom (Martz, Neil, Williams, & Biscaccianti, forthcoming 2005).

2.1 Definition

There seems to be no clear, consistent definition of entrepreneur in the research. At least two scales, the Entrepreneurial Quotient (EQ) and the Entrepreneurial Attitude Orientation (EAO) (Huefner, Hunt, & Robinson, 1996) have been developed to identify potential entrepreneurs. Some researchers simply equate new venture creation with entrepreneurship (Timmons, Smollen, & Dingee, 1985). Others posit that there exists a fundamental distinction between entrepreneurs and small business owners (Carland, Hoy, Boulton, & Carland, 1984). While profitability remains a key driver for both of these groups of business people, confounding personal goals also influence the business owners. Begley and Boyd (1987) draw a distinction between the small business owners who created a new business and those who did not create a new business, but have been hired to run the new business.

Further, several researchers suggest that entrepreneurs and managers differ in areas of basic personality traits, business competence and risk taking. Rowe, Mason, Dickel, Mann, & Mockler (1994) identified four basic decision styles: conceptual, directive, behavioral, and analytic. Reynierse (1997) reported that entrepreneurs were generally more flexible and more open to change than their manager counterparts. For Chandler and Hanks (1994), entrepreneurs excelled in identifying and taking advantage of opportunities while a competent manager did better at delegating and coordinating tasks than did the entrepreneur. With regard to risk taking, Hisrich (1990) found managers operated to minimize mistakes while entrepreneurs were more willing to accept the risks associated with aggressive business decisions. Envick and Langford (2000) used the Five-Factor Model personality model to compare entrepreneurs and managers. Ultimately, they found managers to be more cautious and more team-oriented than entrepreneurs.

In reality, it seems more likely that there are ways to categorize entrepreneurs into subsets. Vesper (1980) uses potential entry strategies as a categorization tool to develop eleven potential categories. These include categories for entrepreneurs such as independent innovators, economy of scale exploiters, and value manipulators. Shuman, Seeger, Kamm, and Teebagy (1986) produced a ten-category classification scheme based around how the entrepreneur gained control of the business. Some of their categories included successor in family business, independent, started from scratch, and acquirer. Rogoff and Lee (1996) synthesized their topology down to three categories: creators, inheritors, and operators. For the purposes of this study, the definition of entrepreneur was simplified to: "a person who starts and runs his/her own business."

2.2 Societal Impact

Returning to the guidelines of Drucker and McClellan mentioned above, there have been several studies that deal with entrepreneurship at a more narrow level of analysis: culture. Fleming (1996) looked at the impact of entrepreneurial education in Ireland over a four-year span. Characteristics such as "attitudes toward entrepreneurship" and "personal and family background" were evaluated. The results indicated that the students surveyed moved slightly toward a more entrepreneurial attitude and the levels of self-employment (and those in smaller firms of less than 50 employees) had increased. Abbey's (2002) cross-cultural study on motivation for entrepreneurship found significant differences between two cultures, one defined as individualist and the other collectivist, on desire for independence and need for economic security.

Box *et al.* (1995) evaluated Thai entrepreneurs by the performance of the companies they ran. This performance was significantly correlated with previous experience in entrepreneurial management; number of previous attempts, successful or not; and industry experience. Koiranen *et al.* (1997) analyzed the risk taking propensity between Finnish and American entrepreneurs and business managers. The results showed that Americans in the study were more willing to take risks than the Finns. Comparisons between American and Egyptian entrepreneurs (Parnell, Crandall, &

Menefee, 1995) showed that American students had greater levels of perceived entrepreneurial education, entrepreneurial opportunities and confidence in taking advantage of the opportunities.

Cultures evolve as a consequence of other changes. Two such changes that impact entrepreneurship are technological change and business organizational change. Shane (1996) suggests the first and supports his contention with research that shows changes in the rate of entrepreneurship can be explained by corresponding rates of change in technology. Schrage (1990) suggests that managers need characteristics of the entrepreneur and the entrepreneur needs characteristics of the manager. He cites Robert Reich's (1987) proposition that challenges the myths about entrepreneurs being the "heroes" in today's business world. Reich suggests that there is no one best attitude or characteristic make-up for entrepreneurs. Furthermore, he argues the dichotomy is even more inappropriate as the business world moves to more of a team-based environment.

So, in total, entrepreneurship has been defined in broad and ambiguous ways. There have been many instruments with many more characteristics used to help categorize and compare entrepreneurs. The comparisons have been conducted at global levels and at country levels. The comparisons have been made looking for unique characteristics of entrepreneurs. Throughout the comparisons, several areas of interest have emerged. These include demographic characteristics such as gender, education level and age and cultural characteristics such as the perceived ability to succeed as an entrepreneur, the overall impression of entrepreneurs, the positive impression of the entrepreneurial lifestyle, and family experience.

2.3 The Global Entrepreneurship Monitor Project

The Global Entrepreneurship Monitor (GEM) program is an ambitious project undertaken to "describe and analyze entrepreneurial processes within a wide range of nations" (Reynolds, Bygrave, Autio, & Hay, 2002). The 2002 GEM report gives some hints to the vastness of the sphere that is considered entrepreneurship. Data for the report were collected from 37 countries representing about 62% of the world's population. Interviews, surveys and compilation of standardized information contributed to the database. The objective of the GEM study is to provide a summary report on differences in global entrepreneurship activity at a national, aggregate level.

The GEM researchers have created a composite index, Total Entrepreneurship Activity (TEA), to help with the comparison of entrepreneurship activity. The TEA is made up of nascent entrepreneurs (those workers involved with a start-up) and of managers in companies that are less than 42 months old. This TEA index has been shown to correlate strongly with a whole battery of alternate measures for entrepreneurship, including, but not limited to, actual number of start-up efforts, start up efforts creating new markets, and opportunity-based entrepreneurship. In 2002, the US rated 11th, France rated 34th, and United Kingdom rated 16th on the TEA.

The 2002 summary report includes a generic profile for an entrepreneur and a discussion of factors that seem to motivate entrepreneurs. In a ratio of 2:1, men are more likely to be involved with entrepreneurship than women. The most active age-span group for those claiming to be entrepreneurs is 25-34 followed by the 18-24 group when looking at those entrepreneurs who choose to enter entrepreneurship (opportunity entrepreneurs). The results of the expert focus groups used in the study show that three areas — government policies, cultural and social norms, and education and training — dominated the discussions. The statistical results of the expert's data showed significant correlations (both negatively correlated) for only two areas: financial support and protection of intellectual property rights. Three socio-demographic characteristics that emerged as indicators of likely entrepreneur activity were: 1.) knowing someone who had started his or her own business in the past two years; 2.) low fear of failure; and 3.) having the skills and ability to undertake a start-up.

3. RESEARCH STUDY

This research study is exploratory in nature. The purpose of this study is to look for cultural differences in the perception of entrepreneurs between American, French and United Kingdom cultures. The subjects are students and so, the primary area of interest centers on their perceptions of entrepreneurs. The perceptions of entrepreneurs will be influenced by the way a culture rewards or encourages entrepreneurship. The basic speculation then is that the more positively a culture supports entrepreneurship the more likely students positively perceive entrepreneurship as a lifestyle and will gravitate toward it as a career choice. This can be translated into more specific conjectures for further study.

> Conjecture: If the GEM, TEA index is an accurate reflection of social characteristics of culture, then students from countries with higher TEA scores should also score higher on their perception concerning entrepreneurs and the entrepreneurial lifestyle.

3.1 Methodology

A questionnaire was developed based upon several of the characteristics from the previous studies mentioned. Appendix A is a facsimile of the questionnaire with question numbers added for referencing purposes. The first section gathers information on gender, age and family experience with entrepreneurs. The second section contains twenty-nine statements requesting the subject to rate his or her level of agreement to the statement. These statements related to entrepreneurial lifestyle, education and ability, acceptance of risk, reputation of entrepreneurs and aspiration to become an entrepreneur. A 7-point Likert scale ranging from low, no agreement, to high, absolute agreement is used to record the rating. When necessary the statements were translated into the student's natural language and checked for consistency.

It is easy to see that the characteristics identified in section 2.3 for our study are more socially oriented than those in the GEM composite measure, TEA. The statements make claims about characteristics concerning the culture of entrepreneurship and were influenced greatly by statements and questions used in the previously cited research. Culture includes norms based around beliefs and perceptions. The questions were intentionally phrased in an attempt to extract the beliefs and perceptions students held about entrepreneurship.

3.2 Subjects

All of the subjects responding to the questionnaire were in business school classes. The subjects included juniors, seniors and first year graduate students representing a wide variety of majors or areas of emphasis. The questionnaire was administered as part of general class discussions around the topic of entrepreneurship. The questionnaires were administered in the three countries at different points in time during 2003 and 2004, making the results susceptible to the timing of significant country specific and world events. In addition, there are some differences in the students' basic educational environments.

The 240 US responses are from students at two different business schools in the United States. Both are four-year, AACSB accredited schools of business. One school is characterized as commuter-oriented while the other is more residential in nature. One is located in a major metropolitan center in the southeast United States and on its webpage claims to be, "a comprehensive, private, urban, coeducational institution of higher education with a predominantly African American heritage." The other is a member of a four-campus, statewide university system and has been ranked as one of the top Western-United States public universities.

There were 541 responses from French students. These students were either 1st or 2nd year students (the US equivalent of junior and senior years respectively in an undergraduate program) enrolled in the course of entrepreneurship at Burgundy School of Business. The school is accredited by Conference des Grandes Ecoles, the French Council of the major Schools of Business and Management. The Burgundy School of Business curriculum is designed to provide students with an exposure to international business cultures, and two thirds of the courses are taught in one of the following three foreign languages: English, Spanish, or German.

The 197 survey respondents from the United Kingdom were 2nd year undergraduate students studying at the University of Plymouth's small rural campus that accommodates the Faculty of Land, Food and Leisure. The University is rated as one of the top "new" universities in the UK and the faculty has received excellent ratings in its independent Teaching Quality Assessments. The students studying with this faculty major in a diverse range of mostly rurally based subjects ranging from agriculture through environmental studies to international tourism management. Thus, their management modules are generally a minor component of their main programs of study. The questionnaire was completed at the time of their final assignment for an autumn semester module entitled "Financial Management 2" which had combined a series of lectures, workshops and invited "expert" guest speakers related to developing a business plan for a new business venture. Thus, whilst the context was enterprise, the content related to business planning, budgeting, risk evaluation and raising financial resources.

4. RESULTS

After allowing for incomplete response sheets and removing those students in these classes from countries other that US, France, United Kingdom, the data set contains 978 usable questionnaires. There were 240 US, 541 French, and 197 UK responses. Overall, 57% of the responses were from females and 85% of the respondents were between the ages of 18 and 23. This age breakdown is slightly different that the GEM-TEA but given the purpose of the study, which is perception of students, it is appropriate.

The data were subjected to a one-way ANOVA and the results are displayed in Table 1. When categorized by nation, the responses for 19 of the questions proved significantly different ($p. < .05$) and their significances have been bolded in the table. This measure of significance means that there is enough difference between at least two of the categories to indicate that the answers from these three groups are different.

Table 1. Mean Values for Three Cultures

Item	US	FR.	UK	Signif.
(Q8) I aspire to be an entrepreneur	4.67	4.49	4.29	.115
(Q6) I believe being an entrepreneur would provide a good living	5.29	5.03	**4.54**<<	.000
(Q7) I believe becoming an entrepreneur would be easy	2.36	2.43	2.30	.498
(Q9) In general, I have heard good things about entrepreneurs	**4.79**>>	4.34	4.33	.000
(Q10) I would be comfortable running my own business	**5.13**>>	4.70	4.68	.005
(Q11) I believe that someone who runs their own business is successful	4.45	**5.05**>>	4.08	.000
(Q12) I believe there is a lot of risk in starting and running your own business	**6.17**>>	5.77	5.76	.002
(Q13) I believe an entrepreneur always has to be an inventor	3.40	**4.42**>>	3.40	.000
(Q14) I believe that entrepreneurs have to suffer a high number of failures before they are successful	3.78	3.70	3.72	.801
(Q15) I believe being a successful entrepreneur is just luck	2.36	2.17	**2.58**>	.002
(Q16) I believe becoming a successful entrepreneur is simply having enough money to start.	3.08	**2.69**<<	3.01	.001
(Q17) I believe it is too difficult for me to succeed as an entrepreneur	2.62	2.84	2.90	.126
(Q18) I believe there exists a standard entrepreneurial profile into which I have to fit	**3.16**>	2.67	2.91	.001
(Q19) I believe the characteristics of entrepreneurs are innate traits and therefore cannot be taught or learned (i.e. initiative, willingness to take risks, creativity, innovative attitude)	3.57	**3.22**<<	3.70	.001
(Q20) I am willing to put the time in that it takes to be an entrepreneur	**5.07**>>	4.43	4.63	.000
(Q21) I would enjoy the lifestyle provided by being an entrepreneur	5.16	**4.33**<<	4.82	.000
(Q22) Being an entrepreneur would better my lifestyle when I retire	**4.87**>	**3.65**<	**4.25**<>	.000
(Q23) Being a successful entrepreneur would increase my wealth	**5.29**>>	4.52	4.79	.000

(Q24) Being an entrepreneur would positively impact my current lifestyle	**5.17>**	**4.19<**	**4.53<>**	.000
(Q25) I believe that being an entrepreneur would have a positive impact on the welfare of the region/country	4.93	4.71	**3.87<<**	.000
(Q26) I do not know anyone who could mentor/help me be an entrepreneur	2.77	2.79	2.93	.616
(Q27) I do not know any institutions within the university that could educate/qualify me be an entrepreneur	3.17	**2.73<<**	3.24	.000
(Q28) I do not know how I would get money to start a business	**3.60>>**	3.22	2.98	.001
(Q29) I believe that one needs a higher level of education than I have to be an entrepreneur.	**3.15>**	**2.16<**	**2.66<>**	.000
(Q30) I believe that one needs a specific education to be a successful entrepreneur	3.03	**3.58>>**	2.72	.000
(Q31) Someone who fails in starting a business is not an entrepreneur	**2.12<>**	**1.67<**	**2.70>**	.000
(Q32) I believe I should not rely too heavily on the government for my retirement	**5.68>>**	4.77	4.82	.000
(Q33) I expect to change jobs and occupation many times before I retire.	4.30	**5.67>>**	4.21	.000
(Q34) I prefer to work for well-established organizations rather than new firms	**4.32>>**	3.57	3.81	.000
>> (or <<) - This category is significantly higher (or lower) than BOTH of the other two				
< or > - This category is significantly different from the category with the lowest/highest value				

However, it is also important to know whether the higher (or the lower) value is significantly different from the other two. With SPSS, a Bonferroni Post Hoc test was run to compare all pairs of categories (US to France; US to UK; and UK to France) and to determine if the values of one category were significantly different from the other two. Twelve of the 19 had one category that was significantly different from each of the other two. In the remainder of the paper these responses will be referred to as double-significant responses. These are identified in the table with a two-caret suffix (<< or >>). The two right-pointing carets (>>) are used to show that the value is significantly higher than both of the other two values when evaluated through the Bonferroni test. Conversely, the two left-pointing carets (<<) are used to designate a value that is significantly lower than both of the other values for that question. For example, the responses creating the 4.54 value in Q7 was compared against the responses creating the 5.29 and the 5.03 values, and was found to be significantly different from both and therefore has the 4.54<< designation. Table 2 identifies the double-significant responses for each culture.

The remainder of the questions are identified with a set of carets (<, >, and <>) showing the order and significance of any differences. In the case of Q15 and Q18, a single caret (>) identifies that the value is significantly different from only one of the other values (the lowest). So, Q24 shows the values from each culture; 4.19 for France, 4.53 for the UK, and 5.17 for the US, and each pair US-UK, US-France, UK-France are significantly different. Similar situations are shown in Q22, Q29, and Q31.

Table 2. Factors Significant to Single Culture

US	France	UK
Q9 - Heard more good things (higher)	Q11 – Running a business is a success (higher)	Q6 – Less likely that entrepreneurship will provide good living (lower)
Q10 – More comfortable running own business (higher)	Q13 – Entrepreneur should be an inventor (higher)	Q25 – Less perceived positive impact on region (lower)
Q12 – Perceived more risk (higher)	Q16 – Success is NOT just having enough money to start (lower)	
Q20 – More willing to put in time needed for success (higher)	Q19 – Characteristics are NOT innate (lower)	
Q23 – Being entrepreneur would increase wealth (higher)	Q21 – Less likely to enjoy entrepreneurship lifestyle (lower)	
Q28 – Do not know how to get start-up money (higher)	Q27 – Less knowledgeable of university resources (lower)	
Q32 – Rely less on government for retirement (higher)	Q30 – Entrepreneurs need specific education (higher)	
Q34 – Prefer well established companies (higher)	Q33 – Anticipate changing jobs more in career (higher)	

In summary, the results show that the responses from 24 questions differ significantly between the three nation categories. In 18 of the 24, the value of one category is significantly different from each of the other two, implying a dominant (or recessive) double-significant response. These characteristics are attributed to a particular culture (Table 2). In 4 of the remaining 6 questions, all three values are significantly different from each other (Table 3). In the final 2 questions showing significant differences, the difference can be attributed to a difference between two (the highest and the lowest values) of the three categories. The responses to these 24 questions provide the information for the discussion that follows.

Table 3. Questions Where Values Differ Significantly Between Each Culture Pair

Q22 – Better lifestyle in retirement
Q24 – Positive impact on current lifestyle
Q29 – People need more education than subject has
Q31 – Failure does not preclude being an entrepreneur

5. ANALYSIS OF FINDINGS

Table 3 identifies four questions on which all culture combinations differ. Simply, this means that the cultures are the most diverse here. Two (Q22 and Q24) specifically deal with lifestyle. In both cases, the US subjects rated their agreement with the question highest, followed by the UK and then the French respondents' scores. Failure as it relates to the definition of entrepreneur was captured in Q31. While all scores are low in agreement, it seems that the French culture is more accepting of failure than US or UK Again with low absolute scores, Q29 shows a lot of disagreement across the three cultures when the amount of education necessary to become an entrepreneur is discussed. While there are significant differences found in all pairs, the extreme values give us some hints as to the cultural perspective. In short: the US subjects see entrepreneurship as a better lifestyle; US subjects feel that a higher level of education is needed; and, UK subjects feel less comfortable calling someone who fails at starting a business an entrepreneur.

More culture-oriented characteristics can be teased out by looking at those questions where one culture's responses are significantly different from the other two as shown in Table 2.

5.1 US Perspective

US responses represent 8 of the 18 double-significant responses. Overall, the US students report more positive perceptions about entrepreneurs than students in the other two cultures (Q9). Clearly, the US students see a high risk in entrepreneurship (Q12) as the 6.17 rating is the highest in the results. However, the same subjects would be comfortable running their own business (Q10) and are willing to dedicate the time necessary (Q20). Although, these students may not know where to obtain financing (Q28) nor do they seem willing to work in entrepreneurial environments as they claim to prefer working in well established organizations (Q34), they seem more willing to put in the time and take the risk because of the perceived lifestyle mentioned earlier (Q22 & Q24). In addition, US subjects report a higher likelihood of a "living good" (Q6) and a higher perception of increased wealth (Q23) with the entrepreneurial lifestyle. Also energizing the US subjects may be their lower comfort relying on their government for retirement (Q32).

5.2 French Perspective

Eight dominant responses were found for the French students: four where the French score is significantly the highest and four where the French score is significantly the lowest. In the highest category, our French subjects believe running one's own business qualifies a person as an entrepreneur (Q11) and that an entrepreneur needs the basic quality of an inventor (Q13). In addition, they feel an entrepreneur needs a specific education to be successful (Q30). The last question that French subjects rated highest was Q33, wherein the French subjects reported they expect to change jobs more than their counterparts during their careers (Q33).

The French subjects reported significantly lowest scores in 4 questions. They are skeptical that an entrepreneur's success is dependent on only money (Q16) or on innate characteristics (Q19). They report they do not know where to go to get the specific education (Q27) they think they need from their response to Q30. The most compelling result for our discussion is with the lower value in Q21. Combining this result with the other discussions on lifestyle above, the French subjects seem to report the lowest enthusiasm (or understanding) for the entrepreneurial lifestyle.

5.3 UK Perspective

The UK answers produced the final 2 double-significant responses: Q6, and Q25. Q6 asks the subjects to respond to the statement that the entrepreneurial lifestyle provides a good living. The results show the UK subjects responding significantly lower than the US or French. In addition, the UK subjects saw fewer ties between entrepreneurship and the local or regional economy. Looking at the UK values from other double-significant responses, the results imply that the UK students see less risk (Q12) and entrepreneurs producing less impact on region/country (Q25). The UK students seem less willing to accept failure for a successful entrepreneur (Q31).

5.4 Comparative Summary of Findings

The results support the basic conjecture. US students report a more positive impression of the entrepreneurship lifestyle. Although they acknowledge the risk of starting a new business and do not seem sure of where to find venture capital, US students find the entrepreneurial lifestyle to be more appealing and they seem to be more willing to put in the time than their UK and French counterparts. UK and French students recorded less positive results on the lifestyle questions in both significantly different responses. French students also believe that entrepreneurs need specific education to be successful and that entrepreneurs will tend to be investors. This could suggest a more limiting view of entrepreneurs by the French students. The UK students reported less acceptance of the entrepreneurial lifestyle as a "good living" and saw less correlation between the local regional/country economy and successful entrepreneurs.

Table 4 summarizes the previous discussion and the next section of the paper provides a short discussion of the key items for each culture.

Table 4. Culture Summary

US	France	UK
Better perception of entrepreneurial lifestyle	Less interest in entrepreneurial lifestyle	Less likelihood of good living
More perceived risk	Entrepreneurship is not innate & needs special education	Less potential positive impact on region
Less reliance on government	Entrepreneurs should be inventors	More reliance on luck
More willing to put in time	Running a business is entrepreneurial	Less forgiving of business failure

6. DISCUSSION

For US students to be more inclined toward entrepreneurship is not unreasonable. The media hypes the entrepreneur in the US culture. Magazines such as *Forbes*, *Inc.*, and *Fast Company* promote the individualism found in entrepreneurs. The icons of successful business entrepreneurs are everywhere. Since the 1990s entrepreneurship has been incorporated into business school curricula throughout the country. Organizations such as Junior Achievement and Students in Free Enterprise help students organize and plan start-up businesses. All of this activity certainly exposes the US student to more positive views of entrepreneurs. In turn, the aspiration level should increase.

The French negative lifestyle scores may show differences based on the fact that an entrepreneur has to work a lot, and must devote his/her best energies to the new venture. This works against the French culture's value of free time, as demonstrated by the 35 hours week working time that was in place during the timeframe of this study. France has now increased the allowed workweek. So, entrepreneurship may be seen as more stressful for the individual and her/his family and therefore less appealing. Historically, the French educational system was organized around the Grandes Ecoles, which aim to train the top managers of the French private and public sector. Since Grandes Ecoles are usually specialized in a very specific field (civil engineering, business and management, agriculture, telecommunications etc.), students may be perceiving that earning a diploma from a famous school specialized in the sector of interest, entrepreneurship, is a necessary condition. Therefore, to be an entrepreneur it would be necessary to be specifically trained in entrepreneurship.

The UK students have probably met wealthy entrepreneurs but have also heard about the difficulties and frustrations involved with the governmental bureaucracy that translate back into quality of life issues. In trying to understand the UK students' low rating on the impact of entrepreneurial activity on their region, the students may have a perception of the general population being taxed to the benefit of the creation of the entrepreneur. This "tax" may come in various forms such of tax incentives for the entrepreneur to locate in the region or other preferential treatment.

6.1 Two Year Impact

The data spans two years and includes students at different levels in their respective programs. This allows us to analyze the data based upon the subjects being in the early part or the latter part of the program. Table 5 presents the analysis of those questions based upon this rudimentary split. Those with a significant difference are in bold.

Twenty-three of the 29 questions showed no significant difference when the subjects were categorized by early and late position in the programs. Four questions (Q6, Q12, Q32, and Q33) remained high, all values being above 5.00. To summarize, regardless of culture students do see the potential for the entrepreneurial lifestyle; do understand that there is a lot of risk in running one's own business and have low confidence in their government's ability to provide for them in retirement.

The three questions with the lowest values, all lower than 2.50, were Q7, Q15, and Q31. These low values indicate students do not believe: that success is tied simply to luck; that a person who fails in a business cannot be an entrepreneur; and that becoming an entrepreneur is not easy. These results seem to demonstrate a good reality check for the students even though it may deter some of them.

The good news is that all seven of the questions with a significant difference moved in a positive direction; one where entrepreneurship is more appealing. Three, Q22, Q23, Q24, show the subject's impression of the entrepreneurial lifestyle improving (remember higher numbers show more agreement). Q25 shows they believe it can have a positive impact on a region's economy. Q20 shows that the students later in the program are more willing to put the time in to obtain the lifestyle they now perceive as "better". The final two questions, Q29 and Q30, show that students increasingly recognize that education is a necessary part of being an entrepreneur. While the need for a specific education is argued within the literature and in the media, the idea that students acknowledge the need to prepare for entrepreneurship and the desire to put in the necessary effort to attain it are positive results.

Table 5. Mean Ratings for Early and Late Students

Item	**Early**	**Late**	**Sign**
(Q8) I aspire to be an entrepreneur	4.45	4.62	.240
(Q6) I believe being an entrepreneur would provide a good living	5.18	5.16	.881
(Q7) I believe becoming an entrepreneur would be easy	2.50	2.47	.769
(Q9) In general, I have heard good things about entrepreneurs	4.56	4.42	.164
(Q10) I would be comfortable running my own business	4.85	4.99	.323
(Q11) I believe that someone who runs their own business is successful	4.88	4.95	.590
(Q12) I believe there is a lot of risk in starting and running your own business	5.73	5.90	.135
(Q13) I believe an entrepreneur always has to be an inventor	3.89	4.06	.270
(Q14) I believe that entrepreneurs have to suffer a high number of failures before they are successful	3.56	3.64	.521
(Q15) I believe being a successful entrepreneur is just luck	2.43	2.24	.082
(Q16) I believe becoming a successful entrepreneur is simply having enough money to start.	2.87	2.95	.447
(Q17) I believe it is too difficult for me to succeed as an entrepreneur	2.95	2.77	.159
(Q18) I believe there exists a standard entrepreneurial profile into which I have to fit	2.70	2.91	.102
(Q19) I believe the characteristics of entrepreneurs are innate traits and therefore cannot be taught or learned (i.e. initiative, willingness to take risks, creativity, innovative attitude)	3.37	3.34	.812

(Q20) I am willing to put the time in that it takes to be an entrepreneur	**4.46**	**4.79**	**.013**
(Q21) I would enjoy the lifestyle provided by being an entrepreneur	4.58	4.70	.318
(Q22) Being an entrepreneur would better my lifestyle when I retire	**3.80**	**4.20**	**.001**
(Q23) Being a successful entrepreneur would increase my wealth	**4.54**	**4.93**	**.001**
(Q24) Being an entrepreneur would positively impact my current lifestyle	**4.20**	**4.55**	**.005**
(Q25) I believe that being an entrepreneur would have a positive impact on the welfare of the region/country	**4.47**	**4.71**	**.038**
(Q26) I do not know anyone who could mentor/help me be an entrepreneur	2.85	2.87	.882
(Q27) I do not know any institutions within the university that could educate/qualify me be an entrepreneur	3.15	2.97	.220
(Q28) I do not know how I would get money to start a business	3.28	3.45	.234
(Q29) I believe that one needs a higher level of education than I have to be an entrepreneur.	**2.23**	**2.66**	**.002**
(Q30) I believe that one needs a specific education to be a successful entrepreneur	**3.04**	**3.60**	**.000**
(Q31) Someone who fails in starting a business is not an entrepreneur	2.08	2.06	.859
(Q32) I believe I should not rely too heavily on the government for my retirement	5.06	5.08	.875
(Q33) I expect to change jobs and occupation many times before I retire.	5.29	5.03	.060
(Q34) I prefer to work for well-established organizations rather than new firms	3.69	3.87	.192

6.2 Limitations

As an exploratory study, these findings are subject to several limitations. The first limitation is also a function of the study's biggest strength: subjects were obtained across cultures and across time. The questionnaires were carefully translated, but subtle distinctions in meaning could still be present. With an eighteen-month time span across the collection period, the results may be susceptible to local events such as the economic shift in the United States. A second concern is the consistency of the identification of subjects within a culture's education system. The identification of subjects as "early" or "late" in the program may be fundamentally different across programs. This would mean that the distinction of "early" and "late" may not be as much an indicator of differences in the student perception as it is an indicator of differences in programs across cultures. A more quantifiable way to identify their point in the program such as the number of business classes completed could prove more useful.

Another issue for this study could be the time span over which the data was collected. As mentioned earlier, significant world business events could influence the findings based upon the time collected. For example, students completing questionnaires prior to the ENRON collapse versus after it have one more negative event influencing their perceptions.

These limitations notwithstanding, the analysis of the aggregate data does indicate there are some cultural differences in the perception of the entrepreneurial lifestyle.

6.3 Operational Impact

The results of the study confirm what most people would expect; teaching entrprenuership will be different in different cultures. What this study identifies better is some of the cultural characteristics that vary across the cultures and in turn, some of the cultural characteristics that educators should pay attention to when designing a curriculum or program. For example, the entreprenuership class that promotes self-sufficiency and ways to reduce "risk" will resonate well with a US audience and less well with a French audience. To capture the interest of a French audience, the program director would be well served to promote the educational components of his or her entreprenueiral program.

Another use of these characteristics would be as "signal towers" into possible changes. For example, since the collection of this data, France has changed from a 35-hour workweek to a 40-hour workweek. With the results of this study as support, one would predict that the average French person's perception of the entrepreneurial lifestyle would become more favorable since their basic work expectation (an identified characteristic) has increased.

For multicultural programs and classes, the questionnaire itself can be used to create discussions. Simply administering the questionnaire to a multicultural class and tabulating the results can expose how the students in the same program think differently. Comparisons of questionnaire data obtained from the same student at the beginning of the program with data at the end of the program can help identify the impact of the program.

Finally, the instructor can use the characteristics that proved significant as "touch points" for a class in entrepreneurship. While understanding venture capital funding, market penetration, and exit strategies are all important topics for the class, their presentation and discussion can be more productive if they acknowledge and address the students' culture.

7. SUMMARY

In summary, a research project was undertaken to look for differences in student perceptions of entrepreneurship based upon culture. The Entrepreneurship Monitoring (GEM) Total Entrepreneurship Activity (TEA) report and other previous cultural research on entrepreneurship provided the foundation for the development of a questionnaire. The basic conjecture was that students in different cultures would show differences in their perception of the entrepreneurial lifestyle. The premise of the conjecture is that the TEA ratings show the level of activity within a country and the higher this activity the more likely the positive perception of entrepreneurs.

Students from three countries: United States, France, and United Kingdom responded to the questionnaire, producing a 978-response data set. Through statistical analysis, significant differences were found between the responses of the three groups on 24 questions. Twenty of the 24 had one of the three groups significantly different from the other two, thereby producing a clear difference. The other four questions had significant differences when each pair of combinations was evaluated. These questions were associated with the three cultures and some observations were discussed.

Future research will need to tease out the relationships between the lifestyle and the other cultural differences suggested by the results. In addition, the finding is simply that a higher TEA level of activity implies a higher perceived value of entrepreneurship. There is no claim that one culture or one level of activity is better than another. Finally, it is left to speculation as to whether the country's culture drives the activity or the country's entrepreneurial activity drives the culture.

APPENDIX A: ENTREPRENEUR QUESTIONNAIRE

This questionnaire is designed to help determine your impression of being an entrepreneur. These are your perceptions and cannot be judged right or wrong. All information is compiled at the aggregate level with no way of determining the identity of respondent.

Demographics:
(Q1) Sex (Circle) M F
(Q2) Age (Circle) <18 18-23 24-29 30-35 36-41 42-47 47+
(Q3) I have relatives who run/ran their own business (circle) [Yes] [No]
If yes, how many (Q3a) ___________
Relationship 1. ______ 2. _______ 3.______ 4. _______
Successful (circle) Y N Y N Y N Y N

(Q4) Number of friends/acquaintances you know who run/ran their own business ______
(Q5) Number of friends/acquaintances you know who would like to run their own business _______

Questions: For our purposes, an entrepreneur is defined as a person who starts and runs their own business. On the scale below, please register your agreement with the statements about entrepreneurs. A one (1) means no agreement; a seven (7) means absolute agreement

Statement	**Agreement** (circle)
(Q6) I believe being an entrepreneur would provide a good living.	1 2 3 4 5 6 7
(Q7) I believe becoming an entrepreneur would be easy.	1 2 3 4 5 6 7
(Q8) I aspire to be an entrepreneur.	1 2 3 4 5 6 7
(Q9) In general, I have heard good things about entrepreneurs.	1 2 3 4 5 6 7
(Q10) I would be comfortable running my own business.	1 2 3 4 5 6 7
(Q11) I believe that someone who runs his or her own business is successful.	1 2 3 4 5 6 7
(Q12) I believe there is a lot of risk in starting and running your own business.	1 2 3 4 5 6 7
(Q13) I believe an entrepreneur always has to be an inventor.	1 2 3 4 5 6 7
(Q14) I believe that entrepreneurs have to suffer a high number of failures before they are successful.	1 2 3 4 5 6 7
(Q15) I believe being a successful entrepreneur is just luck.	1 2 3 4 5 6 7
(Q16) I believe becoming a successful entrepreneur is simply having enough money to start.	1 2 3 4 5 6 7
(Q17) I believe it is too difficult for me to succeed as an entrepreneur.	1 2 3 4 5 6 7
(Q18) I believe there exists a standard entrepreneurial profile into which I have to fit.	1 2 3 4 5 6 7
(Q19) I believe the characteristics of entrepreneurs are innate traits and therefore cannot be taught or learned (*i.e.*, initiative, willingness to take risks, creativity, innovative attitude).	1 2 3 4 5 6 7
(Q20) I am willing to put the time in that it takes to be an entrepreneur.	1 2 3 4 5 6 7
(Q21) I would enjoy the lifestyle provided by being an entrepreneur.	1 2 3 4 5 6 7

(Q22) Being an entrepreneur would better my lifestyle when I retire.	1 2 3 4 5 6 7
(Q23) Being a successful entrepreneur would increase my wealth.	1 2 3 4 5 6 7
(Q24) Being an entrepreneur would positively impact my current lifestyle.	1 2 3 4 5 6 7
(Q25) I believe that being an entrepreneur would have a positive impact on the welfare of the region/country	1 2 3 4 5 6 7
(Q26) I do not know anyone who could mentor/help me be an entrepreneur	1 2 3 4 5 6 7
(Q27) I do not know any institutions within the university that could educate/qualify me be an entrepreneur	1 2 3 4 5 6 7
(Q28) I do not know how I would get money to start a business	1 2 3 4 5 6 7
(Q29) I believe that one needs a higher level of education than I have to be an entrepreneur.	1 2 3 4 5 6 7
(Q30) I believe that one needs a specific education to be a successful entrepreneur	1 2 3 4 5 6 7
(Q31) Someone who fails in starting a business is not an entrepreneur	1 2 3 4 5 6 7
(Q32) I believe I should not rely too heavily on the government for my retirement	1 2 3 4 5 6 7
(Q33) I expect to change jobs and occupation many times before I retire.	1 2 3 4 5 6 7
(Q34) I prefer to work for well-established organizations rather than new firms	1 2 3 4 5 6 7

REFERENCES

Abbey, A. (2002). Cross cultural comparison of motivation for entrepreneurship, *Journal of Business and Entrepreneurship*, *14* (1), 69-82.

Begley, T. H., & Boyd, D. P. (1987). "A comparison of entrepreneurs and managers of small business firms. *Journal of Management*, *13* (1), 99-108.

Carland, J. W., Hoy, F., Boulton, W. R., & Carland, J.C. (1984). Differentiating entrepreneurs from small business owners: A conceptualization. *Academy of Management Review*, *9* (2), 354-359.

Chandler, G. N., & Hanks, S. H. (1994). Founder competence, the environment, and venture performance. *Entrepreneurship: Theory and Practice*, Spring, 77-89.

Drucker, P. F. (1985). *Innovation and Entrepreneurship*. New York: HarperBusiness Publishing.

Envick, B. R., & Langford, M. (2000). The five-factor model of personality: Assessing entrepreneurs and managers. *Academy of Entrepreneurship Journal*, *6* (1), 6-17.

Hisrich, R. D. (1990). Entrepreneurship/intrapreneurship. *American Psychologist*, *45* (2), 209-222.

Huefner, J. C., Hunt, H. K., & Robinson, P. B. (1996). A comparison of four scales predicting entrepreneurship. *Academy of Entrepreneurship Journal*, *1* (2), 56-80.

Martz, W. B., Neil, T., Williams, R., & Biscaccianti, A. (2005). Student perception of entrepreneurs: A cultural perspective. *Journal of Entrepreneurship Education*, (forthcoming).

McClelland, D. C. (1961). *The Achieving Society*. Princeton, NJ: D. Van Norstrand Co.

Parnell, J. A., Crandall, W., & Menefee, M. (1995). Examining the impact of culture on entrepreneurial propensity: An empirical study of prospective American and Egyptian entrepreneurs. *Academy of Entrepreneurship Journal*, *1* (1), 39-52.

Reynolds, P. D., Bygrave, W. D., Autio, E., & Hay, M. (2002). *Global Entrepreneurship Monitor: 2002 Summary Report*. Babson College and Business School, Boston, MA and London, UK.

Reich, R. (1987). Entrepreneurship reconsidered: The team as hero. *Harvard Business Review*, *65* (3), 77-83.

Reynierse, J. H. (1997). An MBTI model of entrepreneurism and bureaucracy: The psychological types of business entrepreneurs compared to business managers and executives. *Journal of Psychological Type*, *40*, 3-19.

Rogoff, E. G., & Lee, M. (1996). Does firm origin matter? An empirical examination of types of small business owners and entrepreneurs. *Academy of Entrepreneurship Journal*, *1* (2), 1-17.

Rowe, A. J., Mason, R. O., Dickel, K. E., Mann, R. B., & Mockler, R. J. (1994). *Strategic Management: A Methodological Approach*. Reading, Massachusetts: Addison-Wesley.

Shane, S. (1996). Explaining variation in the rates of entrepreneurship in the United States: 1899-1988. *Journal of Management*, *22* (5), 747-781.

Schrage, M. (1990). *Shared Minds*. New York: Random House.

Shuman, J. C., Seeger, J. A., Kamm, J. B., & Teebagy, N. C., 1986, An empirical test of ten entrepreneurial propositions, in: *Frontiers of Entrepreneurship Research 1986*, R. Ronstadt, *et. al.*, Babson College, Wellesley, MA, 10 pages.

Timmons, J. A., Smollen, L. E., & Dingee, A., 1985, *New Venture Creation*, 2nd ed., Irwin Publishing, Homewood, IL.

US Department of Labor. (2000). http://www.bls.gov/opub/ils/pdf/opbils37.pdf, accessed on January 8, 2003.

Vesper. K. H. (1980). *New Venture Strategies*. Englewood Cliffs, NJ: Prentice-Hall.

Chapter 13

DEVELOPING LEARNING MATERIALS FOR THE UNKNOWN ONLINE LEARNER

Andrew Ashwin and Kieren Pitts
Biz/ed, Institute for Learning and Research Technology, University of Bristol, Bristol, UK

1. INTRODUCTION — THE NATURE OF E-LEARNING

A Google (http://www.google.com) search for 'e-learning' brings up over 4.8 million results. This reflects the increasing view that e-learning somehow presents answers to a number of major problems facing both further and higher education. Specifically, the challenges that are presented by the rise in student numbers, the failure of funding to keep pace with that increase, the emphasis on meeting targets at all levels, and on the quality of the teaching and learning experience faced by the student learner.

That e-learning is a 'buzz word' in education goes without saying. For some it is a panacea to the problems highlighted above. It is seen as a way of expanding educational horizons by offering students 24-hour access to materials and resources enhancing their learning and a way of partially solving the organizational and administrative problems created by the issues facing education. One revealing factor thrown up by the Google search is that the term 'distance learning' often appears in the same sentence as e-learning and in the various e-learning strategies that are being put forward by universities, colleges, and other bodies, most notably corporate institutions. That e-learning can remove the human interface is not in doubt; whether it is wise to do so is another matter. The promise of e-learning has not always

M.K. McCuddy et al. (eds.),
The Challenges of Educating People to Lead in a Challenging World, 273–290.

delivered the success its proponents promised or expected. The failure of the UKe University project[4] following £62 million worth of investment is testament to the misplaced trust in the ability of e-learning to meet the needs of learners throughout the world.

While such failures seem spectacular, there can be no doubt of the significance of the impact of technology on education over the last ten years and it will continue to be a major factor in developments in education in the coming years. If nothing else, it has meant that the education community has had to think very carefully about the nature and role of e-learning and in so doing, mistakes are bound to be made. As in all learning, it is what we gain from such mistakes that will be important in directing the future of the impact of learning materials for the online learner. This paper will present an overview of one contribution to the e-learning 'revolution' and try to raise some issues to stimulate discussion on the factors involved in developing online learning materials and what the future might hold for such materials.

The reference to distance learning above raises an important point that must be clarified prior to further discussion. Is e-learning a situation where a learner accesses a learning experience remotely from the provider of that learning experience? The answer could be unequivocally 'yes' but it is also something more than that. The recent Department for Education and Skills (DfES) in the UK 'Towards a Unified E-learning Strategy' (2003) interim report attempted to highlight some of the issues facing the development and implementation of the strategy. Interestingly, there were only 430 responses to the consultation document and even more revealing perhaps was the fact that only 19 were from principals or vice chancellors and only 8 from headteachers.[5] The consultation document makes it clear at the outset what e-learning encompasses.

2. WHAT IS E-LEARNING?

> "If someone is learning in a way that uses information and communication technologies (ICTs), they are using e-learning. They could be a pre-school child playing an interactive game; they could be a group of pupils collaborating on a history project with pupils in another country via the Internet; they could be geography students watching an animated diagram of a volcanic eruption their lecturer has just

[4] http://education.guardian.co.uk/elearning/story/0,10577,1204498,00.html.

[5] http://www.dfes.gov.uk/elearningstrategy/uploads/Analysis%20Document.pdf.

downloaded; they could be a nurse taking her driving theory test online with a reading aid to help her dyslexia – it all counts as e-learning" (DfES, 2003, p. 4).

What is clear from this definition is that the provision of the learning material is the interface through which the learner will operate. As such the design and appearance of that interface can be expected to have a significant impact on the success of the learning experience and the amount and level of learning experienced by the learner.

3. WHAT DO WE MEAN BY 'LEARNING'?

A learning experience using such technologies could contribute to a greater degree of understanding and knowledge generation in the learner or an ability to 'do something' following the learning experience. It is important, therefore, to identify what we mean by 'learning.' Surprisingly, in much of the literature, despite numerous references to learning, there are few attempts to define what is meant by the term. Kolb (1984, p. 38) describes learning as 'the process whereby knowledge is created through the transformation of experience.' He emphasizes that learning is about process rather than content and outcomes; transformation rather than just delivery; that learning transforms experience in its objective and subjective forms; and that to understand learning it is necessary to understand knowledge.

Bowring-Carr and West-Burnham (1999) identify a number of factors that contribute to a definition of learning. They see it as being constructive, incremental, co-operative, regulated by the learner, needing a goal, being contextual, and not mandated. They draw the distinction between surface and deep learning and focus on the need to get away from the notion — possibly shared by both teachers and learners — that learning involves the delivery of packets of knowledge or information through a transmission process. They therefore see learning as involving some form of change and that change brings with it the evidence that knowledge itself has also changed.

Senge (2000) discusses learning in the context of the process by which learning takes place, describing it as 'double loop learning.' Single loop learning is characterized by a process involving action, reflection, activity, and response; and it is based on the assumption that our understanding of 'reality' is stable. Double loop learning, however, occurs where these basic assumptions are questioned through the process of reconsidering, re-connecting and reframing our ideas and constructs, allowing us to move onto higher planes of understanding.

Drawing on the brief discussion above, the following definition of learning can be provided. It is not meant to be all encompassing but does provide the salient features; consequently, it is used to inform the outcomes that the development of learning materials seeks to secure.

Learning should be seen as having occurred if the following attributes are present in the learner:

- That new knowledge and skills have been acquired. Knowledge being the 'know why, skill the know how' (Boyett & Boyett, 1998, p. 85).
- That behavior has been changed as a result of the learning characterized by being underpinned by a different set of assumptions about 'reality.'
- That learning, to be deep, must involve and have some meaning to the individual.
- That the learner is able to make some connections between unrelated information and draw informed conclusions.
- That learners are more adept at confronting and coping with change.
- That learning can be characterized by creativity and the ability to solve problems.
- That learners are independent but equally able to work well in communities.

Such a definition is challenging if attempts are made to link the use of an online resource and what the learner goes away with at the end of the process. In developing materials for this environment, however, it is important to have in mind the purpose of the resource in terms of specific learning outcomes. Some of the above may be targeted in some resources while others seek to develop other aspects of what has been defined as 'learning.'

It is pertinent to recognize that e-learning might not only refer to a resource designed to complement a particular course, but also could be any technology utilized to provide a learning experience and or support a learner through that learning experience, however short that experience might be. Assessment methods, assessment monitoring software, student databases, and so on, therefore, could be part of the e-learning framework.

The concern of this paper is in the resources that are designed to provide learners with particular experiences related to courses of study. These could be courses relevant to those in 14-19 education[6] or those pursuing higher education.

[6] 14-19 education in the UK refers to the courses and curriculum followed by students in the 14 to 19 age group. Between 14 and 16 students follow a series of courses leading to examinations that provide the General Certificate in Secondary Education (GCSE). Post

4. THE BACKGROUND OF BIZ/ED

Biz/ed (http://www.bizednac.uk) is a Joint Information Systems Committee (JISC) (http://www.jisc.ac.uk/) funded service charged with developing resources for students following courses of study in business, economics, and related subjects. The aim of the service is to provide both educators and students with access to resources that help in the planning and execution of teaching and learning programs. A number of scenarios could exist in relation to the use of the service. Teachers and lecturers might be using the resources as well as adapting them for use in their own institution. Such practitioners could be from anywhere in the world; indeed, the service receives feedback from educators from all over the globe. This helps to place in context the use of the phrase 'unknown learner' in the title of this paper.

In addition to this use, students might be directed by educators to use particular aspects of the service, or students might use the service having identified relevant information via a search engine in personal or group research projects. In addition, resources could be placed in Virtual Learning Environments (VLEs) for students to access, and these resources could be the basis of seminar or discussion board topics within and external to the institution. Students could be using the site to reinforce or review their learning and understanding of topics or concepts covered at other times during the course. Furthermore the learner could be someone from a corporate body or on a vocational training course studying through a distance-learning program or through their own initiative to further their career or professional understanding.

A team working at the University of Bristol develops the resources. The team consists of two content developers with experience in teaching in colleges, schools, and universities; a content editor; a project manager; and a senior technical researcher. The team receives support from the Institute for Learning and Research Technology (ILRT) at the University in the form of library services, technical support, Web hosting, and systems administration. The team members, therefore, are designing and developing resources that may be used in a variety of ways by a variety of people for a variety of different reasons and purposes that may or may not be known to the team.

Therefore, the design of the materials is crucial to the success of the service. If the resources do not meet the needs of the target audience, they are effectively useless. Such is the dilemma facing researchers in planning

---

compulsory education between 16 and 19 consists of various courses centered around Advanced Level qualifications split into Advanced Subsidiary (AS) taken at the end of the first year of study and A2 taken at the end of the second year. Together the two form an Advanced level qualification.

and designing such resources. This paper focuses on how Biz/ed has sought to approach this problem and identify issues and problems associated with the development of learning materials, and what the underlying pedagogy has been in relation to the recent development of resources and the future plans for the service.

For economics and business-related subjects, the amount of information available via online sources is vast. The sheer volume of information from all manner of sources can be overwhelming for many students. The desire not to 'miss anything' overtakes the skills necessary to select appropriate information and to use that information effectively for the learning task being tackled. Biz/ed therefore provides an opportunity for students to be able to access relevant information in a structured environment that allows them to build their research and selection skills. Biz/ed has a wide range of resources available. The site has basic information in the form of notes and theory explanations and has developed a wide range of resources that are both interactive and can be used in a variety of ways by both educator and student including large scale simulations, RSS news feeds, and games.

In developing these resources, care has been taken to recognize that the unknown user is an individual and that these individuals are likely to have varied learning styles. The term 'learning styles' refers to the preferences that an individual has in carrying out a learning task. It is important to distinguish between 'style' in this context and 'ability.' Ability is assumed to be a given factor — it is not stable in that one can improve that ability through carrying out various learning tasks. For example, the ability of a student to understand the concept of the market mechanism may well improve with use and with experience of using methods and skills associated with that concept. How the student chooses to experience that concept — through verbal means, visual stimulus, hands-on experience, or through the written word — represents the learning style.

The learning style might vary according to the type of activity being carried out and the concept or subject matter being studied and students may happily employ one or more of these styles. The key, however, is that there may be a preference employed that will help the learner access and process information more successfully.

4.1 Learning Styles

Learning styles have been subject to a great deal of research — not all of the research has supported the existence of these styles and some has been critical in the way in which learning styles have been incorporated into teaching and learning programs in schools and colleges (Coffield, Moseley, Hall, & Ecclestone, 2004). The situation is made all the more complex by the number of models in existence, some of which seem to contradict others and which are subject to a temptation to label students as being one or other of an extreme. There is also the danger that the notion of learning styles becomes confused with cognitive styles, learning preferences, learning strategies, and personality types. What follows is a very brief attempt to summarize the main models relevant to 'learning styles' and to highlight the differences between the concepts listed above.

Cognitive styles relate to the way in which an individual processes information. Cognitive styles can be seen as being 'hard wired' at birth and thus are relatively stable compared to the developmental and flexible characteristics of learning style. Rayner and Riding (1998) identify two dimensions to cognitive styles, a wholist/analytic dimension and a verablizer/imager dimension. The former reflects the manner in which an individual organizes information received — for the *wholist*, information is processed in wholes while for the *analytic*, the information is processed in parts. The verbalizer/imager dimension reflects the tendency of an individual to represent knowledge in words (verbalizer) or mental pictures. Rayner and Riding's (1998) work stems from analysis of an array of cognitive styles ranging from Pask's (1976) holist/serialist styles to Witkin, Moore, Oltman, Goodenough, Friedman, Owen, and Raskin's (1977) work on field dependency to Kagan and Kogan's (1970) work on impulsivity/reflectivity. Rayner and Riding (1998) make it very clear that learning performance can be affected to various degrees of significance by the way that material is presented, the mode of presentation, type of content, structure of material including such features as the position of a title, the number and frequency of headings and sub-headings, and size of the visual field of the viewer and the formatting (in large or small steps), the additions of overviews and summaries, and so on.

The processing of information can, in turn, be affected by the approach to study taken by the learner. Entwistle (1983) and Marton, Hounsell, and Entwistle (1984) focus on this as factors influencing the level of learning, whether the level is deep or surface. Their work suggests that learners will approach information differently, depending on what they see as being the intended outcome. The learner's approach may be influenced by what they anticipate the intentions of the information might be. If the feeling is that the material will be used to assess a limited range of the subject matter, the learner might focus purely on what he/she thinks will be asked and the resultant learning will be superficial. If the approach is influenced by the belief that the intention of the learning provider is to assess the understanding of the meaning of the information as well as its factual content, the approach tends to lead to more deep learning with some attempts made by the learner to be able to attach personal meaning to the information.

Biggs and Collis (1982) provide a taxonomy of this idea referred to as the 'SOLO' taxonomy — the Structure of Observed Learning Outcome. The taxonomy categorizes responses as: pre-structural — a mere restatement of the question or an answer irrelevant to the question; uni-structural where one piece of relevant information is presented; and multi-structural containing several pieces of relevant information. At a higher level of outcome responses may be relational where information is inter-related and conclusions are drawn from the analysis and extended abstract where information is not only inter-related but also includes reference to abstract concepts and theoretical ideas to provide a deeper explanation that emphasizes higher order skills. {The preceding sentence is long-winded and confusing. Please rewrite it into at least two sentences so that your meaning is clearly conveyed to the reader.}

Honey and Mumford (1986) took the work of Kolb (1984) and suggested that ineffective learning continues because the solutions being provided focused on the teaching method rather than individual's approach to learning. Much has been written about Kolb's experiential learning cycle. Essentially it consists of a four-stage approach to learning that draws heavily on the work of Lewin (1951), Piaget (1968), Dewey (1938, 1958), and Jung (1977). Kolb (1984) sees learning as a process grounded in experience. The four stages of learning (concrete experience, observation and reflection, abstract generalization, and testing in new situations) are linked to the ways in which individuals will grasp and transform information leading to four structural dimensions. Divergent styles are characterized by being sensitive to other people's feelings, having an open mind, and liking to deal with a wide range of views and opinions. Assimilators organize information, enjoy building conceptual models, testing theories and ideas, and analyzing quantitative data. Convergers enjoy experimenting with new ideas, choosing appropriate solutions, setting goals, and making decisions. Accommodators commit to objectives, enjoy seeking and exploiting opportunities, getting involved, and dealing with people.

These four dimensions therefore can be reflected and accommodated in the way in which information is presented. Honey and Mumford (1986) took Kolb's (1984) approach and developed a test, which is regarded as having more empirical validity. They suggest that learning resources, which are heavily weighted in favor of one particular style, may well benefit those learners whose style matches the presentation of the resource. For example, a resource with a great deal of written material, few images, and questions focusing on comprehension of the text given, may be appropriate for those who are reflectors or theorists — but might marginalize those for whom this type of approach is not suited.

One criticism of the Kolb (1984) and Honey and Mumford (1986) approach is that it appears heavily associated, intentionally or not, with personality styles. It may be that one aspect of personality involves how the individual prefers to process information but there is also a danger in education of labeling people into different categories and confusing personality type with learning style. The latter is a preferred method rather than a given trait. Individuals can utilize different learning styles at different times for different reasons with different resources, albeit one type may be preferred. Personality types suggest some link with genetic makeup or social development, which would be much harder to change or to encourage diversity of approach. Such confusion can also apply to learning preferences. This could relate to the preferred mode of presentation of new information (lecture, group activity, individual study, visual representation and so on) or to the type of environment preferred (bright lights, dimmed light, warm cozy room, airy cool environment, formal desk arrangement, or casual 'laid back' study). There is little that an online resource can do to influence such environmental preferences; however, the learner can be presented with a task and be encouraged to approach it in his/her preferred learning environment. Perhaps the most well known theory of learning styles that encompasses this approach is the Dunn and Dunn (1972) model.

The model identifies five stimuli — environmental, emotional, sociological, psychological, and physiological — with each having various parts, giving a total of 21 elements. The elements all cover a range of preferences such as the degree to which the individual prefers sound when involved in learning activities, to the preference for structure in learning materials, to working on one's own or in groups. As such, much of the model can be said to refer to learning preferences, which might include learning styles, but the whole model could be considered too broad to focus purely on learning styles.

Perhaps the most recognizable manifestation of learning styles is the VAK approach — visual, auditory, and kinaesthetic. Such a model has the advantage of being relatively easy to grasp for many educators and is largely, in its simplest form, devoid of complex psychological or neurophysiological terms. As such it can be argued that it reduces a complex process — learning — to something apparently very simple and leads to a labeling of individuals that creates a greater degree of inflexibility in the approaches adopted by students to a learning task.

One such model that incorporates the VAK approach but which seeks to take the simple VAK categories a little further is that devised by the Felder and Silverman model (Felder, 1993). They assert that learning style is partly defined by answers to five questions:

- How learners prefer to perceive information — through sensory means (sound, sights, physical sensations) or intuitive means (insights, ideas and memories).
- The learner's preferred mode of perceiving information — visual or verbal.
- How such information is organized — inductive (inference of principles or through facts and observations) or deductive (the learner draws conclusions and inferences from the given principles).
- How the learner prefers to process the information — actively or reflectively.
- How the learner prefers to progress towards understanding — sequentially (through logical steps) or globally (through large chunks in an holistic fashion).

The implications of this approach are that the development and use learning materials need to reflect learners' different perceptual preferences. Indeed, Felder (1993) went so far as to suggest that students on science-based courses in some universities in the United States failed to progress to the second tier and fulfill their potential as scientists because they were 'turned off' in the first tier primarily because of a failure to address common learning styles in the teaching and learning program.

If we make the assumption that students and teachers can identify their learning style, then some strategy can be developed to help learners gain the most from their learning experience by providing or devising resources that will maximize their learning potential within that experience. Such strategies could chart a pathway through a particular series of learning outcomes; the preferred method may be to meet with other learners to discuss issues or to maximize the use of images or visual representation in coping with the learning activity. This suggests that the online resource developer must be aware of the necessity of developing materials that do provide such different pathways to maximize the opportunities for learners to select the approaches that most suit their learning style.

4.2 The Pedagogy of Learning Material Development

Given the above discussion, the development of learning materials at Biz/ed has been based on a premise that students prefer to access and process information in different ways in building learning. The outcomes from the various resources produced may, as was explained at the beginning of this chapter, be varied depending on the curriculum being followed and the assessment process used. Biz/ed, however, is seeking to help bring about learning; it is looking to challenge assumptions, to encourage students to question information and knowledge, and to build higher-order skills of analysis and evaluation. The latter is seen as encompassing a number of the features of learning that were highlighted in our definition. To be able to break down information into constituent parts requires the student to confront change, to be confident in making connections between different pieces of related or unrelated knowledge, and to encourage deep learning by making connections with personal meaning for students.

In confronting the tasks produced, students can be in a position to have changed assumptions about the subject matter in question and to have the capability of being able to draw informed conclusions about the issue at hand that is quantitatively different to that which they held before tackling the resource. Such a claim is clearly challenging, but that is the pedagogical basis for the development of materials at Biz/ed.

Resources have been developed to try to highlight the points made above. The site contains notes and plenty of written information on a wide range of topics pertaining to business, economics, and related subject areas. These are designed to underpin other resources, enabling the student to be able to access information that is detailed, yet accessible on the one Web site. Students studying macroeconomics, for example, have access to a wide range of notes about different government policies and economic theory related to macroeconomic policy through the Virtual Economy (http://www.bized.ac.uk/virtual/economy/library/).

However, to generate deep learning and to satisfy the requirements of meeting different learning styles, other resources are needed to support that information and to allow students to be able to experiment with different concept areas to assess the extent of their understanding. Continuing the example of macroeconomics, the Virtual Economy contains a model developed in conjunction with the Institute of Fiscal Studies (IFS) and the ESRC Macroeconomic Modeling Bureau at Warwick University. The model consists of a simple version with limited variables and a full version that incorporates a far greater degree of sophistication and complexity. In developing the resource, a number of issues need to be considered.

The way in which the resource might be used could vary. University lecturers may be setting the task as part of a 'virtual' seminar — students are introduced to the issues relating to government macroeconomic policy and students are then expected to use the model to achieve certain outcomes. The outcomes could then be aired through a discussion board on a VLE or in more traditional seminar settings.

Some students may be looking to build their understanding of the principles of macroeconomics. The resource structure allows the student to follow the process in detail and to receive support throughout with worksheets, information, and help sections. Other users may be those in further education and schools studying the subject at a simpler level for Advanced Supplementary (AS) — taken in the first year of post-16 education in the UK, and at A2 (the second stage of study to gain the full Advanced Level qualification), or a vocational course. The 'easy' version allows the salient point to be covered while at the same time giving the students the feeling that they are in a degree of control over how they are building their learning.

One vital aspect of the way in which resources are developed is the necessity for them to adhere to accessibility guidelines and comply with the Disability Discrimination Act (1995) and the Special Education Needs and Disability Act (SENDA) (2001). Our online resources are developed and accessibility assessed at every stage. The XHTML (eXtensible HyperText Markup Language — http://www.w3.org/MarkUp) pages on the site are all validated to ensure that they are well-formed and adhere to the XHTML standard. In addition, our pages use cascading stylesheets (CSS — http://www.w3.org/Style/CSS/) to separate content from presentation. Furthermore, prior to uploading new resources they are assessed using the Web Accessibility Initiative checklists for Web content (http://www.w3.org/TR/WCAG10/full-checklist.html). We do not rely on online accessibility checkers — such as Bobby (http://bobby.watchfire.com) — since there are some areas that can only be checked and accessibility assured if a human performs it. An example of one of these issues is confirming that a resource uses the "clearest and simplest language appropriate" (http://www.w3.org/TR/WCAG10/full-checklist.html). Most content is reviewed by at least two people before it is made available on the Web site; and larger resources often undergo periods of user testing by both educators and students, depending on the nature of the resource.

The Virtual Economy is an example of a major resource that can be used in a variety of learning environments. The development of other materials of this magnitude will build on the principles outlined here. There is a need for students to be able to use the resource on their own to reinforce or refresh knowledge and understanding. Such resources also have to be capable of being used in a classroom setting for a small group (say up to 20) or for larger groups in a traditional lecture/seminar setting.

Biz/ed is also looking to develop such materials to be used as the basis for group work within the class setting and for groups to be able to interact with each other either within the same institution or between institutions. The thinking behind such a development is that collaborative learning helps widen the opportunities for students to question the information that they are presented, to learn from the mistakes of others, and to gain and give feedback in a learning situation.

Smaller scale resources further underpin the opportunities provided by the major resources like the Virtual Economy. The 'Mind Your Business' (MYB) resource provides an opportunity for students to be able to tackle topical news issues and to be able to look at the theory behind the topic, which will then be assessed through different activities and tasks that may or may not involve traditional 'case study' type questions. This latter scenario is one with which students and lecturers will be familiar, but equally, the presentation of successive case studies tends to lack variety and the challenge soon becomes predictable and tedious.

MYB attempts to avoid such predictability by providing a flexible way in which the resource can be utilized. Students could use the resource without any outside help as a means of acquainting themselves with topical issues and the theoretical background, but the development of the resource is really built around a human interface providing students with different challenges. The tasks given in the MYB might or might not relate directly to the topic in question. The task may ask students to take what they have read in the main news and theory section and to relate it to a different context. The intent is for the students to demonstrate that they can take the concepts and issues covered in one context and apply them to a different but related situation. This helps to satisfy the requirement that students confront their understanding and are able to transfer it to different areas — such a skill is characteristic of deep rather than surface learning.

The assessment methods employed in the MYB resources tend to emphasize to the learner that they are not being expected to reproduce sections of the topic and theory in purely written answers. The way in which the material is assessed has an important link with learning styles. Some students, for example, may prefer to explore the issues through written means (reflectors and theorists) and the opportunity to present information in this way is one possible method suggested. For those who prefer the diverger/accommodator style, the work can be assessed through research, collaboration and discussion, and presentation utilizing visual images and approaches that are more suited to the preferences of such learners.

In addition to this, the major topic areas provided by Biz/ed are accompanied by mind-maps that enable those who prefer the wholist style to see how the different aspects of the subject are linked together. Such a resource can be used and referred to at regular stages throughout a program of study to help the student navigate through the topic area. At the same time, the mind-map is supplemented by a linear representation of the same information to help those who prefer the analytic style.

One specific example where students are provided with a different approach to a problem that encourages a deep approach to learning as opposed to a surface one was based on decision making in a business (http://www.bized.ac.uk/educators/16-19/business/strategy/activity/decision1. htm). The activity is based around a sports club having to make important decisions about its future development — should it stay in its current location and seek to develop its existing facilities, or move to new premises? The activity provides a range of information — some highly relevant some not so, and also incorporates many aspects of other parts of a business studies course as well as the need to consider some risk analysis. Images are used to provide the student with a mental representation of the context and the task (to construct a decision tree) is left deliberately vague. Students have to spend time thinking through the issues. Convergers and analytics, for example, could approach the task in a highly methodical way whereas as wholists and divergers might prefer to spend time discussing the range of different issues the activity presents. Feedback, following the publication of this resource, indicated that there had indeed been a considerable degree of discussion regarding the issues raised and there were some teachers as well as students who seemed to feel there 'must be' a single answer to the activity. The fact that students had to make decisions, judgments, and assumptions in dealing with the task emphasizes the belief that students' learning will develop if they are challenged. The activity builds on current knowledge yet provides opportunities to challenge existing assumptions, change realities, and thus develop learning — all of which we have outlined in our earlier definition of learning at the beginning of section 3.

This approach to the development of learning materials is designed to send a signal to the learner that their approach needs to be one reflecting the deep approach rather than the surface approach to learning. This follows the work of Entwistle (1983) and Marton *et al.* (1984) highlighted above.

Written information needs to be presented in different ways to suit different styles of learning. The suite of materials under the 'Lesson Plan' heading in the Educators section (http://www.bized.ac.uk/educators/16-19/lesson/index.htm) contains resources that are linked but which could be used in different ways. The topic in question is related to a specific syllabus area. The lesson plan gives the educator a suggestion as to how the resources could be used in a classroom context. For the learner, the material is presented in different formats. A mind-map provides an overview in visual format of the topic designed to help those with different preferences as outlined above.

The educator and the learners can then introduce the topic in a variety of ways. There are text-based notes available on the site but these are supplemented by a series of Microsoft PowerPoint (http://office.microsoft.com/powerpoint) presentations on each topic area. The presentations not only summarize the key points but also present them in a step-by-step manner suiting serialist learners, while the combination of visual images provided by photographs and diagrammatic representations further help learners to access the information in different ways.

Once the topic has been presented and developed, the activity provides the opportunity for learners to carry out further research, or to work in groups or individually on tasks related to the topic. The resource is developed with the aim of providing clear instructions and guides to the learners about the task they have to carry out. Links are provided that have been quality checked to help avoid the problem of students wasting considerable amounts of time surfing the net and not finding the information they require. Study guides are included in some resources to help build such study skills where appropriate.

Other resources have been designed to get learners involved in a physical way in the learning process — a kinaesthetic approach. One such example is a resource designed to develop understanding of the concept of diminishing marginal returns (http://www.bized.ac.uk/educators/16-19/economics/firms/activity/dimreturns.htm). The resource begins by describing the actions required and providing the source for recording the results of the activity. Once this initial task has been completed, the resource provides further suggestions for developing the learning by introducing costs and revenues to the production idea to develop understanding of such difficult concepts as marginal cost, marginal revenue, and profit maximization. The pedagogy of involving learners in a concrete experience and then developing the experience to focus on building abstract concepts and testing understanding of those new concepts clearly reflects the Kolb (1984) approach in the design of the resource. This is being supplemented by the development and publishing of a range of games and simulations to be used in classrooms that encourage active learning and help meet the needs of those who prefer to learn by doing rather than through written, verbal, or visual means.

5. SUMMARY

Biz/ed has a range of resources, not all of which could hope to meet every kind of learning style even if we were able to articulate exactly what they were. Some of the materials will be appropriate for educators to use with groups. Some will rely on, or be more appropriate for, learners to approach on their own. Either way, the issue facing the development of such resources is that the learner is an unknown quantity. Regardless of the learners' preferences, engaging them with the resources is paramount if personal meaning is to be developed and learning encouraged.

The use of developing technologies is therefore a feature of future resource development. One such example that has been used to date is animation via Macromedia Flash (http://www.macromedia.com/software/flash/) technology. Development of such materials presents particular problems in terms of accessibility and usability; however, compliance with SENDA (2001) requirements is maintained. The resource used in this example is a representation of the market mechanism (http://www.bized.ac.uk/stafsup/options/supply/interactive_markets_1.htm). The pedagogy behind this development was that there were all too often static diagrammatic representations of the way in which markets operate in textbooks and other online resources. To develop understanding, it was deemed important to involve the student in the process by which market forces, in theory, impact on price and resource allocation.

Such a resource necessitates being built up in clear steps. Learners are introduced to the demand curve, get an early taste of elasticity — without mentioning the term initially — and get opportunities to experiment with different scenarios. The learner is invited to make some sense out of the results from their experimentation and to compare different situations. This is designed to encourage students to work through the learning cycle but in a way that allows them to get involved (or not, as preferred), use visual representations, and find contradictions and outcomes that they are invited to think through. The structured approach was deemed necessary in this instance because of the large nature of the resource and the limitations of the viewing area for most learners.

The importance of the technology is brought to light in the latter stages of the resource where the learner gets to see the dynamic nature of market forces, how surpluses and shortages are developed when demand or supply changes, and how such pressures impact on prices. The students are engaged because they can select the extent to which demand or supply shifts and also the direction of the shift. There are suggestions for those who prefer a more serialist approach to guide them through the process.

The development of this latter resource and the intention to build on the production of games and simulations as well as including more traditional text-based resources reflects the desire to provide for a range of learning styles that will be present in the end users. There is still a debate about the nature of learning styles and the failure of anyone to come up with a definitive categorization or construct (even if that was desirable). An important issue in designing learning materials is, however, to attempt to incorporate the thinking behind these constructs in learning resources so that learners have an opportunity of being able to choose or focus on materials that meet their particular preferences. In addition, educators should be able to present to their students a varied range of materials that they can be confident will enrich their teaching strategies, and which are more likely to meet the differing needs of the learners with which they are faced.

The examples of the resources provided go some way towards trying to cater to a range of style differences. The fact that Biz/ed is a global provider does mean that apart from the suggestions that are given in the resources, there is little control over how the resources might be used by an individual or by a teacher/lecturer. Consequently, this aspect of the 'unknown learner' increases the importance of designing resources with as much flexibility as possible. The resources must be capable of being used in different ways by different and unknown end-users. One could be asked whether the resources are designed with teachers in mind or with students or others in mind? The answer is that each of these must be catered to and borne in mind in the design.

It may be that the next step to building on the success of Biz/ed is to develop programs that explain to unknown users how they can get the most benefit from the use of Biz/ed. A series of case studies reflecting different resources and different end-users is being contemplated as a means of communicating to the business education community the flexibility of the site, and how the same resources can be used and combined to improve the quality of learning outcomes.

The unknown learner may be just that but if the principles of what learning means are at the forefront of thinking in the way in which the materials are designed at all times, then that unknown learner is being catered to in different ways through different and expanding means. The process is by no means complete but Biz/ed has made considerable progress in identifying key aspects of e-learning and pushing the boundary as to what is possible in a coherent and well designed program of resources to help learners everywhere, whoever they may be.

REFERENCES

Biggs, J. B., & Collis, K. E. (1982). *Evaluating the Quality of Learning: The Solo Taxonomy.* New York: Academic Press.

Bowring-Carr, C., & West-Burnham, J. (1999). *Managing Learning for Achievement.* London: Financial Times.

Boyett, J., & Boyett, J. (1998). *The Guru Guide.* New York: John Wiley & Sons Inc.

Coffield, F., Moseley, D., Hall, E., & Ecclestone, K. (2004). *Learning Styles and Pedagogy in Post 16 Learning: A Systematic and Critical Review.* Learning and Skills Research Center, London.

Department for Education and Skills (DfES). (2003). Towards a unified e-learning strategy, Consultation document, DfES Reference Number: DfES/0424/2003, http://www.dfes.gov.uk/consultations2/16/docs/towards%20a%20 unified %20e-learning%20strategy.pdf, accessed April 2004.

Dewey, J. (1938). *Experience and Education*. Kappa Delta Pi Lecture Series. New York: Macmillan.

Dewey, J. (1958). *Experience and Nature*. New York: Dover Publications.

Disability Discrimination Act. (1995). http://www.disability.gov.uk/dda/, accessed April 2004.

Dunn, R. S., & Dunn, K. (1972). *Practical Approaches to Individualizing Instruction: Contacts and Other Effective Teaching Strategies*. West Nyjack, NY: Parker.

Entwistle, N. (1983). *Styles of Teaching and Learning: An Integrated Outline of Educational Psychology for Students, Teachers and Lecturers*. Chichester: John Wiley & Sons Ltd.

Entwistle, N. (1987). *Understanding Classroom Learning*. London: Hodder & Stoughton.

Felder, R. M. (1993). Reaching the second tier: Learning and teaching styles in college science education. *Journal of College Science Teaching*, *23* (5), 286-290.

Honey, P., & Mumford, A. (1986). *The Manual of Learning Styles*. Maidenhead, Berkshire: Peter Honey.

Jung, C. (1977). Psychological types. *Collected Works of C. G. Jung, Vol. 6*, R. F. C Hull, trans., Bollingen Series XX. Princeton, NJ: Princeton University Press.

Kagan, J., & Kogan, N. (1970). Individual variation in cognitive processes. In P. H. Musser (Ed.), *Carmichaels Manual of Child Psychology, Vol. 1*. New York: Wiley.

Kolb, D. A. (1984). *Experiential Learning: Experience as the Source of Learning and Development*. Englewood Cliffs, NJ: Prentice-Hall.

Lewin, K. (1951). *Field Theory in Social Sciences*. New York: Harper & Row.

Marton, F., Hounsell, D. J., & Entwistle, N.J. (1984). *The Experience of Learning*. Edinburgh: Scottish Academic Press.

Pask, G. (1976). Styles and strategies of learning. *British Journal of Educational Psychology*, *46*, 128-148.

Piaget, J. (1968). *Structuralism*. New York: Harper Torchbooks.

Rayner, S., & Riding, R. (1998). *Cognitive Styles and Learning Strategies: Understanding Style Differences in Learning and Behavior*. London: David Fulton.

Special Education Needs and Disability Act. (2001). http://www.hmso.gov.uk/acts/acts2001/20010010.htm, accessed April 2004.

Senge, P. (2000). *Schools that Learn: A Fifth Discipline Fieldbook for Educators, Parents and Everyone Who Cares about Education*. London: Nicholas Brealey.

Witkin, H. A., Moore, C. A., Oltman, P. K., Goodenough, D. R., Friedman, F., Owen, D. R., & Raskin, E. (1977). Role of the field dependent and field independent cognitive styles in academic evolution: A longitudinal study. *Journal of Educational Psychology*, *69* (3), 197-211.

Chapter 14

'CREDIT WHERE CREDIT'S DUE'

Piloting the Accreditation of Experiential Learning — A Case Study

Stewart Falconer and John Troy
Napier University, Edinburgh, Scotland

1. INTRODUCTION

The development of a learning society incorporating the concept of lifelong learning has been discussed in the higher education sector for many years now. The need for individuals to continue to develop personal and technical skills, knowledge, and understanding has been a prominent part of thinking within employment and education. Effective lifelong learning can ensure greater diversity in employability and personal fulfillment while meeting the needs of a changing economic environment. Employers benefit through having human resources at their disposal in the numbers and of the quality they require to meet their objectives. This is particularly demonstrated in the workplace through the desire for continuing professional development both from employer and from employee, and, accordingly, higher education must work hard to develop innovative approaches to the provision of relevant knowledge coupled with attractive and appropriate programs and qualifications.

This need has been addressed successfully within the School of Accounting and Economics in Napier University, Edinburgh, Scotland through the introduction of programs offering direct entry at an advanced stage of the BA Honors Financial Services program to holders of relevant professional qualifications. These 'Pathway' programs, which provide a route from professional qualification to an honors degree through the accreditation of the professional qualification, have proven popular with

M.K. McCuddy et al. (eds.),
The Challenges of Educating People to Lead in a Challenging World, 291–305.

employers and individuals and they meet many of the professional development needs of the sector.

Knowledge derived from accrediting prior learning of part-time distance learner students who are employed full-time in the financial services sector reveals that, through their work experience, these individuals bring a substantial amount of experiential learning and expertise to their studies. This led Napier University to consider ways in which this experience might be recognized through the accreditation of experiential learning. Initial steps have been taken in evaluating this through a study to examine the opportunities for giving each individual full and appropriate credit for those experiences he/she has gained in the workplace.

This concept of accrediting prior experience and learning at University level has assumed increasing importance as institutions address some of the practical and operational issues surrounding entry to programs posed by the lifelong learning agenda (Commission of the European Communities, 2000). For example, how do adults who wish to join programs obtain admission if they have no formal qualifications? In addition, the combination of work and study for a protracted period of between six and eight years can be less than attractive. Institutions are making efforts to take account of this by looking at ways to give credit for forms of learning which have not been accredited previously or which do not fall within traditional accreditation procedures, such as learning that arises from life or vocational experiences (Konrad, 2001). Such accreditation enables experience to be recognized as a form of attainment that others might not have achieved, although it can be difficult from a practical point of view to find an objective method with which to assess and accredit the experience.

2. EXPERIENTIAL LEARNING

If lifelong learning is to be defined adequately, it must incorporate experiential learning, that is, learning which is not simply accumulated by studies that lead to qualifications. Failure to recognize this would appear to restrict significantly our recognition of the benefits of learning throughout life. Learning by experience is an important form of lifelong learning but one which is too often assessed inadequately or not at all.

2.1 Definitions and Descriptions of Experiential Learning

At this stage, it is helpful to consider some definitions and descriptions of what is meant by the term experiential learning and, in doing this, some theory and some practical application in the form of current approaches within Higher Education in the United Kingdom (UK) has been examined.

Konrad (2001) quotes from the Learning from Experience Trust (2000):

> *"Accreditation of prior experiential learning (APEL) is the award of credit for learning based on prior experience – from work, community or volunteer experience – which has not previously been assessed and/or awarded credit. By converting informal learning into certificated learning, APEL provides cost-effective routes to qualifications. It has potential significance for people who, through life and work experience, have learned knowledge, skills and analytical abilities that are comparable to those in a higher education award. APEL offers the possibility for what learners know to be recognized, assessed with the same rigor as any other learning would be at HE level, and awarded credit."*

This description is an appropriate starting point to set out the framework with which Higher Education can begin the process of undertaking an effective analysis of how experiential learning is evaluated and credited. Looking for the moment at the Higher Education sector in the UK, it is useful to obtain some understanding of how a number of Universities have addressed the process (see Table 1). Collectively, these universities focus on evaluating differentially nuanced aspects of work experiences or personal study experiences that create academic value.

The University of East London offers a clear distinction between APL and APEL. **APL** (Assessment of Prior Learning) is the accreditation of previously acquired certificates/qualifications. **APEL** (Assessment of Prior Experiential Learning) is the process by which appropriate learning experience is given academic value. This paper concentrates on APEL, although we have accumulated considerable experience over the past seven years in working with APL. Such experience has demonstrated that it is much more straightforward to accredit certificated learning than to accredit learning gained from experience.

2.2 Challenges of Experiential Learning

Experiential learning cannot be discussed without mentioning Kolb's (1984) model. In examining the possibility of accrediting such learning, the principle that experience is a powerful source of learning and, consequently,

Table 1. Examples of UK Approaches to Evaluating Experiential Learning

University	**Approach to Evaluation**
University of East London	"APEL is the process by which appropriate learning experience is given academic value. Sources of credit might be relevant or related work experience, relevant or related voluntary work and/or relevant or related home work." [www.uel.ac.uk/apel/general_info]
University of Manchester	"APEL is the process of awarding academic credits for uncertificated learning gained from experience." [www.man.ac.uk/policies/3D]
Cardiff University	"APEL refers to learning that has been achieved informally, such as in the workplace or during personally motivated study." [www.cf.ac.uk/ls/guidance/apel]
Middlesex University	"Middlesex University recognizes that learning occurs throughout life, especially through active participation in short courses and in the work place. It also occurs in non-employment situations in the home and in voluntary work. The University believes that these kinds of learning should be accredited … to ensure that, where appropriate, students are enrolled on programmes of study with advanced standing." Academic Policy Statement APS2 (2004)

that individuals must understand how to build on it is acknowledged. That is the basis for much of what Kolb has postulated. However, it is, arguably, not a principal source of reference for this paper. In addition, it is not felt that there is any need to be put off by Michelson's (1996) suggestion that:

> *"experiential learning is, arguably, one of the most significant areas for current research and practice in adult education, and increasingly one of the most problematic."*

Trying to determine what prompts experiential learning or trying to understand the opportunities that are available across different learning environments is clearly a complex business. Such complexity is evident in Fenwick's (2000) description of Schon (1983):

> *"a significant promoter of constructivism to understand workplace learning, arguing that practitioners learn by noticing and framing problems of interest to them in particular ways, then enquiring and experimenting with solutions. Their knowledge is constructed through reflection during and after their experimental action on the... problems of practice."*

We are prepared to watch closely as the academic debates develop, but at the same time, to work within the scope of current approaches and thinking about the learning that can be achieved in what might be called non-formal education. Although it should go without saying that we recognize the importance of knowing both how and what people learn, in terms of our priorities here, the concern is not so much about **how** they have learned but rather **what** they have learned, almost regardless of where the learning has taken place.

Brookfield (1983) comments that writers in the field of experiential learning have tended to use the term in two different senses. On the one hand, it is used to describe the sort of learning that is undertaken by students who are given the chance to acquire and apply knowledge and skills in an immediate and relevant setting. This sort of learning is usually sponsored by an institution and might be used in medicine, social work, or teaching. Alternatively, it might fall into the category of a work-based learning component of an undergraduate degree program. On the other hand, Brookfield (1983), adopting Houle's (1980) conception, also refers to experiential learning as "education that occurs as a direct participation in the events of life." Learning of this sort is not sponsored by some formal education institution but by people themselves. It is achieved by reflection on everyday experiences and is the way that most of us do our learning. Each of these perspectives is relevant to the basic premise of this paper – an acknowledgement that learning can be gained in a variety of different ways and in a variety of different situations, that it does not need to be certificated and that it can be used as a basis for awarding credit which will allow advanced entry to Higher Education programs of study.

2.3 Quality Assurance Issues in Evaluating Experiential Learning

A recent report from the Quality Assurance Agency in the UK highlights the need for vigilance to ensure that accreditation of prior learning is of a sufficiently rigorous standard. The concern is that credit may be given for economic rather than academic reasons and students may be allowed entry to programs without an appropriate background. However, current practice among the institutions that are accrediting prior experiential learning indicates they are well aware of this. The general approach of these institutions to quality assurance is to acknowledge that the accreditation process must be seen to be fair and rigorous by the applicant and by the institution. In this connection there are some basic criteria for acceptability of learning for an APEL claim.

First and foremost, it needs to be clearly recognized that the credit is not being awarded for the experience but, rather, for the learning which has been gained as a consequence of the experience. For example, the University of East London states that:

> *"It is the learning only that can provide a base for credit. Separating learning from experience is a skill in itself. You will not get credit because you have done something or have been on a course, but you could if you demonstrated you learned some thing from it."*

The University of East London position follows logically from experiential learning theory that defines learning as:

> *"The process whereby knowledge is created through the transformation of experience. Knowledge results from the combination of grasping and transforming experience."*
>
> Kolb (1984)

Secondly, applicants must substantiate their claims through the provision of evidence in some form, usually through the submission of a portfolio. The evidence is then examined under four fairly standard headings:

- **Validity** – the evidence must match the learning outcomes for which the claim for credit is being made.
- **Sufficiency** – the volume and level of the learning must match that for which the claim is made.

- **Quality** – the evidence must relate to the applicant's own experience.
- **Currency** – the evidence must not be 'out of date'.

2.4 Evidence of Experiential Learning

It is generally acknowledged that learning must be evidenced and Konrad (2001) suggests that such evidence should cover the following areas:

- The nature of the experiences for which credit is sought.
- Evidence, direct or indirect (letters, testimonials, etc.), to substantiate the experiences.
- The nature, scope, and magnitude of the experiences in terms of learning that occurred.
- The relationship of the learning to the award or program for which entry or advanced standing is being sought.

In many cases, the evidence is submitted in the form of a portfolio that provides an explanation of what has been learned and how it was acquired. The University of East London defines a portfolio as:

> *"A portable collection of items and evidence in a variety of media used for a variety of purposes. For the purpose of academic credit, the portfolio is a reflective compilation which usually includes pieces of writing that demonstrate analysis of one's learning within the context of work and life experiences. The portfolio is where you can record your reflection and learning outcomes supported by evidence to support your learning claim."*

The completion of the portfolio follows a series of stages and is supported by an APEL Co-coordinator. These stages are:

1. Initial discussion of experiences.
2. Reviewing the experiences.
3. Recognizing relevant experiences.
4. Identifying relevant learning.
5. Matching learning outcomes/criteria.
6. Assembling evidence of learning.
7. Recording and organizing evidence.
8. Presenting evidence for assessment.

In assisting applicants to identify what to include in their portfolio, the University of East London suggests that credit claims can be documented by identifying learning experiences in two ways: evidence-driven claims and criteria-driven claims. In *Make Your Experience Count* (2004), the University of East London describes these forms of documentation as follows:

> *"Evidence driven – this is when you look at a piece of evidence, for example, a project you have done for a specific duration or an employment position you have held over a certain period or a particular role you have fulfilled in a specific setting such as work, home, community, and then draw out your own learning outcomes from this piece of evidence.*
>
> *"Criteria driven – this is when you aim to meet a set of criteria, for example, learning outcomes of a specific module in the degree programme you are interested in and then you search for evidence from your learning experiences to meet these criteria."*

In the case study discussed below, we have opted to use the second of these forms of documentation, with the relevant criteria being the program learning outcomes with respect to the levels of study for which credit is sought.

3. THE PILOT STUDY

The School of Accounting and Economics at Napier University in Edinburgh, Scotland has been offering APL to holders of financial services based professional qualifications since 1997. Initially this began with the recognition of the Scottish professional banking qualification (MCIBS) and it has moved on to include the Associateship of the Chartered Insurance Institute (ACII) and the Advanced Financial Planning Certificate (AFPC). In addition, advanced entry is offered to holders of similar qualifications in Hong Kong and to holders of business related National Diplomas in the UK. However, in working on these programs with students who are studying on a part-time, distance learning basis while in full-time employment, it has become clear that they have a variety of experience and skills and the maturity and commitment that they bring to their studies along with their certificated qualifications is impressive.

In the School's early developments in this area, with Banking and Insurance professionals, advanced entry was offered purely on the strength of the certificated qualification. However, with the 'Financial Planning Pathway' for holders of the AFPC, this was not possible; consequently, to admit students at a sufficiently advanced stage to make the program attractive, it was necessary to seek further opportunities to award credit. These students have completed a range of UK financial planning qualifications up to and including the Advanced Financial Planning Certificate. Their certificated qualifications (APL) and experiential learning (APEL) are accredited as shown in Table 2. In the table, one credit is equivalent to ten hours of study during a semester.

Table 2. Accreditation Guidelines for APL and APEL

Level of Study	APL	APEL	Total Credit Awarded	Credit to Be Completed	Accumulated Credit Required	Level of Award
One	30	90	120	None	120	Certificate
Two	30	90	120	None	240	Diploma
Three	60	---	60	60	360	Degree
Four	---	---	---	120	480	Honors

In summary, students are admitted to the program half way through level three with a further 60 credits to complete the Ordinary degree and a further 120 credits after that to complete the Honors degree. Study for the additional 180 credits is on a distance-learning basis, using study guides, e-mail support and optional weekend tutorials.

3.1 Required Evidence and Documentation

Evidence is required to substantiate the accreditation of experiential learning at levels one and two of the program. As indicated above, a criteria-driven approach is used to identify learning experiences. This is achieved through the completion of a Reflective Account in the form of a questionnaire that allows the applicant to map their experiential learning against the program learning outcomes for levels one and two of the BA Honors in Financial Services program. These outcomes are described below:

At the end of level one, students will have:

- developed, and demonstrated, a broad business knowledge;
- developed a number of quantitative and information gathering skills;

- begun to learn to work as part of a team; and
- improved their written and oral communication skills via tutorials, coursework and examinations.

At the end of level two, students will have:

- developed a further knowledge and understanding of economics and financial services which will support their studies at level three and four;
- further developed their information management and quantitative skills;
- learned to collect, interpret and report data on financial services related topics; and
- been introduced to the ways in which knowledge and learning are applied within the financial services environment.

In addition, specific learning incorporated in particular modules at levels one and two of the program, which applicants will not have covered in their certificated learning, is also covered in the Reflective Account.

The key aspects of both the program and module outcomes are described under four key headings.

1. **Business knowledge and awareness:** This incorporates the four key academic disciplines covered within the early stages of the program – economics, accounting, marketing and law.
2. **Information in business:** An understanding of the importance and uses of information in a business environment should be demonstrated along with the ability to interpret data for business use.
3. **Quantitative skills:** Experience should be demonstrated of the use of information technology in the workplace in the collection and use of data, in particular in relation to problem solving.
4. **Other, more generic skills:** A number of generic or transferable skills are incorporated in the program learning outcomes, notably, effective communication, working independently, working in a team, using initiative and researching a topic.

Guidance is provided on completion of the questionnaire, a copy of which is attached as Appendix A. The completed questionnaire is assessed by a member of the program team using an assessment form, a copy of which is attached as Appendix B.

3.2 Initial Experience with the Process

At the moment, the Financial Planning Pathway continues to run on a pilot basis with fifteen students and, so far, performance has been very good. Although two students have deferred their studies, in each case this has been due to work commitments rather than as a result of difficulties with the academic content of the program. Although the program is in its early days, we have concluded that the results thus far provide a good indication that the procedures for accreditation of experiential learning are sufficiently robust.

We have been very encouraged with our progress to date in employing APEL to allow students advanced entry and it is believed that the system, once refined as necessary in the light of experience, has the potential to enable the School to seek students from other financial-related professions. In addition, there seems no reason why the basic model should not have the potential to be used consistently across other University programs, and, perhaps, across other institutions.

APPENDIX A: THE FINANCIAL PLANNING PATH — DEMONSTRATION OF PRIOR LEARNING

(1) Prior Qualifications

Please list your qualifications and the dates when they were achieved.

(2) Business Knowledge and Awareness

In this section, we are looking for evidence of:

- General business knowledge.
- Specific awareness of key business areas and their application within a business environment.

Set out ways in which your work experience to date has provided you with an understanding of the following business areas:

2.1 Economics

What do you understand by the term economics and how do you feel your knowledge of economics is reflected in your work? In what ways have you used economic data at work and how has it helped you to achieve your objectives?

2.2 Accounting

In what ways do you use accounting and finance at work? What do you think is the purpose of a company's annual report and accounts and who would use the report and accounts and for what purpose?

2.3 Marketing

What do you think marketing is? In what ways are you involved in marketing within your organization? Provide some examples of the ways in which your organization's marketing strategy is implemented.

2.4 Law

What legislation governs or has an impact on the way in which you do your job? Provide examples to illustrate your answer.

(3) Information in Business

In this section, we are looking for evidence of:

- Understanding of the importance of and uses of information in a business environment.
- The ability to interpret data for business use.

Use the space below to detail some of the ways in which you use information and information systems at work and the benefits which their use provides. How do you use information and how does it help you to do your job?

(4) Quantitative Skills

In this section, we're looking for evidence of:

- Experience of using information technology in the workplace in
  - collecting and using data.
  - problem solving.

Provide examples of some of the systems and/or programs you have experience of using at work. How do they work, what is their purpose and what have you achieved through their use?

(5) Generic Skills

In this section, we are looking for evidence of your ability to:

- Communicate effectively orally and in writing.

- Work independently and as part of a team.
- Use initiative.
- Research a topic and report on your findings.

Use the space below to demonstrate, using examples, how you have acquired these skills through your work experience to date.

5.1 Effective communication

5.2 Working independently

5.3 Working in a team

5.4 Using initiative

5.5 Researching a topic

(6) Any Other Relevant Information
(Completion of this section is optional)

APPENDIX B: THE FINANCIAL PLANNING PATHWAY — ACCREDITATION OF PRIOR LEARNING

Assessment of Reflective Account

The assessor should consider each section of the applicant's reflective account and comment on the extent to which the responses and any accompanying evidence demonstrate the achievement of learning under each heading. Finally, an overall assessment of the account should be made and a decision taken on the suitability of the applicant for entry to the program. The appropriate entry point should be identified on the basis of the content of the reflective account and the applicant's prior qualifications.

(1) Prior Qualifications

Confirm these are appropriate for entry to the program.

(2) Business Knowledge and Awareness

Look for evidence of:

- General business knowledge.
- Specific awareness of key business areas:
  - Accounting

  - Economics
  - Marketing
  - Law
- Appreciation of the application of these areas within a business environment.

(3) Information in Business

Look for evidence of:

- Understanding of the importance of and uses of information in a business environment.
- The ability to interpret data for business use.

(4) Quantitative Skills

Look for evidence of:

- Experience of using information technology in the workplace.
- The use of technology in collecting and using data and in problem solving.

(5) Generic Skills

Look for evidence of the ability to:

- Communicate effectively orally and in writing.
- Work independently and as part of a team.
- Use initiative.
- Research a topic and report on the findings.

(6) Any Other Relevant Information

Note any points which have relevance to the application and accreditation processes.

Overall Assessment

(1) The applicant's prior qualifications and experiential learning, as demonstrated in the reflective account are sufficient to allow entry to the Financial Planning Pathway with the following level of accreditation:

270 credits   300 credits   330 credits   360 credits (circle as appropriate)

(2) The applicant has not demonstrated a sufficient level of experiential learning to allow entry to the Financial Planning Pathway.

Delete (1) or (2) as appropriate.

REFERENCES

Brookfield, S. D. (1983). *Adult Learning, Adult Education and the Community*. Open University Press: New York: Teachers College, Columbia University and England.

Commission of the European Communities. (2000). *A Memorandum on Lifelong Learning*. SEC, Brussels, p. 1832.

Fenwick, T. J. (2000). Expanding conceptions of experiential learning: A review of five contemporary perspectives. *Adult Education Quarterly*, *50* (4), 243-272.

Houle, C. (1980). *Continuing Learning in the Professions*. San Francisco: Jossey-Bass.

Kolb, D. A. (1984). *Experiential Learning*. Englewood Cliffs: Prentice Hall.

Konrad, J. (2001). Accreditation of Prior Experiential Learning in the United Kingdom. School of Education and Professional Development, Leeds Metropolitan University (working paper).

Learning from Experience Trust. (2000). *Mapping APEL: Accreditation of Experiential Learning in English Higher Education Institutions*, London.

Michelson, E. (1996). Usual suspects: Experience, reflection and the engendering of knowledge. *International Journal of Lifelong Education*, *15* (6), 438-454.

Middlesex University. (2004). *Academic Policy Statement APS2*.

Schon, D. A. (1983). *The Reflective Practitioner*. New York: Basic Books.

University of East London. (2004). *Make Your Experience Count, A Guidance Manual*.

Web Sites

Cardiff University – http://www.cf.ac.uk/ls/guidance/apel

University of East London – http://www.uel.ac.uk/apel/general_info

University of Manchester – http://www.man.ac.uk/policies/3D

PART IV

DEVELOPING COMPETENCIES FOR CAREER SUCCESS: ISSUES AND PRACTICES

Chapter 15

TEACHING FOR LIFE — GENERIC CAPABILITIES THAT LINK UNIVERSITY LEARNING WITH WORKPLACE LEARNING

Jennifer Radbourne
Faculty of Business, Queensland University of Technology, Brisbane, Australia

1. INTRODUCTION

Business schools are under increasing pressure to enhance the learning capability and employability of graduates. Business professional institutes and employer organizations are demanding more than the technical knowledge and skills required to perform discipline/professional specific tasks. They want graduates who can demonstrate capabilities in communication, teamwork, risk taking, decision making, problem solving, critical thinking, analytical reasoning, visioning and innovation, leadership, ethical practices, appreciation of diversity, and a commitment to social justice. Evidence in literature and reports (Karpin, 1995; Kirby, 2000; Commonwealth of Australia, 2002; Nelson, 2002) and in test data (McCowan & Richardson, 1998; Employer Survey, 1998; DETYA, 2000) shows that the employability gap[7] is closed when graduates possess these generic capabilities. What is important, however, is the increasing research showing that the strategies used to develop generic capabilities lead to improved learning, both in university courses and in the workplace. Acquisition of these generic capabilities, or generic skills, engenders a process self-assessment, a desire for effectiveness in performance, and a

[7] The 'employability gap' is the gap between the university's preparation of the student for employment through the award of the degree, and the student's commencement of employment.

M.K. McCuddy et al. (eds.),
The Challenges of Educating People to Lead in a Challenging World, 309–323.

consequent ongoing practice of learning, that is, lifelong learning (Candy, Crebert, & O'Leary, 1994; De Corte, 1996; Mentkowski & Associates, 2000).

The hypothesis for this paper is that *by teaching business students the generic skills and capabilities for effective performance in the workplace, they are being taught learning that lasts*. For the purpose of this paper the term 'learning that lasts' will be used to describe lifelong learning. This hypothesis is built around four questions. Which skills are critical for business students? Which skills should be taught in the curriculum at university? Which skills are best acquired in the workplace? What level of competence in graduate capabilities is required for effective performance in the workplace? The skills identified as critical for business graduates are centered around leadership and management, interpersonal and communication, social justice, decision making, and technical and cognitive. Of these, the research shows that the technical and cognitive skills, the interpersonal and communication skills, and social justice skills are those best learned at university. However, all the skills were rated as requiring high or very high competence in the workplace, replicating the feedback from employers.

2. GENERIC SKILLS EXPLAINED

"The term generic skills is widely used to refer to a range of qualities and capacities that are increasingly viewed as important in higher education. These include thinking skills…; effective communication skills…; personal attributes…; and values…. This diverse collection of qualities and capacities is distinguished from the discipline-specific knowledge and associated technical skills that traditionally are connected with higher education" (Hager, Holland, & Beckett, 2002, p. 3). The Business Higher Education Round Table position paper (Hager, Holland, & Beckett, 2002) in Australia where these generic skills were discussed highlighted the growing demand from businesses and employer organizations for graduates to possess these generic skills. This increased emphasis on employability reflects the shift to a knowledge-based economy where the intangible assets of the employee, such as "creativity, design proficiency, customer relations and goodwill," have become important in the dynamic contemporary job market. Employers responding to a national survey by the Australian government education department (DETYA) in 2000, stated that the greatest skill deficiencies among new graduates were perceived to be in the areas of creativity and flair, oral business communications, problem solving and the capacity for independent and critical thinking. This is disappointing given that Karpin in

1995 and numerous studies in the 1990s (Canadian Corporate Council on Education, 1994; B-HERT, 1991; Hearn, Close, Smith, & Southey, 1992; Employer Survey, 1998; Oregon University C&E Services 1990) had identified the key generic skills and abilities for business graduates, and business schools registered interest in including these in courses as a means of meeting need and demand. Such accountability is typical for business schools that operate in a small competitive market in Australia. Higher Education institutions seeking competitive advantage and intent on quality assurance had willingly incorporated these skills and abilities into their curriculum. These skills were not very different from an earlier set of skills outlined by the Mayer Committee (1992). The Mayer Committee's list was labeled competencies "essential for participation in work, and for effective participation in further education and in adult life more generally" (1992, p. 7). This link from employability to lifelong learning was an argument taken up by Candy, Crebert, and O'Leary (1994). Candy *et al.* suggest that the deeper learning engaged through the teaching and learning of generic skills results in reflection and self-directed learning that fosters lifelong learning capacities.

By embedding generic skills in courses, the "balance between discovery learning and personal exploration, on the one hand, and systematic instruction and guidance, on the other" (De Corte, 1996, pp. 112-113) is achieved. De Corte (1996) provides a valuable model for teaching students to become lifelong learners. He recommended requiring students to progressively increase their self-regulation in the learning environment as they acquired "general learning and thinking skills."

3. RESEARCH PROJECT

The subject of this paper covers four successive projects, executed at the Queensland University of Technology (QUT) in Australia from 1998. The business school, together with the university's careers and employment office, surveyed graduates and employers to identify the importance and competency levels of graduates' capabilities. Using these data, the second project was implemented in 2001/2002 wherein the teaching and assessment of the specific skills and abilities required for business graduates was embedded in the curriculum. A student evaluation provided valuable evidence on how students rated teaching strategies, importance for employment, and levels of competency in these skills and abilities. In Project 3, a further alumni survey was carried out in 2002 replicating the 1998 survey data on levels of importance and competence, but also seeking information on where these skills and abilities were learned: at university, in the workplace, or through other social and community activity. This new part of the survey was designed to provide evidence for further curriculum design and a new focus on teaching learning that lasts. Project 4 concluded the research using focus groups with alumni of post-five years graduation.

3.1 PROJECT 1 — Graduate and Employer Perception Surveys 1998

In 1998 academic staff in QUT's business school and managers in the university's careers and employment office conducted research on employer satisfaction with graduates utilizing the findings of previous studies with special reference to the work of Evers, Rush and Berdrow in Canada who had begun a ten-year skill development project in 1986. Evers, Rush and Berdrow (1998) investigated participants from the early years of university through to their stabilized career stage, identifying four areas of skill competence. They focused on the perceived competence levels of participants, the major elements of change and influence on the skill acquisition process, the change in participants' self-perceptions of skills competencies across time, and the future skill requirements of corporations given organizational change.

QUT's study (McGowan and Richardson, 1998) built on the matrix of skills from previous studies so that comparison could occur. All the skills identified and tested in previous studies were subjected to factor analysis. Five factors for the Level of Competence Scale emerged with strong reliability coefficients. This resulted in the development of five skill categories deemed applicable to this study in the Australian context:

- Leadership/management;
- Interpersonal/communication;
- Social justice;
- Adventurous decision making; and
- Technical/professional/cognitive.

Each skill category included a set of sub-skills or relevant dimensions of a skill category. As shown in Figure 1, each skill category included a set of sub-skills or relevant dimensions of a skill category.

The survey tool included a description of the sub-skill concept to ensure common understanding by respondents. For example: leadership and influence involves the ability to give direction and guidance, and to delegate work tasks in a manner which proves to be effective and motivates others to do their best; coordinating involves being able to coordinate the work of peers and subordinates and encourage positive group relations; risk taking involves taking reasonable job-related risks by recognizing alternative or

1. Leadership/management	**2. Interpersonal/communication**
• visioning and innovation • leadership/influence • creativity and change • coordinating • managing conflict • being positive and resilient • time management	• interpersonal • teamwork • listening/responding • oral communication • written communication • working independently • understanding organizations
3. Social justice — others and self	**4. Adventurous decision making**
• social justice • multicultural • community involvements • career/life management • strengths and weaknesses	• risk taking • decision making • planning and organizing • standards/ethics
5. Technical/professional/ cognitive	
• technical/professional • life-long learning • computing • problem solving/analytic • cognitive research • ability to conceptualize	

Figure 1. Generic Skills Selected for This Project

different ways of constructively meeting objectives; cognitive and research involves the ability to research, process information, think critically, evaluate and develop action plans as well as apply theoretical concepts to practical solutions; lifelong learning involves the ability to gain knowledge from daily experiences, to keep current on new developments and have a strong orientation towards lifelong learning.

Two surveys were developed to obtain dual feedback from supervisors and graduates of the perceived skill level and perceived skill importance in order to measure differences and commonalities in responses. The sample from the Graduate Perceptions survey instrument addresses the skill of teamwork (see Figure 2). Survey respondents circled the number representing their level of competence from 1 to 5 (including Don't Know), and the level of importance from 1 to 5 (including Not Applicable).

Two-fifths or 40% of the 700 graduates with one year of employment responded. Only 14% of employers responded. The graduates rated self-management skills, cognitive skills, innovative skills, interpersonal skills,

Level of competence	Skill/Ability	Importance
1 2 3 4 5 DK	Teamwork Involves the ability to work well in a team through collaboration, cooperation and supporting others in order to achieve team goals.	1 2 3 4 5 NA

Figure 2. Sample of Graduation Perception Instrument

and social justice skills as requiring the highest level of competence. There was a positive correlation between the five sub-scales for level of competence and importance. Therefore, if the skill was seen to be important then the graduate would develop competence in it or vice-versa.

The employers' ratings of the skills and abilities of the business graduates presented the following as most important: innovative leadership, interpersonal skills, social justice skills, decision making, and technical/professional skills. There were significant discrepancies between importance and skill level observed. However, the five important skills identified by both groups were essentially the same with slight differences in priority order.

In addition, the five factors that emerged from the Employer Importance Scale reflected the listings of desirable skills and abilities in contemporary literature — social justice, risk taking, and self-management. The study facilitated the business school's understanding of (1) the skills and abilities that are important for graduates in seeking employment, and (2) the need to incorporate these into the curriculum.

3.2 PROJECT 2 — Embedding Generic Skills in the Curriculum

Following the 1998 survey, the business school conducted a review of the undergraduate curriculum in 1999. The business degree is built on core foundational study in marketing, accounting, economics, business law and ethics, international business, management, government and society, and information analysis and communication. This foundation leads to specialized study in these areas reinforcing a discipline-focused curriculum. The review highlighted the fact that the curriculum was not learner-centered. The disciplines were delivered in silos without integration even at the foundation level. No allowance was made for the reality of the business world where disciplines and departments do not act independently from each other. This discipline-based curriculum did not explicitly embrace student acquisition of the skills and abilities required for employment, such as teamwork, problem solving, critical thinking, leadership, innovation, and communication. It measured the acquisition of knowledge as information, but not knowledge as application. The need for integration and incorporation of the skills and abilities in business were identified as drivers for a new learner-centered model of business education.

The business school sought funding from the central university under a teaching and learning grant scheme for a two-year project "to develop an integrated approach to embedding and assessing generic and identified business specific skills and competencies across each of the eight business core units (subjects)" (Faculty of Business, 2000). The application was successful. It involved utilizing a multi-layered multimedia case study of the Port of Brisbane Corporation to integrate content across disciplines and as the basis for the teaching and learning of a matrix of skills and abilities. The selected skills and abilities were drawn from the earlier QUT research by McCowan and Richardson (1998), and were combined with skills identified in the literature for new business graduates. Through 2001 and 2002 the teachers in these eight subjects progressively included specific skills and abilities in the learning objectives of the sub-cases that were taught in content associated with the Port of Brisbane Corporation case study. In conjunction with this progressive inclusion of skills and abilities they assessed students' acquisition of them. During each semester in 2003 and 2004 new sub-cases were developed such that every undergraduate business student was exposed across all their core subjects — a full year of study — to the emphasis on acquisition of generic business skills.

Figure 3 shows a sample of the five generic skills previously described in concept, the learning tasks designed to instill them, and the means by which they were assessed. These tasks all relate to the subject "Management, People and Organizations." Selected generic skills were included in all subjects, including accountancy, economics, marketing, international business, business law, information analysis, and communication.

The overall performance of students in this subject improved significantly in the semester in which the changes were introduced. The percentage of students acquiring high distinction and distinction grades increased from 23% to 28% and a reduction in lower grades from 42% to 27% in 2001 and 2002 respectively. The distribution of results in Semester 2, 2002, was very comparable with those of the other business core subjects. Previously, the distribution had compared poorly with the majority of these subjects.

Generic Skills	Tutorial/Learning Task	Assessment Methods
Leadership and influence	Tutorial teams have a formal structure overseen by CEO. However, shared leadership is promoted. Each team member contributes to the overall team task and is also responsible for teaching other team members concepts related to her or his area of responsibility.	• Peer assessment • Examination (multiple choice and /or short essay)
Coordinating	There are five designated roles in the team (CEO, Strategic Planning Manager/Deputy CEO, HR Manager,. Org. Design Manager, International Business Manager). Each person is required to contribute specific outcomes to the overall task.	• Team tutorial project assignment • Examination (multiple choice)
Risk taking	The team tutorial project requires students to engage in ill-structured problem solving and decision making. There is no single right decision outcome. The choices they make affect their mark on the project assignment.	• Team tutorial project assignment • Examination (multiple choice and/or short-answer essay questions)
Cognitive and research	Student teams are expected to search electronic databases for recent articles on those topics relevant to the completion of the team tutorial project.	• Team tutorial project assignment — covered by explicit criteria in the assessment sheet
Lifelong learning	At the beginning of the semester students are expected to develop learning goals based on their self-assessment of generic skills and to use opportunities provided in tutorial to meet these goals. Students are provided with an opportunity to reassess their goal achievement efforts at the end of the semester and to set new goals for the following semester.	• Self assessment activity • Personal goal-setting activity at the beginning and the at the end of semester

Figure 3. Learning Tasks and Assessment Methods for Generic Skills

Throughout the project, evaluations were implemented to check teacher and student expectations and levels of satisfaction with the case study and use, with the multimedia delivery, with the learning of skills and abilities, and the relationship of these skills and abilities to employment. Two-thirds (66%) of the sample of 926 students rated the importance of the skills and abilities to employers as very important or extremely important. Moreover, 81% of the sample were satisfied or very satisfied that the skills were taught and acquired in the subject and they preferred explicit teaching by lecturers or tutors. The qualitative comments by students affirmed that this mode of teaching developed "the ability to apply the skills learned to real life situations."

This project stimulated research and reflection in diverse areas of student learning: generic skills and abilities, case method pedagogy, workplace experience, multimedia resources, assessment, curriculum integration, and the teacher as learner. The specific outcomes were that skills and abilities were incorporated into learning objectives, teaching and assessment, and that students' employability may have improved through acquisition of these skills and abilities.

Each stage of research and implementation of ideas from this growing study into the skills and abilities of business students led to the need for further testing and development. This embedding project may not be measured effectively until after the first cohort of students graduate in 2004. At that time the students should be more employable because of their acquired skills and abilities, as shown in previous employer surveys by McCowan and Richardson (1998) and the literature and reports on employer expectations cited earlier in this paper. The gap in the research project, however, was a contemporary study to confirm which skills and abilities should be included in the teaching and curriculum at university, and which skills and abilities are learned in the workplace. There was also a third area of investigation needed. This focused on the level of competence from these university and workplace learning environments, and how skills learned at university were further developed in the workplace. Thus the theory of 'learning that lasts' needed examination in the context of this particular business school.

3.3 PROJECT 3 — Graduate Perception Survey 2002

Late in 2002 the next stage of research was implemented. Building on the 1998 survey by McCowan and Richardson, 526 business graduates who were employed for one year were sent a survey requiring rating of their levels of competence in the five areas of skills and abilities as well as the importance them in the workplace. They were also asked to indicate where these skills and abilities were primarily learned — at university, in the workplace, or through other social and community activity. Part 2 of the survey addressed the graduates' method of recording their achievement of these skills and abilities, who validated their achievement, and how they have practiced and developed these skills and abilities since graduation. The return rate was disappointing at 20%, but there was sufficient convergence of the data to suggest that more returns would have supported the same results.

All the skills in the leadership/management factor (leadership/influence, creativity and change, planning and organization, visioning and innovation, and managing conflict) were rated at high or very high importance in the workplace, the highest being planning and organization. Graduates rated their competence in these skills as average to high, with the highest being in planning/organization and creativity/change. Leadership, visioning, and managing conflict were skills in need of greater more competence. All these skills, other than planning and organization, were primarily learned in the workplace. The implication here is that since these skills and abilities are of high importance in the workplace and learned in the workplace, they need more developmental emphasis for students at university, thereby preparing students for such learning.

Over half the respondents rated their competence as high in the second factor, interpersonal/communication, which includes oral communication, written communication, teamwork, listening/responding, and working independently. The highest rating (93.8%) was for high or very high competence at working independently. All these skills received similar very high importance ratings in the workplace. Oral and written communications were primarily learned at university, listening/responding through social and community activity, and working independently was learned equally at university and the workplace.

Competence in the individual and corporate social responsibility factor was rated as high by the majority of respondents, with very high competence in the skills of appreciation of diversity and lifelong learning. These two skills were also rated as being of very high importance in the workplace, yet primarily learned at university. Social justice and community involvement were identified as being learned through social and community activity. The adventurous decision-making factor had lower levels of competence than other skills, apart form standards and ethics, in which 50% of the graduates claimed very high competence. Again, this skill was deemed of very high importance in the workplace, while risk taking had a lower level of importance than decision making and standards/ethics. The university was identified as the place where standards and ethics were primarily learned, and the workplace for decision making and risk taking.

The final factor, technical/professional/cognitive, which includes content knowledge, research skills, problem solving and analytical skills, and the ability to conceptualize, received high ratings for level of competence, but not very high ratings. Overall these competency ratings were lower than all other skills. This is a significant finding as these are the skills the business school believes it teaches its students. All these skills were rated as of high and very high importance in the workplace and primarily learned at university. This research exposed a gap in the teaching and learning in the business school.

Most graduates used their Curriculum Vitae (CV) to record their achievement of these skills and abilities, and 87.6% validate them by self-assessment. This is also significant, as it indicates that the university must teach self-assessment.

Figure 4 shows how graduates practice and develop their skills and abilities. The most frequently selected responses regarding ongoing skill development were as follows: 93% indicated "observing others in the workplace," 90.7% identified "reading and listening through various media," and 89.2% chose "working independently on projects." The option receiving the lowest response (32%) was "participating in a formal mentoring process."

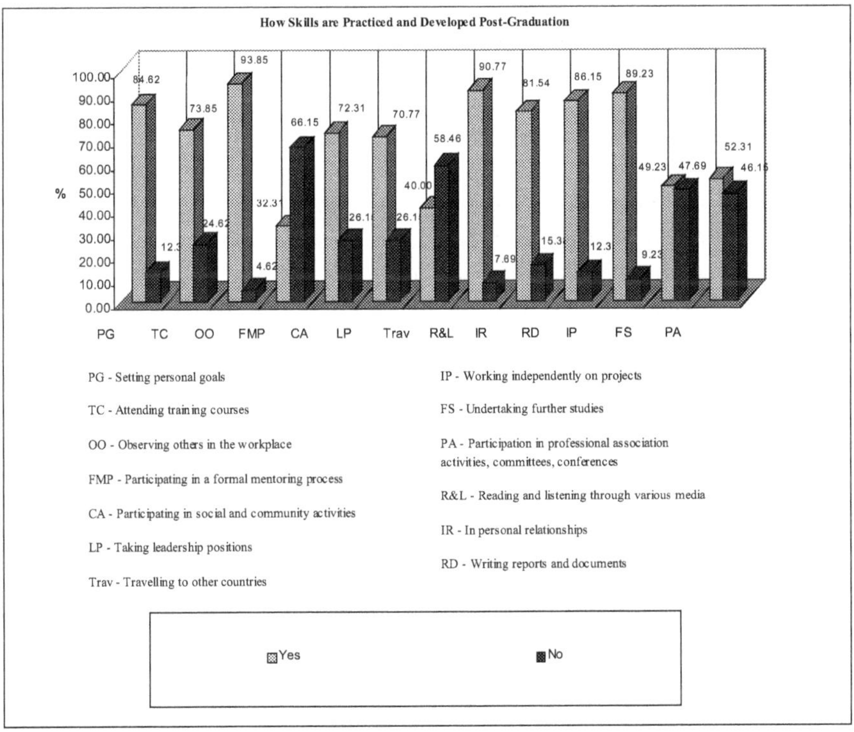

Figure 4. Graduate Response to Ongoing Skill Development

This stage of the study provided invaluable evidence on graduates' competence in a skill or ability when they are one year into employment. It isolated the levels of competence and importance in particular skills, and therefore the need for explicit inclusion of particular skills in the business curriculum and teaching and learning strategies. The university was identified as not preparing students for competence in the workplace in particular skills and abilities and this must be remedied. In relation to the theory of learning that lasts, these graduates reinforced the need for competence in self-assessment as the most important way in which graduates continue to practice and develop their skills and abilities. Observing others and listening and responding through various media as methods for development require individual reflection, assessment, and learning. The university has to accept responsibility for teaching self-assessment skills.

3.4 PROJECT 4 — Post Five-year Graduation Focus Groups 2003

In order to test these findings relating to learning that lasts, two focus groups were conducted in March 2003 with graduates of more than five years. A pool of QUT graduates known to the researcher from diverse courses and business disciplines were contacted by telephone and invited to participate in a focus group to discuss how they used in the workplace the knowledge and skills gained during university. Their length of employment ranged from five years to 15 years, and this employment represented public service, nonprofit organizations; the education sector; and private enterprise. The only screening was that the participant was a business graduate of QUT (or its predecessor institution) and had been employed for five years or more post graduation. They had no knowledge of the project and had not been engaged in any business education research previously. None of the participants knew each other. The focus groups were recorded and notes were taken by a research assistant to support the write-up of the discussion. The focus group participants were asked the six questions that are listed in Figure 5.

The answers to the first question included "research and data gathering," "where to go and search for information," "a framework to build new models," "management and report writing skills," "conceptual development," and "an underlying philosophy of how one does things." Most participants knew that the teaching and assessment had been explicit, but felt their learning of these skills was implicit through writing, research, and discussion. This implicit nature of learning skills was reinforced by the answers of where the skills are best learned. Participants referred to the "toolbox" of skills or framework learned during study, which are then developed in the workplace. Their practice and development of these skills since graduation occurred through training courses, working independently on projects, taking leadership positions, and participating in community and

1. Can you tell me what (if any) skills and abilities, other than the content knowledge of your discipline, you were taught or learned when you studied in the Faculty of Business[8] at QUT?
2. Was this teaching of generic skills explicit or implicit?
3. Where do you think these generic skills/graduate capabilities are best learned? Which ones? Why?
4. How have you practiced and developed these skills and abilities since graduation?
5. What is the best way that the Faculty of Business can link university learning and workplace learning?
6. How would you define or describe "learning that lasts"?

Figure 5. Focus Group Questions

professional committees and events. Importantly they stated that the skills are better learned at university where there is time to learn and a 'safety' in making mistakes in using these skills. The suggestions that participants gave for linking university and workplace learning included the use of real examples and information in the curriculum, assignments based on work and a real context, internships for students with limited work experience, more employer understanding of what a degree means, follow-up skill development or 'debriefing' after graduation, and teaching students how to find and use a mentor. Participants described 'learning that lasts' as "learning fundamental processes that can be universally applied," "the philosophical ability to give people broad and divergent perspectives and maintain their interest in learning," and a cycle of learning and application where "the university equips one with the skills to go through this cyclical learning."

4. CONCLUSION

Graduates of more than five years are clearly able to measure their university learning in application to the workplace. They described going

[8] In Australia, a School is labeled a Faculty. Thus the Faculty of Business is the same as a 'business school.'

back to texts, theories, and university assignments as a reference for new tasks in the workplace. They confirmed that their learning was founded in the explicit nature of knowledge and skill development, and they then subconsciously applied this in everyday work practices. Their ongoing employment and career planning came from the confidence they developed through this application of learning. The toolbox of skills and abilities learned at university provided a critical framework for effective workplace performance.

This final piece of research provided an answer to the hypothesis that *by teaching business students the generic capabilities for effective performance in the workplace, they are being taught learning that lasts*. Fully testing the hypothesis requires a longitudinal study of the students who were involved in the project of embedding skills and abilities in the curriculum through a case study of the Port of Brisbane Corporation. Early findings demonstrate this to be proven, despite the variables in the populations sampled over five years. As universities focus more on reducing the employability gap, this study suggests that teaching generic skills and abilities in the university curriculum will achieve lifelong learning practices, or 'learning that lasts.'

REFERENCES

Business Higher Education Round Table. (1991). *Identifying Key Attributes that Business Sought from University Graduates.* Melbourne.

Commonwealth of Australia. (2002) *Employability Skills of the Future.* Canberra: Department of Education, Science and Training.

Candy, P. C., Crebert, G., & O'Leary, J. (1994) *Developing Lifelong Learners Through Undergraduate Education, Commissioned Report No. 28.* Canberra: National Board of Employment, Education and Training.

Corporate Council on Education. (1994). *Employability Skills Profile.* Ottawa: The Conference Board of Canada.

De Corte, E. (1996). New perspectives of learning and teaching in higher education. In A. Burgen (Ed.), *Goals and Purposes of Higher Education in the 21st Century* (pp. 112-113). London: Jessica Kingsley.

Department of Education, Training and Youth Affairs DETYA. (2000). *Employer Satisfaction with Graduate Skills: Research Report 99/7*, February 2000. Canberra: Evaluations and Investigations Program, Higher Education Division, DETYA.

Employer Survey. (1998). South Australia: Flinders University.

Evers, F. T., Rush J. C., & Berdrow, I. (1998). *The Bases of Competence — Skills for Lifelong Learning and Employability.* San Francisco: Jossey-Bass.

Faculty of Business. (2000). Large Teaching and Learning Grant Application. Brisbane: Queensland University of Technology (QUT).

Hager, P., Holland, S., & Beckett, D. (2002). *Enhancing the Learning and Employability of Graduates: The Role of Generic Skills.* B-HERT Position Paper No. 9. Melbourne: Business Higher Education Round Table.

Hearn, G., Close, A., Smith, B., & Southey, G. (1992). *Developing Generic Professional Competencies in Australia: Towards a Framework for Professional Development*. Brisbane: Queensland University of Technology (QUT).

Karpin, D. (1995). *Enterprising Nation: Renewing Australia's Managers to Meet the Challenges of the Asia-Pacific Century: Report of the Industry Taskforce on Leadership and Management Skills*. Canberra: Australian Government Publishing Service.

Kirby, P. (2000). *Ministerial Review of Post Compulsory Education and Training Pathways in Victoria: Final Report*. Melbourne: Department of Education, Employment and Training.

Mayer Committee. (1992). *Key Competencies* (p. 8-9). Canberra: Australian Education Council.

McCowan, C., & Richardson, A. (1998). *Employer/Graduate Perceptions of the Skills and Abilities of Recent Business Graduates*. Brisbane: QUT Careers and Employment, Queensland University of Technology.

Mentkowski, M., & Associates. (2000). *Learning that Lasts – Integrated Learning, Development, and Performance in College and Beyond*. San Francisco: Jossey-Bass.

Oregon University C&E Services. (1990). *Making the Match, Third Student Survey, and Manager Survey*. Eugene, OR: Oregon University.

Chapter 16

HOW DISTANCE EDUCATION CAN SUSTAIN THE DEVELOPMENT OF COMPETENCIES

Herman van den Bosch
School of Management of the Open University of the Netherlands, Heerlen, the Netherlands

1. INTRODUCTION

During the last decennium, many universities have adopted innovative teaching and learning methods, such as problem-based and project learning. Due to these methods, students are developing skills in bridging the gap between theory and practice. They have exceeded the level of knowledge reproduction and entered the level of knowledge application. Critical success factors for these innovative processes include the use of real problems, the necessity to search for knowledge sources, and the possibility to work cooperatively.

Critical success factors such as the aforementioned seem to be associated with campus universities, which offer ample opportunities for students and teachers to meet at regular intervals. In distance universities, students and teachers only meet incidentally and students proceed at their own speed. Universities without face-to-face communication have to overcome difficulties when dealing with educational innovation.

Like other institutions for distance education, the Open University in the Netherlands (OUNL) and its School of Management have adopted a learning concept that focuses on the development of student's competencies. However, it proves to be quite difficult to realize this mission. First, this is difficult because of the need to design learning methods and assessment tools that enable students to link theory and practice. Second, it is difficult because the prevailing attitudes with regard to the reproduction of prefab content must be changed.

M.K. McCuddy et al. (eds.),
The Challenges of Educating People to Lead in a Challenging World, 325–342.

This chapter will elaborate upon the competency-based philosophy of learning adopted by the School of Management of the OUNL and show the design of the content and the teaching and learning strategies. Section 2 of the chapter briefly describes the shift in thinking with respect to goals and means in higher education. This section produces a shortlist of critical educational design factors for developing academic competencies. Section 3 is an overview of tools and procedures that can be applied in distance education in order to substitute for the above-mentioned critical educational design factors. This section is introduced by a short overview of the opportunities and constraints of using distance learning compared to traditional campus universities. Section 4 of the chapter offers a summary comparison of campus-based education and distance education with respect to the environmental characteristics that sustain competency development. Section 5 shows an example of a competency-based course: the basics of marketing.

2. DEVELOPING ACADEMIC COMPETENCIES

Most applicants for management jobs have obtained a bachelor degree at least. The relevance of this degree with respect to considerations related to the labor market has frequently been questioned. In particular, there are doubts regarding the ability of students to apply scientific theories and methods in a business context and in solving problems (Boyatzis, Cowen, & Kolb, 1995; Porter & McKibbin, 1988). In addition, Gijselaers states that the problem of freshmen is not so much the availability of knowledge, but the ability to create new knowledge within the context of an environment in which complexity prevails and quick changes take place (Gijselaers & Arts, 2003). "Employers demand graduates who are able to operate in complex environments, *i.e.*, environments characterized by ill-defined problems, contradictory information, informal collaboration and abstract, dynamic and highly integrated processes. The concept of competence is strongly associated with the ability to master such complex situations" (Westera, 2001).

In this section we will focus on the features of the curriculum that are critical in the development of the aforementioned competencies. Based upon practice and the current literature on university education, we have identified six characteristics, which together create conditions for students to develop the competencies as mentioned above (Duffy & Jonassen, 1992; Jonassen & Land, 2000; Merrill, 2000; Perkins & Salomon, 1988; Ramsden, 1992; Van den Bosch & Kieft, 2001; Van Merriënboer, 1997). These characteristics are:

- Learning is based on tasks, representing the pursued competencies.
- Learning becomes more realistic by applying cases.
- Giving feedback is a major role of the teacher.
- Learning is a collaborative act.
- Students have to search actively for information.
- Education should afford different learning paths.

2.1 Tasks

In traditional education, students begin with studying the learning materials and later they apply their newly acquired knowledge to problems. In competency-based education students are advised to start thinking about how they will manage tasks. It is only when they have a basic idea on how to approach tasks that they will be offered advice to thoroughly study essential reading materials.

Tasks or assignments invite students to analyze or solve theoretical or practical problems that are remotely or directly related to the relevant field of study. In order to be challenging, tasks will have to generate at least 20 hours of study. Sometimes it is better to subdivide tasks into subtasks. In general, the length of the description of tasks will not exceed 100 – 200 words. The same applies to subtasks.

The handling of tasks usually involves alternation between group work and individual study. For instance, in problem-based learning students meet in order to define a problem and an approach to the problem, and within a few days they meet to report the outcomes of their individual studies.

Tasks will vary with respect to: (1) the prescription of scientific and other sources; (2) the degree of freedom in defining the problem; and (3) the level of specificity. An example of a task with a small degree of freedom with respect to defining the problem and a low level of specificity is "Define three conditions under which increased inflation has favorable economic effects." Tasks not only promote active learning, but also activate prior knowledge.

Accomplishing a task may be facilitated by more or less detailed references to sources, which contain building blocks of the answer.

2.2 Cases

In a competency-based approach, the tasks provide the framework and guidance for working on the problem or situation. This situation is frequently presented with the help of case studies. Cases are useful when students are encouraged to relate theory and practice and when they have to analyze or define solutions by considering realistic circumstances. Cases usually have a high degree of motivational value.

Case studies generally have two components: (1) A description of a problem or situation: descriptions of practice (conflicts, procedures, negotiations). (2) Data: these are case resources that students need to study or apply to the problem or situation, such as statistical data, transcripts of interviews, brochures, etc.

Cases have to be carefully selected or designed with regard to the goal and content of the task. Cases may vary in many respects, including the following:

- Length: depends on the number of tasks or subtasks.
- Linearity: the use of the Internet offers the possibility to broaden the main body of the case in many respects.
- Completeness: a case may contain all needed information; however, the task may also require students to find information themselves.
- Structure: cases may vary from structured stories to seemingly isolated pieces of information; for instance, a selection of statistics.

Cases can be handled in many different ways. The use of realistic data as part of a task is an example of a modest use. Research carried out by students at companies as part of a project may also be considered to be a case approach. In addition to written information, cases can be enriched by guest lectures and company visits. Moreover, the Internet offers useful information about the company under study.

2.3 Feedback

In traditional classes a dominant role of the teacher is explaining the learning content, even before students have made serious attempts to master it themselves. This attitude does not favor active learning behavior. Therefore, in competency-based learning students have to think and to be productive in advance. The teacher can then comment upon their work at a later stage.

Feedback is time consuming and therefore it has to be well organized. A distinction can be made between standard feedback and personalized feedback. Classes or even lectures are appropriate means for delivering standard feedback. For personalized feedback to occur, however, face-to-face contacts with tutors are most appropriate.

The role attributed to feedback is changing the role of assessments. In competency-based learning, students earn a significant part of their marks — if not all — by submitting papers and carrying out other activities such as presentations. Assessments gradually cease to be a nervous and haphazard demonstration of students' knowledge, which often take place in a setting that is not very representative of real life. Assessment is authentic when the performance of students is tested with regard to worthy intellectual tasks. Traditional assessment, by contract, relies on indirect or proxy 'items' — efficient, simplistic substitutes from which no valid inferences can be made about the student's performance (Wiggins, 1990).

2.4 Collaboration

Cooperation between students is promoted for many reasons, including the effects on their motivation and an increasing efficiency resulting from the division of tasks. From a constructivist perspective, cooperation helps in constructing more complete and mature knowledge. Knowledge is considered as resulting from interaction between a person and parts of the environment. The resulting constructs are at least partially unique for one who is observant. Sharing views contributes to constructing a multi-perspective view (Barab & Duffy, 1998; Gunawardena, 2003).

Collaboration in face-to-face education is usually an organic process, which does not require any arrangements and facilities. In the case of inexperienced students, tutors supervise the process of group building. Groups meet on a regular basis, possibly in the presence of a tutor. In general, a tutor monitors the dynamics of the group, which allows him or her to examine the contribution of the individual group members.

2.5 Active Searching in Learning Resources

Academics spend a considerable amount of time searching for relevant literature sources. Students are offered books, reading lists, and readers. However, an active search of scientific and other sources should be part of promoting active learning.

The availability of a broad variety of books, journals, documents, statistics, proceedings, and archives is considered to be a useful commodity in universities for promoting problem-based or project learning. 'Study landscapes' or 'study centers' were constructed as places where students can find sources and have room to think, study, discuss, or write. Such facilities proved to be indispensable in creating a favorable climate for active learning.

2.6 Personal Differences

Students differ in learning styles and prior knowledge. Educational institutions usually select one predominant strategy and group their students accordingly. Traditionally, students went to classes or lectures and spent the rest of their time on individual study. However, competency-based strategies highlighted working in (small) groups. There are only few examples of universities that allow students to choose between separate 'tracks'.

Nowadays differences between students increase. A growing number of students already have work experience. In addition, their average age is also higher. Differences in prior knowledge, abilities and study preferences are also increasing. Educational institutions feel the pressure to find an adequate answer to these challenges.

3. DISTANCE LEARNING

Originally, distance learning was a facility for people who failed to take their chance to study at a young age and at a campus-based university. Nowadays, distance education is a realistic alternative for people, who deliberately choose to combine studying and working. Distance education is a flexible answer for people who cannot or who do not want to spend a considerable time at the campus and adapt their pace to the majority of the students. Distance education creates facilities for students to follow an individual path of study, adapting their learning strategy to prior knowledge and study preferences. Last but not least, distance learning can unite students from different parts of the world, who otherwise would not be able to join a face-to-face program.

The main disadvantage of distance education is that the limited face-to-face contacts can induce feelings of alienation. This can be prevented by:

- Limiting traditional learning, reading, and exams to a minimum. Instead, different more active methods can be explored based on mutual learning at a distance.
- Focusing on the working environments of the students. The students are experienced officials and each student brings a set of 'cases' and experiences into the learning process.
- Combining cognitive and skills training.
- Combining reading, writing, discussions, workshops, and videoconferencing and virtual classrooms.
- Quick response-time for tutors (questions should be answered preferably within one day; rules have to be negotiated).

Distance education has changed during the last decade. Until recently many people regarded distance education more or less as an equivalent of readable and richly illustrated study books, with a built-in guidance. Nowadays distance education has many guises, also as a result of the use of information and communications technology (ICT).

However, the main challenge is the implementation of competency-based learning. This brings us to the question of whether it is feasible to adopt the six characteristics of an active learning environment in distance learning. Below we will discuss how universities may implement this adoption.

3.1 Tasks

Tasks can be used in distance education without drastic adaptations. However, there will be no frequent exchange of results with other students. Students in distance education programs praise the freedom to study at their own speed. Consequently, feedback has to be given by the tutor or through an automatic feedback-generating device.

Because of the absence of regular meetings, it is necessary to have a greater structure in the handling of tasks in distance education than in a face-to-face environment. Tasks in distance education will contain the following information:

- A reference to a (real life) problem.
- A description of the expected activities (what a student should do) and the product the student has to deliver.
- The criteria for an acceptable product.
- Information on how a student should approach the task.
- The time available for finishing the task.
- If and how the task is going to be assessed.
- A description of the learning resources.

3.2 Cases

Cases usually are based on written or digital information of companies and institutions. Consequently, the presentation of cases in face-to-face learning and in distance learning does not differ significantly. In fact, face-to-face learning uses the virtues of the Internet as a tool to find company information.

In addition, digital devices may be used to offer short presentations and lectures of relevant company spokesmen. However, they will not show up regularly in classes.

In addition, some variants of case studies are more or less limited to use in distance education. Among these, the virtual company may be mentioned, although there are resemblances with gaming simulation in face-to-face education. In a virtual company, students deal with business problems in an asynchronous way. Roles are assigned and new data are added regularly.

3.3 Feedback

The necessity of frequent feedback — standardized or personalized — is a major challenge in distance education. Traditional models of distance education generally lacked feedback. The cost structure of distance education focuses on investments in materials that can be studied without any substantial support. High investments are compensated by low variable costs. Competency-based distance learning involves high investments and high variable costs. Consequently, a reconsideration of the production process is necessary. The standard feedback is automated through ICT, by delivering standardized responses to cases. Experienced course developers will be able to anticipate student mistakes or omissions. They can offer sample answers and instructions for correction, which students can compare with the answers of their own. In addition, multiple-choice self-tests are introduced in order to give students the opportunity to monitor the mastery of their subject matter.

Competency-based education requires students to produce non-standardized answers to complex questions and tasks. For this reason, personalized feedback is indispensable. In order to make efficient use of the tutor's time, smart solutions have been introduced. For instance, the system randomly selects a number of assignments, which are commented upon. The tutor offers his or her comments upon a preliminary answer, suggests necessary improvements and subsequently checks the final result. In addition, tutors make use of programs that deliver building blocks for editing feedback.

In order to limit the tutor's time, a bombardment of e-mails by mostly a minority of the students will have to be avoided. Communication through e-mail should therefore be minimal and tutor-student communication should take place in a moderated discussion list. The primary focus of such a list is that students answer each other's questions. The tutor's role is to supervise the process, structure the discussion and step in, in case of evident mistakes. Only when personal affairs have to be discussed, students are allowed to mail the tutor directly.

3.4 Collaboration

Collaboration between distance learning students occurs less naturally than in face-to-face education. Many students cherish the time and place independency offered by distance learning and fear collaboration will affect this freedom in a negative way. On the other hand, and often after initial resistance, some of the students learn to appreciate the social dimension of their studies as a result of this collaboration.

Discussion lists are frequently used in order to regulate interaction between students. In addition, team rooms are created. Team rooms offer facilities for small groups of students to collaborate, for instance to write a group paper (Van den Bosch & Bolluyt, 2001). In a team room students can find discussion facilities and facilities to share and manage documents.

Synchronic communication can be arranged through simple means such as chatting and more sophisticated means such as video conferencing. Asynchronic communication is more adapted to the characteristics of distance learners, particularly when several languages are involved.

3.5 Active Searching in Learning Resources

Traditionally, students carefully study textbooks and then are examined. However, in competency-based learning students apply scientific sources 'just in time' in order to analyze or solve the problems presented to them by tasks and cases. Learning resources, for instance, are textbooks, articles, manuals, and statistical tools. In distance education, active searching does not encounter any limitations. Extensive library services offered many advantages to students in campus universities. The growth of digital sources — the Internet, but in particular digital books and journals — leveled off this advantage.

Some distance learning suppliers even deliver all learning resources via the Web. Consequently, students have to read textbooks from the screen or print them. Generally, students prefer the delivery of essential reading material in printed form.

In the learning resources, a distinction can be made between essential reading material and additional reading material. Essential reading materials are those materials that provide students with the supportive knowledge they need to solve a problem or carry out a knowledge-creation task. These materials provide the basic cognitive structures, methods of procedures. A digital library, electronic journal, and a data base with information objects (Barritt, Lewis, & Wieseler, 1999; Wieseler, 2001) will facilitate this goal.

In addition to essential reading materials, students should be able to find resources on their own in an academic environment. The Internet — in addition to libraries — offers ample useful material. The overwhelming problem is to find this material. It is for this reason that additional training in searching the Internet will be provided to students who need this.

3.6 Personal Differences

Distance learning is suited well to deal with personal differences because of the personalized character of distance learning methods and the availability of ICT tools, which make it possible to combine standardized learning objects in various ways. For example, students who prefer a deductive approach to learning will be offered theoretical knowledge before information on a case is provided. Students with inductive learning preferences like to get acquainted with a case prior to their inventory of relevant theoretical viewpoints.

In addition to adapting learning material to learning styles, intake assessment is another tool that can be adapted to individual differences between students.

Distance learning institutions are only at the outset of delivering tailored-made learning packages. A major contribution to the viability of distance learning will be made, if customization of learning materials is feasible.

4. A COMPARISON BETWEEN CAMPUS-BASED AND DISTANCE EDUCATION

Section 2 of the chapter was a description of the main characteristics of competency development in campus universities. In section 3, an inventory was made of the opportunities and constraints of distance education with respect to competency-based learning. The conclusion was that environmental characteristics favoring competency-based learning in campus-based universities could be adapted to the characteristics of distance learning. This section of the chapter offers a summary comparison of campus-based education and distance education with respect to the environmental characteristics that sustain competency development.

Figure 1 compares features that develop competencies in both educational modes. Working with tasks, cases, and stimulation of active search in scientific sources do not offer major problems. Tasks may need more elaboration, because of the absence of a teacher, who clarifies passages, which evoke questions. If distance education uses the Internet, the use of cases and the active search for information even will be easier, because of the nearly unrestricted availability of data.

However, the introduction of cost-effective solutions for feedback and the implementation of collaboration are more challenging. This is not inherent to distance education, but a consequence of the preference of many distance students to work individually. The merits of a personalized approach, which are characteristic of distance education par excellence, still have to be realized to a large extent. With respect to the creation of individualized learning paths, distance learning has advantages in comparison with campus-based education.

	Tasks	**Cases**	**Feedback**	**Colla-boration**	**Active search**	**Learning paths**
Face to face	•Real problems •Relating theory and practice •Prescribed procedure	•Description of reality •Data and resources	•Main role of the teacher •Standard versus personalized feedback	•Elaboration of tasks in groups •Motivation •Efficiency •Multi-perspective •Skills	•Academic attitude •Broad variety of sources •Academic workplaces	•Tendency towards uniform approach •Separate tracks
Distance learning	•No frequent exchange of ideas •Need of structure	•Multi media •Company presentation	•High degree of standardi-zation in feedback •Answering devices •Efficiency in examination	•Resistance •Team room facilities •Merits of asynchronic work	•Electronic sources	•Place and time indepen-dency •Persona-lization according to learning styles •Intake as-sessment

Figure 1. Features that Develop Competencies in Face-to-Face and Distance Education

5. EXAMPLE: BASICS OF MARKETING

In the final part of this chapter, the reader will be introduced to the OUNL course 'Basics of Marketing' (average study load per student: 200 hours). Most principles mentioned above have been applied. At the time this chapter was prepared, about 450 students have participated in this course in which a handbook was applied as essential reading material. Students greatly appreciated the course and pass-rates are encouragingly high. The proceedings of the course are explained below, based on the characteristics of competency-based learning, introduced earlier, except for collaboration, which did not apply to this course. For illustrative purposes a (limited) set of screen dumps have been added and are explained.

5.1 Tasks

The course is comprised of two pairs of 16 tasks. These are made visible in the left window (Figure 2). One set of tasks is for practice, and the other — equivalent — set serves examination purposes.

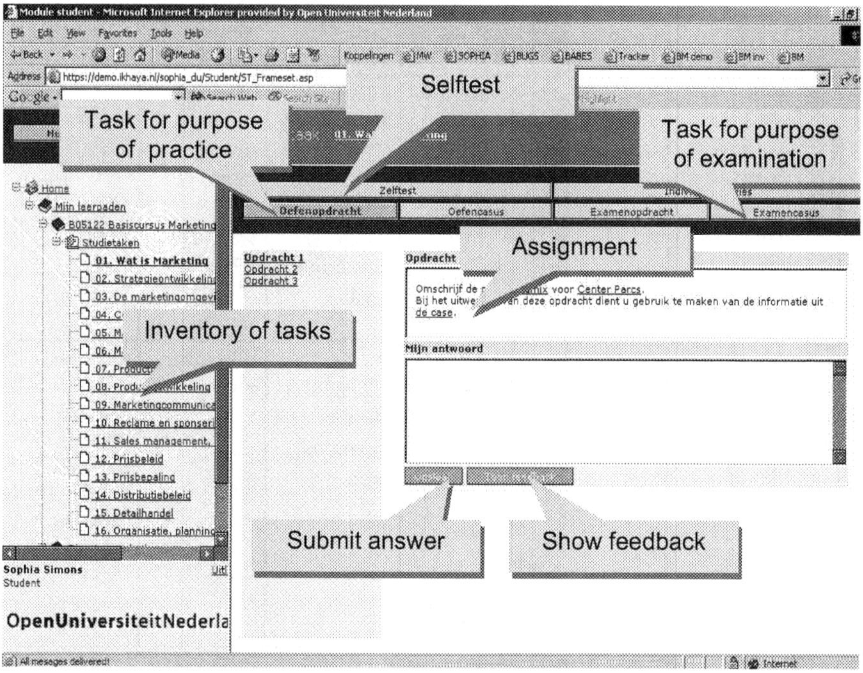

Figure 2. Answering Form

A task covers one chapter of the book. Tasks are subdivided into three to five assignments. Each assignment is made visible in the window called *Opdracht* (assignment). Students have to complete their answer in the window called *Mijn antwoord* (My answer).

One set of tasks has to be carried out for the purpose of practice (*oefenopdracht*). The second group is part of the examination (*examenopdracht*).

5.2 Cases

Each task is associated with a case. The case includes relevant material as facts and figures, links to Web sites and short videos. Figure 3 shows the screen that is made visible after pressing the button *Oefencasus* (task for purpose of practice). Students need the information obtainable from the case when they want to practice the task. From this window students can find relevant information about Center Parcs, visit the official Web site or print a summary of the case materials.

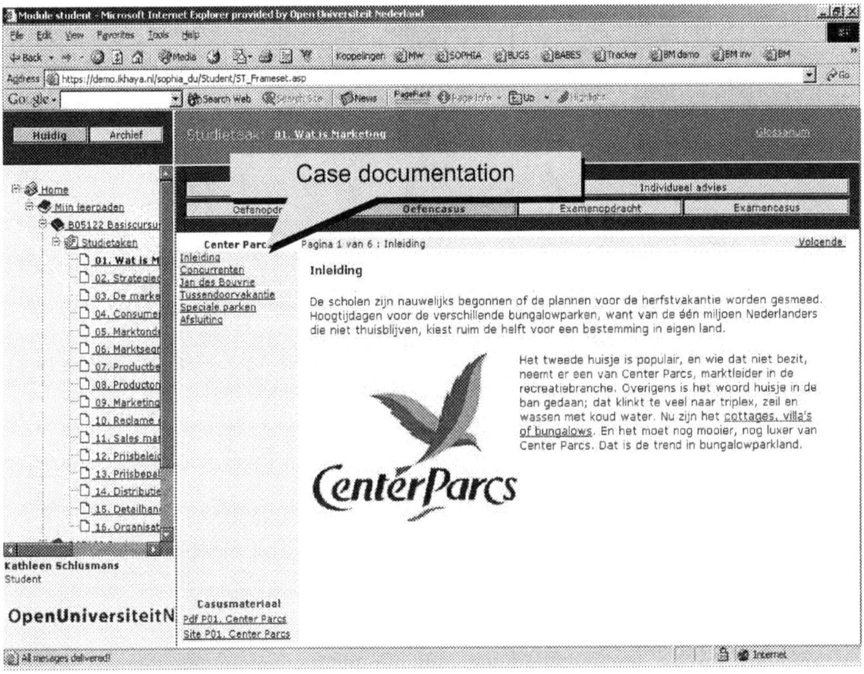

Figure 3. Example of a Case

5.3 Feedback

After finishing an assignment in the practice mode, students can compare their answer with the standard, by pressing the button *Toon feedback* (show feedback) (see Figure 2). In addition, a tutor monitors the process and he or she might call to order students who are not serious enough about the process, although the submission of assignments in the practice mode is voluntary.

In the examination mode all 16 tasks and accompanying assignments have to be submitted. Four tasks are chosen arbitrarily in order to make the process of producing summative feedback more efficient. For purposes of grading, teachers may compare the answers of students and the way their colleagues valued these. Identical answers may create suspicion.

Figure 4 is derived from the tutor's environment. As soon as a student has submitted all answers, the system makes a selection and the teacher can start grading. The selected tasks are offered to the teacher. The ideal answer is made visible when he or she presses the button *Standaardantwoord* (right answer). The button *Antwoordgeschiedenis* (all answers submitted) shows the responses of other students as well as the marks they received.

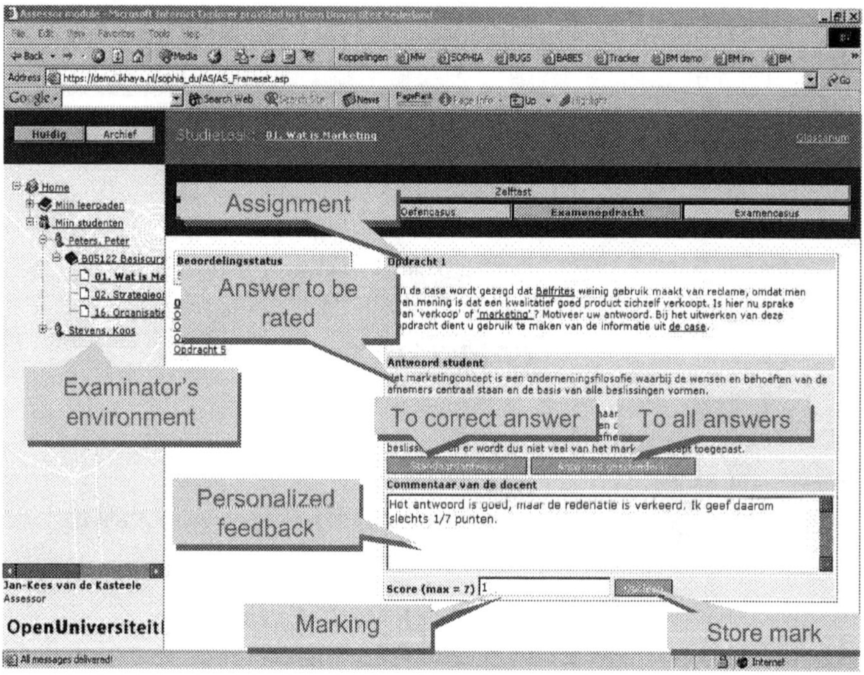

Figure 4. The Grading Environment

The window *Commentaar van de docent* (teacher's commentary) offers room for brief feedback. The grade of the student is shown in the box called *Score* (marking).

5.4 Active search for Learning Resources

In addition to the manual, students have a glossary at their disposal in which 1,000 concepts are explained. The glossary is searchable. Concepts in tasks and assignments and corresponding parts of the glossary are hyperlinked with the glossary. When students activate a hyperlink, a pop-up window appears with the corresponding part of the glossary (Figure 5).

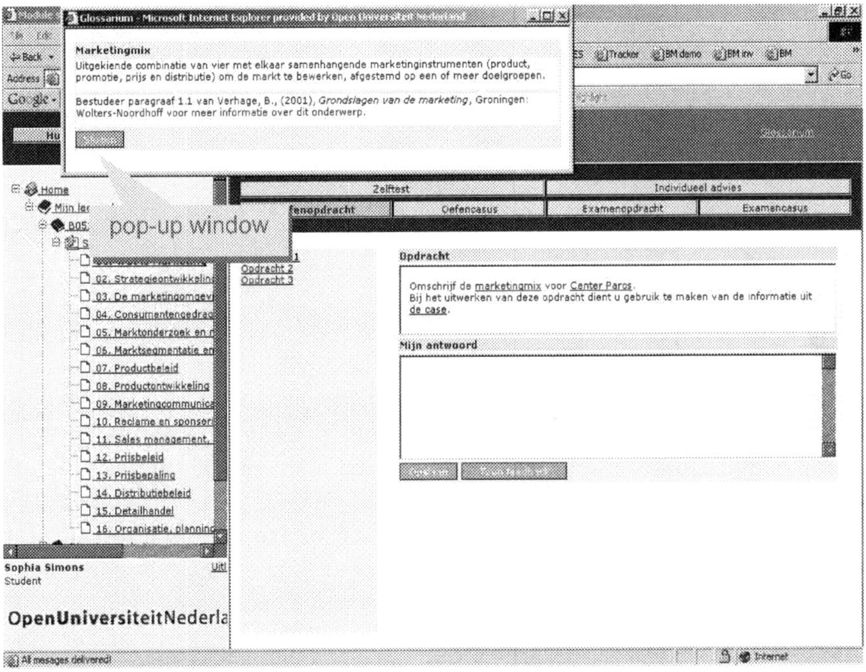

Figure 5. Pop-up Window

This is only the beginning of a promising development. The actual glossary has been obtained from the manual. In the future it is possible that main disciplinary concepts and methods are captured in reusable information objects, which are course-independent.

Active searching is even more requested within the cases. Information about the cases is presented in a non-linear fashion and students will have to scan the material in order to find relevant information.

5.5 Personal Differences

Prior knowledge of participants in the course will differ considerably. For this reason and in order to focus the attention of students on the assignments, a self-test accompanies each task (see Figure 2). Students are advised to test themselves before reading the book. After each (multiple choice) question feedback is generated and when all questions have been completed the students will obtain study advice. Students who answered all questions well do not have to read the accompanying parts of the manual. For them it will suffice to consult the glossary.

As prior knowledge appears to be sufficient and students are more experienced with the proceedings, many stop practicing and turn directly towards the examination mode.

6. CONCLUSION

In the first part of the chapter, an inventory was drawn up of the characteristics of a competency-based learning environment in a face-to-face situation. In the last decade distance education has been revitalized as a result of the growing diversity of students regarding prior knowledge, learning styles and learning goals, and the need to combine study and other activities.

In section 3, an inventory has been made of the opportunities of and constraints on distance education with respect to competency-based learning. Environmental characteristics that favor competency-based learning in campus-based universities can be adapted to the characteristics of distance learning. That means there is no differentiation between competency-based learning and distance education. However, the case 'Basics of Marketing' illustrated that competency-based distance education relies heavily on the support of ICT. This support is needed in at least four domains:

- The organizational frame of the learning process.
- Instruction.
- Interaction.
- Delivery of information.

Working with tasks, cases, and stimulation of active search in scientific sources does not offer major problems. The use of the Internet even stimulates active search for information and the use of cases. The future will likely show that distance learning has advantages in comparison with campus-based education with respect to the creation of individualized learning paths. The introduction of cost-effective solutions for feedback and the implementation of collaboration appear to be more challenging.

The general conclusion is that the advantages of distance education (learning at your own pace and speed and at any place) are not restricted to more traditional learning objectives such as the transmission of information, but also apply to innovative learning objectives as well.

REFERENCES

Barab, S. A., & Duffy, T. M. (1998). *From Practice Fields to Communities of Practice.* (CRLT Technical Report No. 1-98). Bloomington: Indiana University.

Barritt, C., Lewis, D., & Wieseler, W. (1999). *Cisco Systems Reusable Information Object Strategy*. San José, CA.: Cisco Systems.

Boyatzis, R. E., Cowen, S. S., & Kolb, D. A. (1995). *Innovation in Professional Education: Steps on a Journey from Teaching to Learning: The Story of Change and Invention at the Weatherhead School of Management*. 1st ed. San Francisco: Jossey-Bass Publishers.

Duffy, T. M., & Jonassen, D. H. (1992). Constructivism: New implications for instructional technology. In D. H. Jonassen (Ed.), *Constructivism and the Technology of Instruction: A Conversation* (pp. 1-16). Hillsdale, NJ: Lawrence Erlbaum Associates.

Gijselaers, W. H., & Arts, J. (2003). Transfer of knowledge within the managerial workplace. In H. P. A. Boshuizen (Ed.), *Expertise Development: The Transition Between School and Work* (pp. 75-94). Heerlen: Open Universiteit Nederland.

Gunawardena, C. N. (2003). Theory into practice: The challenge of designing inquiry-based online learning environments. In J. R. Kirkley (Ed.), *Learner Centered Theory and Practice in Distance Education: Cases from Higher Education* (pp. 130-146). Mahwah, NJ: Lawrence Erlbaum & Associates.

Jonassen, D. H., & Land, S. M. (2000). *Theoretical Foundations of Learning Environments*. Mahwah NJ: Lawrence Erlbaum & Associates.

Merrill, M. D. (2000). *First principles of education*. Paper presented at the International Conference of the Association for Educational Communications and Technology (AECT), Denver, CO.

Perkins, D., & Salomon, G. (1988). Are cognitive skills context-bound? *Educational Researcher, 18*, 1, 16-25.

Porter, L., & McKibbin, L. (1988). *Management Education and Development. Drift or Thrust into the 21st Century*. New York: McGraw-Hill.

Ramsden, P. (1992). *Learning to Teach in Higher Education*. London: Routledge.

Van den Bosch, H. M. J., & Bolluyt, J. (2001). The use of hypertext in the writing of group papers. *Journal of Computer-assisted Learning, 17,* 4, 355-362.

Van den Bosch, H. M. J., & Kieft, M. (2001). The hybrid curriculum; the acquisition of academic competencies in the university curriculum. In W. H. Gijselaers (Ed.), *Educational Innovation in Economics and Business Administration*, Part V. (pp. 41-56). Dordrecht: Kluwer Academic Press.

Van Merriënboer, J. J. G. (1997). *Training Complex Cognitive Skills: A Four-Component Instructional Design Model for Technical Training*. Englewood Cliffs, NJ: Educational Technology Publications.

Westera, W. (2001). Competences in education: A confusion of tongues. *Journal of Curriculum Studies, 33*, 1, 75-88.

Wieseler, W. (2001). *RIO: A Standards Based Approach for Reusable Information Objects*. San José, CA: Cisco Systems white paper.

Wiggins, G. (1990). *The Case for Authentic Assessment*. Eric Digests, ERIC Identifier: ED328611.

Chapter 17

THE ETHICAL EDUCATION OF FUTURE LEADERS

An Approach for Helping Students Become Authentic Ethical Role Models

Michael K. McCuddy
Valparaiso University, College of Business Administration, Valparaiso, Indiana, USA

1. INTRODUCTION

Over the past few years, ethical scandals have occurred in all too many companies around the world. Some of the prominent ones gaining extensive media attention include Adelphia, Arthur Andersen, Enron, Tyco, and WorldCom, all headquartered in the United States; Adecco and Parmalat in Europe; and Yukos in Russia. The impact of these and other scandals have been felt around the world. Oppenheimer (2001) describes how U.S. multinational companies, including IBM and Citibank, have contributed to corruption in Latin America. Additionally, Spain's Banco Bilbao Vizcya Argentaria has been charged with money laundering, questionable cash transfers, and secret political campaign contributions in its Latin American operations (Dempsey, 2002). Also in Latin America, smaller companies, which represent the majority of businesses there, tend to resist pressures for greater transparency in financial reporting (Dempsey, 2002). Walerius (2004), in a commentary on Middle Eastern nations, observes that businesses are often the source of corruption and sometimes oppose efforts to eliminate corruption. Numerous other examples exist throughout the world — no nation or geographic region seems to be immune to corruption.

The ethical failures at these companies typically have been attributed to a failure of leadership, to the creation and maintenance of an unethical culture, or quite often both. As Trice and Beyer observe, an important "consideration

M.K. McCuddy et al. (eds.),
The Challenges of Educating People to Lead in a Challenging World, 343–359.

in any management of organizational culture is whether such management is ethical" (1993, p. 370). Enron's ethical failure, for example, has been widely attributed to both a leadership failure and a culture that encouraged unethical decisions and actions (Fowler, 2002). Ruettgers (2003) describes Enron as a company with a corporate culture that allowed individual self-interest to run amok. Another example is provided by Tyco's ethical problems, which have been attributed to the need for changes in its corporate culture (Bray, 2004).

There is a saying — "the fish stinks from the head" — that provides an interesting perspective about leadership failure. When a fish rots, the odor emanates from the head. When the top leadership is unethical, the organization is like the rotting fish — it stinks from the head of the organization. Sometimes the top-level executives, through their decisions and actions, are directly involved in these ethical failures; other times, the decisions and actions of other organization members are directly implicated in the ethical failures. Nonetheless, when a significant ethical failure occurs in an organization, the ultimate responsibility for that failure lies with the top-level executives of the organization — even if they have not been direct players in the unethical decisions and actions. Top-level leaders set the moral tone for the organization and have a profound impact on the development and maintenance of an ethical organizational culture (Ruettgers, 2003).

"Ethical leadership is vital in an organization. … it is the leader's ethical conduct guided by moral principles and integrity that gives legitimacy and credibility to the vision and sustains it. Without ethical leadership, the organization is a soulless structure. When the leader's moral integrity is in doubt, then the leader's vision — however noble, well-crafted, and articulated, is viewed with skepticism by the followers, loses its vigor, and is incapable of moving them to work toward its realization" (Kanungo & Mendonca, 1998, pp. 49-50).

While top-level leaders play crucial roles in the ethical successes and failures of organizations, leaders at all levels of organizations — from top-level executives on down to the first-line supervisors and team leaders — must serve as ethical role models and promote and reinforce ethical decisions and actions among their followers. Consequently, all people who would become effective and respected leaders at any level in our global society's economic and social institutions must learn to be *authentic ethical role models* for their followers. Ruettgers (2003) makes the compelling argument that integrity must permeate an organization but that integrity at any level of the organization is limited by the intent and behavior of the top-level leaders.

The author suggests that becoming an *authentic ethical role model* rests on fulfilling four key requirements. First, becoming an *authentic ethical role model* requires people to become acutely aware of their own moral orientation and how they are developing as moral individuals. Second, it requires people to be cognizant of how their personal moral orientation fits with broader community expectations, values, and norms. Third, it requires people to examine how their personal moral orientation affects their decisions and actions on various organizational issues. Finally, it requires people to explore how the decisions they make and the actions they take will affect relationships with and the interests of the organization's various stakeholders.

This paper describes an approach to teaching business ethics that seeks to meaningfully address the preceding four requirements for becoming an *authentic ethical role model*. This educational approach provides content material pertaining to the fundamental theories and concepts that explain and guide ethical thinking, reasoning, decision making, and actions. However, content is not the primary emphasis of this educational approach. Rather, the educational process is targeted toward personal consciousness-raising for each student. Each future leader is challenged to examine the kind of moral being he/she has become and the kind of moral being he/she wants to become in his/her future personal life and professional life, and how his/her personal and emerging professional morality links to the workplace and the broader social community. In addition, the paper provides details regarding how the topical coverage, course assignments, and daily class activities foster student exploration of their ongoing development as moral beings.

2. THE AUTHENTIC ETHICAL ROLE MODEL

Any individual can serve as a role model for other people. The individual's decisions and actions can influence others and provide guidance to them in their own conduct. No individual can force another person to act morally or immorally. Each human being has the free will to choose between what is right, fair, and just and what is wrong, unfair, and unjust. An individual who makes decisions and take actions that are exemplars of that which is right, fair, and just is an *authentic ethical role model*.

2.1 What Is an Authentic Ethical Role Model?

Human beings are imperfect creatures — although some people appear to think otherwise. Since inherently imperfect human beings make decisions and implement those decisions, there is no certainty as to the ethicality of such decisions and actions. Some decisions and actions are likely to be inherently evil and immoral, deliberately seeking to exploit and/or deceive others. Some decisions and actions are likely to be pseudomoral; such decisions and actions create the illusion of morality while enabling the person to covertly act otherwise. Some decisions and actions are likely to be amoral in that ethical considerations and concerns are not on the person's "radar screen." Some — one would hope many — decisions and actions are ethical, reflecting true moral intent in the pursuit of that which is right, fair, and just. This does not mean that all ethical decisions and actions will proceed without flaw or difficulty; mistakes will occur even when people act on the basis of good intentions. But the mistakes are just that — mistakes!

"Ethical leadership can be said to exist when moral intent and principles inform and guide the leader's actions" (Kanungo & Mendonca, 1998, p. 50). The *authentic ethical role model* always strives to make decisions and take actions that are right, fair, and just in dealing with all relevant stakeholders. The *authentic ethical role model* operates on the basis of true moral intent — the unwavering commitment to pursuing right, fair, and just solutions. Another key point is that the *authentic ethical role model* will inevitably make mistakes, but will seek to correct them in a right, fair, and just manner and to learn from them for the benefit of as many stakeholders as possible — and ideally all stakeholders.

Authentic ethical role models often base their moral intent on some understanding of spirituality and spiritual wisdom. In a business context, moral intent based on spiritual wisdom can provide guidance regarding the purpose and pursuit of money (earning profits), establishing partnerships, exercising stewardship, handling multiple responsibilities, developing innovations, being entrepreneurial, and more (Graves & Addington, 2003).

2.2 Why Are Authentic Ethical Role Models Important?

Clearly, the immoral, amoral, and pseudomoral options for making decisions and taking actions are not admirable paths to pursue. The only viable path to pursue — if one wishes to achieve sustainable long-term success and to make genuine and valuable contributions to society — is the moral one. This implies that both means and ends are important. Some people would argue from a *teleological* perspective that the ends, or consequences of one's decisions and actions, constitute the essential criterion by which the morality of decision and actions should be evaluated. Others would argue that a means-based, or *deontological* perspective, should be used in evaluating the morality of decisions and actions. In short, the argument is that as long as the means are moral, even "bad outcomes" can be acceptable. Choosing between the two perspectives constitutes a forced choice — an "either/or" decision. Many phenomena — and morality from a means/ends perspective is one of them — are not purely one-sided. Rather, the evaluation of decisions and actions as being moral or not should embrace criteria reflecting means as well as ends — it is a "both/and" phenomenon, not an "either/or" one. It also provides the justification for arguing that the moral option, rather than the amoral, pseudomoral, or immoral options, is the path to long-term success and genuine societal contributions.

Authentic ethical role models are committed to the moral path. They help others to appreciate the value of moral decisions and actions. They help others learn to make decisions and take actions that reflect fair and just balancing of the interests of all stakeholders. They are positive exemplars of the possibilities — of serving both self and others — that grow out of true concern for doing what is right, fair, and just for all parties concerned, including oneself. In short, *authentic ethical role models* can light the way as others pursue their moral journeys.

As noted in the introduction, leaders at all levels of organizations can and must serve as *authentic ethical role models* for others. While the top echelon of an organization profoundly influences the development and maintenance of an ethical organizational culture, middle-level and lower-level leaders are the ones who translate the culture into the organization's daily operations and activities. Emanating from the top-level leaders, each subsequently lower level of leadership helps operationalize and sustain an organization's culture — whether it is ethical or unethical. Ultimately, the lower-level leaders are the ones who assume substantial responsibility for making the culture come alive for non-supervisory organizational participants. Thus, all leaders throughout an organization should strive to be *authentic ethical role models*.

One might argue that *authentic ethical role models* are important in business because the alternative of more and more Enrons, Tycos, Adelphias, WorldComs, and Parmalats, to name several, is simply unacceptable! Although there are undoubtedly other cases of ethical failure similar to the Enrons and WorldComs, they have received less publicity. Undoubtedly, there are also instances of ethical failure that have not been exposed in the media and are therefore away from the public's consciousness. Nonetheless, the publicized ethical failures have fueled society's expectations of and demand for greater morality, accountability, and transparency in business. This also is a reflection of what might be called a cultural shift in society. Increasingly, business enterprises are expected to simultaneously make genuine contributions to society and operate effectively, efficiently, and profitably (Paine, 2003). There is also a cultural shift in expectations with regard to longer-term implications of business operations. There is more concern about sustainability (Carpenter, 1998; Newton, 1997) and the impact of business decisions and actions on future generations. Understanding and responding to these cultural shifts is an important responsibility of *authentic ethical role models*.

3. REQUIREMENTS FOR BECOMNG AN AUTHENTIC ETHICAL ROLE MODEL

For anyone to be an *authentic ethical role model*, certain requirements must be met. As shown in Figure 1, these requirements follow a logical sequence of development, starting with enhancing awareness of one's own moral orientation, then understanding one's orientation in relation to the different communities of which one is a part, then recognizing how one's moral orientation influences personal decisions and actions, and finally considering the impact of one's decisions and actions on affected organizational stakeholders. Successful progress in meeting all four requirements culminates in an enhanced capacity for the individual to act as an *authentic ethical role model.*

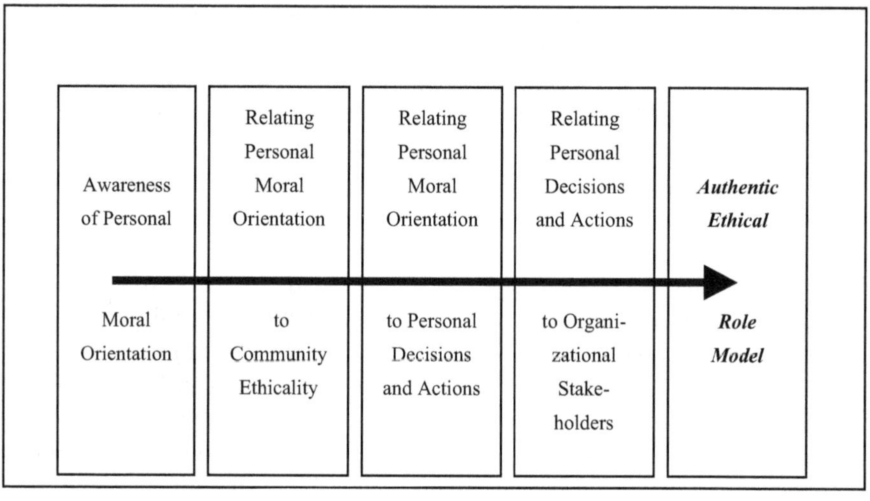

Figure 1. Major Requirements for Becoming an *Authentic Ethical Role Model*

3.1 Awareness of Personal Moral Orientation

The journey toward becoming an *authentic ethical role model* begins with a person's intense awareness of his or her own moral orientation and how he/she is developing as a moral individual. People must be cognizant of their fundamental orientation toward ethical issues. People must recognize the decisions and actions that they regard as ethical and those that they consider to be unethical. They must also know why they consider certain decisions and actions to be ethical and others to be unethical. People must also be aware of how, if at all, their personal view of ethics varies across decision situations and with the use of different analytical or evaluative perspectives.

Individuals must also assess their personal inclinations toward decisions and actions that benefit themselves versus benefiting the community. Are decisions and actions oriented toward selfishness or toward altruism and selflessness? Or, alternatively, is the ethical orientation somewhere between selfishness and selflessness? The *authentic ethical role model* takes a position that combines concern for self and concern for others. This position, known as self-fullness, involves the simultaneous and balanced pursuit of reasonable self-interest and reasonable concern for the common good (McCuddy, 2005; McCuddy & Pirie, forthcoming). The *authentic ethical role model* rests upon the self-fullness moral orientation; the other requirements for becoming an authentic ethical role model build upon the foundation of self-fullness.

3.2 Relating Personal Moral Orientation to Community Ethicality

The second requirement for becoming an *authentic ethical role model* involves recognition of how personal moral orientation fits in with broader community expectations, values, and norms. Individuals must be aware of the convergence and divergence of their own ethical expectations and values with those of multiple social communities. These communities include, but are not limited to, family and friends, the employing organization, professional associations, one's home country, and other countries where the organization's business is conducted. Given these multiple communities, numerous different configurations are possible for balancing concern for self with concern for the broader community.

3.3 Relating Personal Moral Orientation to Personal Decisions and Actions

The third requirement for becoming an *authentic ethical role model* concerns the exploration of how personal moral orientation affects decisions and actions regarding various organizational issues. The *authentic ethical role model*, in pursuing a state of self-fullness, applies criteria that reasonably, fairly, and justly balance personal interests and community interests in dealing with every issue.

3.4 Relating Personal Decisions and Actions to Organizational Stakeholders

The fourth requirement for becoming an *authentic ethical role model* focuses on how decisions and actions influence relationships with and the interests of the organization's various stakeholders. An *authentic ethical role model* considers the implications of decisions and actions on any given issue for all relevant stakeholders. The objective always should be to balance the interests of the various stakeholders in order to achieve a solution that is as right, fair, and just as possible for all concerned.

4. AN EDUCATIONAL PROCESS FOR BECOMNG AN AUTHENTIC ETHICAL ROLE MODEL

Theoretically, there may be many ways by which a person can develop into an *authentic ethical role model*. The author has devised and utilized a particular educational process that, over several semesters, has proven successful in helping students to grapple with and move toward meeting the requirements for becoming an *authentic ethical role model*.

4.1 Basic Nature of the Course

Ethics in Business is the title of the course being discussed in this paper. It is a dual level course, enrolling both undergraduate students — primarily seniors or fourth-year students in the College of Business Administration — and graduate students pursuing a masters degree, typically in either liberal studies or sports management. Enrollment averages around two-dozen students per course section, thus permitting a highly student-centered educational approach.

4.2 Course Objectives

The *Ethics in Business* course rests on six fundamental objectives. Five of these objectives are generalizable to any educational institution, while one of them is relevant to the particular character of Valparaiso University. The five generalizable objectives are:

- To provide students with an understanding of the fundamental theories and concepts that explain and guide ethical thinking, reasoning, decision making, and actions.
- To expose students to ethical and moral issues that people encounter in business settings.
- To foster examination of each student's own ethical principles and propensities as they pertain to his/her personal behavior and perspectives on the role of business in society.
- To help students develop an appreciation for the broad-based role that ethics can (and should) play in business.
- To help students understand ethics in a global context.

The one objective that reflects the special character of Valparaiso University relates to it being a religiously affiliated institution of higher learning, which overtly embraces the Christian intellectual tradition. This additional objective is:

- To help students develop an appreciation for business morality in the context of the doctrine, thinking, and values of Christian faith traditions.

4.3 Basic Approach to the Course

The *Ethics in Business* course uses a seminar approach wherein the students are very actively involved in the learning experiences of every class session. During the first half of the course, the seminar discussion is led and facilitated by the professor, and the students are actively involved in exploring essential elements of the conceptual foundation of personal and professional ethics. This foundation is applied to the various contexts within which ethical dilemmas occur. During the second half of the course, the seminar discussion is led and facilitated by student teams, and the professor along with the other students in the class consider ethical situations as presented by the team. Table 1 provides an overview of the key topics in the *Ethics in Business* course, who facilitates each topic, and the number of 75-minute class sessions devoted to each topic.

The reliance on student facilitation for half of the seminar sessions is based on the philosophy that 'the most powerful way to learn for oneself is to attempt to teach someone else.' Thus, each student is actively involved in facilitating class discussions of various ethical issues. By doing so, the students are likely to learn the material better. The students also gain useful presentation experience — something that is very valuable in preparing for any managerial or leadership position. Interestingly, the facilitation experience is one part of the course that the students nearly unanimously

Table 1. Overview of Content and Facilitation Responsibilities in *Ethics in Business*

Ethical Topic	Session Facilitator	Number of 75-Minute Class Sessions Devoted to Topic
Ethics in personal and professional life	Professor	3
Models of moral decision making	Professor	2
Ethics in the global economy	Professor	3
Christian business ethics in the contemporary world	Professor	3
The morality of capitalism	Student Team	1
Capitalism and biblical values	Student Team	1
Corporate social responsibility	Student Team	1
Employee rights and privacy	Student Team	1
Workplace discrimination and affirmative action	Student Team	1
Sexual harassment	Student Team	1
Advertising ethics	Student Team	1
Product safety and quality	Student Team	1
The environment and economic growth	Student Team	1
Insider trading, mergers, and acquisitions	Student Team	1
Individual moral responsibility	Student Team	1
Creating and encouraging moral corporate cultures	Student Team	1

have ardently supported and asked the professor to retain. In sum, the *Ethics in Business* course is as much about personal ethical awareness as it is about examining ethical theories, concepts, and issues. As one former student put it: "Ethics has been more of a self-discovering adventure than a class."

The efforts of the student facilitation teams are particularly beneficial in providing exposure to multiple viewpoints on any given ethical issue. Rather than taking a particular position on an issue and excluding others, the facilitation teams typically give attention to the arguments associated with the different sides of an issue. This helps broaden the students' understanding of both the diversity of opinion about and the potential complexity of moral issues.

4.4 Learning Activities

The *Ethics in Business* course addresses the requirements for becoming an *authentic ethical role model* through various learning activities. These activities are divided into two broad categories: (1) professor-guided foundation development and (2) student assignments.

4.4.1 Professor-Guided Foundation Development

During the first half of the course, the professor develops a foundation that serves the following purposes:

- Building a basic understanding of the nature of ethics in a person's personal life and professional life.
- Exposing the students to the professor's perspective and thinking regarding ethics in general and business ethics in particular.
- Creating a context for each student's examination of and reflection on his/her personal ethical orientation and philosophy.
- Creating a context for examining a variety of ethical issues that are germane to the workplace.
- Building a climate of openness and trust in exploring sensitive moral issues.

The content of the professor-guided foundation includes theories, concepts, information, ideas, and viewpoints on the following topics:

- Examples of students' ethics in action in the academic setting.
- Examples of people's ethics in action in the workplace.
- Ethical decisions and actions relative to stakeholders.
- Business as a calling.
- Students' concepts of a personal calling.
- Problem solving, decision making, and the moral decision-making process.
- Models of moral development.
- Concepts of self and community in moral development.
- Selfishness, selflessness, and self-fullness as alternative moral journeys in personal life and professional life.
- The global context of ethical decisions and actions.
- Global variations in ethical antecedents (or precursors) and consequences.
- Ethical relativism versus ethical universalism.
- The secular and spiritual natures of stewardship.

- Types of stewardship.
- Constraints and influences on stewardship.
- Stewardship and sustainability.

While some lecturing occurs during the professor-guided sessions, there is much more emphasis on free-flowing dialogue within a supportive and respectful environment. Ideas are challenged but people are not attacked. Active involvement on the part of all students is expected and encouraged. As the initial weeks of the academic term unfold, openness and trust gradually emerge and flourish within the class. This serves as an important bridge to the student-facilitated sessions during the second half of the semester, which relies heavily on student involvement, initiative, risk taking, openness, and trust. Without exception, a climate of openness and trust develops every time this course is offered, though there is some variation between course sections in the levels of these attributes. For instance, it is not unusual for some students, in the course of a discussion, to reveal things about themselves that they would probably never be willing to reveal in any other course context.

4.4.2 Student Assignments

The assignments are intended to actively engage students in exploring and grappling with their own moral perspectives, with important issues in business ethics, and how their moral perspectives relate to dealing with ethical issues in their current and future personal lives as well as future professional lives. The student assignments include the seminar facilitation assignment, active participation in discussion and activities, and three analytical essays — one on ethical foundations, a second on ethical codes, and a third on ethical issues. For the undergraduate students, which constitute the vast majority of enrollees in the course, the seminar facilitation assignment is worth 30 percent of the course grade, participation is worth 25 percent, the ethical foundations essay is worth 12.5 percent, the ethical codes essay is worth 20 percent, and the ethical issues essay is worth 12.5 percent. For masters degree students, the percentage contribution of these components to the course grade is reduced proportionately as there is a required research project that constitutes 22 percent of the course grade.

4.4.2.1 Seminar Facilitation Assignment

Six student teams, consisting of four or five members, are formed to assume responsibility for facilitating the seminar discussion of the assigned topics. In practice, this means that each team is responsible for facilitating discussion on two different topics. Teams are assigned topics, trying to accommodate each team's topic preferences as much as possible.

The purpose of the facilitation activity is to help the seminar participants to profoundly explore and grapple with a variety of ethical and moral issues in business. The facilitation team is expected to actively engage the seminar participants in learning about business ethics from the perspective of the assigned topic. The facilitation team is also expected to challenge each seminar participant to confront his/her own ethical principles, and to examine and understand the ethical principles of others.

4.4.2.2 Active Participation

Active, thoughtful, articulate, quality participation is expected of every seminar member. Every student must be involved for the *Ethics in Business* course to operate effectively, achieve its objectives, and assist the students in becoming *authentic ethical role model*s.

Periodically throughout the semester, each student completes a brief self-assessment of his/her participation activity. The professor expects the students' self-assessments to be completed with total honesty and integrity — clearly consistent with the thrust of the course. The students' self-assessment provides the starting point for the professor's evaluation of the participation component of the course. The self-evaluation is important because it pertains to the student's understanding and practice of his/her moral orientation.

4.4.2.3 Ethical Foundations Essay

The ethical foundations essay draws on the topics covered by the professor. Based on his/her understanding of this material, each student writes an essay addressing the following questions:

- Why are ethical decisions and actions important in business organizations?
- Is it appropriate to base business ethics on a spiritual (or alternatively, religious) foundation? Why or why not?
- What other foundations represent appropriate bases for business ethics? Which of these additional bases is/are most appropriate? Why?

4.4.2.4 Ethical Codes Essay

Each student selects an industry of interest from *Fortune* magazine's "America's Most Admired Companies List" or "Global Most Admired Companies List" — there is, of course, some degree of overlap between the two lists. For the selected industry, the student chooses one of the two companies with reputational ratings at the top of the industry and one of the two companies with reputational ratings at the bottom of the industry. For each of the two selected companies, the student examines the ethics statement, code of ethics, code of ethical conduct, guiding ethical principles, or similarly named document available on the respective companies' Web sites. The student then writes an analytical essay that compares and contrasts the ethical statements of the two companies, giving particular attention to the following items:

- The student's insights regarding the extent to which the top leadership of the organization serves as an ethical role model for other organization members.
- The student's insights regarding the extent to which the organization's culture supports ethical decisions and actions.
- The student's insights regarding the obligations/responsibilities that mid-level and lower-level organization members have for making ethical decisions and taking ethical actions.
- The student's insights regarding the organization's position on stewardship.
- The student's insights regarding the organization's ethical orientation and stewardship orientation within a global context.
- The student's insights regarding the interconnections among the preceding five items.

4.4.2.5 Ethical Issues Essay

The ethical issues essay focuses on the topics covered by the student facilitation teams (refer again to Table 1). Each student selects two of the ten topics covered by the other student facilitation teams (in other words, a student cannot write about the topics for which his/her own team served as facilitators). Given this constraint, each student chooses the two topics that had the greatest impact on his/her ethical thinking. Each student then writes an essay addressing the following questions:

- Why did these two topics have the greatest impact on the student's ethical thinking?
- How did each topic impact the student's ethical thinking?
- How has this information affected (or how does the student anticipate it will affect) the ethical decisions he/she makes and actions he/she takes in his/her professional and personal lives?

4.5 How *Ethics in Business* Addresses the Requirements for Becoming an Authentic Ethical Role Model

Taken together, the professor-guided foundation development and the student assignments constitute a set of learning activities that contribute to the students' potential for becoming *authentic ethical role models*. Table 2 summarizes how each of the six learning activities seems to influence the four requirements for becoming an *authentic ethical role model.* The judgments presented in Table 2 are based on five semesters of experience with all but the ethical foundations essay and the ethical codes essay, and on two semesters of experience with the precise configuration described in this paper. The last class of each semester is devoted to discussion of two questions: What is the most important thing that you learned in this course, or what is the most important insight you have gained, or what has had the greatest impact on your life? What, if anything, would you change in this course, and what would you keep the same? Every student is expected to respond to these questions, and one student, at the professor's request, takes copious notes on the students' contributions. Subsequently, those notes are content analyzed by the professor, with a view, in part, toward assessing how much of an impact each of the learning activities in the course has had on the four requirements for becoming an *authentic ethical role model.*

Of the 24 effects (*i.e.*, six learning activities times four requirements for becoming an *authentic ethical role model*) identified in Table 2, three reflect a moderate impact, four represent a moderate to substantial impact, and 17 reflect a substantial impact. Overall, the professor's experiences and the students' experiences indicate that this set of learning activities does an admirable job of addressing the four requirements for helping students move in the direction of being *authentic ethical role models*.

5. CONCLUDING OBSERVATIONS

The moral failures of some business leaders during the past few years have dramatically focused attention on the need for ethical leaders and ethical role models. Indeed, without moral leadership, the future of business may be at significant risk. Being an *authentic ethical role model* is an important means through which a person can demonstrate moral leadership. In turn, an important — even essential — part of education for future business leaders is helping them learn to be *authentic ethical role models*. Anything less is an injustice not only to them but also to all of civilized society.

Table 2. Summary of How Learning Activities in *Ethics in Business* Influence the Requirements for Becoming an Authentic Ethical Role Model

Learning Activities in *Ethics in Business*	**Requirements for Becoming an Authentic Ethical Role Model**			
	Awareness of Personal Moral Orientation	**Relating Personal and Community Ethicality**	**Relating Personal Moral Orientation to Personal Decisions and Actions**	**Relating Personal Decisions and Actions to Organizational Stakeholders**
Professor-guided Foundation Development	Substantial Impact	Substantial Impact	Substantial Impact	Substantial Impact
Seminar Facilitation Assignment	Moderate Impact	Substantial Impact	Substantial Impact	Substantial Impact
Active Participation	Substantial Impact	Substantial Impact	Moderate to Substantial Impact	Moderate to Substantial Impact
Ethical Foundations Essay	Moderate Impact	Moderate Impact	Substantial Impact	Substantial Impact
Ethical Codes Essay	Moderate Impact	Substantial Impact	Substantial Impact	Substantial Impact
Ethical Issues Essay	Substantial Impact	Substantial Impact	Substantial Impact	Moderate Impact

REFERENCES

Bray, C. (2004, June 3). Lawyer told Belnick Tyco needed "culture" changes, Dow Jones Newswires.

Carpenter, S. R. (1998). Sustainability. *Encyclopedia of Applied Ethics,* 4 (pp. 275-293). San Diego, CA: Academic Press.

Dempsey, M. A. (2002). Transparency: Just like old times. *Latin Trade, 4*, 10, 34-37.

Fowler, T. (2002). The pride and the fall of Enron. *Houston Chronicle.* http://www.chron.com/cs/CDA/story.hts/special/enron/1624822.

Graves, S. R., & Addington, T. G. (2003). *Behind the Bottom Line: Powering Business Life with Spiritual Wisdom.* San Francisco: Jossey-Bass.

Kanungo, R. N., & Mendonca, M. (1998). Leadership, ethics of. *Encyclopedia of Applied Ethics*, 3 (pp. 49-58). San Diego, CA: Academic Press.

McCuddy, M. K. (2005). Moral alternatives and the pursuit of stewardship in business. *American Society of Business & Behavioral Sciences Proceedings 2005, 12*, 1, 1194-1199.

McCuddy, M. K., & Pirie, W. L. In press. Spirituality, stewardship, and financial decision making: Toward a theory of intertemporal stewardship. *Managerial Finance*.

Newton, L. H. (1997). Stewardship. In P. H. Werhane & R. E. Freeman (Eds.), *The Blackwell Encyclopedic Dictionary of Business Ethics* (pp. 606-607). Oxford: Blackwell Business.

Oppenheimer, A. (2001). *Ojos Vendados: Estados Unidos el negocio de la corrupción en América Latina (Blindfolded: The United States and the Business of Corruption in Latin America*. Buenos Aires: Editorial Sudamericana.

Paine, L. S. (2003). *Value Shift: Why Companies Must Merge Social and Financial Imperatives to Achieve Superior Performance*. New York: McGraw-Hill.

Ruettgers, M. (2003). Responsibility lies in leadership. *Vital Speeches of the Day*, *70*, 5, 150-155.

Trice, H. M., & Beyer, J. M. (1993). *The Cultures of Work Organizations*. Englewood Cliffs: Prentice-Hall.

Walerius, R. (2004, May 17). FOCUS: Middle East nations struggle to fight corruption. Dow Jones Newswires.

Chapter 18

DEVELOPING CRITICAL THINKING SKILLS ONLINE TO FACILITATE A DISCURSIVE MULTICULTURAL CLASSROOM

Meredith Godat[1] and Kate Whiteley-De Graaf[2]
[1]*Faculty of Business, Queensland University of Technology, Brisbane, Queensland, Australia;* [2]*School of Advertising, Marketing and Public Relations, Faculty of Business, Queensland University of Technology, Brisbane, Queensland, Australia*

1. INTRODUCTION

The impact of technology in today's teaching and learning has created an impetus on educators to differentiate between the applications of information versus knowledge (Sims, 2000, and Megarry, 1989). It is no longer sufficient to provide access and retrieval processes in online teaching, but more importantly there is an increasing need to facilitate the opportunities and processes for collaboration and complex thinking tasks such as critical thinking in order to ensure that knowledge is learned (Jonassen, 1997). There is minimal evidence to show support for communication and critical thinking learning processes in the classroom among international students where English is not their first language. Computer mediated communication can provide a social aspect to learning where interaction involves an exchange of information and requires participants to formulate arguments or reorganize material to arrive at new relationships or concepts (Graham & Scarborough, 1999). Electronically enhanced course components increase the capacity for scaffolding to take place, allowing students to experience the learning material in various modes and preserving class times for interaction and discourse (Schwartzman, 2002).

This paper demonstrates the use of scaffolding as a critical thinking scheme using an online discussion forum. It provides the results from a pilot study undertaken with post-graduate students enrolled in Media Strategy and

M.K. McCuddy et al. (eds.),
The Challenges of Educating People to Lead in a Challenging World, 361–384.

Advertising Management subjects in the Faculty of Business at the Queensland University of Technology in Brisbane, Australia.

This study discusses and demonstrates the interaction taken place between the facilitator and students. It also provides evidence of individual student responses from their participation in answering questionnaires throughout the duration of the study. A quantitative research method was chosen and surveys in the form of closed questions were implemented. According to Neuman (2002), survey research is a process whereby researchers can translate a research problem into questions and then use this information to create appropriate data. Past studies on the investigation of online teaching strategies — including 'chat room's and 'discussion forums' — have produced findings that indicate they can effectively facilitate interaction and discourse between students of different ethnic groups. Research also implies this can help students acquire critical thinking skills.

This study will provide evidence of some of the teaching and learning needs of university students from ethnic backgrounds within a classroom environment. It will also identify opportunities for future research on the relationship between computer mediated teaching and critical thinking.

The discipline of Advertising requires a number of higher order generic skills such as decision-making, risk-taking, negotiation, and critical thinking skills. These skills underlie effective oral and written communication skills that are essential for graduates to effectively contribute and participate in discursive dialogues in the advertising business arena. Advertising Management and Media Strategy are subjects that demand the acquisition and application of these skills in the real world of Advertising practice. These are post-graduate subjects in the School of Advertising, Marketing and Public Relations, which belong to the Faculty of Business at the Queensland University of Technology. Post-graduate enrolment in these subjects have a 50% rate of students coming from overseas, in particular students from the Asia-Pacific region, and therefore whose first language is not English. Their participation in face-to-face discussion forums have been minimal, with Australian students, whose first language is English, dominating the contributions in the classroom discussions. For this cohort of students, it was difficult to assess the acquisition of critical thinking skills, either as written or explicit behavior (as in discussions), and to ensure that they can be effective contributors to the planning and management of advertising campaigns and projects in the workplace.

In spite of the dedication and refocus towards more learner-centered goals, the issue of parity between goal setting and the achieved learning outcomes, particularly in the area of generic skills acquisition, has not been the basis for assessment and therefore not measured directly. A review of the Faculty of Business assessment shows critical thinking as a generic skill more often assumed to have been acquired based on the marking received by a student (Queensland University of Technology, 2003). This commonly used assessment strategy, however, does not facilitate the development of and the measurement of the student's immediate critical thinking skills that often requires the processing of short-term and long-term memory within a short and limited space of time. Critical thinking (assumed to have been acquired on the basis of high marks) is demanded during discussions and negotiations taking place in the advertising boardroom. Verbally expressing the results of short-term processed critical thinking is the key to their active participation.

This project looked at utilizing computer mediated tools of moderated online discussions and integrated multi-media to provide multiple access and utilization of the subject material, a process of "layering" (Evelyn Wood Technique cited in Schwartzman, 2002). The layering process or scaffolding employed in this study allowed students to preview and review the learning materials, using a number of electronic media prior to the discussions taking place. Information is processed at three levels: individual, online and face-to-face discussions. The focus of this study was the critical thinking processes that were translated from online into face-to-face discussions in the multicultural classroom environment. The study attempted to address the hypothesis: *The use of online discussion forums helps facilitate critical thinking in face-to-face classroom discussion amongst students whose first language is not English.*

2. CRITICAL THINKING IN LEARNING

Critical thinking is a higher order cognitive process that is demonstrated by a range of behaviors from evaluating arguments, expressing judgments, making inferences, analyzing theories, proposing solutions to a problem and analyzing their possible consequences (McKenzie & Murphy, 2000). Astleitner (2002) and Frampton (1994) further refine the definition to include conceptual, methodical, and contextual considerations upon which the judgment is based. Therefore, critical thinking is a skill that is demonstrated by deep learning processes characterized by organized thought, justified argumentation, and the ability to relate new knowledge with previously learned knowledge. This is in comparison to surface learning, which is demonstrated by repetition or memorization of information, lack of integration, and differentiation between principles and example.

Clearly, theorists of cognitive science are in agreement that the simple regurgitation and repetition of information is not intellectual behavior that demonstrates higher order thinking skills. Educational theorists and practitioners alike are in concurrence, as evidenced by a review of the goals and mission statements in discipline-specific curricula and by the extent to which it impacts the development of generic skills and the capacity for lifelong learning (Arons, 1985; Oliver & McLoughlin, 2000; QUT Manual of Policies and Principles, 2003). Critical thinking as an objective in discipline-based curricula is achieved via various teaching strategies such as workshops, problem-based projects, formative assessment activities, criterion-referenced assessment, and discussion forums (QUT, 2003). However, Astleitner (2002) contends that there is still a shortcoming because critical thinking is not explicitly taught especially when it has been shown to have high correlation with student achievements.

We ask the question, how does critical thinking take place in the cognitive domain? To develop critical thinking, core information must first be processed through working memory. Working memory is where current mental activity takes place. Because working memory is short in both duration and capacity, only a limited amount of information can be held and processed (Chandler, Cooper, Pollock, & Tindall-Ford, 1998). When information has been successfully processed in working memory, it becomes part of long-term memory. Information stored in long-term memory can be used as information chunks and drawn upon to help organize and structure new information. Doing this reflects a process of higher intellectual behavior such as problem solving and critical thinking (Egan & Schwartz, 1979; Jeffries, Turner, Polson, & Atwood, 1981).

3. COMPUTER-ASSISTED LEARNING

Computer-based delivery programs and strategies have been used to enhance the teaching and learning processes and experiences in the classroom. Academic researchers assert that the application for learning support management and the use of computer resources as tools for achieving specific learning outcomes has grown in conjunction with the development of online technology. Nevertheless, one only needs a review of the literature to show the benefits that have already been derived.

Online discussion forums and other computer mediated learning techniques have been used and advocated with increasing frequency by teachers and researchers to facilitate the development of problem-based learning (Oliver & Omari, 1995) and collaborative learning (Cecez-Kecmanovic & Webb, 2000), and to increase learning interactions and teamwork (Draper, Cargrill, & Cutts, 2002; Franklin & Peat, 2001; Graham & Scarborough, 1999; McLoughlin, 2002). Evaluations to determine the acquired level of problem-based learning skills and extent of collaboration have differed from the use of surveys, interviews, and focus groups, although such methods have the problem of relying on the level of activity online as indicative of the level of learning acquired (Mason, 1992). The studies of Gunawardena, Lowe and Anderson (1998), Henri (1993), Romiszowski and Mason (1996), and McKenzie and Murphy (2000) have found that in order to assess true acquisition of learning via online mediums, in-depth content analysis should be undertaken of the discussion record. McKenzie and Murphy (2000) used an adaptation of Henri's model (1992, 1993) based on analyzing the rate and type of participation, structure, interactivity, and cognitive and meta-cognitive dimensions to evaluate the effectiveness of online discussion groups in a mainly asynchronous environment.

Interactivity has been a term used to promote the use of computer enhanced learning environments almost callously and without regard to its true role in the learning process. Sims (2000) offers a framework of interactivity constructs that can be used to guide the use of computer-based activity to enhance the learning process; these are the dimensions of the learner, content, pedagogy, and context. The basis for developing an interactive learning activity will most likely rely on the use of one or more of these constructs founded on sound theory. As a social interactive process the framework offered by Sims becomes a teaching support tool for teachers to develop collaborative learning (Cecez-Kecmanivic & Webb, 2000). An online discussion forum, in particular, is an effective medium for developing this social interactive process allowing the participants to organize and reorganize information, create their own conceptual framework based on the threaded discussions from other participants, as well as being able to receive feedback. As claimed by Kaye (1992), the analysis, in-depth processing, and recall of course material in the response-feedback cycle forms the basis for deriving greater benefit through the online discussion medium. Its social dimension is clear in the conversational interchange, allowing for discursive, interactive and reflective communication to take place — a framework that strongly supports the learning process and purposes of educational evaluation (Laurillard, 1993; and Svensson, 2002). How effective online discussion forums are in facilitating a discursive environment is dependent on a number of factors, including making it a key and integral part of the learning structure and environment (McKenzie & Murphy, 2000); the role of the teacher as moderator and in maintaining the student-teacher dialogue (O'Reilly & Newton, 2002); and ensuring that the interface design and hypertext links to resources are intuitive, easy to navigate through, and allow self-directed learning (Brown, 1997), not to mention easy access to the online medium and resources.

4. LEARNING IN THE MULTICULTURAL CONTEXT

Learning behaviors that seem to dominate Southeast Asia, Hong Kong, and China include rote learning (Chan, 1999). According to Biggs (1994), rote learning can be defined as a learning mechanism that does not include thought or meaning *so that* the learner fails to understand the real meaning of the information or material learned. According to Chan (1999), previous studies imply that students who depend on the rote method of learning often lack originality of the thinking process. The research reveals that Southeast Asia and Chinese students attend a majority of lectures that provide minimal discussion or question time during the course of the lecture. Problem solving in a classroom environment also appears to be neglected. It seems that their assessment is largely achieved through written examinations that do not examine the ability to work with others and identify practical problems (Chan, 1999). Chan further questions the benefits of another method of learning known as repetitive learning which enables the students to recall information and attach a meaning to the material presented. Yau (1994) implies that students will feel more comfortable interacting with one another in a classroom environment once relationships between themselves and others within the room have been defined. Biggs (1994) claims that international students, as opposed to western students, are more likely to seek one-on-one interaction with the teacher and with one another once the lecture is over.

Biggs (1994) suggests learning in the western style does include students being taught to: use abstract frameworks when conceptualizing the information, be meta-cognitive when planning and monitoring their progress, and make outcomes well-structured and integrated. For most international students, this process is undertaken silently. According to Chan (1999), long silences in class does not necessarily imply an international student is refusing to participate because he/she may just be thinking more about the question and may need more input or probing from the teacher. According to Tanian (2002), many students feel hesitant to participate in classroom discussion because of communication apprehension. McCrosky (1997) suggests that 15% to 20% of university students throughout Western society suffer from high communication apprehension; 60% suffer anxiety and all students do suffer anxiety to some degree throughout their studies. Merrier and Dirks (1997) imply that students know they must contribute in classroom discussion; however, the fear of failure and nerves can cause them to avoid speaking in front of other students. According to Chan (1999), Westerners need to be more sympathetic to the individual cultural needs and learning differences of international students. Hence, there is a need to design and implement learning materials and methods that would better appeal to this group of learners.

5. METHODOLOGY

5.1 Overview and Study Design

Advertising Management (Class 1) and Media Strategy (Class 2) were taught over a thirteen-week semester. Consent to voluntarily participate in the study was solicited from the students by the researchers. The researchers explained that all subject-specific information and data gathered would be kept confidential. Students were informed that the study was about learning and teaching strategies without any reference to assessing critical thinking between two cultural groups. Learning materials were processed at three levels of the scaffolding scheme: individual, online, and face-to-face. Students accessed the learning materials through handouts, online materials, and video clips of case studies related to the weekly modules. Students were instructed to access the learning materials two weeks prior to the online discussion forums. A series of online discussion forums were set up at intervals with the face-to-face lectures and discussions, and were conducted by posing questions to students in both modes. Students were color coded anonymously, depending on whether or not their first language was English. The color coding was conducted so that students could not identify the group to which they belonged. Figure 1 illustrates the study design process.

The first level of processing was based on individual access to lecture handouts, presentations, and case studies through the Online Learning and Teaching system. The Online Learning and Teaching system is a learning management tool used by students and teachers at Queensland University of Technology. Teachers are able to upload learning materials, set up and develop learning tools, allow assignment upload for students, communicate with students, conduct online conferencing, and provide student information.

Handouts and presentations were uploaded on the Online Learning and Teaching system during the first week of the semester to allow students to review the materials prior to any online or face-to-face activity. These handouts and presentations had clear statements of the objectives for the topic and the requirements for the week. Students were expected to have read and reviewed the learning materials prior to their attendance at online discussions and classroom lectures.

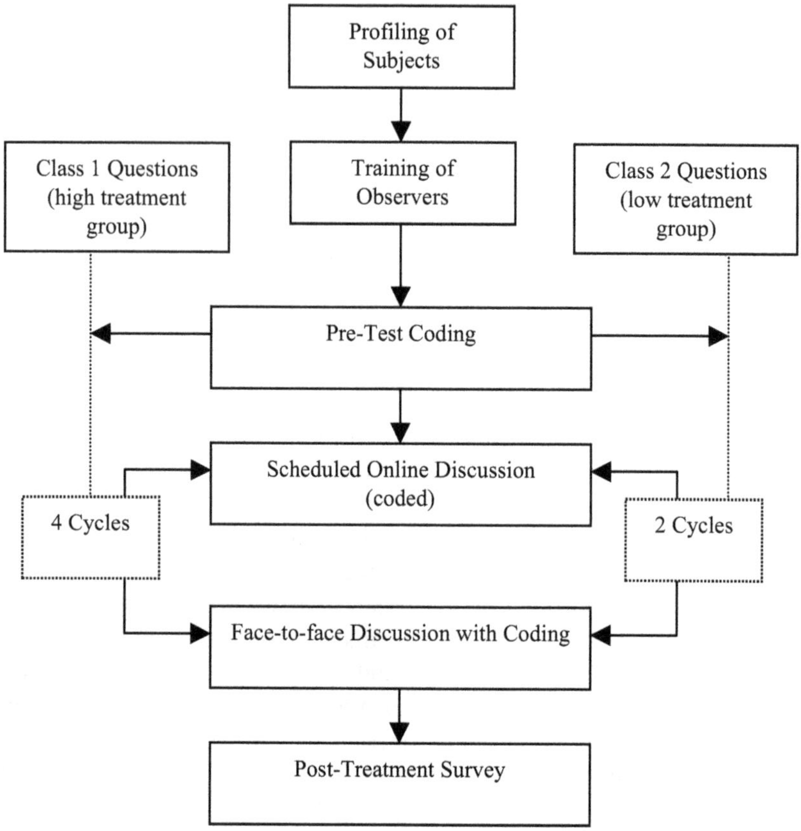

Figure 1. Study Design

5.2 Case Studies and Discussions

In 2002, the post-graduate Advertising program decided to have a common portal on the Online Learning and Teaching system for all subjects being offered in the program. The portal is a virtual advertising firm called "QUT Advertising Consultancy" that provides post-graduate students in Advertising with access to shared resources, learning materials, and expertise. It is a collaborative environment where students undertake the role of employees in the advertising firm through projects, and teachers take on the role of "expert consultants." QUT Advertising Consultancy is a virtual advertising firm that also provides collaborative learning opportunities through its sub-module called the QUT Advertising Classroom, an online environment that allows individual subjects to implement more subject-specific teaching strategies and is used as an extension of the physical classroom. For Advertising Management (Class 1) and Media Strategy (Class 2) it was an online discussion forum. It is here where the case studies were developed and implemented in Semester 1, 2003.

A series of case studies in video format was developed in order to provide a virtual workplace scenario for the students to process two weeks prior to the online discussion forum. Haaken and Christensen (1999) have advocated the use of multimedia technology to allow access to real world scenarios through a virtual workplace boardroom, a medium that was used successfully within the faculty to develop generic skills (Radbourne, 2002). An innovation implemented in this study was to present real world case studies in video clips to portray Advertising managers and their clients negotiating and discussing issues relevant to real advertising campaigns in Australia. The virtual case studies provided students with a number of benefits, including: gaining familiarity with the advertising agencies and their campaigns; understanding the issues relevant to current practices in the Advertising field; access to experts and practitioners in the industry who shared first-hand experience and information with the students; and exposure to discussions between managers of the advertising agency and their clients, which were presented within the context of the topic assigned for the week of the discussions. As an example, one case study video presents the discussions between Personalized Plates Queensland, the client, and Mojo Partners, the advertising agency. Personalized Plates Queensland is a profit-based government organization that sells personalized plates to motorists in Queensland, Australia to help fund road and traffic developments. Mojo Partners was contracted as the advertising agency to promote to motorists personalized number plates, a campaign to appeal to both young and older generation of drivers. The case study describes the campaign issues and evaluation of the campaign and strategies.

Each case study was presented through a series of streaming video clips in order to provide easy access to "chunks" of information that students could easily go back to for review purposes. Information to process can be selected, reviewed, and re-selected as the learner assimilates knowledge and forms his/her conceptual framework.

The teaching of critical thinking requires a context-based approach to the use of strategies and techniques, and demands that teachers providing the instruction participate in the skills development process versus 'seeking the counsel of outsiders with little knowledge of the local context' (Browne, 1999; Golding, Marginson, & Pascoe, 1996; Misko, 1995). For this reason the online discussion forums for Advertising Management (Class 1) and Media Strategy (Class 2) were both teacher-moderated and conducted in place of selected weekly lecture sessions so there was greater incentive for students to login and join the online discussion. Prior to the online discussion forum session, the lecturer, as subject matter expert, prepared a number of questions, ranging from items that required lower-order to higher-order cognitive demand processes. Therefore, students were asked to address questions in an increasing order of difficulty.

Attendance to the online discussion does not mean participative behavior, and therefore content analysis was a better means of measuring student demonstration of critical thinking development and acquisition. Attendance was expectedly high because of the teacher-moderated nature of the instructional design; however, it was the quality of participation and the demonstration of critical thinking that needed to be evaluated.

The online discussion forum was followed by a face-to-face session where a review and summary of the online discussion was provided. The review process was followed by a lecture discussion of the new topic. The same criteria for the online discussion forums were applied in the classroom.

5.3 Online and Face-to-Face Response Coding

Questions asked during the face-to-face and online discussions were classified into two types: declarative (D) and critical thinking (CT) questions. The former are questions that would elicit declarative or elementary responses and therefore initiating surface learning, while the latter elicited in-depth to strategic type responses, initiating deep learning. The number of declarative and critical thinking questions asked during the face-to-face and online discussions was dependent on the topic being presented at the time of the discussion. Online and face-to-face discussions that took place centered on a weekly topic and therefore questions asked during both sessions were related.

The cognitive skills dimension of Henri's model (1992, 1993) was used as the criterion by which responses were coded, based on a demonstration of both surface and deep learning processes taking place (see Table 1). Henri provided a behavioral response matrix for describing surface and deep learning against which contributions to discussion topics were coded.

As two international students had declined to participate, videotaping the face-to-face discussions was not possible. Therefore, observers needed to code the responses manually. Independent observers were appointed, trained, and calibrated to conduct the coding of both the responses during the face-to-face discussions and the transcripts of the online discussion forums. The following training considerations were paramount to ensure reliability of data:

- One-hour workshop on coding critical thinking according to levels followed by a one-hour coding within an actual Advertising lecture.
- Training and calibration process to ensure that all observers would provide congruent coding of their understanding of the meaning of each critical thinking level.
- Resolution of discrepancies between observers' coding formed part of the training. Where a disagreement between coding was found, the reasons were discussed and a consensus of the coding decided.

Table 1. Critical Thinking Skills Coding Levels

Code	Critical Thinking Levels	Behavioral Response
A	Elementary Clarification (surface processing)	Asked relevant questions, clarifications Introduced a problem Pass on information without elaboration Suggesting a solution without explanation
B	In-depth Clarification (deep processing)	Analyzes a problem and identifies assumptions Contributed further information to the discussion AND elaborates on the topic Presents a wider view, shows links and interprets meaning of expressions
C	Inference and Judgment (deep processing)	Provided opposing or supporting arguments to the discussion Providing reasons and grounds for claims Expresses a judgment about an inference, relevance of an argument, theory or solution Evidence of justification
D	Strategy (deep processing)	Proposes a solution; outlines what is needed to implement the solution Provides analysis of possible consequences

Two independent paired observers — one for the online discussion and one for the face-to-face discussion — were each asked to code the responses in the online and lecture discussions (post-online), respectively. Online discussion observers coded the online discussion transcripts while the face-to-face discussion observers attended the lecture discussions, recorded the questions asked by the lecturer and coded the responses to each question presented. Questions raised by the lecturer could vary during the course of the discussion; therefore, when the questions were asked the observers wrote them down. The coding also differentiated between the groups of students who had English as their first language (EFL) and those who did not have English as their first language (ENFL). Each group was coded by colored squares attached to the backrest of student's chairs at the beginning of the class. Four color codes varied between sessions and within groups to avoid students being able to determine their group identity. An Observer Coding

Form (see Appendix A) was used and contained descriptors and examples for each level of critical thinking.

5.4 Research Participants

Two classes, Advertising Management (Class 1) and Media Strategy (Class 2), formed the sample for the study, with both having a mix of Australian and international students. For the purposes of this study, permanent and non-permanent residents were counted as international students. International students whose first language was English were classified under the Australian students group. A greater number of students in Class 1 had English as their first language (37%) compared to 25% for Class 2 that had 8% more international students.

The sample groups were similar in their undergraduate qualifications (83% and 83%) with a smaller proportion of post-graduate (17% and 17%) qualifications. The highest participation of 83% and 92% came from 21– 30 years of age for Class 1 and Class 2, respectively.

In comparing the computer usage of the Class 1 and Class 2 students, they were considered in terms of their language of origin groupings (whether or not English was their first language), with both classes showing similar usage and frequency across various computer mediums. There was a greater difference in terms of news group participation between groups of students based on their language of origin, with Class 2 having 33% more for students whose first language was English versus 19% for Class 1 of the same language group. The use of online discussion forums is average across all groups. A similar level of computer usage is seen in both classes for students whose first language is not English, with Class 2 generally having more frequent users.

The percentage distribution of student experiences in using each medium across Classes 1 and 2 show that only 44% versus 57% have used online discussion forums among students that do not have English as their first language. A very high Internet use of 95% was found across the samples.

Overall, the profiles students participating in this study were similar across classes and groups of students, based on their language of origin.

6. RESULTS AND ANALYSIS

6.1 Class Comparisons of Online and Face-to-Face Discussion Responses Between EFL and ENFL Groups

In order to determine the response behavior of students to critical thinking and declarative question types based on whether or not their first language was English, the mean values of the coded responses were summarized across all sessions for both classes (see Tables 2 and 3).

6.1.1 Online Discussions

The online response behavior shows that critical thinking questions will elicit deeper learning and, therefore, students will respond critically. Contrary to the expectation that declarative questions would elicit surface learning responses, they in fact were shown to encourage deeper learning with the subsequent online discussion forums. Table 2 shows that both groups of students in Classes 1 and 2 did not exhibit higher-level critical thinking in the first online discussion forum. This may have been brought about by adaptation to the new online medium. Overall, students whose first language was English showed more in-depth responses to both critical thinking and declarative questions types.

For students whose first language was not English, elementary to in-depth levels of responses were more evenly spread across the critical thinking levels measured in this study. They also show an increase in CT responses, particularly in the second session. The data also indicate that over time these students show an increased in-depth response to declarative questions. Similarly, for students whose first language was English, specific question types elicited a corresponding response but not without extending to deeper learning processes taking place.

6.1.2 Face-to-Face Discussions

Online discussions were followed by face-to-face discussions. A review of the mean values (see Tables 2 and 3) shows a shift in student response behavior between both student groups for Classes 1 and 2. Because the group mean value is influenced by the online mean (which tends to be high in participation), the post-online mean values are more indicative of what happens in the classroom following an online discussion session. Except for the first face-to-face session in Class 1, the data show a greater level of

Table 2. Class 1 Summary of Mean Values (N = 42, n = 41)

	English First Language*				English Not First Language*			
CT Question Type:	A	B	C	D	A	B	C	D
Pre-Test (06.03.03)	1.00	1.00	0.20	0.00	0.40	0.20	0.00	0.00
Online 1 (13.03.03)	6.00	6.25	0.50	0.13	4.75	4.57	1.63	0.13
Online 2 (10.04.03)	2.00	11.33	2.33	0.00	5.67	6.33	2.33	0.00
Online 3 (01.05.03)	2.40	2.60	1.20	0.40	3.00	1.80	0.20	0.00
Online 4 (22.05.03)	1.80	2.00	1.00	0.00	1.60	1.60	0.60	0.20
CT Online Mean	3.05	5.55	1.26	0.13	3.75	3.58	1.19	0.08
Post-Online F2F 1 (20.03.03)	0.67	1.67	1.67	0.33	1.33	0.33	0.33	0.00
Post-Online F2F 2 (08.05.03)	1.25	0.50	0.25	0.00	1.50	0.50	0.00	0.00
Post-Online F2F 3 (29.05.03)	0.50	0.50	0.17	0.00	0.33	1.00	0.17	0.00
CT Post-Online F2F Mean	0.81	0.89	0.69	0.11	1.06	0.61	0.17	0.00
CT Group Means	2.09	3.55	1.02	0.12	2.60	2.31	0.75	0.05
D Question Type:	A	B	C	D	A	B	C	D
Pre-Test (06.03.03)	1.50	2.00	0.17	0.00	0.33	0.17	0.00	0.00
Online 1 (13.03.03)	9.00	4.00	0.25	0.00	8.75	3.25	0.50	0.00
Online 2 (10.04.03)	3.50	7.17	1.67	0.00	4.83	5.67	1.17	0.00
Online 3 (01.05.03)	2.00	1.00	1.00	0.00	2.00	1.00	0.00	0.00
Online 4 (22.05.03)	2.00	3.00	0.00	0.33	0.67	2.00	0.00	0.00
D Online Mean	4.13	3.79	0.73	0.08	4.06	2.98	0.42	0.00
Post-Online F2F 1 (20.03.03)	1.71	3.13	0.75	0.25	1.29	0.50	0.25	0.00
Post-Online F2F 2 (08.05.03)	1.00	0.50	0.00	0.00	1.00	1.00	0.00	0.00
Post-Online F2F 3 (29.05.03)	0.40	0.60	0.20	0.00	0.80	0.00	0.00	0.00
D Post-Online F2F Mean	1.04	1.41	0.32	0.08	1.03	0.50	0.08	0.00
D Group Means	2.80	2.77	0.55	0.08	2.76	1.92	0.27	0.00
EFL Group Mean	2.45	3.16	0.78	0.10				
ENFL Group Mean	2.68	2.11	0.51	0.02				

*A: Elementary B: In-depth C: Judgment D: Strategy

Table 3. Class 2 Summary of Mean Values (N = 25, n = 24)

	English First Language*				English Not First Language*			
CT Questions	A	B	C	D	A	B	C	D
Pre-Test (05.03.03)	10.00	14.00	8.00	3.00	6.00	7.00	4.00	0.00
Online 1 (19.03.03)	4.33	3.80	1.33	1.00	2.83	2.17	0.33	0.00
Online 2 (09.04.03)	4.00	10.00	9.00	2.00	6.00	6.00	2.00	0.00
CT Online Mean	4.17	6.90	5.17	1.50	4.42	4.08	1.17	0.00
Post-Online F2F 1 (16.04.03)	1.57	0.83	0.29	0.00	0.57	0.00	0.00	0.00
Post-Online F2F 2 (08.05.03)	1.00	0.00	0.00	0.00	2.00	2.00	0.00	0.00
CT Post-Online F2F Mean	1.29	0.42	0.14	0.00	1.29	1.00	0.00	0.00
CT Group Means	2.73	3.66	2.65	0.75	2.85	2.54	0.58	0.00
D Questions	A	B	C	D	A	B	C	D
Pre-Test (05.03.03)	0.25	0.50	0.00	0.00	0.25	0.25	0.00	0.00
Online 1 (19.03.03)	4.67	2.17	0.00	0.00	3.00	0.60	0.50	0.00
Online 2 (09.04.03)	0.00	4.00	0.00	2.00	0.00	3.00	0.00	0.00
D Online Mean	2.33	3.08	0.00	1.00	1.50	1.80	0.25	0.00
Post-Online F2F 1 (16.04.03)	4.00	1.00	0.50	0.00	0.75	0.25	0.00	0.00
Post-Online F2F 2 (08.05.03)	1.00	0.40	0.20	0.00	1.00	0.60	0.00	0.00
D Post-Online F2F Mean	2.50	0.70	0.35	0.00	0.88	0.43	0.00	0.00
D Group Means	2.42	1.89	0.18	0.50	1.19	1.11	0.13	0.00
EFL Group Mean	2.57	2.78	1.41	0.63				
ENFL Group Mean	2.02	1.83	0.35	0.00				

*A: Elementary B: In-depth C: Judgment D: Strategy

elementary responses regardless of whether it was a response for the critical thinking or declarative question types for both student groups. The variation in Class 1 may have been brought about as an after-effect of the high rate of participation during the first online session where there were 65% more responses in the discussion compared to the average number of online contributions. It is interesting to note that students whose first language is

English responded more critically during subsequent sessions as compared to their non-English speaking counterparts in both classes.

By analyzing the mean values according to question type, the response behavior of both student groups can be determined for Classes 1 and 2. Overall, for the critical thinking question type, Class 1 and Class 2 students whose first language was English showed higher critical thinking response levels. Students whose first language was not English tended to respond more at elementary levels when asked the critical thinking type questions, compared to students whose first language was English.

When asked declarative questions, most groups responded more at elementary levels than in-depth levels during face-to-face discussions compared to their responses to critical thinking questions, indicating that students will respond according to the type of question given. However, it was observed that in-depth responses and participation was exhibited over time for both student groups with declarative questions also eliciting critical thinking responses, although the students whose first language was English tended to respond more in-depth. Therefore, it appears that the initiative to respond makes students go beyond the elementary level of processing.

6.2 Does On-Line Discussion Facilitate Face-to-Face Learning?

To test the hypothesis of whether online discussion forums can facilitate or translate to critical thinking in face-to-face classroom discussions, pre- and post-treatment comparisons of post-online discussions were conducted. One group sampling with pre- and post-data analysis using the two-tailed *t*-Test was conducted. Table 4 shows a significant difference between the pre- and post-test response values to the critical thinking type of questions for both groups in Class 2 at a 0.1 level of significance, two-tailed (p=2.353).

These data also indicate that although declarative questions may have been shown to elicit deeper process learning it was not significant. A review of the student distribution showed that Class 2 had a higher percentage of international students compared to Class 1. Therefore, the effects of the online discussion forum in facilitating critical thinking may be greater. For Class 1, the t-Test scores fell below the p-values at the 0.10 level of significance set for this study. Therefore, there was no significant difference between the pre-test and post-treatment data.

In order to determine whether more treatment resulted in better transference of deeper learning processes and the development of critical thinking, a comparison between groups of students across Classes 1 and 2 was conducted, noting that the former had more online and face-to-face discussions. In addition, an overall between-class comparison was conducted. No significant difference was found between groups and classes. The results indicate that it is not the amount of exposure that contributes to students engaging in critical thinking but the style of questions that provoke the appropriate critical thinking type responses.

Table 4. Class 1 and 2 t-Test Values at 0.1 Level of Significance (p=2.353)

Group		Pre-Test	Post-Online F2F	Difference	*t*
Class 1					
EFL CT	Mean	0.55	0.63	-0.08	-0.49
	Std Dev	0.53	0.35	0.30	
ENFL CT	Mean	0.15	0.46	-0.31	-2.16
	Std Dev	0.19	0.48	0.29	
EFL D	Mean	0.92	0.71	0.21	1.10
	Std Dev	0.99	0.62	0.37	
ENFL D	Mean	0.13	0.40	-0.28	-1.76
	Std Dev	0.16	0.47	0.31	
Class 2					
EFL CT	Mean	8.75	0.46	8.29	3.83
	Std Dev	4.57	0.58	4.33	
ENFL CT	Mean	4.25	0.57	3.68	2.84
	Std Dev	3.10	0.67	2.59	
EFL D	Mean	0.19	0.89	-0.70	-1.34
	Std Dev	0.24	1.11	1.04	
ENFL D	Mean	0.13	0.33	-0.20	-1.36
	Std Dev	0.14	0.42	0.30	
Language Group and Between Class Comparisons					
EFL	Mean	1.62	1.85	-0.23	-0.99
	Std Dev	1.42	1.01	0.46	
ENFL	Mean	1.33	1.05	0.28	2.04
	Std Dev	1.27	1.02	0.27	
Class	Mean	1.48	1.45	0.03	0.16
	Std Dev	1.26	1.03	0.44	

6.3 Post-Treatment Survey

A survey was conducted at the end of the semester in order to determine how students perceived their participation in relation to the critical thinking processes that they employed during the discussions and whether their perceptions matched the quantitative analysis conducted in the study.

A majority of students whose first language was not English showed a general lack of confidence in face-to-face discussions (75%), indicating that lack of fluency in the English language and lack of time were predominant reasons. Other reasons given included "Some students seem to know it all and I don't want to get shot down" and timidity. Interestingly, the fear of being embarrassed in front of others was also a reason given by one of the students whose first language was English.

When asked about the perception of their level of response to context-related problems or issues within the subject matter, students whose first language was English felt they generally contributed across all levels of critical thinking, with 100% of the students feeling they sometimes gave in-depth, inference, judgment, and strategic type responses. The students whose first language was not English, although having contributed across all critical thinking levels, felt they were doing so less frequently. More than in the classroom, students in both groups felt that overall they were contributing at higher critical thinking levels during the online discussion forums; this perception was higher amongst the group of students whose first language was not English — 75% compared to 57% for the other group. This is reflected in how all respondents felt more confident in using online forums for discussion.

Again, all students whose first language was not English felt that online discussion forums allowed them to think more critically and provided them with better preparation for classroom discussions. Some students whose first language was English felt the online discussion forums did not make a difference (43%).

Finally, students were asked if the video segments gave a sense of real world advertising. The Australian videos did not seem to be reflective of the practice that international students would encounter in their countries of origin, with only 25% saying that they had no preference. Students whose first language was English felt they could relate better to the videos, with 57% agreeing that it gave them a sense of the real world. In terms of the usefulness of the videos and online discussion forums as a learning tool, 100% of students whose first language was not English versus 43% of students whose first language was English agreed.

7. DISCUSSION

This study aimed to answer the question of whether the use of online discussion forums could help facilitate critical thinking in face-to-face classroom discussion among students whose first language is not English. Although the findings show that the initiative to respond makes students go beyond the elementary level of processing, presenting students with questions that are designed to elicit deep cognitive learning processes during a face-to-face or online discussion is a key factor in ensuring that critical thinking takes place. The scaffolding approach, which uses purposively designed questions for online discussion, as opposed to the frequency of sessions, facilitated the translation of the critical thinking skill into the classroom for both students groups. This finding supports the schema presented by Egan and Schwartz (1979) that demonstrates how information that has been properly processed in working memory can be drawn upon during higher intellectual activities such as problem solving and critical thinking. Although this was more evident for Class 2, the higher number of international students in this class whose first language was not English may have contributed to the difference. This therefore indicates that these are the students who will benefit the most from this approach.

Henri's model (1992), which was used in this study, provided a meaningful framework for evaluating discussion forums via content analysis and the surveying of student perceptions regarding their level and quality of contribution. We suggest that the same framework be used for peer and self-assessment in future studies. However, as implied above, assessment of the acquisition of critical thinking skills should be supported by schemes to ensure that students understand the criteria that define each level of acquisition. While the pre- and post-test comparisons support students' self-perception of having undertaken deeper levels of critical thinking, the high values for the latter indicate the need to provide opportunities and support for increasing capabilities for critical thinking and to allow for more accurate self-assessment.

Online discussion forums can be used to facilitate and engage students in deep learning activities such as critical thinking when the students perceive those forums to be an acceptable communication and learning medium. Despite a lower response rate as compared to their counterparts, there was clearly a strong perception among students whose first language is not English that online discussion forums support critical thinking. This result supports the findings of Chan (1999) that more time may be needed to process information. Importantly, training in the new medium may be a key factor for adaptation; this is suggested by the results that showed the first online discussion forum did not produce higher-level critical thinking for either group in Classes 1 and 2. It is worthwhile to note that participation in the online discussions was not compulsory and did decrease over time for Class 1 and 2, once again indicating the need to include learning design strategies such as peer assessment and group work to encourage greater participation.

This study supports the evaluation conducted by McKenzie and Murphy (2000) who found that to be effective for skills acquisition, online discussions must form an integral part of the program. As shown in this study, the online practice of critical thinking can build confidence and help critical thinking translate into the classroom, particularly where barriers to participation, such as inadequate time to process information, are overcome.

8. CONCLUSION AND IMPLICATIONS FOR FURTHER STUDY

Findings that can be derived from the data analysis can be summarized as follows:

1. To engage students in the process of critical thinking, appropriate instructional techniques such as self and peer assessment must be applied.
2. Questions that prompt the student to analyze, present arguments, make judgments, and provide solutions will elicit critical thinking responses and will initiate the students into thinking critically.
3. Online discussion forums using critical thinking questions can be used to facilitate critical thinking in the classroom environment for students whose first language is English and for those whose first language is not English.
4. Students perceive online discussion forums as useful learning tools that can assist them in developing their critical thinking skills as well as prepare them for face-to-face classroom discussions.

This pilot study provides foundational data that can be used as the basis for further research. Since the sample was discipline specific, use of the same teacher along with convenient and purposive sampling methods served as an effective control for maintaining reliability of treatment. Although this may limit the extent to which these findings can be generalized to a larger population, it provides a framework for investigation that can be applied across any discipline. A larger sampling that represents various sub-disciplines in Advertising and other business disciplines would be more generalizable and applicable to a larger population. Subject maturation due to the application of discussion forums for teaching in the subjects, as well as university equity policies against videotaping students, may have influenced the results. To remove the effects of maturation, we recommend further research using a split-group sampling and a control group within a larger study.

The results of this study imply that there are more aspects of critical thinking that need to be explored within an online environment and how it translates into the workplace. Considerations should be made of the specific cultural context within which critical thinking skills will be applied in the workplace. Long-term studies should be conducted to ensure that critical thinking is actually translated into the workplace where power plays and financial implications tend to have a significant impact on staff interactions.

One principle that can be derived from this pilot study is that the use of a structured approach and purposeful instructional design of discussion forums is a key to facilitating participation and thereby engaging the students in critical thinking.

APPENDIX A: OBSERVER'S CODING FORM

Unit:____________________ **Date:**______
No. of EFL:____________________ **Colors:**_____
No. of ENFL:____________________
Total:__________**(Total Enrolled:**________**)**

*(Write question here)*____________________

Description	EFL	ENFL
Elementary: Asked relevant questions, clarifications Introduced a problem Pass on information without elaboration Suggesting a solution without explanation		
In-depth clarification: Analyses a problem and identifies assumptions Contributed further information to the discussion AND elaborates on the topic Presents a wider view, shows links and interprets meaning of expressions		
Judgment: Provided opposing or supporting arguments to the discussion Providing reasons and grounds for claims Expresses a judgment about an inference, relevance of an argument, theory or solution Evidence of justification		
Strategy: Proposes a solution; outlines what is needed to implement the solution Provides analysis of possible consequences		

REFERENCES

Arons, A. B. (1985). CT and the Baccalaureate Curriculum. *Liberal Education, 71*, 141-157.

Astleitner, H. (June 2002). Teaching critical thinking online. *Journal of Instructional Psychology*, retrieved January 24, 2003 from http://www.findarticles.com.

Biggs, J. (1994). Asian learners through Western eyes: an astigmatic paradox. *Australian and New Zealand Journal of Vocational Educational Research, 2* (2), 40-63.

Brown, A. (1997). Designing for learning: What are the essential features of an effective online course? *Australian Journal of Educational Technology, 13* (2), 115-126.

Browne, M. N. (June 1999). Teaching how to teach critical thinking. *College Student Journal*, retrieved January 24, 2003 from http://www.findarticles.com.

Cecez-Kecmanovic, D., & Webb, C. (2000). Towards a communicative model of collaborative web-mediated learning. *Australian Journal of Educational Technology, 16* (1), 73-85.

Chan, S. (1999). The Chinese learner — a question of style. *Education and Training, 42* (67), 294-304.

Chandler, P., Cooper, G., Pollock, E., & Tindall-Ford, S. (1998). Applying cognitive psychology principles to education and training. Australian Association for Research in Education, retrieved April 17, 2003 from http://www.aare.edu.au/98pap/cha98030.htm.

Draper, S. W., Cargrill, J., & Cutts, Q. (2002). Electronically enhanced classroom interaction. *Australian Journal of Educational Technology, 18* (1), 13-23.

Egan, D. E., & Schwartz, B. J. (1979). Chunking in recall of symbolic drawings. *Memory and Cognition, 7*, 149-158.

Frampton, D. (1994). Analyzing cognitions in a hypermedia learning environment. *Australian Journal of Educational Technology, 10,* (2), 81-95.

Franklin, S., & Peat, M. (2001). Managing change: The use of mixed delivery modes to increase learning opportunities. *Australian Journal of Educational Technology, 17* (1), 37-49.

Golding, B., Marginson, S., & Pascoe, R. (1996). *Changing Context, Moving Skills: Generic Skills in the Context of Credit Transfer and the Recognition of Prior Learning*. Canberra: Australian Government Publishing Service.

Graham, M., & Scarborough, H. (1999). Computer mediated communication and collaborative learning in an undergraduate distance education environment. *Australian Journal of Educational Technology, 15* (1), 20-46.

Gunawardena, C. N., Lowe, C. A., & Anderson, T. (1998). Transcript analysis of computer-mediated conferences as a tool for testing constructivist and social-constructivist learning theories. In *Distance Learning: Proceedings of the Annual Conference on Distance Teaching & Learning* (pp. 139-145), August 5-7, Madison, WI.

Haaken, S., & Christensen, G. (1999). Interactive Case Studies — Enablers for Innovative Learning. Conference paper presented to the 6th Annual EDiNEB International Conference, Bergen, Norway.

Henri, F. (1992). Computer conferencing and content analysis. In A. R. Kaye (Ed.), *Collaborative Learning Through Computer Conferencing: The Najaden Paper* (pp. 117-136). New York: Springer-Verlag.

Henri, F. (July 1993). The virtual university: Collaborative learning through computer conferencing. Workshop, Monash University.

Jeffries, R., Turner, A. T., Polson, P. G., & Atwood, M. E. (1981). Processes involved in designing software. In J. R. Anderson (Ed.). *Cognitive Skill and Their Acquisition*, Hillsdale, NJ: Laurence Erlbaum Associates.

Jonassen, D. H. (1997). Instructional design model for well-structured and ill-structured problem-solving learning outcomes. *Educational Technology: Research and Development, 45* (1), 65-95.
Kaye, A. R. (1992). Learning together apart. In A. R. Kaye (Ed.), *Collaborative Learning Through Computer Conferencing* (pp. 1-24). The Najaden Papers. New York: Springer-Verlag.
Laurillard, D. (1993). *Rethinking University Teaching: A Framework for Effective Use of Educational Technology*. London: Routlege.
Mason, R. (1992). Evaluation methodologies for computer conferencing applications. In A. R. Kaye (Ed.), *Collaborative Learning Through Computer Conferencing* (pp. 105-106). The Najaden Papers. New York: Springer-Verlag.
McCrosky, J. C. (1997). Oral communication apprehension: A summary of recent theory and research. *Human Communication Research, 4* (1), 78-96.
McKenzie, W., & Murphy, D. (2000). I hope this goes somewhere: Evaluation of an online discussion group. *Australian Journal of Educational Technology, 16* (3), 239-257.
McLoughlin, C. (2002). Computer supported teamwork: An integrative approach to evaluating cooperative learning in an online environment. *Australian Journal of Educational Technology, 18* (2), 227-254.
Merrier, P., & Dirks, R. (1997). Student attitudes towards written, oral and e-mail communication. *Business Communication Quarterly, 60* (2), 89-100.
Misko, J. (1995). *Transfer: Using Learning in New Contexts.* National Center for Vocational Education Research (*NCVER),* Adelaide.
Neuman. (2002). *Social Research Methods* (4th ed.). Needham Heights, MA: Allyn & Bacon.
O'Reilly, M., & Newton, D. (2002). Interaction online: Above and beyond requirements of assessment. *Australian Journal of Educational Technology, 18* (1), 57-70.
Oliver, R., & McLoughlin, C., (March 2000). Web-based learning and generic skills development. *Uniserve Science News, 15,* retrieved April 10 2002 from http://science.uniserve.edu.au/newsletter/vol15/oliver.html.
Oliver, R., & Omari, A. (1995). Using online technologies to support problem based learning: Learner's responses and perceptions. *Australian Journal of Educational Technology, 15* (1), 58-79.
Queensland University of Technology. (January 2003). http://www.qut.edu.au/.
QUT Manual of Policies and Principles. (January 2003). http://www.qut.edu.au/admin/mopp/.
Radbourne, J. (2002). From a discipline focused curriculum to a learner-centered curriculum using a multi-layered multi-media case to achieve changes in business education. Paper presented to the 19th International Conference on Case Method Research and Application, WACRA. The University for Public Administration on June 30 to July 3 Mannheim, Germany.
Romiszowski, A. J., & Mason, R. (1996). Computer-mediated communication. In D. H. Jonassen (Ed.), *Handbook of Research for Educational Communication and Technology* (pp. 438-456). New York: Simon & Schuster Macmillan.
Schwartzman, R. (Sept 2002). What can online course components teach about improving instruction and learning? *Journal of Instructional Psychology*, retrieved January 24, 2003 from http://www.findarticles.com.
Sims, R., (2000). An interactive conundrum: Constructs of interactivity and learning theory. *Australian Journal of Educational Technology, 16* (1), 45-57.
Svensson, L. (2002). Discursive evaluation in a distributed learning community. *Australian Journal of Educational Technology, 18* (3), 308-322.

Tanian, S. M. (2002). It's hard for students to participate when they're scared speechless (pp. 1611-1617). ANZMAC 2002 Conference Proceedings.

Yau, O. (1994). *Consumer Behavior in China — Customer Satisfaction and Cultural Values*. London: Routlege.

Chapter 19

COMPETENCE DEVELOPMENT IN ENTREPRENEURSHIP

The Role of University Education

Greet Fastré and Anita Van Gils

University of Maastricht, Faculty of Economics and Business Administration, Maastricht, the Netherlands

1. INTRODUCTION

At present, entrepreneurship is of fundamental importance for our society (Thornton, 1999; Bruyat & Julien, 2000). Entrepreneurial companies contribute to economic welfare as they increase the innovative capacity of the economy. These enterprises also lead to more flexible markets and intensified competition. Moreover, through entrepreneurship, new businesses and jobs are created (De Clerck & De Sutter, 2003), an issue of utmost importance in today's global business environment.

To contribute to societal welfare, an entrepreneur is supposed to be successful. Scientific research relates successful entrepreneurship to three factors: (1) the organization (organizational theory) and its resources (resource-based theory), (2) the environment (strategic management theory), and (3) the individual (psychology, organizational behavior, entrepreneurship theory) (Baum, Locke, & Smith, 2001; Dollinger, 2003). This chapter focuses on the last factor, the entrepreneur. A bulk of studies has tried to identify traits and motives of successful entrepreneurs; however, the concepts identified (internal locus of control, need for achievement, etc.) have produced weak support (Baum *et al.*, 2001). Recently, authors have shifted their research focus from studying entrepreneurial traits to the study of competencies (Man, Lau, & Chan, 2002). More specifically, they try to distinguish those competencies that entrepreneurs need in order to become successful (Mullins, 1996; Baum *et al.*, 2001; Man *et al.*, 2002). The first

M.K. McCuddy et al. (eds.),
The Challenges of Educating People to Lead in a Challenging World, 385–398.

aim of this chapter is to present an overview of the competencies identified in the literature as being critical for the success of an entrepreneur.

As several of the competencies identified in the first part of this chapter can be taught, potential entrepreneurs should be educated in a way that these competencies are enhanced. This has to be done on all levels, from primary school to university education. Some studies have focused on the role of education in stimulating entrepreneurial behavior, but almost no attention has been given to the competency approach for developing university curricula. Therefore, the second aim of this chapter is to examine the role of universities in the process of teaching entrepreneurial competencies.

The remaining part of this chapter is structured as follows. First, the results of a literature review related to entrepreneurial competencies are presented. Secondly, the role of university education in teaching potential entrepreneurs is discussed. Finally, this study examines the curricula of two universities having a different perspective on entrepreneurship education. By comparing these two universities, conclusions can be drawn on the competency development pattern in both cases. Based on this information, useful advice will be formulated with regard to the development of university curricula that would add value to the study of future entrepreneurs.

2. ENTREPRENEURIAL COMPETENCIES

Given the mixed support for the relationship between founder's characteristics and venture performance, Chandler and Jansen (1992) shifted their research focus to entrepreneurial competence research. Based on a questionnaire that allowed founders to provide self-evaluations of their competencies, they concluded that successful entrepreneurs rated themselves as being proficient in the entrepreneurial function (opportunity recognition), as well as in the managerial and technical-functional roles. A follow-up study (Chandler & Hanks, 1994) confirmed the earlier research findings: founder competencies moderated the relationship between the quality of the opportunity and firm performance and the relationship between access to resource-based capabilities and firm-performance.

Since the introduction of the competency concept in entrepreneurship research (Chandler & Jansen, 1992; Chandler & Hanks, 1994), several scientists have selected this approach to study the impact of the individual on firm success criteria. Mullins (1996) attested that competency facilitates responsive behavior to changing market conditions when the firm's performance was not favorable in prior years. He stressed the importance of the entrepreneurs' ability to build relationships with current and prospective customers. Baron and Markman (2000) confirmed the importance of the entrepreneurs' social skills, as it is a specific competence that helps the entrepreneur to interact effectively with others.

Building on job performance theory, Baum *et al.* (2001) introduced the concepts 'general' and 'specific' competencies in the entrepreneurship literature. Competencies are defined as individual characteristics such as the knowledge, skills, and/or abilities required to perform a specific job (Baum *et al.*, 2001, p. 293). Specific competencies are those related to the industry the firm is operating in and to the technological knowledge required within it. General competencies refer to management skills that are independent of the firm context, as oral presentation skills, the use of power, and decision-making ability. They concluded that the entrepreneurs' specific competencies are direct predictors of venture growth, while general competencies have significant indirect effects.

For this research project, the competency perspective as presented by Man *et al.* (2002) has been adapted, as these authors emphasized the process or behavioral approach. According to Man *et al.* (2002, p. 124), entrepreneurial competencies are "higher-level characteristics encompassing personality traits, skills and knowledge, and therefore can be seen as the total ability of the entrepreneur to perform a job successfully." Six major entrepreneurial competencies are distinguished: (1) opportunity, (2) relationship, (3) conceptual, (4) organizing, (5) strategic, and (6) commitment competencies. Table 1 presents the six competency groups, together with their behavioral focus (column 2). In column three, detailed examples of these competencies are presented, as they were identified in this literature review. The last column specifies the references used.

In this research project, we will focus on the six competency areas indicated in Table 1, as these competencies are changeable and learnable (Man *et al.*, 2002). We do not take into account personality traits, as they are mainly fixed at the moment a student enters into university education.

3. UNIVERSITY EDUCATION IN ENTREPRENEURSHIP: A COMPETENCIES BASED-APPROACH?

Although the first entrepreneurship course was introduced in the 1940s at the Harvard Business School (Katz, 2003), it took until the 1970s before the number of universities offering these types of course increased dramatically (Vesper & Gartner, 1997). Institutional, industry specific, and societal changes were at the basis of this major shift in emphasis (Vesper & Gartner,

Table 1: Classification of Entrepreneurial Competencies (Table was adapted from Man, Lau, & Chan, 2002)

Competency Area	Behavioral Focus	Competencies	References
Opportunity competencies	Recognizing and developing market opportunities through various means	Adventurous, driven by ideas, being open for opportunities, opportunity recognition	Casson (1982); McClelland (1987); Mitton (1989); Chandler and Jansen (1992); Chandler and Hanks (1994); Snell and Lau (1994); Gasse (1997); Bartlett and Ghoshall (1997); Baum et al. (2001); Beaver (2002)
Relationship competencies	Person-to-person or individual-to-group-based interactions	Management skills, negotiating, convincing skills, social skills, communication skills, conflict management, building trust, stress management	McClelland (1987); Ibrahim (1987); Mitton (1989); Chandler and Jansen (1992); Durkan et al. (1993); Bird (1995); Mullins (1996); Bartlett and Ghoshall (1997); Gasse (1997); Baron and Markman (2000); Gibb (2002); Baron and Shane (2005)
Conceptual competencies	Different conceptual abilities, which are reflected in the behaviors of the entrepreneur	Generalist instead of specialist, decision skills, creative problem solving, risk taking, innovative, ambitious, pro-activeness	Casson (1982); McClelland (1987); Mitton (1989); Chandler and Jansen (1992); Durkan et al. (1993); Snell and Lau (1994); Bird (1995); Bartlett and Ghoshall (1997); Gasse (1997); Baum et al. (2001); Gibb (2002); Beaver (2002); Morrison et al. (2003); Sternberg (2004)
Organizing competencies	Competencies related to the organization of different internal and external human, physical, financial, and technological resources	Analytical skills, team-building, calculating skills, delegation and organization skills, leading employees, training and controlling	Casson (1982); McClelland (1987); Mitton (1989); Chandler and Jansen (1992); Durkan et al. (1993); Snell and Lau (1994); Bartlett and Ghoshall (1997); Gasse (1997); Baum et al. (2001); Beaver (2002)
Strategic competencies	Competencies related to setting, evaluating, and implementing the strategies of the firm	Strategic thinking, time management, project management	McClelland (1987); Mitton (1989); Durkan et al. (1993); Snell and Lau (1994); Bird (1995); Bartlett and Ghoshall (1997); Gasse (1997); Gibb (2002)
Commitment competencies	Competencies that drive the entrepreneur to move ahead with the business	Willing to work hard	Ibrahim (1987); McClelland (1987); Mitton (1989); Chandler and Jansen (1992); Durkan *et al.* (1993); Bartlett and Ghoshall (1997); Gibb (2002)

1997; Katz, 2003). Nevertheless, even in today's society, sources of friction remain between academia and entrepreneurship education (Klofsten, 2000; Laukkanen, 2000), and several members of the academic community claim that this specific type of education is not required at a university level. Prominent entrepreneurship researchers (Chia, 1996; Gibb, 2002) claim the opposite — at universities the importance of entrepreneurship courses will grow even more in the future. Moreover, entrepreneurship education is becoming an evaluation item for famous accreditation systems such as the Association to Advance Collegiate Schools of Business (AACSB) (Fiet, 2000b).

The academic literature on entrepreneurship education focuses on four subjects: (1) its history and evolution, (2) the content of the programs, (3) the process and pedagogical issues of entrepreneurship education, and (4) the results of these courses or programs.

Several researchers have focused on stipulating the history or evolution of entrepreneurship education (for an overview, see Katz, 2003), but most of the results published refer to the American situation. Much less emphasis has been given to monitoring the achievements of these entrepreneurship programs (Gibb, 2002). However, two Scandinavian studies do report positive results. Kolvereid and Moen (1997), using Norwegian data, indicate that graduates with an entrepreneurship major are more likely to start new businesses and have stronger entrepreneurial intentions than other graduates. Based on a Swedish case, Klofsten (2000) concludes that entrepreneurial behavior can be stimulated and that, as a result, the quality of new projects and firms will be improved. Further research on this topic is mandated. However, as our research project focuses on stimulating entrepreneurial competencies, the next sections of this paper will describe content and process issues in entrepreneurship education.

Within universities, the topics and the types of the entrepreneurship courses offered differ a lot (Vesper & Gartner, 1997; Fiet, 2000a; Gibb 2002). A major issue at the basis of these divergent views is the definition of entrepreneurship (Gartner, 1990; Gibb, 2002). Katz (2003) uses the 'prairie populist' model to describe entrepreneurship, in which he refers to academic disciplines and specialties including entrepreneurship, new venture creation, entrepreneurial finance, small business, family business, free enterprise, private enterprise, high-technology business, new product development, micro-enterprise development, applied economic development, professional practice studies, women's entrepreneurship, minority entrepreneurship, and ethnic entrepreneurship. Given that both the general public and academics perceive the entrepreneurship concept in this way, different views also exist on what constitutes an entrepreneurship program. Fiet (2000a), in comparing 18 syllabi of entrepreneurship academics, concluded that those syllabi encompassed 116 different topics, of which only one third of the topics overlapped. Leading topical coverage areas were strategy/competitive analysis, managing growth, discovery/idea generation, risk and rationality, financing, and creativity. He argues that academics have the responsibility to put more emphasis on teaching aspiring entrepreneurs theory, instead of excessively describing the entrepreneurial phenomenon.

Different researchers have also examined the types of courses included in entrepreneurship programs (Vesper & Gartner, 1997; Gibb, 2002). Courses most frequently offered include entrepreneurship or new venture creation, business plans, small business management, financing entrepreneurial businesses, networks, and family business. Given the current global society, with its many sources of uncertainty and complexity, Gibb (2002) argues to extend the notion of entrepreneurship to one of enterprising behaviors and enterprising organizations. In this way, one could focus on encouraging effective enterprising behavior in all kinds of organizational, social, and economic circumstances. This involves abandoning the functional approach in education, and putting the emphasis on learning 'entrepreneurial capacities.' The capacities described by Gibb (2002) are complementary to the competencies as described by Man *et al.* (2002), and are therefore included in Table 1. According to Gibb, embracing a wider enterprise and entrepreneurship paradigm is a task a university can fulfill more easily than a business school.

With respect to the process of entrepreneurial teaching, most authors plead for a major paradigm shift (Chia, 1996; Fiet, 2000a; Laukkanen, 2000; Nunn & Ehlen, 2001; Gibb, 2002). All agree that the current university's focus on the individual's analytical rigor should be abandoned. However, they all offer different — though not contradicting — pedagogical directions. Chia (1996) indicates that the cultivation of the 'entrepreneurial imagination' is an important task for universities in order to prepare future managers for the complexities of a global environment characterized by heterogeneity, nervousness, and vastly different socio-political and economic network configurations. He further argues:

> *"Paradoxically, for modern management educators, the very attempt to reduce the complex phenomena of successful managers and entrepreneurs in order to facilitate pedagogical priorities violates against the essence of entrepreneurial thinking since,…, it is the very act of breaking away from the dominant frames of thought and established conventions that sets the entrepreneur apart from the others"* (Chia, 1996, p. 415*)*.

In this respect, Chia (1996) emphasizes that entrepreneurship education should be directed at the opening of visions. Fiet (2000a) discusses the development of student approved learning contents in order to stimulate the acquisition of theory-based competencies. Therefore, teachers should delegate responsibility for classroom meetings to students; they themselves should monitor the competency-development process. Laukkanen (2000) indicates that entrepreneurship education should be less focused on the individual mindset; instead universities should become business-generating models.

Shifting the educational paradigm also involves a shift in the knowledge base, attitudes, and behaviors among academic teaching staff. Nunn and Ehlen (2001) propose team-teaching as an approach to overcome lack of competence among teaching staff. Gibb (2002) suggests that universities should integrate in communities of practice, in order to learn from them.

The literature review as presented in the previous sections clearly shows that only a few researchers (Fiet, 2000a; Gibb, 2002) have touched upon the competency-based approach in entrepreneurship education. However, within education sciences and human resource management, the advantages of using a competency approach for learning has been demonstrated in several contexts (see for some overview articles: Canning, 1990; Stewart & Page, 1992; Lawson & Limbrick, 1996; Ellström, 1997; Burchell & Westmoreland, 1999; Nedermeijer & Pilot, 2000; Van der Klink & Boon, 2002). Van der Klink and Boon (2002) applied the competency-based approach to the development of a university curriculum in economics. In their opinion, this approach helps to develop rich competency profiles for specific jobs, thereby including the specific contexts of different job situations. These balanced insights provide a basis for curriculum renewal. Besides, they can be used as an instrument to convince teachers and trainers of the necessity and feasibility of this renewal.

The aim of this paper is to extend competency-based research in the area of entrepreneurship education and university curricula development. More specifically, by analyzing the perception of university staff, students, and alumni on the importance of entrepreneurial competencies and an inspection of their respective university curricula, conclusions can be drawn on the competency development pattern in both cases. Moreover, based on this information, useful advice will be formulated with regard to the development of university curricula that adds value to the study of future entrepreneurs.

4. RESEARCH DESIGN

4.1 Method

As little empirical data are available regarding competency-based curriculum development at universities, we opted for the case design. Yin (1989) claimed that case studies are the preferred strategy when 'how' or 'why' questions are posed, as is the case in this research project. Furthermore, Eisenhardt (1989, 1991) indicated that this research approach is especially appropriate in new topic areas. Different cases often emphasize complementary aspects of a phenomenon, and by putting those aspects together researchers can draw a more complete theoretical picture (Eisenhardt, 1991).

4.2 Research Setting

We selected two universities: the LUC (Limburg University Centre) in Belgium and the UM (Maastricht University) in the Netherlands. These universities were chosen because of the different curricula they offered. At the LUC, a special 'Entrepreneurship' curriculum was developed for graduate students, which consisted of one full academic year dedicated to entrepreneurship courses. The most important courses offered are financial management in the start and growth phases, HRM, strategic innovation management, and business planning. At Maastricht University, developing students' general scientific knowledge is more important than the education of job-related competencies. As a consequence, no specific entrepreneurship curriculum is offered and the number of entrepreneurship or small business courses is very limited. However, through skills courses, some attention is given to the development of general managerial competencies.

Not only is the course content different at both universities, but the pedagogical approach also differs. At Maastricht University, students work in small groups of a maximum 14 students, and the Problem-Based Learning approach is the dominant paradigm. At the Limburg University Centre, the group consists of 15 to 30 students and besides group tasks, lecturing is the traditional teaching approach.

4.3 Sample

In order to get a perspective on the importance of the different entrepreneurial competencies as presented in Table 1 and to evaluate the university curricula, three different groups of respondents were asked for their opinions: alumni entrepreneurs, academic staff, and entrepreneurship students. The advantage is a triangulation of data sources within the different universities.

First, we had four interviews with alumni of these universities in order to ascertain their perception on the importance of the different entrepreneurial competencies, and to investigate — ex post — how their universities had been preparing them for their entrepreneurial tasks. A second group of respondents was the academic staff of both universities. As not all staff members are involved in entrepreneurship courses, only those academics that stipulated a relationship to entrepreneurship in their course descriptions were interviewed. Besides four staff members of the LUC and five of the UM, the deans of both faculties were asked to express their opinion on the role of a university in entrepreneurship education. Finally, twenty-nine students of the entrepreneurship program at the LUC, and twenty-two students that participated in the Advanced Business Innovation course (one of the few UM courses having a strong emphasis on entrepreneurship) received a survey in relation to the topics under study.

5. INTERVIEW AND SURVEY RESULTS

All respondents agree that the entrepreneurship competencies as identified by Man *et al.* (2002) are important for becoming successful as an entrepreneur. However, respondents of the two universities do not agree on the importance ranking of those competencies. Especially the opinion of the entrepreneurs differs a lot. Whereas the Belgian entrepreneurs both emphasize the need for strategic and conceptual competencies, the Dutch entrepreneurs relate their success to their relational and commitment competencies. According to them, for conceptual and strategic competencies, other people can be recruited within the enterprise. Surprisingly, also the academic staff members of the Limburg University Centre and their students do put more emphasis on strategic competencies than do their Dutch counterparts. Furthermore, almost all respondent groups stress the importance of opportunity competencies. They all perceive this competency as a necessary condition to be able to start and become successful as an entrepreneur.

As stipulated before, the university programs the entrepreneurs received differed in content and process. According to the Belgian entrepreneurs, the functional course approach has helped them to enhance their entrepreneurial competencies. However, if they would be able to change the curriculum, they would include courses taught by entrepreneurs and focus more on general problem-solving skills. The Dutch entrepreneurs valued the general course approach within their university program. Furthermore, their entrepreneurial competencies were enhanced by the responsibility they had as students for their learning outcomes (as a result of the PBL method). The emphasis on presentation skills was also perceived as very valuable. If the UM entrepreneurs had to change the curriculum, they would also stimulate the interaction between entrepreneurs and students. Moreover, the development of leadership skills should get a more central role within the curriculum. According to them, this is an important issue not only for potential entrepreneurs, but also for future managers.

The deans of both universities acknowledge the importance of entrepreneurship. They differ however with respect to the impact of it on the curricula of their universities. According to the dean of the LUC, an important task of the university is to professionalize the local economy, and therefore educating potential entrepreneurs has a high priority. According the interim dean of the UM, it is the combination of a general academic education and a focus on certain skills that adds value to the profile of potential entrepreneurs. Within the UM, creativity is important in several courses, and students can also enhance their entrepreneurial competencies by going abroad during a certain time period of their study. However, he doubts if graduated university students will possess enough technological knowledge to enter markets with new products or services. For the future, he would like to increase the entrepreneurial focus within the Masters curricula.

The members of the academic staff within both universities enlarge the perspectives offered by the deans. The LUC professors describe the course content as being very relevant for future entrepreneurs. They also try to avoid too much lecturing, by including case studies and guest lectures in their courses. Most UM academics indicate the lack of focus on entrepreneurial issues in UM courses. However, all agree that the PBL-education system and the different skills trainings enhance the entrepreneurial competencies described in Table 1.

Within the survey, students were first asked to indicate their entrepreneurial intentions. Whereas only about 45% of the LUC students both think about and express a preference for starting his or her enterprise in the future, among the UM students this figure increases to 80%. Both student groups share the perception that their university prepares them most for the organizational competencies an entrepreneur needs, and least for the opportunity competencies. Besides, UM students are dissatisfied with the preparation of the commitment competencies. This result can be interpreted in two ways. First, it can indicate that these students are not prepared for a job situation in which they have to work hard. Another explanation can be that they do not feel committed enough to entrepreneurship, as their study does not confront them with entrepreneurial courses and practice. This last reason seems to be the more realistic. If these students could change the curriculum, they would offer more entrepreneurship and leadership courses. Besides, like their Belgian colleagues, they would stimulate the interaction with entrepreneurs, through guest lectures and internships. The Belgian students would especially change the pedagogical approach to teaching; they prefer an improved focus on creativity, student responsibility, and communication.

6. CONCLUSION

Entrepreneurship and entrepreneurial behavior are of utmost importance in the current global economy. Therefore, education institutions should stimulate this kind of behavior among the individuals within society. Researchers emphasize the central role universities have to fulfill, as they — better than business schools — can offer the conceptual frames needed.

Within the entrepreneurship literature, much debate exists in relation to the content and process approach of university programs in entrepreneurship. The competency approach, as developed within HRM and education sciences, has only recently been introduced. However, competence statements related to specific jobs and contexts that are used in learning situations are a basis of the debate concerning the goals to which learners are aspiring (Burchell & Westmoreland, 1999). Therefore, the competence statements represent an ideal starting point for discussing content and process issues in the development or reformulation of university curricula.

The results of our empirical research project confirm the importance of the six entrepreneurial competencies as identified by Man *et al.* (2002) and presented in Table 1. The case studies also confirm the context specificity of competencies. The Belgian respondents perceive the strategic competencies as far more important than their Dutch counterparts. Dutch entrepreneurs perceive their relational competencies as a basis for their success. These results have important implications for university curricula development. Since the required competencies vary within different contexts (countries, jobs), academics should be very careful in copying international management or entrepreneurship programs. Ideally, competency profiles of groups of alumni having the same job specification should be developed first. Then based on the ambitions of the current students and the competency profiles developed, university programs should be evaluated, discussed, and refocused.

Our study also confirms the necessity to include entrepreneurship courses within university curricula. The UM students, studying at a university that emphasizes general academic development, clearly indicate their lack of opportunity and commitment competencies. Moreover, in order to enhance their entrepreneurial competencies, they would like to integrate entrepreneurship and leadership courses into the curriculum. Both the university dean and UM staff members recognize this problem, and the first steps are being taken to start an introductory entrepreneurship course in the bachelor program. However, according to the authors, more in-depth research should be executed within the faculty in order to study the future job profiles of the students. Given the ambition of many students to start their own enterprises, the education of entrepreneurial competencies should be integrated in all parts of the university curriculum. Moreover, as entrepreneurial behavior adds value, both in small and large organizations, students as well as Dutch firms would benefit from a new educational approach.

Although Limburg University already focuses on entrepreneurship education, our results suggest that entrepreneurship programs should be evaluated continuously. Today's entrepreneurs are operating in a fast-changing knowledge-based environment, and the competencies required to become successful can be dynamic too. LUC students could benefit from creativity and technical-oriented courses in order to improve their opportunity competencies.

In relation to the process of entrepreneurship education, the classical lecturing approach does not seem to satisfy students in these programs. They would like to become more involved in approving the learning content and to get increased levels of responsibility in order to improve their leadership skills, communication skills, and independence. Both students and entrepreneurs would also value increased interaction between themselves. Although guest lectures could be a means to solve this problem, Hayward (2000) claims that involvement of entrepreneurs in university programs often leads to high risks of knowledge being offered as 'anecdotes' or 'war stories.' Offering internship possibilities within entrepreneurial firms or contexts could be a better solution.

REFERENCES

Baron, R. A., & Markman, G. (2000). Beyond social capital: How social skills can enhance entrepreneurs' success. *Academy of Management Executive*, *14* (1), 106-116.

Baron, R. A., & Shane, S. A. (2005). *Entrepreneurship a Process Perspective* Canada: Thomson South-Western.

Bartlett, C. A., & Ghoshal, S. (1997). The myth of the generic manager: New personal competencies for new management roles. *California Management Review*, *40* (1), 92-116.

Baum, J. R., Locke, E. A., & Smith, K. G. (2001). A multidimensional model of venture growth. *Academy of Management Journal*, *44* (2), 292-303.

Beaver, G. (2002). *Small Business, Entrepreneurship and Enterprise Development.* Harlow: Pearson Education Limited.

Bird, B. (1995). Towards a theory of entrepreneurial competency. In J. A. Katz & R. H. Brockhaus Snr. (Eds.), *Advances in Entrepreneurship, Firm Emergence and Growth, Vol.2* (pp. 51-72). Greenwich: JAI Press.

Bruyat, C., & Julien, P. A. (2000). Defining the field of research in entrepreneurship. *Journal of Business Venturing, 16* (2), 165-180.

Burchell, H., & Westmoreland, S. (1999). Relationship between competence-based education and student reflection on practice: A UK case study of initial teacher training. *International Journal of Training and Development, 3* (2), 156-166.

Canning, R. (1990). The quest for competence. *Industrial and Commercial Training, 22* (5), 12-16.

Casson, M. (1982). *The Entrepreneur.* Totowa, NJ: Barnes & Noble Books.

Chandler, G. N., & Jansen, E. (1992). The founder's self-assessed competence and venture performance. *Journal of Business Venturing, 7* (3), 223-236.

Chandler, G. N., & Hanks, S. H. (1994). Founder competence, the environment, and venture performance. *Entrepreneurship Theory and Practice, 18* (3), 77-89.

Chia, R. (1996). Teaching paradigm shifting in management education: University business schools and the entrepreneurial imagination. *Journal of Management Studies, 33* (4), 409-428.

De Clerck, D., & De Sutter, M. (2003). *De Relatie tussen Ondernemerschap en Economische Groei: een Literatuuroverzicht.* Steunpunt Ondernemerschap, Ondernemingen en Innovatie, Belgium.

Dollinger, M. J. (2003). *Entrepreneurship: Strategies and Resources.* New Jersey: Prentice-Hall.

Durkan, P., Harrison, R., Lindsay, P., & Thompson, E. (1993). Competence and executive education and development in an SME-environment. *Irish Business Administration Research, 14* (1), 65-80.

Eisenhardt, K. M. (1989). Building theories from case study research. *Academy of Management Review, 14* (4), 532-550.

Eisenhardt, K. M. (1991). Better stories and better constructs: The case for rigor and comparative logic. *Academy of Management Review, 16* (3), 620-627.

Ellström, P. (1997). The many meanings of occupational competence and qualification. *Journal of European Industrial Training, 21* (6/7), 266-273.

Fiet, J. O. (2000a). The theoretical side of teaching entrepreneurship. *Journal of Business Venturing, 16* (1), 1-24.

Fiet, J. O. (2000b). The pedagogical side of entrepreneurship theory. *Journal of Business Venturing, 16* (2), 101-117.

Gartner, W. B. (1990). What are we talking about when we talk about entrepreneurship. *Journal of Business Venturing, 5* (1), 15-28.

Gasse, Y. (1997). *Entrepreneurial-Managerial Competencies and Practices of Growing SMEs.* Laval, Canada: Center for Entrepreneurship and SME.

Gibb, A. A. (2002). In pursuit of a new 'enterprise' and 'entrepreneurship' paradigm for learning: Creative destruction, new values, new ways of doing things and new combinations of knowledge. *International Journal of Management Reviews, 4* (3), 233-269.

Hayward, G. (2000). *Evaluating Entrepreneurship in Scottish Universities.* Oxford: University of Oxford Education Department.

Ibrahim, A. B. (1987). Perceived causes of success in small businesses. *American Journal of Small Business, 11* (4), 41-51.

Katz, J. A. (2003). The chronology and intellectual trajectory of American entrepreneurship education. *Journal of Business Venturing, 18* (2), 283-300.

Kolvereid, L., & Moen, O. (1997). Entrepreneurship among business graduates: Does a major in entrepreneurship make a difference? *Journal of European Industrial Training, 21* (4), 154-160.

Klofsten, M. (2000). Training entrepreneurship at universities: A Swedish case. *Journal of European Industrial Training, 24* (6), 337-344.

Laukkanen, M. (2000). Exploring alternative approaches in high-level entrepreneurship education: Creating micro-mechanisms for endogenous regional growth. *Entrepreneurship and Regional Development, 12* (1), 25-47.

Lawson, T. E., & Limbrick, V. (1996). Critical competencies and developmental experiences for top HR executives. *Human Resource Management, 35* (1), 67-85.

Man, T. W. Y., Lau, T., & Chan, K. F. (2002). The competitiveness of small and medium enterprises: A conceptualization with focus on entrepreneurial competencies. *Journal of Business Venturing, 17* (2), 123-142.

McClelland, D. C. (1987). Characteristics of successful entrepreneurs. *Journal of Creative Behavior, 21* (1), 18-21.

Mitton, D. G. (1989). The complete entrepreneur. *Entrepreneurship Theory and Practice, 13* (3), 9-19.

Morrison, A., Breen, J., & Ali, S. (2003). Small business growth: Intention, ability, and opportunity. *Journal of Small Business Management, 41* (4), 417-425.

Mullins, J. W. (1996). Early growth decisions of entrepreneurs: The influence of competency and prior performance under changing market conditions. *Journal of Business Venturing, 11* (2), 89-105.

Nedermeijer, J., & Pilot, A. (2000). *Beroepscompetenties en Academische Vorming in het Hoger Onderwijs*. Groningen: Wolters-Noordhoff.

Nunn, L. E., & Ehlen, C. R. (2001). Developing curricula with a major emphasis in entrepreneurship — An accounting perspective. *The Journal of Applied Business Research, 17* (4), 1-8.

Snell, R., & Lau, A. (1994). Exploring local competencies salient for expanding small businesses. *Journal of Managerial Development, 13* (4), 4-15.

Sternberg, R. J. (2004). Successful intelligence as a basis for entrepreneurship. *Journal of Business Venturing, 19* (2), 189-201.

Stewart, J., & Page, C. (1992). Competences — Are they useful to trainers? *Industrial and Commercial Training, 24* (7), 32-35.

Thornton, P. (1999). The sociology of entrepreneurship. *Annual Review of Sociology, 25*, (1), 19-46.

Van der Klink, M., & Boon, J. (2002). The investigation of competencies within professional domains. *Human Resource Development International, 5* (4), 411-424.

Vesper, K. H., & Gartner, W. B. (1997). Measuring progress in entrepreneurship education. *Journal of Business Venturing, 12* (5), 403-421.

Yin, R. K. (1989). *Case Research: Designs and Methods*. London: Sage Publications.

PART V

USING TECHNOLOGY TO FACILITATE TEACHING AND LEARNING

Chapter 20

LMS, LCMS, AND E-LEARNING ENVIRONMENTS

Where Did the Didactics Go?

Marjolein C. J. Caniëls, Anke H. J. Smeets-Verstraeten, and Herman M. J. van den Bosch

School of Management of the Open University of the Netherlands, Heerlen, the Netherlands

1. INTRODUCTION

Web-based education is very popular. Research of the American Ministry of Education revealed that 56 percent of American universities offer their education (partly) by means of distance education via the Internet. Students seem to be very enthusiastic about e-learning; at least the number of students applying for online lectures is growing explosively (Tabs, 2003).

Educational institutes use a variety of software tools to deliver web-based education to students. Broadly, three groups of software systems can be distinguished: (1) Learning Management Systems (LMS); (2) Learning Content Management Systems (LCMS) or authoring tools; and (3) e-learning environments. Each of these systems offers a specific kind of electronic support to educational institutions: a LMS provides assistance with the organization of the education and offers administrative support, a LCMS provides authoring tools for educational materials, and an e-learning environment is the virtual place where students and teachers interact.

Most software producers intentionally distance themselves from didactical issues. They often are indifferent to didactical principles that should underpin their software systems (Govindasamy, 2002). Firidiyek (1999) argues that there is a serious mismatch between the abundance of features in LMS and the lack or total absence of explanation on the didactic principles underlying the inclusion of these tools. As Govindasamy puts it "most LMS providers perceive themselves as mere providers of technology. Consequently, while every technologically possible feature is included in

M.K. McCuddy et al. (eds.),
The Challenges of Educating People to Lead in a Challenging World, 401–421.

LMS, there is an absence of overt pedagogical integration" (2002, p. 288). In our view, the careful integration of didactic principles is a crucial requirement for successful implementation of e-learning.

In this paper, we report on our design and implementation of a web-based e-learning system that was developed as an answer to the shortcomings of the existing software tools for distance education. The system is specifically designed to incorporate various didactic principles. In addition, the system supports the entire range of required educational processes and all the actors involved in them. It provides an all-in-one solution, in the sense that all three of the above named processes are integrated in one software system, *i.e.*, authoring tools as well as administrative tools are integrated with an e-learning environment in which students and teachers interact. The system is currently named Sophia, and is the fruit of a project that is funded by the Digital University of the Netherlands.[9]

The general objective of this paper is to contribute to the knowledge about electronic learning systems, by showing the relation between didactical principles and the design of an e-learning system. Second, the paper will point out how the various issues that should be addressed by e-learning software can be incorporated in one overall system. We will use the newly developed e-learning system Sophia to describe how these two issues can be tackled.

The organization of the paper is as follows. In Section 2 we will go into the fourth generation of distance education and elaborate on the different processes involved in the organization of education. We show how the software packages that are currently on the market only partly fulfill the needs of educational institutions. Furthermore, we will show in this section that it is impossible to translate classroom education to Web-based education without paying close attention to the accompanying shift in didactics. In section 3, we map out the different didactical scenarios that underpin Web-based teaching in our newly developed application. In section 4, we illustrate how educational processes can be supported in an all-in-one system. Section 5 presents preliminary conclusions.

[9] The Dutch Digital University was founded in 2001. This joint initiative of ten Dutch universities aims at developing e-learning content and tools and disseminating these among the Dutch universities.

2. WEB-BASED EDUCATION: WHERE DID THE DIDACTICS GO?

Web-based education constitutes the fourth generation of distance education. In first generation distance education the interaction between students and the educational institution took place solely by means of written educational materials and mail. This form was also called "correspondence education" (Passerini & Granger, 2000; Spooner *et al.*, 1998). The second-generation distance education was characterized by the use of radio and television broadcastings, audio and videotapes in addition to written materials. This kind of distance education was popular in the beginning of the 1970s. Ten years thereafter, CD-roms and other multimedia products entered distance education (the third generation). Presently, e-learning environments prevail. The fourth generation exploits the developments in telecommunication technology and, most importantly, the growth of the Internet.

In the meantime, many universities have adopted innovative teaching and learning models, such as problem-based and project learning. As a consequence, students are developing skills in bridging the gap between theory and practice. They have exceeded the level of knowledge reproduction and entered the level of knowledge application.

These new models aim at the development of competencies that are inherent to students' future professional or academic careers. These new developments cope with doubts regarding the ability of students in traditional universities to apply scientific theories and methods in a business context and in solving problems (Boyatzis, Cowen, & Kolb, 1995; Porter & McKibbin, 1988).

Based upon our practice and the current literature on university education, we have identified six characteristics, which together create conditions that enable students to develop the competencies as mentioned above (Duffy & Jonassen, 1992; Jonassen & Land, 2000; Merrill, 2000; Perkins & Salomon, 1988; Ramsden, 1992; Van den Bosch & Kieft, 2001; Van Merriënboer, 1997).

1. *Learning is based on tasks, representing the pursued competencies.* In traditional education, students begin with studying the learning materials and later they apply their newly acquired knowledge to problems. In competency-based education students elaborate on tasks or assignments, which invite them to analyze or solve theoretical or practical problems that are remotely or directly related to the relevant field of study.
2. *Learning becomes more realistic by applying cases.* In a competency-based approach, the tasks provide the framework and guidance for

working on the problem or situation. This situation is frequently presented with the help of case studies. Case studies generally consist of two components: (1) a description of a problem or situation, *i.e.*, descriptions of practice (conflicts, procedures, negotiations); and (2) data, *i.e.*, case resources students need to study or apply to the problem or situation, such as statistical data, transcripts of interviews, brochures, etc.

3. *Giving feedback is a major role of the teacher.* In traditional classes a dominant role of the teacher is explaining the learning content, even before students have made serious attempts to master it themselves. Therefore, in competency-based learning students have to think and to be productive in advance. The teacher can then comment upon their work at a later stage.
4. *Learning implies collaboration between students.* Collaboration between students is promoted for many reasons, including the effects on their motivation and an increasing efficiency resulting from the division of tasks. From a constructivist perspective, sharing views contributes to constructing a multi-perspective view (Barab & Duffy, 1998; Gunawardena, 2003).
5. *Students have to search actively for information.* Usually, students are offered books, reading lists and readers. However, academics spend a considerable time searching for relevant literature sources. In competency-based learning the active search of learning materials is promoted.
6. *Education should afford different learning paths.* Students differ in learning styles and prior knowledge. Educational institutions usually select one predominant strategy and group their students accordingly. Differences in prior knowledge, abilities and study preferences are increasing. Educational institutions feel the pressure to find an adequate answer to these challenges.

Critical success factors such as the aforementioned seem to be associated with campus universities, which offer ample opportunities for students and teachers to meet at regular intervals. In distance universities, students and teachers only meet incidentally and students proceed at their own speed. Virtual devices can partially compensate for the lack of academic discussions and debates. In addition, most distance learning programs offer residential schools at regular intervals. Here skill training, intense colloquia, discussions and examinations are brought together within relatively short periods of time.

Proper use of the fourth generation of distance learning techniques creates the conditions for adopting competency-based learning in distance teaching. While former generations of distance education were teacher-led, the specific educational needs of individual students can now be put center stage (Downes, 2002; Vermunt, 1992). In fourth generation distance education systems, students can be enabled to determine their knowledge gaps themselves (for instance, by means of a diagnostic test). They have the potential to study or gather knowledge at the exact moment they need it (Al-Nuaimy, Zhang, & Noble 2001; Collis, 1998). Moreover, students should be allowed to decide for themselves the amount of practice materials they need to have before taking the final graded test. However, the realization of these challenges depends upon the proper use of the technological features associated with fourth generation distance teaching.

We argue that current e-learning systems have two prominent drawbacks that hinder the development of fourth generation distance education systems towards competency-based learning. First, didactic underpinnings are neglected. It is striking that most of the existing e-learning environments are places where the teacher will upload study materials that students will download, thereby discarding the many didactic principles that could be supported and enhanced by using e-learning tools. Designers of e-learning polish old fashioned teaching methods due to their lack of knowledge of recent developments in university teaching. Important didactic principles such as just-in-time learning, competence-based learning, and learning aimed at a practical application of theoretical insights are not supported by such systems. Instead, current systems tend to focus almost entirely on the management of the learning process (Ismail, 2002). "They add little or no value to the learning process. Furthermore, they do not provide any means to support internal content production processes, relying instead on commercial courseware" (Ismail, 2002, p. 330). In the currently existing e-learning environments, information and communication technology is used to create a one-on-one translation of classroom teaching to Web-based teaching. Leidner and Jarvenpaa (1995) have shown that "initial attempts to bring information technology to management education follow a classic story of automating rather than transforming. It is primarily used to automate the information delivery function in classrooms. In absence of fundamental changes to the teaching and learning process, such classrooms may do little than speed up ineffective processes and methods of teaching" (1995, p. 265). As a result e-learning tools are not as student-centered as they should be, but they are still very much teacher-led. In this way a traditional classroom setting is mimicked and no advantage is taken of the large educational potential of fourth generation distance education systems.[10]

The second shortcoming of current systems is closely related to the first and has to do with the fact that current software tools only offer point solutions to specific needs. Providing fourth generation distance education calls for the organization of a wide range of educational processes. Each of the current systems provides software solutions for only a subset of these processes. There is no system that supports the entire range. The processes that play a role in the education of students vary from authoring of educational materials; the design of courses and allocation of students and teachers to these; providing study and communication facilities for students; and supervision, evaluation and grading by teachers. Broadly speaking three sets of processes can be distinguished: (1) processes concerning the authoring and managing of educational materials on the task level; (2) processes related to the design and management of information on the course level; and (3) processes connected with the teaching itself (see Table 1). The third column in Table 1 shows some well-known systems that offer software solutions for a particular subset of educational processes.

Table 1. Sets of Educational Processes and Typical Software Solutions

Categories of Educational Processes	**Processes**	**Examples of Current Systems**
1. Authoring (LCMS)	Developing content (tasks) Storing and managing content	Macromedia Authorware, Total LCMS, WebPublisher[11]
2. Management (LMS)	Designing courses (packaging content into courses) Allocating students and teachers to courses Evaluation of students	Blackboard, Lotus LearningSpace, Docent, WebCT[12]
3. E-learning environment	Studying (student-centred) Teacher - student interaction (student support) Grading of tasks	BSCW (Basic Support for Co-operative Work)

[10] Parikh and Verma (2002) note that "a strong opinion has recently emerged that the current practice of using the Internet in teaching has not lived up to the high initial expectations and it even leads to sub-standard education" (p. 28). They believe that appropriate teaching methods and instructional material to support learning activities is a key to improving Web-based learning.

[11] See http://www.clueful.com.au/cgi-bin /cmsdirectory/browse/Products%3aCommercial%20systems for a broad overview of CMS systems.

[12] See http://www.nettskolen.com/in_english/webedusite/used_lms.html for a broad overview of LMS systems.

Educational institutions are under a constant pressure to work in a cost-efficient way (Moonen, 1994). E-learning tools can help in reaching goals of efficiency by coordinating the workflow of all actors involved in the education process. However, this is only possible when one integrated system is used. Until now the creation of e-learning tools has been driven by technology instead of the needs of the learning process itself. Most software tool developers do not recognize that Web-based teaching requires an integrated tool; rather they have focused on providing a solution for a specific subset of educational processes.

We conclude that (1) there is a need to integrate didactical concepts and strategies into the e-learning environment; and (2) there is a clear need for one unifying system to make the entire range of educational processes more efficient and effective (see also Parikh & Verma, 2002). In the remainder of this paper we present our prototype for a multimedia e-learning environment, called Sophia, and we will show how the above challenges can be met in practice. An application of Sophia is demonstrated elsewhere in this book.[13]

3. DIDACTICS INTEGRATED IN AN E-LEARNING ENVIRONMENT

The central objective of developing Sophia was to design an e-learning environment firmly rooted in a number of didactic principles that embody the aforementioned characteristics of competency-oriented learning. These principles are applied in several different instructional strategies. An instructional strategy contains a didactical scenario on how to teach students specific competencies[14] or knowledge. The instructional strategies provide the core of the application around which several other supportive facilities are designed.

The learning process of students contains different stages from mastering basic and essential concepts and methods to applying this knowledge in practical situations (Gonzàlez-Castaño *et al.*, 2001).[15] Sophia provides online

[13] Herman van den Bosch: How distance education can sustain the development of competencies.

[14] In accordance with Ulrich *et al.* (1995) we define competence as a student's ability to handle real-life situations in a professional way by integrating and applying knowledge, skills, insights, and attitude and to reflect on the chosen approach.

[15] Parts of this section draw on Caniëls and Smeets-Verstraeten (2004).

functionality supporting all these stages, *i.e.*, via the Internet one can (a) diagnose the knowledge the student already possesses; (b) provide the student with activities that will help him fill his knowledge gaps; (c) provide the student with assignments on real-life case(s) and let the student apply the theoretical knowledge to a real-life problem; and (d) test whether the student possesses the required level of knowledge or competence.

All instructional strategies cover one or more learning stages (see Table 2). Note that strategies do not always cover all stages, thereby opening possibilities for blended learning. It is possible for an organization to make a deliberate choice about the way in which each learning phase is supported, either by Web-based teaching or by offline methods. For example, some organizations might prefer to take the examination in a classroom environment, while all other learning phases take place online.

Table 2. Overview of Instructional Strategies in Sophia

	Learning Stages			
Instructional Strategies (Task Types)	(a) Detection of Knowledge or Competence Gaps	(b) Acquisition of Knowledge or Competencies	(c) Practice the Application of Knowledge or Competencies	(d) Examination
1. Diagnose	x	x		
2. Diagnose and test	x	x		x
3. Combination +	x	x	x	x
4. Combination			x	x
5. Practice +	x	x	x	
6. Practice			x	
7. Exam +	x	x		x
8. Exam				x
9. Discussion	x	x		x
10. Project				x

Explanation

Practice	In this task type students will exercise their skills by solving assignments that relate to a real-life case. This task type will provide automated feedback to the answers of a student. The purpose of this type of task is providing an exercise environment for the students; the answers of the student will not be rated.
Exam	This task type is very similar to the practice task, only now students will not receive automated feedback in response to their answers. This type of task is designed to provide an examination environment for the students; a teacher rates the answers given.
Combination	This task type combines the practice task and the exam task. Students will be able to practice exercises and the examination online.
+	Refers to the addition of a diagnostic test to a specific type of task. The diagnostic test shows the student whether he has the required level of knowledge to successfully fulfill the task or whether the student should study some more before trying to answer the assignments.

Note that while some instructional strategies cover an identical set of learning stages, they differ in the adopted didactical scenario. For example, instructional strategies 2, 7, and 9 all provide e-learning materials for processes (a), (b), and (d). Below we will explain the distinct didactical principles guiding each task type. In the design of e-learning materials authors can choose to develop a task that adopts a certain instructional strategy. Therefore, instructional strategies are also called task types. The entire study environment is structured around tasks.

Task types 1 and 2 (or instructional strategies 1 and 2) focus on the idea of providing knowledge to students on exactly those areas where they experience gaps. In this way the system accommodates differences in prior knowledge of students (characteristic 6 — accommodate for individual differences). Tasks of these types are used to determine the level of prior knowledge of students by means of sophisticated multiple-choice questions.[16] After completing the test the student receives advice for further

[16] To provide sophisticated multiple-choice questions Sophia is partly integrated with Question Mark Perception (QMP). QMP is a computer assisted assessment system, which allows several distinct forms of multiple choice questions and incorporates several mechanisms for differentiated feedback. Empirical evidence indicates that simply showing students the correct answer has less effect on learning than providing elaborate feedback on the correct and incorrect elements of the given answer (Dempsey, Driscoll, & Swindell, 1993). Moreover, the motivation of students is positively influenced when the feedback that is given is tailor made to the answer of the student (Ross and Morrison, 1993).

study that is conditional on the mistakes made in the test. One will usually employ tasks of type 1 at the beginning of a course. Based on the knowledge gaps, the students are directed towards tasks (of another instructional strategy) that will provide them with knowledge, insights, skills, and attitudes on specific subjects. Tasks of type 1 can be used in combination with a real-life exam in a classroom, while tasks of type 2 are specifically designed for online evaluation of students on their level of knowledge and competence. Type 2 tasks are typically used as a conclusion to an entire course.

Task types 3 to 8 are firmly rooted in constructivist ideas on just-in-time learning (Schoening, 1998) and case-based learning. After detecting and filling the knowledge gaps, the student starts out with a problem relevant for a specific firm provided in a case description. Assignments will lead the student to both relevant theory on this problem and background information on the firm (characteristic 1 — assignments as a point of departure; characteristic 2 — the use of cases). It is up to the student to determine which information to use for solving the assignments. Often the student will need to search actively for additional information (characteristic 5 — active search for information). Students are immersed in a real world context and discover how to use certain theoretical concepts and methods. Theoretical insights are gathered at the exact moment they are needed to solve the assignment (just-in-time). Type 3 tasks provide online facilities for all phases in the learning process, whereas tasks of types 4 to 8 leave room for fulfilling one or several learning stages offline.

Finally, task types 9 and 10 find their origin in problem-based learning (Birch, 1986; Norman, 1988; Dolmans *et al.*, 1994) and project-based learning (Blumenfeld *et al.*, 1991) respectively.[17] Project-based learning differs from problem-based learning in several ways. An important difference is that problem-based learning is directed more towards acquiring knowledge, while project-based learning strongly emphasizes the application of knowledge (Leroy & Van den Bosch, 2001, p. 10). In the problem-based tasks (type 9) students typically start with an online discussion on a specific case description, which is designed to seduce students into the investigation of problems. Students ask and refine questions and debate on ideas for possible solutions (characteristic 4 — collaboration). This stage is concluded with identifying what is lacking in the collective knowledge and then setting learning objectives. In a subsequent session (usually in a classroom),

---

[17] For a detailed description of the benefits of project-based learning we refer to Blumenfeld et al., 1991, pp. 372-372.

students will communicate their ideas and findings to each other and ask new questions until finally all learning objectives have been reached to the full satisfaction of all students. In Sophia this task-type is concluded with an individual assignment for each student, which will be graded by the teacher. The project-based tasks (type 10) follow a similar approach. The point of departure is an online project-assignment, which leads to an online discussion among students on how to manage the project. The final goal is to produce a certain artifact (*e.g.*, a model, a report, a videotape, or computer program) in a group effort. The final artifact is handed in online to a teacher who grades the end result.

From the perspective of a learning content designer, a course usually contains several tasks. A designer of e-learning materials starts out by choosing an instructional strategy suitable for the specific objective he wants to reach with a certain task. One has to choose which stages of the learning process will be supported online and which will be provided in another way (by classroom lectures, books, videos, etc.).

We can conclude that on the task level students are treated as active agents in the learning process instead of passive recipients of knowledge. In addition, the system provides an intake assessment. In this way the entire course (and even the entire program) can be exactly matched to the educational needs of students. Intake assessments can test either knowledge or competencies. Sophia provides knowledge assessments on several levels and in various areas, *e.g.*, history, mathematics, and English. Competencies are assessed with the "Intake Assessment for Competencies" (IAC), which contains three phases: self-assessment, portfolio, and interview. The self-assessment describes first of all the competencies that will be assessed. This is followed by a survey, based on the well-known STARR method (Situation, Task, Action, Result, Reflection), which consists of statements relevant for the specific competency.[18] The student ticks off his level of skill for each statement, which is then checked against the minimum required level of skill for the specific competence. In the portfolio phase of the IAC the student supplies documents that provide evidence of his personal skills.[19] These can be certificates of qualifications or descriptions of situations in

[18] The STARR method stems from behavioral interviewing and is based on the idea that past performance is the best predictor of future performance in a similar situation. If a student is able to describe a positive experience in which he demonstrated leadership skills in the past, it is likely that this student can duplicate this behavior in the future (Janz, 1986; Janz *et al.*, 1989).

[19] A portfolio can be defined as "a collection of evidence, usually in written form, of both the products and processes of learning. It attests top achievement and personal development, by providing critical analysis of its contents" (McMullan *et al.*, 2003).

which the student had to use a specific skill. An assessor will evaluate the quality of the provided documents and if they prove to be convincing, the assessor will schedule an interview with the student. The interview creates the opportunity to check whether the student is as competent as was indicated by the self-assessment and the portfolio. Based on the interview the assessor decides whether the student will be enrolled for the education program at all, and if so, which courses and tasks will be suitable.

4. ONE INTEGRATED SYSTEM

An important shortcoming of current software systems is that they provide solutions for only a limited set of educational processes. Sophia was designed to join all educational processes in one system. In this way all actors involved in the education of students can easily access tasks and student information. Moreover, one integrated system facilitates the managing of educational processes and increases the specialization of actors, thereby enhancing efficiency.

In Section 2 we argued that educational processes could be divided into three groups: (1) processes concerning the authoring and managing of educational materials on the task level (usually organized by an LCMS); (2) processes related to the design and management of information on the course level (usually supported by an LMS); and (3) processes connected with the teaching itself (e-learning environment). Our newly developed system provides support for all these groups of processes. It distinguishes different roles in each group. Each role gives the user of the system access to specific possibilities. In addition, each role defines several responsibilities for the user.[20]

4.1 LCMS

The author role takes a prominent place in the LCMS counterpart of our system. Authors are responsible for the creation of tasks and the storing of learning objects in the library. As already mentioned in Section 3, Sophia provides an author with a limited set of building blocks to construct a task. The building blocks ensure a sensible didactic approach and pave the way for a further specialization in the authoring process. Several blocks do not require expert content knowledge in order to be filled, *e.g.*, the inclusion of Websites that are relevant for cases. A (low-wage) student assistant can

[20] Parts of this section draw on Caniëls & Smeets-Verstraeten (2004).

execute this work. This specialization within the authoring process opens many possibilities for cost efficient content production, since easy tasks can be directed to lower-wage content designers. Content experts can focus on filling those building blocks that require expert knowledge.

Figure 1 presents a screenshot of the workspace of the author. The dark blocks on the right hand side of the screen correspond to the building blocks for a task. In this screenshot the building blocks for a task of type 3 (combination+) are shown. In this specific view, only one of the building blocks is unfolded, namely the one in which the assignments can be designed.

As soon as authors co-operate digitally and tasks are re-used, a content management system becomes vital to manage different versions of educational materials. Updating and revising learning objects introduces the danger of having different versions of the same object operational simultaneously. A content management system assures that tasks used by students cannot be altered or removed unintentionally by other actors in the system. Sophia introduces a life cycle for tasks to tackle this problem. Only legitimate authors can edit tasks during certain phases of the life cycle of a task.

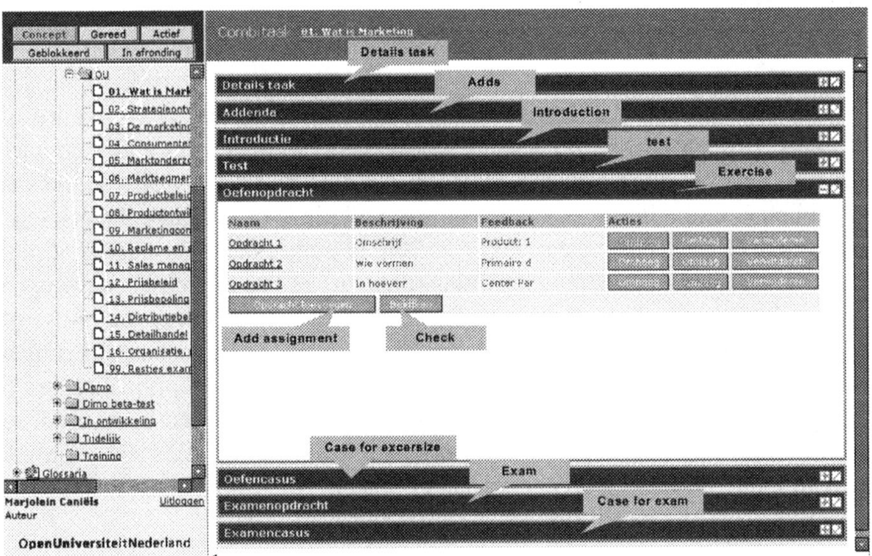

Figure 1. Screenshot of the Workspace of the Author

A task is subject to five life-cycle phases. In the upper left of Figure 1 the five life cycle phases are visible. As can be seen from the slightly darker color of the "concept" button, the author is currently working in the draft phase. In this phase the author develops a task. As soon as the development of a task is completed, the author will give the task the predicate "ready-for-use".[21] The task now enters the second phase of its life cycle. An author is allowed to withdraw the task from this phase, as long as the task has not yet been added to a course by the supervisor.[22]The third phase in the task life-cycle is called "active". Active tasks have been added to a learning path and therefore cannot be altered by authors. An addendum function allows supervisors and authors to add recent information to the tasks in this stage of the life-cycle. All students using these tasks will immediately be notified of this additional information. Large revisions of active tasks are only possible by copying an active task to the draft phase (in which the task can be revised). Once the task is revised it will be declared "ready-for-use" by the author and hence it can be included in new courses by the supervisor. However, in this example the unrevised tasks remain in circulation. To remove an outdated task, the author can "block" it, and thereby the task will reach its fourth stage in its life cycle. Active learning paths containing a blocked task will still be operational. However, a supervisor cannot include blocked tasks in new learning paths. Only "ready-for-use" and "active" tasks are available for the creation of new learning paths. Blocked tasks, which are not used in any course, automatically enter the final phase of their life-cycle. These so-called "closed" tasks are obsolete and may be deleted from the system by the author.[23]

An efficient LCMS is characterized by many possibilities for re-use of objects. Objects can be (a) resources, (b) tasks, and even (c) entire courses (learning paths). One of the facilities that enable re-usability of resources is the library. In the library, authors can store all kinds of learning objects, *e.g.*, images, cases, Websites, and text files. Other authors can be granted access to certain libraries, thereby enabling them to re-use materials developed earlier by other authors. A glossary is another facility enabling the re-use of objects. In this case an object is a specific glossary term, accompanied by a description and study advice about where to find a more elaborate discussion of the term in the literature. Just as a single glossary item can be re-used, so can entire glossaries pertaining to specific content fields be re-used. Conditional access protects content objects in Sophia against being

[21] Ready-for-use" corresponds to "gereed" in Dutch, see Figure 1.

[22] The supervisor role will be discussed under the heading "LMS". It is obvious though that the activities of supervisors have an influence on the environment of authors. Therefore, in practice it is impossible to make a strict demarcation between the LCMS and the LMS.

[23] "Closed" corresponds to "in afronding" in Dutch, see Figure 1.

overwritten unintentionally. Editing of objects is only allowed for authors within one content group (authoring in a specific content field). Authors of other content groups may be granted use of existing resources, but the only way for them to make adaptations is to copy the original objects to their own resource library before editing it.

4.2 LMS

The supervisor accommodates the functionality that is usually provided by an LMS role and an administrative role. In the supervisor role one is responsible for composing the educational program (*i.e.*, the course, or the learning path). Furthermore, the supervisor monitors the progress of all students in the learning paths he has created. When the course period is over, he closes the learning path by sending students their final grade. To compose a course the supervisor can either (a) choose an instructional strategy (or mix of strategies) that is considered useful for the course, and subsequently instruct authors to make tasks of this type; or (b) create a learning path with already existing tasks (developed by authors for another course). The latter is called re-use. Tasks can be (re-)used in an unlimited number of courses. This is sensible because a task is a learning object, which is created to fulfill a specific educational objective. One specific task could very well be useful in several different courses. A supervisor is able to compose different courses by (re)combining tasks. All tasks designed by authors within a certain content group can be used freely in learning paths. In order to facilitate re-use, tasks are stored in a content management system. Moreover, entire learning paths can be re-used as well (for instance for another group of students)[24]. A common function of an LMS is the administration of students and teachers. Sophia distinguishes a separate administrator role, in which one can add or remove users. An administrator can also design homepages for general use. These contain information on the educational institution or the company that offers the courses. In addition, the administrator can provide role-specific information that will be displayed in the system. For instance, students are welcomed to the training facility and are instructed about the use of the system. Similarly, authors are instructed about the process of creating educational materials with the application.

[24] Learning paths undergo a somewhat different, though similar life-cycle to tasks. The life-cycle of a learning path has the following phases: draft, active, and closed.

4.3 E-Learning Environment

The e-learning environment in Sophia provides a virtual space where students and teachers work and interact. The student role is quite straightforward. A student visits the Sophia Website and logs in with a unique and personal login name and password. The learning paths will direct the student to his/her tasks on different subjects. Questions on the tasks can be posed to the mentor. Usually, learning paths are concluded with tasks testing the competencies of the student.[25] Assessors will grade these tasks and subsequently the supervisor will grade the overall performance in the learning path. A student is still able to access his study materials after his assignments have been graded, but obviously he is not allowed to make changes.

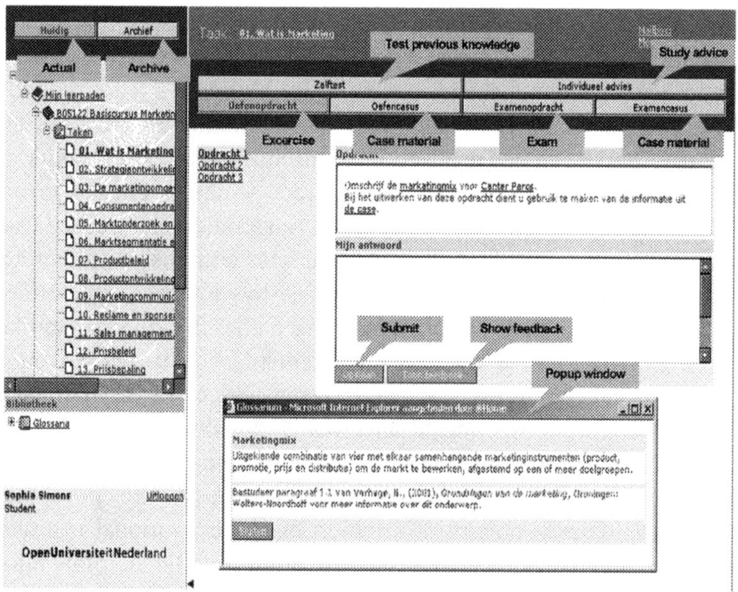

Figure 2. Screenshot of the Workspace of the Student

Figure 2 shows the workspace of the student. In this particular view a student sees the first assignment of a combination+ task. In the box below the assignment the student can type his analysis of the problem. Note the two hyperlinks in the assignment that lead the student to: (1) the theory about the

[25] This is not to deny the possibility for blended learning in the system that enables a choice for offline examination.

marketing mix (the link has been clicked and the small window in the lower part of the figure resulted); and (2) the case specific information about the firm Center Parcs. The button "Toon feedback" in the middle of the screen gives instant feedback on the assignment to the student. The upper right of the screen shows the mailbox of the mentor. By following this link the student can pose a question to the mentor of the course.

The teacher role is divided into several sub-roles. The *mentor* supports students by answering questions on the education material and uses facilities such as e-mail and a FAQ (Frequently Asked Questions). A mentor has access to progress overviews of the students, which enables him to focus on students who need assistance. *Assessors* are responsible for grading tasks of students. Sophia supports assessors in a number of ways. First, assessors can make use of answer models, describing the essential elements that a correct answer contains. Second, the system assures objectivity across assessors in grading the same assignments for different students. Depending on the task type, assessors have access to an overview of the grading behavior (and rationale) of other assessors for a specific assignment. The *moderator* role is created for instructional strategies that incorporate discussion groups related to a certain subject. The moderator monitors the discussion groups, deletes improper contributions and undertakes action against contributors who abuse the system. The role-differentiation allows for specialization within the teaching staff. Course development usually is performed by the professor; all other roles are performed by lesser-qualified individuals.

In the above we allocated each role to one of the three subsystems identified in Section 2. It becomes clear that it is nearly impossible to make such a clear demarcation of LCMS, LMS and the e-learning environment. Actors in all the subsystems co-operate and communicate. This is underscored by Figure 3. This figure shows how the Learning Content Management System (LCMS), the Learning Management System (LMS) and the e-learning environment are related and integrated within one system.

The tasks published by authors are used in courses (learning paths) designed by the supervisor. The supervisor allocates students and teachers to the course and monitors the progress of students and the behavior of teachers. Students communicate with other students, the teacher (in case of questions about learning content) and the supervisor (in case of planning problems). The teacher controls the progress of his students on detail level (by motivating them in the absence of progress) and he coaches them as they are working on the assignments. Eventually, the teacher grades the work of the student. This grade is instantly visible for the supervisor. When additional offline assignments exist, the supervisor inserts the grades for these offline assignments into the system and finalizes the course for the student. The grade will now be instantly visible for the student.

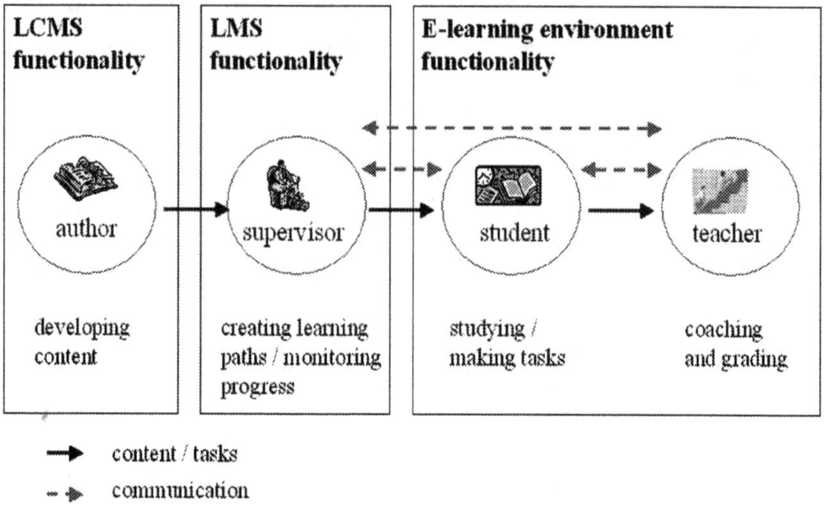

Figure 3. Organization of the Education in Sophia

The various overviews in the system provide valuable information to all the users. For instance, supervisors who want to design a course have an instantly updated overview of all tasks that are marked ready-for-use by the authors. This is only possible because of the integrated system that couples the LCMS to the LMS. Additionally, supervisors can instantly see whether teachers have graded the student assignments in time. The integrated system makes sure that information generated by the e-learning environment is always immediately visible within the LMS.

Real students in real courses currently use the system. The first preliminary evaluations of the implementation of Sophia indicate that the system meets all expectations. Sophia is fast and can be accessed easily through the Internet. The system is easy to use for students as well as teachers and managers of educational institutions. They highly appreciate the didactic principles incorporated. The system proves to be very effective in organizing educational processes such as the development of educational materials (especially by large teams of authors), the distribution of materials to students, and the maintenance of content.

5. CONCLUSIONS

The fourth generation of distance education calls for (a) the integration of didactical principles in an e-learning application, and (b) the development of one unified system that supports all actors involved in educational processes. Practical applications that tackle both issues are scarce. This paper demonstrated the design of an all-in-one system called Sophia. It showed how such a system could support the various educational processes that are usually separately attended to in an LCMS, LMS, and an electronic learning environment. The adoption of Internet technology in education does not automatically mean that principles of competency-oriented learning are followed. On the contrary, modern technologies are often used to revitalize out-dated learning principles. This paper showed that it is very well possible to adopt competency-oriented education and integrate these didactic principles in an e-learning application. Moreover, it gave a practical illustration of how the instructional strategies can support teachers in translating classroom education into Web-based education, thereby adopting and joining several distinct didactic principles and creating possibilities for students to develop competencies.

The underlying study is based on field research and is explorative in nature. Further research will be directed towards a detailed evaluation of the system. Different groups of users will be systematically questioned on different aspects such as ease of use, usefulness, timeliness of response, convenience, format and layout, accuracy, conformance to the knowledge gap, and satisfaction.

ACKNOWLEDGMENT

The authors thank Iwan Wopereis for valuable comments on earlier versions of this paper. The usual disclaimer applies.

REFERENCES

Al-Nuaimy, W., Zhang, J., & Noble, A. (2001), Web-based learning environment for a communications module. *Computer Applications in Engineering Education*, *9*, 114-121.

Barab, S. A., & Duffy, T. M. (1998). *From Practice Fields to Communities of Practice (CRLT Technical Report No. 1-98)*, Bloomington: Indiana University.

Boyatzis, R. E., Cowen, S. S., & Kolb, D. A. (1995). Innovation in professional education: Steps on a journey from teaching to learning, *The Story of Change and Invention at the Weatherhead School of Management*, 1st ed. San Francisco: Jossey-Bass.

Birch, S. (1986). Towards a model for problem-based learning, *Studies in Higher Education*, *11*, 1, 73-82.

Blumenfeld, P. C., Soloway, E., Marx, R., Krajcik, J., Guzdial, M., & Palincsar A. (1991). Motivating project-based learning: Sustaining the doing, supporting the learning, *Educational Psychologist*, *26,* 3,4, 369-398.

Burgess, J. R. D., & Russell J. E. A. (2003). The effectiveness of distance learning initiatives in organizations, *Journal of Vocational Behavior, 63,* 289-303.

Caniëls, M. C. J., & Smeets-Verstraeten A. H. J. (2004) How to integrate didactic principles in an e-learning environment (Management Sciences Working Paper gr04-01), Heerlen: Open University of the Netherlands.

Collis, B. (1998). New didactics for university instruction: Why and how? *Computers & Education, 31,* 373-393.

Davis, J. H. S. (2000). (Spring), Traditional vs. online learning: It's not an either/or proposition. *Employment Relations Today*, 47-60.

Dolmans, D. H. J. M., Schmidt, H. G., & Gijselaers, W. H. (1994). What drives the student in problem-based learning? *Medical Education*, *28*, 372–380.

Downes, S., (2002). *TheLearning Object Economy*. Moncton, Canada: National Research Council.

Duffy, T. M., & Jonassen, D. H. (1992). Constructivism: New implications for instructional technology. In T. M. Duffy & D. H. Jonassen (Eds.), *Constructivism and the Technology of Instruction: A conversation* (pp. 1-16). Hillsdale: Lawrence Erlbaum Associates.

Gonzàlez-Castaño, F. J., Anido-Rifón, L., Vales-Alonso, J., Fernández-Iglesias, M. J., Llamas Nistal, M., Rodríguez-Hernández, P., & Pousada-Carballo J. M. (2001). Internet access to real equipment at computer architecture laboratories using the java/CORBA paradigm. *Computers & Education*, *36,* 151-170.

Govindasamy, T. (2002). Successful implementation of e-learning – Pedagogical considerations, *The Internet and Higher Education*, *4,* 287-299.

Gunawardena, C. N. (2003). Theory into practice: The challenge of designing inquiry-based online learning environments. In T. M. Duffy & J. R. Kirkley (Eds.). *Learner Centered Theory and Practice in Distance Education. Cases from Higher Education* (pp 130-146). Mahwah : Lawrence Erlbaum & Associates.

Ismail, J. (2002). The design of an e-learning system: Beyond the hype, *The Internet and Higher Education*, *4,* 329-336.

Jonassen, D. H., & Land, S. M. (2000). *Theoretical Foundations of Learning Environments.* Mahwah: Lawrence Erlbaum & Associates.

Leidner, D. E., & Jarvenpaa, S. L. (1995). The use of information technology to enhance management school education: A theoretical view. *MIS Quarterly*, *19*, 3, 265-291.

Leroy, P., & Van den Bosch, H. (2001). The role of project-based learning in the "Political and Social Sciences of the Environment" curriculum at Nijmegen University. *International Journal of Sustainability in Higher Education*, *2*, 1, 8-20.

Merrill, M. D. (2000). First principles of education, paper presented at the International Conference of the Association for Educational Communications and Technology (AECT), Denver.

Moonen, J. (1994). How to do more with less? In K. Beatie, C. McNaught, & S. Willis (Eds.), *Interactive Multimedia in University Education: Designing for Change in Teaching and Learning* (pp. 155-163). Amsterdam: Elsevier.

Norman, G. R. (1988). Problem-solving skills, solving problems and problem-based learning. *Medical Education*, *22*, 279-286.

Parikh, M., & Verma S. (2002). Utilizing Internet technologies to support learning: An empirical analysis. *International Journal of Information Management*, *22,* 27-46.

Passerini, K., & Granger, M. J. (2000). A developmental model for distance learning using the Internet, *Computers & Education*, *34*, 1-15.

Perkins, D., & Salomon, G. (1988). Are cognitive skills context-bound? *Educational Researcher*, 18. 1, 16-15.

Porter, L., & McKibbin, L. (1988). *Management Education and Development: Drift or Thrust into the 21th Century*. New-York: McGraw-Hill.

Ramsden, P. (1992). *Learning to Teach in Higher Education*. London: Routledge.

Ross S. M., & Morrison, G. R. (1993). Using feedback to adapt instruction for individuals. In J .V. Dempsey & G. C. Sales (Eds.), *Interactive Instruction and Feedback* (pp. 177-195). Englewood Cliffs: Educational Technology Publications.

Schoening, J. R. (1998). Education reform and its needs for technical standards. *Computer Standards & Interfaces*, *20*, 159–164.

Spooner, F., Spooner, M., Algozzine, B., & Jordan, L. (1998). Distance education and special education: Promises, practices, and potential pitfalls. *Teacher Education and Special Education*, *21*, 2, 121-131.

Tabs, E. D. (2003). *Distance Education at Degree-Granting Postsecondary Institutions: 2000-2001*, Washington, DC: US Department of Education, National Center for Education Statistics.

Van den Bosch, H. M. J., & Kieft, M. (2001). The hybrid curriculum; the acquisition of academic competencies in the university curriculum. In W. H. Gijselaers (Ed.) .*Educational Innovation in Economics and Business Administration, Part V* (pp.41-56). Dordrecht: Kluwer, Academic Press.

Van Merriënboer, J. J. G. (1997). *Training Complex Cognitive Skills. A Four-component Instructional Design Model for Technical Training*. Englewood Cliffs: Educational Technology Publications.

Vermunt, J. (1992). *Leerstijlen en Sturen van Leerprocessen in het Hoger Onderwijs. Naar-Procesgerichte Instructie in Zelfstandig Denken*. Lisse: Swets & Zeitlinger.

Chapter 21

ADOPTION OF BLENDED LEARNING BY FACULTY

An Exploratory Analysis

Marc Humbert
Grenoble Ecole de Managemement, Grenoble, France

1. INTRODUCTION

Grenoble Ecole de Management (GEM) was created in 1984. Since its creation, considerable focus has been placed on the use of Information and Communication Technologies (ICT), which now is an integral part of the "culture" of most faculty members and students. As a matter of fact, laptops became mandatory for students 18 years ago.

With the development of the Web, management decided to move more and more into "e-learning," like in many other Higher Education (HE) institutions. In fact, it is more accurate to speak of "blended learning" because in such a traditional "bricks and mortar" institution, ICT acts more as a complement to traditional courses than as a complete distance learning tool. Among faculty members, some innovators began to put course content on Web sites as early as the 1990s, developing online interactive learning based on collaborative software to offer additional support to their lectures.

In 2001, GEM's Management decided to accelerate this process and to engage in a strategy of generalized blended learning. GEM's definition of blended learning was: a flexible combination of traditional education (Face-to-Face) and use of all kinds of ICT available to enhance learning. The 5-year plan defined for all courses was to progressively decrease the number of face-to-face sessions. The first action was to replace part of the lectures with multimedia content either online or on CD-ROMs. The second action was to create online activities to complement traditional face-to-face activities. To

M.K. McCuddy et al. (eds.),
The Challenges of Educating People to Lead in a Challenging World, 423–436.

meet these objectives, an e-learning lab was created in order to provide a set of services to students and faculty members alike.

An incremental approach was used to build this lab so that cost and resistance to change could be minimized. With a limited budget, it was necessary to develop faculty members' autonomy. In order to provide this autonomy, technology had to be kept simple and a lot of time had to be invested in training faculty members.

Work was carried out in two main areas: content creation and use of a Learning Management System (LMS) to manage content and to organize online activities for students. To begin with, most faculty members preferred simple software that they were used to (Word, Excel, and PowerPoint) in order to create content by attaching the corresponding files to the Learning Management System (LMS). Today, a lot of these instructors have moved on to use multimedia tools. Most of the multimedia content is developed using Microsoft Producer to obtain a combination of video and PowerPoint slides. This software has the advantage of being free and user-friendly, hence facilitating the change from traditional lectures. The remaining developments have been done using Macromedia Flash. Some instructors are able to develop content using this tool on their own, although most work in a team with a developer.

The choice of LMS was also based on an ease-of-use criterion. In this school, Lotus collaborative software (Lotus Notes and Quickplace) had been used for nearly 10 years with a lot of success for content management and collaboration, but it was not a real LMS. In 2003, among other Learning Management Systems, Lotus Learning Space was tested but Blackboard was chosen because it was more user-friendly. In 2004, the decision was finally made to migrate to an open-source LMS (called Moodle), which offers more functional features for collaborative activities while keeping the necessary ease-of-use (McMullin & Munro, 2004).

Now, it is time to evaluate the outcome of this plan regarding the faculty's adoption of learning technologies. The evaluation is based on a sample group of 37 faculty members and is divided into three phases: the first phase describes the online achievements of the professors surveyed; the second, based mainly on a questionnaire, analyzes the barriers to technology adoption; and the third phase focuses on an exploratory analysis of personal factors liable to explain the variations observed in the phase two analysis.

The following section provides a brief survey of literature on faculty members' adoption of technology. Section 3 presents the methodology behind exploratory research, based mainly on a survey conducted on a sample of 37 faculty members. In Section 4, the results of this survey are presented and discussed, while Section 5 presents some conclusions.

2. THEORETICAL BACKGROUND

2.1 Diffusion of "Innovation"

The first phase of this research is aimed at providing a description of the diffusion of innovation among faculty members. A highly conventional model is the diffusion of innovation model proposed by Rogers (1995), where people are categorized into five groups based on the time they "jump" into the innovation: Innovators, Early Adopters, Early Majority, Late Majority, and Laggards. This model was used by Padgett and Conceicao-Runlee (2000) to better understand faculty reaction to a development program on technology integration. In this study, a similar approach has been followed in order to identify whether it was a good model to describe the online behavior of GEM faculty members. This is the first descriptive phase of this research.

2.2 Barriers to Adoption

Many studies have dealt with the potential barriers to ICT adoption by faculty but these studies were mainly in the realm of distance learning. Less has been written about the specific case of blended learning but it can be assumed that the barriers are similar.

In these studies (Legget & Persichitte, 1998; Freeman & Capper, 2000; Pajo & Wallace, 2001; Cho & Berge; 2002; O'Quinn & Corry, 2002; Schifter, 2002; Parker, 2003; Giannoni & Tesone, 2003), the same groups of barriers can be identified:

- Concerns about workload, time spent online, and adequacy of payment for this time.
- Concerns about effectiveness and quality of e-learning.
- Concerns about technology (access to technology, technical expertise, technical support).
- Concerns about career development.

2.3 Influence of Personal Factors

Two interesting sub-areas of research have been identified.

2.3.1 Research into the Personality of instructors

Using the Myers-Briggs Type Indicator (MBTI), Chan (2001) investigated the impact of tutors' personalities on their teaching effectiveness in a distance learning institution in Hong Kong. The results revealed that tutors characterized by a high degree of extraversion were more effective in the classroom environment. Tutors with a high degree of introversion preferred online interactions. No statistically significant difference was found with respect to other personality dimensions.

2.3.2 Research into Teaching Styles

Grasha (1994) defines teaching style as a "pattern of needs, beliefs and behaviors that faculty display in their classroom." He identified five teaching styles that represented typical orientations and strategies implemented by college instructors. He claims "these styles converge into four different clusters (see Table 1) that, like colors on an artist's palette, make up the characteristic ways professors design instructional settings." The Web sites of Indiana University and the University of Alabama (2004) propose a brief description of each cluster and an online test (the Teaching Style Inventory) to "categorize" instructors.

Table 1. Grasha's Categorization of Instructors

Cluster	Description
Cluster 1	The expert/formal authority cluster tends toward teacher-centered classrooms in which information is presented and students receive knowledge.
Cluster 2	The personal model/expert/formal authority cluster is a teacher-centered approach that emphasizes modeling and demonstration. This approach encourages students to observe processes as well as content.
Cluster 3	The facilitator/personal model/expert cluster is a student-centered model for the classroom. Teachers design activities, social interactions, or problem-solving situations that allow students to practice the processes for applying course content.
Cluster 4	The delegator/facilitator/expert cluster places much of the learning burden on the students. Teachers provide complex tasks that require student initiative, and often group work to complete.

According to their findings, the first cluster of teachers should favor e-Lectures, Hyperlinking and Video–recorded lectures. The online requirements are "Read this electronic document" or "View this PowerPoint or video." The second cluster should prefer streaming video lab demonstrations, virtual Laboratories and Whiteboards. The third cluster should focus on Virtual Laboratories, Virtual Field Trips, Discussion Boards and Chat Rooms, while the last should opt for Electronic Portfolios and WebQuests.

3. METHODOLOGY OF THE SURVEY

The study was conducted on a sample group of 37 professors at Grenoble Ecole de Management (about half the staff), all of whom had at least some basic experience in one type of online work or another. All of these professors were volunteers and were responsible for at least one blended course on the "Sup de Co" (Master in Management) program.

The study was divided into the following three phases.

3.1.1 Phase 1

A detailed analysis of their online work was conducted in order to test the Rogers' (1995) model. This analysis was based mainly on the online achievements of these professors and was performed by a group of three experts. These experts built up an analysis grid using different criteria and measurements: speed of reaction; quality and quantity of online content; quality and quantity of online activities and assessments, site visits, etc. The grid made it possible to draw up an initial classification which was then slightly adjusted following interviews with faculty members.

3.1.2 Phase 2

A questionnaire about barriers to ICT adoption was designed in two stages. During a preliminary short interview, faculty members provided a first list of main barriers according to them. This list was supplemented with information from literature on the subject, and then a final questionnaire was designed. This final questionnaire contained 20 questions. In each question, participants were invited to evaluate the strength of a barrier. A five-point Likert scale was used with responses ranging from 1 = "This barrier is not important at all" to 5 = "This barrier is very important." All 37 faculty members completed the questionnaire. Finally, after collecting the results of the questionnaire, additional follow-up interviews with some faculty members provided additional information for the analysis.

3.1.3 Phase 3

Faculty members were asked to take the MBTI test (if they did not already know their profile). Nineteen subjects submitted their profiles. These profile results were correlated with the groups obtained in the first phase and also with the item "Risk of decreasing the richness of interactions" from the questionnaire in the second phase. Finally, the subjects have been asked to answer a test helping to identify their teaching style using the "Teaching

Styles Inventory" (TSI) available on the Indiana University Web site. This involved 18 people and the results were interpreted in relation to the descriptive analysis performed in the second phase.

4. RESULTS

4.1 Description of Adoption Process

After the classification process described above, the subjects were placed in the following groups:

Innovators: Three instructors could be seen as innovators. All their content has been online for many years; they have made significant efforts to propose online activities. They use online assessment. They are always ready to test a new technology to try to improve the online part of their courses. They are usually self-taught and learned to use technology before the training was organized.

Early adopters: Seven instructors were classified as early adopters. They used e-learning before it was a school requirement. All their content is online and based on multimedia technology. They have played an important role in the diffusion of ICT by encouraging their colleagues to adopt these technologies.

Early majority: Twelve instructors were categorized as early majority. They have been influenced by early adopters to move towards blended learning. They need suitable support, both from a technical and educational point of view. They also need rewards and incentives to be comfortable with this change.

Late majority: Fifteen instructors constitute the late majority. They have begun blended learning but only did so when it became mandatory. They want to be convinced that their current work will be enhanced with this approach.

Laggard: No instructor was placed in a "laggard" category, which is not surprising because our survey focused on faculty members who already had experience with these technologies. Laggards, if any, might be found in the rest of the faculty.

An interesting point to note is that in the questionnaire we asked these instructors to identify the category to which they thought they belonged. Not surprisingly what they perceived was different from what was actually observed: they tended to overestimate their category, ranking themselves more on the innovative side of the scale (most of them considered themselves as early adopters).

Table 2 reports the means and standard deviations for responses to each of the questionnaire items. These results were analyzed using the categories identified in literature.

Table 2. Results of the Questionnaire

Rank	Item	Mean	Standard Deviation
1	Risk of decreasing the richness of interaction	3.81	1.49
2	Lack of time to prepare online content and activities	3.70	1.27
3	Difficulty dealing with online interactions	3.15	1.20
4	Control of time spent in online interactions	2.95	1.43
5	Adequacy of payment for time spent online	2.92	1.53
6	Effectiveness of multimedia to replace traditional lectures	2.79	1.49
7	Fear of lower learning level for students	2.78	1.20
8	Lack of understanding of institution's vision and strategy	2.65	1.49
9	Appropriation of content developed by other people	2.50	1.43
10	Fear of having a less effective course	2.49	1.53
11	Fear of students' rejection	2.25	1.49
12	Difficulties involved in online assessment	2.19	1.42
13	Fear of being a victim of fashion	2.11	1.42
14	Technical problems	2.08	1.27
15	Fear of loss of recognition	1.84	1.39
16	Fear about legal issues	1.84	1.01
17	Fear about status and role	1.69	1.24
18	Difficulty achieving quality design	1.65	1.37
19	Global lack of trust	1.62	0.92
20	Difficulty of moving on to a learner-centered approach	1.58	1.33

Legend: all items reflect adoption barriers. They are measured using a Likert scale from 1 = "this barrier is not important" to 5 = "this barrier is very important."

4.1.1 Time and Adequacy of Payment

Time issues (perceptions of a high workload for online teaching) are the most cited barriers in the literature (see for example, Legget & Persichitte 1998; Pajo & Wallace, 2001; O'Quinn & Corry 2002; Naidu, 2004). In this survey, time issues were cited by nearly all faculty members during preliminary interviews and when asked open-ended questions. In the questionnaire, items 2, 4, and 5 are time-related and may be analyzed as described below.

"Lack of time to prepare online content and activities" has a mean score of 3.70 and "Control of time spent on online interactions" is graded a little lower at 2.95. This points to a difference in relation to the early results presented in literature. The early results cited from the literature are mainly based on Anglo-Saxon experiments and may therefore be due to cultural differences. According to Anglo-Saxon feedback, more importance is given to the workload involved in interactions with students than to the time spent on preparation (Sellani & Harrington, 2002). This could be explained by the fact that Anglo-Saxons may be more used to adopting existing content while French instructors will think about developing new material for teaching online.

These figures correspond to perceptions, not objective reality. Indeed, it would be interesting to have a more objective means of measuring time. Perception can be misleading: instructors may feel they are losing control over time because online time is not bounded. This is illustrated in item 4 in the survey relating to 'time control' (mean score = 2.95). In fact, real time measurement is still an open research question with a lot of controversial results. For example, Lazarus (2003) reports a study of time measurement for three courses and concludes that the time periods are very similar to those of traditional courses. In contrast, Schifter (2004) reports numerous studies indicating more time spent in distance education. Using time logs, Cavanaugh (2005) compares two courses, one taught online and the other based on traditional teaching methods, and shows a significantly higher workload for the online course. He concludes that this difference is explained by the time spent in communicating with students. On the contrary, Thompson (2004) performed an in-depth analysis of the workload of six faculty members in an online environment and she concludes that their workload, with time measurements based on each task, was comparable or slightly smaller than that involved in face-to-face courses. According to her, a differential "chunking" of productive time contributed in some cases to a perception of increased workload.

Another important issue is how that time is valorized by the administration: with blended-learning, it is necessary to define efficient compensation systems. Item 5 relating to "adequacy of payment for time spent online" scored an average of 2.92 but obtained a high standard deviation (1.53). This is certainly due to variations in real time spent online but also to variations in compensation found across programs. Indeed, different compensation systems have been reviewed at GEM but there is as yet no clear norm. According to Schifter (2004), this variation in compensation models is a general problem and as such could influence our findings.

4.1.2 Quality and Effectiveness

Not surprisingly, quality and effectiveness issues are a big concern for the faculty members surveyed. Although there is a substantial amount of literature on this subject, there is still a lot of discussion about whether e-learning or blended learning methods are as effective as traditional education (Olson & Wisher, 2002). Generally speaking, the two items about effectiveness have a low to medium-level score ("fear of having a less effective course" at 2.49 and "fear of a lower level of learning" at 2.78) and after three years of experimentation, faculty members are generally confident about e-learning effectiveness (item relating to a "Global lack of trust" is ranked 19th with a score of 1.62). However, an analysis of the different online components of a blended course (content, online activities and interactions, and online assessment) shows some interesting variations.

Interaction appears to be the main concern of faculty members ("Risk of decreasing the richness of interaction" is ranked in first position at 3.81 and "Difficulty dealing with online interactions" is ranked third at 3.15). The instructors maintain a strong belief in the richness of face-to-face interaction and are afraid that if traditional sessions are reduced, the loss of interaction will not be compensated by online interaction. Some of these instructors do not even use online interactions, preferring instead face-to-face sessions to interact with their students. Those who try to use online interactions encounter many difficulties. These perceptions are highly consistent with the results of surveys conducted on students where a low rate of satisfaction with online interaction has been observed. (Student satisfaction surveys about e-learning are performed on a yearly basis and questions about online interactions usually score around 2.5 on a 5-point scale where 1 indicates a very low level of satisfaction and 5 a very high level of satisfaction).

Concerns about content and design of online courses are less noteworthy. "Difficulty achieving quality design" scores 1.64 (ranked 18) and "Effectiveness of multimedia to replace traditional lectures" is graded at 2.79. Again, this is in accordance with students' perceptions (in the annual satisfaction surveys questions about quality of online content usually get a score of over 4). Among the 37 instructors, 28 had already created and used multimedia content while nine had not yet tried this. It is interesting to note that the average score is 2.55 for the first group and 3.44 for the second group. With these small samples, the difference is not significant ($p = 0.06$) and the assumption that the barrier is lower for instructors who have already tried out multimedia tools would need to be checked with larger samples.

"Difficulties involved in online assessment" has a mean score of 2.19. This is low but there is certainly a bias in the answers because instructors use online assessments for self-assessment purposes (non-graded) in most cases. It is not really significant since the question itself was somewhat ambiguous according to post-questionnaire interviews. In fact, many faculty members use online postings of papers but do not consider this as online assessment, and those who use online tests (about half of them) again use these for self-assessments (without grades) in most cases. Thus the main problem of online assessment, the question of integrity (Olt, 2002), was not covered by the question. During interviews, this question of integrity was introduced and caused many questions to be raised by faculty members.

4.1.3 Technical Expertise

An organization cannot successfully implement e-learning or blended learning without proper infrastructure. Technical expertise is often reported as an important barrier to technology integration (Cho & Berge, 2002) and technical support must be easily available. In GEM, where there is a high level of technical culture, this was not the case. Access to technology is not a problem in this environment. All faculty members have a laptop and benefit from high speed Internet access in the school and at home. Technical support is good, numerous training sessions are organized and plenty of assistance is available. As a consequence, item 14 concerning "technical problems" scored 2.08. However, during the initial interviews technical problems were found to be more important in the late majority group. A difference could be observed in the results of the questionnaire (2.33 for the late majority group and 1.82 for the other groups) and was found to be significant with a t-test ($p = 0.047$).

4.1.4 Evolving Role and Status and Vision of the Future

Frequently, e-learning requires modifications in faculty work processes and in the roles played by faculty members within the institution. Many aspects of the roles played by faculty members are changing.

The idea of moving on to a learner-centered approach is not perceived as a big barrier by our faculty; the corresponding item is ranked as the least important (rank of 20 with a score of 1.58). As lecturers in management, the instructors have been trained in this approach and may be reluctant to give a conservative image of themselves.

According to this survey, recognition does not appear to be an important issue: "Fear of loss of recognition" is only graded at 1.84, and "Fear about status and role" at 1.69.

Analyzing concerns about the vision for the future is an interesting venture. "Lack of understanding of institution's vision and strategy" obtained a low to medium-level score (2.65) but had a high standard deviation of 1.49. One important reason for developing e-learning for Higher Education institutions is to try to deal with the increasing student population and decreasing funding while improving productivity. This can be perceived as contrary to improving quality, which is another objective proposed. During interviews, many faculty members admitted feeling uncomfortable with these dual objectives. According to Jones, Lindner, Murphy, and

Dooley (2002), faculty who are "philosophically in agreement" with distance learning have a higher perceived value of this process and are more motivated to participate. This is a clear indication that administrative departments should provide faculty with valuable perspectives of blended learning to promote a successful program.

4.2 Analysis of Personal Factors

The last phase of the study was aimed at explaining the differences observed in faculty members' behavior. Two characteristics were analyzed: instructors' personality and teaching style. Since the sample is small, this is only a first exploratory analysis, one which needs to be extended in the future.

4.2.1 MBTI

A first analysis was performed to try to confirm Chan's results (2001) on Introversion/Extraversion. Among the 19 faculty members who provided their profile, ten are extraverted (E) and nine are introverted (I). As shown in Table 3, these data were compared with the adoption process results where the first 3 categories have been grouped together. Unfortunately, these data are not sufficient to prove any statistically significant relationship.

Table 3. MBTI Analysis

	Innovators, Early adopters, Early Majority	Late majority
Extraverted	4	6
Introverted	5	4

With the same objective, the results for item 1 on the "Risk of decreasing the richness of interaction" were compared according to whether the instructors were extraverted or introverted. The overall score for this item was 3.81. It was 3.42 in the group of 19 MBTI profiles. It is 3.67 for the extraverted group and lower (3.33) for the introverted group. These results (extraverted are less attracted by online interactions) are in accordance with Chan's results but are not significant. As Chan did, we found no significant relationship between online behavior and other personality dimensions provided by MBTI.

4.2.2 Influence of Teaching Styles

Eighteen faculty members answered the TSI. Eight of them were in the first cluster, three in the second, four in the third and three in the fourth. Again with so few data, it was impossible to perform a quantitative analysis. A first exploratory analysis was conducted on the eight people belonging to the first cluster and was based on Web site analysis and interviews.

Six cases from the eight "expert/formal authority" cluster were in accordance with the hypotheses given at the Universities of Indiana and Alabama (2004). Their Web sites contained sophisticated e-content and online communication with students was very directive. Online exchanges were very poor.

5. CONCLUSION

After the first three years of this "blended learning" project, the results obtained in this study are globally encouraging concerning faculty adoption of e-learning.

In the future, identification of barriers to acceptance should now help both the e-learning lab and school management to improve support to faculty. For the e-learning lab, much work remains to be done to improve online activities and encourage instructors to place more trust in them. The results suggest that school management must deal with time and workload issues. To better analyze these findings, it is now necessary to establish more precise measurements of the time spent in development and online activities; and it will be the role of management to set up effective norms regarding adequacy of payment for time spent online. Finally, school management must also define a clear vision of the future.

After this first exploratory phase, which is very descriptive, further research using larger sample groups must be conducted to explore personality and teaching styles. A better understanding of these factors will lead to increased flexibility of the overall system.

REFERENCES

Cavanaugh, J. (2005). Teaching online — A time comparison. *Online Journal of Distance Learning Administration, 8* (1): available online at http://www.westga.edu/~distance/ojdla/spring81/cavanaugh81.htm, checked on July 15, 2005.

Chan, B. (2001). *An Empirical study of the relationship between tutor's personality and teaching effectiveness: Implications for management of tutors in distance education.*

International Conference on Offshore Education and Training in an e-Learning World, Australia.

Cho, S. K., & Berge, Z. L. (2002). Overcoming barriers to distance training and education. *USDLA Journal, 16* (1): available online at http://www.usdla.org/html/journal/JAN02_Issue/article01, checked on July 15, 2005.

Freeman, M. A., & Capper, J. M. (2000). Obstacles and opportunities for technological innovation in business teaching and learning. *The International Journal of Management Education, 1* (1), pp 37-47.

Giannoni, D. L., & Tesone, D. V. (2003). What academic administrators should know to attract senior level faculty members to online learning environments. *Online Journal of Distance Learning Administration. 6* (1): available online at http://www.westga.edu/%7Edistance/ojdla/spring61/giannoni61.htm, checked on July 15, 2005.

Grasha, A. F. (1994). A matter of style: The teacher as expert, formal authority, personal model, facilitator, and delegator. *College Teaching, 42*, 142-149.

Indiana State University. (2004). *CTL Teaching Styles*. Available online at http://www.indstate.edu/ctl/styles/tstyle.html, checked on July 15, 2005.

Jones, E., Lindner, J., Murphy, T., & Dooley, K. (2002). Faculty philosophical position towards distance education: Competency, value, and educational technology support. *Online Journal of Distance Learning Administration, 5* (1): available online at http://www.westga.edu/~distance/ojdla/spring51/jones51.htm, checked on July 15, 2005.

Lazarus, B. D. (2003). Teaching courses online: How much time does it take? *Journal of Asynchronous Learning, 7* (3), 48-53.

Legget, W. P., & Persichitte, K. A. (1998). Blood, sweat, and tears: 50 years of technology implementation obstacles. *Techtrends, 43* (3), 33-36.

McMullin, B., & Munro, M. (2004). Moodle at DCU, (DUBLIN CITY UNIVERSITY). EdTech 2004, Fifth Annual Irish Educational Technology Users' Conference, Tralee, Ireland, June 3-4 2004: available online at http://odtl.dcu.ie/wp/2004/odtl-2004-01.html, checked on July 15, 2005.

Naidu, S. (2004). Trends in faculty use and perceptions of e-learning. *Asian Journal of Distance Education, 2* (2): available online at http://www.asianjde.org/2004v2.2.Naidu.pdf, checked on July 15, 2005.

Olson, T. M., & Wisher, R. A. (2002). The effectiveness of web-based instruction: An initial inquiry. *International Review of Research in Open and Distance Learning*, October 2002: available online at http://www.irrodl.org/content/v3.2/olsen.html, checked on July 15, 2005.

Olt, M. (2002). Ethics and distance education: Strategies for minimizing academic dishonesty in online assessment. *Online Journal of Distance Learning Administration, 5* (3): available online at http://www.westga.edu/~distance/ojdla/fall53/olt53.html, checked on July 15, 2005.

O'Quinn, L. & Corry, M. (2002). Factors that deter faculty from participating in distance education. *Online Journal of Distance Learning Administration, 5* (4): available online at http://www.westga.edu/~distance/ojdla/winter54/Quinn54.htm, checked on July 15, 2005.

Padgett, D., & Conceicao-Runlee, S. (2000). Designing a faculty development program on technology: If you build it, will they come? *Journal of Social Work Education, 36* (2), 325-341.

Pajo, K., & Wallace, C. (2001). Barriers to the uptake of web-based technology by university teachers. *Journal of Distance Education, 16* (1): available online at http://cade.icaap.org/vol16.1/pajoetal.html, checked on July 15, 2005.

Parker, A. (2003). Motivation and incentives for distance faculty. *Online Journal of Distance Learning Administration, 6* (3): available online at http://www.westga.edu/~distance/ojdla/all63/parker63.htm , checked on July 15, 2005.

Rogers, E. M. (1995). *Diffusion of Innovations*. New York: Free Press.

Schifter, C. C. (2002). Faculty participation in asynchronous learning networks: A case study of motivating and inhibiting factors. *Journal of Asynchronous Learning, 4* (1), 17-22: available online at http://www.aln.org/publications/jaln/v4n1/pdf/v4n1_schifter.pdf, checked on July 15, 2005.

Schifter, C. C. (2004). Compensation models in distance education: National survey questionnaire revisited. *Online Journal of Distance Learning Administration, 7* (1): available online at http://www.westga.edu/~distance/schifter31.html, , checked on July 15, 2005.

Sellani R., & Harrington, W. (2002). Addressing administrator/faculty conflict in an academic online environment. *The Internet and Higher Education, 5* **(2)**, 131-145.

Thompson, M. M. (2004). Faculty self-study research project: Examining the online workload. *Journal of Asynchronous Learning Networks, 8* (3), 84-88: available online at http://www.sloan-c.org/_publications/jaln/v8n3/pdf/v8n3_thompson.pdf, checked on July 15, 2005.

University of Alabama Website. (2004). *Exploring excellence in teaching.* Available online at http://www.teachingweek.ua.edu/learningstyles.html, checked on July 15, 2005.

Chapter 22

DIGITAL MEDIA U, THE SECTORAL UNIVERSITY

Applying the Concept of a Corporate University to a Business Sector

Tim Cappelli and David Russell
Manchester Institute of Telematics and Employment Research, Manchester Metropolitan University, Manchester, UK

1. INTRODUCTION

Digital Media U (DM-U) is a European Union assisted project, run by MITER[26] at Manchester Metropolitan University (MMU). It responds to the demand for skills development in Digital Media, a sector considered vital to the economy of the North West[27] of England. Project partners include IBM, FD Learning, and Macromedia.

The first conceptual challenge is related to the discrete nature of the industry, which would seem to preclude setting up a corporate university. Conversely, there is no professional association to represent the numerous micro enterprises and to organize training and qualifications.

DM-U is predicated on a 'cluster' view of digital media in the region, as applied by the North West Development Agency (NWDA) Regional Strategy 2003, and our knowledge of the sector and the relationships among its members induced us to see it in terms of a supply chain, leading to the idea of a 'sectoral university.' DM-U's development is influenced by examples of:

[26] Manchester Institute of Telematics and Employment Research

[27] This spelling reflects NWDA, the North West Development Agency in the United Kingdom.

M.K. McCuddy et al. (eds.),
The Challenges of Educating People to Lead in a Challenging World, 437–453.

- Corporate universities' extension of services to supply chain partners.
- Continuous Professional Development (CPD).
- Work-Based Learning (WBL).
- Knowledge capture linked to learning in organizations.

DM-U will provide a Continuous Professional Development (CPD) service for professionals in the sector, who will join as members. The emphasis will be on easy and instant accessibility and the service will be both personalized to the member and customized for specific sub-sectors — for example, e-learning or games. Members can enter at various levels and choose their own pathways through the materials and resources.

DM-U will offer a blend of online and offline courses, enhanced and supported by a range of learning and support facilities. The CPD Framework will be underpinned by external and internal accreditation, allowing credits towards MMU awards. DM-U is built on an innovative conceptual model, where the learning and knowledge management functions interact to offer learning programs and sharable resources, such as case studies and project rooms.

It is intended to exploit the relationships among members and project partners to create a 'sectoral learning community,' which will influence curriculum development. This sectoral learning community will be formed by MMU, MITER and its networks, project partners, educational institutions, and learners and their organizations.

This paper provides a work in progress report, focusing on:

- The Digital Media sector and the demand for learning.
- Adapting the Corporate University (CU) model.
- Building the curriculum and acquiring content.
- Building a model to link assessment and accreditation.
- Progress on the project to date.

2. BACKGROUND

MITER's EU funded projects over the past five years have focused on the creative and digital industries. The project benefits, in terms of experiences, expertise, networks and research results, are now being combined in our two main projects, DM-U and Digital Media Watch (DM-W), an industry monitoring and intelligence gathering service. DM-W, through its annual survey and news service, will be a key provider for DM-U's information resources.

The Single Programming Document[28] recognizes the Digital Media Sector as a determinant of economic prosperity and sustainability and the digital and creative industries have been identified as priority sectors in the North West Development Agency Regional Economic Strategy 2003. There is, however, no trade body or single source of specialized support.

The sector is fast moving and difficult to define, but the Digital Industries North West (DINW) Strategy Document (2002, p. 3) includes within it *"web design, multimedia, hardware and software consultancy and supply, networking installation, 3D visualization and product design, Internet service provision, data processing and mining, digital gaming, digital broadcasting and e-learning."* The sector is also difficult to quantify and businesses appear under several Standard Industrial Classification (SIC) NWDA categories, meaning that datasets overlap. DINW (2002) estimates that there are around 5,000 businesses employing 50,000 to 60,000 people in the region. Three quarters of these businesses employ fewer than 10 people, a figure corroborated by the 2003 Annual Survey carried out by DM-W.

The strategy for the Digital Industries in the North West (2002) highlighted a shortage of management and technical skills, as well as 'soft skills.' These findings were echoed in the 2003 DM-W survey and many small firms, by necessity, are seeking staff with the ability to work in several areas. The earlier CLIME project[29] workshops evidenced demand among creative businesses for the sort of training and advice common to all micros and Small and Medium Sized Enterprises (SMEs), regardless of sector.

DINW (2002) identified weaknesses and threats to the industry, including a shortage of experienced managers and shortcomings in the supply of technical skills. The DM-W survey of 2003 raised some criticisms of current training and education. It identified some 'soft' skill shortages such as problem-solving and social skills while some respondents saw a lack of specialist IT knowledge as a key barrier to growth. Others were seeking combinations of skills, such as technical and business ability, that would allow people to work in more than one area.

DM-W found a lack of awareness of existing support mechanisms and previous MITER research (SMILE[30]) had suggested that although many

[28] The North West England Objective 2 Single Programming Document, http://www.eurofundingnw.org.uk/DocDetails.asp?DocumentId=30&section=documents.

[29] Creative Leaders in Media Enterprises, a one year European Social Fund project undertaken by MITER, 1999-2000.

[30] Report of the Skills for the Missing Industry's Leaders and Enterprises (SMILE) Project, a one year European Social Fund/ADAPT project undertaken by MITER, 2000-2001

companies rely on sub-contractors rather than recruiting full-time employees, there is difficulty in finding subcontractors with the relevant skills. These two areas come within the scope of DM-U's resources.

DM-U sees its members as the equivalent of a supply chain and the partners form part of our community. Corporate universities have widened their scope to include supply chain partners and we thought that features of the corporate university model would be appropriate.

3. CORPORATE UNIVERSITIES

A corporate university (CU) has been defined as a "centralized strategic umbrella for the education and development of employees ... [which] is the chief vehicle for disseminating an organization's culture and fostering the development of not only job skills, but also such core workplace skills as learning-to-learn, leadership, creative thinking, and problem solving," (Meister, 1998, p. 38). Examples of corporate universities in the USA and UK, respectively, are Motorola U and Unipart U. Motorola U provides learning to staff, customers, suppliers, and partners across the world and accredits course delivery through other institutions. It has now extended its services into consultancy.

Unipart U was originally designed to improve employee performance and centers on a physical facility where staff both learn and teach. It too is now open to customers and suppliers, and a main principle is to get the learning into practice quickly. A Unipart U innovation is 'Faculty on the Floor,' which enables workers in production cells to solve problems using computer-based problem-solving tools and Web-based examples of best practice.

3.1 Applying the CU Model to DM-U

Some of the CU themes adopted by DM-U are short, 'just-in-time,' courses, opening up to the supply chain and selling of additional services. We are mapping the CU idea across to DM-U in several ways, including small chunks of learning, a focus on business issues, and a range of topics and delivery. There are other themes reflected in the CU concept, as exemplified in the Businesslab project, that have been carried into the development of DM-U and will enable it to transcend the role of course provider. These are:

- Using technology to deliver just-in-time learning programs.
- Developing strategic partnerships with suppliers and clients.
- Developing the CU as a branded profit center.

- Raising knowledge levels in individual firms and across the sector.
- Using technology for knowledge capture and management.
- Harnessing the intellectual capital of the workforce.
- Using tools to integrate learning with intellectual capital.

3.2 A Sectoral Learning Community

At the heart of DM-U is the creation of a 'sectoral learning community,' building on theories of Communities of Practice and applying them in the light of MITER's work on 'Integrated Learning Communities.' The Learning Community will be made up of MITER's existing digital media network, project partners, educational institutions, and members and their organizations. Definitions of 'learning community' vary; Brosnan and Burgess (2003) quote Wenger (1998, p. 215) who says that it is a community of practice that "includes learning, not only as a matter of course in the history of its practice, but at the very core of its enterprise." For us, the term is used to describe "the interactions between the collection of communities of practice integral to the firm and the range of external experts, clients and end users implicated in the creation of an e-learning product" (Russell, Calvey, & Banks, 2003, p. 35).

Brosnan and Burgess (2003) noted how social networks and trust developed in the community they created around a Web-based course for learners from different organizations. Russell *et al.* (2003*)* noted that the e-learning firms they studied generated a dynamic among learners who were encouraged to share experiences and stories. They too were from different organizations and their learning is situated in the professional arena, rather than in their own firm.

As members contribute information and case studies to DM-U resources and respond to 'ask the expert' questions, DM-U will have to capture and manage this knowledge. Earl (1994, p. 62) provided a model of knowledge management specifying that "for a business to build a strategic capability in knowledge, the proposition is that at least four components are required. [These are] Knowledge systems, networks, knowledge workers and learning organizations."

DM-U will be able to draw on the people and the networks; and its capture systems form part of the technical architecture. It intends to create the learning organization by combining Work-Based Learning (WBL) with the other necessary components, which are 'team work, training demand and knowledge as a strategy' (Earl, 1994).

4. DM-U ARCHITECTURE

The representation in Figure 1 shows the various elements of the environment and the way they interconnect.

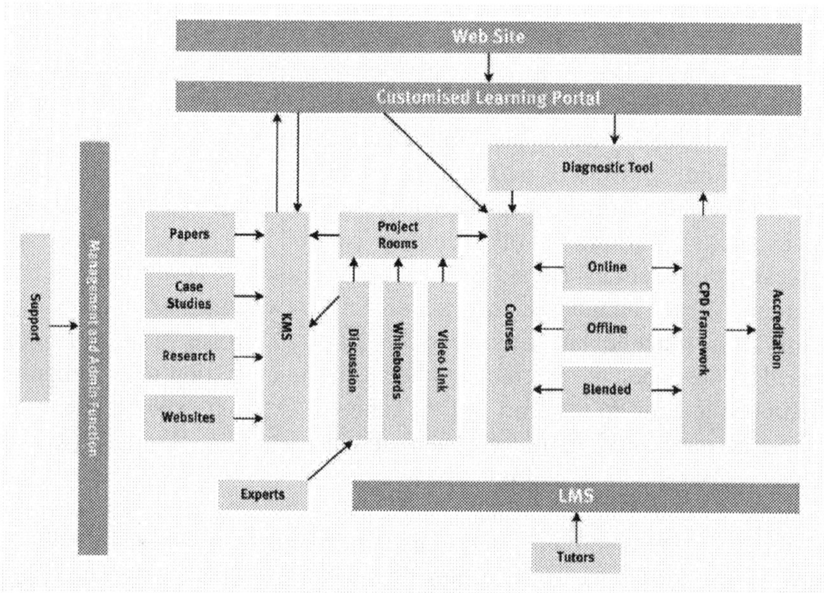

Figure 1. Elements in the Environment and Their Interconnection

This architecture was derived from an examination of the needs of the digital media industry as described previously. The most crucial of these was the need for relevant, immediate training and information, which was accessible to a technically sophisticated audience. In addition, empirical evidence from the SMILE Project demonstrated the lack of awareness that existed in the Digital Media Constituency in relation to the training and professional development needs of managers. The previous work by MITER also demonstrated the need for a better exchange of best practice within the sector set against an environment where knowledge was a commodity and therefore closely guarded. Hence, the provision of an online curriculum of courses alone was insufficient to cover the needs of this expanding and economically important sector. Instead a 'Whole Development Model'[31] was

[31] Term and methodology used by David Bird, now of MMU Business School, 2002.

required which supported the learning and transfer of knowledge within the sector.

The Whole Development Model states that learning is not confined to the provision of courses or the gaining of awards. Learning is instead a continuous process, which derives from experience, and relies on the flow of knowledge within a Learning Community. The Whole Development Modality is achieved through the facilitation of this process together with coaching learners through this knowledge, enabling them to 'mine' each other as well as providing information on demand to support performance. Hence, the five elements of achieving the Whole Development Modality are:

- Learning.
- Knowledge Management.
- Learning Community Support.
- Coaching.
- Performance Support.

Using the Corporate University Model, these elements of Whole Development Modality were then incorporated into the architecture for DM-U as shown in Figure 2.

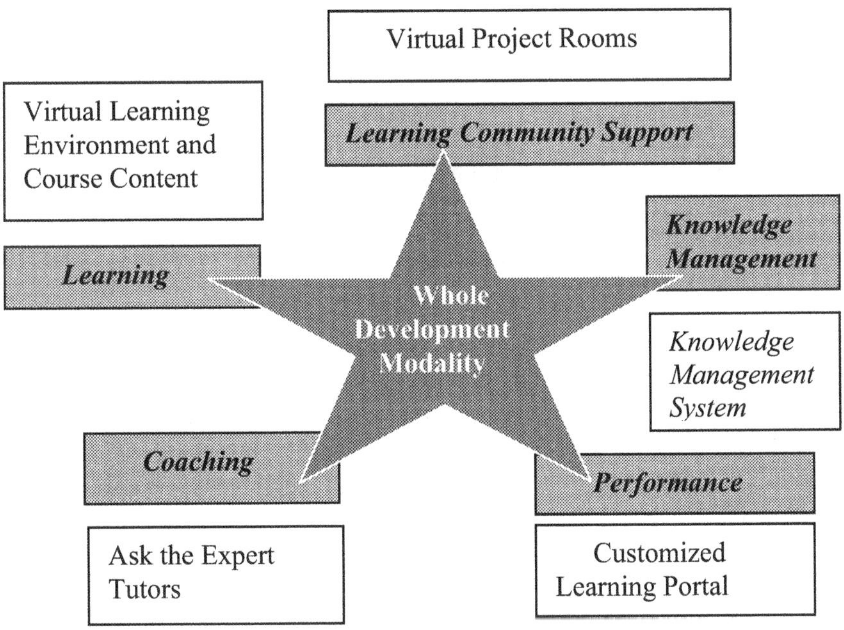

Figure 2. Whole Development Modality

5. LEARNING

DM-U provides access to a range of courses — on-line, instructor-led and 'blended' — all accessed and managed by a Virtual Learning Environment.

5.1 Knowledge Management System (KMS)

The KMS of DM-U is the heart of the functionality and the part that adds much of the value to this environment. The KMS links with the users' information and preferences and is be able to:

- Work as a searchable database allowing users to find information based on key words.
- Link with keywords from each of the courses, to provide resources for learners when they enroll.
- Track users' previous requests for information and courses and flag up new, relevant information.
- Highlight linked resources based on requests for courses and information and users' job roles. The information coming from the KMS's tracking and collating of user preferences drives the personalization of the portal.
- Customized Learning Portal.

This part of the architecture provides the overarching portal, which interfaces with all other aspects of the architecture. Its function is to provide a seamless service to the user; and by integrating the KMS with the Learning Content, provide on-demand information and learning.

5.2 Ask the Experts

This allows users to pose questions to a group of 'experts' from the wider learning community, for instance, in technology, business, or legal subjects. Other members may also reply to questions and become identified as experts themselves, thus growing the size and capacity of the community. Tutors assigned to the various courses also facilitate this guidance towards relevant knowledge.

5.3 Project Rooms

The virtual rooms provide a focal point for users to work together in a collaborative environment, sharing applications and resources synchronously and asynchronously; and, in effect, acting as the tool through which the learning community can communicate. By providing secure, virtual rooms with access to a range of online applications, users can meet and collaborate on common issues, exchanging best practice and facilitating the flow of knowledge between theoretical courses and practical applications.

5.4 CPD Framework and Accreditation

This element will be discussed in more detail later but the framework and accreditation model are being developed especially for DM-U.

6. LEARNING IN DM-U

DM-U's emphasis is on Work-Based Learning (WBL) and the principal idea behind the learning environment is to establish links across learning, application, value, accreditation, and business performance improvement. WBL is founded on the educational principles that much learning activity at work can be recognized and accredited as part of a qualification.

The whole basis of the curriculum is to enhance and enrich the performance of the individual or the employee, but, through WBL, this carries through to the business as well, increasing performance of the business community. Because of the small size of many of the businesses in the sector, we would argue that, in development terms, the individual and the business become synonymous.

Theories and company procedures often differ from actual workplace practice and real competence results from combining them in practice-based learning (Lave & Wenger, 1990; Brown & Duguid, 1991). Staley and MacKenzie (2001, p. 16) emphasize the value of Work-Based Learning and suggest the question: "What opportunities can we create for students to put theory into practice?" They point to the use of 'substitute experiences' for students in Higher Education, but, in DM-U, we want the members to build on real experiences.

6.1 DM-U Curriculum

DM-U will offer a choice of courses or learning units of varying lengths — instructor-led, on-line, and off-line. We recognize that some topics are better suited to an instructor-led approach, and, where certificated industry standard products are available, we see no advantage in developing competing products.

6.2 Design of the Curriculum

DM-U is founded on the principle that learning undertaken in the workplace can be treated in the same way as formal or traditional learning. WBL can be accounted for and recorded, building up an e-portfolio of career-long learning, independent of employers' records. WBL can also be used to count towards a formal qualification. The development of the DM-U CPD framework was influenced by the examples of the Chartered Institute of Management, the Institute of IT Training, and other professional bodies. Because of the close relationship between individual and business development, CPD and WBL will combine to improve professional practice and commercial performance.

7. LEARNING DELIVERY

DM-U needs to recognize the constraints faced by SMEs and micro businesses: they are disparate, they are pressed for time, and they are usually under financial pressure. Small firms look for 'absolutely-last-minute' training (Attwell, 2003) and our own research (MITER, 2004) found that they want material to be modified to address small firms' needs and those of particular sectors; 'Just-in-Time/Just Enough' (JIT/JE) training could also be 'Just for Me.'

Some topics, particularly technical, are usually delivered in a classroom setting and are often described as better suited to an instructor-led approach but, where possible, we would like members to be able to choose from face-to-face, online, and offline. Many small firms tell us that they cannot afford face-to-face training and that they are excluded from the sort of discounts available to corporations.

We also found an ambivalent attitude to course completion and accreditation (MITER, 2004); some course participants saw value in directly relevant sections but not in formal completion, and only around half expressed an interest in qualifications or certification. Again, we are offering a choice.

7.1 Learning Content Domains

All the DM-U learning content is acquired from outside suppliers (as opposed to the university) and is organized into three 'domains': *Professional*, *Entrepreneurship*, and *Personal Development*, which we will explain further.

7.2 Professional

The DINW strategy document of 2002 emphasizes the role of technology in the creation of the digital industries sector and the topics in this domain concentrate on technical skills, especially with 'industry standard' tools, and keeping up to date with changing technology.

Although people are often recruited on the strength of industry reputation, portfolios of work and demonstrable skills, feedback from MITER's Wired City Cheshire networking meetings shows that freelancers and micros enhance their credibility with clients by using 'vendor specific' certificates and qualifications.

7.3 Entrepreneurship

The content in this domain addresses the management and business issues that the developing firm encounters. Most businesses in this sector are between two and five years old (MITER, 2003) so we concentrated on developmental rather than start-up issues. This is not only a critical period for survival in business terms, it is the stage at which the individual proprietor has to move beyond his or her own, usually technical, area of expertise and adopt a managerial role. Although digital media is specialized, businesses face 'generic' issues regardless of sector and courses will include financial awareness; project management; sales and marketing; the legal environment, including intellectual property and employment law; and management techniques.

7.4 Personal Development

This domain is aimed at helping the individual acquire a broader range of personal and interpersonal skills that can be applied within the business organization to help the development of owners and staff. Topics in this domain include communication, leadership, coaching, interviewing skills, business presentations, and time management.

8. SELECTION AND ACQUISITION OF CONTENT

Morrison and Meister (2000) raised the prospect of companies going direct to 'the sources of what they want taught' (for example, publishers) and bypassing universities altogether. With the need to satisfy the JIT/JE needs of small firms, we considered that the standard university course structure would be inflexible and too slow, with lengthy planning periods and long lead times even for short courses. We were also seeking content with more emphasis on practice as opposed to theory.

The criticism of inflexibility applies in part to the main providers of technical training where instructor-led sessions run to a fixed timetable. However, they are internationally known and sell certificated industry standard courses and we found several of them willing to enter into 'brokerage' contracts that offer DM-U members 'consortium purchasing' advantages with discounts normally available only to corporations.

Some online learning content is located on our own servers and other programs involve granting access to remote servers, again after booking and payment. Eventually, we are planning to move on to commissioning content to address specific business needs and use learning objects to create our own programs.

9. DM-U ASSESSMENT AND ACCREDITATION

Most of the learning programs available to DM-U members will have built-in assessment, but formal assessment in DM-U is voluntary for members; they are free to do as much or as little of the courses as they choose. We know that within this sector most people are graduates and we acknowledge the findings of Owen (2002) that there is relatively little business and professional demand for postgraduate qualifications. However, DM-U is based on choices and we offer an accredited CPD framework. We wanted to accommodate those who wish to acquire MMU qualifications and to create in DM-U a model applicable to other business sectors where formal qualifications are more important.

The decision to offer to DM-U members the opportunity to gain university qualifications raised two challenging issues: creating a work based assessment system and accreditation of 'outside programs.'

The work-based assessment approach, adopted by DM-U, attempts to avoid the dangers that Wolf[32] sees in 'the language of competence based assessment, learning outcomes and quality audit,' when this is linked to courses without an element of workplace application.

We argue that added richness and value derive from the application of learning and DM-U will be giving credit to application in the workplace. This carries through the link to business performance and needs. Sanchez

[32] Alison Wolf, Professor of Education at The Institute of Education, London, writing in the Times Higher Education Supplement, April 4th 2003

(1996) suggests that there are three types of knowledge that may exist in firms: know-how (practical), know-why (theoretical), and know-what (strategic). By concentrating on WBL and the application of learning, DM-U's programs are intended to help generate all three types. Our intention is that DM-U will offer conceptualization of learning, real practice, evaluation, and reflection.

Many of the units of learning offered by DM-U will come from outside providers or be 'vendor specific': that is, based on particular software applications. For these to lead to MMU qualifications, we would need to put numerous courses from disparate sources through the MMU accreditation and quality procedures. Although some credit levels are mappable across schemes, this would be a process with enormous resource implications.

Thinking about these two issues prompted the idea of aggregating the learning units and assessing of members' work through online 'Wraparound Accredited Assessment (WAAs) Units (WAAs),'[33] matched to university qualification levels. These assessment units will be used to demonstrate how the learning has been applied, reviewed, and evaluated within the work/business context. These units will bring together assessment and accreditation by 'wrapping around' learning and its application providing evidence of evaluation and reflection on practice.

10. DM-U ACCREDITATION MODEL AND OPERATION OF WAAS

A Credit Framework is described by the UK Credit Equivalence project as 'a set of minimal specifications for valuing, measuring, describing and comparing achievement in a common way.' Credits are awarded to learners for the achievement of learning outcomes at a level determined by level descriptors. The values are usually based on learning times attached to the learning outcomes and credit level.[34] Some levels can be mapped across schemes (NICATS, 2002, p.98[35]) and Credit Accumulation and Transfer Schemes (CATS) allow learners to accumulate credits in an awarding

[33] Name and units developed by Les Selby, DM-U Curriculum and Accreditation Manager, 2003.

[34] In Higher Education, the general approach is that 10 hours = 1 credit, 1 year = 1200 hours of study, so that a course involves 360 credits. In Further Education, credits are more closely related to learning outcomes and measurable achievements.

[35] NICATS, the Northern Ireland Credit Accumulation and Transfer System developed to develop a credit framework across all post-16 education and training, linking FE and HE.

institution and transfer those credits both within that awarding institution and in other bodies and schemes.

In using WBL and the workplace application of learning, the framework must accommodate assessment procedures incorporating systematic reflection on experience and an element of self-assessment. DM-U intends to use versions of Accreditation of Prior Learning (APL) and Accreditation of Parallel Professional Learning Experiences (APPLE). APL normally relates to learning and experience gained from a formal program and APPLE may include formal or informal programs and/or professional work experience undertaken during the period of registration.

APL, in its various forms, is often used in practice as a prerequisite for admission to courses (Wallis, 2000) or to gain exemptions, but this is not the approach that DM-U will adopt. Ecclestone (1992) highlights the flexibility of credit systems and the ways in which assessments can become part of the learning. This latter point is important, because DM-U's model of WAAs will be much closer to APPLE. The experiential learning will be contemporaneous with the program. On this point, we see this use of APL as something more than replicating university course requirements or finding and measuring equivalencies between work experience and established academic courses. Starr-Glass (2002, p. 229) sees a danger of reducing APL to a "sterile, norm-related examination of the status quo." He recommends ways of taking APL beyond the "concurrent validity (which) looks for a similarity between APL outcomes and those who are presently identified as possessors of this kind of knowledge (presently enrolled students or job incumbents)" (Starr-Glass, 2002, p. 223). We want to keep close to what goes on in the workplace and tailor the curriculum to present and future business needs; and we hope that the partners' involvement in the DM-U community members might bring some of the 'predictive validity' that Starr-Glass (2002) seeks.

The MMU Approval Documentation requires logical links among units, cohesion, progression, and an approved level. The WAAs would be under our control and would fit with MMU approval procedures, giving structure to the CPD framework. In the absence of an external professional body, MMU would act as the benchmark by which the CPD activities could gain validity and reliability.

In creating WAAs as freestanding modules under our control, we had to apply level descriptors from existing courses to ensure that learning outcomes are consistent with the University's existing programs and levels. To set up the WAAs, there had to be a linkage of external learning activities with the rigors of the MMU system. Although we were not seeking to accredit all the DM-U learning content, we had to organize learning units into blocks at recognizable levels so that they fit with the WAAs. Again, this was done using existing level descriptors.

The elements of the actual WAA modules require evidence of:

- Personal development.
- Research and action planning.
- Integration of learning into practice.
- Evaluation of learning and application.
- Reflection and review.

By undertaking WAA, learners can demonstrate achievement of these 'approved' outcomes.

11. CONCLUSION

The project's main objective is to increase the productivity, creativity and competitive performance of SMEs in the Digital Media Sector, through the provision of support and the creation of a learning community and network. While the development was funded until the end of 2004, the overriding aim was for DM-U to become self-sustaining at the end of that period.[36] The membership levels and take up of courses will show that DM-U is responding to the market. There are specific annual targets for outputs, results and impacts, measured in terms of SMEs assisted, sales increases, and jobs created. Achievements will be measured against these targets quarterly. Overall, critical success factors and key performance indicators drive DM-U. It is guided by MMU program approval and quality procedures but it is not part of the mainstream of the university. It can therefore be seen as a business venture and while not highly speculative, there are risks. As such, a business model has been developed for DM-U which aims to take the initiative from an EU funded project to a full self-sustaining venture with its own value chain and financial model.

At the time of writing, the DM-U portal has been built (see http://www.dm-u.co.uk) and we have set up agreements with course and content providers. Several tranches (or slices) of learning content have been loaded and all the forms for registering for CPD and explanatory material are available. The project rooms are operational. The accreditation model and WAAs are still under development and there will be a two-stage

[36] In fact self-sustainability was never achieved since the project started late and the marketing campaign failed to recruit the level of members required by the end of the project. Given a longer timescale and a more effective marketing strategy, the model would prove sustainable.

development of the CPD Program with the pathway established first and the accredited CPD pathway to follow by mid 2005.

This paper is very much a work-in-progress report and is quite descriptive. However, we have shown that we are developing a model that responds to current research and, perhaps more importantly, to market needs. DM-U responds to the UK Government intention to encourage stronger partnerships between Higher Education institutions and regional development agencies. The concept and architecture are innovative and the project is building CPD and accreditation models from scratch. DM-U will generate partnerships and exploit them in innovative ways. It is also envisaged that, when fully developed, the DM-U model could be used in other sectors.

REFERENCES

Attwell, G. (2003). E-learning and Small and Medium Enterprises. Elearningeuropa.info, http://www.elearningeuropa.info/doc.php?lng=1&id=4329&doclng=1, accessed November 9, 2004.

Brosnan, K., & Burgess, R. C. (2003). Web-based continuing professional development — a learning architecture approach. *Journal of Workplace Learning*, *15* (1), 24-33.

Brown, J. S., & Duguid, P. (1991). Organizational knowledge and communities of practice. *Organization Science*, *2* (1), 40-57.

Businesslab, Corporate Learning Environments: Research Program Prospectus, http://www.businesslab.co.uk/popup/downloads/CLE_Prospectus.pdf, accessed November 9, 2004.

Digital Industries North West (DINW). (2002). A Strategy for the Digital Industries in the North West of England: SWOT Analysis, Strategic Framework an Action Plan. SQW Ltd. for Digital Industries North West, Warrington.

DM-Watch Project. (2003). DM-Watch Project Industry Intelligence Annual Survey of the Digital Media Sector 2003, to be published by MITER, Manchester (awaiting publication).

Earl, M. J. (1994). Knowledge as strategy: Reflections on Skandia International and Shorko Films. In C. Ciborra & T. Jelassi (Eds.), *Strategic Information Systems* (pp. 53-69). Chichester: Wiley.

Ecclestone, K. (1992). *Understanding Accreditation: Ways of Recognizing Achievement*. London: Further Education Unit.

Lave, J., & Wenger, E. (1990). *Situated Learning: Legitimate Peripheral Participation*. Cambridge, UK : Cambridge University Press.

Manchester Institute of Telematics and Employment Research (MITER). (2003). Digital Industries in the North West, http://www.dm-w.co.uk/downloads/industry/research/NWreport311.pdf, accessed November 9, 2004.

Manchester Institute of Telematics and Employment Research (MITER). (2004). Perceptions of Online Marketing Training using Broadband, report prepared for Multimediamarketing.com, manager of project on behalf of North West Development Agency Broadband Fund, available from MITER.

Meister, J. (1998). Ten steps to creating a corporate university. *Training and Development, 52* (1), 38-43.

Morrison, J. L. & Meister, J. C. (2000). Corporate universities: An interview with Jeanne Meister. *The Technology Source,* http://ts.mivu.org/default.asp?show=article&id=785, accessed November 9, 2004.

NICATS (Northern Ireland Credit Accumulation and Transfer System). (2002). Designing Learning Programs: A Credit Based Approach, (a guide to the NICATS Credit Scheme, available on request from NICATS, Belfast).

Owen, J. (2002). A Report into Current and Future Skills Development Requirements in the Digital Content Sector, for Digital Dynamics, a North West Development Agency Skills Development Fund project (a report into the findings of the Digital Dynamics project, available on request from NWDA, Warrington UK).

Russell, D., Calvey, D., & Banks, M. (2003). Creating new learning communities: Towards effective e-learning production. *Journal of Workplace Learning, 15* (1), 34-44.

Sanchez, R. (1996). Managing articulated knowledge in competence-based competition. In R. Sanchez & A. Heene (Eds.), *Strategic Learning and Knowledge Management* (pp. 163-187). Chichester: Wiley.

Staley, A., & MacKenzie, N. (2001). *Computer Supported Experiential Learning.* Birmingham: University of Central England.

Starr-Glass, D. (2002). Metaphor and totem: Exploring and evaluating prior experiential learning. *Assessment and Evaluation in Higher Education, 27* (3), 221-231.

Wallis, M. (2000). *Pathways to Accreditation for Lifelong Learning: Guidelines for Using the Open College Network.* Leeds: West and North Yorkshire Open College Network.

Chapter 23

DESIGN AND IMPLEMENTATION OF VARIOUS WEB-BASED COURSES WHICH INVOLVE A DIDACTIC TECHNIQUE

The ITESM Model

Aurora González Turnbull, Rubén D. Santiago Acosta, and Blanca J. Garza Flores

Monterrey Institute of Technology, Campus Estado de México, México

1. BACKGROUND

The Instituto Tecnologico y de Estudios Superiores de Monterrey (ITESM or Tec de Monterrey) is an educational institution with the goal of contributing to the development of the country and its society. In order to accomplish this, every ten years the ITESM gives an opinion poll to various companies, the ITESM graduates, the alumni employers, and the professors. Considering the national and international context, the employment situation in the country, the international education tendencies, and the most recent technological advances, the ITESM System establishes its mission.

The ITESM *Mission towards 2005* is to educate individuals who are: (1) committed to the social, economic, and political improvement of their communities; and (2) internationally competitive in their areas of specialty. Carrying out research and extension programs relevant to Mexico's sustainable development is also part of the Mission of the Institute.

The ITESM Education Model has emerged within this context.

M.K. McCuddy et al. (eds.),
The Challenges of Educating People to Lead in a Challenging World, 455–474.

2.THE ITESM MODEL

To fulfill the ITESM Mission, the students must acquire and/or develop certain attitudes, abilities, and values (known by the Spanish acronym of HAVs), which are now explicitly written in each of the courses. In this sense we are moving from a traditional teaching methodology (see Figure 1) to one in which the students play the main role in the learning process (see Figure 2). There is a combination of individual and group learning, teachers' lectures, and student's independent learning. This will allow the graduates to best respond to the needs of society.

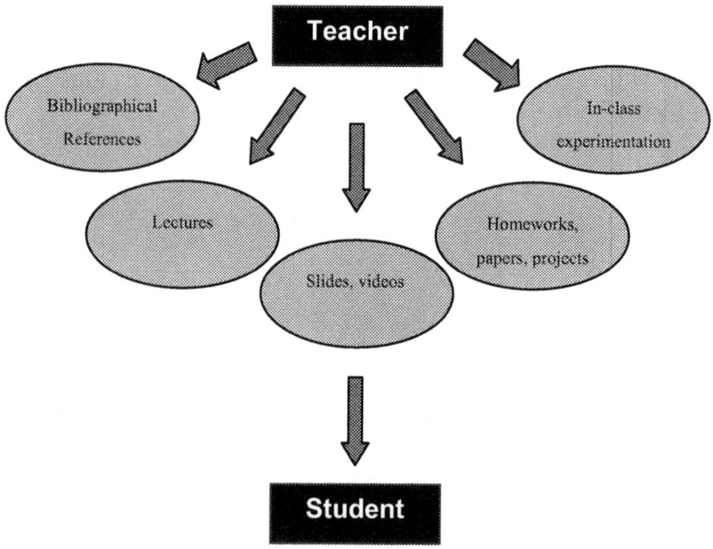

Figure 1. Traditional Educational Model

The challenge now is for the teacher to incorporate some of those HAVs in each of his/her courses based on the instructional design prepared at the Institute for this purpose. In this instructional design three main factors have been considered: the course design; the planning of the course, which includes objectives, content, activities, materials, and evaluation; and a combined traditional and on-line strategy that moves the professors' role from lecturer to facilitator of the learning process.

The main differences between the traditional and the redesigned model are shown in Table 1. We can observe that this model enhances self-learning because it is student-centered, so students play a more active role and the professor's intervention works in relation to the students' requirements.

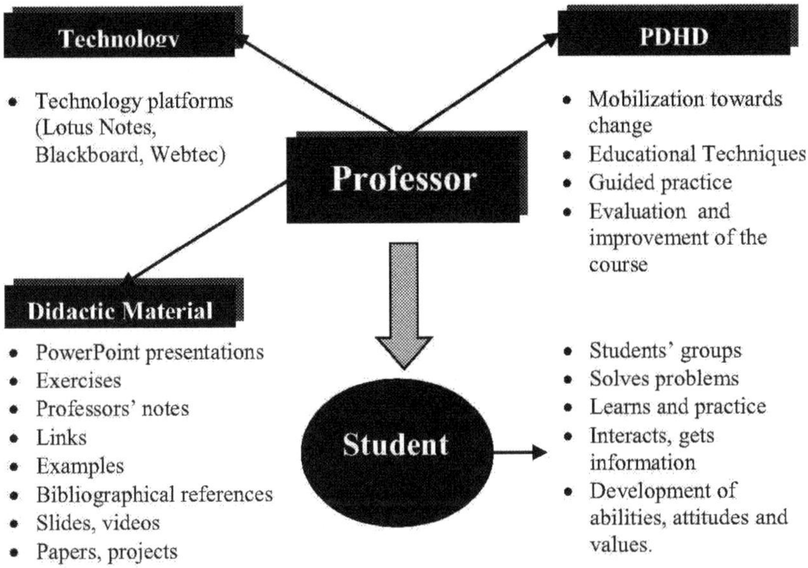

Figure 2. Professor and Student Roles

Table 1. Differences Between the Traditional and Redesigned Model

Traditional Model	Redesigned Model
Teacher-centered	Student-centered
Centered in teaching	Centered in learning
It develops attitudes, values, and abilities accidentally	It develops attitudes, values, and abilities in a programmed way, and they are evaluated
Teacher's lectures	Variety of didactic techniques, such as problem-based learning, case methodology, project-oriented learning, collaborative learning
Reduced use of technology	Use of various technological resources

Two more elements are incorporated into the redesigned model: collaborative learning and a more efficient use of technology. In this sense, we have to emphasize that the entire process of the educational model at the ITESM is based on the most recent educational technology. The courses are supported by a Web-based platform. The ITESM has designed its own platform, Webtec, which is a response to the specific needs and requirements indicated both by the teachers and by the students, after previously using two other platforms: Learning Space and Blackboard.

As we have seen, the challenge is for the teacher to guarantee the continuous educational preparation of the students, as well as an efficient development in new knowledge. In order to obtain these results, the Institute supports the academic staff with national and international training programs in didactics, philosophy, technology, and education evaluation systems. As shown in Figure 2, the professor and the student play different roles than they do in the traditional educational model shown in Figure 1.

2.1 Training Program at the ITESM

All full-time and part-time members of the faculty are required to take some mandatory training courses that comprise the Program for the Development of Teaching Abilities (PDHD in Spanish). This program has two specific objectives: (1) To offer a variety of courses, workshops, and activities that train the professors in the knowledge, abilities, and attitudes that must be incorporated in the educative model, as well as in the methodologies and didactic techniques required to do it. (2) To use a centered educational methodology, such as the one the professor applies in the educative model, with its inherent characteristics. This will allow the professor to assume a new role as s/he is building his/her own training process in which s/he plays a central role (Martin Perez, 2002, p. 147). The program's purpose is to promote the same learning environment as the one the students are going to experience, so, among its characteristics, the program intends to motivate the professor so s/he will be involved in the ITESM Mission and in the changes it implies.

To better understand the process, we are going to describe the PDHD (see Figure 2), which has four stages:

- STAGE 1 — Mobilization towards change: At this stage, the professor is introduced to the educational model of the Institute, its Mission, the changing process within the Institute, the desired profile of the graduates and professors, world-wide educational tendencies, etc.
- STAGE 2 — Educational Techniques: As part of the reengineering of the learning process, teachers have to participate in the redesign process of their courses. To do so, s/he has to be trained in didactic techniques, instructional design, and the use of a technology platform. This stage will be explained in more detail in the following section.
- STAGE 3 — Guided Practice and Evaluation: At this stage, the teacher participates in guided practice during the implementation of the course that s/he teaches. This process involves the evaluation and reflective process of the redesigned course with the

implementation of a didactic technique. The results are documented and the participants are encouraged to continue with this process even after concluding the next stage.

- STAGE 4 — Improvement of the Course: Based on the observations and comments done at Stage 3, the teacher is responsible for making necessary changes. This process will be very useful in the future because the redesigned courses are going to be validated every two years.

2.2 The Changing Process in the ITESM MODEL

We have observed the transformation of the professor into a facilitator of the process; now we will describe the elements that have to be considered in redesigning a Web-based course that incorporates a didactic technique as a global strategy for the teaching-learning process. The Educational Model of the ITESM is based on some characteristics that must be included in all of the courses, regardless of the level or discipline (Martin Perez, 2002, p. 45). These characteristics make the student learn to work collaboratively, acquire relevant and deep knowledge, direct his/her own learning, and improve his/her learning through additive and formative evaluation.

2.2.1 The Education Committee

To assist in the process at ITESM, Campus Estado de México (CEM), an Education Committee was formed (Comité Educativo, CE). It is an entity that was created to assist the academic staff in developing and implementing their courses on a Web-based platform. The elements and relationships of the Education Committee, shown in Figure 3, are described below.

- *Tutor CE.* Each member of the academic staff of the Committee is called a tutor. A tutor is a professor who: has already redesigned his/her course and the course has been approved by the Academic Vice-presidency of the Institute; has been trained in instructional design as well as in one of the main didactic techniques mentioned above; has accomplished the PDHD program; and collaborates in other academic activities at the Campus in order to contribute in the development of the Educational Model between full time and half time professors. Some of the tutors have a high proficiency in English so they can tutor the process of the courses that are being redesigned in English.

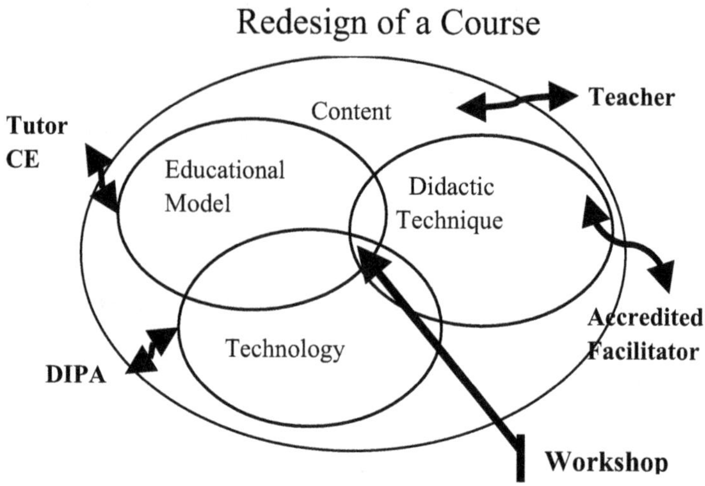

Figure 3. Elements and Relationships of the Education Committee

- *DIpA* is the Spanish abbreviation of Direction of Informatics for the Academy. It is the entity in charge of the technology training programs for the academic staff and it also provides assistance to the professor in the redesigning process.
- *Accredited Facilitator* is the professor who has already accomplished an international program in one of the didactic techniques.
- *Professor* is the faculty member who will redesign her/his course. S/he must have taught the subject at least two times; s/he must have all the didactic material of the course.
- *Content of the course* consists of learning units, topics, objectives, and the program of activities to obtain each unit goal. It also considers the abilities, attitudes, and values to be developed in the course, as well as the evaluation system.
- *Workshop.* The Education Committee has developed a workshop in order to accomplish all the above, namely: tutoring the teachers in the redesign process; assisting them in incorporating the Educational Model characteristics in their courses; facilitating the process of deciding the best didactic technique for the course and its implementation; and supervising the process of developing the course in the platform.

2.2.2 Elements of a Course

The general information of the course incorporates the following documents: introduction, educational intentions, objectives, content, conceptual map, didactic strategy, expetations of teacher and student, evaluation system, information sources, and technology sources. The elements of each learning unit are: title, introduction to the unit, objectives, unit activities, didactic material related to the course content, and the adopting teacher's guide and didactic documentation. Each learning unit has one or more activities. The elements of an activity are: title, objectives, in-class and outside-of-class activities, evaluation formats, and student materials.

2.2.3 Didactic Techniques

All the courses incorporate a specific didactic technique that enables students to develop some of the attitudes, values, and abilities established in the Mission of the ITESM, depending on the characteristics of the course. These techniques are used in combination with traditional methodologies such as lectures, problem solving, individual work, etc. The ITESM has declared that the following techniques will be used: Problem-Based Learning (PBL), Case Methodology, and Project-Oriented Learning (POL), as well as Collaborative Learning, which gives support to the others. These are explained in more detail in section 3 below.

2.2.4 Technology

Informatics provides support for the courses. Students interact with one another using the following computerized sources: Internet, e-mail, virtual groups, special software for some of the courses, and the Digital Library of the System.

3. DIDACTIC TECHNIQUES

Table 2 shows the differential characteristics of each one of the Didactic Techniques. Collaborative Learning is not included in the table because, even though some courses have it incorporated as the main strategy, it is considered as complementary to the other three.

Table 2. Characteristics of the Main Didactic Techniques

Technique	*Detonator Element*	*Differential Characteristics*
PBL	*A problem or a non-ordinary situation that implies time to make a solution proposal.*	*The teacher writes the scenario. The objectives of the activity are unknown for the student.*
POL	*A project must be made.*	*The result is a product.*
Case	*All the case information must be given to the student.*	*The case is real; the teacher only changes some relevant information of the case or company to protect its security.*

3.1 Problem-Based Learning

There are three main principles in PBL (Torp & Sage, 1998):

- There is an understanding of a situation or a real problem based on interactions with the environment.
- Learning is stimulated when facing a cognitive conflict.
- Knowledge is developed when recognizing and accepting the social processes and when evaluating different individual interpretations of the same situation.

The elements considered in our PBL activities are: presenting the scenario and clarifying terms; definition of the problem; identifying what we know and what we need to know; listing possible solution strategies (actions, suggestions, hypotheses, etc.); carrying out the selected strategy, presenting and establishing the bases of the solution; and evaluating the solution and providing feedback.

Table 3 shows a scenario used in the course, *Energy Transfer*, created by Sofía Faddeeva. The problem incorporates ethic issues in an engineering course.

3.2 Project-Oriented Learning

Project-Oriented Learning is a didactic technique that can be characterized in the following ways:

- It is done with a real project that contains the learning objectives of the curricula.
- The students, working collaboratively, develop their knowledge to obtain a solution to a real problem.
- The students are responsible of their own work.
- The students are responsible for the outcome of the project.

Table 3. Example of a PBL Activity Incorporated in a Course

Course: Energy Transfer **Name:** Sofia Faddeeva Sknarina **Activity**: Ethical questions

Implicit scenario: Winter Woes

For nearly a week the Eastern seaboard had been blasted by what weather forecasters euphemistically called a 'wintry mix': snow, sleet, and freezing rain. The resulting ice-glazed streets and sidewalks sent residents scurrying for aid in the form of shovels, ice choppers, salt, sand, dirt, cat litter — anything to make possible some mode of transportation. Chris and Lee, the only two of a group of housemates left in Newark during Winter session, tried to avoid the problem for a while, until their dwindling supply of Doritos and Diet Coke made a shopping trip imperative. They gingerly made their way out to the car and, after two hours of hacking away ice from the door and windows, managed to get in. Twisting the key in the ignition, Chris was delighted to hear the battery turn over immediately, and mentally posted a note of congratulations for taking advantage of a battery sale just a few weeks earlier.

The engine, however, didn't 'catch' for a while and, when it finally did, ran very roughly, surging and chugging. "It acts like it's not getting enough gas," Lee noted. "Have you added any 'dry gas' recently?" "Huh?" Chris responded. "It's some stuff that you can add to the fuel tank of the car — it's supposed to keep the fuel lines from freezing up," Lee said. "You just toss a bottle's worth in when you tank up, and it eliminates the chugging. My folks swear by it — kept our old car running forever in the winter. We can get some at the gas station." "But that doesn't make sense," said Chris the theoretician. "Gasoline doesn't freeze at these temperatures — 5°F is cold, but that isn't enough to freeze gasoline — is it?" "I think it has something to do with the gas getting wet — at least, I thought that's why they called it 'dry gas.' I don't know — I just know that dry gas always worked for us — whatever the reason, it can't hurt to try."

After tanking up at the gas station, Chris and Lee slide down to Agway on Main Street to pick up some salt for deicing their sidewalk. They've lucked out — a new shipment just came in. The board over the counter reads:

Rock Salt $5.00/ 100 lbs.

Calcium Chloride $18.95/ 80 lbs.

Urea $8.00/ 100 lbs.

"Now what?" Lee said. "I thought salt was salt; I didn't know there were different kinds!" "Beats me," Chris agreed. "I heard the traffic guy saying something about it being too cold for salt to work — maybe one of these other things would work better."

© Susan Groh, Univ. of Delaware, 2001, PBL Clearinghouse.

Evaluation of activity

This scenario involves questions related to engineering ethics in the PBL-based engineering courses. The engineering PBL scenarios have two ethics categories: scenarios that involve ethics explicitly and those that involve ethics implicitly. This classification is of special interest and helps in understanding the mechanism of teaching values in the PBL-based courses.

This technique is based on reaching the learning objectives through a project, teamwork, the application of the scientific method to solve a project, the active and responsible participation of the students, and the development of social skills such as tolerance, communication, conflict solving.

The teacher's role is very important; in fact, s/he plays three roles or there must be three people involved: examiner or main supervisor, who will oversee the assessment, and be a guarantor that the assessment is fair towards the students; facilitator; and evaluator, who can be internal (from the university) or external (from other institutions or from the industry) (Icaza, Heredia, & Borch, 2004).

3.3 The Case Method

The case method considers three stages in the learning process (Leenders, Mauffette-Leenders, & Erskine, 2001):

1. Individual preparation
   - Detailed reading of the case
   - Analyzing the case
2. Small group discussion
   - Defining the group
   - Establishing the guidelines
   - Discussion
3. Large group discussion
   - In-class/pre-class phase
   - Pre-case or "warm-up"
   - Discussion
   - Post-case or closing

Cases are field-based and they have to be taken from a real situation "involving a decision, a challenge, an opportunity, a problem or an issue faced by a person (or people) in an organization" (Leenders, Mauffette-Leenders, & Erskine, 2001, p. 2).

3.4 Collaborative Learning

All didactic techniques mentioned above are enhanced by cooperative learning, the basic components of which are: positive interdependence, individual accountability, group processing, social skills, and face-to-face interaction (Johnson, Johnson, & Holubec, 1993). In collaborative learning it is very important to determine several factors, including: the appropriate collaborative group for each activity; the role played by each group member;

how each basic component will be programmed; evaluation of learning of collaborative work and skills and attitudes; rubric formulation so the students know the evaluation criteria from the beginning; materials needed for the activity; how group processing will be done; previous activity; the teacher's role; and a step-by-step description of how the activity will be developed.

Table 4 shows an example of a collaborative activity designed by Consuelo García for a *Human Resources* course. The main characteristics of collaborative learning are illustrated in this table: objective, activity, methodology, and evaluation. The instructions for the required work during the course are given to the students in a special section of the technological platform.

These techniques allow structuring the courses deliberately, according to the values, abilities, and attitudes promoted in the ITESM Mission.

4. EVALUATION

As part of the reengineering of the learning process, teachers have to participate in the redesign process of their courses. In this section we provide an evaluation of what happened at our campus with regard to the process described in the preceding section of this chapter.

4.1 The Process

The redesign process began on August 1997. Since then, many courses were put in a Web-based platform. The first used was Learning Space, then in August 2000 Blackboard was incorporated, and in August 2002 Web-Tec was implemented. As mentioned in the first part of this chapter, the teachers are being trained to work with the most recent educational technology as well as with some specific didactic techniques.

At ITESM CEM, the Education Committee was created in February 2002; so, as of the writing of this paper, it has been working for three semester periods and one summer period. The main function of this committee is to facilitate the redesign process, so evaluating the process itself is necessary.

Table 4. Example of a CL Activity Incorporated in a Course (Taken Literally from the Human Resources Course)

Course: Human Resources **Name:** Consuelo García Álvarez

Activity "THE NATURE OF PEOPLE DILEMMA"

When you were promoted to Human Resources Director in the company you worked for last year, you truly believed it was the best thing that could have happened to you. After all these years your effort was finally rewarded with a recognized position and attractive economic compensations.

However, last Monday your boss, the CEO of the company, assigned you a task that maybe is the most difficult one you have had to perform in your career so far. In this moment you wish you were not in the position to decide, but you are.

The economic situation of the world has been unstable, and a downsizing has been decided to optimize the resources of the company. You have to fire 3 of your 5 direct subordinates because you have to search for "healthy numbers" for your organizations.

You have taken some notes to define the profile of your subordinates. Who would you fire?"

Objectives

To understand the elements integrating the nature of people and to share information and opinions working on their social skills and positive interdependence.

Methodology

Group discussion, one student from each team will have to express their position, justifying their decision on possible consequences. The teacher will introduce the concepts about the nature of people, based on what happened in the teams.

Evaluation of activity

This exercise allows students to identify individual elements that affect decision making, and that are part of the nature of people. Most of the times, students tend to go for economic arguments that support their decision and forget about the value of humans in organizations, firing Barbara Wallace "because she is deaf" and Julie James "because she is old." This trend allows the instructor to orient the final group discussion toward ethics and social responsibility (that are parts of the "nature of organizations"), linking this topic with the following one. This also enriches the activity with a personal ethical reflection.

Table 5 presents the evaluation statistics for courses approved at the System and Campus level, from a total of 1,089 courses offered each semester at Campus Estado de México. The courses are evaluated by the academic vice-president. S/he uses an evaluation rubric that considers three attributes: use of the platform, use of the didactic technique, and the academic content of the course. The vice-president classifies the course either as "Approved at the System Level," "Approved at the Campus Level," or "Rejected." The courses at the Campus level accomplish all the requirements but they have issues to improve. The courses at the System level are those that accomplish the requirements with high quality standards, so they can be transferred from one campus to another.

Table 5. Courses Approved at the System and Campus Level

Courses in the ITESM Model	
Approved at the System level	*264*
Approved at the Campus level	*326*
In process	*203*
Total	*773*

We have not yet established a good parameter for measuring the Committee's effectiveness. Table 6 presents the historical data regarding the number of courses approved in both levels: system and campus, before and after the foundation of the Education Committee.

Table 6. Courses Approved at the System and Campus Level, Before and After the Education Committee

Courses in the ITESM Model	**Before Committee**	**After Committee**
Approved at the System level	120	144
Approved at the Campus level	165	181
Total	285	225

Between August 1997 and December 2000, approval was gained for 285 courses that were redesigned in Learning Space without incorporating the didactic technique. From January 2001 to December 2002, 225 courses were approved but the rate of approval increased substantially, thereby demonstrating the effectiveness of the Committee in the production and quality-level of courses approved under the ITESM standards.

4.2 The Course

Prior to incorporating a didactic technique, all courses designed according to the ITESM model were evaluated with no criteria or vague criteria.

The philosophy for the present criteria consists of giving students responsibility for their own learning — that is, a student-centered model in which they have to participate rather than only attending the professor's lectures.

The nine criteria that have been incorporated into the redesigned courses are:

1. *Educative intentions.* These have to do with the formative profile of the student. The course has to incorporate the abilities, values, and attitudes (HAV in Spanish) established in the ITESM Mission.
2. *Course objectives.* These focus on what the student is going to be able to do at the end of the course.

3. *Contents* are established and/or modified every three to five years by the academic staff of the specific area in order to adapt to society's specific needs.
4. *Activities* are the specific actions the professor must execute to cover the contents and reach the objectives that are prepared by the professor. Mainly they consider the didactic technique declared for the specific course. Nevertheless, all the courses have collaborative activities to promote teamwork as a specific ability declared in the Mission. The activities must incorporate the schedule in which they are going to take place, the conditions needed, the required materials (bibliography, documents, Internet links, etc.), as well as the way to present the information.
5. *Sources of information* have to be updated.
6. *Technological resources*. In some courses there are specific technological programs that are needed for the development of the course.
7. *Evaluation* covers the percentages of the activities, exams, projects, presentations, and any other activity or work done by the student.
8. *Expectations of the professor and the students* include the policies of the course and the academic rules of the ITESM.
9. *Use of the technologic platform* wherein the students find an explanation about Lotus Notes, Blackboard, or Webtec.

Afterwards, other criteria are used that are related to the learning units and the didactic technique. In general, the unit has to incorporate activities that could be done inside or outside of class. There is a site at the technologic platform in which the content material is located so the students can reach it whenever they require it.

4.3 Implementation

The process followed in Stage 3 of the PDHD consists on a series of steps having the goal of determining the opportunity areas of the course. In this process:

- The professor self-evaluates the design of the course, including objectives, activities, materials, didactic technique, and the way it is delivered to the student. (This is not an assessment of the program because this is institutional as we have mentioned above.)
- There is a diagnostic exam at the beginning of the course in order to detect the student's level in previous knowledge, abilities, attitudes, and the didactic technique. With the results, the professor considers what s/he can expect about the students' performance and

determines the actions that will lead students to achieve the courses' goals.

- After the first of four class periods, the students answer a survey in which they express their opinion about the contents, material, program effectiveness, and relationship with the professor, among others. With this information and the professor's reflection s/he can adopt new guides to continue the course.
- Another professor assists by observing one class, paying special attention to the way in which the didactic technique is used. S/he then provides feedback to the professor.
- At mid-term, the professor can document the changes s/he considers necessary to have better performance.
- S/he administers the survey once more after modifications are made. Once more s/he can be observed and with all these elements s/he establishes improvements s/he can make in the course.

The documentation of this process lets the professor go into the last stage of the PDHD in which, formally, s/he is going to carry out the improvements to the designed course.

4.4 The Professors' and Students' Opinions

At the end of the semesters, August-December 2003 and January-May 2004, 158 students and 53 professors, at the professional level, answered a survey about how they perceived the impact of the ITESM model in the classroom.

The students' survey consisted of 18 questions divided into four categories: student's work, professor's work, didactic technique, and use of technology. On the other hand, the professors' survey had 16 questions related to his/her role at the classroom, students' results, use of technology, and use of the didactic technique.

Figure 4 shows how the students and professors perceived themselves in using the technology. The professors' perception is better than that of the students in the items related with their interactions; on the contrary, the students' perception is better than that of the professors regarding the item of exams application.

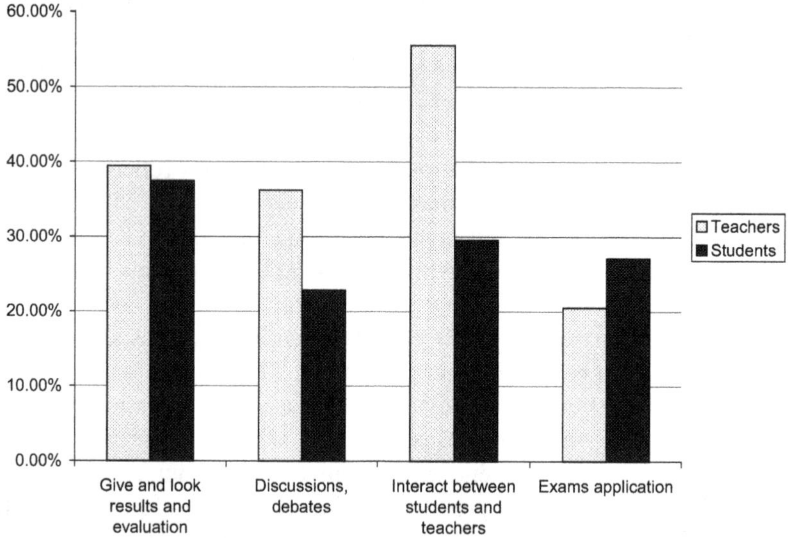

Figure 4. Uses Given to the Technological Platform

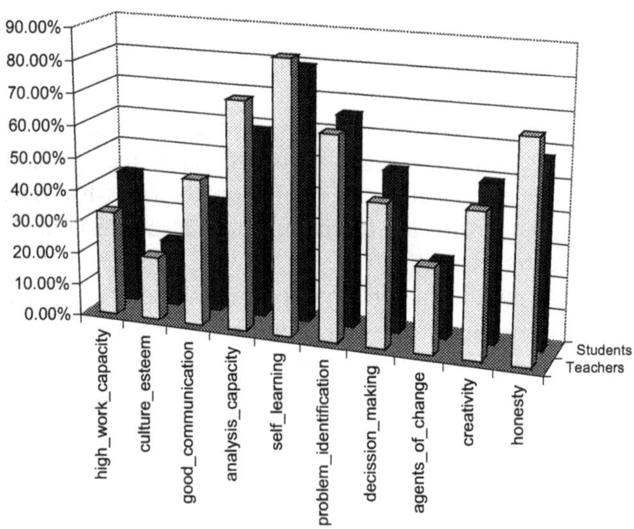

Figure 5. Abilities, Attitudes and Values Developed in the Courses: Professors' and Students' Perception

Figure 5 shows the developed HAVs according to the professors' perception and students' perceptions; the outstanding abilities identified by both groups are self-learning, analysis capacity, and honesty.

In other survey results, the students indicated, that: they aid their learning with books and the use of the World Wide Web; they dedicate three to five hours weekly to complementary activities or study; and they feel they have their professors' support. The professors told us that the implementation process was fine, but could be improved and that they needed more support in their specific fields of knowledge. Implementation consists of putting into practice the activities planned for the course. Figure 6 shows the results obtained, in two consecutive semesters, regarding the professors' perceptions about the implementation process.

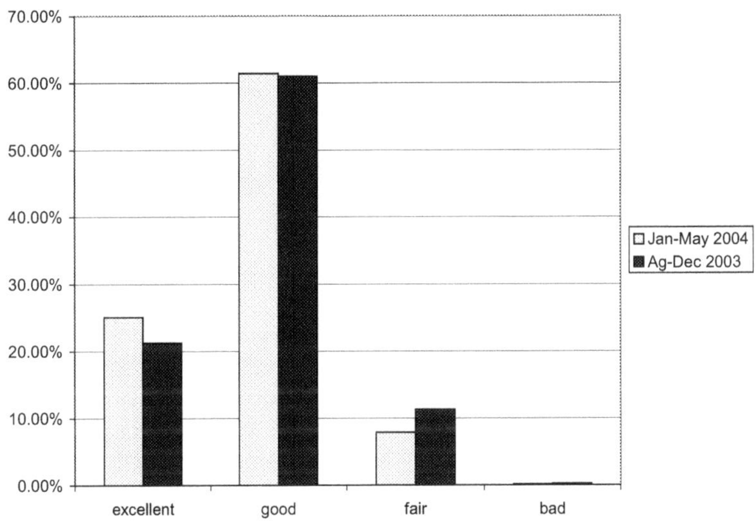

Figure 6. Professor's Opinion about the Implementation Process

4.5 Graduates' Opinions

In 2004, a survey was administered to 2,625 graduates of Engineering, Computer, Business, and Social Sciences, based on the bachelor programs offered at the Campus. The objective of this survey was to learn their opinions about the effectiveness of the Education Model of ITESM. In this survey, four items were considered: C1 — general knowledge; C2 —

collaborative work; C3 — self-learning ability; and C4 — ability to self-evaluate and evaluate others' work. The measurement scale went from 1 to 5 where 5 represented the best situation. The outcomes are presented on Figure 7.

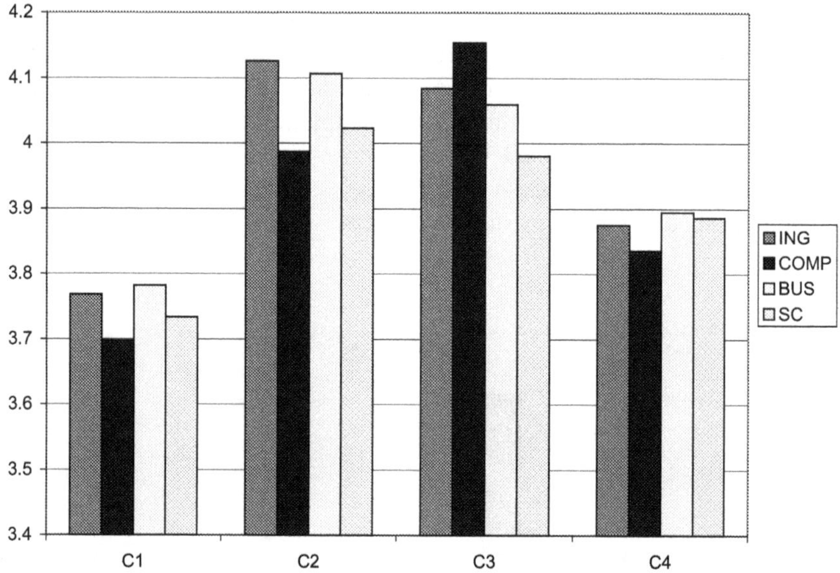

Figure 7. Results About: How effective do you think the ITESM Educative Model has been in developing in you the issues C1, C2, C3, C4?

Both the graduates who work (1,792) and those who don't (849) evaluated the Educative Model positively (there was no statistical difference in both groups' perceptions). Almost half the graduates (1,270 out of 2,625) indicated that at least 50% of the courses in their study plan were redesigned ones. In the same survey mentioned above, using a 1 to 5 scale, where 5 was very important, the working graduates evaluated the work relevance of some of the abilities they developed under the Educative Model. These outcomes are shown in Table 7.

These results reflect only part of what the ITESM enquires about at the end of each semester; however, they are the most relevant for the purpose of this paper. They provide information about the advantages and disadvantages of the Model and what is going on in the classroom. Also, considering that the Model emerges from the *Mission towards 2005*, the results recognize, in an explicit and conscious way, the achievement of certain abilities, values, and attitudes.

Table 7. Relevance of Abilities in the graduates' Work

Ability	Evaluation
Self-confidence	4.71
Ability to relate with others	4.61
Ability to communicate	4.54
Collaborative work	4.51
Ability to find and analyze information	4.42
Knowledge of their field	3.94
Performance in English	3.75

5. CONCLUSIONS

The ITESM Model has incorporated the main elements in the learning process: the professor, the students, and the courses.

The professors have had to modify their teaching techniques, based on the characteristics of modern education. In doing this they have been trained at the PDHD, a task that has been very hard. First, the professors had to become adequately familiar with modern worldwide educational tendencies. Second, they had to adopt and incorporate new technology and theories in instructional design and didactic techniques, while at the same time updating the content material of their courses. Third, the professors reflect on their teaching activity using the new model and engage in ongoing improvement of their courses.

The students also have had to be at the vanguard of the learning process, incorporating into their activities more defined techniques that require more responsibility, teamwork and collaboration, analysis and synthesis, and compromise with others. All these are attitudes and abilities were explicitly promoted in the different courses, as part of the Model.

As an aid to this process, the Educative Committee played an important role, assisting the professors both in their training as well as in the process of redesigning their courses. The objective of it has been to generate an environment of change that allows the professors to improve the implementation process. We know that there is a lot more to do and the Educational Committee will continue working with the training of professors and ongoing improvement of their courses.

The results of graduates' surveys show favorable perceptions regarding the Model. The graduates reported that they had acquired most of the abilities, attitudes, and values established in our Mission. Moreover, the graduates indicated that these abilities, attitudes, and values had been useful in their professional work.

The experience presented in this paper shows that when updating the education model of an institution, the creation of an education committee is important. Such a committee should be formed with professors from different areas who will assume leadership in pointing out the advantages, disadvantages, risks, and improvement areas that must be addressed in order to reach high quality standards in their courses.

REFERENCES

Icaza, J. I., Heredia, Y., & Borch, O. E. M. (2004). Project oriented immersion learning. *Building Online Digital Products for a Cyberspace Publishing House.* Tecnológico de Monterrey and Aalborg University. http://www.control.auc.dk/preprint/4728.pdf, retrieved November 10, 2004.

ITESM. (1999). El modelo educativo del Tec de Monterrey. http://www.sistema.itesm.mx/va/dide/modelo/home.htm, retrieved November 10, 2004.

Johnson, D., Johnson, R., & Holubec, E. J. (1993). *Circles of learning. Cooperation in the classroom* (4th ed.). Edina, MN, USA.

Leenders, M. R., Mauffette-Leenders, A., & Erskine, J. A. (2001). *Writing Cases* (4th ed.). Ivey School of Business Administration, The University of Western Ontario, London, Ontario.

Martin Perez, M. (2002). *El modelo educativo del Tecnológico de Monterrey.* Tec de Monterrey, Monterrey, Mexico.

Torp, L., & Sage, S. (1998). *Problems as Possibilities: Problem-based Learning for K-12 Education.* Association for Supervision and Curriculum Development, Alexandria, VA.

Chapter 24

ACTION E-LEARNING

An Exploratory Case Study Examining the Impact of Action Learning on the Design of Management-level Web-based Instruction

Deborah DeWolfe Waddill
Restek Consulting, Vienna, Virginia, USA

1. INTRODUCTION

Web-based instruction is this century's most-talked about educational and training media. In an attempt to actualize the power of this tool, organizations are experimenting with innovative methods to improve their learning processes (Yoo, Kanawattanachai, & Citurs, 2002). The resulting courses offered over corporate and educational Intranets — also called Web-based instruction or WBI — present what can be a cost-effective alternative to face-to-face training (Fornaciari, Forte, & Mathews, 1999; Phillips, Phillips, Duresky, & Gaudet, 2002; Roberts, 1998).

On the balance sheet, WBI that is high volume and low margin can be cost effective (Forman, 2002). Conversely, however, those cost efficiencies are partially eroded when the class size is small and the development costs high. In the latter case, Fornaciari, Forte, and Mathews (1999) point out that organizations with a strategy for differentiation — where the firm's product or service offering creates something that is perceived as being unique — can demand a higher price and sustain smaller, more individualized classes. In so doing they can realize the cost benefits.

When WBI was first implemented in the 1990s it was defined and designed for the capabilities of the technology, not the type of adult learning environment or experience provided (Driscoll, 1998, 1999, Hall, 1997). Typically, those creating WBI courseware were experts in a subject matter or in the technology but had little or no understanding of how to design

M.K. McCuddy et al. (eds.),
The Challenges of Educating People to Lead in a Challenging World, 475–497.

instruction to accommodate the way adults learn (Khan, Waddill, & McDonald, 2001). In the latter part of the 1990s new developments took place, particularly in the area of education.

Educational institutions have begun to rely more heavily upon e-learning delivery using a variety of applications. Some creative design applications and features for Web-based instruction include implementation in an interpersonal skills course (Human, Kilbourne, Clark, Shriberg, & Cunningham, 1999), project-based instruction online (DeFillippi, 2001; Rhodes & Garrick, 2003), problem-based online learning (Dolmans, Gijselaers, Moust, & Grave, 2002; Gijselaers, 1995; Kanet & Barut, 2003), and online discussion rooms. The latter is particularly popular as a method to increase interactivity, community, and the meaningfulness of the courseware (Brower, 2003; Yoo, Kanawattanachai, & Citurs, 2002).

These approaches to Web-based instruction have been employed in the management education and management training environments in an effort to increase the quality of online courseware. To date, however no studies have been conducted measuring the impact of the powerful management development process called Action Learning as a WBI delivery method. Action learning has been offered over the Internet as a course (Reeve, 1998) and as an online tutoring approach (Sandelands, 1999). In both cases its impact on the learning process was favorably reported. However, the action learning process has not been applied as a Web-based instructional method.

Reg Revans was the creator and "father" of action learning (Dilworth, 1998b). He developed this method originally as he worked with the British government for the nationalization of the coal industry. In that situation, the action learning participants visited each other's work sites and consulted with each other to solve real, "live" problems. Later he refined his action learning approach and relied upon those who were considered to be part of the problem to solve the problem. Revans went on to use this process in other parts of the world.

In the 1990s, Marquardt (1999) formalized the action learning process when he distilled the elements of action learning. Marquardt identified six essential features of action learning: (1) a problem in need of resolution; (2) a group of four to eight people called the action "set"; (3) a commitment to the use of a questioning and reflection process; (4) a commitment to taking action (by one with the authority to do so); (5) a commitment to learning; and (6) a facilitator to enable the process. Marquardt's approach is advantageous because it provides workable actions and conditions that specify exactly how action learning can succeed. Marquardt's action learning method was used in this study.

Action learning differs from other management education methods such as experiential, problem-based, project-based, or workplace learning

(Marsick & O'Neil, 1999). Unique to action learning is the convergence of these criteria: the problem must be a "live," urgent problem; the problem presenter must have the authority to enact a solution; and the group/set members must participate in a questioning process called reflective inquiry. As a result of the reflective inquiry process the presenting problem may be "reframed" or may change in nature (Marquardt, 1999, p. 2004).

2. THE STUDY APPROACH

The research reported in this chapter examined how action learning impacted the effectiveness of one management-level online course. The research idea was spurred by the awareness of design challenges for Web-based instruction. Reportedly, WBI needs to spur interactivity in order to increase learning. The action learning approach addresses these needs.

2.1 Research Question

An exploratory case study method was used to approach the research question: *How does the action learning process impact the effectiveness of one management-level e-learning course?* According to Yin (2003), case study research is most appropriate as a method when the question to be answered is a "How" question. It was chosen as the methodology for this study because the exploratory case study "tries to illuminate a decision or set of decisions: Why they were taken, how they were implemented, and with what result" (Schramm in Yin, 2003, p. 12).

3. THEORY AND WBI

Since adult learners were the target audience, adult learning theory provided the theoretical underpinnings for the research. Knowles (1973) examined characteristics of adult learners that are still relevant for training design in the 21st century (Shandler, 1996). Knowles noted that adults tend to prefer self-direction. This implies that training, at least in part, needs to allow for choice, input, and decisions by participants. Learning should encourage the communication, reflection, and evaluation of adults' experiences in light of the educational content and goals. Additionally, adults appreciate methods that simulate the work environment because they want to acquire knowledge and skills that can be immediately applied to real life situations. Later, Knowles added two more characteristics to his description of the adult learner (1984, 1998). First, adults are externally motivated by incentives like promotions, new knowledge, better pay, etc. Second, adults identify their own learning needs based upon real-life events. When they identify their own skill deficiencies they will be more participatory and open to learning that addresses the knowledge gaps.

3.1 Adult Learning Theory and WBI

Web-based adult learning must be designed with the adult learner in mind and should address these needs. Consequently, WBI should allow adult learners to interact with other learners (Saba, 2000), work with others (Bandura, 1977, 1986; Cho and Berge, 2002; Dewey, 1916), have control of their learning (Rotter, 1954; Rotter, Seeman, & Liverant, 1962), have incentives to learn (Keller & Kopp, 1987; Martins & Kellermanns, 2004; Rossett, 2000), and have time for reflection to help them make meaning of their learning experiences (DeFillippi, 2001; Marsick, Cederholm, Turner, & Pearson, 1992; Schon, 1987). Adult learners differ significantly from most undergraduates who have had neither the life experiences nor the responsibilities of an adult (Nadkarni, 2003). The target audience for this study was managers who demonstrated potential for the executive track.

While the need for some learner control is a characteristic of the adult learner and should be designed into the WBI (Rotter, 1954; Rotter, Seeman, & Liverant, 1962), learner control can inadvertently undercut the learner's own goals. Adult learners may remain engaged in Web-based instruction until they have learned what they feel they need to improve a specific skill or to learn a certain task (Zielinski, 2000, p. 66). They may drop the course when other priorities and responsibilities seem more important (Parker, 1999). Along those lines, Carr (2000) states that because many WBI learners are older and have more competing obligations, they may drop out of the course when other obligations claim priority. In these cases, learner control is both an asset and a liability. Adult learners have control over their learning in a WBI environment such that they can drop out when the WBI no longer serves their purposes. Consequently, the designer of WBI must distribute relevant learning activities throughout the course to keep the learner involved.

3.2 Instructor/Facilitator and WBI

Web-based instruction rocks the very core of instructional design largely because "The Internet has blurred the distinction between who is a content user and who is a content provider, throwing off-balance another pillar of training — the role of the instructor" (Galagan, 2000, p. 29). Rather than deal with the modified role of the instructor, some organizations have simply eliminated the instructor/facilitator from the delivery of WBI. This type of training is pre-programmed instruction that is delivered over an Internet connection. The impact of that decision upon the learner may be increased isolation (Cho & Berge 2002).

Specifically, this study addressed management training and development as opposed to entry level, new-hire, or front-line training and development. The selection of the management construct allows examination of a management development method called action learning. Action learning assumes that the learner must have the power to make decisions and the authority to implement solutions to business problems, two things which undergraduates, new-hires, and entry-level personnel may not normally have.

3.3 Evaluating WBI

Kirkpatrick's Four Levels of Evaluation served as the foundation for measuring effectiveness in terms of the ways in which participants' knowledge and behavior changed. According to Kirkpatrick, it is important to capture an initial reaction to the course. Kirkpatrick (1994) states, "Positive reaction may not ensure learning, but negative reaction almost certainly reduces the possibility of its [learning] occurring" (1994, p. 22).

Other tools for evaluating WBI exist, but Kirkpatrick's method is accepted and endorsed in the e-learning literature as a viable process for evaluating the effectiveness of online instruction (Hall & LeCavalier, 2000; Hughes & Attwell, 2003; Mayberry, 2005; Singh, 2001). Further, in comparison to other more prescriptive evaluation tools, these Four Levels of Evaluation provide the flexibility that is necessary to assess a constructivist design where participants develop their own learning goals and objectives.

In the action learning online course, there were only twelve volunteer subjects; this number of participants/respondents does not satisfy conditions necessary for quantitative research. Thus the parameters of the research, the environment, the target audience, the number of participants, the philosophical underpinnings (constructivism) as manifested in the course design provide the conditions necessary for implementing Kirkpatrick's Four Levels of Evaluation. Kirkpatrick's four levels are:

- Level One — What were the students' perceptions of the learning approach to the course?
- Level Two — What was learned?
- Level Three — Was the learning being used and if so, how?
- Level Four — Did the learning have a positive effect on the host organization?

4. METHOD

This study examined the impact of the action learning process upon a management-level web-based instruction course. In order to accomplish this end, the selection of host organization and the identification of courseware for modification were critical. With regard to the host organization, it had to be one that embraced adult learning principles and allowed for increased learner control, as well as the infrastructure to support WBI (Marquardt, 1999). These were available through the host organization. The host site, a for-profit training consulting organization, agreed that an action learning approach was a viable Web-based instruction methodology and allowed the researcher (and author of this chapter) to use their server to pilot a WBI action learning course using action learning as the method.

4.1 Host Site

The host site for this research will be referred to as "Management University" (MU); this is not the actual name. MU is an educational organization that provides training to United States federal government employees. Management University delivers hundreds of face-to-face and online courses on a wide variety of topics.

The Director of Training at MU agreed to the action learning online research because of its relevance to and potential impact on their present offerings, however the researcher received no remuneration for the services provided. MU's Leadership Development Program (LDP) grooms managers for upper-level management. It is a yearlong management development program. Managers who wish to participate in this training must be nominated by their own management and then must go through a rigorous selection process that includes a pre- and post-program performance review by peers, subordinates and superiors, a personality test, and other evaluative measures. At the conclusion of the program, managers create their own Management Development Plan (MDP).

4.2 Participants

The participants in the Action E-Learning course were management-level individuals who were graduates of MU's Leadership Development Program. A recruitment letter was sent out to LDP Alumni requesting volunteers to participate in this groundbreaking research. Twelve recent graduates of the program volunteered and participated in the action learning online course.

The twelve volunteers had the following common characteristics: they were all senior managers working in a federal government position, they each had completed the LDP, they worked in a variety of locations nationwide, they had Internet access and typically used the Internet in daily business transactions, they were familiar with computer-based learning, and they were committed to rendering positive change within their organizations. During the LDP, they each had developed their own Management Development Plan (MDP).

The volunteers were grouped into three sets. Since the online environment often changes and even reverses personal assertiveness and communication styles (Weasenforth, Biesenbach-Lucas, & Meloni, 2002), participants were not grouped by personality type. However, a gender balance was intentionally established (Arbaugh, 2000).

4.3 Propositions

A management-level course on the topic of action learning was modified to include action learning methods, yet conform to the same curriculum purpose, goals, and content. The unit of analysis was the individual within the action learning set. The propositions (Yin, 2003) to be examined were:

- Proposition 1: The action learning component will prompt each learner to examine at least one troubling, business/workplace problem related to the course content.
- Proposition 2: The learner will take action and report the results of the action as a learning opportunity for the other participants in the set.

The results of this case study demonstrate the impact of using action learning as an effective approach for the design of management-level WBI.

4.4 Course Strategies

The course included strategies to:

- Capitalize on the learners' Management Development Plans and give them an opportunity to customize their learning to their own development plans.
- Allow the learners to, consequently, establish their own, personal goals and learning objectives relative to their Management Development Plans.
- Provide resources relative to the components of the action learning process.
- Introduce participants to the processes, principles, tools, and skills to lead and/or participate in open-group action learning sets.
- Provide practice scenarios.

- Immerse the learners in real life scenarios by allowing them to submit their own "live" problems for the course discussion and personal action.
- Introduce the learner to the reflective inquiry (questioning and reflection) processes unique to action learning.

4.5 Action E-learning Courseware Design

The design for this WBI course included steps to modify the face-to-face version of the course to create an online offering using action learning as the method. A redesign process must occur in order to adapt to the assets and liabilities of the online environment (Brindle & Levesque, 2000). Design changes were made to accommodate asynchronous delivery online. The areas impacted by these design changes are the following:

- The learning environment provided the most dramatic difference. The Action Learning Course was conducted face-to-face in a classroom whereas the Action E-Learning (AEL) Course was conducted in a Web-based (virtual) environment using asynchronous communication and Blackboard as the Learning Management System.
- The face-to-face course was conducted over fourteen weeks where participants met in a classroom every two weeks for eight-hour sessions. At the client's request, the Action E-Learning Course was shortened to five, continuous weeks.
- The audiences differed; for the face-to-face version the students were masters or doctoral level students. For the Action E-Learning course the participants were all graduates of the Leadership Development Program.
- The purpose and goals/objectives for the face-to-face offering were very specific and based in the behaviorist approach to course design; on the other hand, in the AEL Course the participants developed their own learning goals and tied them to the Management Development Plan (MDP) that they designed while enrolled in the Leadership Development Program.
- In the face-to-face class, the topics progressed from a simple to complex approach whereas in the Action E-Learning information was arranged in blocks; the learners provided their own sequencing.
- The face-to-face course did not require the participant to consider reframing the problem, though it may have occurred. The Action E-Learning threaded discussion required, after the first week, that the participants either restate or reframe (modify) their problem statement at the beginning of each week-long cycle of questions.

- In the classroom course, there was a teacher and towards the end of the course participants rotated the action set facilitation. In the Action E-Learning Course the teacher was a set facilitator who offered resources and facilitation expertise and could only ask questions; participants did not rotate set facilitation.
- In both classes each participant presented an urgent issue/problem. This is called the open-group approach as opposed to the single problem approach where the entire set works on one problem with the sponsor (the one responsible for implementing the solution) participating in the set (Marquardt, 2004).
- In the face-to-face AL Course, the students were assessed based upon their active participation, journal log, and research papers. The Action E-Learning Course participants assessed their own learning by: creating personal goals tied to their Management Development Plan, presenting a business problem, setting norms, generating questions and answering those posed, submitting a learning log that recorded what they had learned, reframing their own problem, assessing and reporting whether or not they met their goals, and completing the end-of-course interview. Another unique facet of the AEL course was that the facilitator conducted a follow-up inquiry within six months of course completion. The purpose of the inquiries was to identify the status of the participants' solutions and subsequent actions to resolve the problem.

4.6 Action E-learning Cycle

This course introduced a unique tactic for Web-based, asynchronous discussion. Participants were required to follow a pre-specified discussion approach. The facilitator set the guidelines for the sequence of activities while the participants in each set established the norms. The WBI literature attests to the wisdom of having predetermined rules of interaction in order to limit the chaos that can occur online. Brindle and Levesque (2000, p. 453) state, "What might be spontaneous in an on-campus setting spells confusion at a distance, so care should be taken to be extraordinarily organized and clear." Figure 1. The Action E-Learning Cycle depicts the required discussion sequence of action e-learning.

Participants posted their urgent problem in the threaded discussion on the first day of the weeklong session. There were five one-week sessions in the course. Relevant readings were cited under the References button in Blackboard. The Announcement page that appeared when participants logged in to Blackboard provided direction and activities for the weeklong session. Participants were required to pose at least three questions for their

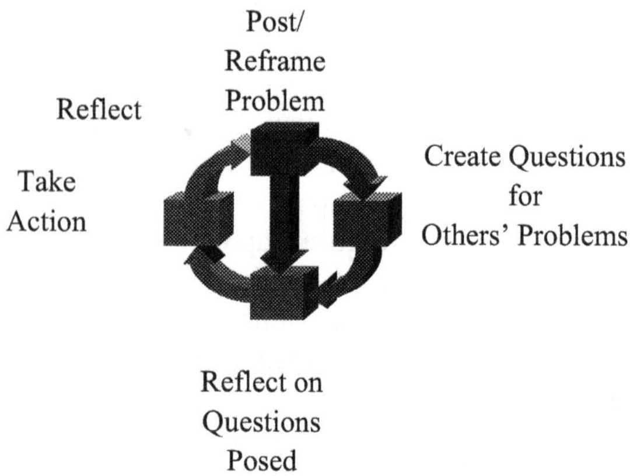

Figure 1. The Action E-Learning Cycle

other set members before midweek. Then they reflected on the questions about their own problems, made a commitment to action, and reported on the results of actions taken. Since this course was only five weeks long, many participants did not take action until the end, if at all, but a majority of the participants did identify actions they would take.

On the first day of the next one-week session, participants either "reframed" or restated the urgent problem. Reframing occurs when the person presenting the problem feels that the core problem has changed. Set members asked questions of each other and the cycle continued until the participant came to a solution and actions to implement or the course ended. There were no phone conferences or face-to-face sessions with the participants. Most of them did not know each other. The researcher/facilitator never met the participants face-to-face. The purpose of conducting this course entirely as WBI, not blended learning, was to determine if the WBI action learning method could result in learning. Throughout the five-week course, the facilitator was available by phone for questions regarding the process, problem selection, or Blackboard related issues. There was a flurry of calls at the beginning having to do with login and passwords; aside from that there was very little phone contact.

4.7 The Research Domain

Each individual brought what he or she perceived to be a difficult, urgent problem to the table. All participants worked in federal agencies and participated as volunteers for this research while they continued to perform their full-time jobs within the government. The participants knew the course timetable and made a commitment to complete the course within the allotted five weeks as well as participate in the end-of-course interviews.

4.8 Data Sources

The Leadership Development Program (LDP) offered through Management University is a competency-based executive training program. Participants are required to be managers under consideration by their organizations for executive responsibilities. Their superiors acknowledge their potential to become executives and must nominate them to participate in the LDP. The goal of the LDP is to build on the competencies needed to become successful leaders and possibly executives in the federal agency. The LDP participants' organizations provide the necessary funding and release time to complete the yearlong program. All participants in the LDP complete a competency inventory, and a review by selected peers, subordinates, and superiors to gain feedback on the essential behaviors of a successful leader in preparation for the design of their Management Development Plan (MDP) that they had to have as a result of their enrollment in the program.

The LDP alumni had the prerequisite skills to access and participate in an online course because they had used a Web-based discussion room in the LDP program. However, most had not taken any online instruction. For many of the volunteers in this research, their primary exposure to Web-based instruction occurred when using a learning management system, Blackboard, for project work and communication during the Leadership Development Program.

4.9 Data Collection

In the evaluation of course effectiveness, the specific data collection approach was to: (a) Gather and evaluate reflections by the participants using the data in email records, online threaded discussions, and the end-of-course interviews; (b) Examine the logs (journals) for learnings; (c) Examine the commitments to action; (d) Collect feedback from the learners on the outcomes of their actions taken during the course; and (e) Follow up by email two and six months after course completion to elicit data regarding the impact of their commitments to action and actions, either on themselves or the organization.

4.10 Interview Protocol

Upon completion of the management-level, Action E-Learning Course, each participant was interviewed. For qualitative research, Stake (1995, p. 25) refers to the questions within this protocol as "topical information questions." Participants were encouraged to provide anecdotal information in support of their responses to the interview questions. All of the twelve interviews occurred at the participant's convenience, within two weeks of the course termination and were initiated by phone. All telephone interview responses were transcribed and resubmitted to the interviewee for confirmation, correction, or additional comments. If corrective feedback was not received from participants within three weeks after their receipt of the transcribed interviews, the interviews were finalized and coded.

The set participants had access to all of the threaded discussions. They reviewed their own bios and write-ups of the problems. They provided their own words regarding actions taken and follow-up activities. Additionally, a professor of qualitative research methods reviewed the research methodology. Each of these procedures minimizes threats to trustworthiness.

4.11 Data Analysis

Atlas TI was used for data analysis; it is a qualitative analysis software tool that is designed for textual coding and analysis. All of the documents, threaded discussions, personal emails (to the facilitator and submitted outside of the public forum of Blackboard), participant journals, meeting notes, and transcribed interviews were converted to text files in order to select, code, annotate, and compare data segments.

When coding the segments and sentence fragments within each of the documents, some of the codes emerged (open-coding) from the documents' contents; others were predetermined by the research questions and constructs of the study. The codes captured the variety and range of "input" that came directly from the participants. The content and context of the sentences within the text drove the process of code assignment. A peer reviewed the raw data and the assigned codes to examine their validity.

The theoretical basis for the course modifications emerges from the constructivist school of learning where meaning and knowledge are socially constructed (Duffy & Jonassen, 1992; Jonassen, Peck, & Wilson, 1999; Savery & Duffy, 1996; Weasenforth, Biesenbach-Lucas, & Meloni, 2002). The modifications that occurred to the course were very specific and involved the use of action learning as the delivery method. Evidence of the impact of this innovation was viewable from the pattern of student persistence in the learning effort and measurable from the standpoint of the effectiveness of the courseware to achieve its stated purpose and participant goal(s), the account of participant learnings and their reported behavior changes.

Being both researcher and facilitator permitted the viewing of the postings to the threaded discussion as well as all files to which a facilitator normally has access. Online set facilitation is not for the faint of heart. Neither is it a role to be taken lightly. In the Action E-Learning process, the facilitator must: (a) Be vigilant of the online dialogue to intervene when the process gets off track; (b) Enable and enforce the reflective inquiry process; (c) Ask questions; and (d) Inform participants of any relevant exchanges or events involving the facilitator and participants that occur outside of the threaded discussion.

Design documents related to the course before and after its modification were relevant to this effort. Other documents included, but were not be limited to the course syllabus, all participant assignments, organizational memos, emails, policy changes, printouts of threaded discussion, etc., that bore relevance to the course content or process. The online threaded discussions, documents, and emails specific to this course, and generated both by the facilitator and the students were saved and subjected to rigorous analysis, as were the transcribed interviews. In total thirty-four textual files were analyzed.

5. FINDINGS

Table 1 summarizes the participants' commitments to action and actions taken as reported in the follow-up interviews and later in email updates.

5.1 Support for Propositions

Were the propositions for this research supported? The two propositions were:

- Proposition 1: The action learning component will prompt each learner to take constructive action on at least one troubling, business/workplace problem related to the course content.
- Proposition 2: The learner will take action and report the results of the action as a learning opportunity for the other participants in the group.

As can be seen in Table 1, a majority of the participants who completed the course took action on their problems during or after the course. It appears that the propositions were supported because a majority of the learners who completed the course did take action and reported the results of the action.

Another way to examine the propositions is through evaluating the effectiveness of the course.

Table 1. Action E-learning Participant Problems and Actions

Action E-Learning Participant Problems and Actions					
Partici-pant	**Problem Type**	**Level of Risk**	**Re-frame?**	**Commitment To Action**	**Action Taken During and After the Course (Designated "Later")**
Male #1	Team building	Low	No	Dropped	Dropped-None
Male #2	Merging organizations	High	Yes	Consensus and collaboration	Visiting other department heads; conducting an off-site strategic planning session, later
Female #1	Association member participation	Low	Yes	Call members about member benefits from participation	None
Male #3	Computer updates, will be outdated before complete	High	Yes	Alternate channels to propose suggestions	Pursued alternate channels, later
Female #2	Unresponsive superior causing disruption/ Classes	High	Yes	Pursue an early intervention program with superior	Began early intervention, later
Female #3	Pursue Ph.D.	Low	Yes	Give up; later, decided to pursue CPA	Researched CPA programs, later
Male #4	Retirement or not	Low	No	Dropped	Dropped--Prepared for retirement
Male #5	Brand recognition	Low	Yes	Logo, standardized report cover, survey	Discussed with staff
Male #6	Homeland security emergency efforts	High	Yes	Be prepared icon; article to inform; use a general agency-wide communication	Met with Web Master
Female #4	Team building/ management development	High	Yes	Include team members, meeting with facilitator for dispute resolution center	Individual meetings; included team members
Male #7	Career derailment	High	Yes	Wait and see	Applied for the job, later
Male #8	Career derailment	High	No	Talk with superior	Asked to stay in position; Remained

5.2 Kirkpatrick's Four Levels of Evaluation

The impact of the Action E-Learning approach and its effectiveness as an online method were evaluated using Kirkpatrick's (1994, 1996) Four Levels of Evaluation. A complaint of Kirkpatrick's is that organizations often stop at the first level, reaction, and never get beyond that. This research examined all four levels.

5.2.1 Level One Evaluation: Reaction

Kirkpatrick's Level One evaluates reaction. The majority of the learners reacted positively to this course. One learner stated in response to the question of how he felt about action learning being offered online, "I don't know if this [the action learning process] could be done any other way." The two who initially preferred the face-to-face training environment stated their preference for the face-to-face venue at the beginning and maintained it to the end. However, one of those two said that she could see some application for AEL in the regional offices of her organization. The other saw the value of Action E-Learning regarding its application with virtual teams. This was evidence that she began to soften toward the online approach regardless of her personal preference.

The Level One responses to the Action E-Learning Events were not all positive. Negative reactions could be grouped into two areas of concern: (a) the open-group approach (where each individual presents a problem); and (b) formation of a sense of community. With regard to the former, four of the participants had less favorable reactions to the open-group approach. One participant, for instance, imputed his own confusion on all of the participants when he said, "We felt really confused if it was a single issue or multiple issues, if we were supposed to vote on it or what; there was no leadership within the group itself to make that determination; it was very awkward getting started."

Although no one else indicated a similar confusion, it is worthy of note. Certainly the single-issue approach would be more straightforward and more easily handled online. This individual was never able to discern if we were working on one problem or multiple problems. He found the open-group process very confusing online. In the second week, that same individual dropped the course.

The facilitator assumed that learning communities would form through the process of discussing the individual problems that were presented. It would seem that learning communities should develop from social learning situations. However, one can query, "Can learning communities develop when people cannot interact socially in the same room, face to face?" This question addresses the dynamics of distance learning in general and WBI in particular. Given the literature on WBI and learning communities, the assumption was that communities would form.

In the final analysis, the assumption that learning communities would emerge was incorrect. All of the participants indicated that they did not develop any on-going relationships of any type from the course. Any relationships that existed were residual from the Leadership Development Program. This is a surprising finding for the facilitator, who was convinced that the action learning process itself would bond the individuals and build a sense of community. That did not happen.

5.2.2 Level Two Evaluation: Learning

Kirkpatrick's Level Two evaluates learning. In the threaded discussion online, all of the participants learned and used the reflective inquiry method. None of the participants were familiar with the questioning and reflection approach prior to the AEL Course. In order to use reflective inquiry, they had to learn the AEL Cycle.

The act of reframing is evidence of learning. When the originator looks at the context differently, he or she may find that the problem becomes a different problem. Reframing occurs when the problem presenter changes the crux of the problem. Each time the problem was reframed in the context of this course at the beginning of each session, it indicated that the participant had changed his or her perception of the problem. Nine of the twelve participants reframed their problem at least once. Changed perceptions also indicate learning. Consequently, reframing is an indicator that learning has taken place.

By their own testimonies, all participants who completed the course said they learned something from the course, either about action learning or about their problem or both. The first and second levels of evaluation determined course effectiveness. The value to the organization appears at Kirkpatrick's Third and Fourth Levels of Evaluation.

5.2.3 Level Three Evaluation: Behavior

Kirkpatrick's (1994, p. 22) Level Three evaluates changes in behavior where behavior is defined as follows: "…the extent to which change in behavior has occurred because the participant attended the training program." The prerequisite condition to the problem selection for the course was that the participants each identify and present what he or she perceived as a real problem in their workplace. Most of the participants' business problems required some novel solutions that the majority of the participants found during the course. According to the participants who took action, those solutions and the implementation plan emerged as a result of the course. The actions taken by the participants during or after the course *may* indicate a change in behavior, but they do not provide conclusive evidence.

5.2.4 Level Four Evaluation: Results

Kirkpatrick's (1994, p. 25) Fourth Level is defined as "the final results that occurred because the participants attended the program." This level is more difficult to evaluate (Kirkpatrick, 1994, p. 65), especially for management development issues. However, there were indications of personal and organizational results occurring due to the impact of the Action E-Learning Course.

Kirkpatrick indicates that the results should be measurable. When it is a management development or personal development issue, the measurement would be to interview those around the participant to identify reactions to the changes in behavior resulting from personal development. Tools such as feedback from subordinates, peers, and supervisors would be appropriate as a measurement of results. One participant received some benefits of the results during the course as she involved her subordinates in more of the critical decision-making processes. One of her team members commented, "Wow, that felt good to hear and be a part of the decision making."

In the above-mentioned anecdotal case, the AEL Course participant's new management behaviors and attitudes evoked a positive response from a subordinate. However, in general the researcher/facilitator neither had access to nor the authority necessary to obtain feedback and/or gather follow up information on all of the other participants. Without this important data, it is difficult to ascertain if the course rendered lasting behavioral changes.

The results and impact of the actions taken requires more passage of time to evaluate. The feedback received from the participants relative to long-term results was that they were moving forward with their plans and had no major obstacles preventing implementation. One participant recommended that future Action E-Learning offerings include a step where the participant states, alongside the problem, recommendations for measuring the effect of the actions on the organization. Then the researcher would know what to examine for impact.

If the participants had worked on a single problem (rather than the open-group approach), the results would probably be easier to measure. Action learning has a reputation as an organizational learning tool. The power of action learning to impact organizational learning is that participants are not merely producing reports or making recommendations for another person to implement. Participants or sponsors implement solutions they have developed themselves. This ultimately has an impact on the organization.

The results for the organization are not measurable because of the open-group approach and the use of volunteers. If this research had focused on a single live problem that was presented by a sponsor, then the facilitator could exercise more control over the problem selection process. The facilitator can, in a single problem approach, ensure that the problems that are chosen result in measurable outcomes. Additionally, given the fact that in the AEL course the participants were volunteers from various agencies in the U.S. federal government, the researcher did not have access to performance and personnel records to examine long-term changes in behavior.

6. IMPLICATIONS, LIMITATIONS, AND FUTURE DIRECTIONS

A discussion of this research brings us to the topic of the virtual, asynchronous learning environment. The participants themselves touted the strengths of the application. One participant stated in the interview, "To me the advantage was the ability to get the point across without being interrupted, it gave you time to think. It also gives people a good chance to 'listen.'" The positive feedback provided by the participants about the asynchronous technology focused on its strengths. Participants were less likely to jump to conclusions in an asynchronous environment because they had time to consider a response. The asynchronicity allowed the set members to think and "listen" to what others were saying. It enabled the learners to get a point across without getting interrupted. They had the opportunity to reflect and fashion questions for other set members as well as to consider and design the answers to the questions they received.

This research has some significant and practical implications. First, it demonstrates the usefulness of the action learning approach conducted in an online instructional situation. Second, it provides insights on how to facilitate an action learning session online. Third, it demonstrates a successful online design approach that could be used for future design efforts. Fourth, this research demonstrates specific and repeatable techniques such as the AEL Cycle for the implementation of action learning online.

This study focused on the segment of e-learning courseware that can be labeled medium fidelity. Medium fidelity courseware requires a greater reliance on student/teacher contact because this type of training typically has a more direct influence on job performance. According to Nucleus Research (2002), medium fidelity courseware is acknowledged to be the least effective as online courseware. Implementing action learning in a medium fidelity course offered online will impact the development of Web-based instruction for that segment of courseware. The results of this study and the significance of the study can influence the approach used by organizations and higher-level institutes of learning as they develop management-level programs for delivery on line. Additionally, it further demonstrates another significant application of the action learning process.

The limitations to this study are noted here. Participants in the Action E-Learning Course were all volunteers. Intuitively, participant volunteers are less involved and committed than paying participants. Two of the twelve participants in this study dropped out of the study. One stated this in his email notifying me of withdrawal from the course, "It appears from my workload at the present time, I will not be able to [complete the course]. Consequently, much to my embarrassment, I am forced to withdraw as a member of your study group." The other withdrew saying, "Both my family, and our Church, are requiring more time than I have to give." As a volunteer, this course and the research were not as critical as the participants' personal responsibilities.

The length of the course was reduced at the client's request. Thus a fourteen-week course became a five-week course. A five-week course does not provide enough time and data to draw conclusions about the participants' changed behaviors resulting from the course.

This study was conducted and analyzed by a single individual. The use of a single judge is appropriate when the goal is to create "an in-depth understanding of a whole event, but it increases the need for further research" (Gersick, 1988).

Eisenhardt (1989, p. 537), in her article on building theory from case study research, states, "Selection of an appropriate population controls extraneous variation and helps to define the limits for generalizing the findings." This Action E-Learning approach targeted a specific population, management-level leaders. Thus, we know that AEL can be used with management-level individuals who have the authority to implement the solutions they develop during the action learning process. However, it is not clear that this same Action E-Learning instructional method would work with undergraduates, front-line, or entry-level personnel.

The conclusion is that online courses involving management-level individuals may find the Action E-Learning method an effective instructional design approach. In action learning, the person who owns the problem must have the authority within their organizations to implement the solutions they develop as a result of the action learning process. Thus, the target population for this research was the management-level individual.

Finally, participants must have reliable Internet access. The online approach will only work with those who have reliable access to the Internet.

Two powerful reactions of the participants evidenced learning and offered a commentary on the Action E-Learning approach. One person said, "I don't think a face-to-face approach would work with this [action learning] course!" Another stated, "I'm not sure this [action learning] process could be done any other way" [speaking about the asynchronous aspect]. These two reactions totally contradicted the expected response by critics of this study who said that action learning could not be conducted successfully online.

In the future, a longitudinal approach to the action learning process would be appropriate. When a course is compressed into such a short time frame (five weeks instead of fourteen), there should be allowance for follow-up. Ideally, the course should take place over a six to twelve month period where the long-term effects of the action learning process could be accurately assessed.

A future enhancement to the open-group approach (where each individual brings a unique problem) would be to have the owners of the problem identify at the beginning of the course if there is any way to measure impact of their problem-solution on their organizations. The owner or sponsor of the problem should establish, at its inception, the metrics to measure the impact on the organization. Then, after the action learning event, the evaluators would know where to start in the organization to assess the impact.

7. SUMMARY

In summary, this study demonstrates the power and effectiveness of the action learning method when applied online. Action learning can be implemented as an e-learning course delivery method. Management-level participants can learn the action learning online approach and use it to take action on urgent problems. It is an effective methodology for delivery of a management-level, virtual asynchronous course.

REFERENCES

Arbaugh, J. B., J. B. (2000). An exploratory study of the effects of gender on student learning and class participation in an internet-based MBA course. *Management Learning, 31* (4), 503-549.

Bandura, A., A. (1977). *Social Learning Theory*. Englewood Cliffs, NJ: Prentice-Hall.

Bandura, A., A. (1986). *Social Foundations of Thought and Action: A Social Cognitive Theory*. Englewood Cliffs, NJ: Prentice-Hall.

Brindle, J., J., & Levesque, L., L. (2000). Bridging the gap: Challenges and prescriptions for interactive distance education. *Journal of Management Education, 24* (4), 445-419.

Brower, H. H., H. H. (2003). On emulating classroom discussion in a distance-delivered OBHR course: Creating an on-line learning community. *Academy of Management Learning and Education, 2* (1), 22-36.

Carr, S., S. (2000). As distance education comes of age, the challenge is keeping the students, http://chronicle.com/free/v46/i23/23a00101.htm, retrieved January 30, 2002.

Cho, S. K., S. K., & Berge, Z. L., Z. L. (2002). Overcoming barriers to distance training and education. *Education at a Distance —The USDLA Journal, 16* (1), 1-15.

DeFillippi, R. J., R. J. (2001). Introduction: Project-based learning, reflective practices and learning outcomes. *Management Learning, 32* (1), 5-10.

Dewey, J., J. (1916). *Democracy and Education*. New York: The Free Press.

Dilworth, R. L., R. L. (1998a). Action learning in a nutshell. *Performance Improvement Quarterly, 11* (1), 28-43.

Dilworth, R. L., R. L. (1998b). Setting the stage, *Performance Improvement Quarterly, 11* (1), 5-8.

Dolmans, D., D., Gijselaers, W. H., W. H., Moust, J., J., & De Grave, W., W. (2002). Trends in research on the tutor in problem-based learning: Conclusions and implications for educational practice and research. *Medical Teacher, 24* (2), 173-180.

Driscoll, M., M. (1998). *Web-based Training: Using Technology to Design Adult Learning Experiences*. San Francisco: Jossey-Bass/Pfeiffer.

Driscoll, M., M. (1999). Web-based training in the workplace. *Adult Learning, 10* (4), 21-25.

Duffy, T. M., T. M., & Jonassen, D. H., D. H. (Eds.). (1992). *Constructivism and the Technology of Instruction, A Conversation* (1st ed.). Hillsdale, NJ: Lawrence Erlbaum Associates.

Eisenhardt, K., K. (1989). Building theories from case study research. *Academy of Management Review, 14* (4), 532-550.

Forman, D. C., D. C. (2002). Benefits, costs, and the value of e-learning programs. In A. Rossett, A. (Ed.),*The ASTD E-Learning Handbook: Best Practices, Strategies, and Case Studies for an Emerging Field* (pp. 398-413). New York: McGraw-Hill.

Fornaciari, C. J., C. J., Forte, M., M., & Mathews, C., C. (1999). Distance education as a strategy: How can your school compete? *Journal of Management Education, 23* (6), 703-719.

Galagan, P. A., P. A. (2000). The e-learning revolution. *Training & Development, 54* (12), 24-30.

Gersick, C., C. (1988). Time and transition in work teams: Toward a new model of group development. *Academy of Management Journal, 31* (1), 9-41.

Gijselaers, W. H., W. H. (Ed.). (1995). *Educational Innovation in Economics and Business Administration*. Dordrecht, The Netherlands: Kluwer Academic Publishers.

Hall, B., B. (1997). *Web-Based Training Cookbook*. New York: John Wiley & Sons, Inc.

Hall, B., B., & LeCavalier, J., J. (November 2000). The case for Level 3, http://www.learningcircuits.org/2000/nov2000/hall.htm, retrieved May 20, 2005.

Hughes, J., J., & Attwell, G., G. (February 2003). A framework for the evaluation of e-learning, http://www.theknownet.com/ict_smes_seminars/papers/Hughes_Attwell.html, retrieved May 20, 2005.

Human, S. E., S. E., Kilbourne, L. M., L. M., Clark, T., T., Shriberg, A., A., & Cunningham, B., B. (1999). Using Web-enhanced instruction in an interpersonal skills course. *Journal of Management Education, 23* (5), 584-607.

Jonassen, D. H., D. H., Peck, K., K., & Wilson, B. G., B. G. (1999). *Learning with Technology: A Constructivist Perspective*. Upper Saddle River, NJ: Merrill, Prentice-Hall.

Kanet, J. J., J. J., & Barut, M., M. (2003). Problem-based learning for production and operations management. *Decision Sciences Journal of Innovative Education, 1* (1), 99-118.

Keller, J. M., J. M., & Kopp, T. W., T. W. (1987). Application of the ARCS model of motivational design. In C. M. Reigeluth, C. M. (Ed.), *Instructional Theories in Action: Lessons Illustrating Selected Theories and Models* (pp. 289-320). Hillsdale, NJ: Lawrence Erlbaum Associates.

Khan, B. H., B. H., Waddill, D. D., D. D., & McDonald, J. A., J. A. (2001). Case studies of Web-based training sites. In B. H. Khan, B. H. (Ed.), *Web-Based Training* (pp. 367-374). Englewood Cliffs, NJ: Educational Technology Publications.

Kirkpatrick, D., D. (1994). *Evaluating Training Programs: The Four Levels*. San Francisco: Berrett-Koehler.

Kirkpatrick, D., D. (1996). Great ideas revisited: Revisiting Kirkpatricks's four-level model. *Training and Development Journal, 50* (1), 54-58.

Knowles, M., M. (1973). *The Adult Learner: A Neglected Species*. Houston, TX: Gulf Publishing.

Knowles, M. S., M. S. (1984). *Andragogy in Action*. San Francisco: Jossey-Bass.

Knowles, M. S., M. S., Holton, E. F. I., E. F. I., & Swanson, R. A., R. A. (1998). *The Adult Learner* (5th ed.). Woburn, MA: Butterworth-Heinemann.

Marquardt, M. J., M. J. (1999). *Action Learning in Action: Transforming Problems and People for World-Class Organizational Learning* (1st ed.). Palo Alto, CA: Davies-Black Publishing.

Marquardt, M. J., M. J. (2004). *Optimizing the Power of Action Learning*. Palo Alto, CA: Davies-Black Publishing.

Marsick, V. J., V. J., & O'Neil, J. A., J. A. (1999). The many faces of action learning. *Management Learning, 30* (2), 159-176.

Marsick, V. J., V. J., Cederholm, L., L., Turner, E., E., & Pearson, T., T. (1992). Action-reflection learning. *Training & Development, 46* (8), 63-66.

Martins, L. L., L. L., & Kellermanns, F. W., F. W. (2004). A Model of business school students' acceptance of a Web-based course management system. *Academy of Management Learning and Education, 3* (1), 7-26.

Mayberry, E., E. (2005). Kirkpatrick's level 3: Improving the evaluation of e-learning, http://www.learningcircuits.org/2005/may2005/mayberry.htm, retrieved May 19, 2005.

Nadkarni, S., S. (2003). Instructional methods and mental models of students: An empirical investigation. *Academy of Management Learning and Education, 2* (4), 335-351.

National Educational Association (NEA). (2000). Quality on the line: Benchmarks for success in Internet-based distance education, http://www.nea.org/ technology/onlinecourseguide.html, retrieved May 17, 2005.

Nucleus Research. (2002). E-learning delivers consistent returns, http://www.NucleusResearch.com, retrieved October 16, 2002.

Parker, A., A. (December 1999). A study of variables that predict dropout from distance education, http://www.outreach.uiuc.edu/ijet/v1n2/parker, retrieved January 30, 2002.

Phillips, J. J., J. J., Phillips, P. P., P. P., Duresky, L. Z., L. Z., & Gaudet, C., C. (2002). Evaluating the ROI of e-learning. In A. Rossett, A. (Ed.), *The ASTD E-Learning*

Handbook: Best Practices, Strategies, and Case Studies for an Emerging Field (pp. 387-397). New York: McGraw-Hill.

Reeve, S. D., S. D. (1998). Action learning and management development: Lesson for Web-based education. Paper presented at the 9th International Conference on College Teaching and Learning.

Revans, R. W., R. W. (1980). *Action Learning: New Techniques for Management* (1st ed.). London: Anchor Press Ltd.

Revans, R. W., R. W. (1982). *The Origin and Growth of Action Learning*. London: Chartwell Bratt.

Rhodes, C., C., & Garrick, J., J. (2003). Project-based learning and the limits of corporate knowledge. *Journal of Management Education, 27* (4), 447-471.

Roberts, B., B. (1998). Training via the desktop. *HRMagazine, 43* (9), 98-104.

Rossett, A., A. (2000). Confessions of a Web dropout. *Training, 37* (8), 100.

Rotter, J. B., J. B. (1954). *Social Learning and Clinical Psychology*. Englewood Cliffs, NJ: Prentice-Hall.

Rotter, J. B., J. B., Seeman, M., M., & Liverant, S., S. (1962). Internal versus external control of reinforcements: A major variable in behavior theory. Paper presented at the Decisions Values and Groups. Proceedings of a conference held at the University of New Mexico, New Mexico.

Saba, F., F. (2000). Research in distance education: A status report. *International Review of Research in Open and Distance Learning, 1* (1), 1-9.

Sandelands, E., E. (1999). Cyber tutoring and learning: How to facilitate action learning online, http://www.mcb.co.uk/imc/news/academic/cyber-tutoring.html, retrieved January 28, 2004.

Savery, J. R., J. R., & Duffy, T. M., T. M. (1996). Problem-based learning: An instructional model and its constructivist framework. In B. G. Wilson, B. G. (Ed.), *Constructivist Learning Environments: Case Studies in Instructional Design* (pp. 135-148). Englewood Cliffs, NJ: Educational Technology Publications.

Schon, D. A., D. A. (1987). *Educating the Reflective Practitioner*. San Francisco: Jossey-Bass Publishers.

Shandler, D., D. (1996). *Reengineering the Training Function: How to Align Training with the Corporate Agenda*. Delray Beach, FL: St. Lucie Press.

Singh, H., H. (2001). Online implementation of Kirpatrick's four levels of evaluation using Web databases. In B. H. Khan, B. H. (Ed.), *Web-Based Training* (pp. 523-529). Englewood Cliffs, NJ: Educational Technology Publications.

Stake, R. E., R. E. (1995). *The Art of Case Study Research*. Thousand Oaks, CA: Sage Publications.

Weasenforth, D., D., Biesenbach-Lucas, S., S., & Meloni, C., C. (2002). Realizing constructivist objectives through collaborative technologies: Threaded discussions. *Language Learning & Technology, 6* (3), 58-86.

Yin, R. K., R. K. (Ed.). (2003). *Case Study Research Design and Methods* (3rd ed.). Vol. 5. Thousand Oaks, CA: Sage Publications.

Yoo, Y., Y., Kanawattanachai, P., P., & Citurs, A., A. (2002). Forging into the wired wilderness: A case study of a technology-mediated distributed discussion-based class. *Journal of Management Education, 26* (2), 139-163.

Zielinski, D., D. (2000). Can you keep learners online? *Training, 37* (3), 64-75.

Chapter 25

ONLINE INTERNET TESTING

Lower Perceived Performance by Students

Wm. Benjamin Martz and Morgan M. Shepherd
University of Colorado at Colorado Springs, USA

1. INTRODUCTION

This chapter reports on a research study that looked at the differences between online students and traditional classroom students taking a quiz. The study examined differences in actual test performance, perceived performance, test satisfaction, study habits, and time pressure.

There has been a lot of research comparing distance education students to traditional students. Student performance, student satisfaction, student retention, trust, stress and feelings of isolation have all been analyzed. However, most of these have been looked at on a high level, specifically overall grades. We used this study to drill down to one specific element of student grades, specifically the quiz.

We compared two groups of students with similar backgrounds, similar study habits, and similar grades. Both groups were taking an introductory MBA level course in Visual Basic© programming. The course content, instructor, syllabus, lecture materials, notes, assessments and semester (time of year) were the same. We had both groups fill out a survey, and found that the online students had lower levels of satisfaction with their perceived results than the traditional on-campus students.

M.K. McCuddy et al. (eds.),
The Challenges of Educating People to Lead in a Challenging World, 499–511.

2. PREVIOUS RESEARCH IN DISTANCE EDUCATION

Distance education is big business; over 1.6 million students enroll in distance education classes annually. The Institute for Higher Education (2000) predicts that by 2004 over 90 percent of all two and four-year colleges will offer some sort of online courses. By the end of 2003, the virtual education market will grow in excess of $21 billion (Svetcov, 2000). New technologies and improvements in networking capabilities are enabling distance education instructors to come closer to providing the traditional learning environment for their students. However, there are still many issues that need to be resolved; and according to recent research studies, it does not appear that these will be resolved anytime soon (Russell, 2003).

Interestingly, the research in distance education goes back into the late 1920s when the first studies were published comparing the test scores of students in a classroom to their counterparts in a correspondence course (Crump, 1928). Since then, hundreds of journal articles, studies and reports have been published with similar comparisons with TV, radio, video tapes, computer-based training, audio-conferencing, groupware, and now the Internet, representing the technology compared to the traditional classroom (Moore, 1995).

Much of the research compares the distance education approach to the traditional classroom approach, looking for areas where the results from the distance education approach equals or exceeds those from the traditional classroom approach (Allen, Bourhis, Burrell, & Mabryl, 2002). There are many confounds involved, making this type of research difficult. One of these confounds is the definition given to "distance education." These definitions range from correspondence courses, to satellite classrooms where the instructor travels to lecture to a group of students meeting face-to-face, to courses that are held via email, to courses that are held via two-way full motion video with other technological support. The definition debate will probably never end, as some definitions do not include the use of any technology (correspondence courses), while others require several technologies to be implemented (full motion video with chat rooms, listservers and e-mail). For the purpose of this study, our definition of distance education involves a student body who never see each other or the instructors; who communicate via email, phone or chat; and who hand in assignments via e-mail or via posting to a common work group area.

Other confounds arise due to the nature of the dependent variables that are studied, and the interaction effects among them. Some of the dependent variables studied have been student performance, student satisfaction, and student retention (Russell, 2003). Within each of these three variables, socialization is thought to play a significant role. For example, Kling (2000) defines the study of complex issues around the interaction of information technologies with an institutional and cultural perspective as "social informatics." With the proliferation of the Internet, distance education is becoming a legitimate arena for social informatics. Kling's definition guides us to look at social issues brought on by the use of the Internet technology with education in general.

Other researchers (Shipley & Veroff, 1952; Papert, 1980; Hills & Francis, 1999) suggest that learning requires a social context to be effective. Bandura (1977) relies heavily on the interaction of people with their environment in his Social Learning Theory. Gunawardena and Zittle (1997) use results from their study to conjecture that "social presence is a strong predictor of satisfaction" in a computer-based environment. Tu (2000) goes even further by suggesting that the main driver of learning is the "consciousness of another person in the environment." Each of these studies indicates the importance of social issues in distance education. However, for each study that claims to show a significant difference between the distance and the traditional classroom environment, there seems to be one that claims to show that there is NO significant difference between the two environments. TeleEducation NB has helped compile two lists of research with regard to distance education. Russell (2003) summarizes those studies that found "no significant difference" between students in distance education and students in traditional classroom environments. Those findings demonstrating a significant difference are available through the TeleEducation (2003) Website.

Some studies have found significant differences in favor of the distance learning environment. For example, in a study on participation, Colorito (2001) found online students participating more than traditional students. Schutte (1997) found online learners tested 20 percent better than similar students in a traditional classroom setting. Nesler and Hanner (2001) surveyed students from different nursing programs about their level of socialization and were surprised to find online nursing students showed more socialization characteristics than their peers in the traditional classroom environment. Gagne and Shepherd (2001) found online students less satisfied than their peers in the traditional classroom with the availability of the instructor in a distance environment. However, this does reinforce the importance of some type of social interaction to distance education students. Maki, Maki, Patterson, and Whittaker (2000) found satisfaction with a lecture course to be lower for online students than for traditional students. Chen, Lehman, and Armstrong (1991) found that the attitudes of students in a computer-based class were less positive than those attitudes from students in a conventional classroom.

By design, much of distance education is a solitary experience. In this light, Hogan and Kwiatkowski (1998) argue that the emotional aspects of teaching large groups with technology have been ignored. Hearn and Scott (1998) concur and suggest that before adopting technology for distance teaching, the technology must be able to address the social context of learning. This idea is somewhat borne out by Hills and Francis's (1999) work with Computer Based Training (CBT) wherein they found that students were more successful in the CBT environment when more social interaction occurred.

Several researchers suggest that there may be problems inherent with the distance environment. The most bothersome may be student retention where course drop out rates as high as 50 percent are reported (Carr, 2000). Brown and Liedholm (2002) found that students in the virtual classroom performed worse than their traditional counterparts on examinations. Without the hands-on supervision inherent in the traditional environment, cheating and plagiarism take on added concerns (Agger-Gupta, 2002).

Other social factors also are being examined. Kirkman, Rosen, Gibson, Etsluk, & McPherson (2002) identified two social factors, creating trust and the feeling of isolation, as key factors for students to succeed in the distance environment. Hara and Kling (2001) research and report on the concern that distance courses may create new anxiety and stress for the student. Haythornthwaite, Kazmer, Robins, & Showmaker (2000) found that the distance environment limited the number of social cues and in turn, this limitation reduced the participation found in a distance environment.

This study looks more closely at student satisfaction, specifically student satisfaction with the testing process in our distance education program. To help reduce the threat of cheating, all student tests are timed. A timer starts when the student begins the test. The timer counts down the time, and is clearly visible in the corner of the screen. After the timer is started, the student can view the questions and take the test. Should the timer expire, the students' work up to that point is automatically submitted.

One potential problem with this method is the increased stress that might arise. Building on the work of Hara and Kling (2001) and Haythornthwaite *et al.* (2000), we hypothesize that this stress comes from two sources. The first source is the fear of not performing well, and the second source is the fear of not performing as well as your peers. Both fears exist in a traditional classroom, although the latter fear may be somewhat lessened due to the fact that the student can receive some visual clues as to how well they are doing compared to their peers.

3. STUDENT FEEDBACK CUES IN THE TESTING ENVIRONMENT

In the traditional test-taking environment students get feedback from the other students in the room. This feedback takes several forms. The first is in the form of pre-quiz "working" of the room. Students ask each other how much they studied for this quiz and how difficult/easy they think it will be. A second form of feedback occurs during the actual taking of the test. In the role of a student, suppose I see that time is running out and I'm only 75 percent of the way through the quiz. If I notice that 90 percent of my peers are still taking the quiz, I may realize that at least we are all "tanking" this quiz together (misery loves company). This socialization cue will help to dampen my fear. Yet another cue is in the form of the post-quiz "working" of the room. Students get a chance to see how well the others thought they did (albeit perceived performance) on the quiz. The distance student does not have easy access to any of these socialization cues. Hence, we decided to explore the effects of these socialization aspects on student satisfaction in the distance test-taking environment.

We hypothesized that *due to this lack of socialization cues in the distance education environment, the distance students would be less satisfied with their performance on the quiz than the traditional classroom students*. We devised an experiment to test this hypothesis.

Like many of the other studies discussed earlier, this research study was undertaken to explore the possibility of differences between the traditional classroom environment and the distance education environment (see Figure 1). However, the unit of analysis for this study is the common learning activity of test taking. Most studies noted earlier use the complete course as the unit of study, *i.e.*, student performance over the span of an entire course. This study uses a subset activity of a course, a test. The rationale of using this lower level of granularity is that differences that may occur at the test level may well be "washed out" when the aggregate unit of measure, the course, is used.

The subjects in this study were drawn from two Masters of Business Administration (MBA) level classes. Both classes were introductory, information systems classes teaching Visual Basic© programming. One was offered through an established distance program while the second was taught in a traditional classroom. Both courses were offered in the same 16-week semester format, by the same instructor, using the same book, same lecture material including slides, same assignments, and the same grading scale. The weekly assignments and order of topics was the same. The distance class had nine students and the on-campus class had ten students.

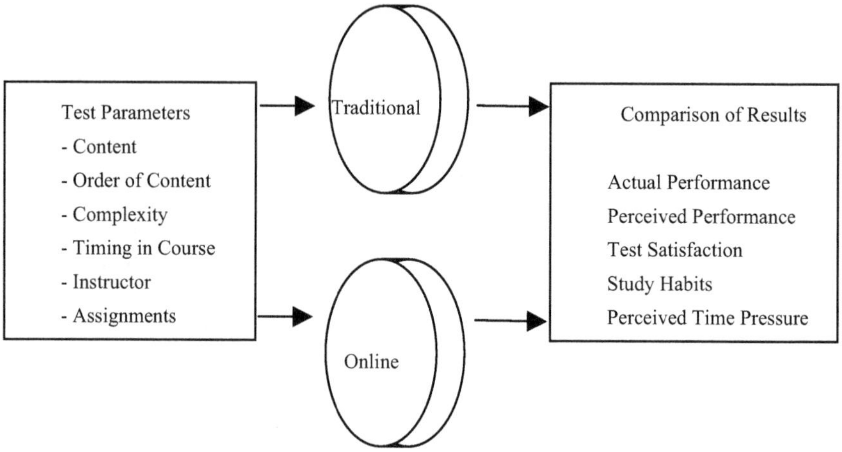

Figure 1. Research Design

The actual test used in the study was the first test of the semester for both classes. The distance class took the test using an automated, online testing program provided by the course content package that was accessed over the Internet. The on-campus class took its test on paper. The tests had the same questions with the same weights and the same order. The test was divided into three sections so as to minimize the potential problems in the distance environment. Both environments imposed the same time limit; the online test automatically enforced the time limit while a timer was used to enforce the on-campus class time limit. In both cases, a multiple-choice format was used to test students' understanding of basic programming knowledge.

A 15-item questionnaire was developed using the themes of interest from previous distance education research. Questions were developed to explore the areas assumed to be fundamentally different between distance and traditional classroom education. The questions were developed to look for potential differences in actual performance, perceived performance, test satisfaction, study habits, and time pressure.

In both cases, immediately after the test, the questionnaire was distributed to the class members. The distance class received the questionnaire as an email attachment. All questionnaires were returned within three days. The on-campus class filled out and turned in the questionnaire before leaving the classroom. All students in both classes returned their questionnaires.

4. A COMPARISON BETWEEN DISTANCE LEARNING AND FACE-TO-FACE LEARNING

The responses from the two groups were tabulated and are shown in Table 1. The columns show the number of online and on-campus students who agree or strongly agree (denoted in the A column) and who disagree or strongly disagree (denoted in the D column). In addition, Table 1 shows the significance of a statistical test, the Fisher Exact Test (Siegel, 1958), comparing the results of the online students to the on-campus students for each question. Siegel (1958, p. 96) offers this test as "an extremely useful nonparametic technique for analyzing discrete data (either nominal or ordinal) when two independent samples are small in size" and the results "fall into one or the other of two mutually exclusive classes" as we have here.

The first important observation is that two of the questions (Q4 and Q12) show a significant difference. Q4 hints at a social interaction difference between the two groups. Clearly, online students do not want to take tests with other students around while the on-campus students seem to prefer to have other students around.

Question 12 proves a little more interesting. Q12 shows that the two groups of MBA students report a significant difference in their satisfaction with their own performance. Remember, this is really perceived performance, as the results were not yet returned in class or available on line. This finding becomes more noteworthy because the actual test scores were not significantly different.

Questions 1, 2, and 3 deal with the issue of time pressure. Did the two groups feel pressure to complete the test? No, not really. Both groups disagreed that they felt time pressure and they disagreed that the time pressure helped their performance. While not statistically significant, the results for Q3 show that more of the online students would have preferred more time. Combined, these results show that a time limit did not induce the feelings of pressure, but the online group would be more receptive to an extension of the time limit.

Questions 4 and 5 tried to determine differences in the social aspect of having others in the room when taking the test. Certainly, being able to see when others complete and hand in the test could induce comparisons. In turn, these comparisons, if negative, could induce higher levels of anxiety. The results of these questions track well with what would be expected. Those students who have chosen a distance education class report little interest in having other students as a reference group and those choosing an on-campus environment like having other students as a reference group.

Table 1. Comparison of Online to On-Campus Groups

Statement	Online		On-Campus		Sign.
	A	D	A	D	(1)
Q1 I felt a lot of time pressure in taking this test.	3	6	2	8	.444
Q2 The time pressure helped me to perform well on this test.	0	9	2	8	.263
Q3 I would have scored higher with more time for the test.	4	5	1	9	.173
Q4 I prefer taking tests with my other classmates in a traditional classroom.	**0**	**9**	**6**	**4**	**.008**
Q5 I prefer taking tests by myself w/o other classmates in the room.	6	3	3	7	.128
Q6 The test was a fair way to evaluate how well I knew the subject matter.	6	3	9	1	.360
Q7 I studied for this test more than I usually do for tests.	0	9	1	9	.526
Q8 I studied with others (study group, non-classmate, etc.) for this test.	1	8	0	10	.474
Q9 I prefer studying with others for tests.	3	6	2	8	.444
Q10 I believe that I finished sooner than 50% of the others taking this test.	2	7	5	5	.220
Q11 I believe that I scored better than 50% of the others taking this test.	2	7	5	5	.220
Q12 Overall, I was satisfied with my performance on the test.	**2**	**7**	**8**	**2**	**.019**
Q13 Overall, I was satisfied with the format of the test.	6	3	8	2	.444
Q14 I waited until the last possible time to turn my test in.	3	6	1	9	.249
Q15 I studied between the sections of the test.	2	7	0	10	.211
Non-questionnaire Objective Measures					
Correct Prediction of Position (CPP)	5		8		.259
Correct Prediction of Score (CPS)	5		4		.414
Actual Test Score — ATS (average)	127		133		.211 (2)

(1) Fisher's exact Test (2) Mann-Whitney Test — (Siegel, 1958)

Question 6 asks directly for an assessment of the fairness of the test. Both groups thought the test was a fair evaluation. This can be interpreted to mean that neither the technology nor the test seemed to impact on the students' perception of fairness.

Questions 7, 8, and 9 concentrate on the students' study habits. Questions 8 and 9 try to determine if there is a difference in a student's preference for studying with others. There was none. Question 7 was asked to see if there was any difference in the perceived difficulty of the test. Neither group studied more than they normally do. This is significant for the online group as it implies that they did not envision the distance exam to be harder than that to which they were accustomed.

Questions 10 and 11 were designed to test for the potential social impacts of the on-campus environment. As suspected, the on-campus students did better than the distance students when they were asked to predict in which half of the class — top or bottom — that they (1) had completed and handed in their test, and (2) had scored. The on-campus students were very accurate with their assessment of whether they turned their test in with the upper 50th percentile, or the lower 50th percentile. Half estimated that they finished in the first 50th percentile, and half estimated that they finished in the second 50th percentile. This indicates that the social cues were providing significant feedback. Also of interest is their estimate as to whether they scored in the upper 50th percentile or the lower 50th percentile was 50-50.

Questions 12 and 13 deal with a student's satisfaction. The first question looks at his or her performance and the second asks about the format of the test. As stated earlier, the perceived performance proved significantly different between those students in the on-campus class and those in the online class. This difference does not carry through on Q13 as no difference was found related to the format of the test.

Questions 14 and 15 compare each student's behavior with respect to when they handed in the test and to whether or not they studied between the sections of the test. One could expect the on-campus students to wait until the last moment while the distance students do not. The results imply otherwise. Question 15 is truly unique to the distance environment. It indicates that two students found it necessary to study between the sections of the test.

5. ANALYZING THE DIFFERENCE IN PERCEIVED PERFORMANCE

First, why would there be a difference in perceived performance? A further analysis of the data did not find any of the other questions (Q1 through Q15) significantly correlated to Q12. So, none of the typical concerns looked at such as "time pressure" (Q1-Q3), "fairness of the test" (Q6), "study habits" (Q7-Q9), nor "format of the test" (Q13), help us understand the perceived performance difference exhibited.

However, one interpretation of Q10 and Q11 may provide a hint. While the differences between the subjects in these two classes are not statistically significant, it is interesting to note that the estimates of finishing position in the on-campus class better match the actual results than do the estimates in the distance class. This hints that the students in the on-campus class have a better reference point. Obviously, they can see the other students handing in their exams and compare their relative position. This reference point was not available to the distance class. Could it be that the reference point provided in the traditional classroom helps students understand their relative position and lead to better "perceived satisfaction"? This might also explain the decidedly negative impression that the distance students felt, concerning both whether they turned in their test in the upper or lower 50th percentile, and whether they scored in the upper or lower 50th percentile.

The second area of interest is with time pressure. Again, without statistical significance, this is conjecture only. The numbers for the time pressure questions hint at time pressure impacting the online students more than the on-campus. This is especially true when a student was asked if he/she would have scored higher with more time (Q3). The two groups had the same amount of time. But we need to realize that a key difference was the "enforcer" of the deadline. In the distance case, the software counts down using a displayed clock and when zero is reached, the software closes down the test and locks the student out. This is a very rigid and impersonal activity in that there is no arguing with the computer. In the classroom environment, the "enforcer" is a human being. A student may feel it easier to push the time limit. Even as the instructor is saying, "It is time to turn the tests in," a student may feel comfortable finishing a sentence. Extrapolating then, could it be that the "impersonalness" of the automated testing environment influences perceived pressure.

The results raise one concern and provide two conjectures for understanding differences between on-campus and distance environments. The concern is for why would online students report lower perceived performance than on-campus students. Several keys factors suggested by the literature, such as test fairness and study habits, did not help explain the difference. However, one conjecture consistent with the data is that an on-campus student has a built-in reference group when handing in tests — those students who have already handed the test in before him/her. The second conjecture consistent with the data is that "time pressure" may be inherent to the distance testing environment simply because the testing software is an impersonal enforcer of the time limit.

Lack of social cues may very well account for the more pessimistic attitudes of the distance students, even though there was no significant difference on the test. Now we need to look at various ways in which we can infuse the distance education environment with similar social cues. One way may be to put an "average time to complete quiz" number up on the screen for the distance students when they start their quiz, along with a "you are the XXth person to take this test" number so the students can better make sense out of the two. We may need to hold a special chat session prior to the quiz to allow the distance students to get some of these socialization cues. If we can infuse some portion of these social cues into the distance environment, we may be able to improve the satisfaction levels of the distance education students taking timed quizzes.

6. LIMITATIONS OF THE STUDY

The major limitation of this study is the sample size. With only 19 subjects spread over two classes, any differences found between the two groups will be sensitive to statistical prejudices. It should be noted that the Fisher Exact Test, which was used to designate any differences as significant, is the appropriate test for analyzing a two by two result. Also, it is a very conservative test meaning that if a significant difference is noted, it is more likely a true difference.

7. CONCLUSION

The distance education environment is big business. As such, there is much interest in understanding any differences inherent between these environments. The literature has a long list of researchers concerned with understanding these differences. Many hard, objective issues have been raised, such as performance, retention and participation. Lately, softer, subjective social issues, such as time pressure, anxiety, stress, and trust, have been thrown into the debate. All in all, the results have been ambiguous. There are studies showing significant differences between the two environments and there are studies showing no significant differences. The latter ones imply that the distance environment is "just as good" as the traditional environment.

The study reported here adds one more issue to the significant difference side of the equation. Using two classes, equivalent on many of the confounding variables such as instructor, test format, time constraints, etc., data were gathered on issues such as perceived performance, study habits, and actual performance. The limitations of a small sample size notwithstanding, the results show that the distance students rated their satisfaction with perceived performance significantly lower than the on-campus students.

The attempt to interpret the implications of these findings suggested two conjectures consistent with the data. One, the testing process in the distance environment uses more of an impersonal enforcer of the time limit. As such, the distance student may feel more time is needed and be less positive about his or her performance as the time limit runs out. Two, the on-campus environment provides students with a built-in reference group for analyzing their performance. As students hand in tests, they "know" where they fall in relation to others that have and have not yet handed in the test. Possible methods for adding the reference group to distance classes and for removing the personal confound from the on-campus environment were suggested.

The results of this study suggest one more area of concern for those looking to implement a distance environment: students in distance environments may exhibit lower perceived performance.

REFERENCES

Agger-Gupta, D. (2002). Uncertain frontiers: Exploring ethical dimensions of online learning. In K. E. Rudestam & J. Schoenholtz-Read (Eds.), *Handbook of online learning* (pp. 125-148). London: Sage Publishing.

Allen, M., Bourhis, J., Burrell, N., & Mabry, E. (2002). Comparing student satisfaction with distance education to traditional classrooms in higher education: A meta analysis, *American Journal of Distance Education* , *16* (2), 120-125.

Bandura, A. (1977). *Social Learning Theory*. Englewood Cliffs, NJ: Prentice-Hall.

Brown, B. W., & Liedholm, C. E. (2002). Teaching microeconomic principles: Can web course replace the classroom in principles of microeconomics? *American Economic Review*, *92* (2), 1-15.

Carr, S. (2000). As distance education comes of age the challenge is keeping students. *Chronicle of Higher Education*, February 11, pp. 11-21.

Chen, H., Lehman, J., & Armstrong, P. (1991). Comparison of performance and attitude in traditional and computer conferencing classes. *The American Journal of Distance Education*, *5* (3), 51-64.

Colorito, R. (2001). Learning online. *Indiana Alumni Magazine*, *64* (1).

Crump, R. (1928). *Correspondence and class extension work in Oklahoma.* Doctoral dissertation. Teachers College, Columbia University.

Gagne, M., & Shepherd, M. (2001). Distance learning in accounting: A comparison between distance and traditional accounting class. *T.H.E. Journal*, *28* (9), 58-60, 62, 65-66.

Gunawardena, C. & Zittle, F. (1997). Social presence as a predictor of satisfaction within a computer-mediated conferencing environment. *American Journal of Distance Education*, *11* (3), 8-26.

Hara, N., & Kling, R. (2001). Students' distress with a web-based distance education course. *Information, Communication and Society*, *3* (4), 557-579.

Haythornthwaite, C., Kazmer, M., Robins, J., & Showmaker, S. (2000). Community development among distance learners: Temporal and technological dimensions, *Journal of Computer-mediated Communication*, *6* (1): available at http://www.ascusc.org/jcmc/vol6/issue1/haythornthwaite.html.

Hills, H., & Francis, P. (1999). Interaction learning. *People Management*, *5* (14), 48-49.

Hearn, G., & Scott, D. (1998). Students staying home. *Futures*, *30* (7), 731-737.

Hogan, D., & Kwiatkowski, R. (1998). Emotional aspects of large group teaching, *Human Relations*, *51* (11), 1403-1417.

Institute for Higher Education Policy. (2000). Quality on the Line: Benchmarks for Success in Internet Distance Education, Washington, D.C.

Kirkman, B. L., Rosen, B., Gibson, C., Etsluk, P., & McPherson, S. (2002). Five challenges to virtual team success: Lessons from Sabre, Inc. *The Academy of Management Executive, 16* (3), 67-79.

Kling, R. (2000). Learning about information technologies and social change: The contribution of social informatics. *Information Society*, *16* (3), 217-232.

Maki, R., Maki, W., Patterson, M., & Whittaker, P. (2000). Evaluation of a web-based introductory psychology course: I. Learning and satisfaction in on-line versus lecture courses. *Behavior Research Methods, Instruments and Computers*, *32* (2), 230-239.

Moore, M. (1995). American distance education: A short literature review. In F. Lockwood, (Ed.), *Open and Distance Learning Today* (pp. 32-41). London, New York: Routledge.

Nesler, M., & Hanner, M. (2001). Professional socialization of baccalaureate nursing students; Can students in distance nursing programs become socialized? *Journal of Nursing Education*, *40* (7), 293-302.

Papert, S. (1980). *Mindstorms*, New York: Basic Books.

Russell, T. (2003). The no significant difference phenomenon. http://teleeducation.nb.ca/ nosignificantdifference/, accessed March 30, 2003.

Schutte, J. (1997). Is there a title to this work? http://www.csun.edu/sociology/virexp.htm/, last accessed on October 29, 2004.

Siegel, S. (1958). *Non-parametric Statistics*. New York: McGraw-Hill.

Shipley, T., & Veroff, J. (1952). A projective measure of need affiliation. *Journal of Experimental Psychology*, *43*, 349-356.

Svetcov, D. (2000). The virtual classroom vs. the real one. *Forbes*, *166* (7), 50-52.

TeleEducation. (2003). http://teleeducation.nb.ca/nosignificantdifference/, accessed on March 30, 2003.

Tu, C. (2000). Online learning migration: From social learning theory to social presence theory in the CMC environment. *Journal of Network and Computer Applications*, *23* (1), 27-37.

PART VI

TEACHING AND LEARNING INSIGHTS FROM UNIQUE APPLICATIONS

Chapter 26

BRIDGING THE KNOWING-DOING GAP

Powerful Ideas for Innovative Learning Design and the Use of IT in Corporate Education

Sergio Vasquez Bronfman
ESCP-EAP (European School of Management), Paris, France

1. INTRODUCTION

In the field of professional, continuous, and corporate education (PCCE)[37] there is a recurrent complaint concerning the effectiveness of the educational process (Mintzberg, 1988; Mintzberg, 1996; Schön, 1983). Effectiveness is "the ability of a system to produce what it must produce." Therefore, in an effective PCCE system people should learn to do what they must do when working in their companies. Unfortunately this is not what one can observe; actual PCCE systems produce people who get a lot of knowledge but who are unable to put it into practice.

One of the main reasons for this knowing-doing gap (Pfeffer & Sutton, 2000) is *infocentrism*, which is a wrong interpretation of what learning is. Infocentrism says that learning is a kind of information system: knowledge is transmitted to learners through lectures and/or accessed through readings; then learners must retain this knowledge; and finally professors organize

[37] Professional education refers to university education (either undergraduate or postgraduate) of architects, engineers, doctors in medicine, business professions, etc. (see Schön, 1983). "Continuous and corporate education" refer to all educational activities (either performed in-company or not) that do not lead to a degree. Although the scope of this paper is on PCCE in general, the argumentation and the examples shown here apply mainly in the corporate education field.

M.K. McCuddy et al. (eds.),
The Challenges of Educating People to Lead in a Challenging World, 515–531.

tests of knowledge retention that we call exams.[38] In good educational settings, exercises and case studies are also performed. Implicitly, the infocentric perspective makes the hypothesis that if knowledge is transmitted properly (*i.e.*, lectures are clear) then application (practice) is obvious. In fact this hypothesis is falsified. Hence the knowing-doing gap comes into existence.

When turning to the use of information technologies (IT) in education and training we observe another important problem: *technocentrism*. In Seymour Papert's words, "technocentrism is the fallacy of referring all questions to technology" (Papert, 1987; Papert, 1990). In the field of educational technologies, technocentrism leads to focus on questions about the number of computers per student, the number of computers connected to the Internet and the functionalities of an e-learning platform. In educational technology research, technocentrism leads to questions such as: "Will the Internet have this or that effect on management learning, by comparison with a traditional classroom?" or "Will a CD-ROM lead to a mechanical method of thinking in accounting?" Scholars then run evaluation studies comparing, for instance, a course delivered via the Internet with a traditional face-to-face course, identifying information technology as the only variable, and assuming that the hypothesis "all else being equal" (*ceteris paribus*) is true. Of course it is false, because in fact everything changes: the professor, the students, the classroom, and the technology.

What is missed in infocentric and technocentric perspectives is a correct interpretation on how people learn, and in particular on how people learn to become and develop themselves as professionals. This discussion is clarified if we make some distinctions on learning. Jerome Bruner made the distinction between *learn about* and *learn to be*, to which this paper adds *learn to do*. We then have three kinds of learning:

- Learn about ... (*e.g.*, negotiation, communication, history, medicine, software design, etc.).
- Learn to do ... (*e.g.*, how to negotiate, how to communicate well, how to run a research in history, how to diagnose illnesses, how to design software, etc.).
- Learn to be ... (*e.g.*, a negotiator, a communicator, a researcher in the field of history, a doctor, a software designer, etc.).

One can love history and be interested in medicine or in human communication. By reading books on these topics, attending conferences, doing courses (online or face-to-face), etc., one can learn a lot *about* history,

[38] To be rigorous, "information" rather than "knowledge" should be written here (see Brown and Duguid, 2000).

medicine, and human communication, but that does not mean that one will be able to conduct research in history, to diagnose illnesses, or to communicate effectively. In other words, one will not be able to *do*.

Following the same logic, if one has been successfully conducting a first piece of research in history, has diagnosed some simple illnesses, or has solved a communication problem, that does not mean that one will be considered a historian, a doctor, or a professional in the field of human communication. In other words, one will be able to do, but one will not yet *be* (a professional recognized as such by his/her peers). To reach this level one must be involved in recurrent practice inside the proper professional community (historians, doctors, human communication practitioners, etc.).

Bearing in mind these learning distinctions and the knowing-doing gap, it can be said that one of the causes of this gap is that the vast majority of PCCE systems satisfy only the "learn about" kind of learning, and that professionals and companies expect at least "learn to do". Educational practices needed in order to "learn about" are not sufficient when one needs to "learn to do". Hence, there is an important discrepancy between supply and demand in professional, continuous, and corporate education. One can observe this confusion in face-to-face training and even more in e-learning.

Of course, to "learn about" things and topics is necessary. Maybe the majority of what we learn consciously in life is "about" things. But in the field of corporate education we need a new kind of educational practice in order to allow people to "learn to do" and "learn to be". This paper will describe some ideas that, in addition to infocentrism, technocentrism, and the learning distinctions above, will allow us to design this new kind of educational practice and, therefore, to bridge the knowing-doing gap. These are well known ideas in the field of educational research but (unfortunately) most often unrecognized in educational practices.

2. A PEDAGOGICAL FRAMEWORK FOR INSTRUCTIONAL DESIGN

Not surprisingly, the thinking in this paper has been influenced by John Dewey's ideas on learning by doing (Dewey, 1933) and by Jean Piaget's ideas on constructivism (Piaget, 1985; Piaget, 1992). The paper also builds on pedagogical perspectives such as constructionism (Papert, 1990; Harel & Papert, 1991), and on the work of Vygotsky (1985). Constructivism is based on the assumption that knowledge is created by learners, rather than transmitted by teachers like information in a pipeline, and that they discover and *construct* meaning from their environments. Constructionism suggests that learners are particularly likely to create knowledge when they are actively engaged in *making* something that is also personally meaningful and that they can *share with others*, such as video games, robots, computer animations, written stories or, closer to corporate education, e-commerce Web sites or a bank branch's business plan.

Constructionism is also close to the work of Vygotsky, in the sense that learning is a *social* process and stems from cooperative activities, from making something collectively. Moreover, Vygotsky states that effective learning occurs when this process happens within transactions between learners and members of their culture more experienced than them, hence leading to concepts like coaching, mentoring, etc. This is why Vygotsky's ideas are often called *social constructivism.*

The Russian educational thinker is also known for the concepts of *zone of proximal development* (ZDP) and *scaffolding*. ZDP refers to the distance between what a learner can perform by himself and what he/she can perform with the help of an experienced practitioner, while scaffolding refers to the need for step-by-step progress in learning and to constructing new knowledge on the basis of what one already knows.

On the basis of these ideas we now have a first framework for educational design in order to allow people to "learn to do". Summarizing this framework we can say that "learning to do" needs a learning by doing environment where students make things collectively, tackling problems under the guidance of experienced practitioners, where they can share ideas with others, hence working in teams, where coaching helps students to perform what they have to do, where lecturing and reading give people the information they need to perform their learning activities.

Nevertheless, if we want to bridge the knowing-doing gap in PCCE, course design based on the above educational framework will not be sufficient. Of course, people need to learn by doing, but this "doing" must also be significant, *i.e.*, activities that deal with important issues for learners. In professional and continuous education, and in particular in corporate training environments, significant activities are those that are related to learners' daily work practices. This is called the *everyday coping* of learners with the subject of the course. "Everyday coping" — which is a concept adapted from Hubert Dreyfus' interpretation of Heideggerian philosophy (Dreyfus, 1991; Wrathall & Malpas, 2000) — means the way learners cope every day with some subject or topic, the way they face it every day at the workplace.[39] Therefore, if one wants to bridge the knowing-doing gap, the

[39] Hubert Dreyfus calls skilful coping not only the way people deal with daily work situations, but mainly the smooth and unobtrusive responses to those situations (Wrathall and Malpas, 2000).

main question for learning design should be: *what is the learners' everyday coping with regard to the subject of the course?*

This framework for a "learn to do" design can be represented by the following model:

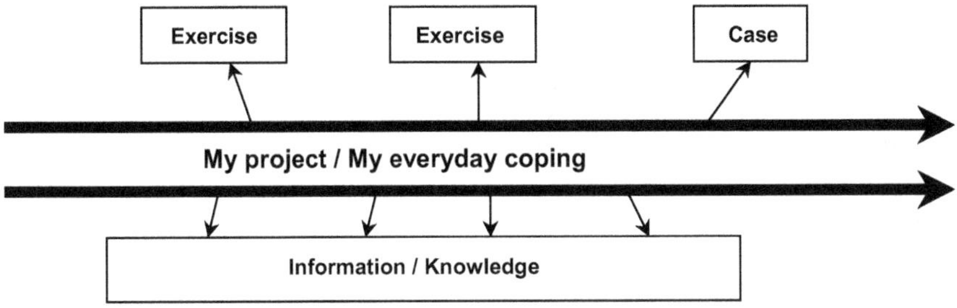

Figure 1. Model of the "Learn to Do" Design

The structure of a course is a sequence of activities for which information and knowledge come in support of these activities, rather than a sequence of "pieces of content" with exercises and case studies in order to apply the content. Hence, the spinal column of a course is a sequence of situations based on the learners' daily work and the way they cope every day with these situations, or a real project they have to plan and manage. Learners will access information and knowledge *from* the activities in which they are involved.

In our design model, "theory" or "content" (which of course remains very important) is now called "information/knowledge" or even "documentation" in order to strengthen the similarity with real work. As a matter of fact, when we are at work we never start by looking at theoretical content, then moving to do some exercises and in the end coming to real work. In fact we just work, we do things, and only when there is something we don't know how to perform do we look for information or knowledge. We find this information in the documentation we have at the office, in books, on the Internet, … or in colleagues' minds.

Nevertheless, in our model there are also exercises and cases that are not necessarily linked to the everyday coping of the learners. These exercises and cases are often relevant in order to progress step-by-step in the mastering of a certain skill. Following Vygostky's concept of *scaffolding*, it is necessary to have many intermediate steps in the learning process similar to when we climb stairs: we have to go up step-by-step. But it is from being involved in a significant activity (*e.g.* a work project) that it becomes interesting to have access to exercises and cases that are not necessarily linked to our daily practice at work.

In the next section we will look at some examples of this framework that have been designed and implemented in a Spanish savings bank.

3. THE VIRTAULA PROJECT

La Caixa is one of the most important Spanish financial institutions. It is a savings bank that has around 20,000 employees, spread all over Spain, and that has a strong reputation of commitment in the training of its employees.

Over the past years la Caixa has recruited many new employees (around 5,000) in order to replace people going into retirement and to ensure the expansion of the bank all over Spain. New employees must complete a compulsory training program during their first year at la Caixa. This program includes management skills such as communication and negotiation, and courses typical of the banking profession such as investments, taxes, insurance, etc. In the past, the training of the new employees was done face-to-face and on a traditional distance training delivery mode (printed materials plus post office). But in the new scenario this was too expensive. Moreover, it became impossible to update the material, which was a big handicap in a changing environment like financial services. Therefore, the Human Resources Department of the bank (which is in charge of the project) decided to move to e-learning, and launched the Virtaula project.

Virtaula started in January 2000 with two virtual classrooms of 25 new employees with one online tutor (or coach/trainer) each.[40] As of May 2004 more than 5,800 new employees have done or are doing their first year training program in Virtaula.

In the beginning of the project the design of the e-learning material did not encourage learner-tutor interaction or learner-learner interaction. Moreover, new employees complained that the learning material was "boring" and "not very practical". Thus, in September 2001 the author suggested[41] redesigning the learning material with two goals in mind: a) learning activities should be interactive in nature, and b) the gap should be

[40] Online tutors are la Caixa's employees, generally branch managers (the bank has almost 1,000 people who perform training tasks in addition to their daily tasks). They were face-to-face trainers who, voluntarily, became online trainers.

[41] From September 2000 until February 2002 the author has been the project manager of Virtaula at GEC S.A., the company that was in charge of the project as a provider. After February 2002 the author became responsible for pedagogical innovation in the project.

reduced between what is taught in training courses and the real situations that learners face at their workplaces (in other words, bridging the knowing-doing gap).

How can we structure a course around a sequence of activities and how can we design significant activities? Using participative course design methods, the design team worked with end-users of Virtaula, *i.e.*, the new employees and their managers. For instance, when designing a course on insurance for new employees, we asked them: What is the everyday coping of la Caixa's new employees on insurance? The answer helped us to focus on the skills that new employees must come to master when dealing with insurance (for instance, to selling insurance that takes care of customers' concerns). Then we asked for recurrent situations faced by the new employees in this field, which led us to write a sequence of mini-cases. At the end of each mini-case learners have to answer questions like: "What would you do in this situation?" or "What kind of products can you offer to this client?" or "What would be your advice to this customer?", etc. Answers must generally be sent to a moderated forum for discussion with the online classroom colleagues. Relevant information necessary to perform these activities is suggested to learners (which they can access on the Web pages of the courses).

The first targets of the e-learning project were the new employees. Nevertheless, as top management in the bank started to see that e-learning was a successful move, new target audiences were included, *e.g.*, branch managers (there are more than 4,500 branches of la Caixa).[42] In groups of 300-400 every year (since October 2000), branch managers have started a traditional one year face-to-face program aimed at the management of branches. In all, more than 1,500 branch managers have done or are doing this course via Virtaula. This is a program designed by la Caixa's HR Department and done in partnership with 14 Spanish universities. But the HR Department wanted the whole group to do a common course whose main goal was to design a kind of business plan for a branch of la Caixa. This course is done via Virtaula.

Instead of starting by asking the branch managers to read some theoretical content on business plans, then to do some exercises and case studies and, in the end, to apply this knowledge to their own branches, the course starts by asking them to write 10 lines with their first ideas on their branches, how they see it three years in the future, and to send these 10 lines to their tutors (or coaches). As a consequence, branch managers are involved from the beginning in the main activity of the course: to make *their* business

[42] Also, more than 2,500 financial advisors have been trained via Virtaula.

plan, the business plan of the branches they are managing. From there, tutors will coach them in the design of their business plans and, as part of this process, they will suggest relevant material to the branch managers, material that is available in Virtaula as Information/Knowledge.

The action research we have done on the uses and results of Virtaula showed that this framework and model for instructional design is of great help in bridging the knowing-doing gap.[43]

4. REFLECTIVE LEARNING

Until now we have discussed a kind of learning that is related to concepts like *assimilation*. Assimilation refers to the idea developed by Piaget of a process that involves incorporating new information into an already existing cognitive structure (Piaget, 1985). But there is another kind of learning that happens when there is a need to change the cognitive structure to make sense of the environment. Piaget called *accommodation* the learning process which starts when something happens that leads us to change our assumptions. This concept is close to what Donald Schön calls *reflection*.

Schön says that "reflection" starts when there is a "surprise" (good or bad), when there is a breakdown: something produces unexpected results, an error resists correction, or we begin to look at something in a new way. We may respond to this situation by reflection and we may do so in one of two ways (Schön, 1987).

We may reflect *on* action, thinking back on what we have done in order to discover the causes of the unexpected outcome. And we may reflect *in* action, *i.e.*, in the midst of action without interrupting it. Reflection then has a critical function, questioning the assumptional structure of our knowledge. Therefore we learn in the sense of Piaget's accommodation.[44]

Reflective learning literature deals mainly with reflection-*on*-action. Nevertheless, we think that the real challenge is to design learning situations that allow for reflection-*in*-action. This is mainly because the huge majority of the situations we face every day when we find a surprise are not situations

[43] During the year 2002 the author directed a research team that conducted an action research study on how people were using Virtaula, what they appreciated and what was going wrong. Data came from the statistics of the Virtaula e-learning platform, the analysis of what people were saying in electronic forums, and from semi-structured interviews that we performed with 129 Virtaula users.

[44] The author strongly believes that this interpretation of the concept of reflection is also related to the Heideggerian concept of "breakdown" and its consequences for learning (Dreyfus, 1991).

that allow us to stop and think. We have to think on the situation while dealing with it. As Schön says, "what distinguishes reflection-in-action from other kinds of reflection is its immediate significance for action" (Schön, 1987).

We now give an example of an online reflective course on Communication that has been designed for la Caixa's employees.[45] The course is structured in six learning units, every unit having the same structure as below:

- First, trainees read a reflective story (a mini-case that tells a story with a breakdown, a surprise, that can be interpreted in terms of human communication) and participate in an online discussion of this story in a forum.
- Second, trainees are encouraged to access some readings on communication theory that allow for a new interpretation of the reflective story. Then follows an online discussion of the participants' *own* examples of the same kind of story.
- Third, following a given procedure, trainees must run a face-to-face exercise on human communication (with a colleague, a friend, etc.), then report the results via e-mail, and finally participate in an online discussion on what happened in this exercise. While doing the face-to-face exercise, participants must reflect *in* action; when they participate in the related online discussion they are allowed to reflect *on* action.
- Finally, trainees must write an evaluation report of the above exercises, in light of what they have learned.

As we can see, this course is not a completely online course. Participants must do some face-to-face activities. This is because human communication is an embodied phenomenon. As human beings, we are not like minds in a vat, we have bodies and our bodies play an important role in the communication process. Therefore, if one wants to learn *to communicate* (which is not the same as to learn *about communication*) one must also train his/her body to communicate and reflect on what happens to the body in the face-to-face exercises. Moreover, it may be asserted that in human communication courses face-to-face exercises are the only way to allow people to reflect *in* action, the subsequent online discussions allowing them to reflect *on* action.

[45] In fact, this course on Communication has been designed by a company whose members were trained in the applications of Hubert Dreyfus' ideas, among others.

We will now turn to some new ideas that can allow us to design and implement "learn to be" educational activities.

5. SITUATED LEARNING AND COMMUNITIES OF PRACTICE

In order to "learn to be" one must go beyond teaching. The works of Jean Lave and Etienne Wenger (Lave & Wenger, 1991), John Seely Brown and Paul Duguid (Brown & Duguid, 1991; Brown & Duguid, 2000) and, in some aspects, that of Lev Vygotsky, have clearly shown that learning is a social process and takes place whether there is any intentional education or not. At least, some kind of incidental learning takes place through interaction between peers on their common job practice. Moreover, this kind of learning takes place in a *situated action* (in space and time). The above authors make a breakthrough in the theory of learning by shifting the focus from the individual as learner to learning as participation in the social world, from a cognitive process to a social practice.

All of this means that nobody can learn a job outside of a community of practitioners. If one wants to learn the job of a doctor (*i.e.*, to learn *to be* a doctor), one must practice inside a community of doctors; if one wants to become an entrepreneur, one must practice entrepreneurship inside of a community of entrepreneurs.

Lave and Wenger created the concept of *Legitimate Peripheral Participation* (LPP) to draw attention to the point that learners inevitably participate (more or less) in communities of practitioners and that the mastery of knowledge requires newcomers to move toward full participation in the sociocultural practices of a community. Therefore, they stress the point that, in order to facilitate learning, one must create an environment that facilitates LPP and access to practice, ongoing work activities, and practical expertise.

Building on situated learning, Etienne Wenger developed the concept of *Communities of Practice* (Wenger, 1998), which reflect informal structures that gather people linked through *a common practice*, which is also recurrent and stable in time. Communities of Practice (CPs) always develop around what matters to its members; therefore, if one wants to facilitate LPP and to "learn to be", a CP is a good candidate.

Following this logic, la Caixa has started to *cultivate* (rather than to *create*) some emergent communities of practice. The term "to cultivate" emphasizes the point that a CP cannot be created intentionally or overmanaged. An effective CP should rise almost spontaneously.

Nevertheless, that does not mean that nothing can be done in order to help CP development (Wenger, McDermott, & Snyder, 2002).

In this sense, "to cultivate" is a good analogy. One cannot really "create" a plant but much can be done in order to help an existing plant to grow. Thus, rather than trying to create a community of practice, one must help to cultivate the already existing communities (even if they are in an embryonic state). In order to do this, the first thing to do is to identify those emerging CPs.

We have identified two main CPs at the bank: the new employees' online tutors and the branch managers. More than 45 online tutors are spread all over Spain. In the beginning they felt very isolated and complained that this was a very new job and that they needed more training. We started to work with them in order to create a *community* of online tutors rather than having 45 individuals; therefore, we organized a two-day (and night) residential work session that has taken place every six months. After the first one, fruitful online work could start mainly through discussions in electronic forums, where people worked on topics like new employees' participation in virtual classrooms, online coaching, etc. Moreover, when asked, the online tutors made substantial contributions to course design for their trainees.

Concerning the branch managers, in order to facilitate their access to the Virtaula system before the beginning of their online course, we created an online forum where they could have discussions on their ongoing problems at work, thus sharing their practical knowledge. Following Etienne Wenger's advice, a prestigious branch manager moderates this forum in order to give credibility to the discussion and to build trust.

The research we have done on the uses and results of Virtaula has shown that the branch managers value greatly the possibility of having contacts and asking for help outside of their own branches. Even more, some of them started to have informal but regular face-to-face meetings, or expressed the will to do this. For instance, 26 branch managers of a Spanish region decided to meet for lunch the first Friday of every month in order to have discussions on their ongoing problems. Hence, in addition to the cultivation of the electronic branch managers' community of practice, we started to cultivate local CPs.

Usually, discussions in a CP start when someone poses a question to the community, most often a problematic question. A member of the community who knows the answer then gives the solution. People learn from each other by sharing existing knowledge. In order to share this knowledge, storytelling is an interesting technique.

Stories are important for learning for at least two reasons. First, stories are the "natural" way in which our brain structures our memories (Bruner, 1996). We all remember better the "story" of a project than just some data on it. Second, in the structure of a story there is always a breakdown. A typical story starts with a situation where there is a breakdown: something does not work anymore and unexpected facts are observed. Therefore something new appears as a goal. But, in order to reach this goal there will be many difficulties — people who will fight to reach the goal and other people who will be opposed to the goal (Christian & Boudès, 2000). In other words, starting from a main breakdown — what worked before does not work anymore — there will be new breakdowns until the "heroes" reach the goal.

What is relevant here is that when we face a breakdown we put ourselves "automatically" in the mood for learning. As a matter of fact, when everything is going well we believe that we know; and when one believes that he/she already knows, it is impossible to be in the proper mood for learning. On the contrary, when we see that we do not know anymore we put ourselves in a good mood for learning.

In a CP's discussion, we can also find cases where nobody in the community has the answer to a question. People have nothing to share but ignorance and confusion. Therefore, CP members must work together in the search for answers. Here we have another idea that can help us to find the answers, hence creating new knowledge. This is the *action learning* perspective and methods.

Action learning was invented by Reginald Revans when he was leading the training department at the National Coal Board in the United Kingdom. It is based on two important points: a) work on the *real* problems faced by learners, and b) work on problems where there is confusion, ignorance, and where nobody has the answer. This is done in a "learning set," *i.e.*, a group of 5-8 people whose main goal is to learn from their own experience through questioning and reflecting (Revans, 1980; Pedler, 1991).

The group decides on the common problem/opportunity on which to work. People look for new interpretations, new ways of settling the problem/opportunity. A good guide to doing this is to work on the following questions:

- What am I trying to do?
- What is stopping me from doing it? What is the problem?
- What action will I take in order to overcome the obstacles?

It is in this process that people learn from each other and create new knowledge.

In this school of thought, learning involves programmed knowledge (knowledge one gets from outside the set through lectures, seminars, books, etc.), but the majority of the learning occurs through fresh questions that help the person addressing the problem to look at it in different ways so that better solutions can be found.

Another important point here is that *learning means implementation* (stopping at the analysis and recommendations phase will not be sufficient). Action learning is then a cyclical process: it starts with problem discussion; people look for new ways of seeing the problem, finding solutions, implementing solutions, and observing results, ... and the process starts again with the discussion of problems with implementation.

6. CONCLUSIONS

This paper has described a set of powerful ideas aimed at bridging the knowing-doing gap in professional, continuous, and (mainly) corporate education. Starting from *infocentrism*, a distinction is made between "learn about", "learn to do", and "learn to be", a distinction that helps us to understand the miscommunication between supply and demand in PCC education.

The thinking presented in the article draws on well-known ideas such as learning by doing, constructivism, social constructivism, zone of proximal development, and scaffolding, in order to construct a framework that allows for the design of "learn to do" environments. Nevertheless, a design based on a sequence of activities supported by pieces of content will not completely allow for bridging the knowing-doing gap; in addition, the concept of learners' everyday coping is needed.

All of this allowed the construction of a model that is a guide for course design, a model that we have implemented in the Virtaula project at la Caixa. The action-research we have done on the uses and results of Virtaula showed that this model is a powerful one in helping design a "learn to do" environment and therefore to bridge the knowing-doing gap.

The above ideas proved to be very useful for learning purposes that involve incorporating new information into an existing cognitive structure (*i.e.*, assimilation). But when there is a need for learning that can change the cognitive structures (*i.e.*, accommodation), one shall also base the instructional design on concepts such as reflection-in-action and reflection-on-action. These concepts have been put in practice in a course on Communication that has been designed for the Virtaula project.

Nevertheless, although course design has been improved, learning does not stop there. At least in corporate settings, learning can (and should) happen almost every time through Legitimate Peripheral Participation. Communities of Practice are, in this sense, excellent arenas that allow people to "learn to be" by facilitating access to practical expertise. The rise of CPs at la Caixa[46] and its encouraging results show that these ideas are powerful ones for professional and organizational development, while storytelling and action learning are the ideas that allow the discussions that are the vitality of CPs to materialize.

On the basis of these ideas for learning innovation, a new version of this pedagogical framework can be offered:

- People should be in a learning-by-doing environment where the activities must be based on the learners' everyday coping.
- Their "doing" must be coached by experienced practitioners.
- The learning environment must promote interactions between peers in the proper communities of practice.
- Professors and educational material provide information and are open to new and more powerful interpretations.

Within this framework one can design learning environments and activities that can bridge the knowing-doing gap.

It is only within this framework that the question of the uses of information technology in education should be posed. Far from technocentric thinking, we can now think about: how IT can help us to distribute this kind of learning on large territories; how IT can allow for personnel time flexibility of access; how it can help to design environments that create breakdowns hence opening to reflective learning (see Schön, 1996); how technology can help to organize the huge amount of available educational material; how we can design microworlds and "tools to think with" (Papert, 1981); how the Internet allows for distributed communities of practice; etc. While doing this, we have to keep in mind the limits of information technology as well as its possibilities (Dreyfus, 2001).

We can call *practicentrism* our pedagogical perspective for educational design. Table 1 summarize practicentrism as opposed to infocentrism in corporate education. Practicentrism is what is necessary when one needs to learn "to do" something and/or learn "to be" somebody, while the infocentric approach can apply when one just needs to learn "about" something.

This paper has also shown some examples of these uses of IT in education. This is what occurred in the Virtaula project and in other settings (see for instance Vasquez Bronfman, 2000; Vasquez Bronfman, 2003). Finally, the author has done this work not only as an observer but also as a

[46] In June 2004, 135 eGroups of around 15 people each, and 51 virtual communities in different territorial areas, concerning around 70 people each, have been created. That means that more than 5,500 people in the bank are learning through discussions of their everyday problems at work. Further research should be done in order to evaluate the results of these activities.

practitioner (in order to better transform reality). Otherwise, learning on how people learn would not be possible.

Table 1. Infocentrism Versus Practicentrism

	Infocentrism	**Practicentrism**
Interpretation of learning	Learning is essentially transmission of information and retention of this information by learners.	Learning by doing, and learning by sharing with peers.
Course design structure	Course structure is a sequence of theoretical content with exercises for application.	Course structure is a sequence of activities with content in support of these activities.
Activities	Activities should be generic and detached.	Activities should be based on learners' everyday coping.
Role of content	Content is the core of learning material.	Content must inform on how to perform activities (which are the core of the learning process), and be open to new interpretations.
Exercises and cases	The role of exercises and cases is to apply theory.	Exercises should help to master a skill step by step. Cases should describe practice in other settings, thus bringing diversity in professional practice.
Role of professors	Professors deliver knowledge.	Professors coach/guide learners in the activities they have to perform.
Professional development	Professional development happens through individual learning in courses.	Professional development happens essentially through access to practice into the proper communities.
Role of IT	IT is a channel or a platform for content delivery.	IT helps to distribute innovative learning on large territories; allows for personnel time flexibility of access to learning; helps to design environments that create breakdowns, hence opening to reflective learning; allows asking for help in a community of practice regardless time and space, etc.

REFERENCES

Brown, J. S., & Duguid, P. (1991). Organizational learning and communities of practice: Toward a unified view of working, learning and innovation. *Organization Science*, *2* (1), 40-57.

Brown, J. S., & Duguid, P. (2000). *The Social Life of Information*. Boston: Harvard Business School Press.

Bruner, J. (1996). *Education, l'Entrée dans la Culture*. Paris: Retz.

Christian, D., & Boudès, T. (2000). Du reporting au raconting dans la conduite des projets. *Gérer et Comprendre*, (March issue), 52-63.

Dewey J. (1933). *How We Think*. Chicago: Regnery.

Dreyfus, H. L. (1991). *Being-in-the-World*. Cambridge: MIT Press.

Dreyfus, H. L. (2001). *On the Internet*. London: Routledge.

Harel, I., & Papert, S. (Eds.). (1991). *Constructionism*. Norwood, NJ: Ablex.

Lave, J., & Wenger, E. (1991). *Situated Learning. Legitimate Peripheral Participation*. Cambridge, UK: Cambridge University Press.

Mintzberg, H. (Winter 1988-1989). Formons des managers, non des MBA! *Harvard-L'Expansion, (51)*, 84-92.

Mintzberg, H. (1996). Musings on Management. *Harvard Business Review*, *74* (4), 61-67.

Papert, S. (1981). *Le Jaillissement de l'Esprit*. Paris: Flammarion.

Papert, S. (1987). Computer criticism vs. technocentric thinking. *Educational Researcher*, *16* (1), 22-30.

Papert, S. (1990). *A critique of technocentrism in thinking about the school of the future*. E&L Memo No. 2, Epistemology and Learning Group. Boston: MIT Media Laboratory.

Pedler, M. (1991). *Action Learning in Practice*. Gower: London.

Piaget, J. (1985). *Psychologie et Pédagogie*. Paris: Gallimard (Collection Folio).

Piaget, J. (1992). *La Naissance de l'Intelligence chez l'Enfant*. Paris: Delachaux & Niestle.

Pfeffer, J., & Sutton, R. (2000). *The Knowing-Doing Gap*. Boston: Harvard Business School Press.

Revans, R. (1980). *Action Learning: New Techniques for Management*. London: Blond & Briggs.

Schön, D. A. (1983). *The Reflective Practitioner*. New York: Basic Books.

Schön, D. A. (1987). *Educating the Reflective Practitioner*. San Francisco: Jossey-Bass Publishers.

Schön, D. A. (1996). Reflective conversation with materials: an interview with Donald Schön by John Bennett. In T. Winograd *et al.* (Eds.), *Bringing Design to Software*. Reading, MA: Addison-Wesley.

Vasquez Bronfman, S. (2000). Le practicum réflexif: un cadre pour l'apprentissage de savoir-faire. *Sciences et Techniques Educatives*, *7* (1), 227-243.

Vasquez Bronfman, S. (2003). Linking Pedagogical Innovation and Information Technology to Enhance Business Education. In R. Ottewill, L. Borredon, L. Falque, B. MacFarlane, & A. Wall (Eds), *Educational Innovation in Economics and Business VIII* (pp. 77-91). Dordrecht: Kluwer Academic Publishers.

Vygotsky, L. (1985). *Pensée et Langage*. Paris: La Dispute.

Wenger, E. (1998). *Communities of Practice: Learning, Meaning and Identity*. Cambridge, UK: Cambridge University Press.

Wenger, E., McDermott, R., & Snyder, W. M. (2002). *Cultivating Communities of Practice.* Boston: Harvard Business School Press.

Wrathall, M., & Malpas, J. (2000). *Heidegger, Coping, and Cognitive Science: Essays in Honor of Hubert L. Dreyfus* (Volume 2). Cambridge, MA: MIT Press.

Chapter 27

EDUCATING PROFESSIONALS

Leveraging Diversity in Globalizing Education

Ard Huizing[1], Rik Maes[1], and Thomas J.P. Thijssen[2]
[1]*Universiteit van Amsterdam Business School, Department of Business Studies, Information Management Section, Amsterdam, the Netherlands;* [2]*Via Nova Academy and PrimaVera Research Group, Universiteit van Amsterdam, the Netherlands*

1. INTRODUCTION

Surrounded by complicated issues, globalization is heavily debated. Some critics, for instance, equate it with worldwide capitalism and focus on the unrestricted movement of capital and the increasing domination of nation-states by global financial markets and multinational corporations (Greider, 1997; Soros, 2002). They also warn against market values infiltrating domains of social practice where they do not belong, and ultimately against cultural homogenization resulting in the gradual disappearance of local cultures. What the critics envisage is a *strong* form of globalization that asks for the production of similar kinds of human beings on a global scale (Friedman, 1994).

Others, however, assert that the strong form of globalization underemphasizes the adaptive and creative role of all the actors involved — countries, governments, firms, and other existing or emerging institutions and local practices. They see globalization as a multi-pronged development suggesting that economic forces are sometimes reinforced and sometimes contested by social, political, and cultural processes (Held, McGrew, Goldblatt, & Perraton, 1999). Also, globalization affects each actor in a different way due to each actor's individual history, traditions, culture, resources, and priorities (Lash & Urry, 1994; Yang, 2003). Local actors operating in situated contexts, therefore, always influence the uptake and use of globalization processes. Moreover, they are not confined to the passive

M.K. McCuddy et al. (eds.),
The Challenges of Educating People to Lead in a Challenging World, 533–553.

assimilation of the outcomes of globalization processes, but can actively exploit the opportunities offered by globalization to carve new spaces of their own and make use of the changing conditions for reaching their own ends (Trompenaars & Hampden-Turner, 1998; Kloos, 1999).

In this alternative view on globalization, the terms of the new world order will not be simply imposed 'from above,' but rather be negotiated by a diverse multitude of social practices and institutions. What globalization is and will become is dependent upon the dynamic interplay between top down forces and bottom-up initiatives, between 'globalization from above' and 'grassroots globalization' (Appadurai, 2000). This *weak* form of globalization is reflected in the definition of globalization as "the intensification of worldwide social relations which link distant localities in such a way that local happenings are shaped by events occurring many miles away *and vice versa*" (Giddens, 1990, p. 64; italics added). In other words, globalization simultaneously affects and is affected by many localities and, therefore, by cultural diversity.

The mutual relationship between globalization and cultural diversity presents a major challenge for all the actors involved. The reasoning is as follows. Ashby's law of requisite variety (1956) states that the complexity and speed of an actor's response has to increase with the complexity and speed of change in the environment. Due to globalization, most, if not all actors are faced with growing complexity and dynamism in their environments (Wilson, 2003). Hence, more is required from their learning capabilities to keep up with the changing conditions. According to Ashby's law, then, these actors need more variety or diversity as a constant source of critical inquiry, learning, and innovation to be able to reach the demanded higher levels of complexity and speed. This relationship between diversity and critical inquiry, learning, and innovation is of special interest to the subject of this chapter: higher education.

Defined as the intensification of worldwide social relations linking distant localities, globalization will result in greater cultural diversity in education institutions. Cultural diversity can be described (*cf.* Dewey, 1927; Swann, Polzer, Connor Seyle, & Jin Ko, 2004; April, 2004) as the amount of inter-individual variability across several demographic and functional categories (*e.g.*, value systems, sex, education, work, and socio-economic background). Following Ashby's law of requisite variety, this chapter is based on the premise that this cultural diversity can be leveraged into enhanced learning capabilities for all those involved. However, whereas globalization enables closer contacts among different cultures, it does not inform us regarding how to leverage diversity in the classroom; that is, how to exploit cultural differences in concrete educational settings. Since taking advantage of diversity requires learning with and from each other, the challenge posed by globalization is how to actually combine the varied ideas, knowledge, and skills of different cultures in such a way that diversity can indeed be seen as a constant source of critical inquiry, learning, and innovation? Furthermore, how can higher education institutions leverage diversity most productively and, in that way, help shape globalization?

This chapter reports on how the Section of Information Management, as part of the Business School of the University of Amsterdam in the Netherlands, has prepared itself for the effects that globalization has and will have on higher education. This Section has a long record of experimentation with educational design and the organization of learning processes, both relating to regular bachelor and master programs as well as to postgraduate life-long learning and continuing education initiatives. The learning by sharing concept, which is based upon a social learning theory, has evolved out of these experimentations and innovations. The purpose of this chapter is to show how diversity can be leveraged through learning by sharing.

The chapter is organized as follows: First, five categories of globalization implications for higher education are identified and explained in further detail. Next, the learning by sharing concept is presented as the bottom-up response of one part of one university. Its six guiding principles indicate how the challenge of globalization and leveraging diversity can be met. Three recent education initiatives of the Information Management Section are subsequently discussed, showing how the portrayed categories of globalization effects on higher education can be explored and exploited in concrete educational settings. These initiatives also indicate that leveraging diversity is a learning process in itself. The lessons that can be derived from the three initiatives are therefore explicitly discussed in the final section.

2. GLOBALIZATION AND HIGHER EDUCATION

Globalization impacts higher or tertiary education. We see five categories of implications that higher education institutions can address and potentially enhance in their efforts to create a sustainable future: (1) a need to harmonize education structures, programs, procedures, and agreements across countries; (2) a need to meet more varied and changing learning needs; (3) a need for generative learning; (4) a need for grounding education upon a social learning theory; and (5) a need for identification. Together, these categories of implications show that a weak form of globalization is more likely to evolve, because they leave ample room for all the actors involved to construct unique responses, which on their turn will shape the future course of globalization. The five categories of implications are further detailed below and summarized in Table 1.

Table 1. Globalization Implications for Higher Education

A need for harmonization	• Internationalize education structures, programs, procedures, and agreements • Face growing competition and establish alliances on the global education marketplace • Take a stand on globalization issues
A need to meet varied and changing learning needs	• Increase flexibility and variation in curriculum design and implementation • Include learning and learning-to-learn capabilities in curricula • See the learners' ability to take responsibility for their own lives and learning processes as the point of education
A need for generative learning	• Combine knowledge transfer with knowledge creation • Focus on learning capabilities to foster confidence and trust in students' sense-making abilities and abilities to deal with real-world issues • Use fundamental theories • Apply an interdisciplinary approach • Use real-world complex issues to practice action learning • Apply open staffing to bring in different perspectives, ideas, and insights
A need for a social learning theory	• Ground learning programs upon a social learning theory • Translate the community of practice idea to educational settings • Provide a common frame of reference • Remove boundaries between the roles of teacher, student, researcher, and practitioner
A need for identification	• Enable personal and social identification • Shape learning environments serving economic and non-economic needs • Compete for the attention of students

2.1 A Need for Harmonization

To play a role in a globalizing world, education structures, programs, procedures, and agreements need to be harmonized across countries so that students, teachers, and researchers can move freely and choose the organizations, networks, and communities of their liking. Examples of harmonization are: the creation of international student exchange programs: the adaptation to a unified course-credit system; the conformation to international quality assessments; and for many universities outside the Anglo-Saxon academic world, the implementation of the bachelor-master structure as well as teaching in English, in particular in academic disciplines related to international business where English is the dominant language.

Another implication of harmonization is the emergence of a global education marketplace where each institution has to compete for funds, faculty, and students. This growing competition increasingly takes place on a worldwide scale, as is indicated by joint degree offerings among institutions in two or more countries ('twinning'), off-shoring through franchising or branch openings, and using the Internet as a new delivery channel. As a result, higher education is ever more seen as an economic sector in itself and treated as a business enterprise, which attracts new and often private providers to the market and sometimes results in public-private alliances.

Exemplary in this regard is the attempt of multinational corporations and some government agencies in the developed countries to include higher education in the framework of the World Trade Organization through the General Agreement on Trade in Services proposal. The idea behind this proposal is that knowledge is a *commodity like any other product*, which should be traded freely around the world while ensuring protections for the owners of knowledge products. In this economic view, the value of higher education is determined by market forces.

Prospective benefits of this marketization of higher education — sometimes referred to as 'McDonaldization' or 'Americanization' (Appadurai, 2000, Altbach, 2004) — are a strong motivation for traditional institutions to innovate and generate new academic environments, increase the supply of education, improve access for students, and diminish their dependency on public funding. However, as many critics contend (Yang, 2003; De Vita & Case, 2003; Altbach, 2004), tensions between academic and commercial-based motives are rising as market-driven globalization does not necessarily serve non-economic yet basic human needs. Other issues involve, among others, the compromised sovereignty of nation-states to establish national education policies, the global dominance of the English-speaking education institutions, and the inequality between the developed and developing countries. Globalization requires each participating actor to take a stand in these issues.

2.2 A Need to Meet Varied and Changing Learning Needs

Due to globalization, higher education institutions need to display more flexibility and variation in curriculum design and implementation to meet the increasingly varied and changing needs of learners. Learning needs become more varied because the student population attracted worldwide will show more diversity in terms of their education and socio-economic backgrounds, value systems, and preferred learning styles. Moreover, as a result of the dynamic developments in most academic disciplines and the requirement to remain well informed, many people will engage in life-long learning. Another reason for experienced workers to regularly return to the university is that most organizations are involved in almost constant change programs leading to many vertical and horizontal career shifts over the workers' professional years and, thus, to specific and changing learning needs.

Furthermore, in dynamic and complex environments the purpose of education is no longer simply to transfer knowledge. Such environments require a different education that emphasizes learning and learning-to-learn capabilities so that people are better prepared to take responsibility for their own lives and learning processes. According to Rowe (2004, p. 5), taking responsibility is the point of education, because if "...people do not assume authority over themselves, they cannot use their creativity and curiosity to the full, nor discover the art of living wisely."

2.3 A Need for Generative Learning

As globalization causes greater dynamism and complexity, people, organizations, and societies are increasingly confronted with problems, issues, and dilemmas that are neither clear-cut nor well defined. Much of social and organizational life today is uncertain and ambiguous. Nevertheless, in large parts of the academic world education is still seen as a formal process of instruction to convey formal, existing knowledge. A typical example would be business schools relying on case-based education in which lessons learned elsewhere are copied, cloning students and professionals. Another example from the fast developing practice of management and organization is education proceeding from hype to hype, which results in the accumulation of rapidly deteriorating knowledge.

In uncertain and ambiguous environments, however, learning should be generative, implying that education should change from 'looking in the rear view mirror' to 'exploring horizons for new developments,' from imparting existing knowledge to experimentation and exploration allowing learners to create knowledge and meanings for themselves. Generative learning also means that learners become familiar and comfortable with abstract, fundamental theories and with crossing the borders of the often-rigid academic disciplines to develop interdisciplinary understandings and insights. By offering fundamental theories in an interdisciplinary approach, learners improve their conceptual capabilities, which aids in the continuous need to make sense in uncertain and ambiguous realities and in facing such realities with confidence and trust. Such education can be enhanced by practicing in action learning environments in which real-world fundamental issues are explored for which there are no a priori answers available. Moreover, generative learning can be promoted by open staffing, meaning that 'outsiders' — teachers, researchers, and practitioners — are invited to complement faculty and bring in different cultures, perspectives, ideas, and insights.

2.4 A Need for a Social Learning Theory

Leveraging diversity is more than enabling close contacts between diverse people. In comparison to homogeneous groups, members of culturally diverse groups can be less committed to each other and to their employers, communicate relatively poorly, experience more conflict, and take more time for decision-making (Swann *et al.*, 2004). These causes of ineffective behavior show that learning is not just a cognitive and individual activity, but also a social and sensitive process in which new meanings are collectively negotiated. They also illustrate that learning is just as dependent upon social qualities such as tolerance, reciprocity, trust, and a sense of belonging as upon personal cognitive skills. Turning diversity into a genuine source of inspiration, critical inquiry, and learning is therefore a real challenge requiring more than bringing people together. For higher education this implies that learning programs preferably should be based upon a social theory of learning. In many academic institutions, however, students are approached as individuals solely seeking cognitive content, skills, and personal development, even if group assignments are a regular part of the curriculum.

A social theory of learning is nowadays strongly associated with the idea of communities of practice. Communities of practice are "groups of people informally bound together by shared expertise and passion for a joint enterprise" (Wenger & Snyder, 2000, p. 139). Academic institutions can translate this idea to educational settings by establishing platforms on which diversity can be expressed, both on-line and off-line, and to guide learners to leverage this diversity into creative and motivated performance. Part of this guidance can be the provision of a common theoretical frame of reference, as a shared point of departure, to help shape learning as an interactive journey exploring new horizons. Moreover, in education communities the traditional boundaries between the roles of teacher, student, researcher, and practitioner blur as all participants are challenged to integrate these roles as part of their learning.

2.5 A Need for Identification

To a large degree, people derive their identity from the networks and communities in which they participate and to which they belong. When globalization makes them aware that they live in one big world that is capable of directly influencing their local practices, identity issues can arise. Questions such as 'Who am I?' and 'Where could I, or should I, go?' inevitably challenges one's identity (Kloos, 1999). As Bauman (2001, p. 126) portrays, the issue "…is not so much how to obtain the identities of their choice and how to have them recognized by others, but *which* identity to choose, and how best to keep alert and vigilant so that *another* choice can be made."

As a result of its sheer size, the emerging global economy inherently lacks possibilities of personal and social identification. Markets are impersonal; they spur neither commitment nor engagement. Even worse, market-driven globalization may undermine the social conditions of social networks and communities (Adler, 2001). From this perspective it is not surprising that identity and communities of practice as 'homes of identity' (Wenger, 1998) have recently attracted so much attention. "Just as community collapses, identity is invented" (Young in Bauman, 2001, p. 128).

In the global economy, there is a need for institutions enabling personal and social identification. Unlike this economy, universities can contribute to this need as they provide identification possibilities related to professional and knowledge domains. Implications are that they have to serve economic as well as non-economic human needs such as social engagement and mutual commitment among students, teachers, researchers, and practitioners to create invigorating learning environments, not just in the classroom but also during the other hours in the week. We are only just beginning to learn how such demands can be reconciled with mass student recruitment and decreasing public funding. The answers we can imagine, however, could very well be a major factor in the growing competition among education institutions competing for the attention of students who are constantly evaluating a multitude of interesting 'distractions' in their efforts to balance personal, social, and economic value (Thijssen & Vernooij, 2004). Higher education is just one of them.

3. LEARNING BY SHARING

The five categories of globalization implications discussed in the previous section offer significant degrees of autonomy and initiative for all the actors involved to carve a space of their own on the emerging global education marketplace. As shown above, much of the literature on globalization is focused on the marketization or 'Americanization' of local cultures and the attendant fear of cultural homogenization. Globalization, however, is a much broader issue. As to higher education, the harmonization of its institutions will inevitably lead to closer contacts among cultures. The resultant cultural diversity in the classroom on its turn will influence how local education will evolve. Local education institutions will differ in their responses to these developments, not only because of their varying individual histories, traditions, cultures, and resources, but also because they will actively differentiate themselves while competing and cooperating globally.

We posit that leveraging diversity can and will be used as a major distinguishing factor in the search of a unique position in the global education marketplace. That is, universities, their faculties, business schools, and sections will differ in the way they will address the portrayed needs for meeting varied learning needs, generative and social learning, and for institutions facilitating personal and social identification with professional and knowledge domains. The ultimate effects of globalization on higher education are dependent on how such bottom-up globalization initiatives interact with the relevant top-down forces.

'Learning by sharing' is the social learning framework upon which the grassroots initiatives of the Information Management Section of the University of Amsterdam in the Netherlands are based. Providing education to academic students ranging from first-year newcomers to experienced life-long learners, the Section's ambition is to build a lively community with a global presence with which those sharing an interest in information management can identify. The Section is involved in regular, publicly funded bachelor and master programs. For 18 years now, it additionally has provided a privately financed, two-year postgraduate executive program on information management that offers practitioners with at least five years of experience the opportunity to acquire an accredited executive master degree. Currently, this MBA-like program is also offered in-house at the Dutch police. The maximum enrollment of 24 students annually underlines the small-scale nature of the program, thereby allowing all participants to build personal and social commitment, while private funding enables worldwide recruitment of renowned teachers (open staffing). The more than 350 students who have attended this program are united within the Amsterdam Association of Information Management. On top of that, graduated students can participate in the Fellows program, a new initiative on which we will report later in this chapter. Finally, information management researchers — faculty and practitioners as well as foreign and local researchers — channel their projects and publications through the PrimaVera research program. All these initiatives are supported by Web sites and Intranet technology enabling all participants to share ideas, work on projects, and expand their community.

The learning by sharing framework (see Figure 1) has emerged out of these education and research experiences and will continue to evolve as new initiatives and experiments lead to adaptations and refinements of its guiding principles (Thijssen, Maes, & Vernooij, 2002; Maes, 2003). These guiding principles illustrate how diversity can be leveraged in concrete educational settings and, therefore, how the portrayed implications of globalization can be exploited. We distinguish six guiding principles to construct education curricula and programs: (1) use a common theoretical frame of reference; (2) include students, teachers, researchers, and practitioners in every educational setting and promote role-switching; (3) combine business and university in action learning programs to study real-world fundamental issues; (4) apply fundamental theories to diverse and complex practices; (5) focus on cognition, skills, and attitudes to stimulate generative learning and learning-to-learn capabilities; and (6) shape learning as a social process to explore and exploit the potential value of diversity.

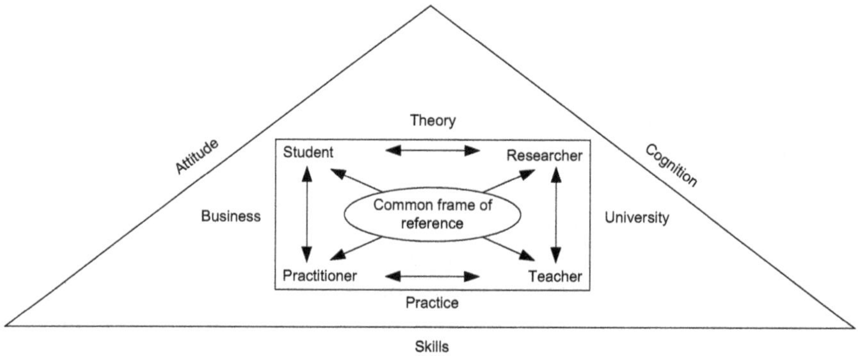

Figure 1. Learning by Sharing

All education programs of the Information Management Section are constructed upon these six principles. They are all based upon a common theoretical frame of reference that is used as a shared starting point to discuss and reflect on information management theories and practices. This frame of reference is the focal point of attention in the community's research activities (for those interested in this common frame of reference, see Maes, 2003 and http://primavera.fee.uva.nl). With regard to this theoretical framework, community members can play four roles: student, practitioner, teacher, and researcher. The arrows between these roles indicate that the boundaries between them blur as members proceed from the periphery of the community towards its center; that is, there is a direct relationship between participation, engagement, and learning. The arrows also show that learning involves close interactions among fundamental, interdisciplinary theory and culturally diverse practices as well as among business and university that are jointly engaged in action learning, exploring new horizons that are both theoretically and practically relevant. Furthermore, 'cognition, skills, and attitudes' reflect the emphasis put on generative learning capabilities that enhance the participants' abilities to take responsibility for their own lives.

They express that learning is about personal and social change aimed at improving individual and collective meaning-making capabilities, which are increasingly needed to continually make sense out of a rapidly evolving and globalizing world. Finally, there is value in diversity. As taking advantage of diversity in educational settings requires learning with and from each other, one way to realize this value is to shape learning as a social process in a critical yet committed community. Membership of this community is open to all those who want to identify with information management in a broad sense and who wish to participate in the community's activities in one way or another.

4. EXPERIMENTS IN EDUCATING PROFESSIONALS AND THE ORGANIZATION OF LEARNING

As mentioned, learning by sharing is the overall learning theory of the Executive Master in Information Management program, as discussed in Maes (2003); of regular programs at the bachelor and master levels; of derived, targeted programs; and of initiatives in continuing education. This section shows three recent initiatives, taken respectively from regular programs (Course Information Management in Practice), continuing education (I+M Fellows), and derived programs (Investigative Course in Experience Economy). Each experiment is briefly described after which it is related to the distinguished categories of globalization implications for higher education. For each experiment, Table 2 highlights the concrete measures taken, all of which are based upon the learning by sharing principles discussed earlier. Together, the three initiatives prove that consistency in curriculum design in itself contributes to the preparation of professionals who can operate in an open, global, and diversified world.

4.1 Experiment I: Information Management in Practice

This course, part of the master programs in Business Information Systems and in Business Studies (80% and 20% of the students respectively), was organized for the first time in the academic year 2003-2004. Its unequivocal objective is to confront master students with professionals working in real-life *and vice versa* (note the unmistakable reciprocity): learning by sharing between students, reflective practitioners, and the accompanying teaching staff.

Table 2. Summary of Three Experiments

	Information Management in Practice	**I+M Fellows**	**Investigative Course in Experience Economy**
A need for harmonization	Diverse acts of harmonization at Dutch universities. Increasing diversity due to harmonization.	Extra-curriculum initiative counterbalancing the trend towards harmonization. Combination of private funding with academic and human values.	Initiative showing that the uptake of global issues is culture-dependent requiring local interpretations.
A need to meet varied and changing learning needs	Individual learning needs drive learning methods and style. Personal learning in a social context. Learning relates to cognition, skills, and attitudes. Project teams based on maximal diversity.	Participants set their own learning agenda and their own projects. Emphasis on professional and personal growth. Learning relates to cognition, skills, and attitudes. Participants coming from multiple backgrounds.	Diverse group of international participants coming from multiple backgrounds. Learning needs related to varied business and research objectives in diverse contexts. Learning relates to cognition, skills, and attitudes.
A need for generative learning	Ill-defined real-life projects. Problem- and participant-driven content; no formal program. Open confrontation among all participants. Open staffing.	Innovation and intrapreneurship are rooted in personal development. Few pre-programmed activities. Out-of-the-box, real-life topics requiring an interdisciplinary and fundamental approach. Open staffing.	Interactive, generative workshop. Real-world complex issue. No pre-defined but co-constructed outcomes. Interdisciplinary and fundamental approach. Open staffing.
A need for a social learning theory	Unite all participants in a community. Continuing efforts to promote an open and trustworthy climate. An electronic learning environment.	Collegial learning in a community. Blurring of boundaries between the roles of student, teacher, researcher, and practitioner. An electronic learning environment.	Co-construction of local interpretations of the issue at hand. Shared learning in a community. An electronic learning environment.
A need for identification	Identification with community, projects, and information management in general. Open discussion of students' diverse backgrounds.	Identification with community, projects, and information management in general. Emphasis on personal engagement and participation.	Working on modern society's identity. Cross-national and local identification with globalization issues. Community and social learning.

Traditionally, students from Business Information Systems and Business Studies at the University of Amsterdam have diverse ethnic and social backgrounds; the 31 students taking part in this experimental course represented 12 different nationalities, ranging from Surinam and India to the former Yugoslavia and the Netherlands. Including the teaching staff, there were 14 nationalities working together. The professional organizations involved were municipal services from the city of Amsterdam, in itself a growingly multi-cultural city. The projects undertaken were equally unusual: projects *together with* the city services *for the benefit of* the citizens.

The course got unanimous approval. Practitioners as well as students, the municipality as well as the teaching staff were enthusiastic about the outcome of the projects, but even more about the personal lessons learned through this open confrontation at the edge of the thinkable (brought in by the students), feasible (idem, by the practitioners) and achievable (to be realized in cooperation). It was generative learning from diversity in optima forma.

As to the *need for harmonization* mentioned in Table 2, it can be said that the University of Amsterdam has implemented the bachelor-master structure in 2003. Moreover, the already common practice of giving specific courses in English was extended to full bachelor and master programs in 2005. While conducting new experiments, the Information Management Section takes such acts of harmonization as a given. However, whereas increasing diversity is expected as a result of further harmonization, the Section has already gained much experience with diversity for a considerable time now as the Netherlands has become a multi-cultural country over the past decades. In that sense, globalization is not a new phenomenon for the Section.

One way to make use of diversity is to *meet the varying individual learning needs* and engage students and other participants to help each other in fulfilling these needs. This aspect was overtly addressed in this experiment, in terms of clearly deviating learning methods and style, being driven by the individual learning needs of all participants involved (including those of the non-students). Students collaborated in small project teams that were composed in such a way that diversity was maximized. Moreover, this experiment was aimed at personal above professional learning. In fact, this aspect was the *raison d'être* of this experimental course.

Generative learning also played a central role in the course. The projects chosen were all ill-defined, most of them basically existing in the mind and experience of the (badly understood and highly diverging) citizens and other participating actors. A great part of the expended efforts were in making sense out of these divergent signals and in dialoguing with practitioners as well as with citizens. The course was completely problem- and student-driven. There was no formal program, meaning that meetings were organized according to the emerging needs of the participants. Staffing was open: university teachers, including faculty from other universities, practitioners, and students brought in quite different perspectives.

The need for community building based on a *social learning theory* needed great care. In particular at the beginning of the course, the social aspects of learning required specific attention due to the different backgrounds of the participants and the university culture, where 'staying in your own comfort zone' is both reassuring and safe. Having project teams based on maximal internal diversity was helpful in this regard, as well as the efforts put in creating an open and trustworthy atmosphere. For instance, students not showing up were called, even in the middle of the night, and told that they deprived other participants of their own input. Heavy use was made of a QuickPlace electronic learning environment, where personal and social learning as well as gossip and joking were an integral part. The end result was a warming feeling of a community of practice as well as of togetherness, which is quite different from normal practice at the University of Amsterdam.

As to the *need for identification*, this aspect is partly dealt with in the foregoing discussion on social learning theory and community building. Besides, students were overtly and positively consulted on their social and racial background. This open encounter was highly appreciated by the participants, contrary to common belief.

4.2 Experiment II: I+M Fellows

I+M Fellows is the continuing education sequel to the postgraduate Executive Master in Information Management (EMIM) program mentioned earlier. In the first year of this experiment, 20 alumni participated. These are professionals being employed as information managers, consultants in information management, and so on. In many instances, their careers were boosted by successfully finishing the EMIM course.

The Fellows initiative is aimed at professional and personal growth and at close cooperation with the PrimaVera research program of the organizing Information Management Section. It is highly participant-driven, where participants are actively invited to set their own learning agenda, to go around together in shared learning projects, and to find each other in collegial learning. Apart from the alumni, external experts and teachers from the EMIM course are participating. In addition, two teachers operate as dedicated learning facilitators. Topics chosen in the first year were, for example, learning from your own mistakes, the Socratic dialogue, and personal power in relation to professionalism. Apart from the bimonthly meetings, active study groups (*e.g.*, on 'the lively organization') and reading groups are stimulated, a study tour is organized, and so on.

The initiative faced some start-up problems, especially due to the uncommon approach directed at personal growth and group initiatives, and the fact that only a few pre-programmed activities had been scheduled. Professionals operating in a highly competitive environment clearly have difficulties in overcoming barriers of time and they face loyalty issues. Nevertheless, the experiment has experienced a fruitful year, where the second year endeavored to obtain more concrete output to achieve greater balance between professional and personal learning. The driving idea behind this experiment, that personal development is at the heart of professional success, however, was not questioned at all.

Reflecting on the implications of globalization on higher education, I+M Fellows is an extra-curriculum initiative counterbalancing national and university acts of *harmonization*. It is an example of how private funding can be combined with academic motives and basic human needs. Moreover, it suits the *need to meet varying learning needs* in that alumni with a special interest in personal growth were given an extra learning opportunity in addition to the other education offerings of the Section. Furthermore, as there was no formal, pre-planned program and students could set their own learning agenda, the variation of learning needs that could be expressed within the 'curriculum' design was optimal. The combinations of professional and personal learning as well as the personal initiatives that were expected addressed learning and learning-to-learn capabilities. Participating professionals apparently needed to overcome serious barriers in taking up that responsibility. This could be due to the fact that the EMIM program in which they were previously involved, was more supply-driven. Closer investigation, however, reveals that there is an area of tension between personal learning and growing needs (individualized) and expectations from the employer (more standardized). To a certain extent, one could say that present-day organizations, as a result of the immense pressure under which they are supposed to attain short-term results, are not exploiting the full potential of their high-level employees. It is our belief that innovation and intrapreneurship are deep-rooted in personal development and creativity as sought after in this Fellows program.

The objectives of personal development and creativity indicate that *generative learning* is at the heart of the Fellows initiative. Subjects dealt with are by definition interdisciplinary and cross the boundaries of cognitive learning. Two examples are: (1) the subject of information infrastructures was tackled by inviting the participants to actively develop ideas for the crucial and real-life start-up of a major cultural infrastructure — a former industrial plant transformed into a cultural breeding ground; and (2) the first meeting of the second year, dedicated to coping with major transformations, was centered around the eventuality of the Netherlands being inundated due to a major natural disaster. In both cases there are no pre-defined answers to the challenges posed. Participation, therefore, requires creativity and out-of-the-box thinking to create new knowledge and meanings.

Next, the Fellows program is set up as a *community of practice* of and in itself, including the use of a QuickPlace digital environment for intermediate communication and collaboration. Individual and group evaluations, however, showed that all participants subscribed to the idea of learning by sharing, but found it difficult to implement it; a number of initiatives (working groups in particular) started enthusiastically but were not continued after the first period of thrill. All participants agreed that this initial zeal could probably be better sustained by fixing clear and tangible targets for each of the initiatives taken, which might be opposite to the original aim of open-ended learning.

As to the *need for identification*, this aspect was taken up hesitantly. Only at the end of the first year, did participants identify themselves with the personal, transgressing and even confrontational learning style of the Fellows program. This common identity, transcending the day-to-day solicitudes, is nevertheless experienced as one of the main reasons to participate; we believe that we just need more time to establish it.

4.3 Experiment III: Investigative Course in Experience Economy

This course is organized by the European Center for the Experience Economy, a center associated with the initiating Section of Information Management through the PrimaVera research program. The purpose of the Center is to conduct research and to organize courses in order to ground the practice of the Experience Economy (Pine & Gilmore, 1999; Prahalad & Ramaswamy, 2004) in theory and to build a community of practice around this emerging concept.

The four-day course is organized according to the learning by sharing principles, where each of the participants successively plays the different roles involved. Participants are executives interested in introducing elements of the experience economy in their organization, university researchers, Ph.D. students, consultants, etc. The ‘course,’ which was organized twice, is more than a course in the strict sense of the word in that common meaning building, developing new ideas, and grounding the concepts of the experience economy in theoretical research are integral parts of the experiment. A large part of the course is in the form of a highly interactive, generative workshop.

The underlying idea of the course is that the current state-of-the-art in providing experiences as a business proposal is too limited, as customers increasingly demand authenticity and true value. Understanding the value-seeking process of individuals is considered key in positioning the experience offering. The quest for this authentic need asks for innovative approaches to both research and teaching.

In relating this course to the implications of globalization for higher education as mentioned in Table 2, a first observation is that the experiences with the course reflect the point that local actors operating in situated contexts always influence the uptake and use of globalization processes. At first glance, the experience economy seems to be a global issue that is part of globalizing world trends. Again and again, however, it appears that new business concepts and ideas, which often originate in the USA, cannot be exported to other cultures on a one-to-one basis. The idea underlying the course is therefore to make the experience economy concept adaptable to the European scene. In fact, the very existence of and apparent need for a European Center proves this point. Paradoxically perhaps, by translating the concept of the experience economy to local contexts, the global application of this concept increases. This observation puts the *need for harmonizing education programs*, and in particular the fear of Americanization and cultural homogenization in a different perspective.

Participants in the course come from different European countries. The diverse composition of the participating group, ranging from 'hardcore' business people to equally 'hardcore' university researchers, implies very *different learning needs and styles*. The complementary nature of the learning goals is nevertheless experienced as an essential component of the course that can be leveraged by approaching the experience economy through critical inquiry, as a business opportunity, a research subject and part of the globalizing world where cultural variety and identity play a prominent role. This approach emphasizes *generative learning*, as the outcome of the course is not established beforehand but is co-constructed during the investigative course. To promote knowledge creation, the approach taken also entails the participation of a wide range of experts; for instance, a professional chef introducing the role of the senses in designing experiences, and a group decision support system as part of the technical support for the course.

As to the *need for a social learning theory*, the investigative nature of the course could not be attained without the explicit adherence to the learning by sharing format. Building up the feeling of a real community of practice is, given the divergent composition of the group, an integral part of the course, though not always easy to realize from the very beginning onward, as traditional attitudes regarding participation in a course are at right angles to the generative way of social learning.

Finally, with regard to the *need for identification*, the experience economy is addressed as an economic, social, and cultural phenomenon, going beyond the original intentions behind the concept and hence as a part of the identity of modern society.

5. CONCLUSIONS AND LESSONS LEARNED

The five categories of globalization implications on higher education summarized in Table 1 leave ample room for individual universities, faculties, business schools, and sections to construct responses of their own to globalization. Learning by sharing is the bottom-up response of one section of one university that expresses how this section is preparing itself for a globalized world. Globalization leads to an intensification of worldwide social relations linking distant localities (Giddens, 1990) and as such leads to greater cultural diversity in educational settings. A basic assumption behind learning by sharing is that this diversity can be leveraged into enhanced learning capabilities, which, following Ashby's law of requisite variety (1956), every system needs when it is confronted with growing complexity and dynamism in its environment. The Section of Information Management of the University of Amsterdam sees its responsibility as helping shape education in such a way that diversity does result in improved learning and learning-to-learn capabilities of individual participants, and hence of the organizations for which they work and the societies in which they live. The learning by sharing concept shows how this can be achieved.

The three recent initiatives of the Section of Information Management discussed in this chapter show in more detail how the six guiding principles of learning by sharing can be applied in concrete educational practices to face the challenge of globalization and leveraging the potential value of diversity. They also illustrate that exploiting diversity is a learning process in itself. The lessons learned relate to all the categories of globalization implications described.

As to the *need for harmonization*, harmonizing education structures, programs, procedures, and agreements should be viewed as a necessary yet insufficient condition to embrace diversity. Harmonization enables closer contacts among different cultures, but does not tell how to exploit such differences. That is where the other implications of globalization come into our discussion showing that harmonization is not the end of globalization, but rather the beginning of major transformations in higher education. Requiring much time and energy, such transformations need to be balanced with the speed of change that is considered necessary to keep up with the changing conditions. Although individual universities, faculties, business schools, and sections have their own responsibilities in this and can pro-actively prepare themselves, preserving this delicate balance is primarily a task for national and international higher education institutions and governmental agencies.

Another implication of harmonization is the emergence of a global education marketplace, which, according to many (Adler, 2001; Yang, 2003) would result in the marketization of education, thereby undermining the social conditions of networks and communities. Market-driven globalization would predominantly serve economic needs and disregard human and academic values such as integrity, disinterestedness, and trust. This chapter shows how the Section of Information Management attempts to reconcile both kinds of needs. Although there is an economic motive involved in extending the supply of education with continuing education initiatives and derived, targeted programs, the three recent initiatives indicate that the human and academic values dominate in learning by sharing. The dominance of these values becomes clear in the explicit recognition of the need to provide opportunities for *personal and social identification* that markets simply cannot deliver and in organizing *learning in communities* with which people can identify themselves. As globalization proceeds, we expect these elements of learning by sharing to become even more important than they already are.

With regard to the growing *need of identification and use of communities* to shape learning processes, additional lessons learned can be derived from the three experiments described. Most importantly, the building and maintenance of communities require constant care. As all three experiments indicate, there is a tension between professional, personal, and social learning, between individual learners having their specific learning needs and employers who are paying for their education, and between career and private life that every learner has to balance. The lessons learned are that the value added of every education initiative must be clear in advance and that a learning rhythm (Wenger, 1998) should be created that fits the community members. This latter point relates, amongst others, to the regularity of physical meetings, the time and effort needed to participate, and the support of on-line facilities. The right rhythm can only be discovered through experimentation and fine-tuning programs according to the feedback given. Moreover, the knowledge and experience gained through experimentation help tremendously in achieving the Section's ultimate ambition of building a lively community around information management with a global presence.

Compared to communities creating a sense of belonging, increasing flexibility and variation in curriculum designs to *meet varied and changing learning needs* is relatively easy to implement. The lesson learned here is that it is increasingly rewarding to see students as life-long learners and offer them a large variety of education programs in an inspiring academic environment. The extra funding generated by privately financed initiatives can be used to continuously improve this environment.

Furthermore, the three experiments discussed show that *generative learning* always meets great enthusiasm on behalf of all participants — students, practitioners, researchers, and teachers alike. However, such learning is particularly suited for master students who have finished their bachelors degree and for experienced managers returning to the university. As learners proceed from first-year academic education to postgraduate programs, the emphasis can increasingly be put on generative learning, on learner-guided education in which the learners themselves are responsible for their own learning agendas, and on blending learning and working. It is the combination of being familiar with existing knowledge and being challenged in generative environments that enhances people's learning capabilities and their abilities to take responsibility over their own lives.

REFERENCES

Adler, P. S. (2001). Market, hierarchy, and trust: The knowledge economy and the future of capitalism. *Organization Science*, *12* (2), 215-234.

Altbach, P. G. (2004). Globalization and the university: Myths and realities in an unequal world. *Tertiary Education and Management*, *10* (1), 3-25.

Appadurai, A. (2000). Grassroots globalization and the research imagination. *Public Culture*, *12* (1), 1-19.

April, K. (2004). Leveraging diversity: Weaving strong fabrics from different threads. *Convergence*, *3* (4), 54-55.

Ashby, W. R. (1956). *An Introduction to Cybernetics*. Chapman & Hall, London.

Bauman, Z. (2001). Identity in the globalizing world. *Social Anthropology*, *9* (2), 121-129.

De Vita, G., & Case, P. (2003). Rethinking the internationalization agenda in UK higher education. *Journal of Further & Higher Education*, *27* (4), 383-398.

Dewey, J. (1927). *The Public and Its Problems*. Athens, Ohio: Swallow Press.

Friedman, J. (1994). *Cultural Identity and Global Process*. London: Sage.

Giddens, A. (1990). *The Consequences of Modernity*. Cambridge, UK: Polity Press.

Greider, W. (1997). *One World, Ready or Not: The Manic Logic of Global Capitalism*. New York: Simon & Schuster.

Held, D., McGrew, A., Goldblatt, D., & Perraton, J. (1999). *Global Transformations: Politics, Economics and Culture*. Stanford: Stanford University Press.

Kloos, P. (1999). The Dialectics of Globalization and Localization. In D. Kalb, M. van der Land, R. Staring, B. van Steenbergen, & N. Wilterdink (Eds.), *The Ends of Globalization: Bringing Society Back In* (pp. 281-298). Lanham: Rowman & Littlefield.

Lash, S., & Urry, J. (1994). *Economies of Signs & Space*. London: Sage.

Maes, R. (2003). On the alliance of executive education and research in information management at the University of Amsterdam. *International Journal of Information Management, 23* (3), 249-257.

Pine, B. J., & Gilmore, J. H. (1999). *The Experience Economy*. Boston: Harvard Business School Press.

Prahalad, C. K., & Ramaswamy, V. (2004). *The Future of Competition: Co-creating Unique Value with Customers*. Boston: Harvard Business School Press.

Rowe, D. (2004). *RSA Journal*, April, 5.

Soros, G. (2002). *George Soros on Globalization*. New York and London: Public Affairs.

Swann, W. B., Polzer, J. T., Connor Seyle, D., & Jin Ko, S. (2004). Finding value in diversity: Verification of personal and social self-views in diverse groups, *Academy of Management* Review, *29* (1), 9-27.

Thijssen, J. P. T., Maes, R., & Vernooij, A. T. J. (2002). Learning by sharing: A model for life-long learning. In T. A. Johannessen, A. Pedersen, & K. Petersen (Eds.), *Educational Innovation in Economics and Business VI, Teaching Today the Knowledge of Tomorrow* (pp. 189-198). Dordrecht, the Netherlands: Kluwer Academic Publishers.

Thijssen, J. P. T., & Vernooij, A. T. J. (2004). Bridging the gap between academic degrees and life-long learning processes: Designing life-long learning processes. In R. G. Milter, V. S. Perotti, & M. S. R. Segers (Eds.), *Educational Innovation in Economics and Business IX, Breaking Boundaries for Global Learning* (pp. 137-156). Dordrecht: Springer.

Trompenaars, F., & Hampden-Turner, C. (1998). *Riding the Waves of Culture: Understanding Cultural Diversity in Business*. London: Nicholas Brealy Publishing.

Wenger, E. (1998). *Communities of Practice —Learning, Meaning, and Identity*. Cambridge: Cambridge University Press.

Wenger, E., & Snyder, W. (2000). Communities of practice: The organizational frontier. *Harvard Business Review, 78* (1), 139-145.

Wilson, D. N. (2003). The future of comparative and international education in a globalized world. *International Review of Education*, *49*(1-2), 15-33.

Yang, R. (2003). Globalization and higher education development: A critical analysis. *International Review of Education*, *49* (3-4), 269-291.

Chapter 28

SOCIAL ENTREPRENEURSHIP AND CULTURAL CHANGE

The Relevance of a Public Sector Experiment for Innovative Education

Thomas J.P. Thijssen[1] and Fons T.J. Vernooij[2]
[1]*Via Nova Foundation, Hamilton International and PrimaVera Research Group, University of Amsterdam, the Netherlands;* [2]*Vrije Universiteit, Amsterdam, the Netherlands*

1. INTRODUCTION

This chapter reports on collaborative learning and innovation in the social sector in the Netherlands. It is aimed at the design of a methodology to better combat social exclusion and poverty. The research comprises a literature study on innovation and culture in the private sector. The transformation to the public sector leads to the concept of social entrepreneurship (Thompson, Alvy, & Lees, 2000; Thompson, 2002). The research is supported by an experiment in the area of social services for the poor in the Netherlands. This experiment is part of a longitudinal study on social entrepreneurship and culture change in the social services sector.

The relevance of this research for education is to be found in the use of collaborative learning as an essential part of a new approach to get social service counselors ready for a role as a social entrepreneur. Instead of behaving like a bureaucrat who follows the rules of the system, social service counselors should behave more like entrepreneurs trying to grasp opportunities to support the individual development of clients. This requires a reorientation of counselors where they not only acquire knowledge about entrepreneurship and skills to perform that way, but where they develop an attitude to take initiatives related to individual qualities of clients. Collaborative learning requires them to build bridges between clients and

M.K. McCuddy et al. (eds.),
The Challenges of Educating People to Lead in a Challenging World, 555–579.

managers in a way that results in successful integration of clients into society.

This research is part of a longitudinal study in monitoring innovations in the Netherlands Social Services System. Starting with the results of studies on entrepreneurship in the private sector and presenting a view on the culture within organizations as formulated by Quinn (1995), a transformation is made to the public sector. Emphasis is placed on the relevance of private sector innovation characteristics and Quinn's model of Competing Values for the social services sector in the Netherlands. This leads to the concept of social entrepreneurship as a new methodology for counsclors in the social services sector, aiming at the integration in society of poor people who are socially excluded.

An experiment in Zeeland (the Netherlands) is used to test and explain this new approach. The research is based on criteria found in current literature on innovation, culture, entrepreneurship and learning. The new vision and methodology developed in this experiment show promising results for the transfer of experiences from the private sector to innovation in the social services sector. However, a second phase in the research project must elaborate on the question of whether a generalization can be made about the success of social entrepreneurship and cultural change in a context of collaborative learning.

2. THE PROBLEM IN THE NETHERLANDS: OVER ONE MILLION POOR PEOPLE TODAY

Innovation in the public sector through experimentation may lead to social inclusion and thereby to the alleviation of poverty. However, according to the manifest against poverty and social exclusion (Alliance for Social Justice, 2002), the Netherlands account for over 1 million individuals in a situation of poverty. This is out of a population of 16 million, approximately 6 million of whom are active workers. The 1 million can be divided into several categories, such as immigrants, refugees, patients and handicapped, children (one out of 10!), single parents, homeless people, and finally individuals who draw on social security.

This paper focuses on the last group. In the summer of 2003 over 360,000 individuals were dependent upon social security (General Support or Algemene Bijstand) in the Netherlands. They had no or limited prospects to ever leave the current system of social services. The question arises: Is it acceptable, in a welfare country such as the Netherlands, that individuals are excluded from social participation and live in a state of poverty?

The Social Cultural Planning Bureau (SCP, 2000) defined poverty as follows: *"a forced shortage of requirements, which are deemed socially necessary. The shortage is not a voluntary choice, individuals would rather take care of their own needs."* According to project leader J. Tas (2003), who headed an experiment in the province of Zeeland in the Netherlands, poverty is not so much an income problem, but a problem of dependency, loss of self-respect, isolation, and lack of self-sufficiency. Therefore, an approach is required that aims at giving people self-esteem. Stimulating the ambitions of poor people and supporting them to perform accordingly should be the main focus of social security counselors. Entrepreneurship with the focus on the needs of the clients is required instead of the focus on bureaucratic rules.

The main research question is: *What experiences from the private sector can be used for innovation within the social security system to offer new perspectives to individuals in a situation of poverty?*

First, a literature study is conducted to discover the characteristics of innovation and culture in both the private sector and the public sector. In the public sector the focus is limited to social security and poverty. By comparing the private sector literature with the public sector literature, criteria will be identified that may be used to describe and explain experiments in practice.

The research is limited to the first three phases of the research cycle defined by Van der Zwaan (1999). He identifies four phases: explore, describe, explain, and test. The choice implies that this research project will focus on: exploration, description, and explanation. The testing will take place in the next phase of the longitudinal study. For that purpose the research findings of the case study (the Zeeland experiment) are analyzed and the conclusions and recommendations are formulated. Finally, the implications for education are formulated.

3. INNOVATION AND CULTURE IN THE PRIVATE SECTOR

In exploring the contribution of private sector innovations in entrepreneurship for the social services sector it is important to find the key factors for success and failure in the field of organizational culture. In today's global economy approximately 80% of all business activities (both small and large businesses) are service activities and most employment is in this sector (Pine & Gilmore, 2001).

In the Netherlands, 84% of the business organizations actively pursue a design approach for change, yet 76% of those organizations pursuing change fail to achieve the intended results. Moreover, 80% of change processes that do work are initiated from the bottom up (Bennebroek Gravenhorst, Werkman. & Boonstra, 2001). As far as the key factors for success innovation are concerned, De Jong, Kemp, and Snel (2001) identify the following: innovative ability, organizational structure and culture, access to means and creativity, network activities and collaborative learning, and market characteristics.

3.1 Innovative Ability

Based on research by EIM Business and Policy Research (De Jong, Kemp, & Snel, 2001), there are a number of important determinants of innovative ability in service companies. These are people characteristics, strategy, structure, availability of means, network activities, firm characteristics, innovation infrastructure, and market characteristics. The research is not representative for all sectors but it gives an idea of what to look for when exploring innovative ability. De Jong, Kemp, and Snel (2001) tested 38 determinants over 8 categories and showed that most categories are suitable to explain part of the innovative ability of service businesses. There are two important criteria for innovation to occur. The first is the willingness of employees to take risks (creativity, willingness to co-operate, adaptability, and flexibility). The second is the formulation of a strategic mission statement that includes a focus on innovation and setting innovation objectives.

3.2 Organizational Structure and Culture

The same study shows that the organizational structure is best tailored by working in multidisciplinary teams to support innovation and that employees who are autonomous have higher innovative abilities. The culture is most conducive to innovation when it is result-oriented and professional in an *entrepreneurial* manner. Companies that apply this rule, give their employees greater freedom of action. There should be few rules and procedures for carrying out the work. People should be held responsible for their own results.

3.3 Access to Means and Creativity

In the *Origin and Evolution of New Businesses*, Bhidé (2000) describes the ability to secure resources as an important competence of entrepreneurs.

That is in line with the EIM study where the determinant of the use of creative techniques to secure means was supported.

3.4 Network Activities and Collaborative Learning

Service businesses attempting to improve innovative ability by means of network activities focus on their external orientation (contacts with suppliers, competitors, and knowledge institutions) and transfer knowledge in exchange for money (De Jong *et al.*, 2001). When employees maintain frequent, intensive contacts with the environment, additional information that stimulates idea generation is provided. Developing and implementing an external orientation in each job constitutes a major step in creating and maintaining an innovative organization. The enterprise should be open for knowledge that is developed outside of it.

3.5 Market Characteristics

Service businesses that operate in markets with a high intensity of non-price competition will have more innovative ability. De Jong *et al.* (2001) conclude that in a situation of non-price competition, service businesses will have more innovative ability. The same counts for markets where the demand is highly uncertain.

4. ORGANIZATIONAL CULTURE

Robert E. Quinn (1995) describes organizational culture in his 'Competing Values Model.' It enables us to describe and visualize a particular culture in an organization. Also, it allows us to compare the organizational culture in the private sector with the public sector. Quinn's model is presented in Figure 1. The model describes flexibility and control from an internal and external perspective.

The description of the Competing Values Model should to be interpreted as follows:

1. *Purpose Culture*: the focus of this type of culture is on innovation, personal freedom, intuition, creativity, vision, and growth. It can be described as 'entrepreneurial.'
2. *People Culture*: the focus of the people culture is on the development of employees, collaboration, acceptance, consensus, teambuilding, appreciation, and respect.

3. *Process Culture*: the focus of the process culture is on rules and regulations, procedures, and the avoidance of mistakes.
4. *Performance Culture*: the focus of the performance culture is on market orientation, decision-making, goal setting, production, and performance.

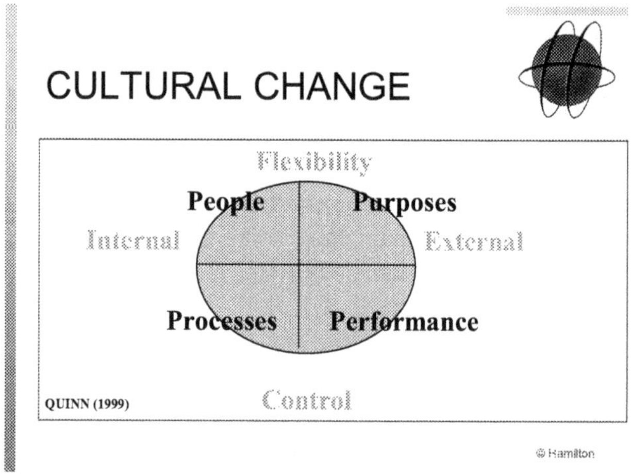

Figure 1. The Four Cultures of the Competing Values Model (Quinn)

Quinn recommends that organizations should aim to strike a good balance in an organization among each of the above named cultures in order to be successful. This is supported by empirical research by Ghoshal and Bartlett (1997). Figure 2 shows a balance between cultures of purpose, people, processes, and performance (by the blue square in the middle). Looking at the main characteristics of innovative organizations in the private sector and their innovative ability, it can be stated that these organizations are externally oriented, have a purpose, and align the internal organization (people) and processes in order to perform well in the marketplace.

According to De Jong (2001) the main criteria for innovations in service businesses in the private sector are:

1. Creative recombination;
2. Strategy and mission for innovation;
3. External orientation on customers, suppliers, competitors and knowledge institutions;
4. Multi-disciplinary teams and employee autonomy;
5. Creative techniques for securing means; and
6. Idea generation through network activities and collaborative learning.

Further, these findings indicate that non-price competition and an uncertain demand foster innovative ability.

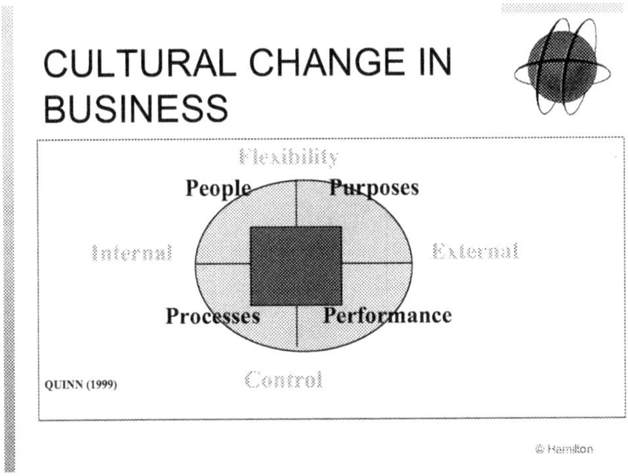

Figure 2. The Required Balance Among the Four Cultures

The above criteria reflect an entrepreneurial approach to serving customer needs in a market-oriented way. Entrepreneurship can be defined as *the active pursuit of opportunities, as a result of which value is created.* The entrepreneur starts with the opportunity and then seeks the resources to exploit it (Molian & Leleux, 1996). The hypothesis is that the above criteria reflect the innovative ability of service organizations in the private sector. The question is: "What can service organizations in the public sector learn from these private sector insights?"

5. INNOVATION AND CULTURE IN THE PUBLIC SECTOR

Traditionally the social services sector is governed by rules and regulations and can be typified as a process-oriented culture as is shown in Figure 3.

Only very recently has the government realized that an approach of 'one size fits all' is not productive in the social activation of individuals who are dependent on government support for a longer period of time, such as individuals in a state of poverty (Serail & Van de Pas, 2002). Instead, the citizen should be treated as an unique individual and all processes of support (political, managerial, and operational) should be redesigned and tailored to offer new perspectives for social inclusion and psychological well-being to the non-active individuals. This fits with an approach where the public sector is redefining its role in society as an answer to rapid changes and to the requirements of citizens, nongovernmental organizations (NGOs) and businesses.

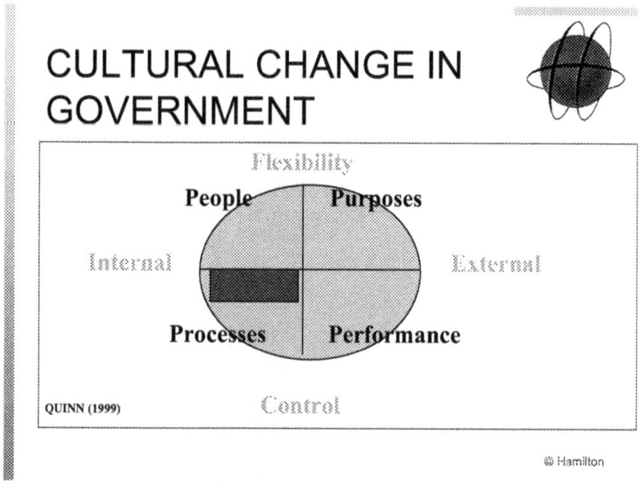

Figure 3. Processes Are the Main Focus of Interest in the Public Sector

The Ministry of Social Affairs and Work in the Netherlands passed a law in 1996 with a specific article (144Abw) for local governments to experiment on social inclusion and labor participation. The experiments were monitored and the first findings were reported in 1999 (Serail & Van de Pas, 2002). The time period for the experiments was extended until 2002. Both project leaders and clients were interviewed in 32 municipalities. The research objectives were to identify the effects of the experiments on lowering social exclusion and the effects on increasing labor participation. The methodology included conducting personal interviews (500) and telephone inquiries (32), as well as distributing questionnaires (373).

5.1 Key Experimental Results: The Clients' Perspective

The main findings of these experiments are as follows (Serail & Van de Pas, 2002):

1. *The client must be the starting point.* It is important to match services to what the client abilities are and to what the client's

aspirations are. Understanding of the client's social system (children, partner, neighbors, friends, etc.) is important.

2. *Social activation should aim for realistic goals for the client.* The concept of the integration ladder must be introduced, starting with social inclusion, activating to work, structural voluntary work, temporary paid-for work, and finally, regular work. It is considered better to formulate an in-between goal than to aim too high from the start. Otherwise the client could respond by leaving the program. The experiments have shown that clients can climb more steps on the ladder as they change their objectives parallel to their personal development.

3. *Clear understanding of the client's characteristics.* The better the understanding is of the client's characteristics in terms of social exclusion and distance to the labor market, the easier it is to deliver tailor-made services.

4. *Mandatory or voluntary participation.* Project leaders are divided on the issue of whether voluntary or mandatory participation of clients in programs is required. Some are in favor of mandatory participation in the initial phase of the program (research through in-depth interviews), and leave the participation in a program open to the client. Others are in favor of total voluntary participation and yet others prefer total mandatory participation. The conclusion that researchers (Serail & Van de Pas, 2002) reached is that once the client is committed to a program, the commitment is two-way. The social service and the client are mutually committed.

5. *A long but valuable road to social activation.* The experiments show that programs of social activation take from six months to two years. During this time a step-by-step approach between the social counselor and the client, and clear agreements on the specific actions to take, will help ease the client ahead to social inclusion, more psychological well-being, and in a number of cases to voluntary or paid-for work. Even if work is not a realistic prospect, the effects of an individualized approach on personal development and a sense of well-being are positive.

6. *Continuity, intensity, and trust are important criteria.* The experiments indicate that the continuity of the counselor is an important factor for success and the intensity of guidance to avoid

having individuals drop out of the program. Trust between the client and the counselor is of key importance. To establish trust is not always an easy matter, as many clients have had negative personal experiences with institutes and their representatives. A counselor must be trustworthy in his behavior and not make any promises that cannot be realized. If such promises are made, the client will only become more distrusting. At the end of a program, clients cannot be aborted. Follow up is an essential part of the program.

7. *Social activation calls for close collaboration and communication.* In most cases more than one organization is involved in social activation programs. Communication about what activities should be performed by whom is important. Periodic assessment of the process and clear commitment to contributions are essential. Social activation should be part of a planned process where all steps are connected both in time and in content. It is realized that in this respect much can be improved in current programs for social activation and a case manager is needed to monitor progress and align contributions to the process.

Besides the main findings, which are stated above, there are also other lessons to be learned from these experiments (Serail & Van de Pas, 2002). Not all of the clients were fully enthusiastic. Indeed, 34% of the clients (research base of 500) identified one or more negative points about programs of social activation. Of these 500, 10% considered the imposed duties as negative and 6% were disappointed about the content of the program. This indicates that a better connection between the client's capabilities and the program is necessary. Also, 5% of the 500 considered the time spent in the program as competing with time spent on leisure activities, social contacts, and/or housekeeping. Finally, 67% of the clients indicated no negative points at all (more than one answer was possible).

Some of the clients did offer suggestions for improvement of the program; 36% of them made one or more suggestions. Among these suggestions were the following:

- The duration of the program should not be limited to a set period.
- The clients would prefer more intensive individual coaching and extra help in finding employment or education.
- Clients suggested better financial remuneration for expenses such as travel, better tools and materials, better child support, and better administrative procedures.
- Clients think that better coaching and better financial support are the main criteria for improvement.

5.2 Key Experimental Results: The Counselors' Perspective

In total, 48 counselors responded to questions about key success factors. There was an overlap with the lessons learned from clients. The counselor respondents cited the following key success factors:

- An individualized approach should be tailored to the individual's capabilities and desires.
- A local support base needs to invest in target group.
- Willingness to collaborate between organizations must exist.
- Employees must have expertise and be experienced, self-motivated, and committed.

The counselors also named a number of factors for failure. The same respondents named the following failure factors:

- Lack of communication.
- Lack of supporting facilities and the existence of waiting lists.
- Problems with client selection and steering towards programs.
- Lack of continuity through personnel turnover.
- Client problems becoming more intense.

5.3 General Experimental Effects

The general effects of the experiments can be described succinctly. Starting with 12,000 clients in 43 experiments, 54% ended participation within the programs — of these, 29% passed on to work (paid and unpaid) and 19% ended the program in advance of the end of the planned period. At the time of reporting, 46% of the clients were still part of various programs. The sustainable effects of the programs are high, whereas the relapse to social security is 12%. The experiments prove that work is an excellent social integrator.

The researchers, Serail and Van de Pas (2002), conclude that more attention is needed for different outcomes of social activation programs. Valid outcomes other than work are possible, such as voluntary unpaid work. If paid-for work would be the only criterion, many individuals would not be eligible for participating in the program and would remain in a situation of social exclusion. An integration ladder, such as mentioned earlier, may assist in establishing realistic objectives for each client.

Figure 4 indicates the desired outcome — the required cultural change in government policy is from the small square (bottom left) to the large square (center of the model). The experiments described in this section of the chapter show a progression towards a better balance among the four types of cultures by putting the client at the center of attention, setting realistic goals, aiming at a clear understanding of the client, and searching for collaboration and communication between service organizations. The cultural changes thus far have taken place from process-oriented (bottom left) to people-oriented (top left) and performance-oriented (bottom right). Many experiments still lack an overall vision, or equivalently a purpose-oriented culture (top right).

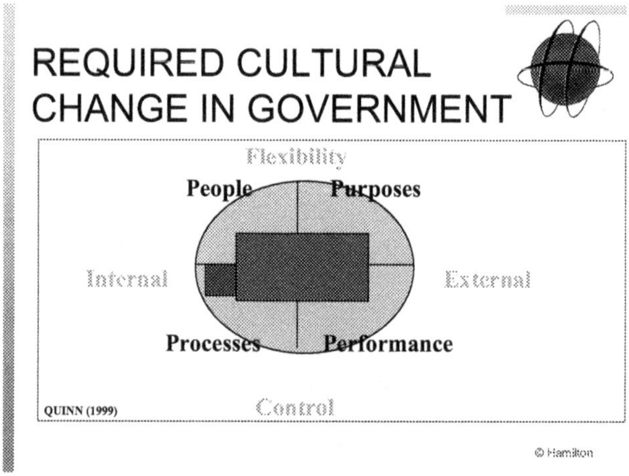

Figure 4. The Desired Outcome of Government Policy

The cultural change is taking place from a focus on bureaucracy (process culture) to a more entrepreneurial culture (purpose culture) focusing on clients' needs and involving the organization (people culture) in working together to serve clients better (performance culture).

Based on the above information of approximately 43 experiments (Serail & Van de Pas, 2002) we can list the following criteria for innovation in the social services:

1. The client must be the starting point.
2. Social activation should aim for realistic goals for clients.
3. A clear understanding of client's characteristics is required.
4. Continuity, intensity, and trust are the key factors.
5. Close collaboration and communication between service organizations is required.
6. An individualized approach should be tailored to the individual's capabilities and desires.
7. Better coaching and financial support is needed.
8. Child support is necessary.

9. A connection must exist between client's capabilities and the program.
10. Employees must possess expertise and be experienced, self motivated, and committed.

In addition, the following external criteria are important:

1. A local support base to invest in target group is required.
2. A willingness to collaborate between organizations must exist.
3. Political and managerial responsibility is a requirement for taking the problem of social exclusion and poverty seriously and to support experiments to learn and to innovate.

6. SOCIAL ENTREPRENEURSHIP

Organization culture is changing from being bureaucratic to being more entrepreneurial. In the case of not-for-profit enterprises, the term *social* entrepreneurship (Thompson, Alvy, & Lees, 2000; Mordecai, 2002) can be introduced as compared to entrepreneurship in commercial organizations. The main object of social entrepreneurship is a social cause (*i.e.*, to improve social cohesion, combat poverty, defend human rights, improve health services, etc.). When social entrepreneurship is practiced, it involves all levels of the organization; political, managerial, and operational levels are all in need of alignment, focusing on a particular social cause.

If social service organizations are to be more client-oriented, a cultural change is required (Hibbert, Hogg, & Quinn, 2002). Experiments in social services practice are helping the cultural change process. A comparison between the private sector and the public sector, as shown in Table 1, offers information on innovation and culture, which can be translated into criteria for an experiment in social services practice. The criteria are regrouped in Table 2, starting with broader aspects such as dynamics and strategy and finally coming to more detailed aspects as employees, clients, and networks. The purpose of the regrouping is to follow a managerial flow from external dynamics, to organizational culture, to strategy and on to structure and implementation.

Based on the comparison of Tables 1 and 2 between the private and the public sectors of social services, it is possible to make the following observations:

1. *Dynamics*: the dynamics of the private sector and of the public sector are inherently different.
2. *Autonomy and complexity*: private service companies enjoy great freedom to design and implement their own strategy, whereas laws and regulations, which are fixed over time, govern social service

organizations. The role of political parties, NGOs and the political system is not easily geared to reform.

3. *Strategy and vision*: an overall strategy is lacking for social service organizations. There is no clear connection among strategy, organization, and operations. Current experiments focus more on a tactical and operational level. A vision to guide actions is lacking.
4. *Orientation and networking*: social service organizations generally are internally oriented. Working in partnerships and networks is a relatively new phenomenon.
5. *Innovativeness and employees*: employees in the social sector work with strict guidelines and are not rewarded for creativity, self-steering, and risk taking.
6. *Client and trust*: truly getting to know clients' characteristics is not part of the usual work process.
7. *Networking and learning*: counselors have a heavy workload and little time is allowed for networking and learning.

Recently an experiment was started in the province of Zeeland (the Netherlands) to mirror the above observations. The aim of the experiment was: *Develop an overall vision and strategy to guide an experiment where all participants involved learn and actively collaborate to acquire innovative ability for the benefit of clients who are socially excluded and are in a state of poverty.*

Table 1. Private Culture Versus Public Culture in the Services Sector

Private Services Sector Culture	**Public Sector (Social Services) Culture**	**Observations**
Innovative service organizations strike a good balance among purpose, people, processes, and performance.	Experiments in the social services sector show a migration from bureaucracy (process culture) towards a more client-oriented and employee-oriented culture (people culture and performance culture).	Social service experiments are helping to change the culture. An overall vision (purpose) is absent in many experiments.

Table 2. Criteria for Comparing the Private Service Sector and the Public Service Sector

Private Services Sector	Public Sector (Social Services)	Observations
Market dynamics and change	• Political and managerial responsibility for taking the problem of social exclusion and poverty seriously and supporting experiments to learn and to innovate. • Increasing influence from NGOs active in the field of combating poverty and social exclusion.	• Governments (including local governments) are monopoly players, and clients of social services are in a relation of dependency. • The dynamics of a political system and a market-driven system cannot easily be compared. • The role and influence of NGOs and political parties in defending the public interest need to be taken into account.
Employees, creativity, and risk taking	• Employees have expertise and are experienced, self-motivated, and committed.	• Employees in the social sector work with strict guidelines and are not rewarded for creativity, self-steering, and risk taking.
Adding value for citizens as clients	• The client must be the starting point. • Clear understanding of client's characteristics.	*• Rules and regulations are more often the staring point.* • Truly getting to know clients' characteristics is not part of the usual work process.
Network activities and learning	• Close collaboration and communication.	• Counselors have a heavy workload and little time is allowed for networking and learning.
Organizational structure and culture	• The organizational culture is changing from bureaucratic to more entrepreneurial through experimenting.	• Social service organizations are generally internally focused and partnerships between various organizations are relatively new. • Staff turnover is high and experiments lack continuity. • Law and regulations govern actions; building trust is not at the core of activities.

The experiment was intended to accomplish the following:

1. Create an overall strategy and vision on how to assist clients in becoming socially integrated.
2. Solicit commitment from all participants involved on the strategy and vision.
3. Design, develop, and implement innovative work processes enabling all organizational levels to align in supporting clients.
4. Truly get to know each individual client as a unique individual and build a relationship on a foundation of mutual trust.
5. Place autonomy on all levels of the organization and stimulate collaboration, communication, and learning through social entrepreneurship.
6. Allow time for counselors, management, and council officials to reflect and learn, thereby creating a cultural change from a focus on rules and regulations (process culture) to a focus on development and growth of unique individuals (purpose culture in terms of social entrepreneurship).

6.1 The Methodology of the Zeeland Experiment

In this section we report on an experiment in three cities in the province of Zeeland (the Netherlands) as the first phase of a longitudinal study on innovating social services trough social entrepreneurship and cultural change. The cities are: Vlissingen, Reimerswaal, and Sluis. The steps in this first phase are summarized in Table 3.

The first phase of the experiment started in August 2000 and was completed and evaluated in June 2003. The method of working is based on participatory research and collaborative learning. Each step in the process is based on critical inquiry, description, and representation of the answers found. The participants — such as administrators, managers, counselors, and clients — are all actively involved in the process, allowing them to reflect on current working methods and innovative new working methods. The participants are enabled to learn through collaboration, communication, and practice. The learning effects are evaluated during every step of the process. J. Tas headed the experiment and the authors of this paper conducted the action research aspect.

In phase 2 of the longitudinal research, the experiment will be expanded to a larger scale in Zeeland. The aim is to increase the number of cities and participating clients.

Here we present briefly some of the highlights of the first phase of the longitudinal study in Zeeland on the innovation and cultural change of social services. The initial ***trigger*** for change is an action of a NGO named

Splinter. Splinter, an organization defending the rights of the poor in the province of Zeeland, summoned provincial government and cities in the region to take responsibility for the inhabitants of the province living in a situation of poverty and social exclusion. The province responded by furnishing funds for participatory research and for collaborative learning. An expert practitioner in the field of social security was appointed to design and implement the practical research. The choice was made to interview 30 clients to describe the situation, analyze the competencies, the personal ambitions, the constraints and the effects of the organizations involved.

The interviews were presented in December 2001 to Splinter, to the province of Zeeland, and to city officials. The form chosen was a 'Photo Book.' This book contains a narrative description of each client and a preliminary vision outlining how to deal with clients who are socially excluded and in a state of poverty. This document was well received and accepted. The association of cities adopted the preliminary vision and took responsibility for the further steps (step 2 –4) in phase 1 of the research (see Table 3).

Three cities (Vlissingen, Reimerswaal, and Sluis) volunteered to adopt the program for participatory research and collaborative learning. Administrators, managers, and counselors participated actively in clarifying the vision, officially adopting the principles of the vision on the city council, and collaborating in designing and developing a new methodology to serve clients better.

The team worked together in working conferences to discuss and develop a document describing the elements of a new methodology, sharing knowledge, and seeking consensus in the process. The initial resistance changed over time with the unfolding of a collaborative process of seeking new and more entrepreneurial ways to address the problems of clients. The deliverable in the form of a full description of the proposed new methodology and the requirements from the organization in terms of competencies and resources was ready in September 2002. It was adopted by local city councils and the implementation of the new methodology started at the same moment. The collaborative learning continued through training in communication with the participants as clients. The actual selection of 31 clients began and the method was brought into real practice. Monthly 'inter vision sessions' (where counselors reflect on their mindsets, actions, and results) and project meetings offered time for reflection and collaborative learning.

Table 3. Steps Taken in the First Phase of the Experiment

Step/Period	Aim	Description	Deliverable
1: August 2001 to December 2001	• Identify the problem and develop a vision.	• In-depth interviews with 30 clients to gain a deep under-standing of the individuals, problems, ambitions, and possibilities. • Developing a vision and overall strategy based on the findings, and done together with all participants in pilot cities.	• Photo Book on 30 clients and a preliminary outline of a vision and overall strategy.
2: December 2001 to September 2002	• Design and develop an innovative practice.	• Organize working conferences to design and develop a new practice. • Participatory research and collaborative learning.	• Description of a new practice.
3: September 2002 to June 2003	• Implement new practice in a pilot.	• Select and invite 30 clients, 8 counselors, 3 managers, and 3 administrators to actually implement the new practice and reflect monthly on progress made.	• Detailed description of the new practice and implementation with 30 clients.
4: June 2003 to July 2003	• Evaluate the pilot.	• Evaluate the pilot through client interviews and evaluation activities of all participants involved.	•A final description of the new practice. • An evaluation report, including conclusions and recommendations.

6.2 Results of the Zeeland Experiment

The main research question stated at the start of this paper was: *What experiences from the private sector can be used for innovation within the social security system to offer new perspectives to individuals in a situation of poverty?*

In June 2003 the Zeeland experiment was evaluated and the first results became available. The deliverables were:

1. A vision on how to tackle the innovation of the public sector by introducing the concept of social entrepreneurship.
2. A full and detailed description and explanation of the methodology.
3. A detailed evaluation of the effects for clients, the process, and collaboration on all levels of the organization.
4. Conclusions from phase 1 and recommendations for phase 2 of the longitudinal study.

The experiences from the private sector were transferred to the public sector through participatory research and collaborative learning. In the process, participants learned to understand and gain an overview on the existing bureaucratic culture. They acquired a vision on the possibilities of a culture of social entrepreneurship that balances purpose, people, processes and performance. The involved participants gained insight, overview, and foresight as well as new practical competencies. They now know how to shape the future of social services to serve clients better and direct their own actions. The results were presented on a conference in the province of Zeeland in September 2003, where clients, counselors, managers, and administrators of the pilot cities each presented part of the outcomes.

Participatory research and collaborative learning proved to be effective instruments to involve all participants in designing and developing a new vision and a new methodology on social entrepreneurship. Participants, through collaborative learning, acquired and shared fresh insights regarding client's problems as well as new and more effective ways of assisting clients in improving their own situations. The process of creation, learning, practice, reflection on actions, and description of findings facilitated the team of participants who were involved. The findings emerged from collaboration. Each participant is an *owner* of the new vision and the method and knows what is *required* to act as a *social entrepreneur,* based on a client-driven approach.

More specific results were the narrative descriptions of 30 clients in the 'Photo Book.' This book presented real life information, with which participants could identify. A highly qualitative instrument triggered social entrepreneurship as an active pursuit of opportunities to better serve clients in a situation of poverty and social exclusion. The vision (main principles) outlined in the 'Photo Book' has proven to be a guide for all further actions and for evaluation.

We noted earlier that previous experiments in the Netherlands lacked an overall vision and strategy. The Zeeland experiment is the first one to describe an explicit vision that can be split up regarding the roles of all participants.

The *vision for clients* consists of: (1) The client is at the center from start to finish. (2) The client is the architect and builder of his/her own future. (3) The profit (performance) for the client is clearly defined and includes more than a position of paid-for work. In fact, participation in a social network, elimination of specific problems, and participation in voluntary activities were included in the performance as well.

The *vision for counselors* consists of: (1) The counselor has excellent coaching abilities to guide clients from start to finish. (2) Counselors form a social contract with clients, including mutual rights and obligations. (3) The counselor acts as a social entrepreneur, who is client centered, flexible, and creative in the pursuit of opportunities to help clients improve their situation themselves.

The *vision for organizational support* consists of: (1) The city administrators take full responsibility for improving the perspective of citizens who live in poverty and social exclusion. (2) Organizational efforts are directed towards stimulating the ability of self-sufficiency of clients, social participation, taking away obstructions, and connecting to individual competencies, ambitions, and actions of individual clients. (3) Actions of any organization involved in the social integration process are guided by a personal development plan that clarifies specific roles and contributions of all participants involved. Clear contracts establish professional relationships for the benefit of the client.

6.3 Social Entrepreneurship as a Guide for a New Methodology

All participants engaged in the participatory research and collaborative learning process experienced how a vision can guide creation, learning, and performance. It inspires and provides a clear guide for communication and collaboration.

The new methodology can be visualized as a matrix with methodological steps on the vertical side and client results on the horizontal side. The methodological steps for the counselor are: (1) identification and selection of the clients; (2) approach of the clients; and (3) in-depth interviews. These steps are aimed at creating interest, insight, and trust. Once this is achieved the first milestone of a relationship based on mutual trust is attained. The next steps in the methodology are: (4) analysis of the situation and formulation of advice, and (5) an independent diagnosis. These steps are aimed at creating ambition and perspective. They also are aimed at the development of competencies required to become successful. Once this is achieved the second milestone of a personal development plan and commitment to pursue it are attained. The last two steps of the methodology are: (6) working on the personal development plan, and (7) inserting the client as a participant in society. This must lead to the third milestone: social integration on the basis of self-esteem and self-support and with fighting spirit.

The above method was tested and evaluated on 31 clients, and an overview of the results is presented in Figure 5. Apart from two clients who appeared to be capable of self-sufficiency from the beginning, all clients started from a situation of social exclusion and inability to engage in social activities and progressed to adding value to their daily lives and building their self-esteem and psychological well-being and the competencies they need to cope.

The vision developed during the pilot was operationalized in terms of the client results at top of Figure 5. The success criterion that the client should be the starting point was translated to the 'person as an individual.' The success criterion that people should be inspired to design and construct their own lives were translated to 'the person as architect' and the 'person as builder.'

To explain Figure 5, it is to be noted that six clients left the pilot group due to various reasons, including transfer to another geographical location and medical treatment. The remaining 25 clients (represented by the blue circles) have been assisted, 16 of whom are building their own future and are becoming socially integrated. They are taking positive actions to improve their situation through education, voluntary work, engaging in social networks and, in three cases, paid-for work. Five clients are still in the process of constructing a personal development plan and four clients have just started and are still at the stage of building a relationship with their counselors.

All clients were selected from a group of clients (category 4 in the Dutch system) who are considered impossible to integrate. In fact, they were considered a write-off. The results show that this opinion is incorrect and that individuals in a state of poverty and social exclusion can be guided to improve their situation, provided the relationship is built on trust and focuses on the uniqueness of the individual and their competencies, ambitions, and specific actions according to a personal development plan.

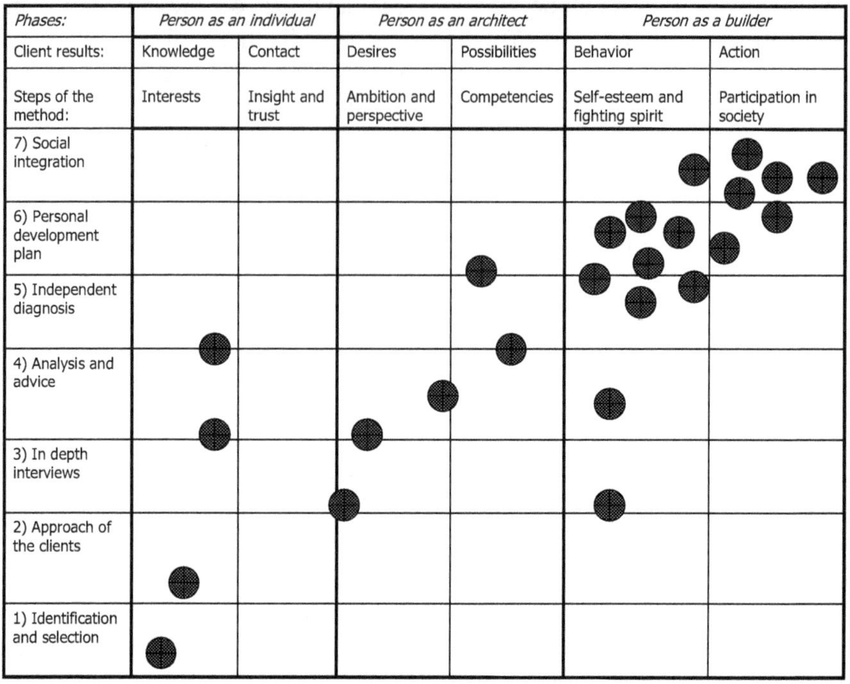

Figure 5. The Improvement of Client's Perspectives in Six Months Time

Without organizational support (communication, collaboration, coordination, and resources) on all levels of the organizations, counselors and clients would not have been able to progress as they did. The initial way of working was top down through rules and regulations. The administrators instructed managers, who in turn instructed counselors to enforce rules and regulations. Clients had to comply. In the new methodology the client is at the center and very soon is at the steering wheel of activities. All organizational levels act in concert and in support of the client's endeavors. In this way the organizational culture has balance among purpose (vision), people (role of all participants for the benefit of the client), processes (clear steps towards social integration), and performance (the improvement of the perspective of individual clients).

In evaluating the pilot program it became clear that local government and local society benefit from the clients as well the clients benefiting themselves. Local government gets a more human face and gets closer to those in need. For them it is important to make a difference between a relationship based on trust and collaboration, as opposed to the application of rules and regulations. Simultaneously, clients make a contribution to society in several ways, including: less use of state facilities such as health services; less use of social services; contributions to the bringing up of children; contributions to mutual aid in social networks; contributions to voluntary activities; and contributions through paid-for work.

7. DISCUSSION

Participatory research and collaborative learning appears to be an effective way in the practice of engaging participants in intensive processes of cultural change if there is a significant **trigger** for such change. However, the results reported in this chapter derive from a research base that is limited to a small number of clients (31), counselors (8), managers (3), and administrators (3). Also, the actual period of implementation covered by this method is only six months.

The results of the research are indicative of the population taking part in the research. It is not expedient at this time to generalize the results to be representative of a larger population. On the other hand, the results are so promising that the vision and methodology developed will be tested on a larger scale in the second phase of the longitudinal research on social entrepreneurship and cultural change in the social services sector.

The first phase of the longitudinal research in the Netherlands showed some promising results. In the next phase it is recommended that the research base be expanded to a larger scale and that also the imbalance of power (between social security services and the client) and the limitations of empowerment be taken into account.

Another aspect that should be explored further is the effect of mutual trust between client and counselor. This seems one of the major reasons why the new methodology may differ from existing experiments in social security and why it may work better for clients. Taking into account the uniqueness of each client, taking time to listen to their life's story, and being there to encourage the client to take hold of their own lives are aspects that certainly demand further exploration. In the Zeeland case, there was a significant trigger for change from NGO Splinter. It should be explored how, in other situations, the influence of (outside) triggers can be used to improve social entrepreneurship and cultural change in social services for the benefit of clients in a state of poverty.

A note of caution, however, is required. In our research we did not pay full attention to the possible effects of imbalance in power and the limitations for empowerment. Every individual has his or her limitations and these limits should be respected. There may always be an imbalance between those in power and those who are not in power. Seeking a delicate power balance according to rules of mutual respect and humanity will be necessary. Self-steering and self-development seem to be good ideas, but individuals do need the basic competencies and ambitions to act accordingly. If not, they need to be nurtured and guided to reach a state at the maximum level of their abilities.

8. IMPLICATIONS FOR EDUCATION

A first implication is about the nature of collaborative learning. Collaborative learning is more than working in teams. The essential characteristics are to be formulated in competencies. A competence is a combination of knowledge, skill, and attitude. Knowing how to be a good social entrepreneur is not enough to be a competent social entrepreneur. Neither is the acquisition of skills, like holding an in-depth interview or stimulating people to formulate a personnel development plan. The attitude is what really matters: the way relations are built by participating in a mix of processes, as described by Quinn (1995). Attitude requires a certain amount of freedom for counselors to behave to their own intuition. Attitude must be a personal drive to succeed in supporting clients so they develop the fighting spirit required to take their destiny in their own hands.

A second implication is about teachers in schools. Educational institutions in practice do not differ much from bureaucratic social service organizations. Organizational processes are similar in that decision-making is often top down, management and employees work with strict guidelines, and there is no room for entrepreneurship. Based on the experiment reported in this chapter, educational institutions can learn the following:

- Empowerment of individuals is possible when a relationship is based on a clear vision of mutual trust, commitment, and development of empowerment.
- Individuals are able to perform and improve their situation if guidance on all levels of the organization (managers, teachers, researchers, and other staff) is aligned and re-directed in ways that support the student's efforts to become young professionals.
- Participatory research and collaborative learning seem powerful instruments to help shape the future of all participants involved if there is a significant *trigger* for change. They become owners of the vision and method, and in this way they become owners of their own destiny.

REFERENCES

Alliantie voor sociale rechtvaardigheid. (2002). *Hoogste Tijd voor Sociale Rechtvaardigheid: manifest tegen armoede en sociale uitsluiting*. Utrecht.

Bennebroek Gravenhorst, K. M., Werkman. R. A., & Boonstra, J. J. (2001). Change capacity of organizations. *Journal of Applied Psychology*, *52* (1), 83-105.

Bhidé, A. V. (2000). *The Origin and Evolution of New Businesses*. Oxford, New York: Oxford University Press.

De Jong, J. P. J. (2001). *Determinants of Innovative Ability: An Empirical Test of a Causal Model*. Zoetermeer: EIM Business & Policy Research.

Ghoshal, S., and Bartlett, C. A., 1997, *The Individualized Corporation: A Fundamentally New Approach to Management*, Harper Business, New York.

Hibbert, S. A., Hogg, G., & Quinn, T. (2002). Consumer response to social entrepreneurship: The case of the Big Issue in Scotland. *International Journal of Nonprofit & Voluntary Sector Marketing*, *7* (3):288-301.

Molian, D., & Leleux, B. (1996). European Casebook on Entrepreneurship and New Ventures. Prentice Hall, Upper Saddle River, New Jersey.

Mordecai, L. (2002). Non-profits and social entrepreneurship: Taking the good, avoiding the bad. *PA Times*, *25* (8), 4.

Pine, D. J., & Gilmore, J. H. (2001). *The Experience Economy: Work is Theatre & Every Business is a Stage*. Boston: Harvard Business School Press.

Quinn, R. E. (1995). *Becoming a Master Manager: A Competency Framework*. New York: John Wiley & Sons.

Serail, S., & Van de Pas, I. (2002). Bijstandsexperimenten: Impulsen tot Activering: Stand van Zaken na Zes Jaar Experimenteren in de Algemene Bijstandswet, Ministerie van Sociale Zaken en Werkgelegenheid, Elsevier Bedrijfsinformatie, Doetinchem.

Social Cultural Planning Bureau. (2000). Definition of poverty.

Tas, J. (2003). Photo Book on People in a State of Poverty, Cities of Reimerswaal, Sluis & Vlissingen.

Thompson, J., Alvy, G., & Lees, A. (2000). Management Decision, Social entrepreneurship — A new look at the people and the potential, *Decision*, *38* (5/6), 328-338.

Thompson, J. L. (2002). The world of the social entrepreneur. International Journal of Public Sector Management, *15* (5), 412, 21 pages, 2 diagrams.

Van der Zwaan, A. H. (1999). Van geval tot geval; ontvouwen of beproeven? Over onderbenutting van gevalstudies. In M. J. Riemsdijk (Ed.), *Dilemma's in Bedrijfskundige Wetenschap* (pp. 62-82). Assen:Van Gorcum.

Chapter 29

INTEGRATING LANGUAGE LEARNING WITH PBL

Principles and Practices

Raymond Ruijten[1] and Nicole van Emmerik[2]

[1]*Research & Evaluation Office, Breda Business School, Hogeschool Brabant, Breda, the Netherlands;* [2]*International Business School, Hogeschool Brabant, Breda, the Netherlands*

1. INTRODUCTION

Breda Business School is one of seven faculties in Hogeschool Brabant, an institution providing education for nearly 12,000 students. The Business School offers a broad, practically oriented education to students wishing to prepare for middle and senior executive positions in both business and not-for-profit organizations.

Breda Business School offers a four-year course, consisting of a one-year foundation phase and a three-year main phase where students choose from a number of programs — Accountancy, Finance and Accounting, Small Business and Retail Management, Marketing, International Business School (International Business and Management Studies), Management, Economics, and Law. Year 1 is common to all programs, except for International Business and Management Studies (IBMS), and acts as a bridging course from previous study as well as providing the basis for selection and referral before progression to the next phase.

In International Business School Breda, all classes are taught in English, as it is a partner in a number of exchange programs with students from most European countries, the USA, and mainland China. Besides, it offers students the possibility of dual qualification. This means that in addition to the Bachelor degree they obtain at IBS Breda, they will obtain a second Bachelor degree of a partner business school abroad.

M.K. McCuddy et al. (eds.),
The Challenges of Educating People to Lead in a Challenging World, 581–598.

2. BACKGROUND

2.1 The Educational Model

Breda Business School made the decision to adopt a problem-based approach to learning. In September 1994, the Finance and Accounting Department was the first to transform its curriculum from being subject-oriented to problem-based, followed by the IBMS program in 1996. Important changes to the educational model were:

- The use of problem-based learning was supported by training.
- The reduction of contact hours from 22 to 11 per week, and increasing self-study time from ± 20 to 30 hours per week.
- The reduction of average student group size from 30 to 12 students.

Two main objectives of this change were:

- The need to change the students' participation in the learning process from a passive to an active role.
- The need to prepare students for professional functions in a continuously changing environment with access to an increasing number of information sources.

The academic year is divided into four 10-week quarters, or 'blocks', which are designed to be structured around themes derived from the nationally agreed upon educational requirements for a particular occupational/vocational area.

Within the whole Breda Business School, the PBL-based content courses are supplemented by foreign language courses. English is offered in all programs, varying from 2 to 4 years of classes, while the Marketing and Small Business and Retail Management programs offer the students the opportunity to study French, German, or Spanish as a second foreign language. In the IBMS program, finally, all students study three foreign languages, with those from outside the Netherlands studying at least English and Dutch as well as having the opportunity to study French, German, or Spanish at various levels.

2.2 Evaluation Results and the Need for Changing the Educational Approach to Language Teaching

Following the introduction of PBL in 1994, numerous evaluations, in the form of written questionnaires and focus groups, were carried out and reported to several conferences (Brouwers & MacDonald, 1996; Brouwers & MacDonald, 1997; Broersma & MacDonald, 1998; Broersma & MacDonald 2000). While there were always very many positive comments and an appreciation of the value of the problem-based approach, a number of areas of concern were identified, including the problem of languages. This was especially the case in the IBMS program, where students reported an increased workload because of the language courses they had to take simultaneously, thus seriously impacting the effectiveness of the PBL approach.

Until then, the questionnaires that were used did not include the language courses. Given that they made up a substantial part of the student learning experience and restricted the ability of the groups to meet at certain times, this was the next aspect to be addressed. As such, the languages were to be looked at as an integral part of the system.

Consequently, a research study was undertaken, aimed at increasing the efficiency and effectiveness of the foreign language courses offered by Breda Business School (Ruijten, 2000). One of its findings was that, until 1998, most of these courses were highly traditional in the sense that they were usually based on the Grammar-Translation Method and on rote learning of structural and lexical elements. There was no consistency between the objectives of the language courses and those of the PBL courses, or between the content offered by both. Moreover, it appeared that there was little uniformity between the language courses of the different programs. The language staff was becoming quite dissatisfied, since they felt that the position of the languages had become marginalized after the introduction of PBL and that student motivation for language learning was rapidly declining.

These findings, combined with the results of the earlier PBL evaluations mentioned above, created a further pressure for change in the educational approach for language teaching.

During the academic year 1998/1999, an agreement was reached about the desired characteristics of any model and, in particular, that Breda Business School would move away from traditional language teaching methods to an approach based on integration with the PBL core content of the program. Furthermore, to optimize the internal consistency of the program, it was of the utmost importance to base the foreign language courses upon the same educational principles as those underlying problem-based learning. In the spring of 1999, a policy document was therefore issued, outlining the choice for Content-Based Instruction (CBI) as the Breda-model for second language teaching.

When the idea of CBI was first proposed, it received a warm welcome from the senior management of Breda Business School as well as from the foreign language teaching staff. Even so, the process of implementing CBI has been much harder than we expected at that time, as will be shown later in this chapter. In the next section, we will first provide a definition of CBI, outlining various models and setting out the differences with traditional language courses.

3. CONTENT-BASED FOREIGN LANGUAGE INSTRUCTION (CBI)

3.1 Characteristics

Over the last two decades or so, Content-Based foreign language Instruction has attracted a great deal of attention. There is an ever growing bulk of literature reporting on CBI experiments at all levels of second language proficiency, from beginners to advanced learners, and at all levels of education, from primary schools to university-level education. The work of Brinton, Snow, and Wesche (1989) is probably still the best book for readers interested in getting an overview of CBI applications at the university level and the rationale underlying the content-based movement. In this book, CBI is defined as:

> "the integration of content learning with language teaching aims. More specifically, it refers to the concurrent study of language and subject matter, with the form and sequence of language presentation dictated by content material. The language curriculum is centered around the academic needs and interests of the students, crossing over the barrier between language and subject matter courses which exists in most secondary and postsecondary institutions" (Brinton, Snow, & Wesche, 1989, p. vii).

A language program comes under CBI if it meets three criteria discussed below (Stryker & Leaver, 1997).

3.1.1 It Is Based on a Subject-Matter Core

Language proficiency is acquired by using the target language as a medium for learning new content material (*e.g.*, culture, business, economics). CBI is characterized by a top-down approach in which the emphasis is on *meaning*, whereas in traditional language courses the emphasis is usually on *form* (bottom-up). That is to say, in bottom-up programs students first have to learn grammatical and lexical elements before they can master the content. In top-down programs, on the other hand, students first have to look at the overall meaning of a text (oral or written) before studying formal elements at the sentence level. In other words, meaning and form, content knowledge and language proficiency go together like horse and carriage.

3.1.2 It Uses Authentic Language and Texts

In CBI programs, materials are used that are selected as much as possible from those produced for native speakers of the language, rather than materials that are specially developed for language instruction purposes. Language learning activities should be designed in such a way that they help students to understand and convey *meaningful* messages and accomplish *realistic tasks* using authentic language. Of course, it is every teacher's experience that students often find such authentic materials far too difficult. This does not mean that CBI teachers should restrict themselves to only the simplest materials. On the contrary, it is not so much the level of difficulty of a text (oral or written) that determines the suitability of a text, but the level of difficulty of the *task* that students are asked to accomplish on the basis of that text. Much depends on the ability of the teacher to effectively "shelter" the text, that is, to make it accessible to the students at their level of proficiency.

3.1.3 It Is Appropriate to the Needs of Specific Groups of Students

The content and learning activities that are selected fit the linguistic, cognitive and affective needs of the students to suit their personal and professional interests. By systematically assessing the students' opinions and learning results, CBI teachers should be able to select materials and learning activities to fit the students' level of proficiency (differentiation), their learning styles (*e.g.*, analytical versus global), and their affective characteristics (feelings and emotions, *e.g.*, how they cope with insecurity, how they react to overt correction). Learning activities can be meaningful and realistic for students if they are taken from their future profession or if they help them in their present study (concurrent content course).

As Stryker and Leaver (1997) point out, 'there is no singular formula for CBI.' Instead, over the last two decades, all kinds of models and variations on models have been implemented, precisely because the three criteria left designers much room to develop language programs that fit their own specific context. For example, it may be necessary to include explicit grammar lessons in a content-based language program. In another context, the CBI teacher may decide to abridge or edit authentic texts for beginning language learners (novice level), or to use the students' mother tongue in the initial phase and only later switch to the use of the target language.

3.2 Models

In the literature on CBI, seven models are often distinguished. Each of these models is discussed below.

3.2.1 Immersion

Immersion is probably the most prototypical CBI model in the sense that content learning objectives are fully integrated with language learning objectives by teaching non-language subjects through a foreign language. Immersion programs are becoming increasingly popular in higher education, with more and more institutions offering entire programs or parts of it in a foreign language. In a PBL context, for example, this means that either within the whole program or within one or more blocks, all tutor group sessions, all training sessions, and all the tasks and study materials are in this target language, which is either the instructor's mother tongue or a second language for the instructor.

There is quite some debate among researchers about whether or not immersion has any negative effects on the students' content learning results. According to Brinton, Snow, and Wesche (1989) there is extensive evidence showing that immersion programs at the primary and secondary school levels are highly effective when it comes to scholastic achievement. There are, however, also articles about university-level immersion programs that report a considerable loss of learning results and an increased workload for the student (Jochems, Rijns, Smid, & Verweij, 1991).

Immersion programs have been shown to have a positive effect on the students' linguistic development. Especially in the field of the receptive skills, immersion students reach a level resembling that of native speakers more quickly than students from traditional language programs. However, this is not true for their productive skills and in particular their grammatical accuracy.

In the most common variant of immersion, there is one content teacher who is responsible for the content course (*e.g.*, in a PBL context, this may be a tutor) in the target language (Direct Content Model). In another, less common variant, known as the Team Content Model, there are two instructors, a content teacher and a language teacher, who are together responsible for the content course (*e.g.*, in a PBL context, both a language teacher and the tutor are present during tutor group sessions).

3.2.2 Adjunct Model

In this model students enroll in two linked courses simultaneously. A content course (or a PBL block) is offered in the target language T1, and parallel to this, students take a language course, also in the target language T1. The main objectives of this language course are to help them to master the content material and to develop transferable academic skills, with *mutually* coordinated assignments. The language learning aims and activities should be attuned to the content learning aims as carefully as possible *and vice versa*; ideally, students should only be required to apply certain skills in the content course after these have been trained in the language course. For example, a complex skill like writing an analytical report can only be practiced after the basic writing skills have been trained sufficiently.

3.2.3 Subsidiary Content Model

In this model the content course (*e.g.*, a PBL course) is taught by a content teacher in a target language T1. The main objectives are to help students to master the content material and to enhance their foreign language skills. Parallel to this, there is a target language course T2, which deals with subject matter that is *related to* that studied in the content course. In a PBL context this may mean, for example, that in the language course, students are given a discussion task that follows the problem task they were asked to solve during their tutor group session.

3.2.4 Supplementary Content Model

The Supplementary Content Model differs from the previous one in that the target language course T2 deals with subject matter that is *the same as* that dealt with in the content course taught in T1. In a PBL setting this may simply mean that students have to give a presentation in the target language about the topic dealt with in their PBL sessions or that they are given an application task for which they need the knowledge they acquired in their PBL sessions.

3.2.5 Theme-Based Language Instruction

In Theme-Based courses, classes are organized around topics or themes. Either such topics have little relation with one another or they are all related to one central theme (*e.g.*, Marketing), which is subsequently split into subthemes (*e.g.*, product development, consumer behavior, distribution). The primary objective of such courses is to help students to develop their target language proficiency within a specific topic area. Theme-Based Language Instruction may be linked to content courses, but usually is not. Just like traditional language courses, it often incorporates a systematic study of grammatical elements, with these elements determining the choice of texts rather than the other way around. Theme-Based Language Instruction is a CBI model that can be implemented in almost any educational setting.

3.2.6 Language for Specific Purposes (LSP)

Language for Specific Purposes is probably the best known example of CBI. LSP courses aim to prepare students for the language demands made in a certain professional field. It is therefore particularly useful for adult learners with clearly identifiable functional/professional language needs. The more homogeneous the characteristics and language needs of the students, the better the chance of success of such courses. However, the syllabus of a language course is often determined rather arbitrarily by the teacher or dictated by tradition. Besides, LSP courses are never directly linked to content courses.

3.2.7 Foreign Languages Across the Curriculum (FLAC)

The rationale behind FLAC programs is that students should be offered as many opportunities as possible to employ their foreign language competencies. In this approach students are asked to read primary sources in languages other than their mother tongue, which helps them to make meaningful use of their language skills and enhances their (cross-cultural) content knowledge. Such assignments can either be set by a content teacher alone or by a content teacher in consultation with a language teacher. One of the major attractions of this approach is that no separate language classes are necessary.

Table 1, which has been adapted from Brinton, Snow, and Wesche (1989), summarizes the seven models described.

3.3 CBI and PBL at Breda Business School

As was described above, from the results of the research study reported in Ruijten (2000) it was concluded that CBI, and specifically the models that aimed at explicitly linking language objectives and content objectives, was an effective approach to teaching foreign language skills in any institution for higher education. No evidence was found to suggest that implementing CBI programs was more difficult if the main educational model used in a university was Problem-Based Learning. For Breda Business School it was

Table 1. Distinguishing Features of 7 CBI Models

	Primary Objective(s)	Instructional Format	Instructional Responsibilities	Focus of Evaluation
Immersion	Help students to master content material	Content course in target language	Content teacher for content class, sometimes helped by language teacher	Mastery of content knowledge
Adjunct Model	Help students to master content material Train students in academic skills	Content course with language course linked to it	Content teacher for content course; language teacher for language course	Mastery of content knowledge in content course; language proficiency in language course
Subsidiary Content Model	Help students to enhance their foreign language skills Help students to master (related) content material	Content course in target language T1, with language course in T2 linked to it	Content teacher for content course; language teacher for language course	Mastery of content knowledge in content course; language proficiency in language course
Supplementary Content Model	Help students to enhance their foreign language skills Help students to master (the same) content material	Content course in target language T1, with language course in T2 linked to it	Content teacher for content course; language teacher for language course	Mastery of content knowledge in content course; language proficiency in language course
Theme-Based Language Instruction	Help students to enhance their foreign language skills within specific themes	Language course is usually not linked to content course	Language teacher for language course with content aspects	Language proficiency
Language for Specific Purposes	Help students to enhance their foreign language skills in a professional field	Separate language course	Language teacher for language course with content aspects	Language proficiency
FLAC	Offer students the opportunity to use foreign language skills to deepen their content knowledge	Content course using (extra) sources in target language	Content teacher for content course, possibly including foreign language sources	Mastery of content knowledge

therefore not so much a question of whether to go for CBI or not, but rather how and to what extent. As the differences between the various CBI models were relatively large, we carefully judged each model on its pros and cons, so as to be able to choose the most appropriate model for each program. First of all, we had to decide whether we wanted full integration (immersion) or separate, but linked language classes. If we were to go for the first option, would we adopt immersion for a whole four-year program or for only parts of it, that is to say, one or more PBL blocks? If so, how many blocks, and which ones, would then be a minimum choice? And if we were to keep separate language classes, how should we integrate them with the PBL blocks? Should we link to the individual tasks within a block, to the theme of the block as a whole, to the projects that form part of these blocks? Should we also incorporate foreign language assignments in blocks that did not have any language courses linked to them?

Bearing in mind Stryker and Leaver (1997)'s remark, quoted above, that 'there is no singular formula for CBI,' it should not therefore come as a surprise that now, three years later, Breda Business School has examples of (variants of) at least 3 CBI models, which have all come up with their own answers to the questions posed in this section. It is, however, beyond the scope of this paper to describe each one of them. Instead, in the remaining part of this paper we will concentrate on some of the innovations made to the language courses within International Business School Breda, as these have been evaluated most extensively.

4. IMPLEMENTING CBI IN INTERNATIONAL BUSINESS SCHOOL BREDA

4.1 The Year 1 English, French, and German language Courses

In 1999, Content-Based foreign language Instruction (CBI) was introduced as the new instructional model for all the language courses within the four-year, English-language IBMS program, with the exception of Dutch and Spanish. There was little sense in linking the Dutch courses to PBL blocks, because their main objective was to help non-Dutch students to survive in the daily practice of living in the Netherlands. Spanish was not linked to the PBL blocks either, on account of research evidence suggesting that students needed to have a certain minimum proficiency level to be successful in CBI courses (Stryker & Leaver, 1997).

The Year 1 English, French, and German language courses were the first to be innovated. As English was used as the medium of instruction for the PBL blocks, the English courses were linked to them in the form of Adjunct courses, their primary objectives being to help students to master content material and develop transferable academic skills. On the other hand, German and French were based on the Subsidiary Content Model, their primary objective being to help students to master the content material by using related subject matter.

For reasons of personnel and organization, this new language model was not formally evaluated at the end of the academic year 1999/2000. In the following academic year, however, this evaluation did take place (Ruijten, 2001). The purpose was to evaluate the content and form of the language courses so as to assess the effectiveness of the CBI model. The three main research questions were:

- How well did the innovated language courses link up with the PBL courses?
- How well did the courses fit the functional needs of students of various linguistic backgrounds?
- How well did the courses stimulate a self-directed learning approach from the students?

4.1.1 Methodology

The evaluation was carried out in two rounds. The innovated English, French, and German courses of Quarters 1 and 2 were evaluated at the beginning of Quarter 3 (February 2001). The questionnaire we used was the same for all three languages and consisted of 30 closed questions, requiring responses on a five-point Likert scale, and 5 open questions. The closed questions were grouped into five areas: course content, course load, teacher, course materials, and course assessment.

For the evaluation of the courses of Quarters 3-4, a few adaptations were made to the questionnaire, the main change being the omission of the closed questions on the written examination, as the students were asked to fill in the questionnaire before the examination took place (end of Quarter 4, June 2001). This questionnaire therefore consisted of 27 closed questions and 4 open questions. By using (basically) the same written questionnaire, we were able to draw comparisons between the three languages and between those of Quarters 1-2 and those of Quarters 3-4.

The total Year 1 population consisted of 52 students at the start of the academic year: 36 Dutch students, 15 Chinese students and 1 Swedish student. The Dutch students enrolled from three different types of secondary education. Twenty-two students completed HAVO (senior general secondary education), 8 VWO (pre-university education), and 6 MBO (senior secondary vocational education). Appendix A provides more information on the Dutch educational system.

All these students were asked to fill out the questionnaire on English, while the Dutch and the Swedish students also had to fill out the questionnaire on either French or German, depending on the language they had chosen (19 students took French, 17 took German, and one took both French and German). As the Chinese students did not have French or German, they needed to fill out only the English questionnaire. During the year, 3 students dropped out, giving a total population of 49 students for the Quarter 3-4 questionnaire.

The response rate is shown in Table 2.

Table 2. Response Rate

	Quarter 1-2		Quarter 3-4	
	Number of Respondents	Response Rate (%)	Number of Respondents	Response Rate (%)
English	48	92	34	69
French	16	76	10	53
German	17	94	9	56

4.1.2 Results

It is beyond the scope of this paper to discuss all the evaluation results in detail. That's why we will focus on those results that are pertinent to the three main research questions posed earlier.

4.1.2.1 Research Question 1: How well did the innovated language courses link up with the PBL courses?

As Table 3 shows, students felt that the Q1-2 English and German language courses were poorly linked with the block courses; the Q1-2 French courses were more clearly linked. When these research findings became available, adaptations were made to the content of the Q3-4 courses of all three languages (a closer link with the blocks, more focus on business communication skills and less on grammar). As a result, students evaluated the Q3-4 courses much better than the Q1-2 courses. Even so, linking the courses to the block courses remained a subject of concern, as they appeared to have only limited success in helping students to understand the content courses, and vice versa.

Table 3. Link Between Language and PBL Courses

	English		French		German	
	Q1-2	Q3-4	Q1-2	Q3-4	Q1-2	Q3-4
5. The content of the two courses was clearly linked with the block courses.	2.3	3.1	3.3	3.5	1.8	2.6
6. The courses helped me to understand the block courses better.	2.1	2.4	2.4	2.5	1.5	1.9
7. The block courses helped me to understand the language courses better.	2.4	2.7	2.5	2.6	1.9	2.1
10. How would you rate the course content overall?	2.5	3.3	3.4	3.8	2.1	2.6

4.1.2.2 Research Question 2: How well did the courses fit the functional needs of students of various linguistic backgrounds?

The main finding in this respect was that students of various educational and linguistic backgrounds evaluated the fit between the language courses and their functional needs very differently. Not only was there a big difference between the Dutch and the Chinese students, but also among the Dutch students, as illustrated by Tables 4, 5, and 6.

Table 4. Fit Between English and Functional Needs at Subgroup Level

	Q	Dutch Students			Chinese Students	Total
		HAVO	VWO	MBO		
2. The content of the two courses was	1-2	2.0	2.8	2.5	3.0	2.5
interesting.	3-4	2.8	3.8	3.5	3.5	3.3
4. The content of the two courses	1-2	2.2	2.5	1.8	3.2	2.6
expanded and improved my knowledge of English.	3-4	2.8	3.2	2.5	3.9	3.3

The research findings served to corroborate the teachers' experience that the Year 1 student population was highly heterogeneous. The various groups of students all had different levels of proficiency and different types of language learning styles and needs. Clearly, the French courses fit the students' functional needs much better than the English and German courses, while the Q3-4 courses were more successful than the Q1-2 courses.

Table 5. Fit Between French and Functional Needs at Subgroup Level

	Q	Dutch Students			Total
		HAVO	VWO	MBO	
4. The content of the two courses expanded	1-2	3.1	4.5	-	3.2
and improved my knowledge of French.	3-4	3.3	4.0	-	3.5
12. The level of difficulty of the courses was	1-2	2.7	3.5	-	2.7
just right.	3-4	2.9	4.0	-	3.2

Table 6. Fit Between German and Functional Needs at Subgroup Level

	Q	Dutch Students			Total
		HAVO	VWO	MBO	
4. The content of the two courses expanded	1-2	1.6	2.0	1.8	1.8
and improved my knowledge of French.	3-4	1.8	2.7	3.0	2.3
12. The level of difficulty of the courses was	1-2	2.4	2.3	2.2	2.3
just right.	3-4	2.3	2.3	3.0	2.4

The adaptations made to the Q3-4 courses paid off in the sense that they increased students' interest in the language courses and led to a better performance.

4.1.2.3 Research Question 3: How well did the courses stimulate a self-directed learning approach from the students?

From the results of the questionnaire, the tentative conclusion was drawn that the innovated language courses had a positive effect on the students' participation in the learning process, moving from a passive to an active role, especially in Q3-4, as illustrated by Table 7. Being first-year students, they obviously needed some time to get used to the new approach to language learning and to understand what they were expected to do.

Table 7. Effect of Language Courses on Self-directed Learning Approach

	English		French		German	
	Q1-2	Q3-4	Q1-2	Q3-4	Q1-2	Q3-4
3. The content of the two courses stimulated me to work hard and regularly.	2.3	2.9	3.4	3.6	2.0	2.3
15. The teaching method used by the teacher was effective.	2.6	3.3	3.3	3.8	1.8	3.0
17. The teacher stimulated me to participate actively in classes.	3.1	3.6	3.4	4.0	2.7	3.1

5. LESSONS LEARNED

The results of our evaluation show that the implementation of Content-Based foreign language Instruction has been quite a difficult process. The innovated language courses obviously did not have the desired effect in at least two important aspects.

First of all, we clearly had problems striking the right balance between language and content learning objectives. From the comments of the students as well as the language staff, with whom the evaluation results were discussed, it appeared that both had the feeling that the language objectives were undermined by the content objectives. We feel, however, that achieving an optimum link between language courses and block courses is not the sole responsibility of the language teachers, but also of the content teachers. In our view, CBI is fundamentally different from traditional language programs, in the sense that it requires a degree of coordination between the content lecturers and the language staff that is highly unusual. They both have to give up part of their autonomy to fine tune their common objectives and select appropriate materials.

Secondly, because of the heterogeneity of the Year 1 student population, we did not fully succeed in making the program suitable to the needs of all the students. The original idea to have one undifferentiated model in which we expected from students a self-directed learning approach, especially to the subject and use of grammar, proved impracticable. Differences in the entrance level of students, especially in an international program like IBMS, with students of many different nationalities coming from highly different educational backgrounds, seem to require a well thought out transition period from the traditional language approach students are used to in their secondary schooling to the content based approach used in Breda Business School.

At the same time, however, we felt that we were definitely on the right track. The adaptations made to the Quarter 3-4 courses showed that efforts to design language courses that link up with content courses and fit students' language needs as well as possible do pay off. Just like problem-based learning, CBI is an innovation that is at once radical and gradual. It is something students and teachers alike have to get used to. Later innovations in our Business School, which we have not formally evaluated yet, seem to point in this direction, if we may believe the students' informal comments.

Finally, if you wish to implement CBI models there are a number of necessary preconditions.

5.1 Funds

Language staff and content staff have to meet before the joint development of CBI language courses can be initiated. The content staff will have to translate the learning objectives of their courses into accurate language products. The language staff will need time to get acquainted with the professional vocabulary and the basic knowledge of the subject concerned. After having done all this, they will need a substantial number of hours to develop new courses. After implementation, quarterly evaluation with both staffs is required as well as time to update the language courses. For if you choose to link the language courses with the fast changing content of, for example, Consumer Marketing, you need to bring in recent newspaper articles and research findings. Although funds are strongly related to the culture and the allocation models of the educational institutions, we believe that introducing CBI requires an investment of 25% extra funds on top of the actual funds spent on language courses and staff.

5.2 ICT facilities

Changing the scope and objectives of the language courses (*i.e.*, leaving grammar and vocabulary instruction to the individual needs and pace of the student) implies a change in educational material. Students will need computers and software programs for self-study and guidance. The Internet will also play a crucial role in the development and updating of the courses. Students should be enabled to use computers for their group or individual work, because CBI language courses result in language products for which they have to look for, share, and give feedback on information by means of reports, presentations, or e-mail correspondence.

5.3 Support from Management, Language Staff, and Content Staff

Although Breda Business School endorsed the choice for CBI, the senior management found it difficult to financially and organizationally facilitate CBI implementations. If a university decides to introduce such a large-scale innovation as CBI, you have to make it very clear from the very start what the financial and organizational consequences are.

Language teachers said ‘yes’ wholeheartedly, too; nevertheless, some of them tended to continue in the old way. Although it has been our experience that CBI is something teachers have to learn by doing, it would therefore, be advisable to provide some form of training to help language teachers to learn to adapt their approach to language teaching.

Finally, this also applies to the content teaching staff. They have to understand that they are responsible for the whole program in which they teach, not just for their own classes. CBI language courses are not something that only causes extra complications and extra work, but, instead, will definitely have a positive effect on the effectiveness of their content classes.

5.4 Expertise

The more knowledge language teachers have of the content core of the program in which they teach, the better able they are to integrate their courses with the core content courses.

5.5 Concluding Note

In summary, the introduction of CBI has been very worthwhile, even though we have not got it completely right yet. The value of the innovation, we believe, comes from the fruitful cooperation between language staff and content staff members to share responsibility for learning outcomes and the positive effect this interdisciplinary approach has on the students' (language) learning behavior. It is something we hope to learn by doing. It has been a radical change that we have been implementing gradually and will continue to do so.

AUTHOR'S NOTE

Since 2004, Hogeschool Brabant has changed its name to Avans Hogeschool after a merger with another institution for higher professional education. Avans Hogeschool now consists of 18 academies, one of which is the International School, offering the International Business and Management Studies program. Avans Hogeschool now provides education to nearly 20,000 students.

APPENDIX A: DUTCH EDUCATIONAL SYSTEM

Higher education in the Netherlands is offered at two types of institutions: universities of professional education (HBO) and research universities (WO). Hogeschool Brabant offers four-year courses at the HBO-level. Students are eligible for admission to HBO-courses if they have completed one of three types of secondary education:

- Senior secondary vocational education and training (MBO).
- Senior general secondary education (HAVO).
- Pre-university education (VWO).

Senior secondary vocational education and training (MBO) programs vary in length from one to four years as well as in level (1 to 4). Completion of MBO programs at level 4 qualifies students for access to HBO. HAVO is a five-year program and prepares students for higher professional education (HBO). VWO takes six years and is the minimum requirement for access to university (WO).

REFERENCES

Brinton, D. M., Snow, M. A., & Wesche, M. B. (1989). *Content-Based Second Language Instruction*, 1st ed. Boston: MA: Heinle & Heinle Publishers.

Broersma, J., & MacDonald, R. (1998, unpublished). *Developments in problem-based learning: The students' perceptions of their learning.* 10th Annual Conference of the European Association for International Education, Stockholm, Sweden.

Broersma, J., & MacDonald, R. (2000, unpublished). *Evaluating the student experience of PBL to improve the student experience of PBL.* 2nd International Conference on Problem-Based Learning in Higher Education, Linköping, Sweden.

Brouwers, M. P., & MacDonald, R. (1996, unpublished). *Transition from a subject-oriented to a theme-oriented curriculum.* 3rd International Educational Innovation in Economics and Business Conference, Orlando, FL.

Brouwers, M. P., & MacDonald, R. (1997, unpublished). *Alternative assessment methods in a problem based learning environment.* 4th International Educational Innovation in Economics and Business Conference, Edinburgh, Scotland.

Jochems, W., Rijns, Y., Smid, H. J., & Verweij, A. 1991. Onderwijs door middel van een vreemde taal, *TvHO*, *9* (3), 165-172.

Ruijten, R. (2000, unpublished). De Didactische Keuze van het Vreemde-Talenonderwijs van de Hogeschool Brabant FEM, Hogeschool Brabant, Breda, the Netherlands.

Ruijten, R. (2001, unpublished). Evaluation Year 1 Language Courses International Business and Management Studies program 2000/2001, Hogeschool Brabant, Breda, the Netherlands.

Stryker, S. B., & Leaver, B. L. (Eds.). 1997, *Content-Based Instruction in Foreign Language Education*, Washington, D.C.: 1st ed. Georgetown University Press.

Chapter 30

ANY PROBLEMS?

PBL Experience with First Year Business Undergraduates

Rysia Reynolds and Graham Benmore
Southampton Business School, Southampton Solent University, Southhampton, UK

1. INTRODUCTION

Within higher education it would appear that a consensus is emerging which suggests that traditional methods of teaching and assessment are failing to impart to students the skills and abilities that they need to be effective employees in the modern world. Most careers in the modern economy place considerable emphasis on the application of knowledge rather than mere possession of that knowledge. Thus, staff who work in higher education need to find means of promoting learning that equip their students with the ability and confidence to apply their knowledge in a variety of circumstances. Problem-based learning (PBL) has evolved within this context. It is based on the understanding that the range of qualities required by students includes individual hard skills such as the ability to communicate effectively, to have confidence in manipulating numbers, and to use modern tools of information technology. In addition to these hard skills, attributes desired of graduates include taking responsibility for one's own personal development, working with and for other people, and the ability to solve problems in a systematic way. It is the last attribute that is seen as particularly important for students in higher education since they are the people who are most likely to move into positions that will require them to develop innovative solutions to complex problems.

Why problem-based learning has spread both among disciplines and continents is generally explained by reference to the contrast it offers to more traditional teaching and learning practices that exist in higher education and its potential to deliver some of these desirable attributes. By

M.K. McCuddy et al. (eds.),
The Challenges of Educating People to Lead in a Challenging World, 599–619.

the time that students come to higher education many are set in their ways of learning and have already developed strategies for learning that are most comfortable and convenient for themselves. This chapter considers the PBL and enquiry-based learning (EBL) approach and outlines the changes introduced to the BA (Hons) in Human Resource Management at the Southampton Business School. It details the unit where EBL was first introduced and discusses, in the light of literature, the experiences of students and staff. Finally it looks at further developing this approach in the future.

2. WHY CONSIDER PBL/EBL?

Problem-based learning is being increasingly adopted within higher education. It is an approach that the course leader and members of the course team have investigated through literature, conference attendance, visits to other institutions, and membership of the Southampton Solent's PBL Interest group. The perceived benefits of this approach are reported as being:

- The student experience is enhanced because students are more involved with their learning.
- Independent learning is supported, as students need to undertake more research.
- Learning outcomes are met through PBL.
- Students improve skill acquisition through PBL and by implication these skills are sought by employers.
- Boud and Feletti (1998, p. 11) articulate the view that although PBL is not the solution to all curriculum design problems, "It is the most fully articulated and trialed alternative to traditional practices and it can provide a means of tackling some of the challenges of (education) which have appeared to date to have been quite intractable".

Schuell (1986, p. 49) offered the premise that effectively achieving desired outcomes relies on students engaging with the learning activities. Biggs (2001) postulates in his quality model that Schuell's premise is relevant to PBL. In order to achieve the desired outcomes, Biggs argues that through solving "…unseen problems" students will not only acquire the requisite knowledge, but also will have their understanding of that knowledge stretched in challenging situations.

Barrows (1986) identified the objectives of PBL within clinical disciplines. It is not to say that these cannot have a more general application to other disciplines. The first two objectives he identified could be generalized as structuring of subject specific knowledge and an effective reasoning process. The other two objectives are clearly generic and relate to the development of self-directed learning skills and increased motivation in learning.

Camp (1996) asserts that problem-based learning is more effective in getting students to learn, remember, apply and continue to learn beyond their formal education than the traditional methods. Woods (1995) is emphatic on the potential of PBL by stating that it is a learning environment that improves learning. Students are forced to learn the fundamentals of the subject and develop processing skills. He contends that PBL is about learning subject knowledge in the context of using and developing process skills.

When contemplating the introduction of a PBL curriculum, the needs of the students have to be addressed. As a result of students' previous learning experience it would appear that there is a general reluctance on the part of most students to actively participate in the learning process. Furthermore the focus on learning outcomes mitigates against learning anything that is not being assessed. Such attitudes are clearly incompatible with the actuality of problem-based learning and need to be addressed. Other limitations of PBL are also reported. When examining Boud's (1985) characteristics of what students actually do during PBL and Schwartz, Mennin, and Webb's (2001) analysis of student activities, it becomes apparent that many of these skills are not commonly possessed by new undergraduates and that, for example, 'to interact with others and to explore existing knowledge' would imply a level of maturity, confidence, and trust in colleagues, which are relatively rare among those having recently left school. Crux Consulting (2000) echoes these reservations. Crux Consulting also suggests that immature students have few clear goals, other than gaining grades and certificates and therefore find PBL frustrating. MacDonald (2001) acknowledges this but also implies that the skills required for students to use PBL effectively can be learned 'on-the-job.'

Allen and Rooney (1998) highlight the need for a shift in student, faculty and staff assumptions about the tutor's role as lecturer to the tutor's role as a provider of constructive feedback in order to facilitate the success of PBL. Little (1998) reported on the results of action research where he identified a range of important factors determining implementation of PBL, including an acceptance of the role change, the ability to model process skills, and an understanding that students will need time to change their assumptions about learning.

3. PBL/EBL—WHAT IS THE DIFFERENCE?

This chapter reflects on first-year experience with a particular focus on the "HRM in Context" unit which was delivered for the first time during 2002/2003 using an approach we refer to as enquiry-based learning (EBL) approach. We define *enquiry-based learning as similar to problem-based learning, an approach that has been long used in many medical and business schools*. However, in our view, PBL focuses on *getting students used to finding solutions to problems* whereas *enquiry-based learning is concerned with investigating phenomena or topics or issues rather than a problem*. In attempting to unravel whether this method of teaching and learning can be considered as falling within the realm of PBL, a number of definitions of PBL were examined and it was found that this approach to teaching and learning was encompassed within these definitions.

Boud (1985) noted that developments in PBL drew on a number of ideas in addition to problem-centeredness, the most important of these being student-centeredness. He identifies eight characteristics of many problem-based courses, which include an emphasis on students taking responsibility for their own learning and a focus on the process of knowledge acquisition. These characteristics are reflected in the approach that we have been using. In his analysis of PBL, Edens (2000, p. 55) argues that all in higher education face a challenge to teach students to link theory with practice and to solve problems in a professional manner. To achieve this, the learning environment has to be redefined to one where students' are active in constructing knowledge and are actively engaged in collaborative inquiry and problem solving. Edens thus incorporates inquiry, as does Woods (2002) who sees PBL as any learning environment in which the problem drives the learning. The problem is therefore posed so that the students need to learn some new knowledge to solve the problem. The key point here, according to Woods (2002), is that the problem is posed before learning takes place. This, not only hands the ownership of the learning process over to the students, but also acts as a significant motivator. In essence, PBL is student-centered and faculty-facilitated. The tasks and issues given to our students were posed to stimulate them to consider what they needed to learn and to undertake that learning prior to resolving the issue, an approached arguably encompassed within PBL.

Savin-Baden (2000, p. 3) makes a clear distinction between problem-solving learning and problem-based learning. She believes that misunderstandings of PBL have resulted in an underestimation of its value in equipping students for a complex and changing professional life and the opportunities that can be gained through it to improve student learning. It can therefore be argued, as Savin-Baden concedes, that PBL is not about solving problems but it is about is an approach to learning that is affected by the structural and pedagogical environment into which it is placed, in terms of the discipline or subject, the organization, and the staff concerned. It is such an approach that was indeed used in the HRM in Context unit, and the terms PBL and EBL are used interchangeably. On the basis that PBL and EBL can be used interchangeably, the aim of this study is to investigate whether, in the experience of students and staff, the perceived benefits of PBL are being achieved.

The expectation is that subsequent to this study the course team will use the indicators listed below in order to continue to evaluate the extent of perceived benefits. These indicators are based on the sources of feedback available to course leaders in the course evaluation and monitoring process.

- Monitoring the effectiveness of the Personal and Professional Development and HRM in Context units at level one.
- Students' first time pass rates, mark distribution, and trailing unit rates (*i.e.*, the existences of outstanding units from the previous year/s which the students have not managed to pass).
- External examiner reports.
- Student feedback questionnaires on course and unit.
- Student feedback at course management meetings and student representative meetings.
- Annual course report.
- Quality Assurance Agency (QAA) visit.
- Unit reviews and reports.
- Teaching and learning projects, at Southampton Solent University and Business School.

4. THE CONTEXT

4.1 The Course

Southampton Business School (SBS) is one of the largest business schools in the United Kingdom. The School of Management is located within the Business School and consists of two subject groups: Strategic Management and Human Resource Management. The Human Resource Management subject group has academic and managerial responsibility for the BA (Hons) Human Resource Management, BA (Hons) International Business, Post-Graduate Certificate and Diploma in Personnel and Development, MA Human Resource Management, and MA Personnel and Development. The unit discussed in this paper is within the BA (Hons)

Human Resource Management. In line with the shift in philosophy in higher education in general, Southampton Business School subscribes to the paradigm that students should no longer be passive recipients of knowledge but should be active participants in their own learning. The School has therefore reviewed the delivery of the BA (Hons) Human Resource Management to incorporate units that are conveyed through PBL.

The BA (Hons) Human Resource Management was originally validated in 1994 and reviewed in 1997. The 1997 revalidation aimed to provide a vocationally oriented course with emphasis on the students' ability to analyze, evaluate, and apply theoretical concepts within the context of business and society. As a result of changes in the external environment, the course team felt it was appropriate to re-examine the degree during 2000/2001 to reflect changes within the HRM field. Such a review provided the opportunity to reconsider the content and delivery of the curriculum and to implement a hybrid curriculum that includes PBL. PBL had been adopted in a few business education courses within higher education in the UK, but not in the undergraduate human resource management programs. Thacker (2002) implemented a broadly similar approach to the one that we decided to introduce at Southampton Solent University. Thacker introduced a project-based action learning approach, involving real organizations, where students have to gather information, discover what they do not know, and collaborate with each other to arrive at a solution.

In undertaking these reflections (or course review) the course team, which consists of the course leader and the unit (module) leaders, decided to increase the focus on skill preparation and student learning in the first year. The team therefore introduced a Personal and Professional Development unit at this level that built on the previous Business Communications unit; it encompassed more study skills and group development skills in order to help students develop both as independent learners and team members. The Human Resources in Context unit, upon which this paper is based, aims to provide students with a broad-based background to the study of human resources and gives them an opportunity to apply some of the new skills through PBL/EBL. The overall philosophy of the course team was to prepare students early for the challenge of the degree as well as providing the foundation for 'lifelong learning' and 'knowledge based work.' In order to achieve this, the course team also diverted an additional 48 hours of class contact to the first year and a further 30 hours of directed study. An increased emphasis on Research Methods in the second year, and the introduction of Contemporary HR Issues and an addition of 20 Credit Accumulation Transfer (CAT) points to the dissertation, which is now equivalent to one third of the final year's marks, characterize the changes to the later years of the degree. The team intends that among other changes,

Contemporary HR Issues and Work Psychology will be delivered through PBL/EBL.

The degree offers two pathways that give students the opportunity to either specialize further in an aspect of HRM or to diversify into broader areas of interest, these being the BA (Hons) HRM with Management of Change and the BA (Hons) HRM with Business Psychology. The course team was committed to the enhancement of student learning as a central philosophy and issues relating to learning, teaching, and assessment are primarily the responsibility of the course and unit teams. As well as directing more resources to the first year, the course team had extensive discussions and development sessions on PBL and EBL and decided to embed this approach to learning in a number of units.

4.2 Unit Design and Delivery

At the simplest level, the contrast between the traditional format of university education and a more progressive approach such as PBL lies in the notion of the student being a passive receptor of knowledge as implied by the traditional format, or the student being an active participant in a learning process as implied by the progressive approach. Perhaps this describes the qualitative difference between the modern usage of the terms "teaching" and "learning" to the extent that in "teaching" it is the teacher who is active and in "learning" it is the student who is active. Moreover, it is the issue of responsibility that underlies this distinction in that "teaching" implies that the responsibility for the outcomes of the teaching process lies with the teacher. In contrast, our use of the word "learning," as for example in the term "life-long learning," implies that the responsibility is shifted to the learner. Within this context the unit information issued to students stated that we were attempting to equip them with the skills necessary to enable them to make a contribution to organizations that are operating in uncertain times, and that the focus of the unit is always on the process of activities rather than the content. In other words, the emphasis is on undertaking tasks rather than listening and remembering.

The unit was organized around six HRM issues, which were: the historical development of HRM, the employment relationship, individual differences, organizational cultures, employee well-being, and managing people effectively. Students tackled all issues by working tasks that required them to investigate these topics within the context of small groups. The topics were addressed through a four-week cycle and guidance was given for each assignment. Introductory materials were issued when students first encountered the task. There was no other prior preparation provided for the area of the study encompassed by the issue. During the first week, students formed small groups and were given some direction as to which resources to access. In weeks two and three, group work took place with staff available to facilitate meetings. Work was submitted at the end of week three with feedback and review in week four. The format of the submission differed on each occasion and varied from the production of a collage to the presentation of a scripted drama. Each piece of work was evaluated with assessment criteria that were related to the issue being addressed.

In addition to the six tasks, students were required to keep reflective diaries where they were encouraged to think about their learning and identify strengths and weaknesses. Students were encouraged to develop creative skills and to use a variety of formats in their creative diaries. The unit design encouraged students to go through the same process as described by Schwartz, Mennin, and Webb (2001) regarding what students actually do while working with a problem. This included encountering the problem 'cold,' without undertaking any preparatory study and interacting with each other to explore their existing knowledge in relation to the issue. Having done that, students had to form and test hypotheses, identify further learning needs, undertake self-study between group meetings to satisfy the identified learning needs, and return to the group to integrate newly gained knowledge and to apply it. Reflection on the process and the content were undertaken through reflective diaries.

Staff expectations of the HRM in Context unit reflected some of Schwartz *et al.*'s (2001) process; staff expressed their goals as:

- Helping students to develop into independent learners by encouraging them to enjoy taking responsibility for their own learning through the exploration of existing knowledge and by equipping them with the skills to be able to do so.
- Encouraging students to develop self-study skills so as to become creative thinkers who are comfortable with ambiguity and able to think of innovative solutions to problems. Increasingly organizations report that they are seeking employees who are capable of 'thinking outside of the box' and this aim was included with this contextual factor in mind.
- Encouraging students to become skilled at assessing their own strengths and weaknesses through reflection.
- Enabling students to become effective team workers through interactions with each other.

It was apparent that these aims would be harder to achieve through the single unit whose philosophy they represent than if they reflected the ethos of the whole course. However, as indicated earlier, there are particular reasons why the course is only partially EBL in nature and so we were aware that the ways of working in the HRM in Context unit might be quite different to the practices adopted in others.

The assessment of the unit consisted of each piece of work relating to a particular issue being weighted at 10%, totaling 60%. The reflective diaries contributed the remaining 40% to the overall mark of the unit. The methods of assessment are an issue within PBL. In deciding on the format of assessment, the unit team was informed by some of the issues raised in PBL literature; for example, those raised by Major and Palmer (2001, p. 4). They argue that PBL poses some unique challenges for assessment in that traditional methods such as examinations may not be effective. They go on to identify principles of good assessment, which include: having a clear idea of what the students are expected to achieve, comparing educational goals and expectations with performance, and assessing on a continuous rather than a summative basis. Reynolds (1997, p. 272), in discussing the requirement for students to produce an authentic product in degree-level Psychology using PBL, states that, "Assessment needs to fit the philosophy of active learning." Woods (1995, Section 5.12), who reviewed a variety of methods of assessment, also uses, as part of the coursework, journals that are marked by tutors.

5. METHODOLOGY

The research that is reported here is part of a longer study that aims to explore the student\tutor experience with a wider range of PBL/EBL units in this particular degree program. Perhaps the most interesting data will be obtained when students have finished their degree and reflection upon the complete experience will be possible with the gathering of course monitoring data.

The thinking behind our approach to both the whole research program, and this initial stage of it, is essentially that of an interpretivist (Saunders, Lewis, & Thornhill, 2003) or phenomenological (Collis & Hussey, 2003) nature as we are interested in probing the detail of how students and tutors perceive the EBL experience. Most of the data are therefore of a qualitative nature, taking the form of written and spoken statements. However, the qualitative data are complemented by quantitative survey data that were gathered in order to gauge general patterns in the thinking of student participants.

Our research was conducted between two cohorts of students who studied this unit. The first group from 2002/2003 was comprised of a sample of 11 students from a group of 18; the second group from 2003/2004 contained 18 responses from 29 students. All of the students, except two who were more mature, were aged between 18-25 and were embarking upon their first year in higher education. Most had come directly from secondary education but a significant proportion (20%) had worked for at least one year. An EBL approach to learning was unfamiliar to all but one of the students at the outset of the course.

Four different data collection methods were used in this research: student surveys, student focus groups, extracts from students' reflective diaries, and tutor interviews. The survey asked 16 questions and enabled us to identify general views and collect further short statements of opinion. The issues that the survey investigated included the students' understanding of the objectives of EBL, their perceptions of the effectiveness of learning, and their views on assessment and group work. The 30-minute focus group sessions consisted of seven or eight students and were conducted by an independent trained focus group facilitator. They were recorded on video and gave students an opportunity to discuss in depth the issues associated with their experience of EBL. We obtained permission to extract data from the reflective diaries completed by students as part of their unit assessment. This proved to be a very rich source of information and we discovered some very detailed commentaries on the EBL learning experience. Finally, tutor views were sought in brief (20-minute) interviews. These combined methods enabled us to gather some rich and detailed data from which we were able to gain interesting insights into the EBL experience from both student and tutor perspectives.

Among the issues that students and tutors were asked to consider were: the effectiveness of the EBL unit in developing independent learning skills and understanding of subject material; the nature of the group work experience; the perceived fairness of assessment methods; and the strengths and weaknesses of the EBL unit. Using four different research methods enabled us to accumulate a considerable amount of data for analysis. As the EBL program and tutor team for both cohorts of students was the same and the data provided by each cohort was not substantially different, we have therefore not distinguished between the two in our analysis. We hope that by doing so we have been able to present our findings in a way that is not unnecessarily complicated.

We looked for key themes in the qualitative data that appeared to be featured most frequently and powerfully in the written and spoken detail. Clearly, we made subjective choices about what we thought these were but we accept this as a weakness with most interpretivist research. Hence, we used 'informal methods' (Collis & Hussey, 2003, pp. 254-255) to identify these themes by searching for the 'clustering of ideas' (Miles & Huberman, 1994, pp. 248-250) which could be translated into 'meaning units' Cresswell, 1998, p. 150). Following Silverman (2000, p. 145), we sought regularities, patterns, and explanations to 'make sense of our data.' We would have ideally liked the time to have involved the research participants in the analysis of the qualitative data as practiced by some postmodern researchers such as Boje (1994) and Kilduff and Mahra (1997) but hope to make use of this technique at a later stage in our research program. The quantitative data was handled by converting student responses into some simple tables and diagrams that reflect overall percentage results.

6. WHAT WE FOUND

Here we review some of the quantitative and qualitative data generated from our research. Some of the quantitative data gives an insight into the student's perception of their learning experience. The survey findings provided a trigger for further exploration through qualitative research and are discussed under the themes identified from qualitative research. Some illustrative statements made by students and tutors have been included. The students have been identified by numerical codes (1-30) and the tutors by the letters (A) and (B). Twenty-nine students from the two cohorts responded to the questionnaires. The results indicate that 82% of students felt that PBL was clearly explained. As Figure 1 illustrates, the most prevalent student response (76%) considered that one of main objectives of this method of teaching and learning was to get people to work in teams; a additional 55% of responses saw it as an aid to student understanding.[47]

The data derived from the focus group sessions, reflective diaries, and tutor interviews generated three principal themes. The issues that these themes embrace occurred with most frequency within the data and were also signaled as the most significant.

6.1 Working with Others

The first theme concerns the emphasis within the unit upon working with others. As indicated in Figure 1, this was the most popular response in relation to the perceived objective of PBL/EBL. The focus groups and reflective diaries clearly indicated that many students enjoyed working with their peers and welcomed the opportunities to get to know each other better at the outset of their course. This remained true for several individuals even when particular group dynamics presented challenges. So, for example, one student commented that she had benefited from 'working with others that I

[47] Respondents could choose more than one option.

wouldn't choose to' (student 22). Benefits were variously reported as including fun, building effective working relationships, feeling more confident and sharing ideas to develop better responses to assignment questions. Examples of statements reflecting these views include:

- "I do very much enjoy working in groups. I like being around people and feel it can be an excellent way of producing work" (student 9).
- "…I built a sound relationship with my fellow course mates which I feel is extremely helpful and important as it allowed us to help each other out in other modules" (student 8).

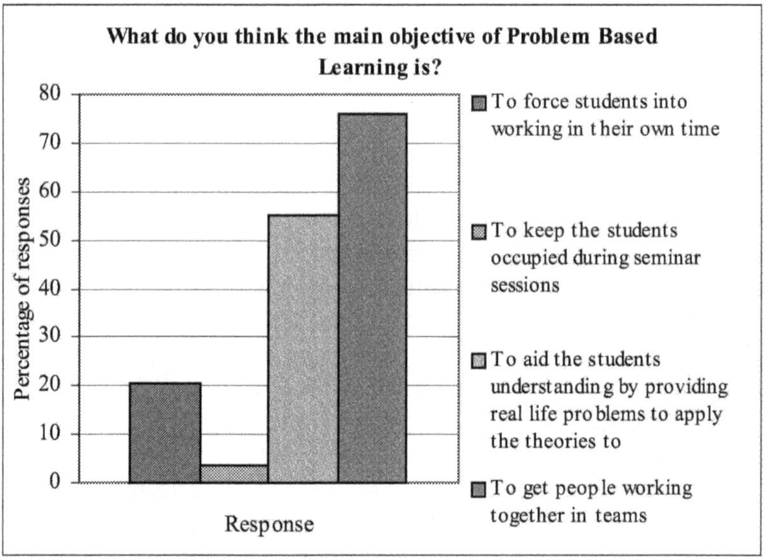

Figure 1. Main Objectives of Problem-Based Learning

Beyond this, some students reported that they also enjoyed working with their tutors in a more participative way and felt that the EBL approach engendered a more relaxed learning environment that helped to develop confidence. The tutors also saw this as a benefit and felt that it was possible to get to know more about student perspectives by working in this format.

However, working in groups also gives rise to many tensions and these were also reported. A minority of students surveyed (20%) thought this form of learning was less effective than other units. Of these students, 55% identified difficulties with group work as the chief barrier to effectiveness followed by lack of guidance. The principal issue arising out of the focus groups and reflective diaries concerned perceptions of unequal contributions from group members towards the assignment work; this engendered feelings of discontentment and irritation if groups were given the same mark for an assignment (which was usually the case). This, of course, is a recurrent concern for students who are required to work in group situations and so it was no surprise that it arose in our data. Most students referred directly to this issue including student (4) for whom the only downside of group work was 'if you got stuck with one of the lazy and bad attendees.' Also, student (3) recognized that 'there are certain class members that aren't so bothered about getting a high grade.' The problem of inequity is always going to be difficult to resolve, particularly at a time when the customer culture continues to make inroads into the HE sector. Perhaps a possible way forward here would be to engage students in self-assessment — a suggestion offered by both of the unit tutors.

6.2 Independent Learning

The second issue to emerge from our research was the scope that EBL facilitates for independent or self-learning. As illustrated in Figure 2, when students were asked about skill development through PBL/EBL, the most frequently identified skill was collaboration (86%) and the lesser identified skills were exploration of new knowledge (62%), integrating/synthesizing new knowledge (50%), and independent learning (50%).

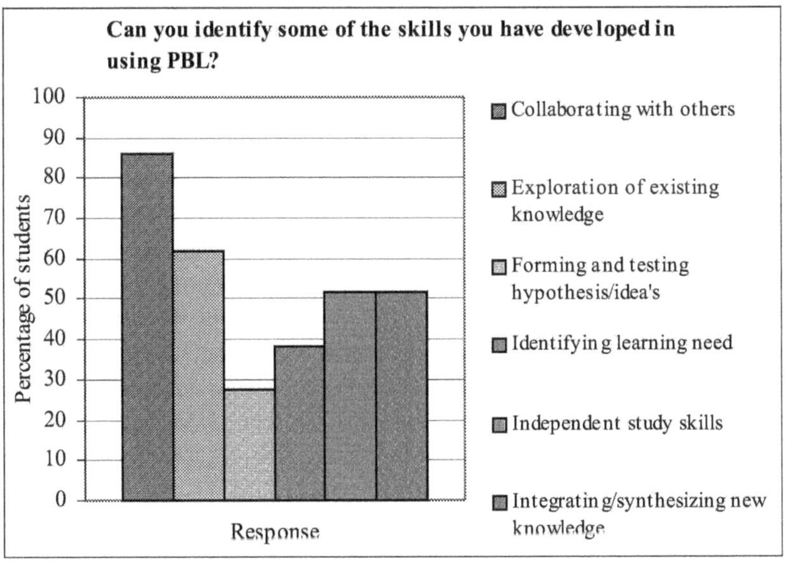

Figure 2. PBL Skills Identified

This quantitative result is supported by the qualitative data, as many students remarked that this unit enhanced learning because the responsibility for finding information was placed with them. One student suggested that it was preferable not to be 'spoon-fed' (student 25), while another stated that self-learning meant that knowledge 'sticks in your head better' (student 17). A further observation argued that the opportunities for learning through EBL were perhaps greater than through traditional approaches: "We were forced to go out and ensure that we understood the topics. Having lectures doesn't always mean we understand everything" (student 19).

6.3 Greater Potential for Learning

The tutors similarly indicated that EBL offered greater potential for learning. Tutor (A) contended that EBL was rather similar to dissertation work where the onus for achieving learning outcomes was transferred from the lecturer to the student. This served to heighten motivation and interest. Indeed, in our survey sample overall 61% of the students reported better motivation in this unit than in others that they studied. A number of students also observed that the EBL unit offered plenty of potential for learning because the assignment tasks were like real life situations and offered opportunities to use creativity (deliberately encouraged on the basis that increasingly creative thinking is seen as a critical precursor to organizational change). This view is reinforced with the result that 82% of the surveyed students perceived the assessment as fair. Of the 18% who considered assessment as unfair, issues relating to group work were again cited by 67% who said it was because their marks depended on others in the group. A further 33% (two students) cited the reason for unfairness as being having more work to do than in other units.

Many of the tasks did require the completion of practical activities such as writing a newspaper article on a current industrial relations dispute, or the use of creative skills, as in the completion of a collage, to depict the historical development of human resource management. Clearly, such tasks required the application of theoretical knowledge, but the opportunity to demonstrate knowledge in practical and creative formats was found to be both more relevant and enjoyable by many students. However, it must be acknowledged that this view, although popular, was not universal; a minority of students expressed concern that their natural inclination was not to be creative and so they struggled with this aspect of the work.

6.4 Process or Content?

Our third principal finding concerned the debate that EBL continues to fuel as to whether curricula should focus upon process or content. The move towards the former within HE is not without resistance. This was demonstrated by several comments made by students. Examples include:

- "Is it really possible to pass a course without learning any of the core material?" (student 6).
- "Although I have really enjoyed this unit I feel a bit disappointed that I haven't learnt as much about HRM in content as I would have liked" (student 11).
- "The only thing that I feel was a problem is the fact that I don't think I've learnt anything apart from how to present things" (student 3).

These statements endorse the traditional notion that learning essentially requires an understanding of a specific body of knowledge and that a focus upon the process of learning merely facilitates the development of skills. This thinking can only be challenged with evidence that the ability to find relevant information is more useful than the absorption of knowledge. It was difficult for tutors to achieve this on the Level 1 of the HRM degree where only the HRM in Context unit was delivered through EBL. Both unit tutors strongly contended that the EBL philosophy needed to extend over a significant part of the Level 1 program rather than be confined to just a small proportion of the course, as was envisaged when the degree was revalidated in 2002. The reiteration of the philosophy across the course would enable the rationale for EBL to be reinforced and provide further opportunities for evidence to emerge about the benefits it entails.

Notwithstanding the difficulty of promoting the advantages of EBL through one solitary unit, it was still possible for some students to perceive them. Figure 3 illustrates the students' responses when they were asked to summarize the unit in one word. Interestingly, the responses were evenly split between 41% of students who perceived the unit as either motivating or encouraging (23% and 18% respectively) and a further 41% who found the unit frustrating.

The views expressed in the focus groups and dairies were, however, much more positive. Comments have included the following:

- 'I have very much enjoyed this course (unit).
- 'I feel that I have learnt a lot, my creativity skills have definitely developed and I feel much more confident in using these skills.'
- 'I like the way that it is different to (*sic*) other subjects in that we do not just sit around and listen but we have to get very much involved in each assignment. For this reason I have found many of the

assignments fun and enjoyable but still feel that I have learnt a lot about the subject' (student 1).

These seemingly contrary views appear to suggest that students have found this both an enjoyable and, at times, a frustrating experience — possibly due to having to work in an unfamiliar territory and deal with ambiguity.

In this discussion we have reviewed the three major themes that emerged from our research. We have tried to show as many examples as possible while leaving space for discussion of some of the implications these results entailed. There has not been the space here to consider some of the subsidiary issues that surfaced through our research. These included the value of reflection, opportunities to learn about oneself and others, approaches to assessment, and the role of tutors in the EBL process. However, as we have indicated, this research represents the early stages of a longer project. We hope to explore the student/tutor experience on further EBL units located on subsequent levels of the HRM degree and so build a more detailed picture of the issues associated with this approach to learning and teaching.

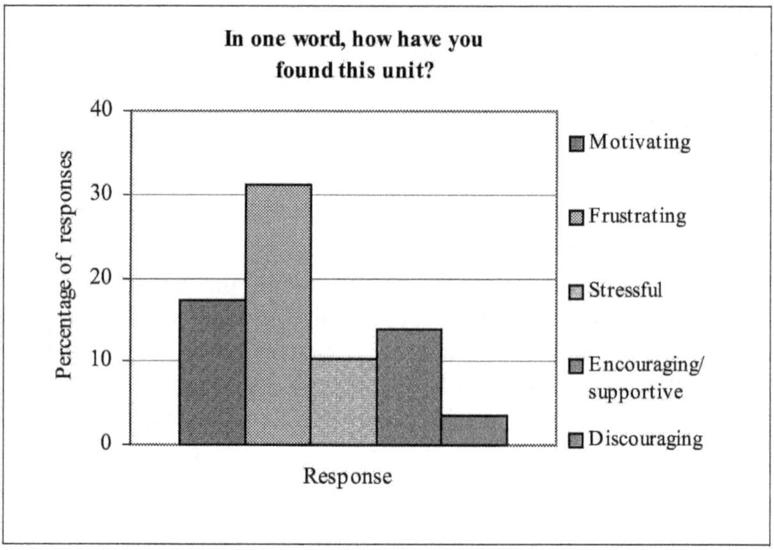

Figure 3. Perceptions of the Unit

7. WHAT WE LEARNED?

Although students seemed to be largely aware of some of the purposes of PBL/EBL, the most popular response in terms of the objectives of PBL was 'to get people working together in teams.' The staff saw cooperation as a technique through which other objectives, which aid student understanding and help develop a range of skills, would be achieved; cooperation was not seen as the principal goal. This suggests that as we move towards delivering more EBL/PBL units, staff have to be aware of these differences in perceptions and ensure that students are cognizant that group work is aimed at enhancing their learning experience and, therefore, is a means to an end and not the end itself. Having said that, as our findings indicate, students, on the whole, enjoyed the experience and found the environment more conducive to learning. The majority also concurred with the goals articulated by staff in that they perceived the main objective as being an aid to understanding. When Woods (1995) analyzed the potential of PBL he embraced active cooperation as a principle that improves learning. In relation to this analysis, students had clearly been working in an environment of active cooperation and had developed many of the processing skills that Woods identified, such as problem-solving, interpersonal, and group and team skills. It could therefore be argued that although students saw the main purpose of the EBL unit as group work, they had in fact developed generic skills that are essential to successful problem solving.

The difficulties that a minority of students had with teamwork seem to support the observation of Crux Consulting (2000) that students who lack maturity are looking for certificates rather than knowledge. Indeed, the two more mature students in the group thought they had gained the most from this approach. The focus that students place on assessment also contributed to this problem; and it does seem that peer assessment would, at least to some extent, mitigate against these difficulties.

As reported in the findings, many students perceived the purpose of PBL/EBL to be learning the fundamental principles of the subject and thereby achieving the learning outcomes, a perspective that is consistent with that of Woods (1995). The concerns regarding lack of content gave opposing views. It may well be that they had gained depth of understanding of a few topics and issues at the expense of breadth of knowledge. Alternatively, if, as Boud (1985, cited in Savin-Baden, 2000, pp. 17-18) outlined, the focus is on "...the process of knowledge acquisition rather than the product of such process," then our objectives have been achieved.

One of the objectives of the team was to foster independent learning in students. Half the students recognized independent learning as a skill they had acquired; others acknowledged that their learning had been enhanced, and the use of terms such as 'self-learning' and not 'spoon-fed' indicated that independent learning had largely taken place. Some students also reported that they had developed specific skills such as how to address the tasks set and how to access information. They had, in the main, accepted responsibility, not only for their own learning, but also for the learning of others. In this way we feel that they are well on the road to independence. In the words of one of the students: 'I think they have done it quite well and it will help next year.'

(Student 3) further acknowledges that students recognize that they have gained skills that will help them to deal with future challenges. It was interesting to note that only a minority of students identified the forming and testing of hypotheses as a skill that they had enhanced as a result of their experience on this unit. This concurs with Schwartz's (2001) assertion that it is difficult to imagine young undergraduates being able to 'form and test hypotheses.' MacDonald (2001) makes similar points and implies that the skills required for students to use PBL can be learned while they are taking part. However, Allen and Rooney (1998) emphasize that students and faculty need to adjust to this facilitating style. Similarly Woods (1995) offers a guide for a weeklong preparatory course for students about to embark on their first experience with PBL. Although we anticipated this problem and attempted to prepare students for EBL through the Personal and Professional Development unit, the two units run concurrently and it may be beneficial to have a longer preparatory period before embarking on EBL tasks.

The format of assessment generally fit well with the principles of PBL in that it followed the principles outlined by Major and Palmer (2001) and Reynolds (1997). Assessment reflected the philosophy of active learning and students were required to make an authentic product related to the issue and to make judgments on their performance through their diaries. The tutors, as noted in their reflections, are reviewing the exact format of assessment and have reduced the number of assessment tasks for 2004/2005. This will be evaluated at the end of the appropriate academic year.

The positive overall comments that students made on the unit in the reflective diaries and during the focus group discussions are tempered by the 41% of students who reported that they found the experience frustrating. This reported frustration seems to be linked to the difficulties that first-year undergraduates have with ambiguity, as noted by MacDonald (2001) and Woods (1995), and the issues of all members equally contributing to group work. It also again highlights the process versus content debate; some students seem to be critical of their acquisition of subject content, but fully aware of the skills they had acquired as part of the process and the frustrations that had arisen in completing their assessment tasks.

Nevertheless, the vast majority of students had successfully completed their assessed tasks — thus, their learning outcomes — and had reported the acquisition and integration of knowledge as some of the skills they had acquired. This contradictory view can perhaps be explained by the students' subjective view of their experience; in the past they had only been exposed to the 'transmission' of knowledge which, for the first time, was being challenged. It is hoped that further exposure to PBL/EBL units will heighten awareness of the benefits of this method of learning.

Since this study is part of a longer project we acknowledge that its scope is limited both in relation to the number of students and its focus on one unit. The response rate to the survey (60%) could also have been improved upon had the questionnaires been distributed on a number of occasions in the course of a week or two rather than just on one day, as was the case. The interpretivist nature of three methods of data collection is by its nature accompanied by an element of subjectivity. There may also have been some hesitation on the part of the students in being overly critical in the reflections entered into their diaries as this formed part of their unit assessment.

8. THE NEXT STEP

We will continue with our evaluation of this unit and the course as it progresses and as the students experience more EBL/PBL in units at levels two and three. Since completing this research, one more unit is being delivered via EBL with two further units planned for 2005/2006 academic year at levels two and three. The unit team of the HR in Context unit is also currently implementing some of the proposed changes discussed in this paper and we plan to evaluate these later in the 2004/2005 academic year.

The first years' experience on this unit has nevertheless gone some way towards achieving its stated aims in that students had worked cooperatively and were, on the whole, more involved with their learning. There was evidence of greater opportunities for self-learning and independent learning, as well as conspicuous evidence of skill acquisition. The research reported in this paper has also highlighted a number of issues that have led us to consider further refinements.

In order to ensure that students are aware of the link between the skills developed in the Personal and Professional Development unit and those used in the HRM in Context unit, we propose that greater emphasis be placed in the Personal and Professional Development unit on the role it plays in preparing students for learning through EBL/PBL. Staff who teach this unit are aware that they are preparing students for the EBL approach and of the course philosophy. Nevertheless, as we work towards introducing this way of learning more comprehensively throughout the HRM course, further staff development would be a means of continuing to raise awareness of the benefits and problems encountered by students.

Spending more time during induction and the first week/s in preparing students for EBL is an additional way forward that is likely to mitigate against the difficulties and frustrations some students experienced with group work. Assessment issues were also raised in relation to workload and notions of 'fairness' related to group work. Our recommendation aimed at overcoming these problems is to review the number of tasks and the format of assessment and to give consideration to peer assessment. Providing students with a more comprehensive resource package, and reinforcing the relative importance of process and content, should provide students with a clearer vision of outcomes and improve their awareness of their achievements in terms of knowledge and skills. We anticipate that as other EBL/PBL units come on-stream we will not only further explore the student/tutor experience, thus building a more detailed picture of the issues linked to this approach, but also will use the indicators identified in section 3 of this chapter in order to benchmark student performance against the 'traditional' approach to teaching and learning. We hope that we will continue to extend this philosophy as further research and experience provides additional knowledge of the issues and implications associated with EBL. Ultimately, we would like to be in a position to deliver the whole course through EBL and PBL units. However, to achieve this aim we require the full staff, student, and institutional support.

In conclusion, we believe that we have made some inroads in equipping our students for the roles that they will face in the modern economy in that they will be better able to apply their knowledge in a variety of circumstances. This, in turn, will enable them to make a valuable contribution to the challenges that they will face as professionals.

ACKNOWLEDGEMENT

The authors would like to thank David Saxon, Senior Lecturer at Southampton Solent University for his contribution and thoughts.

REFERENCES

Allen, R., & Rooney, P. (1998). Designing a problem-based learning environment for ESL students in business communication. *Business Communication Quarterly, 61* (2), 48-55.

Barrows, H. (1986). A taxonomy of problem learning methods, *Medical Education. 20* (6), 481-486.

Biggs, J. (2001). The reflective institutions: Assuring and enhancing the quality of teaching and learning. *Higher Education. 41* (3), 221-238.

Boje, D. (1994). Organizational storytelling: The struggles of premodern, modern and postmodern organizational learning discourses. *Management Learning, 25* (3), 433-61.

Boud, D. (1985). *Problem-based Learning in Education for Professions.* Sydney: Higher Education Research and Development Society of Australasia.

Boud, D., & Feletti, G. (1998). Changing problem-based learning. In D. Boud & G. Feletti (Eds.), *The Challenge of Problem-based Learning*, 2nd ed. (pp. 1-14). London: Kogan.

Camp, C. (1996). Problem-based learning: A paradigm shift or a passing fad? *Medical Education Online.* http://www.med-ed-online.org/f0000003.htm, accessed November 15, 2002.

Collis, J., & Hussey, R. (2003). *Business Research: A Practical Guide for Undergraduate and Postgraduate Students.* Basingstoke: Palgrave Macmillan.

Cresswell, J. (1998). *Qualitative Inquiry and Research Design: Choosing Among the Five Traditions.* London: Sage.

Crux Consulting. (2000). http://www.bgsu.edu/colleges/as/pcc/resources.html, accessed January 10, 2003.

Edens, K. (2000). Preparing problem solvers for the 21st century through problem based learning. *College Teaching, 48* (2), 55.

Kilduff, M., & Mahra, A. (1997). Postmodern and organizational research. *Academy of Management Review, 22* (2), 453-481.

Little, S. (1998). Preparing tertiary teachers for problem-based learning. In D. Boud & G. Feletti (Eds.), *The Challenge of Problem-based Learning*, 2nd ed. (pp. 117-124). London: Kogan.

MacDonald, R. (2001). Problem-based learning: Implications for educational developers. *Educational Developments, 2* (2), 1-5.

Major, C., & Palmer, B. (2001). Assessing the effectiveness of problem-based learning in higher education: Lessons from literature. *Academic Exchange Quarterly, 5* (1), 4.

Miles, M. B., & Huberman, A. M. (1994). *Qualitative Data Analysis.* London: Sage.

Reynolds, F. (1997). Studying psychology at degree level: Would problem-based learning enhance the student experiences? *Studies in Higher Education, 22* (3), 263-275.

Saunders, M., Lewis, P., & Thornhill, A. (2003). *Research Methods for Business Students.* Harlow: Prentice-Hall.

Savin-Baden, M. (2000). *Problem-based Learning in Higher Education: Untold Stories*, Selected publications from the Society for Research into Higher Education (SRHE) and Open University Press, Buckingham.

Schuell, T. J. (1986). Cognitive conceptions of learning. *Review of Educational Research, 56*, 411-436.

Schwartz, P. , Mennin, S., & Webb, G. (Eds.). (2001). *Problem-based Learning: Case Studies, Experiences and Practice.* London: Kogan.

Silverman, D. (2000). *Doing Qualitative Research: A Practical Handbook*, London: Sage.

Thacker, R. A. (2002). Revising the HR curriculum: An academic/practitioner partnership. *Education and Training, 44* (1), 31-39.

Woods, D. (1995). *Problem-based Learning: Helping Your Students to Gain the Most from PBL.* Ontario, Canada: Waterdown.

Woods, D. (2002). Problem-based learning especially in the context of large classes, http://www.chemeng.mcmaster.ca/pbl/pbl.htm, accessed January 22, 2003.

Index

Educational Innovation in Economics and Business

1. W.H. Gijselaers, D.T. Tempelaar, P.K. Keizer, J.M. Blommaert, E.M. Bernard and H. Kasper (eds.): *Educational Innovation in Economics and Business Administration*. The Case of Problem Based Learning. 1995 ISBN 0-7923-3272-5
2. D.T. Tempelaar, F. Wiedersheim-Paul and E. Gunnarsson (eds.): *Educational Innovation in Economics and Business II*. In Search of Quality. 1998 ISBN 0-7923-4901-6
3. R.G. Milter, J.E. Stinson and W.H. Gijselaers (eds.): *Educational Innovation in Economics and Business III*. Innovative Practices in Business Education. 1998 ISBN 0-7923-5001-4
4. J. Hommes, P.K. Keizer, M. Pettigrew and J. Troy (eds.): *Educational Innovation in Economics and Business IV*. Learning in a Changing Environment. 1999 ISBN 0-7923-5855-4
5. L. Borghans, W.H. Gijselaers, R.G. Milter and J.E. Stinson (eds.): *Educational Innovation in Economics and Business V*. Business Education for the Changing Workplace. 2000 ISBN 0-7923-6550-X
6. T.A. Johannessen, A. Pedersen and K. Petersen (eds): *Educational Innovation in Economics and Business VI*. Teaching Today the Knowledge of Tomorrow. 2002 ISBN 1-4020-0478-8
7. A. Bentzen-Bilkvist, W.H. Gijselaers and R.G. Milter (eds.): *Educational Innovation in Economics and Business VII*. Educating Knowledge Workers for Corporate Leadership: Learning into the Future. 2002 ISBN 1-4020-1064-8
8. R. Ottewill, L. Borredon, L. Falque, B. Macfarlane and A. Wall (eds.): *Educational Innovation in Economics and Business VIII*. Pedagogy, Technology and Innovation. 2003 ISBN 1-4020-1787-1
9. R.G. Milter, V.S. Perotti and M.S.R. Segers (eds.): *Educational Innovation in Economics and Business IX*. Breaking Boundaries for Global Learning. 2004 ISBN 1-4020-3170-X
10. M.K. McCuddy, H. van den Bosch, Wm. B. Martz (Jr.), A.V. Matveev and K.O. Morse (eds.): *The Challenges of Educating People to Lead in a Challenging World*. 2007 ISBN 1-4020-5611-7

CPSIA information can be obtained
at www.ICGtesting.com
Printed in the USA
LVHW051326220221
679631LV00008B/307